Deliberately Divi

To Susan —

Deliberately Divided

Inside the Controversial Study of Twins and Triplets Adopted Apart

Nancy L. Segal

Best wishes —
Nancy Segal.

ROWMAN & LITTLEFIELD
Lanham • Boulder • New York • London

Published by Rowman & Littlefield
An imprint of The Rowman & Littlefield Publishing Group, Inc.
4501 Forbes Boulevard, Suite 200, Lanham, Maryland 20706
www.rowman.com

86-90 Paul Street, London EC2A 4NE, United Kingdom

British Library Cataloguing in Publication Information Available

Library of Congress Cataloging-in-Publication Data Is Available

ISBN: 978-1-5381-3285-2 (cloth)
ISBN: 978-1-5381-3286-9 (electronic)

To the Twins, Triplets, and Families
Whose Lives Were Touched by the
Events Described Herein

Contents

Acknowledgments

There is a moment at the end of writing a book that I truly relish. It is the chance to acknowledge the many people who have helped and supported me along the way. All books take their authors on journeys of highs and lows, but *Deliberately Divided* has been exceptional—more highs than I could have imagined and more lows than I care to recall. I knew from the start that writing this book would be a challenge, but I have no regrets. I have grown as a scholar, as an author, as a researcher, and as a human being, and for all those things I am grateful.

Lori Shinseki, director of the 2017 documentary film *The Twinning Reaction*, first encouraged me to write the inside story of the Louise Wise Services-Child Development Center twin study. Her wonderful film motivated me to delve deeply into the lives of the twins and their families who had been so horribly hurt by that controversial undertaking. Lori graciously bequeathed to me many of the materials she had gathered for the making of her film. Becky Read, producer of the award-winning documentary film, *Three Identical Strangers*, was also a source of inspiration, information, and support, often conveyed through text messages sent at odd hours, given our UK-US time difference.

My boyfriend, philosophy professor Dr. Craig K. Ihara, read every chapter as I wrote them, bringing sharp insight and keen understanding to the topics at hand. His scribbled remarks in the margins were often illegible, but we reviewed them together and I agreed with him 99.9 percent of the time. My psychology department colleague, Dr. Cheryl Crippen, read every chapter as well, while handling her huge teaching load. I am indebted to her and have urged her to take on editing as a second career. My freshman roommate at Boston University, Bianca Carter, offered to read the entire manuscript upon completion, and I was thrilled to accept. As a former journalism major, Bianca was the perfect person to provide the finishing touch.

I wish to sincerely thank Francisca (Franci) J. Niculae, Lindita Djokovic, Elizabeth Pratt-Thompson, and Dina Arch, graduate students at California State University, Fullerton (CSUF). Franci performed searches for articles and addresses, and helped me decipher a number of Dr. Bernard's handwritten entries. Lindita and Elizabeth skillfully transcribed many of the interviews that appear throughout the different chapters. Dina gave me a leather-bound notebook for recording my thoughts as the book moved forward. A notebook may seem like a strange gift in our digital age, but I used it and accumulated a valuable assortment of ideas at the end. My colleague and friend, philosophy professor Dr. John K. Davis, handed me helpful sources on legal and ethical issues, marking key passages of importance. I read them while taping a segment for *60 Minutes–Australia* when the producers wanted to record me doing "real work."

I am deeply indebted to Stephen E. Novak, Head of Archives and Special Collections at Columbia University's Health Sciences Library. His patience with my countless questions and numerous requests for and about Viola Bernard's materials was impressive. Christine Weideman, Director of Manuscripts and Archives at Yale University, provided valuable information about the process of accepting and managing archived collections. I also wish to acknowledge the library staff at CSUF for finding articles and books despite closure of the campus from the coronavirus. Michael Bedford, CSUF information technology consultant, expertly and remotely solved the computer problems that occasionally threatened my progress. Kelly Donovan, graphic artist, turned figures and photographs into works of art. Liz Mazlish, younger sister of one of the separated twins, offered extraordinary insights and valued support throughout.

My fraternal twin sister, Anne, and her husband, Mark, forwarded a constant stream of articles and other resources that related to the issues I was addressing. My own twin relationship with Anne gave rise to my passion for twins and for what twin studies reveal about the origins of human behavior. Being a twin has sensitized me to what it might mean to learn late in life that one is a twin and to have had that relationship denied.

My former postdoctoral mentor and now valued colleague, Thomas J. Bouchard Jr., was available to answer questions at any time. He did so with his usual wisdom and clarity. Many other colleagues and friends offered advice and assistance, namely Maurice W. Dysken, Leonard L. Heston, John M. Davis, Francie Gabbay, and Kevin Haroian.

I am grateful to the many individuals who agreed to be interviewed—especially one who "so did not want to do it." It was important to tell this story, and everyone who spoke to me understood that. I remain ready to listen to anyone who has new insights to share, even individuals who did not wish to speak to me previously. As I said in the final chapter, this is a story that is over, but not finished.

My literary agent, Carol Mann, head of the Carol Mann Agency in New York, did a terrific job by bringing my book proposal to Rowman & Littlefield and to editor Suzanne Staszak-Silva. This is the second time that Carol has come through for me, having managed my previous book, *Accidental Brothers*. I am grateful to Hannah Fisher, associate production editor, Deni Remsberg, assistant acquisitions editor, and Susan Hershberg, publicity manager, who performed their respective tasks so intelligently and efficiently. I am also indebted to Sean McDonagh in Rowman & Littlefield's British office for answering my questions about rights and permissions.

I saved my greatest appreciation, admiration, and awe for the twins and their families. Reliving past hurts and current heartaches was not easy, but you understood that we had a common goal—to bring transparency to the twin separations, the Louise Wise Services-Child Development Center twin study, and the minds of the people behind it. I hope and believe that you have gained strength in the telling of your stories which you trusted me to tell. Your personal narratives are powerful—for those in control of the data, they are a mighty force to reckon with.

Preface

$\mathcal{U}$nlike most multiple birth babies, these newborn twins and triplets did not grow up together. In accordance with the policy of a New York adoption service, the members of at least nine infant twin pairs and a set of triplets grew up apart, raised in different families.[1] Desperate for children, their adoptive mothers and fathers were thrilled to be offered a newborn baby—only they never knew that they welcomed just part of a twin or triplet set into their home. The mystery surrounding the birth and placement of these children by the agency staff was intentional, a decision they validated by claiming to support the best interests of each child. But the tale does not end there—because the twins' separate rearing allowed them to be secretly studied by investigators bent on unraveling the effects of nature and nurture on behavioral development.

This book tells the story of a twin study that does not go away. This project has been strongly justified and defended by some, but vehemently attacked and opposed by others. I am riveted by the controversy and feel compelled to explore all sides of the nature and consequences of this work.[2] Digging deeper into the purposeful separation of twins and triplets, and what proved to be the covert observation of their growing up years, is the most challenging task I have faced in my career. I say that as a twin researcher and as a fraternal twin.

It began in the late 1950s with the notion that twins were better off growing up in separate families as they would not be competing for parental attention with a same-age sibling. This claim, conceived by Columbia University psychiatrist Dr. Viola Bernard, informed the placement policy of the Louise Wise Adoption Services in New York City. How long this policy remained in place is a matter of some debate, but we know that twins were adopted into different families, and that the development of each identical twin was tracked and compared for twelve years. Parents were never told that they and their children were unwitting subjects in a long-term study of multiple birth children that was launched to settle the nature-nurture debate. The investigators also reasoned that telling the parents about their child's multiple birth status would interfere with the experiment. Fraternal twins were separated, as well, but they were not part of the project.

The study, known as the Louise Wise Services (LWS)-Child Development Center (CDC) Twin Study, was orchestrated by psychoanalyst and psychiatrist Dr. Peter B. Neubauer, beginning in the early 1960s. Neubauer was a clinical professor of psychiatry at New York University and a supervising analyst at the psychoanalytic institutes of Columbia and New York Universities. He was also a member of the Jewish Board of Guardians, now the Jewish Board of Family and Children's Services. Known for his studies of one-child families, the meanings of play, and the effects of television violence on children's dreams, his views were often presented in the media, as well as in *The Psychoanalytic Study of the Child*, a journal he edited since the 1970s.[3,4]

I did not know of the study's existence until the early 1980s because so much about it was kept secret. It's still news to some of my colleagues and friends, and to many in society who trust professionals to act in their best interests. Information on the infant twins' earliest days prior to placement and the data that were later gathered on them continue to be shrouded in secrecy. Prior to his death in 2008, in 1990 Neubauer's research material was deposited in the Yale University archives, to be concealed until 2065.[5] The year 2066 is widely cited, but it is actually on October 18, 2065, that the copyright passes to Yale University, and on October 25, 2065, that the records can be released. The collection includes sixty-six boxes of material.[6]

Some of Neubauer's former associates and others positioned to address the twins' grievances refused to speak on the record. The twins' adoption histories, bequeathed to Spence-Chapin Services after LWS closed its doors in 2004, have been difficult if not impossible for the twins to obtain. According to many people I spoke with, the Jewish Board of Family and Children's Services has placed innumerable barriers between the twins and their study records.[7]

Why did I agree to do a book-length treatment of a controversial twin research project conducted over half a century ago? The years 2017 and 2018 saw the release of two documentary films related to this study, *The Twinning Reaction* and *Three Identical Strangers*. These films gripped the public to a degree that even the directors and producers had not anticipated—because purposefully sending multiple birth babies to different homes and recording their behavior undercover challenged belief in the sacredness of family ties and shattered trust in scientific integrity. People everywhere were talking about this study. At anniversary parties and birthday celebrations, I was suddenly the center of attention because of my ongoing twin research. In southern California where I live and work, casual conversations at social gatherings were often replaced by dialogue and debate. "How could this happen?!" guests demanded to know. "What more can you tell us?" It was no different among my professional colleagues. "There's so much more that needs to be written about it!" "I wondered if you had been consulted."

There *is* a lot more to say about the twins from this study, as well as its origins, methods, challenges, and outcomes that fifty- to ninety-minute films cannot capture. In the weeks following their release, people insisted that I was the "best person" to write a book because of my past association with the Minnesota Study of Twins Reared Apart, and my more recent work with switched-at-birth twin pairs and young Chinese twins adopted apart.[8] Lori Shinseki, director of *The Twinning Reaction*, was especially encouraging and offered to make many of her materials available. My boyfriend, philosophy professor Craig K. Ihara, argued that despite its dark side, the study warranted a place in the history of twin research. And when I gave lectures on my various twin research projects, audience members bombarded me with questions and comments about the LWS-CDC study. I knew that the twins' stories needed to be told to help them gain information about their past, to help them understand their present, and to prevent such an episode from happening in the future. The twins and their parents have been angry, hurt, and confused since learning that their lives had been so callously tampered with. Ultimately, I did not have to decide to write this book because I knew I was going to do it. In February 2019, editor Suzanne Staszak-Silva at Rowman & Littlefield Publishers gave me that chance.

As thrilling as it was to be offered a contract when competition for such opportunities was (and is) high, I felt a vague unease about this undertaking, a feeling I had never experienced while writing my previous books on twins. I would be reaching out to Neubauer's former colleagues who might talk to me defiantly, reluctantly, or not at all. Many of them were defending him, after the films' release, believing Neubauer had been unfairly vilified in the press and on film. The book I would write was clearly not going to satisfy everyone—television programs, radio interviews, newspaper articles, and internet blogs were teeming with different opinions about the twins' rights to their birth histories, the appropriateness of the Louise Wise adoption policies, and the issue of researcher responsibilities. The book was going to be divisive, and I would be in the cross hairs. Then, a month after signing on with Rowman & Littlefield, I met up with my colleague, Dr. Robert Plomin, a psychologist and geneticist at Kings College, London. I was in London to tape a reared-apart twin segment for the BAFTA award-winning television series, *Long Lost Family*. Plomin and I shared a three-tiered tray of "savouries and fancies" during high tea at the National Portrait Gallery. It was an opportunity for me to hear his views on the LWS-CDC twin study, the two recent films, and related topics.

Plomin is accustomed to controversy. As a leader in the field of behavioral genetics since the early 1970s, he has consistently defended the role of hereditary factors ("nature") in shaping human behavior, challenging the long prevailing view that environmental influences ("nurture") are paramount. His 2018 book, *Blueprint: How DNA Makes Us Who We Are*, describes the potential use of polygenic scores, values that combine small genetic effects allowing predictions about each person's intelligence, personality, and disease predispositions. He calls these scores "fortune tellers," a claim that has been both strongly embraced and hotly contested.[9] Plomin recalled being consulted for a 1982 *60 Minutes* exposé of the Neubauer study that was ultimately cancelled, a curious turn of events I will revisit later in the book. Without asking, I was hoping Plomin would say what I knew already—that this book project was exciting, timely, and important. I was not disappointed because his enthusiasm and encouragement were immediate. When I hinted at the likely controversies that would erupt once the book was out, he unknowingly settled that point, too—"Why write a safe book? Write something that people will talk about!" I trust (and hope) I have done exactly that.

Illustrious and Ignoble

Twin Studies

*I*dentical twins captivate us like no other pair of humans. Seeing two identical infants, children, or adults is irresistible, causing people to peer into baby carriages, stare into playgrounds, and even pose personal questions: Who was born first? Who is smarter? Do you ever switch places? I believe that the universal fascination with twins comes from our appreciation and expectation of individual differences in appearance and behavior—thus, the sight of two people who look and act so much alike challenges these strongly held beliefs. Moreover, most identical twins insist that the love, understanding, and trust that they share with their sibling surpasses that of all other social connections. Their intimacy evokes admiration and envy in most non-twins, but to some it suggests overdependence and confinement. Regardless, we find ourselves intrigued and drawn into twins' lives, trying to understand them. At the same time, scientists study twins for insights into the origins of behavioral and physical traits.

There are also dim sides to twin research, studies that have cast a frightening gloom over this popular and well-respected approach to human development. Twins and their families have been physically hurt and emotionally damaged in the process. Fortunately, there are only a few such investigations, but their effects have been far-reaching, provoking public outrage, distrust in research scientists, and disdain for public servants. There is Dr. William Blatz's scientific abuse of the identical Dionne quintuplets in Canada (1937).[1] There is Dr. Josef Mengele's horrifying twin research conducted at the Auschwitz-Birkenau concentration camp in Poland (1943–1945).[2] There are the tortured medical experiments performed on conjoined twins Masha and Dasha Krivoshlypova in the 1950s by Russian state scientists.[3] And there is Dr. John Money's attempt to turn an accidentally castrated male twin into a

Figure 1.1. Drs. Viola W. Bernard (L) and Peter B. Neubauer (R). Photo of Viola Bernard by Lynn Gilbert, 1977, Courtesy of Columbia University Archives. Photo of Neubauer by an Unnamed Source (Neubauer).

female (1967–1980s).[4,5] These unfortunate studies continue to be examined for the grievous missteps that were made and the important lessons that can be learned.

There is another contentious episode in the twin research field that has not disappeared from discussion. It is New York's Louise Wise Services (LWS)-Child Development Center (CDC) study that tracked the development of separated twins without informing their families about the nature of the investigation. The study began in 1960 and lasted approximately twenty years.[6] It was a collaboration between LWS consultant Dr. Viola W. Bernard and the director of the Jewish Board of Guardians' Child Development Center, Dr. Peter B. Neubauer. This book is the inside story about the policy that separated the twins and the study that tracked them. It is also a venture into why their plan was so seductive, but disturbing, and why it still concerns us. Their work was an attempt to resolve the relative contributions of nature (genes) and nurture (environments) to the ongoing nature-nurture debate.

NATURE-NURTURE DEBATE

Ever since Sir Francis Galton's 1875 twin research persuaded him that "nature prevails enormously over nurture," the nature-nurture debate has held the attention of countless people.[7] Everyone wants explanations for why they are average or astute, short or tall, outgoing or shy, risk-taking or cautious. Twin research brings clarity to these questions, explaining why identical and fraternal twins are valued participants in psychological and medical research. Twin studies have also infiltrated fields as diverse as economics, political science, and religious studies, revising their explanatory landscapes to include genetic effects. Twin studies help us understand why we are lavish or frugal, liberal or conservative, pious or profane.[8]

The LWS-CDC study came at a time when nature-nurture debates were raging worldwide. Most researchers considered nurture, or environmental influences, to be decisive in shaping the way a child developed. "Refrigerator mothers," characterized by high intellect, emotional distance, and inability to "defrost," were blamed for the development of autism in their young children.[9] A similar constellation of traits defined "schizophrenogenic parents" whose coldness, rejection, and hostility were thought to cause psychopathology in their children as they approached adulthood.[10] But those times were changing—genetic findings from non-human animal experiments, twin and adoption studies, and medical research were challenging that wisdom. There was just enough buzz in the air to question the prevailing environmental theories, bringing genetic factors (heredity) into the mix.[11]

It was an exciting but contentious time. People could accept that physical traits, such as height and weight, were partly affected by the genes. However, evidence that behavioral traits, especially general intelligence, had a genetic underpinning was hotly debated, with accusations of sexism and racism brought against many who supported that claim. However, individual differences (e.g., variation among people of the same gender or ethnicity) are distinct from between-group differences (e.g., variation between people of different genders or ethnicities), so it is not possible to draw conclusions about one based on the other. For example, the reasons for differences in rough and tumble play *among* females in one culture are not always the same as those *between* females from different cultures. Prenatal exposure to higher levels of testosterone have been linked to higher rates of rough and tumble play among young girls.[12] However, girls from more egalitarian societies are socialized to be more aggressive than girls from more male-dominated societies.[13] Nevertheless, this crucial difference was not always recognized by proponents or opponents of genetic effects. Careers were crushed and research plans were derailed.[14]

Interestingly, three of Neubauer's New York medical colleagues, Alexander Thomas, Stella Chess, and Thomas Birch, had been following the development of 141 infants since 1956.[15] In 1970 they published their conclusion, chiding physicians who had lost sight of what every mother knows, namely that each child shows a characteristic temperamental style from birth. They found "no consistent or predictable relation between the parents' treatment and the child's specific symptoms." For example, a domineering parent might appear to make one child anxious and another child defiant. Left out of the equation was the child's "own temperament, that is, his own individual style of responding to the environment."[16] Never once did Thomas and company mention the words "heredity," "genetic," or "genes," but their meaning was clear. Separated twins are the perfect way to test ideas like these. Neubauer and Bernard knew this and seized an opportunity that came their way—or some might say that they created.

WHY TWINS?

The logic of the twin research method is clever and elegant, yet amazingly straightforward and simple. It rests on the presence of two types of twins: identical and fraternal. Identical (monozygotic or MZ) twins result when a single fertilized egg, or zygote, divides between one and fourteen days after conception to create two. Further division of one or both of those zygotes results in identical triplets and quadruplets, known as higher order identical multiples. Consequently, identical twins and these "multiple multiples" share all their genes in common, and all members of these sets are either male or female.[17] Fraternal (dizygotic or DZ) twins occur when a woman simultaneously releases two eggs that are fertilized by two separate spermatozoa. These twins share half their genes, on average, which is exactly the same genetic relationship shared by non-twin brothers and sisters born years apart. Fraternal twins can be either same-sex or opposite-sex. The release and fertilization of more than two eggs at a time yields fraternal triplets, quadruplets, or more. It is also possible to have mixed sets, such as a trio composed of an identical pair with a fraternal co-triplet.[18]

The classic twin method involves comparing similarities between pairs of identical twins and pairs of fraternal twins. If identical twin partners, or co-twins, are more alike than fraternal twins in any measured trait, such as visual skill, running speed, or back pain, the conclusion is that genetic factors affect the development of that trait. Environmental influences also play a role because, although identical twins are more alike than any other pair of people, they do not show perfect resemblance.[19] A 2015 survey of twin studies showed that nearly 50 percent of the individual differences among people across

Figure 1.2.   **Types of twins, from L to R: identical, fraternal same-sex and fraternal opposite-sex. Identical twins, Josie (L) and Jessi (R); fraternal same-sex twins, Becky (L) and Abigail (R); and fraternal opposite-sex twins, Ethan (L) and Nami (R). Courtesy of the twins and their families.**

numerous traits are explained by their genetic differences.[20] If environmental factors were not important, that figure would approach 100 percent.

TWINNING RATES

Twinning rates in the United States rose dramatically in recent years, from 18.9 per thousand births in 1980 to 33.3 twins per thousand births in 2017.[21] This upswing, which mostly involved fraternal twins, was largely explained by the increased use of fertility procedures, such as in vitro fertilization (IVF). IVF involves the creation of multiple embryos in a reproductive laboratory and their implantation in the womb. Fraternal twinning is also more common among older mothers, beginning at about age thirty-five. Because some women were delaying their child-bearing years to complete an education or pursue a career, their lifestyle decisions further amplified fraternal twinning rates. These trends have been observed in other Western nations. However, the 2019 rate declined to 32.1 twins per thousand births. This may reflect improved reproductive techniques involving implantation of just one fertilized egg.[22]

Identical twins were also becoming more common, but to a lesser extent. Surprisingly, IVF has also been linked to identical twinning, in that manipulating a fertilized egg outside the body may cause it to divide. In fact, identical twinning rates after reproductive treatment are between two and twelve times higher than the natural identical twinning rate of 0.3–0.4 percent. Improved detection and management of multiple pregnancies also explain why more identical twins were being born than ever before.[23]

However, twinning rates change with the times. The newest report shows a 4 percent *decline* in US twinning rates, starting in 2014 and lasting until 2018.[24] The revised figures of 32.6 and 32.1 twins per thousand births are the lowest since 2002. These updated figures make sense if we look at women over age thirty, but especially at women over age forty whose falloffs are greatest. Older prospective mothers are more likely to seek reproductive assistance (e.g., IVF) than younger mothers, making multiple conceptions more likely. However, given recent improvements in reproductive technologies, fertility specialists are now able to limit the number of implanted embryos to just one with high success rates.[25] This was less true in the past when several embryos were required for favorable outcomes.

TWINS RAISED APART AND TOGETHER

More convincing and more dramatic than twins raised together are the rare twins who have been separated at birth and raised by different families. The scientific significance of these pairs is that they provide a pure estimate of genetic influence, because the twins did not share their parents, schools, friends, or communities. There have been several major studies of reared-apart twins, conducted at the University of Chicago (1937);[26] the University of Odense, Denmark (1965/1980);[27, 28] the Maudsley Institute, London (1966);[29] the Karolinska Institute, Stockholm, Sweden (1984, 1992);[30] and the University of Minnesota (2012).[31] Other reared-apart twin studies have taken place, or are ongoing, in Finland, China, Japan, and the United States.

The Minnesota Study of Twins Reared Apart, directed by Dr. Thomas J. Bouchard Jr., was the most exciting professional opportunity I have ever enjoyed in my career. The week-long assessment of each separated set was filled with tests measuring the twins' mental skills, personality traits, medical characteristics, and more, all of which matched more closely among the reared-apart identical than fraternal pairs. It was also stunning to see the unusual similarities displayed by many separated identical twins—Jack and Oskar washed their hands before and after using the toilet; Jim Lewis and Jim Springer endured severe migraine headaches beginning in their late teens; Barbara and Daphne, the "giggle twins," laughed constantly at nothing in particular; and Bridget and Dorothy arrived in Minneapolis each wearing seven rings, three bracelets and a watch. Such similarities were rarely displayed by the separated fraternal twins, demonstrating that even unusual habits and behaviors are under some degree of genetic control—although the precise pathways from genes to behavior remain murky.[32] However, since the early 2000s geneticists have made some impressive strides in linking specific genes to intellectual, educational, and physical measures.[33]

An area of twin research I find especially engaging concerns the comparative social closeness of identical and fraternal twins, and what the differences tell us about human social relationships, in general. Before arriving in Minnesota as a postdoctoral fellow, I completed my doctoral degree at the University of Chicago. A paper based on my doctoral thesis compared cooperation and competition between seven- to eleven-year-old identical and fraternal twins while they worked together on various tasks, such as puzzle completion.[34] The short films I made of them are still among my favorites because they show how much twins tell us about human performance, just by acting naturally. I found that the identical twins were generally more cooperative and more generous toward one another than the fraternal twins. Thus, it appeared that behaviors important for completing a puzzle (e.g., information-processing skills, temperamental tendencies, and work styles) are more closely aligned and perceived as such by the members of identical than fraternal pairs, explaining their differences in my experimental tasks. Beyond the twins, I believe these findings also tell us why certain pairs of relatives, friends, and co-workers get along better than others—matching on relevant intellectual, personality, and work-related traits may facilitate cooperation.

TWIN RELATIONS

There are countless examples of extraordinary selflessness between twins. It is touching to hear about a female twin who bore a child for her infertile sister, and a male twin who donated a vital organ to assist his brother.[35] Thus, the next part of my story takes an important detour into twin relationships and family ties. It is important to know this as a backdrop to how the LWS-CDC twin study managed such twin and family matters, topics I will also visit in the next chapter.

When I arrived in Minnesota, I was eager to know if the reared-apart identical twins experienced greater closeness and familiarity with one another than the reared-apart fraternal twins, mirroring what was known about twins raised together. They did—both when they met each other and when they participated in the study. More remarkable perhaps, twins of both types generally felt closer to the twin they had recently met than to any unrelated siblings they had known all their lives. Again, perceptions of similarity may have been driving this finding.[36]

Most twins remained in touch with one another long after leaving Minnesota, although there were exceptions. Regardless, every reunited twin we studied was variously pleased, gratified, even overjoyed to have met his or her brother or sister. Most of the twins had been raised in unrelated adoptive families, so it was their first chance to meet a biological relative and to see someone who had the same crooked finger (inward bend of both pinkies), used the same unusual toothpaste (the Swedish brand *Vademecum*), or favored the same quirky cocktail ("Twin Sin" that blended vodka, Blue Curaçao, crème de cacao, and cream). It was also the twins' first opportunity to learn about their medical history. Gaining ten pounds for no apparent reason, losing visual acuity, and suffering from food allergies suddenly made sense, rooted partly in their shared genes. In the process of these discoveries, the twins gained new family members including in-laws, nieces, nephews, and cousins. It was an invigorating, life-changing experience.[37]

In the midst of their celebrations, many twins were angry, hurt, and disheartened that they had been cheated out of significant growing up years together. Perhaps that is why some of these adult twins wore matching t-shirts or played tricks on the Minnesota team, trying to create the common, fun-filled childhood they had missed. Most twins had met before taking part in the study, but some were reunited at the Minneapolis airport. All of them were grateful to Bouchard for bringing them together for a foray into their past, present—and future.

SEPARATED AT BIRTH

Nearly all the twins in the Minnesota Study of Twins Reared Apart study and in the previous reared-apart twin studies had met one another as adults. Therefore, questioning their mothers, fathers, teachers, and friends was not possible because most, if not all, of these people were unavailable or deceased. This also meant that aspects of the twins' growing up years, such as school grades, early friendships, childhood diseases, and parental relationships, were recollected, rather than obtained in real time. Memory is fragile, subject to lapses and errors, but one of our studies revealed an intriguing finding along these lines.

In the Minnesota study, it turned out that recollected measures of the twins' different home atmospheres, like family cohesion, were more alike for the identical than fraternal twins, even though all the twins had been raised in different homes. Two interpretations of this finding were possible: (1) The identical twins' more similar personalities may have explained their matching memories. For example, upbeat people may focus on pleasant events, thereby minimizing the impact or recollection of turbulent times. (2) Alternatively, the twins may have tailored their actual environments to be more compatible with who they were. People upset by warring family members may try to calm the conflicts, converting tension into tranquility. The researchers weighing these possibilities went on to say, "The ideal experiment to compare these two interpretations is not ethical to conduct; one cannot raise infant twins apart in systematically different circumstances, measure those circumstances as they occur, and follow the twins to adulthood."[38]

Or can they? Bernard, Neubauer, and their colleagues did exactly that. It was a dazzling idea—the ideal experiment—the kind researchers dream about, but would not dare to conduct because disrupting human lives is a dangerous endeavor with unforeseen consequences.

In 1993, about fifteen years since the project ended, Dr. Peter Neubauer agreed to be interviewed by *New Yorker* magazine staff writer Lawrence Wright who was researching an article on nature-nurture questions.[39] Neubauer boasted that the prospective design of his study was "unique," elevating it above the other reared-apart twin projects that had relied on the recollections of adults. When I met Neubauer at his home in 2004 he expressed similar satisfaction that his team "was there at the birth." And he was open about his attempts to persuade another adoption agency to place twins apart.[40] His study ended when the twins turned twelve, but if controversies over his work had not been played out so publicly it may have lasted longer.

WHY SEPARATE TWINS?

Twins are separated for many reasons. In the past, unwed women wishing to avoid the social stigmas of out-of-wedlock birth were usually counseled to give up their twins for adoption. (Of course, many societies around the world now accept single mothers, but some do not.) Parents who are financially and/or emotionally unable to care for two babies at once may be forced to relinquish one or both newborns. These separations are mostly decided with the children's best interests at heart. Giving away newborn babies can be heart-wrenching for parents who can only hope that their sons and daughters will enjoy better lives than those they could provide. Adoption agencies have sometimes allowed prospective parents to adopt just one twin if they cannot afford to adopt both. The eagerness of these agencies to place children in good homes and the desperation of some childless couples to have a baby may desensitize them to the twins' best interests, one of which is the special significance of the twins' relationship. Some agencies benefited from acquiring two adoption fees if twins were placed apart.[41]

Over the years I have learned about some unusual social and political events that have conspired to keep twins apart. Divorced spouses have each taken one twin when they parted ways. A couple determined to create the "ideal American family"—mother, father, and two children—gave one twin away when the birth of twin sons followed the birth of a daughter. In a strange twist, one twin child in Romania was given to an infertile couple because families with at least one child enjoyed tax exemption.[42, 43] And in another part of the world, political tensions in mainland China during the Civil War (1945–1949) prevented a young twin from returning home after visiting her grandmother.

Years later, China's 1979 One-Child Policy was indirectly responsible for separating an unknown number of infant female twins.[44] Family size restrictions and the prizing of male over female children led thousands of parents to abandon their baby daughters, some of whom were twins. Bundled in baskets and left at orphanages and police stations, twins were sometimes found apart, then adopted by different families in the United States, Canada, Europe, and Australia. With the full knowledge and cooperation of their families, I have been following the behavioral development of twenty-two of these pairs who ranged in age from three to twenty-five years when they joined the study.[45] I am certain that there are more separated sets whose families are unaware that they are raising a lone twin.

Sometimes newborns are accidentally handed to the wrong mothers by careless or overworked staff members. I have documented ten cases of twins who grew up apart because one twin was switched with an unrelated infant in the baby nursery.[46] The most dramatic case of this kind occurred in Colombia, South America, in 1988, when an identical infant male twin in one set was accidentally exchanged with an identical infant male twin in another set, creating two unrelated "fraternal" pairs in the process. I was privileged to have visited Bogotá in 2015 and 2017 to study these twins as young men in their twenties, and to help them cope with their drastically revised lives once they learned the truth.[47]

There is another reason why some twins have grown up apart, and it is the one behind the LWS-CDC study. It was the belief that twins are better off being raised as singletons in separate families. LWS was the only adoption agency to deliberately divide twins according to this reasoning.

COMING TOGETHER

Separated twins find each other in many ways. Some come together because of mistaken identity, when someone familiar with one twin encounters the other twin by chance, thinking it was the friend that they knew. This happened to identical triplets, Robert (Bob) Shafran, David (Dave) Kellman, and Edward (Eddy) Galland, who were separated by LWS and the focus of the 2018 film, *Three Identical Strangers*. In contrast, some twins, especially fraternal twins, meet only after extensive searching because they do not look physically alike and are rarely confused. I have also studied twins who did not know that they were part of a pair, but as adoptees were in search of their biological parents. Once they discovered they had a twin, their quest to find their brother or sister became all-consuming, reducing the importance of finding their biological parents. A separated twin from Connecticut even hired a private investigator who located her sister in Kentucky.[48]

Being a twin is a celebrated circumstance of birth in most places around the world. The International Twins Association, founded in 1932, promotes the intellectual, social, and spiritual welfare of twins worldwide. In the United States, the annual Twins Days Festival, launched in Twinsburg, Ohio, in 1976, attracts hundreds of twins for exhibitions, games, and contests.[49] The Yorùbá of western Nigeria honor twins with special rituals and statues called *ibeji*.[50] And in 2019, fifty pairs of young twins marched along the Yalta embankment with their parents as part of the Crimean Twins Festival.[51] But twinship has grim sides, as well. The inhabitants of Calabar in southeastern Nigeria believed that twins carried evil spirits, therefore killing them and disowning their family members.[52] Japan once frowned upon the presence of twins, equating human multiple birth with non-human litters. Interestingly, during feudal periods in Japan (1185–1868 CE) the leading lords separated twin sons, keeping one and secretly giving one away to a courtier to raise. The relinquished child retained a token of his true background so that if his brother should die, he could easily fill his place.[53]

I have a DVD that holds a series of twin reunions variously taped by the twins' families or the media. The first moment of connection between reunited twins is indescribable to those who witness it, because the twins' joy and laughter seem boundless. Some twins circle each other in wonder and disbelief, alternately touching their own face and their twin's as if to assure themselves that they are not looking in a mirror. Others shield their faces because the sight of "themselves" is an emotional rush too strong to bear. Some twins embrace more quietly, but the happiness and contentment in their faces can make anyone weep.

No one really knows how often twins grow up apart, but based on available studies and case reports, I have estimated the total to be 1,904 pairs or 3,808 individual twins. That is a small number, given that 1.6 million twins are born each year worldwide.[54] Surely, there are other separated sets that we will never know about, because these twins have no inkling that they are part of a pair. In fact, we really do not know how many twins were separated in

New York City by LWS, although we do know that four identical twin pairs and one identical triplet set were the subjects of Neubauer's study. I also know that at least five additional pairs—three fraternal sets, one identical set (initially followed, but dropped), and one set of undetermined type—were separated, but not studied, making it likely that the number is probably higher.

TWIN STUDIES GOOD AND BAD

Studying twins is exciting for new investigators, as well as for seasoned veterans of the field. My late Minnesota colleague, Dr. David T. Lykken, used to say that any psychological study one conducted would be better with twins.[55] Twins bring new dimensions to most research programs, often challenging traditional interpretations of behavior and generating new ideas. It was once thought that religious interests were due mostly to upbringing, but twin studies tell a genetic tale, as they do for social attitudes and sports participation. The timing of these studies is critical because young identical and fraternal twins living at home generally accept the practices and beliefs of their parents. Thus, both twins will attend religious services, embrace gun control, or compete in tennis matches. But as twins approach adolescence and young adulthood, with its greater freedom of choice, identical twins' attitudes and activities generally remain the same, whereas those of fraternal twins tend to diverge. Greater identical than fraternal twin similarity indicates genetic influence.

Researchers admit that once twins enter their lab, they have a desire to study everything about them. Enthusiasm runs understandably high, but this should never blind researchers to twins' welfare and best interests. I sometimes wonder if twins and other multiples are more likely to experience such wrongdoing because of their vast research potential and universal appeal.

Twins usually enjoy being in research because they are eager to learn more about themselves and are happy to advance scientific understanding in the process. Therefore, it is hurtful for twins, families, and researchers to know that there have been some unfortunate sides to twin studies, like the ones I mentioned at the start of this chapter. Every semester I share several such episodes with my students as a way of preventing wrongdoings in future twin studies. But now it is time to step inside the controversial study of twins and triplets adopted apart.

· 2 ·

Policies and People

Separated by Design

The story of the Louise Wise Services (LWS)-Child Development Center (CDC) twin study has all the ingredients of an academic drama. Even as a work of fiction, it would strain the imagination. As one of the mothers who unknowingly adopted a lone twin so persuasively—and indignantly—put it to me, "If God gives you twins, you don't mess with nature."

Reared-apart twins have appeared in a vast number of fictional works, most likely because they are useful devices for exploring human character, identity, and circumstance. The first known example is Plautus's *Menachemi*, an amusing drama of the mistakes and confusion that ensue when young twins grow up apart. This work was followed by Shakespeare's plays, *Twelfth Night* and *Comedy of Errors*, that also depict the hilarious happenings involving separated twins and everyone around them. No doubt, Shakespeare's fascination with twins can be traced to his having fathered an opposite-sex pair, Judith and Hamnet.[1] I often marvel at the fact that the presence of reared-apart twins in the arts proceeded their presence in the sciences.

Contemporary dramatic treatments of separated twins include films, such as *The Parent Trap*, and television series, such as *Sister, Sister*. A recent fictional reference to separated twins also surfaced in the 2017 novel *The Girl Who Takes an Eye for an Eye*, the fifth installment of Stieg Larsson's popular Millenium series.[2] At the center of the story is a project that purposely placed children into selected environments to determine the effects on their growth. One of the characters mentions an article, "Born Together—Raised Apart," about a "scientific investigation by some people at the University of Minnesota [that used reared-apart twins]." Here we have art mimicking real life as the article is fictitious, but my book by that title and the Minnesota Study of Twins Reared Apart (MISTRA) are not.[3]

LOUISE WISE SERVICES AND DR. VIOLA BERNARD

The Louise Wise adoption agency began as New York's Free Synagogue Child Adoption Committee, located at 48 West 68th Street in Manhattan. It was founded in 1916 by Louise Waterman Wise, wife of the prominent Rabbi Stephen S. Wise. Louise Wise worked tirelessly on behalf of childcare and protection, despite her family's disapproval of a career putting her in contact with people whom they judged to be of questionable background. She persisted nevertheless, efforts that earned her recognition as a "Jewish Eleanor Roosevelt."[4] In 1946, a year before her mother's death, Wise's daughter, Justine Wise Polier, the first female justice in New York State, assumed the presidency of the committee's Board of Directors. In 1949, Polier renamed the committee the Louise Wise Services in honor of her mother. LWS became a well-respected, highly reputed agency, offering a range of individual and family counseling programs and social services. Polier held the presidency until

Figure 2.1. Justine Wise Polier, standing before a portrait of her mother, Louise Waterman Wise, in the boardroom of Louise Wise Services. The location of the painting is currently unknown (L). Board Meeting at LWS. Justine Wise Polier is at the head of the table; to her left is Florence Brown Kreech, former executive director of LWS (R). Arthur and Elizabeth Schlesinger Library, Radcliffe Institute for Advanced Study at Harvard University, Cambridge, MA.

1981 when she was replaced by Sheldon Fogelman, but she continued to serve as honorary president.[5]

Under the leadership of Justine Polier, efforts were made to incorporate the latest mental health findings in decisions regarding legal matters and child placement. Polier worked closely with, and depended upon, psychological and psychiatric experts, among them psychiatrist Dr. Viola Bernard who was her close friend since childhood. LWS also dedicated itself to serving Native American and African American orphans, adoptees, and families, as well as Jewish parents and children.[6] Polier challenged other agencies' practices of placing siblings with different families if children had different skin tones or other physical features, calling these decisions unjust and tragic. These practices, applied by other agencies through the 1960s, were predicated on the belief that raising different-looking brothers and sisters would be difficult for their parents. Instead, Polier felt it was acceptable to place these children together in the same family, and did so. And she blocked the separate adoption of African American brothers when opinion suggested that the darker-skinned boy would be difficult to place. She also believed it was appropriate for siblings to be raised by parents whose religious affiliation differed from that of their birth parents, a decision for which she was criticized.[7] A play, *The Grain of the Wood*, produced by Polier's granddaughter Debra Bradley Ruder, highlights Justine Wise Polier's contributions to fairness and justice for disadvantaged children.[8] Polier and LWS were ahead of their time in many ways.

Above all, LWS was *the* agency to go to for Jewish couples wishing to adopt a child in the 1950s and beyond. By then, its location was an unassuming brownstone building on Manhattan's wealthy upper east side, at 10–12 East 94th Street. The Lakeview Home, a residence for unwed pregnant women, was maintained on Staten Island to house expectant mothers until the time of their delivery at Staten Island Hospital.[9] In fact, "Lakeview Home" is part of the LWS letterhead. Some women resided at a similar facility in New York City before delivering their babies at Mt. Sinai Hospital.[10] Arrangements were then made by LWS to place the babies with the childless couples so eager to adopt them.

In 1942, LWS engaged the well-known Columbia University psychiatrist, Dr. Viola W. Bernard, mentioned previously, as their Chief Psychiatric Consultant and Board Member.[11] Bernard's background was interesting, enviable, and exceptional, made possible by her upper-class family and her own independent spirit. She was born in 1907, in New York, to a wealthy Jewish couple, Jacob Wertheim and his second wife, Emma Stern. Bernard enjoyed certain privileges, such as attending a private high school and enrolling in college courses, but she also studied eastern philosophy while living in an ashram called the "Clarkstown Country Club" in Nyack, New York.[12] She married the Tibetan scholar Theos Casimir Bernard but divorced him four years later. The couple did not have any children.

Bernard completed her psychiatric training in 1936 at New York's Cornell Medical School, followed by various residences and psychoanalytic training. After joining Columbia University's Department of Psychiatry in the 1940s, she steadily ascended the academic ladder to clinical professor of psychiatry in 1963. Her outstanding professional reputation as a psychiatrist and psychoanalyst came from her contributions to child psychiatry, child adoption, and community service.

Bernard's humanitarian efforts were far-reaching. During the second World War, she opened her summer home in Nyack to refugees from Nazi Germany. She was also affiliated with the Wiltwyck School for Boys, an institution offering education, counseling, and other assistance to troubled youth from Protestant African American families.[13] Over the course of her career Bernard received numerous professional awards, among them the 1996 Presidential Commendation from the American Psychiatric Association, for her "compassion, creativity, and courageous intervention in human pain."

Viola Bernard ("Vi" to her family and friends) enjoyed an active social life in addition to a successful career. Friends and colleagues found her "charismatic" and "sparkling," but also "opinionated" and "intimidating." When asked to list her interests and hobbies on an LWS form she wrote, "varied, but include[s] tennis."[14] Surprisingly, she failed to list her well known love of dogs. Her archived material at Columbia University that is open to the public includes one rather extraordinary photo from the American Psychiatric Association collection. Seated around a table enjoying drinks, the guests, including Bernard, are highly amused by an elderly gentleman who placed the bottom of a baby bottle at his mouth while a small live pig sucked hungrily from the nipple on the other end.

Bernard held her position as LWS's chief consultant for forty years, followed by ten years as an ad hoc senior psychiatric consultant. She resigned from the Board of Directors in April 1992, about the same time as her consultancy ended.[15]

TWINS MUST BE SEPARATED

There are two opposing views about how the LWS-CDC twin study got started. I will present both views, saving my own opinion until the final chapters:

- Dr. Viola W. Bernard claimed that twins would benefit from growing up apart. Her colleague, professor and psychoanalyst, Dr. Peter B. Neubauer, learned that this policy had been implemented and decided to follow the newborn twins' development over time.[16]
- Dr. Peter B. Neubauer was interested in exploring the relative contributions of nature and nurture during child development. He determined that the best way to do this was to study separated newborn twins and persuaded Dr. Bernard to propose this policy to LWS.[17]

Contrary to the belief that twins were first separated in the early 1960s when the study began, there is evidence that LWS placed twins apart in the late 1940s and early 1950s. However, it was not until the late 1950s that the LWS developed their formal policy of placing newborn twins in separate homes.[18] The exact date that board approval was given cannot be known because Bernard's twin research documents, dated 1953–1997, remain under seal at Columbia University until 2021, although selected materials may remain restricted beyond that date.[19] There had been recent discussion of delaying the availability of some materials until 2065 to coincide with the release of Neubauer's papers currently stored at Yale.[20]

As I indicated, LWS separated twins prior to the start of the study. Tim and Ilene, a pair of male-female twins placed apart by LWS, were born in 1947 and raised by different families in the New York City area. Their twinship was discovered after Tim's mother did an exhaustive search with the help of various adoption workers and organizations.[21] Kathy and Betsy, a pair of female twins born in 1952, were also separated by LWS and raised by different families in New York. According to Kathy's older sister, counseling psychotherapist Liz Mazlish, neither set of parents had been told that their adopted daughter was part of a twin pair.[22] This information remained unknown until Betsy reviewed records revealing the truth about her birth. The twins' reunion at age thirty was a generally warm, loving affair, but ended in tragedy, as I will later explain.

It is curious that Bernard's hidden files start in 1953, not in 1947 or 1952 when Tim and Ilene, and Kathy and Betsy were born, respectively. After all, Bernard was an LWS consultant beginning in 1942. Resolving this discrepancy may only be possible when her sealed materials can be reviewed. It is also worth noting that LWS claimed to have placed twins both apart *and* together in the 1940s and 1950s, before the agency's board formally approved Bernard's separation proposal in the 1960s.[23] Twins placed together have never come forward.

The most crucial and vexing question is: *why?* What prompted Bernard to formulate and advocate separating infant twins and placing them in different homes? Bernard's first published mention of the benefits of separating twins can be found in a 1963 encyclopedia article on adoption. In the only sentence mentioning twins she asserted that each twin would have a "more advantageous life opportunity from placement with 'his own' parents." This comment is set within a larger paragraph in which she states that "it is usually in the best interests of sibling groups to be placed together," although she notes that there may be exceptions. She does not cite literature to support her claims.[24]

Bernard expands on her thinking about this issue over the years, in her own words, written in 1982:

> I was instrumental in formalizing that policy with the Executive Director and senior staff.[25] Actually, such placements of twin pairs had been being made as part of professional casework since the 1950s and into the latter 1960s without any formalizing as a board-approved policy. Up to 1960, when this policy was adopted, the agency made every effort to place sibling groups together, unless there was some contraindication, but with the young infant twins, they were sometimes placed together and sometimes in separate placements, depending on a constellation of factors involving the adoptive parents, the wishes of the birth parent at times, and the state of the twins.[26] Because there was a great deal in the literature by 1960, the advantages of separate placements for the very young twins seemed sufficiently strong and documented that what had been an informally recognized part of placement practice was formulated into a more formal policy.[27]

A 1997 interview with Bernard by journalist Lawrence Wright offers further insights into her reasoning.[28] She claimed that twin children did not enjoy undivided attention from their parents and, consequently, had difficulties forming separate identities. However, Bernard's conclusion was *not* a research-based conclusion, nor was it endorsed in the psychological journals of the 1950s and 1960s as she has claimed. The unique developmental features of growing up as an identical twin—confusion by others, co-twin dependence, delayed language development—that affect some, but not all pairs were recognized by psychologists[29] and parents in those years.[30] Strategies for managing these situations included dressing twins differently, having each twin spend time alone with one parent, and/or enrolling twins in different classes. However, no one suggested raising twins apart from birth.

In her 1997 interview, Bernard insisted that, "the child psychiatry literature at the time we are talking about was of the opinion that the placement of twins who are identical, in separate homes, had advantages for the children into the adoptive families. The advantages including they had more of a chance to develop their own identities." Exactly what studies was Bernard referring to? Her views may have originated from five select case studies, published in the psychoanalytic literature between 1951 and 1961. These particular sources are cited in a 1986 article by Neubauer's twin study colleague, Dr. Samuel Abrams, as justification by "an adoption agency" for placing twins apart.[31] One of them was a book by the psychologist Dorothy Burlingham that described the ongoing early development of three sets of identical twins raised together. It is a classic in the field because of its depth and detail.[32] Later, I will take a closer look at the five studies Abrams cited.

Abrams was quite clear that these papers justified purposefully placing twins apart, allowing the first such twin research investigation in real time. Studying the twins was irresistible: "It soon became clear that an extraordinary research opportunity had presented itself, the study of identical twins reared apart in *prospect*. For the first time—and as far as anyone knew this was really the *first* time—it would be possible to follow systematically children with shared biological heritages as they grew up in different households."[33] Abrams's words echo those of a former research assistant, one who was not connected to the twin study. The assistant had overheard several CDC colleagues discussing the twin project. "It was a monumental study, a once in a lifetime opportunity to put to rest the dilemma of nature and nurture forever."[34]

Abrams did not mention Viola Bernard's contributions to the twin research in his paper. Nor did he provide descriptive details, such as the twins' age at separation and the methods used to determine that the pairs were identical.

IDENTICAL TWINS ONLY

Fraternal twins do not have the visual interest that identical twins do, but their similarities, differences, and twin-to-twin contacts are fascinating and vital to the research enterprise. Bernard and Neubauer omitted fraternal twins from the study to focus exclusively on identical pairs. However, identical twins' similarities alone are less compelling than their similarities relative to other kinships, and fraternal twins are the perfect comparison.

Nevertheless, identical twins are ideal genetic controls for one another, enabling researchers to link environmental differences to differences in co-twins' development. Twins subjected to different environments, training, or treatment result in what is called a co-twin control experiment. If, for example, one twin was raised by an anxious mother and the other was raised by a calm one, the first twin could possibly be more apprehensive in new situations. Of course, the environment is so much more than what we experience after birth, encompassing the effects of prenatal nutrition, maternal health during pregnancy, and other factors that occur in utero.[35] The random variation in prenatal developmental processes affecting brain development, such as interactions among genes and how mutations affect neuronal connections, also underlies individual differences in intelligence, personality, and other traits.[36]

By not including fraternal twins in the LWS-CDC study, the researchers forfeited an informative comparison group. However, Neubauer, Bernard, and their colleagues were first and foremost clinicians, not researchers. Reflecting back over his ten months as Neubauer's assistant, Dr. Lawrence (Larry) Perlman admitted, only part jokingly, that "they didn't know what they were doing."[37]

I tracked down Dr. Esther R. Goshen-Gottstein, a practicing clinical psychologist in Israel, who had come to New York in the 1960s with her husband during his sabbatical. I recognized her name instantly because I had read her paper on the mothering of twins, triplets, and quadruplets when I was a graduate student.[38] Dr. Goshen-Gottstein had worked on the LWS-CDC twin study for two years. "As I understand it, it was a golden opportunity to learn the influence of nature and nurture. They had separated twins at the adoption agency, so Dr. Neubauer, a prominent psychoanalyst, was given a sort of present," she told me. At the same time, Dr. Goshen-Gottstein acknowledged the importance of the twin relationship and believes that the idea of raising twins separately for their psychological benefit is wrong and lacks a solid basis. She also noted that child development theories and practices change over the years, suggesting that what may have been acceptable years ago is no longer tenable. I will address these issues in later chapters.

ENTER PETER NEUBAUER

Bernard's colleague, the New York psychoanalyst Dr. Peter B. Neubauer, clearly recognized the advantage of studying the behavioral development of separated identical twins and triplets, as it unfolded in real time. This situation was unique—it was a goldmine. However, as I explained, their mothers and fathers never knew until years later that they were raising one member of a multiple birth set, and the twins never knew they were part of a pair. The adoptive parents, to whom LWS purposefully reached out, were only told that their child was enrolled in an ongoing developmental study of adopted children. Most of these families were chosen because they had adopted children in the past from LWS, although the twins' families were intentionally matched in certain ways. For example, Bernard believed it was important for children to have a sibling who was several years older.[39] It has also been suggested that the social status of the family was intentionally varied to see how these factors affected genetically identical children, but this has not been confirmed.[40]

A condition of the adoption was that families had to agree to take part in a "developmental study," meaning that researchers would visit their home periodically to test the children. The twins' parents hardly needed convincing—as one mother put it, she would have "learned to fly" if it meant receiving a child, so desperate were she and her husband to have a second baby in their home.[41]

Most, if not all, families would have happily adopted twins, and some couples had even requested them. As one mother confessed to me, "We told LWS that we wanted twins. My husband and I wanted lots of children—growing up, I regretted having only one sibling. We had plenty of money. We would have taken the triplets." A CDC associate said she had heard that no couples were willing to adopt more than one baby, but that was apparently not so.[42]

TALKING ABOUT THE TWIN STUDY

Not everyone agreed to talk with me, even some people who were highly recommended as potentially informative sources regarding Dr. Neubauer's intellect and character. Explanations for their reserve were limited personal contact, discomfort with involvement in a book project, absence of knowledge about the twin study, weariness from controversies surrounding the research, and/or suspicion of journalistic inquiries—even though I clearly explained that I am a professor, not a journalist. One psychologist routinely refused interviews because patients might guess her identity, but agreed to talk as long as I did not report the conversation. Another individual, a close colleague and personal friend of Peter Neubauer, found himself in an "awkward position," unable to comment on the study because he could not be objective. "I have my own issues with the study, tinged with the long-standing closeness we shared." Regardless, he invited me to meet him in New York when I was on the East Coast. He had enthusiastically endorsed Neubauer's 1990 book, *Nature's Thumbprint*, in a congratulatory comment on the cover.

In July 2019 I sent a letter to the Jewish Board of Family and Children's Services, in New York, requesting a meeting. I also requested limited access to the archived records of one twin pair, citing a 2019 article stating that "researchers may gain access to the material [at Yale University] if they obtain written authorization from the Jewish Board."[43] In my request letter I indicated that twins' names and other identifying information could be redacted and that I was interested in just a small portion of the material. I also stated that "I believe the public would benefit from knowing the kinds of observations and tests that were performed, and if the data shed any new insights on what we currently know from twin studies." A reply was issued on September 17: "We had a meeting today to discuss your request and we have concluded that we are not ready to speak with you." I was invited to revisit this matter in the spring when the situation might be different. I sent a note of thanks and asked again about access to the archives. "Check with us in the spring on that also."[44]

Some people never replied to my invitations to contribute to this book despite several attempts on my part. The individuals I did interview were very familiar with Neubauer's work in diverse areas of child psychology. However, the twin study was news to most of them.

Researchers are eager to share their latest ideas, findings, and challenges with colleagues, myself included. We speak at length and with enthusiasm about our ongoing projects, hoping for feedback, encouragement, and even praise. But Neubauer was silent about his twin research, even as he spoke and wrote extensively about his work on childhood fears, mental disorders, child neglect, and single parenting. Many, if not most, people I interviewed—even those who knew him well—were either dimly aware or fully unaware of the study until the release of the documentary film *Three Identical Strangers* in 2018. Psychiatrist Dr. Eugene Mahon met Neubauer in 1972 or 1973 when he was thirty-two and Neubauer was sixty. Neubauer was his supervisor on a psychoanalytic child case. The twin study had been ongoing for twelve years by then and would continue for at least five more. Mahon recalls a series

of meetings, seminars, and dinners over the years as their collegial and social relationship grew. Most dinners, which sometimes included other couples, took place at Hanratty's (now Tre Otto), located between 97th and 98th Streets on Madison Avenue in Manhattan. I asked Mahon what he knew about the twin study. "Given your interest in twin studies I have no great comments for you since Peter did not discuss it with me too much. But I do remember his sharing with us his amazement that twins separated at birth and reared apart might still have the same opening moves in a chess game, suggesting how powerful the role of nature was despite the quite different nurtures."[45]

Figure 2.2. Florence Brown Kreech, former executive director of LWS. Courtesy of Dr. Andy Tanenbaum, Florence Kreech's nephew.

Apparently Neubauer and Bernard also demanded silence from their associates. Paula Kreech, the stepdaughter of LWS's Executive Director Florence Brown Kreech, knew nothing about the twin study or her stepmother's involvement in it until she saw *Three Identical Strangers*. In fact, Paula only saw the film because she had heard that it involved LWS, the agency over which Florence had presided. She was shocked by what she learned since they had been close since Paula's teenage years and had worked in related fields.[46]

Some key players are deceased, namely Dr. Samuel Abrams, but an interview with him conducted by the author Lawrence Wright in the mid-1990s was made available to me. Psychologist Christa Balzert, "one third of the team, an integral part,"[47] left me a phone message saying that she had nothing new to share and referred me to a 2019 article that discussed the study.[48] "Everything I could say is in that article," but she is never mentioned. She also referenced a single interview she had agreed to, one that I would see in late 2019 or early 2020.[49]

PETER B. NEUBAUER, MD: COLLEAGUE AND FRIEND

The way our lives unfold can be drastically derailed by apparently innocent or accidental events with unintended results. Policies carried out by people with seemingly good objectives, but who lack the foresight to consider the implications or consequences of their deeds, can inflict irrevocable damage on individuals, families, science, and society. The LWS-CDC twin study of the 1960s and 1970s took small, incremental steps toward helping unwed mothers find homes for their babies, but twins were separated in the process. I wondered: How could Dr. Neubauer, who was so dedicated to the well-being of families and children, justify leading a study of separated twins and hiding it from their families? Who was he really?

A complex picture of Neubauer as a colleague and friend emerged out of the interviews I conducted with those who knew him. He was described as kind-hearted and smart, a brilliant scholar who cut to the intellectual chase. He apparently cared deeply about the children of the CDC, impressing his colleagues with his rare ability of "childspeak"—speaking the language of children as if he were a child himself while maintaining his identity as an adult. At the same time, he was a terrible researcher in the eyes of those well versed in scientific investigation. The study's structure and procedures were "shaky," and he provided "little support or guidance."[50] Socially, Neubauer could be congenial and charming. During dinners with colleagues, he loved to tell a funny story about a particular chef—a story that grew with each telling. But he was also known for being narcissistic, distant, and obstinate. "Let's just say I wouldn't want to have dinner with him," one colleague admitted.[51]

Peter Bela Neubauer was born on July 5, 1913, to an Austrian Jewish family in the scenic town of Krems an der Denau. Krems is the oldest town in Lower Austria with a history that dates back over one thousand years to 995. Perhaps as a sign of things to come, Krems is the twin town of Stein, first mentioned in 1072.[52]

Details from a self-report questionnaire for Austrian Jewish immigrants offer insights into Neubauer's early and later life.[53] He grew up in an apartment with his mother Rose, a housewife; father Samuel, a teacher; younger sister Ruth; and older brother Yehuda. The family also employed a servant. German was the only language spoken in the home. The family followed Orthodox Jewish traditions, such as eating kosher food and attending synagogue services every Sabbath. Most of his close friends were his Jewish classmates, although he counted some non-Jewish children as friends during his early years.

As a teenager and young man, Neubauer cared about social issues. He was part of an organization called Blue-White (Blau-Weiß), one of the first and most influential Jewish youth movements founded in Germany in 1912, but later active in Austria and Czechoslovakia. Blue-White promoted a Zionist program and provided a social outlet for Jewish youth who felt alienated in their respective countries.[54] Neubauer later joined Hatzomer Hatzair (The Young Guard), a European Zionist youth movement founded in 1913.[55] He noted that he was the "leader of the group," but his actual standing in the organization is unclear. His involvement in important social issues of the day would be evident throughout his lifetime.

Neubauer's hometown of Krems had a population of seventeen thousand in which the Jewish community remained largely isolated from the town's non-Jewish inhabitants and activities. There was some contact between the Jewish community and the socialists, but most were Catholic conservatives. Krems and the entire country of Austria shunned and demeaned their Jewish citizens, such that Neubauer recalled continuous antisemitism in the town. "I was always aware that I was an outsider. The gymnasium teacher [made] more openly antisemitic statement[s],"[56] and most, but not all, of his non-Jewish childhood friends severed their associations with him. When Hitler came to power in 1933, the Neubauer family hoped to find a solution in Israel, to be proud of their Jewish tradition. Aware of the danger posed to them by Hitler, they saw Zionism as their means of "rescue from being a victim."[57]

Neubauer left the University of Vienna in June 1933 at the age of twenty to complete his medical studies at the University of Bern, Switzerland, which he did in 1938. He claimed that what saved him was his father's fate—Samuel Neubauer had lost his job and had been forced by the Nazis to destroy the temple.[58] The family's apartment was also confiscated. None of Neubauer's immediate family members was sent to a concentration camp, but many of his uncles, aunts, and cousins were. His mother, Rose Blau, passed away in 1931 when Neubauer was eighteen, but his father, brother Yehuda, and sister Ruth left Austria for Palestine. His sister became a member of Kibbutz Dalia, located in northern Israel, while his brother joined the Israeli contingent of the British army and later died in Northern Africa.

Neubauer left Switzerland for the United States in April 1941, beginning his new life in New York City and becoming a US citizen in 1946. He married the late Susan Raskin and raised two sons, Alexander (Sandy) born in 1954 and Joshua born in 1959.[59] As a psychiatrist with psychoanalytic training he became immersed in the lively field of child psychiatry and thrived on the professional and social excitement that New York had to offer. He trained at the New York Psychoanalytic Institute and studied with Sigmund Freud's daughter Anna, a distinguished psychoanalyst in her own right.[60] He and Anna Freud became friends as well as colleagues. Anna Freud also joined the Yale Child Study Center where their mutual colleague, Albert J. Solnit, was a prominent member.[61]

From 1951 until 1985 Neubauer served as director of the Child Development Center of the Jewish Board of Guardians, renamed the Jewish Board of Family and Children's Services in 1978.[62] From the 1970s on he edited, or co-edited, *The Psychoanalytic Study of the Child*, as well as volumes on child development and kibbutz rearing.[63] He also held leadership positions in professional organizations. In 1977 Neubauer helped launch Zero to Three, an organization dedicated to improving the lives of babies and toddlers, a sequel to his earlier social involvements.

Neubauer served on the boards of the Sigmund Freud Archives, Anna Freud Foundation, and Viola W. Bernard Foundation.[64] His publications include the 1990 book *Nature's Thumbprint*, co-authored with his son Alexander, as well as numerous articles and commentaries on child development. Among them is his 1980 foreword to Professor Niels Juel-Nielsen's second volume on separated Danish twins—short, sweet, and suspect. I will return to this particular work later. At the time of his death in 2008, Neubauer was a clinical professor of psychiatry at New York University and a training and supervising analyst at the psychoanalytic institutes of Columbia University and New York University. He also maintained a private clinical practice in Manhattan.[65] One of his most famous clients was Harry Belafonte.[66] In his memoir, Belafonte wrote that "Peter was wise and warm, perhaps the most empathetic person I've ever met." Belafonte convinced his best friend Sidney to engage Neubauer as his therapist, but his wife Julie convinced him that they were too close, that he was part of Sidney's story. Julie suggested her own psychoanalyst—Dr. Viola Bernard.

Throughout his lifetime, Neubauer continued to speak and write in German as well as in English, and while he was no longer religious, he remained "deeply identified with Jewish life and causes." He returned to Austria several times as an invited speaker at psychoanalytic conferences and other professional events. He is known for his views on the effects of television violence and horror films on children's behavior, the impact of rearing in one-parent families, and the many meanings of play.

TALKING TO LAWRENCE WRIGHT

The Pulitzer Prize–winning author Lawrence Wright is credited with discovering the connections between LWS, the LWS-CDC twin study, and the separation of the identical triplets, Robert Shafran, Edward Galland, and David Kellman.[67] His 1993 interview with Peter Neubauer presents a complex character, a blend of brilliant scholarship, and hardheaded investigation when it came to the twins.

To my mind, Neubauer was ahead of his time in thinking critically about the contribution of genetic factors to individual differences in behavior. Behavioral genetics—the discipline concerned with the genetic and environmental influences on individual differences in behavior—while entering the mainstream of psychology in the 1980s, was contentious in some circles and still is.[68] Genetics was not something that most psychoanalysts considered in their clinical settings. The finding that identical twins reared apart were as alike as identical twins reared together in personality, religiosity, attitudes, and interests, and nearly as alike in general intelligence, was unexpected and counterintuitive. But these results were reported consistently by independent investigators working in different laboratories around the world, including the MISTRA.[69]

These findings were misconstrued by some as evidence that parenting didn't matter. My colleagues and I never said this, nor did we diminish the critical role played by mothers and fathers. We explained that warm, sensitive parenting within the normal range of human development was critical for positive child outcomes. We also showed that different parental features and background characteristics did not significantly alter individual differences in the behavioral outcomes of the separated twins we studied in Minnesota. For example, fathers' socioeconomic status, mothers' education, and physical facilities in the home were unrelated to how similar the twins' IQ scores turned out to be.

It appears that reared-apart identical twins create their own environments from the opportunities available to them, compatible with their genetically influenced predispositions—that is how they end up being so alike even when they grow up far apart, sometimes in different countries. The reared-apart identical British twins, Dorothy and Bridget, were raised in homes that differed in educational resources and values. However, the less advantaged twin had a natural passion for reading, obtained a library card, and visited the library often. When the twins met at age thirty-four, they discovered a shared love of the same historical novels by the same author. All of us have a similar role in selecting the people, places, and events that surround us.

The same objective family environment is *not* the same subjective family environment for all children. One child may thrive on electronic gadgets, while his or her sibling may delight in bats and balls. Two hours of story-telling each night may thrill one child and bore another. Of course, children exposed to harsh, abusive environments, enough to overwhelm their genetically based predispositions, will not thrive socially or intellectually. Despite good physical care, orphanage-raised children deprived of playful interactions use their hands as toys, do not laugh or smile, and show stereotypical behaviors such as head banging and body rocking. Educationally impoverished environments do not allow children to fully develop their interests and talents.

Neubauer had an intuitive grasp of these developmental processes. "Because you have a certain makeup, therefore, you responded to this kind of a father and this kind of a mother in your own way when your sibling may have acted differently." And "the fact that many people do not reach their potential does not mean that [the behavior] is not genetically influenced—[it means] the environment interferes with the potential."[70]

MEETING DR. NEUBAUER

I met Dr. Neubauer just once, in December 2004, in his New York City apartment. Clinical psychologist Dr. Larry Perlman, who had arranged this visit, and I were escorted into a room decorated with interesting artifacts acquired during Neubauer's travels. Casually but stylishly dressed for the occasion in a gray shirt, navy sweater, and dark slacks, Neubauer was a gracious host. He was excited to learn that his younger cousin, Liliane Neubauer, was one of my high school friends. But he kept some distance. Perlman and I were there to learn more about the twin study, and he knew that. He didn't smile in the photos we took that day.

"They must be studied!" This was Neubauer's declaration upon hearing that newborn twins were being separated. He expressed considerable pride, even pleasure, in the fact that he and his team had been "there from the birth." Without hesitation, he volunteered that he had tried to solicit the participation of Catholic Charities, another adoption agency in New York City. Sister Bernard—no relation to Viola—refused to cooperate at first, saying that twins had been put together naturally and should not be placed apart. Neubauer countered that adoption agencies separate mothers and babies all the time, and these relationships, too, are formed naturally. Sister Bernard eventually agreed to help him, but she never provided the promised pairs.[71] Other adoption agencies were approached to be part of the study, as I will explain in the next chapter.

Looking back, how did Dr. Neubauer feel about the twin study? He firmly believed that what he had done—studying the twins without their knowledge or the knowledge of their parents—was completely acceptable. He appeared surprised that his work had been questioned, especially by the media. He was also untroubled by having denied the twins the truth about their biological beginnings and the opportunity to experience the closest of human social relationships.[72]

It is worth noting that the health benefits of having a genetic duplicate are lost when twins are separated. Genetically identical twins are ideal when it comes to tracking disease risk or needing an organ.[73] In fact, the first successful kidney donation and transplantation took place between identical male twins. This case was reported in major medical journals, initially in 1956, with a progress report in 1960, several years prior to the start of the LWS-CDC twin study.[74] Surely Neubauer and Bernard would have known about this case. They were clearly aware of identical twins' shared disease predispositions—a passage from *Nature's Thumbprint* describes a pair of separated identical twins whose spontaneous convulsions were treated differently by their respective physicians. "If each pediatrician had known that his patients' convulsions were shared by an identical twin, they each might have approached the condition differently." The source of this report was not given.[75]

I wonder—if the researchers had observed a serious condition in one separated twin, would they have alerted the other twins' family who could have taken precautions? Or would that have derailed the study? I regret not having asked Neubauer that question. I did pose it to one of his former research assistants who replied, "I don't remember."

Neubauer and I sparred a bit over the nature of the triplets' placentae. Neubauer questioned whether the three were truly identical because there had been two placentae, not one.[76] I reminded him of the well-documented fact that identical twins and triplets can have a single shared placenta, separate placentae, or fused placentae. Neubauer did not and would not accept this. I also explained that in 1980 the triplets had participated in the MISTRA and had undergone extensive serological (blood group) analyses, physical measurement (height, weight, body mass index), and dermatologlyphic (fingerprint) studies. Results from these tests, when combined, indicated that the triplets were identical with over 99.9 percent probability.[77] Again, he dismissed these scientific data. According to Dr. Aaron Esman whom I spoke with in 2019, "He [Peter] did things the way he wanted to—his way."[78] Esman knew Neubauer "reasonably well" from their associations with the Jewish Board of Guardians, but they worked independently. Esman had heard about a "twin study," but not about twins being separated.

Neubauer mentioned Walter Cronkite of CBS's *60 Minutes* as an example of his interrogation by the media. Two attempts at presenting the twin study on that program were called off suddenly, incidents I will describe later.

THROUGH THE EYES OF OTHERS

I began this phase of my research in earnest in June 2019. My first contact was a psychiatrist turned publisher, Dr. Arnold (Arnie) Richards. Richards is a member of the Contemporary Freudian Society and Editor-in-Chief at ipbooks.net, an agency that publishes books on psychoanalysis. He was referred to me by Dr. Ilene Serlin, a San Diego psychologist and fraternal member of a triplet set that includes identical twin sisters, Barbara and Erica.[79] Richards admired and stood up for Neubauer, who was twenty years his senior. "An excellent psychoanalyst, devoted to Freud, got a bum rap. Viola Bernard was the true villain—she decided to separate the twins. He was doing his research."[80] Richards's defense was not unqualified. "Once twins were separated it was not okay—he could have told the parents—the lack of transparency was not okay."

Referrals from Richards turned up other sources in an ever-expanding circle. Richards told me about a letter of protest against the film *Three Identical Strangers*, initiated by Dr. Lois Oppenheim. Oppenheim chairs the Department of Modern Languages and Literatures at Montclair State University in Montclair, New Jersey. She and I had been in touch since February 2019, but she had not mentioned this letter. She had been preparing an article about the twin study with psychoanalyst Dr. Leon Hoffman for the *Journal of the American Medical Association* (*JAMA*), and had contacted Dr. Larry Perlman for an interview. Perlman had passed her contact information to me, leading to a series of telephone calls and email exchanges between us.

Oppenheim had known Peter Neubauer for many years having met him "decades and decades ago. . . . He was incredibly kind and smart. He loved what he did, and his work was so important to him." Though Oppenheim had known Neubauer for a long time, she said she had little to tell me. I asked her about the protest letter that had been sent to the American Academy of Arts and Sciences and to CNN. I contacted all but one of the fifty-two signatories and will share their views later in the book.

Both Hoffman and Oppenheim were generous in offering their assistance during our email exchanges and telephone conversations. Hoffman forwarded several articles of interest and suggested one or two people for me to interview. Oppenheim offered to contact several people on my behalf, such as Samuel Abrams's widow Barbara, who had helped organize the twin study data, but suggested that it was unlikely any of them would be willing to talk to me. I contacted several of these people on my own who did agree to talk.

Curiously, the *JAMA* article indicated that "Bernard had no substantive connection to Neubauer or the Child Development Center and influenced the agency's policy without any interest in research opportunities." In contrast, the Columbia University archive finding aid states that, in addition to many of her [Bernard's] personal papers, "There are also records of her participation in the 'Twin Study,' a long-term study of identical twins reared apart that was jointly sponsored by the Child Development Center, Louise Wise Services, and Columbia University." Bernard's handwritten notes, such as "Neubauer / Twins," "Neubauer } Twins," and "Neubauer (Twins)" are scattered throughout her daily calendar entries. Bernard placed a letter explaining the reasons for separate placement in the files of each individual twin in the event that this information would be helpful to staff members and to the twins in the future.[81]

THE END OF LOUISE WISE SERVICES

LWS closed its doors in February 2004, a decision their administrators explained by reductions in public funding and a yearly deficit of one million dollars. New York University Professor Emeritus Trudy Festinger, daughter of Justine Wise Polier, gave me a more complete account of what had happened. Financial issues were involved, but the main reason LWS closed was that the agency provided many mental health services and mental health consultations that the city was unwilling to support. Rather than eliminating these services, the agency preferred to close. "That's what I was told by various board members," Festinger added.[82] LWS's closing did not please several of their social workers who objected to the short notice and to their reduction in severance pay. In addition, union sources faulted the agency for selling off four of its

Manhattan properties for millions of dollars. Still, many in New York City mourned the loss of the agency which had served children and families for years and had consistently received high ratings.[83]

LWS's records were transferred to Spence-Chapin, a nearby New York adoption agency established at about the same time. This transition meant that "thousands of people whose lives were affected by adoptions will continue to have limited access to birth records and other material that might aid them with reunion efforts or health crises."[84] In accordance with legal considerations in the early 2000s, information identifying biological parents could not be given to adoptees, but medical data could be disclosed. However, if both mother and child joined a state or local registry, they would be notified of the match and could decide if they wished to meet. Two New York state laws, passed in 2019, overturned this restriction, enabling adoptees to obtain both a certified copy of their birth certificate *and* information about their biological parents when they turn eighteen. These changes ended over eighty years of secrecy surrounding the backgrounds of children relinquished for adoption. The original law, enacted in 1935, was signed by Herbert Lehman, then-governor of New York state and the father of an adopted child.[85]

It seems that New York State had denied the agency the ability to open their files to adoptees. That was before June 2019 when the new laws were passed, so the situation should have changed. Managing the vast accumulation of records would overwhelm the staff, given that the twins' records were not kept separate from those of the hundreds of non-twin adoptees.[86] Interestingly, Bernard had consulted for Spence-Chapin at one time, but her association with that agency is noted in only one life history interview conducted in 1985.[87]

Given the controversies surrounding the LWS-CDC twin study, and the fact that the data were never published, this project is not cited in the scientific literature. But in the 2019 *JAMA* article there is mention of a "little known" approximately two-hundred-page manuscript, "Becoming Mind: Identical Twins Reared Apart," unpublished to "protect the families' privacy."[88] In response to my question about the nature and whereabouts of this draft, Oppenheim paused. "I cannot tell you anything now. I can't tell you any more, [but] before you finish your book you will know more." I have finished my book, and I do not know more.[89] I had never heard of this manuscript because it had never been mentioned in any prior publication. Oppenheim chastised the two documentary filmmakers for implying that no comprehensive report was available.

Dr. Viola Bernard's 1998 obituary in the *New York Times* did not mention her affiliation with LWS or the study of twins. Neither did Peter Neubauer's, following his death in 2008.

A CELEBRATION OF "TWINSHIP"

The psychologist Dorothy Burlingham, the younger sister of identical twins, authored one of the five references Abrams cited to support LWS's twin separation policy. Later in the book I will show how this source was taken largely out of context and did not advance the policy. For now, it is interesting that having older twin sisters, Julia and Louise (called by her middle name Comfort), is thought to explain Burlingham's interest in twins and her desire for the same close connection that her sisters enjoyed.[90] As a child she felt excluded from their close relationship, writing to her grandson Michael of her loneliness after their deaths in 1973 and 1974. Michael did not think of his aunt as someone who felt lonely.[91]

Burlingham maintained a close professional and personal relationship with Anna Freud, whom she had met in 1924 when both women were in their thirties.[92] Recall that Freud and Neubauer were close colleagues and close friends. One of Neubauer's professional associates joined Neubauer and Freud at informal meetings where many different topics were discussed, including twin research.[93] At first, this individual believed that Freud would have known about the study, but then expressed some uncertainty; despite his own close association with Neubauer, he had been unaware of his colleague's twin research until the release of *Three Identical Strangers*. He had also met Dorothy Burlingham, but said that she never mentioned the twin study either. But Burlingham did know Neubauer, even though there is no mention of him in her detailed biography authored by her grandson, Michael Burlingham.

Burlingham knew Neubauer well enough to arrange for her granddaughter Randi Scott and grandson Michael to secure jobs at the CDC. Randi was a fellow at the CDC in her capacity as a nursery schoolteacher. She arrived in 1966 after having taught at the Hampstead Nurseries in London, founded by her grandmother and Anna Freud. Michael taught woodworking skills to prekindergarten children in 1973. He dimly recalled meeting Neubauer once or twice, while admitting he knew nothing about woodworking. Michael stayed on the job for a few weeks during his work-study term. The twin study was ongoing in 1966 and 1973, but neither of Burlingham's grandchildren was aware of it.[94]

The question remains: Did Burlingham and Freud know about the LWS-CDC twin study? Surely Neubauer was cognizant of Burlingham's seminal 1952 study of three identical twin pairs, cited by Abrams as one of five sources supporting the separate placement of twins. Perhaps if he had read it, Neubauer overlooked or misread Burlingham's closing remarks. She concluded that identical twins experience more intense rivalry than non-twins, even while they are supposed to get along. She also noted that some parents try to alleviate the situation by severing the twin relationship, separating the twins as much as possible or sending one twin away to be raised elsewhere, although she provided no source for these extreme and rare decisions. Is it possible that these remarks belie her hidden knowledge of the twin study? Regardless, Burlingham was against such practices, asserting that, "This [ending the twins' relationship or sending one away] seems an inadequate method of solving the situation. Twins cannot avoid the difficulties which are inherent in their twinship, just as ordinary children cannot help being influenced by the fact of their being an eldest, youngest or a middle child."[95]

Correspondence exchanged between Burlingham and Freud show that they enjoyed an "ideal friendship" as each other's "twin." Dorothy wrote, "I had such pleasure in your letter about the identical twins. It makes me happy and proud that we have such a bond."[96] The intensity of their relationship did not escape notice. Anna's nephew, W. Ernest Freud, noted that his aunt may have "recreated a sibling, if not a twin relationship" with Dorothy.

Burlingham and Freud were friends and "twins" for a lifetime, enjoying a relationship that is legendary. The advantages of twinship were apparent to Burlingham—companionship, intimacy, completeness. A 1979 photo shows Dorothy and Anna seated across a table at London's Maresfield Gardens Library, smiling at one another.[97] When it came to the LWS twins the bond was broken. When it came to adoption, playing God was "inevitable."[98]

• 3 •

How Did It Work?

Inside the Twin Study

𝒯here is a claim that twenty-one children had been intentionally separated from their twin brother or sister by Louise Wise Services (LWS)—the members of nine twin pairs and one triplet set—but that the final study sample

Figure 3.1. Sterling Memorial Library at Yale University, in New Haven, CT. The library holds the twin study data in the Child Development Center's archives, circa 1960–1980. Photo by Dr. Nancy L. Segal.

included thirteen.[1] The accuracy of these numbers cannot be fully confirmed without access to the twins' adoption records maintained by Spence-Chapin or Viola Bernard's papers held by Columbia University. However, Yale University's archives, located in the Sterling Memorial Library, hold a few clues.[2]

Information for eleven children is variously stockpiled within Dr. Neubauer's sixty-five containers. The different twins are labeled Child-1 to Child-11. The one set of triplets might be Child-7, Child-8, and Child-9, as these individuals are listed several times as a group of three. As I indicated earlier, some fraternal twins were separated but were omitted from the study. I can account for the remaining eight children in four sets, but this does not prove that no other pairs were placed apart. For example, there is Justin Goldberg, an entertainment executive from Los Angeles whose incredible look-alike was spotted by his daughter in 2017.[3] This chance encounter would normally arouse interest, not suspicion, but became extremely significant in light of the twins' separate placements and Justin's birth in 1966. Could Justin be a separated twin? His story and the life histories of all the twins are explored in later chapters.

IDENTICAL AND FRATERNAL TWINS REARED APART

The identical twins and triplets who were separated and studied are:

- Susan and Anne[4]
- Ellen and Melanie
- Doug and Howard
- Sharon and Lisa[5]
- Robert, David, and Edward

A fifth identical set, Paula and Elyse, were followed briefly before being dropped from the study. At first, I wondered if the missing set was a pair of seven- or eight-year-old twin boys raised apart in New York and New Jersey who supposedly met through a chance encounter. I heard two slightly different versions of this story, one told to Lawrence Wright by Viola Bernard. According to Bernard, "What we did there was, as long as one family knew about it, one twin, because of recognition through a neighbor, we felt obligated to tell the other one." Bernard said that she worked with both families after the discovery and still received phone calls from the two twins. She chuckled when she came to the end of the story.[6] The general storyline is correct, but many details are not. I know this because I discovered that the twins were girls—Susan and Anne—who shared their story with me for the first time. They were dropped from the study once their twinship was discovered at age six or seven, but their early data are in Neubauer's archive.

These young twins were omitted from the study because of their parents' surprise knowledge of their daughters' twinship and the social contacts that were likely to follow. According to Bernard and Neubauer, these factors would have interfered with the study's rigid parameters—parents could not know that their adoptive child was a twin because of the "mystique" surrounding identical twins, the effects such knowledge might have on the parents' treatment of their children, and the twins' inevitable feeling of a need to meet.[7] The study staff also believed that prior reared-apart twin studies failed because the twins and parents knew there was an identical sibling out there somewhere.[8] But they were wrong because in many cases the families of twins in prior studies were unaware that their child had a twin.[9]

The separated fraternal twins who were not studied are:

- Tim and Ilene[10]
- Paula and Marjorie
- Michele and Allison

The twins whose twin type is undecided and who were not studied are:

- Kathy and Betsy

The psychological and social situations of fraternal twins differ considerably from those of identical twins who differ from all other sibling pairs. This twin type difference, acknowledged by some early psychoanalysts,[11] is largely because fraternal twins share 50 percent of their genes, on average, whereas identical twins share 100 percent. Consequently, same-sex fraternal twins generally do not look physically alike, nor do they show the same degree of behavioral resemblance as identical twins. There is overlap, of course, in that some fraternal twins look and/or act alike in certain ways—both twins may have blonde hair and blue eyes, or both may love reading and dislike math, much the same way any set of siblings might share those traits. I have observed many fraternal twins, including some pairs that look nearly identical, and other pairs that look almost unrelated.[12] Kathy and Betsy looked very much alike, but just different enough, to make their twin type uncertain; I will say more about them in chapter 5. Paula and Marjorie and Michele and Allison showed enough physical differences in hair color, eye color, and/or facial structure to be confidently classified as fraternal. Tim and Ilene were classified as fraternal due to their sex difference. The dramatic occurrence of fraternal twins who appear unrelated is now called "biracial twinning"—fraternal twins born to parents of different ancestry. In such cases, each twin shows more of the physical characteristics of one parent, due to the different genes passed on to each child. Biracial twins have aroused considerable public and professional fascination.[13]

It is difficult to understand how Bernard's reasoning about the need to place twins apart applies to fraternal twin pairs. These different-looking, different-acting twins would have less trouble than identical twins in developing separate identities if raised together, at least little more than ordinary siblings close in age. Perhaps Bernard's concern over twins having to share parental attention and/or overburdening their parents if raised together were decisive factors. Or maybe their twin type (identical or fraternal) was inconclusive early on, so the investigators erred in the direction that would add cases to the study.

Most modern twin studies use DNA analysis to assign twin pairs as identical or fraternal. Agreement across fifteen to eighteen short tandem repeat markers (STRs) assigns twins as identical with 99.9 percent certainty. STRs are uniquely repeating patterns in certain regions of the DNA. Given their high degree of individuality, it would be highly unlikely for two people to match across fifteen markers and to not be identical twins. Of course, any STR differences between twins means that they are fraternal.[14] Such procedures were not available when the LWS-Child Development Center (CDC) twin study was ongoing so twin researchers, including Bernard and Neubauer, relied on blood typing, placental examination, and dermatoglyphic similarities (fingerprint and footprints) for answers.

According to Bernard, placentae and blood were transported to Columbia University's genetics department for analysis. She recalls hauling a pail full of placentae there herself "to see whether there were one or two."[15] Recall that one-third of identical twins have separate placentae, as do all fraternal twins. Moreover, 55 percent of identical twins with separate chorions and 49 percent of fraternal twins have fused placentae,[16] information known in the 1960s and discussed in a major 1970 book on the biology of twinning.[17] This situation would have complicated diagnosing the twin type based on placental inspection alone. And fingerprints are notoriously uncertain indices of whether twins are identical or fraternal, because they are significantly affected by events in the womb, such as temperature and fetal positioning.[18] Very extensive blood-typing, involving about eighteen blood groups, would have been the most accurate measure of twin type in the 1960s and 1970s, as it would be extremely unlikely for fraternal twins to match across the full series.[19] Whether this was done may only be known by reviewing the hidden files.

How soon the twin-typing results were made available to Bernard and Neubauer is unknown, but they seem *not* to have been considered with respect to separation. They only seem to have made a difference with respect to whether the twins were studied.

Are there other reasons behind the separation of the fraternal twins? In addition to Bernard's worries over parental burdening, some psychoanalytically oriented clinicians believed that the identity and relationship problems shown by identical twins also characterized some fraternal twins.[20] It is hard to judge such cases because the methods by which twin type was determined are not given in the published reports. Regardless, it is possible that LWS justified separating fraternal twins if they never developed "the twinning reaction."

THE TWINNING REACTION

The *twinning reaction* is a psychoanalytically derived concept that first appeared in publication in 1961. However, it was described before that, in 1960 and in 1961, at several psychoanalytic association meetings, including those held at the New York Psychoanalytic Society and Institute. It is likely that Bernard and/or Neubauer attended many of these sessions, given their affiliation with the society. The New York Psychoanalytic Society and Institute has a record of the 1961 meeting, but it does not have a list of attendees. Note that while this concept was formally named and defined *after* the 1947 and 1952 separations of the first two fraternal pairs, its features were described in psychodynamically oriented publications *before* that time, as early as 1933.[21] Therefore, it is possible that Bernard was aware of what she considered to be the problems of being raised with a twin before these problems had a name.

The *twinning reaction* consists of (1) "mutual identification, and (2) part fusion of the self-representation and the object representation of the other member of the pair. This leads to a diffuseness of ego boundaries between the two people."[22] It is not exclusive to twins, but may characterize near-in-age siblings and spouses. The more current, commonly used terms for the social ties between twins are *twin bond* or *twin relationship*, which variously refer to the unusual closeness, intimacy, and selflessness that characterize mostly identical twinships, but extend to some fraternal twinships.[23] These terms are not necessarily tied to any particular theoretical framework as is the twinning reaction.

Bernard spoke of the twinning reaction as an "attachment between the two twins." She explained that newborn twins relinquished for adoption were kept together and cared for by a foster family until suitable adoptive parents were found. During their time in foster care, if it was determined that a twinning reaction had developed between them then the twins were not separated, due to possible psychological trauma. If, however, the twins did not show any special attachment to one another, it was felt that they could be safely separated. Who decided the twins' fate and by what methods are not known. Given that there is no evidence that any LWS twins were adopted together, one might conclude that *none* of the twins showed close attachment to one another. But that would be wildly incorrect. What is known about infant twins' social development, and what we know from observations of the separated twins Howard and Doug, suggest otherwise.

Infants as young as six months of age show social interest in one another, but this can occur even earlier for twins.[24] Observations by the late renowned pediatrician T. Berry Brazelton reveal that at three to four months of age, an identical female twin appeared disoriented when her twin sister was taken from the room. When separated like this, the infant stopped moving or feeding when she heard her twin sister's vocalizing.[25] Neubauer recognized Brazelton as one "who has studied infancy with so much insight."[26] Here is a brief look at Doug and Howard's early days together, although more will be said about them in chapter 9.

Doug and Howard, born in 1963, were separated at six months of age. As early as four months of age, they were observed interacting with one another while in foster care, consistent with Brazelton's accelerated social timeline for twins. Notes made during their first half-year together describe their pattern of interplay—which twin started the contact and which twin responded. They were judged to be "stable human objects" in each other's lives.

THE TWINS' MOTHERS

Relinquishing a child for adoption is a painful process, but it is usually done with the children's best interests at heart.[27] According to Bernard, when twins were born the LWS staff members met with the birth mother to explain the advantages of separation. If this plan was not agreeable to the mother, then it was not supposed to be done. However, there is evidence to the contrary.

At age twenty, Hedda Abbott delivered fraternal twin girls in November 1960, the end of a difficult pregnancy that kept her bedridden. She still refers to them fondly as "my twins," but she never regretted giving them up. "I wanted them, but I was young and immature and could not keep them, so I gave them a better life." But Hedda wanted her twins to stay together. "They were not supposed to be separated. I would not sign any adoption papers [with LWS] until I saw them." She insists that she eventually signed papers with this understanding, but the documents disappeared from her mother's house.

When one of the twins found her years later, Hedda asked her how her sister was. "I became unglued when I learned they had been separated."[28]

Hedda keeps a picture of her twin girls close by, taken whey they were three months old. They were kept together in the same crib until at least that age. When a home was then found for one of the twins, her twin sister was left alone for a month.[29]

In 2018 and upon request, Michele Mordkoff, a separated fraternal twin from a different pair, received a letter from Spence-Chapin, the agency that now manages the LWS records. The letter stated that Michele's birth mother had agreed with the plan to separate her twins, but Michele, who has met her birth mother, claims that the opposite is true. Michele believes that a proper translation of Spence-Chapin's words is that "no one was deceived." In other words, mothers were never asked if they preferred placing their twins together or apart, so placing them apart was not truly a deception. Michele insists that her mother was "told, not asked [about the separation]." LWS had explained (to her mother) that it was not possible to keep the twins together, and/or that no family was willing to adopt them both. But we know that some families were willing and eager to take two twins, even three triplets. A mother I spoke with had specifically requested a pair of twins to adopt, but unknowingly received just one. In fact, she and her husband had asked LWS for twins twice, when they adopted their son, and again when they adopted their daughter—who had been separated from her twin.[30]

ATTEMPTS TO RECRUIT TWINS:
BEYOND LOUISE WISE SERVICES

It appears that all of the twins who were studied were separated through LWS. Recall that Neubauer's attempt to solicit the cooperation of Catholic Charities was unsuccessful. However, reviewing available documents from Bernard's archives suggests that other agencies were aware of LWS's interest in separated twins, and tried to be helpful. Interestingly, a few clinicians interested in studying twins that had already been separated sought assistance from LWS for furthering their own work. Communications between then LWS Executive Director Mrs. Florence Brown and Viola Bernard show this to be the case. And aside from their letters, meetings, and memos, Bernard's notation "Florence / Twins" can be found throughout many of Bernard's calendar entries.

Florence Brown was LWS's executive director for nearly thirty years, from the late 1940s until her retirement in 1979 at age sixty-six or sixty-seven. Clearly, she held this position during the 1960s and 1970s while the twin study was underway. As executive director she would have been responsible for all operations of the various programs—professional, financial, hiring, and policy. Photographs show her at meetings with Viola Bernard and other members of the board, as well as at staff meetings and holiday parties. She enjoyed meeting clients. Official LWS stationery included her name in the letterhead. Florence Brown—later Florence Kreech upon remarrying—was recognized for her work by a LWS symposium held in her honor. The October 1969 event was titled "Unmarried Parents and Their Children: Trends, Challenges, Concerns."[31]

Brown was a forward thinker when it came to adoption. Through an extensive series of papers, she wrote sensitively and persuasively about the significance of care for all children and the practice of transracial adoption. During her tenure, the Louise Wise Agency became a pioneer in such practices. Her contribution to an edited volume, *Social Work and Ethnicity*, is impressive and informative in this regard. In 1952, LWS amended its by-laws, enabling the provision of care for all children regardless of race, color, and creed. [32] LWS also placed more children for the Indian Adoption Project than any other American agency.[33]

Brown's role as a central figure in LWS operations is further underlined by her testimony in Arthur ROSS et al., Respondents-Appellants, v. LOUISE WISE SERVICES, INC.[34] The case, decided by the New York Court of Appeals in May 2007, was brought by a couple who had adopted a son from LWS in 1961.[35] The boy showed serious behavioral disturbances—hitting and cursing at his family, threatening people with objects, experiencing night terrors—beginning at age nine and escalating over the years. His adoptive parents had not been told that their son's biological family had a history of schizophrenia. According to Brown, "psychiatrists 'felt for many, many years we knew so little about schizophrenia and they felt very strongly about not putting labels on people.'" Kreech knew that studies were underway, but the agency's psychiatrists "knew too little about hereditary factors," and had no certain information that a child of a parent or parents who had schizophrenia had a greater risk of developing it. "[T]here were children that may have come from parents—and, again, they wouldn't put labels on them—whose parents were disturbed, but it did not necessarily follow that the children were going to be disturbed." An expert for the plaintiffs, Dr. Dolores Malaspina, testified that while American psychiatrists theorized that the roots of schizophrenia might lie in dysfunctional family dynamics, genetic influences on schizophrenia were known by 1911.

Unfortunately, Brown's story has received little attention even though she played significant roles in LWS activities and in the adoption community at large.

Florence Brown, née Goldman, was born on November 26, 1912. Conversations with Brown's stepdaughter, retired hospital administrator Paula Kreech; her nephew, computer science professor Dr. Andy Tanenbaum; and nieces, Carolyn Stern and Eleanor Pine, give the impression of a lovely, kind, and generous woman. I met Tanenbaum in his office at the Vrije Universiteit in Amsterdam, The Netherlands, in the summer 2018. He had only positive memories of Brown, albeit based on family gatherings such as Passover dinners and other holiday events.[36] He was a young boy at the time and had little knowledge of what his Aunt Florence did for a living. He always thought that Edwin, the child that Brown and her husband Bernie brought along, was their common son. However, later genealogical research revealed that Edwin was Uncle Bernie's son and Brown's stepson and that they had never had children together. "She was very kind to him [Edwin] and treated him like her son," Tanenbaum recalled. Brown very much regretted never having had children of her own.

Brown was not happy in her marriage to Bernie, and the couple divorced in 1962. She became Florence Kreech following her second marriage in 1965 to attorney, social worker, and widower Alfred (Fred) Kreech. The two met through Kreech's secretary who had left Fred's office to become Brown's personal assistant at LWS.

Years after his Aunt Florence's death, Tanenbaum learned about her LWS connection, became obsessed with knowing more, and did some searching. He discovered a woman he was certain was Florence Brown's stepdaughter, Paula Kreech, and someone who might be her stepson. As it turned out, Florence Brown did not have another stepson, but a second stepdaughter, Paula's sister, Diane, now deceased.

I returned to California and got to work immediately because of Tanenbaum's urging—he worried that Kreech's stepchildren might be aging and their memories fading. I left a message on Paula's phone machine and several weeks later when she returned from vacation, she called me. We had several lengthy telephone conversations and meetings after that. It was clear that Paula, now in her seventies, was baffled—because Florence had *never* mentioned the twin study to her, nor had she mentioned two of the main researchers, Drs. Peter Neubauer and Samuel Abrams. But Paula and Florence often spoke of an interracial adoption study and of Viola Bernard.

Upon seeing *Three Identical Strangers*, Paula was shocked, angered, and "torn apart" by what might have been the possible portrayal of her stepmother as a cold, unfeeling individual, downing champagne with other LWS administrators after an uncomfortable visit from the triplets' parents. Neither Paula, nor I, are certain that Brown was one of the staff members shown in the reenactment of this event, but she might have been—Brown did have a taste for champagne, but Scotch was her drink of choice. A photograph of an LWS board meeting that included then-president Justine W. Polier and Florence Kreech was included in the film and appears in chapter 2 of this book. Paula loved her stepmother a great deal and struggled to reconcile her kindness with her tacit approval of separating twins.

Paula reflected, "I would like to think that she would want to be a part of the furtherance of the field she so loved, even if posthumously. I only wish she could explain and defend her actions herself and shed more light on why they did what they did. In any case, it will fall on others to explore it further. Actions have consequences and so many people's lives have been affected. Much as I might wish otherwise, there is no turning back."[37]

Perhaps Brown was told to never discuss the study publicly since *the truth had to be kept from the twins' families*. This makes sense because of another incident described to me by one of the newly surfaced twins. When her parents and her twin's parents realized that they were each raising a separated twin sister, they confronted LWS, demanding to know more. The agency staff admitted to having separated the twins, *but made no mention of the twin study*—the staff's silence on this issue suggests that they were urged not to speak about it. My high school friend, Liliane Neubauer, recalled that her elder cousin Peter "studied twins," but that is all she could say. Of course, she was a young girl at the time and visits between her working-class family and his professional, white-collar family were infrequent. But the words of many others I have interviewed convey the secrecy surrounding the study, as does Bernard's correspondence with Brown. Interestingly, a 1978 document sent to one of the twins, explaining the separation policy, referred twice to the 1960 "Joint Study of Louise Wise Services Agency and . . . ," with the identity of the collaborator redacted in both places.[38]

Whether Brown agreed with the practice of separating the pairs, went along with Bernard's "wisdom," or opposed it but did not want to jeopardize her job as LWS's executive director will never be known. Perhaps she believed that since twins were being separated anyway, why not study them? Some of her co-workers were uneasy about the separations, but said nothing, perhaps for the same reasons. Florence Brown Kreech passed away in 2008 at the age of ninety-six.

Letters exchanged between Brown and Bernard reveal the extent to which Brown was involved in the inner workings of the twin study. The portrait of a loving, caring stepmother, aunt, and social worker is hard to reconcile with the dispassionate, business-like tone of her correspondence. In November 14, 1961, Brown wrote a letter focused on the hiring of consultants, but added a postscript: "Hold your breath! Esther Levitt tells me we are going to have some more twins. I do not know any of the details, but it is my understanding that this is a new referral and the girl is in her eighth month. And now will you please stop it! We have enough twins."[39] The 1961 date seems too early to have secured "enough twins," as most twins were separated during or *after* 1961, although two twin sets had been placed apart before then. Levitt's name also appears in a July 1963 note in Bernard's handwritten records as "Esther Levitt / Twins." A November 30, 1961, letter to Bernard concerns items to place on the agenda for a meeting of new psychiatric consultants. A report on the "CDC-LWS Project" was suggested, but no further details were given.

In Brown's March 25, 1965, letter to Bernard, she acknowledged the difficulties of placing white, non-Jewish children, then wrote, "I think we need to concentrate on helping the other agencies that are willing to participate in the CDC study. . . . As long as we are not urging them to separate the twins, I really do not understand why the 'higher ups' should raise so many objections." Kreech sent a March 4, 1971, memo to "Professional Staff" about a meeting with Drs. Robert Reich and Elizabeth Kleinberger concerning several abused child referrals. "He and Dr. Kleinberger will meet with us Tuesday morning, March 10, from 10 to 11 A.M." There is a circle around this date drawn in Bernard's hand, with a line extending to the name Reich scribbled below—a second line connects Reich to a square enclosing the terms "identical twins, fraternal twins placed."[40]

There is a curious twist to this story. As I indicated, several psychiatrists from other locations were themselves interested in studying separated twins and sought cooperation from LWS. These requests were met with silence and concern. Memos variously passed among Brown, Bernard, and Mignon Krause, executive assistant for publicity and public relations, in late 1964 and early 1965, refer to a Dr. Kliever, whom Bernard nicknamed "the psychiatrist in pursuit of a twin study."[41] Kliever was interested in the origins of personality traits in ten-year-old twins reared apart. According to a memo from Krause, "I told him most agencies place twins together and it is only very recently that we have done otherwise . . . thinking had been in earlier years twins should be adopted together—tie with blood relatives, but some thought now there may be some disadvantages to the children and better they be reared separately. I did not know how many sets had been so placed." A subsequent note that appears to be written by Brown, because it refers to Krause, ends by stating, "I am beginning to feel paranoid . . . any chance he is trying to get information from us on behalf of one of our families in study who may have become suspicious?" A handwritten entry by Bernard appears on that note: "Thanks—please keep it till we hear again from Krause."[42] Bernard's consultation with an outside source determined that Kliever was not qualified to engage in collaborative research with LWS. As far as Bernard was concerned the matter was closed, as she so stated. It is uncertain if and what Kliever knew about the LWS-CDC twin study.

A March 9, 1976, inquiry was sent to LWS by Dr. J. Winston Sapp, a psychiatrist associated with Philadelphia's Hahnemann Medical College and Hospital. Sapp referred to a March 4 letter he had received from Bernard in which she mentioned her consultancy with LWS. He also mentioned that he had presented a psychoanalytic case study of twins at Dr. Edward Joseph's American Psychoanalytic Association discussion groups in 1974 and 1975. He was requesting information about whether to separate twins.

Bernard could not locate his letter—I found it in her archives—but she had written a note to Brown (Kreech) about this matter, based on her recollections, saying that, "My main point was to tell him that there were no publications on the subject." She continued, "Dr. Edward Joseph does know of our research through Peter [Neubauer] and may have mentioned it to the seminar which Dr. Sapp attended. We are still being very careful about the research and do not want to share information about it, especially in these days of informed consent concerns."[43] Dr. Sapp passed away in the mid-1990s.[44]

Curiously, a March 4, 1976, letter from Bernard to Sapp is also in Bernard's files, so perhaps their letters crossed in the mail.[45] Here, she apologized for her delayed response to his letter of February 13. She regretted that there had not been any publications from the earlier work, certainly nothing on the topic of treatment. She acknowledged the fascinating nature of the topic and wished him well. A 1976 publication in the *Psychoanalytic Quarterly* by Abrams and Neubauer cited Bernard as a consultant on this longitudinal study of "matched samplings," which was presented at psychoanalytic society meetings in 1974 and 1975.[46] I will say more about this particular paper that holds several clues to several questions.

Prior to the internet, a fruitful way to find twin study participants would have been at academic conferences. These events offer speakers a captive audience whose members enjoy overlapping interests and unique resource access. Opportunities for collaborations are often forged during coffee breaks and cocktail hours where veterans of such meetings know that the "real business" take place. Neubauer attended national gatherings of psychoanalytic associations, as well as many local seminars, workshops, and discussion groups. He was well-positioned to find new cases from among his colleagues. Fruitful venues would have been the Behavior Genetics Association, founded in 1970, and the International Society for Twin Studies, founded in 1974, whose members recruit large numbers of twins for their projects. Organizations and societies centered around newborns, such as the American College of Obstetricians and Gynecologists, might have also provided separated sets. My own views on separating twins will come later in the book; here, I am pointing out that Neubauer did not solicit subjects outside adoption agencies and did not discuss the study or his findings outside select psychoanalytic circles. "It's hard to believe that they would have done a public presentation on the twin data because it was such a big secret," a former twin study assistant and CDC intern told me. The assistant wished to remain anonymous.[47]

In contrast, soon after the Minnesota Study of Twins Reared Apart was launched in March 1979, its director, Professor Thomas J. Bouchard Jr., and colleagues delivered three talks at the Third International Congress on Twin Studies, held in June 1980, in Jerusalem, Israel. These talks were later published as three papers in the conference proceedings in 1981.[48] The point of Bouchard's attendance was based partly on the possibility of locating new participants from attendees who might know of them. Most importantly, this was an opportunity to hear from experts who could have ideas about moving the study forward in the best way possible.

Stephanie Saul, now a staff writer for the *New York Times*, published a stunning article in *Newsday* in 1997, focused on the separated triplets. Bouchard is quoted as saying that he would never approve of separating subjects. "It just does not feel right to me." Because of that he never requested data from Peter Neubauer. The triplets from the Neubauer study did take part in the Minnesota study in 1980 when they were nineteen, many years after their families' association with the LWS-CDC study ended. Their voluntary and informed participation was arranged through an attorney.

FINDING THE TWINS HOMES

The twins' families were selected from among couples who had already successfully adopted a child from LWS. The positive outcomes gave the agency confidence that the singleton twins would also enjoy good and happy homes. As explained, these adoptive mothers and fathers were only informed that their child was enrolled in a developmental study of adopted children that required regular testing, interviews, and observations during home visits. Agreeing to this arrangement was a precondition for the adoption, but the families were delighted to be offered a second baby. Some parents were actually surprised when the offer came in because they had been told that no other children were available.

There was another reason why care was taken to place each identical twin with a family who already had a child. Some LWS staff felt that being an only child would be a drawback and that having a sibling would protect against that. The approximate age gap between the two children was three to five years. Ironically, these twins already had a sibling.

There was a suggestion in the film *Three Identical Strangers* that the triplets had been purposefully placed in families that differed socioeconomically. Robert, whose father was a physician, grew up in a professional family in the upscale New York suburb of Scarsdale; Eddy, whose father was a teacher, grew up in a middle-class family in the Long Island village of New Hyde Park; and David, whose father ran a small business, grew up in a lower-middle-class family in Howard Beach, Queens. Identical twins Sharon Morello and Lisa Banks were also placed in homes that differed considerably in financial status.[49] Perhaps it was reasoned that placing genetically identical individuals in these different settings might, or might not, affect their abilities, temperaments, and talents. Bernard denied that this was the case, explaining that these placements were accidental and made by social workers who had no knowledge of such family factors. She admitted that she was consulted about some placements, but she insisted that they were decided without reference to the research.[50]

A summary of Bernard's remarks at a staff meeting held on January 20, 1964, reflect her conflict regarding the disclosure to prospective adoptive parents of ethnic admixture in children, as well as information about mental illness, mental retardation, and other matters. Would staff discomfort be relieved by sharing such information and letting parents decide? Would parents grow unnecessarily anxious upon learning that mental disorders ran in their child's birth family? Bernard suggested addressing these misgivings through research and follow-up in order to identify meaningful issues, rather than finding the best ways to communicate this information to parents. "Relative to examination of experience is the CDC study of the development of twins in whose background there is a good deal of psychopathology." Bernard noted that two separated three-year-old adoptees—she does not say twins—were doing well.[51] But this news could not have been completely reassuring; even in the 1960s, it was known that psychiatric symptoms in a child at risk are usually not evident until they enter their late teens or twenties.[52]

Academic departments at universities are great resources. A stroll down the corridor or a trip to a nearby building takes one to experts in related areas who can offer valuable advice and guidance, literally for free. Dr. Franz J. Kallman, an authority on schizophrenia, was a member of Bernard's Department of Psychiatry at Columbia University from 1956 until his death in 1965, at which time he was chief of psychiatric research.[53] Kallman was located in the department's Institute of Psychiatry; still, they overlapped from 1956 to 1963 and Bernard would have benefitted from consulting with Kallman. His 1946 paper, "The Genetic Theory of Schizophrenia," showed that the chance of developing the disorder increased with the closeness of the genetic relationship. This conclusion, published fifteen years before the twin study began, was based on studies of schizophrenia across a number of informative kinship pairs—parents and children, brothers and sisters, and identical and fraternal twins.[54] At the same time, Kallman stressed the compatibility of genetic and psychological theories of schizophrenia while recognizing their complex interplay. But perhaps his final statement, that a genetic perspective on the disorder "was equally compatible with the psychiatric concept that schizophrenia can be prevented as well as cured," would have made the greatest impression on Bernard had she read it.

Bernard knew Dr. Niki Erlenmeyer-Kimling as a professional colleague in Columbia University's psychiatry department.[55] Erlenmeyer-Kimling was a leading behavioral geneticist in the 1960s and 1970s, who was tracking the development of children born to schizophrenic parents. Erlenmeyer-Kimling told me she was certain that Bernard would have known of Franz Kallman.[56] I wonder if Bernard or Brown had ever taken that stroll to Kallman's lab.

The question of whether the twins were studied to disentangle the effects of nature and nurture on child development, or whether they were studied to see if good parenting overcame potential behavioral difficulties, due to psychopathology in the biological parents, was also raised. These issues may not have been mutually exclusive, a topic I will consider later on. However, in 1961 as the LWS-CDC study was starting, Bernard was in touch with Dr. David Sobel, a psychiatrist in her department at Columbia University.[57] Sobel was tracking the development of a small group of adopted away children, born to two schizophrenic parents. His aim was to see if the children were "endowed with any special features in their behavior" which, if found early, could help adoption agencies and parents promote healthy outcomes. Sobel assumed that schizophrenia was not an inherited disorder, but reasoned that knowledge of any relevant "endowed features" may have allowed more informed parenting.

Also relevant to the question of the aims of the twin study are LWS Adoption Committee notes from 1960.[58] The Jewish Child Care Association (JCCA)[59] was cited as the largest child referral source for LWS: "most of the JCCA situations are those in which mothers have absconded, or mothers are in mental hospitals; or there are two parents, one of whom is unavailable to surrender." A case is described in which a mother had had several hospitalizations for advanced epilepsy, but refused to relinquish her newborn twins.

"The father is ready to sign surrender but something has to be done legally to free the twins from the mother."

FUNDING SOURCES

Notes in Bernard's files unveil her concern over sources of funding. A March 29, 1961, note reminded her to telephone "Feldman" from the National Institute of Mental Health (NIMH). Another entry prompted her to work on "Dave's draft" of the NIMH grant application, but the date is not given. Bernard received NIMH grants for community psychiatry programs so these notations may have referred to those awards.

Over the years, the twin study was financed by both federal and private sources. Neubauer's colleague, Dr. Arnie Richards, suggested that I begin to identify these sources by consulting another of Neubauer's colleagues, Dr. Henry Nunberg. Nunberg is a psychiatrist still in practice in New York City despite his eighty-six years, albeit with reduced hours.[60] I was excited to learn that he was living in Riverdale, the northern part of the Bronx where I grew up. He and Neubauer had known he each other professionally and socially, their shared Austrian heritage no doubt underlying their mutual attraction. Nunberg's memories of his former friend were that of a man who displayed congeniality, intelligence, and good humor.

Nunberg confessed to knowing nothing about the twin study's financial backing. Both men had been involved with the Psychoanalytic Research and Development Fund, but Nunberg was certain that no awards had come from this source. In fact, Nunberg wasn't even aware of the twin study until he saw *Three Identical Strangers* in the summer 2018 in Williamstown, Massachusetts. He was "shocked and stunned," prompting him to do some reading about the project. He was not surprised that Neubauer had never spoken of it. Nunberg was one of the signatories on the protest letter I referenced earlier and that I will discuss again.

Recall that Neubauer helped found the organization Zero to Three in 1977. Another founding member was Leon J. Yarrow, a psychologist and branch chief of the National Institute of Child Health and Human Development (NICHD), a post he assumed in 1965. Neubauer and Yarrow were colleagues. Andrew L. Yarrow, senior fellow with the Progressive Policy Institute in Washington, DC, and son of Leon Yarrow, confirmed the working relationship between the two when I met him in 2019.[61] Together, Neubauer and Yarrow participated in a series of conferences on infant, child, and toddler development, in 1964 and 1996, sponsored by the NIMH and Committee on Day Care of the Maternal and Child Health Section of the American Public

Health Association. A conference volume resulting from those meetings was published in 1968 and reprinted in 2017. Both Yarrow and Neubauer were contributing authors.[62]

In an article published in 1965—the same year Yarrow joined the NICHD—Yarrow urged more carefully designed studies of foster mothers and infants to find factors linked to favorable and unfavorable child outcomes. He continued, "An intriguing possibility would be to study twins placed with different mothers. Although twins are usually placed together in foster and adoptive homes, they are occasionally separated."[63] In 1965, Neubauer was awarded an NICHD grant in the amount of $9,642 for a project, "Longitudinal Study of Monozygotic Twins Reared Apart," number HD012625-1. This award is listed in the *Research Grants Index*, Fiscal Year, 1965.[64] NICHD dispensed a total of $38,906 in grant money that year.[65]

My efforts to locate a copy of the grant proposal and associated documents, such as correspondence with NICHD officers or final study reports, led me to NICHD's clearing house. I was told that this was a very old grant and a copy was not in their possession.[66] The efforts of ethicist Adam Michael Kelmenson and attorney Barry Coburn were also unsuccessful[67]—no doubt, such materials were discarded prior to digital storage. I believe that the right NICHD administrator, possibly one with a personal interest in twin studies, might exert leverage. Sometimes that's all it takes. However, it is possible that a copy of the grant and related materials have been placed in Neubauer's and/ or Bernard's archives. I know from experience that such proposals require a great deal of work and are rarely discarded by their authors. Papers belonging to Yarrow did not turn up at NICHD, nor did they surface in his home— Leon Yarrow's son Andrew kindly looked for these materials at my request.

Federal funding currently requires grant recipients to disseminate findings in a timely manner. Researchers who fail to comply risk rejection of their applications for future grant renewal. It is uncertain how firmly this policy was in place when Neubauer received his single NICHD award in 1965.[68] I explore the controversies surrounding publication of the twin study data in chapter 12.

A project titled, "Child Development and Adoption Study," listed as 18-U-29 in a government catalog, *Research Relating to Children (1963–1964)*, names Peter B. Neubauer, MD Director, Child Development Center, and Vera D. Bernard—name misspelled—Clinical Professor of Psychiatry, Columbia University, as the investigators. The purpose of the study was to examine "differential interactions between different types of mothers and children."[69] The definition of "different types" is not given, but most likely meant twins reared by different parents. The research design was longitudinal in nature, with repeated interviewing of mothers, plus filming and psychological testing of children. The duration of the study was given as 1960–indefinite.

Many, if not most projects in the catalog variously listed their funding sources, publications, presentations, and cooperating institutions, yet this information was not provided for the Neubauer-Bernard project. Subjects in that study were described only as "children adopted in infancy," with no reference to twins. Another project, identified as 18-Y-15 (1964–1965) and listed in the same catalog, cites Herschel Alt, MA, Peter B. Neubauer, MD, and John Mann, MD, as investigators, with the Jewish Board of Guardians as Research Advisor in a study of child separation and placement. Subjects were not described, although the US Department of Health, Education, and Welfare was listed as a cooperating group. Neubauer is also listed as sole investigator of a follow-up study 18-L-5 (1964–1966) of preschool children in a therapeutic nursery.[70] The subjects were children who had attended the CDC or outpatient therapy department, but no publication or related information were provided.[71] These projects were ongoing during the early years of the twin study, but if they overlap, and by how much, with 18-U-29 is unknown.

The letter dated March 2, 1965, from Florence Brown also congratulated Bernard for getting a "renewal of funds for the CDC-LWS study."[72] The 1965 date matches that of the NICHD grant, possibly the renewal that Brown referenced, although the projects have different titles. Thus, the renewed funding source to which Brown refers is unclear.

Longitudinal studies that follow subjects over several decades are expensive and time-consuming, incurring costs for materials, equipment, and staff. The CDC twin study lasted for nearly twenty years, from the early 1960s until at least 1978 when the youngest set turned twelve; the twin study records are listed in the archives as circa 1960 to 1980.[73] In addition to the NICHD award, the work was partly funded by the Viola W. Bernard Foundation (formerly the Tappanz Foundation) and the Philip A. and Lynn Straus Philanthropic Fund.[74] The Viola W. Bernard Foundation shut down in 2016 over internal disagreements I will air at the end.

The Philip A. and Lynn Straus Philanthropic Fund is part of the larger Straus Foundation, Inc. The foundation was founded in the 1950s and gained charitable status in 1958. Based in Mamaroneck, New York, it was established by the late Philip A. Straus Sr., a businessman, traveler, arts lover, and supporter of early childhood education. The foundation's purpose has been to support education for children and youth from birth to twenty-one years of age, as well as the arts and culture, libraries, civil rights, and social and human services. Straus passed away in 2004 at the age of eighty-eight. He had been married to Lynn Gross Straus and was the father of three children and four grandchildren.[75] His wife Lynn Straus is currently listed as the sole trustee of the foundation. She and her late identical twin sister, Mrs. Robert Lazarus, were the first of three generations of twins in her family.[76]

Straus's financial support had backed many educational and cultural institutions, among them the Jewish Board of Family and Children's Services (JBFCS) and Zero to Three. Most recently, awards of five hundred thousand dollars to $2,049,594 were given to the JBFCS by the Straus Foundation in 2002, 2004, 2005,[77] and 2008.[78] In 2020, I spoke with Lynn, now ninety-four years old. I learned that Lynn had volunteered at the JBFCS in their infancy care program and had served on the board for a while on a voluntary basis. She had been aware of the twin study when it was ongoing. She had been interested in the project, but was uninvolved, even though her foundation had been a source of support. I requested records of Straus Foundation donations made to the twin study, but Lynn is uncertain if they are available.

Private fundraising for the twin study also took place. Neubauer sometimes solicited funds that he channeled to the Jewish Board of Guardians.[79] Securing support for ongoing projects through personal contacts is not an uncommon practice.

DR. SAMUEL ABRAMS

Samuel Abrams, MD, is considered one of the three key contributors to the LWS-CDC twin study, the other two being Peter Neubauer and Crista Balzert. Like Neubauer, Abrams agreed that children's unique genetic predispositions interacted with their environments to produce developmental outcomes.[80] He sensed that the collaboration focused on the twins' similarities, but noted that when inherent programs for growth are "impaired," perhaps due to adverse birth events or childhood illnesses, then environmental opportunities that might make a difference are limited. Given that all the twins were adopted into warm, loving, and financially secure homes, it is not surprising that any differences between them were small—their favorable environments allowed their natural abilities and interests to be expressed.

Once again, Lawrence Wright showed himself to be a skilled questioner.[81] Abrams seemed surprised at Wright's reference to the twin study as "consequential." But of course, no one had ever closely studied identical twins from the time of their separation. Abrams did allow that the twin findings "broaden the therapeutic repertoire" of clinicians, meaning that therapists can help their patients by knowing that environments can modify genetically influenced tendencies. His comment that "children create parenting styles," exemplified forward thinking during a time when parenting styles were considered to be primarily responsible for child outcomes. "The same mother discovers herself behaving very differently with different children."

Abrams also alluded to "developmental lags" in the separated twins, behaviors that he said were not characteristic of all twins. The nature and source of the lags were unclear; as he correctly points out, they might reflect artifacts of the study design or small sample characteristics. However, we know that twins, on average, show delays in growth and in some behaviors more than others, such as language development.[82] Ironically, the CDC twins were separated to avoid difficulties found in twins reared together, but some problems still emerged.

Abrams claimed to have entered the study a little bit late, perhaps in the late 1960s or early 1970s. He explained that the study had been in progress for a while when he was offered the chance to become involved, in order to observe and understand children in a new way. There was more. "Dr. Neubauer was a recognized profound thinker in the field and the opportunity to work with him was one that I was not going to turn down." With regard to how twins were found he replied, "Well that happened long before I got there so I don't really know all the fineries and details." "How many people were involved?" Wright asked. "Again, that's something that I—I just came once a week for a few hours." Abrams indicated that he attended the researchers' periodic meetings, did some writing, and discussed findings with Neubauer, but he could not recall who attended these meetings. He thought of himself as a consultant, someone who reviewed the data, and tried to understand it both theoretically and practically. When it came to questions of funding, he had "no idea." Both the Philip A. and Lynn Straus Foundation and Tappanz Foundation are cited in his 1986 paper for providing support.

The twin study "drastically" changed Abrams's view of human behavior. As of 1993, about fifteen years after the twin study had stopped collecting data, Abrams thought of the development of the mind from childhood to adulthood as a hierarchical series of minds, influenced by "drives, dispositions and the environment, intermixing with one another."[83] It is curious that his views were "drastically" altered by results from a study in which he minimized his involvement.

Abrams passed away in 2016, leaving behind a rich legacy of contributions to the field of child psychoanalysis. Among them are his organizing the Hampstead Clinic Colloquia, chairing child analytic study sessions and founding the research group "Searching for Child Analysis in the 21st Century." Abrams's *New York Times* obituary didn't mention his research with twins.[84]

DATA COLLECTION

There are potential biases inherent in twin studies, as in all studies, that researchers try their best to control. For example, if the same researcher tests both twins in an identical pair, there is the possibility of "seeing" or "looking for" the behaviors in Twin 2 that were first observed in Twin 1. Interpreting a particular behavior might also be compromised. This problem, known as an *assimilation effect*, can be overcome by assigning different investigators to assess each twin. In the case of fraternal twins, there is the greater possibility of exaggerating their differences, known as a *contrast effect*.[85] Another way to handle these situations is to keep researchers blind to twin type. For example, in the Minnesota Study of Twins Reared Apart, the same two periodontists examined both co-twins, but a cloth was draped over the face of one of the twins to conceal facial similarities or dissimilarities that might reveal clues to their twin type.

With respect to standardized tests, such as the Wechsler Intelligence Scale, questions of bias may not be problematic if examiners faithfully follow the administration and scoring rules. To test this idea, I compared the IQ similarity of identical and fraternal twin pairs I had tested on my own, with the IQ similarity of twin pairs in which I had tested only one twin. The results were nearly identical. My colleague and friend, Dr. Len Heston, recorded the medical life histories of the separated Minnesota twins. Heston defended his method. "I presented the questions in the same way to each individual—doctors learn to do this during their second year of medical school. There was a possibility of bias, but if so it did not operate in an important way." Heston's reasoning, coupled with my IQ results, most likely extend to findings in other behavioral and physical domains, especially those that are measured objectively. Regardless, in the Minnesota study we tested twins separately whenever possible, as do most twin researchers wishing to protect their work against bias and the possible appearance of bias.

According to Neubauer, in discussion with Lawrence Wright, the researchers typically sent teams of at least three individuals—among them, a psychologist, pediatrician, observer, and testers—to each twins' home for periodic visits. He explained that this would allow independent assessments by representatives of different disciplines who would not influence each other. When pressed, he said that different teams were used to study each twin. "Why didn't you go into this more in [your book] *Nature's Thumbprint*?" Wright asked. "For the same reason I hesitate to give you an update," Neubauer replied.

Perhaps Neubauer misunderstood some of the questioning, because we know from several sources that the same researchers *did* see both members of a twin pair. Clinical psychologist Dr. Larry Perlman was associated with the study for ten months. He recalled visiting and testing twenty-eight-day-old twin girls while they were in foster care and interviewing their foster mother. He also outlined the research schedule: Once adopted apart, twins were seen every three months during the first year, every six months during the second year and once each year after that. Visits included a Wechsler IQ test, a filmed sample of play behavior, and an interview with the mother. "The visits were scheduled one week apart, so that the observations would be made at the same developmental moment and by the same staff members." Perlman recalled that there was little worry over biased assessment; in fact, it was reasoned that using the same tester for both children eliminated a source of variance. For example, if one tester was more friendly, meticulous, or discerning than the other tester, this could potentially sway the findings. Still, Perlman allowed for the possibility that characterizations of the twins might have been biased to some extent.[86]

The former graduate student CDC intern I quoted earlier substituted as a tester on several occasions.[87] In our interview, she affirmed that she had tested both twins in one male set and both twins in one female set. Accompanied by an interviewer, a videographer, and an anxious driver, she administered the Wechsler Intelligence Scale, Thematic Apperception Test (TAT), Rorschach, Draw-a-Person Test (DAP), and Bender-Gestalt to the twins.[88] There is considerable subjectivity in scoring the TAT, Rorschach, and Bender-Gestalt, and some subjectivity in scoring the DAP. Some portions of the Wechsler also require administrator judgment, such as the vocabulary and information subscales. The prudent approach would have been to have had each twins' protocols analyzed by more than one person, but whether that was done is unknown. She finds it hard to believe that the testing was not biased.

The assistant also found it striking that one of the female twins she tested spoke with a distinct Brooklyn accent that her Westchester-raised twin didn't have, showing how different environments can produce different results. She also recalled her great discomfort at the time, *because she knew what the twins' mothers and fathers did not know—that their adoptive child had an identical twin living with another family.* "A week later you would see the exact same kid. It was disturbing, it did not feel right. Put yourself in that situation." Thinking about *Three Identical Strangers*, she remembered that one of the triplets said he "felt like a lab rat," and she "totally gets" what he meant. Even now, decades later, she feels extremely upset about her connection to the twin study. "I am not proud of that and I have told no one."

There is one more source that should be mentioned. There exists a partial list of investigators and the twins whom they tested, beginning in 1961. It was compiled by Lori Shinseki, director of *The Twinning Reaction*, based on materials given to her by some of the twins. Almost every person on the list tested both twins.

I have worked on many twin studies and have always known the other researchers involved. This was even true of the Minnesota Study of Twins Reared Apart that relied on a large team of psychologists, physicians, and assistants. Part of my job was to escort twins from one office or laboratory to another, a task that facilitated contacts with the study associates. There were also people I saw rarely—the ophthalmologist, the allergist—but I knew who they were. Therefore, I was surprised at first to learn that some people who worked on the LWS-CDC study had no idea about who else was involved, even people whom they actually knew. A former student assistant was stunned to learn that four people on Shinseki's list had tested twins—she had been in class with one of them and had rented office space from another. When I mentioned LWS-CDC Project Director Dr. Nancy Edwards, who was not on the list, the assistant said she was "shocked" to hear of Edwards's involvement in the study. They did not know each other well, but both had graduated from New York University's analytic training program and later had offices in the same building. Dr. Edwards is deceased. My attempts and those of Dr. Larry Perlman to learn more about Edwards's work from her husband Bill and daughter Julie were unsuccessful.[89] Bill knew that his wife had worked on a reared-apart twin study and was intrigued by it. She did not speak much about the study, but she didn't seem to worry over whether the twins might find each other. Julie was too young at the time to know much about her mother's work. Perhaps having to shield information from the families made supervisors and assistants reluctant to talk.

The lives of some of the twins and their parents, the discovery of the twinship, and its impact on the years that followed are described in the next few chapters. I will then present events surrounding Mike Wallace's attempts to explore the twin study on *60 Minutes*, as well as more of the study's inner workings—researchers, publications, and meetings—before returning to the life histories of other separated pairs of twins and the set of triplets.

Twin Brothers with Twin Sisters

Familiar Strangers

In November 2012, I traveled to Madrid, Spain, to speak at *El Ser Creativo: Congreso de Mentes Brillantes* (The Creative Being: Congress of Brilliant Minds). This two-day public gathering offered presentations by experts in areas ranging from molecular biology and human robotics to judicial reform and international cuisine. I discussed my studies of reared-apart twins, focusing on an extraordinary case of switched-at-birth twins I had recently studied who came from the Spanish island of Gran Canaria.[1] The congress was enriching and engaging, and some of us were thrilled to have our pictures emblazoned on Pepsi-Cola cans.[2] However, none of this was as compelling as what I learned at a post-conference party held for local and foreign guests. It was a twin story of secrets, reunions, and family loyalty.

The Twins, Their Family Members, and Friends*

Tim

Tim M. Ilene's reared-apart twin
Susan J. Tim's former wife
Mrs. M. Tim's adoptive mother
Drew M. Susan and Tim's son

Ilene

Ilene Tim's reared-apart twin
John Ilene's husband

---

* Names have been altered in the interest of privacy.

People circulated through the host's crowded living room holding glasses of wine, hoping to join interesting conversations. I was describing my twin studies to a young Spanish woman, Debbie Siegfried, when she suddenly became energized and excited to share a story. Debbie, who specializes in travel, explained that her Aunt Susan (Susan J.) in New York City had been married to Tim M., a Louise Wise adoptee, who had been reared apart from his twin sister, Ilene. I was instantly captivated because this was the first set of separated opposite-sex twins from Louise Wise Services (LWS) I had heard of. I scribbled Susan's phone number on the back of a business card and called her when I got home.

Beginning in 2012, Susan and I spoke over the phone a number of times and had a long meeting in the summer of 2018. We met in her New York City apartment on Manhattan's upper west side. Susan is an attractive blonde and was stylishly dressed, with a warm and vivacious manner. She also admitted that she was reluctant to relive this part of her life yet again (that is, the search for her husband's twin and its aftermath), but was willing to do it for me. The story of Tim and Ilene has never been told publicly prior to this book.

TIM AND ILENE

Tim and Ilene were born in March 1947 to a Russian Jewish mother and Catholic father from the south Bronx in New York City. The couple was unmarried. The two newborns remained with their mother until she relinquished them to LWS when they were six months old. They were separated from one another shortly after that—Ilene was adopted in October and Tim was adopted in November; Tim's delayed adoption was due to an illness. Why the twins were given up, why they were separated, and whether they were together in foster care during the month preceding their adoption is unknown. Recall that their records and those of countless LWS adoptees are in storage at Spence-Chapin's offsite facility, and are both inaccessible and unorganized.

The twins' birth in 1947 is important. They were born nearly fifteen years before the LWS twin separation policy was purposefully practiced in the early 1960s, and about twenty years before it was officially approved by the board of directors. Again, until the early 1960s some twins were allegedly placed together and some twins were placed apart, depending on the circumstances of the pair in question.[3] And in accordance with agency policy, neither Tim nor Ilene's parents were told that their newly adopted child had a twin sibling. Fraternal twins were not part of the LWS-Child Development Center twin study, but the agency contacted their families from time to time until the twins turned five to see how things were going.[4] Twenty years later, Dr. Bernard, who proposed the policy to LWS, reflected back on why parents were never told that their child was a twin:

> Along with this [twin separation] went the decision that adoptive parents in the case of such separate placements should not be informed of the twinship since it would, in terms of clinical judgment, seem to obviate the advantages for individuality of the children's and parents' relationship. At that time in 1960, the information given to adoptive parents about background was selective, and this decision to withhold the information of twinship in separate placements was in accordance with other information that was not given, and was in accordance with general adoptive practice.[5]

THE SEARCH

Tim and Ilene did not meet one another until August 1982 when they were thirty-five. However, a search for their biological family began several years earlier, initiated by Tim's mother, Mrs. M. In 1972, when her son was twenty-five, Mrs. M. contacted staff member Barbara Miller at LWS to request information about his birth mother. She had obtained such data for an older privately adopted son, and wanted it for Tim, as well. The information was not forthcoming from LWS. By 1979, Mrs. M. had discovered on her own that her son had a twin, and she was eager to arrange a reunion between the two siblings. Her discovery came about after Susan had obtained her husband's birth certificate number from a private investigator she had hired through the Adoptees' Liberty Movement Association (ALMA). During a visit to New York from her home in California, Mrs. M. searched through birth certificates maintained by the New York Public Library. She was puzzled to find two consecutively numbered documents for a male and female with the same family name. "A coincidence?" she asked the librarian. "No, it's not a coincidence. It's twins." When Tim asked his mother at a family dinner if she had discovered anything interesting in her search she simply said, "yes." By then Mrs. M. knew that her son's birth name was Robert Raffs, which everyone found extremely funny.

But Mrs. M. was also distraught upon learning that Tim had a twin, insisting that she would have adopted both infants—as it was, she had adopted Tim and his older brother, and went on to conceive another son and a daughter. In August 1979, Mrs. M. met personally with Miller and informed her that she had not yet told her son that he had a twin. Apparently, Tim was ambivalent toward anything having to do with his biological family, so his mother decided to leave things as they were. But then the situation changed suddenly.

A year later, Mrs. M. died from cardiac failure, leaving a pile of search-related letters documenting the existence of her son's twin sister. Miller's memo to Viola Bernard and Morton Rogers, who was then executive director of LWS, give the impression that Tim discovered his twinship from reading the letters himself, but that's not how it happened. Susan told me the story as she remembered it.

Three months before her death in 1980, Mrs. M. told Tim's wife Susan that she had put together a file with papers documenting the search for her son's birth family. Susan's name would appear on the file and she was to open it when her mother-in-law was no longer around. "Tim will never look at it," Mrs. M. said. "The only mother he recognizes is me, the one who raised him." Susan was reading the file on the day of her mother-in-law's funeral when Tim entered the room. She told him that he had a twin sister. Tim left the room without comment, too overcome by the death of his mother. When he returned several hours later, he told her, "I want to meet my twin sister, but only if you will come with me." He was not interested in meeting his biological parents. According to Susan, "I was off and running [to find his twin.]"

The internet was not publicly available until 1991, and not widely so until several years after that. Therefore, people searching for kin in the 1980s relied on reunion registries, adoption professionals, hospital records, and even door-to-door inquiries.[6] Some ongoing twin research projects also held promise. By 1981, the Minnesota Study of Twins Reared Apart, launched in March 1979, was receiving widespread attention in professional journals and in the press.[7] Susan contacted the study's director, Dr. Thomas J. Bouchard Jr., for assistance in finding Tim's twin.[8] Bouchard was "intensely interested" in the case, but was unable to locate her. I vividly recall a drawer in one of Bouchard's cabinets that held the thin files of twins in search. I was hoping to look through Tim's file while writing this book, but Bouchard was uncertain if these files had been retained once he retired.[9]

Susan also embarked on an ambitious letter-writing campaign to find the twin sister, one that lasted for well over a year. She contacted Florence Fisher, a well-known adoption advocate at ALMA, and Arthur Sorosky, senior author of the classic work *Adoption Triangle*.[10] She had petitioned the Westchester Surrogate Court to open the records, but was denied.[11] She even wrote to New York state adoption officials posing as an adoptive mother hoping to obtain her child's medical history before succumbing to cancer.[12] And between September 1980 and July 1981, Susan called Miller at LWS who complained, "I was deluged by frequent angry calls . . . all demanding the identity of the twin. During this period [Susan] spoke with Steve Tulin [attorney for LWS], at my suggestion, who confirmed the agency policy was in conformity with New York State adoption law.[13] Amongst other threats

[Susan] informed me that she had paid for a costly investigation of me and my family (obviously for purposes of blackmail)."[14] Susan has no recollection of speaking to Tulin, asserting that she has a good memory for most things.[15]

In September 1980, Miller had located Tim and Ilene's biological uncle, their birth mother's brother. He revealed that his sister had been deceased for a number of years, that they had severed their relationship, and that he was uninterested in learning about his nephew. Miller suspected that the brother was unaware that his sister had delivered twins, possibly mistaking Tim for his sister's second son born out of wedlock.[16]

The long-awaited news of Ilene's whereabouts came in a 1982 telephone call from Susan's private investigator. At the time Susan, Tim, and their seven-year-old son Drew were celebrating the Fourth of July holiday at Lake Tahoe, located at the juncture of California and Nevada. It was left to Susan to phone Ilene. According to Susan, Tim said he could not do this, and she agreed. She said that her first words to her husband's twin—her new sister-in-law—were, "This is the strangest call you will ever have. I am married to your twin brother if you have birth certificate number _____." Susan recalled that Ilene screamed when she returned and saw the number and that fact that the birth dates matched. Ilene didn't know she was a twin, and her two children didn't know she had been adopted. Obviously upset, she told Susan that the call was disturbing her dinner. "I was very kind," Susan told me. "I said to Ilene that I did not wish to upset her and that it was okay if she preferred not to speak." Two hours later Ilene's husband John called, but he was not surprised. He told Susan that he always "knew" that his wife had a twin brother.[17] There was already a family connection—John had worked for Tim's father for twenty years. Tim's father had died before his son's twinship was discovered, so he never knew the truth about Tim's birth. And John's "knowing" that his wife Ilene had a twin brother was just a feeling without a solid basis.

Tim was very emotional about meeting his twin. In a telephone conversation overheard by his son Drew, he choked up when he had his sister on the line. He told her that he was her twin. It seems she hung up, but he called her right back. He cried. "It was a big thing to watch him be so demonstrative," Drew recalled. For most of his life Tim felt abandoned by a mother he never knew. He told his son that all this was a struggle.[18]

THE REUNION: A MEETING IN PRIVATE

By August 1982, both twins had both been separately interviewed by CBS's *60 Minutes*, a story Susan had pitched a year or so earlier in the event that Ilene was found. She had written to the network out of desperation, reasoning that a public airing of the story might help locate Ilene. Susan first contacted CBS Producer and Executive Don Hewitt who showed her letter to correspondent Mike Wallace and both were excited. It would be a while, but the timing worked out well because when Wallace called Susan later for an update Ilene had just been found. The next step was for the twins to meet. They chose the Beverly Hills Hotel, so CBS sent a crew to southern California to capture the reunion live. It was a wise decision on the producers' part because twin reunions are powerful. As I described earlier, there is usually a fleeting joyful moment when the twins look at each other and experience that first feeling of recognition that comes from seeing a familiar other. This is typically accompanied by a shared emotional connection that I believe comes from knowing that a broken bond has finally been restored. However, the moment is often tinged with sadness and regret at the shared loss of growing up together. Regardless, that first meeting overwhelms the twins and anyone who witnesses it, and the CBS producers clearly knew what makes for compelling television stories. One of the producers was the late Madeline Amgott, a media pioneer and visionary whom I will say more about later in relation to this pair and another.

LWS did not greet the news of television exposure favorably. In an August 6, 1982, memo taken by LWS staff member named Kelly, "*60 Minutes* thinks there's a twin pair the agency knows nothing about, who *60 Minutes* knows about. They told the couple about the 'study' the twins were involved in—Miller reassured the wife [Susan] that her husband was never part of any study."[19] Ultimately, the twins' reunion was not recorded, and the segment was not completed. That is because eighty minutes prior to filming, Ilene changed her mind and refused to take part in the program. Based on my only telephone discussion with Ilene, I suspect that she suddenly worried about losing her privacy by going public.[20] Susan was furious, calling her sister-in-law's behavior a "deception." She insisted that *60 Minutes* would still produce a piece that would "vilify" the agency, although that never happened. Still, as late as October 1982 this segment was under consideration by CBS.[21] Both twins were angry at having been raised apart.

Viola Bernard was out of town while these events were taking place. Miller and an assistant decided that nothing was urgent, but if Bernard should contact them they would tell her what had transpired. Bernard did call and asked that the information be sent to her, but she was not going to get involved at the moment.[22]

Tim and Ilene first met at a private dinner at Ilene's friend's home, just the two of them, and it lasted for hours. The length of their meeting is not surprising. Twins' anticipation of their first reunion is often daunting as they wonder what they will say to each other and how they will be perceived. But reared-apart twins are familiar strangers before they get together, and conversation tends to come easily. Easing into a close relationship is more characteristic of identical twins than fraternal twins because of their genetic identity that underlies many of their matched behavioral and physical features.[23] Thirty-five-year-old identical twins, Elyse Schein and Paula Bernstein, also adopted apart through LWS, first met at a café in April 2004 while the sun was shining and did not part ways until after midnight.[24] However, fraternal twins usually share some recognizable traits.[25] For example, Tim and Ilene have been described as artistic and visually skilled, with the same veiny skin and similarly shaped hands.[26] Both knew they had been given up by the same mother and adopted away under the same circumstances. They liked each other and felt like family. When Drew met Ilene's two children—his new first cousins—he was delighted to discover that they both played soccer and suffered from asthma "just like me." Susan was stunned to see the physical similarities between Ilene's children and Tim. "They looked a lot like him, much more so than their own two parents," she remarked.[27] In fact, the twins' familial tie explains why they respectfully declined my invitation to contribute to this book. This is a story worth telling, but it is important to know all sides to my entry into this saga and when it began.

GOING PUBLIC

I called Tim's son Drew in November 2012 to see if he had a phone number for his father. We spoke very briefly, but the first thing he said was, "it's a crazy story." When I learned that Tim dislikes the spotlight, I decided to postpone further contact until the time seemed right—nearly seven years later. By then, the two films about the New York twin study had been released in 2017 and 2018, I had spoken with Susan and Drew, and I had signed a book contract. So I phoned Tim in early October 2019. He was pleasant, but cautious, not really certain of who I was and how I had found him. Once I explained my project, he seemed willing to cooperate, but wanted to give the idea some thought, and suggested I call him again in a week. I did.

Tim, now in his early seventies and retired from the entertainment industry, is enjoying life. He and Susan divorced due to irreconcilable events that followed Tim's reunion with his twin sister. He and his second wife directed and produced a wonderful film that deals with a woman's separation from her twin brother and her attempts to reconnect with a new family and culture. But adoption and separation are now part of a distant past that Tim does not wish to dwell on. He decided that for these reasons he could not grant me an interview, but if his sister agreed that was her decision. I was disappointed, but I understood. The story does not end there.

The next day was a Friday, which I reserve for working at home in the morning and meeting with research students in the afternoon. Just as we were finishing our projects for the day Tim called. He had done some research on me, listened to my lectures online, was convinced that I was a respected college professor, and realized that my contacting him was not a scam. We talked a bit about his twin film and about my background—he was impressed that I had taken eight years to complete my doctoral degree because it reflected a serious mind set. Tim was now willing to cooperate with the project and promised to send me his sister's cell phone number. He and his wife were about to leave for a vacation outside the United States, so we agreed to meet in New York City in mid-December 2019. We would talk over sushi and sake. The date of that call was October 11.[28]

I called Ilene on Saturday, October 19. Like her twin brother, Ilene was pleasant but cautious because she has been approached before, and asked me for details about the book and who I was, all of which I provided. Over the weeks and months of my interviews I learned that prospective interviewees may feel threatened by journalists, but are generally more receptive to academics. I explained my professional background and qualifications to Ilene. I also mentioned that I am a twin and was raised in New York City, by way of forging common connections. Nevertheless, my knowledge of her adoption and twinship understandably surprised her. She wanted to talk to her brother and think it over. She also asked for more information about me, so I texted my website link and promised to be in touch soon.

Meanwhile, I had travel plans taking me to New York City, New Haven, and Washington, DC, to conduct additional research for this book. I would be on the East Coast from October 22 to November 2. This twelve-day period was heavily scheduled with just one social event, a dinner on October 28 with my twin sister at my favorite New York City restaurant, Canaletto, located on Manhattan's east side. En route to the restaurant, I stopped briefly at an optical store to have my eyeglass frames adjusted. This turned out to be a very fortunate decision because Tim called at that moment and I was able to speak easily in this quiet place that was insulated from the noisy traffic. He expressed his regrets that his twin sister did not wish to cooperate and so he would not be cooperating either. Hoping to persuade him otherwise, I gently told him that I was including a twin from another pair whose co-twin would not be participating, but he was not swayed. He and his twin sister were family. Again, I understood.[29]

DIGRESSION: GENETIC SEXUAL ATTRACTION

Given that LWS separated twins for about twenty years, it is important to consider the implications of twin and sibling separation. The adoption community recognizes a phenomenon known as *genetic sexual attraction* that sometimes evolves between opposite-sex siblings raised apart, and between parents and the biological children they did not raise. Genetic sexual attraction has been described as a desire for close physical contact with a separated relative that may escalate into feelings of sexual desire.[30]

There are five documented cases of reared-apart opposite-sex twins who became romantically involved with one another, either becoming engaged or getting married after meeting as adults. Attraction between reunited male-female twins is no different than the attraction that develops between some separated brothers and sisters. However, the fact that twins are involved amplifies interest in the situation because twins are a rare sibling set. The pairs in question come from the United States,[31] Bulgaria,[32] Australia,[33] Switzerland,[34] and the United Kingdom,[35] and there may be others. In none of these cases were the twins aware of their relationship before becoming close. Their biological connections were, respectively, discovered by a birth mother's search for the twins she adopted away, a birth mother's feelings of familiarity toward her new daughter-in-law, receipt of adoption records by both adopted spouses, and a wife's picture of infant twins that matched one in her new husband's aunt's home. Information about the British case remains confidential.[36]

The most recent case, reported in 2008 in Great Britain, ended in heartbreak and annulment of the relationship at a secret hearing of the High Court. Lord David Alton of Liverpool, an Independent (Crossbench) Peer, called attention to the pair during a debate on the 2008 Human Fertilization and Embryology Bill. Reasoning from this case, Lord Alton argued that children have the right to know the identity of their birth parents.[37] After several attempts that year to pass an amendment to that effect, it was withdrawn. On a related issue, Baroness Royall of Blaisdon committed the government to conducting "a review of practices in informing donor-conceived children of the fact of their donor conception."[38] A review was completed in 2013. A 2020 statement indicated that no further legislative action would be taken, and that parents were encouraged to be open with donor-conceived children regarding their genetic background.[39]

Genetic sexual attraction can be best understood in the context of the Westermarck effect (incest taboo), proposed by the Finnish philosopher and sociologist Edvard Westermarck in 1891. He asserted that because people cannot identify relatives with certainty it is logical to presume that individuals raised together are genetically related. Thus, as an evolutionary adaptation to avoid inbreeding or incest—which raises the chances of genetic defects in children—individuals raised together develop a sexual aversion to one another.[40] Support for this idea comes from the infrequency of romantic ties between unrelated males and females raised together on Israeli kibbutzim where they live and sleep together apart from their parents. Other evidence comes from an old Taiwanese custom in which young females are raised with the males they will eventually marry—such unions are often unsuccessful and infertile, most probably linked to the cohabitation and familiarity of the individuals involved. In contrast, full and half-siblings reared apart can, and have, found one another sexually desirable and formed romantic relationships, as explained previously.[41] This is not so surprising, given human preferences for partners who share behavioral and physical traits, a phenomenon known as positive assortative mating.[42] Friends also show greater similarity in their attitudes and abilities than people chosen at random,[43] and are as alike as fraternal twins in their political views and cognitive structure.[44]

Reared-apart opposite-sex twins took part in the Minnesota Study of Twins Reared Apart, some meeting for the first time on campus. Staff members observed flirtatious behavior between some of these co-twins, prompting a more systematic assessment of their relationships as part of the sexual life history interviews; however, data were available for only a few pairs so conclusions could not be drawn. Likewise, although very rare, romantic connections have also been observed with separated gay twins. The members of an identical reared-apart male pair who participated in the Minnesota Study of Twins Reared Apart developed an intimate relationship—the only known case involving same-sex twins raised apart. However, sexual attraction toward one's twin was expressed by a twin brother in a second separated set, and sexual advances by one separated twin toward the other were reported in an earlier study. The bases of such relationships are complex, but it is likely that they are rooted partly in the twins' perceptions of their behavioral similarities and their lack of a shared social history.[45] It is also possible that such occurrences between same-sex twins are unreported because of the double stigma.

Knowledge of ones' biological background may be more important now than in the past because of possible chance meetings between the growing number of half-siblings conceived by a common sperm donor.[46] If such meetings eventuated in social attraction and marriage between opposite-sex half siblings, the children conceived from such unions would face an elevated risk of having a genetic defect. (This assumes that both half-siblings had inherited the same detrimental gene from their shared mother or father.) All of us carry unfavorable recessive genes, but we are unaffected if we have just one copy.[47] The exact frequency of such chance unions is unknown. Furthermore, in the United States and other Western countries sperm donor identity is not uniformly protected, facilitating searches for half-siblings and fathers. There are also services such as Ancestry.com, 23andme, and various donor sibling networks that can match half-siblings prior to meeting if both individuals register.[48] However, in France where sperm donor identity is concealed, the estimated frequencies of unions between sperm donor-conceived half-siblings and children affected by genetic conditions are considered marginal.[49] This seems surprising, given that France is a much smaller country than the United States, increasing the chances that half-siblings would reside in closer proximity.

LWS separated an unknown number of twins, and presumably there were other male-female pairs among them. All these infants were placed with families in the New York area, a practice that *was* responsible for chance meetings between several identical twins, due to their physical identity, which I will describe later. In contrast, opposite-sex pairs do not look exactly alike and were they to meet they might form close social attachments, produce children with a genetic defect—the risk is 25% if the parents are full siblings—and discover a shocking truth that would derail their lives at many levels. An underappreciated consequence to the discovery, so aptly expressed by one of the reared-apart triplet's wives, is that the effects reach far beyond the twins, disturbing the happiness and well-being of their families.[50]

· 5 ·

"The Biggest Thing in My Life"

Kathy and Betsy

$\mathcal{T}$he title of this chapter is a line from Kathy's 1991 letter to her longtime friend and former boyfriend, Bruce. Kathy is expressing her thoughts about her twin sister, Betsy, whom she had discovered and met for the first time when she was nearly thirty. Betsy was the "biggest thing" in Kathy's life. As if to avoid hurt feelings, Kathy insisted that Bruce was the "next biggest thing" in her life. The letter was written ten years after Betsy allegedly ended her life in 1982, after the twins had enjoyed less than one year together.[1] Kathy was a singleton twin once again until her death in 2018 from leukemia.

Kathy Jo Mazlish and Betsy Caren Leon were most likely fraternal twins according to Kathy's mother, Elaine. However, their twin type was not

The Twins, Their Family Members, and Friends

Kathy

Kathy Mazlish Betsy's reared-apart twin
Elaine Mazlish Kathy's adoptive mother
Robert (Bob) Mazlish Kathy's adoptive father
Liz Mazlish Kathy's younger sister
John Mazlish Kathy's younger brother
Bruce Mayo Kathy's friend

Betsy

Betsy Leon Kathy's reared-apart twin
Edith (Edie) Leon Betsy's adoptive mother
Seymour Leon Betsy's adoptive father

established by the standard scientific methods of the 1950s, such as extensive blood-typing and placental examination; I will say more about this issue later in the chapter.[2] The twins were placed apart by Louise Wise Services (LWS), but the exact reasons are unknown. Their birth on April 2, 1952, preceded the agency's twin separation policy, implemented in 1960, intended to foster each twins' identity and prevent parental overburdening. However, this policy was not formally approved by the agency's board of directors until the late 1960s. But as we know from the story of Tim and Ilene, twins were separated as early as the 1940s.

As I indicted in chapter 3, after 1960, LWS decided that if twins were becoming socially attached to one another, showing the so-called twinning reaction, they would remain together. But as will be evident from the different twins' life histories, it is unlikely that this practice was followed. Furthermore, since the two documentary films were released in 2017 and 2018, not a single reared-together pair placed by LWS has ever come forward or been identified. However, an ambiguous 1962 note in Bernard's handwriting reads, "1 took twins."[3] Perhaps "1" means *one family*. She also drew a line from a note in the margins toward that entry: "Twins were 2 when placed but had always been together in FH [foster home]" and also noted "1 on referral /p ariz." The word "ariz" might mean *Arizona*. Perhaps these twins stayed together, but it is impossible to know for sure.

THE ADOPTIVE FAMILIES

There is more to say about Kathy Mazlish than Betsy Leon. Kathy grew up with two younger siblings, Liz and John (who were not adopted), who could provide information about Kathy, whereas Betsy was an only child. Liz was an especially knowledgeable informant who connected me with Kathy's former boyfriend, Bruce Mayo, who had known Kathy for many years. I also had access to a rare record of Kathy's birth history, summarized in a letter from Spence-Chapin, the agency that took over the LWS files. Some details in that letter also apply to Betsy. However, because Betsy grew up as an only child, there were no siblings for me to consult. Her placement as an only child is a clear departure from LWS's later practice of placing individual twins in families with an older sibling, once the study began.[4] Of course, as the eldest child, Kathy was also placed alone, so it seems that the presence of a sister or brother in the adoptive home was not essential until 1960 when the twin study began. Even then, it was only a prerequisite for the identical twins who were separated and studied in order to keep the family structure constant across cases.

The two sets of adoptive parents, Robert (Bob) and Elaine Mazlish, and Seymour and Edith (Edie) Leon, are deceased. The Mazlishs were a well-to-do couple with a comfortable home in Roslyn Heights, Long Island, located outside New York City. Bob owned and operated Riteway Laundry, a laundry and dry-cleaning business, started by his father after the elder Mazlish emigrated from Poland to the United States.[5] With its fleet of sixty trucks, the Brooklyn-based plant serviced New York City's five boroughs, Long Island, and parts of New Jersey. Elaine was famous for her best-selling books on communication skills with children, co-authored with Adele Faber.[6] Deeply desiring a family, the couple tried to conceive for four years, but were unsuccessful.[7] Like other couples in their situation, they decided to adopt and turned to LWS for help—because LWS was *the* agency to go to for prospective Jewish parents wishing to raise a Jewish baby. They were given a baby girl with dark hair, a dark complexion, blue eyes, and a fine bone structure. She was alert, smiled, and "gooed."[8]

Seymour and Edie Leon lived in Brooklyn, New York, when they adopted Betsy. Seymour was nearly thirty and Edie was nearly twenty-eight years of age at the time. They relocated to West Orange, New Jersey, when Betsy was seven or eight years old.[9] In the early 1950s and 1960s, these communities were largely middle class, but lacked the affluence of Roslyn Heights. Elaine speculated that this difference might have played a role in the conclusion to the twins' final meeting, to which I will later return. Seymour worked in the garment industry in New York City, in a business established by his father. The Leons' reason for adopting their daughter was infertility. The couple moved to Verona, New Jersey, when Betsy was a young adult and on her own.

BIRTH PARENTS

A four-page letter was sent by Spence-Chapin to Kathy Jo Mazlish in 2008, in response to her request for information about her birth family.[10] It is rare to have such detailed information on the birth parents of an LWS-separated twin. In fact, this letter was a surprise to me because I had been told that these records were in storage and unorganized, and also unavailable due to New York State regulations.[11] Perhaps the records were on site at Spence-Chapin before that and in an accessible format. It is also possible that the person who composed Kathy's letter, identified as a member of the adoption counseling team, was a compassionate sort. In the future, Spence-Chapin may be more forthcoming with twins seeking information, due to Governor Andrew

Cuomo's November 2019 approval of legislation allowing adoptees to examine their pre-adoption birth certificates.[12]

Kathy Jo Mazlish, née Ruth Crain, was born at 3:29 p.m., three minutes ahead of her twin sister, Betsy Caren Leon, née Renee Crain.[13] Kathy's birth weight was four pounds, three and a half ounces, below the average weight of five pounds, two and three-quarter ounces typical of female twins.[14] Nevertheless, there is no indication that Kathy showed any physical difficulties. Of course, due to their unique birth circumstances—early delivery, shared intrauterine environment—twins' birthweights cannot be judged with reference to non-twins' standards.

The pregnancy seems to have lasted nearly full term because the twins' birth mother was three months pregnant in early October 1951 and delivered her twins in early April 1952. The birth of two babies "surprised and delighted" their mother who found both twins "very cute," and held and fed them in the hospital.[15] She was twenty-eight years old at the time, single, slim, physically healthy, with brown eyes and reddish-brown hair. Her features were sharp, but attractive, and she dressed with style. She had a high school degree, had worked briefly in textile design, and had enjoyed painting and crafts. However, she suffered from an emotional disorder requiring three hospitalizations, the first in 1946, about six years before her babies were born. Two medical reports from different physicians indicate diagnoses of "manic depressive psychosis with some schizophrenic traits," and a suggestion of "psychosis more indicative of schizophrenia than manic [depression]." She had received both individual therapy and shock treatments during her hospital stays, and psychotherapy after release.

The twins' birth father was a high school graduate and a professional dance band musician. The twins' birth mother described him as "intelligent and sensitive," but also "neurotic."[16] Their relationship was brief, and when she called to tell him about the birth, he said he would visit, but no further information about this was recorded. The social climate of the 1950s was unsympathetic to single mothers. The pregnancy greatly upset the birth mother's father, who said his daughter had to leave their home. She moved to a furnished room, paying a rent she could barely afford. At the advice of her sister, a social worker familiar with LWS, she sought the agency's assistance in October 1951. Being in the early stages of her pregnancy she was unable to enter the maternity residence, so LWS found her a room, provided her with an allowance, and arranged for her prenatal care. During this time, she worked in a factory and continued receiving outpatient psychotherapy.

Upon transfer to the maternity residence in January 1952, she experienced increased anxiety and nightmares. She was moved to the hospital on

Staten Island on March 30, 1952, where she delivered her babies three days later.[17]

BECOMING SEPARATED

The newborn twins and their mother returned to the maternity residence after being discharged from the hospital. Over the next several weeks, their mother tried to put together a plan that would allow her to raise her two daughters. She considered applying for public assistance and asking her sister to assist on weekends. Ultimately, her escalating anxiety over the prospect of raising two newborns left adoption as the only viable option, especially given her requests for psychiatric treatment at this time. Consequently, both twins remained in the baby nursery until May 20 before moving together to an LWS temporary boarding care family.[18] Kathy's foster mother described her as a "good baby and easy to care for . . . alert and responsive to smiles and attention." The foster mother also noted that Kathy required "a lot of feedings because [she was] always hungry." Details about Betsy's early development were not given to Kathy because of confidentiality concerns.[19]

Kathy's progress in her foster home continued to be monitored by LWS. By two months of age, her development appeared normal in terms of eating, sleeping, vocalizing, and socializing behaviors. Meanwhile, her birth mother continued her psychiatric treatment and visits with a social worker from LWS. She was interested in the two babies, asking questions about them and requesting photographs. Finally, on August 6, 1952, Kathy and Betsy's mother relinquished her twins and signed legal documents allowing them to be adopted. Whether she asked LWS to keep her daughters together or was told they would be placed apart because families were unwilling to take two newborns are unknowns.[20] It is also possible that she was "informed" that twins fare better psychologically if they are separated. Other unwed LWS mothers of twins who wished to keep their twins together later discovered that their requests had been denied.[21] Which twin, Kathy or Betsy, was adopted first is unknown.

The twins' birth mother eventually married and delivered a son, fourteen years younger than her twins. Raising him proved to be difficult, so she placed him in foster care and then a group home. Throughout her marriage she underwent several hospitalizations, but according to her husband was generally doing well. Her husband indicated that she had died in 1969 when she was forty-six years old, but the cause of her death was not stated in the Spence-Chapin letter.[22]

As of 2019, Kathy's sister Liz has been a counseling psychotherapist in private practice. She is also a talented sleuth, having found Kathy's younger paternal half-brother, Steven, through the personal genomics and biotechnology company 23andme.[23] Steven is pursuing a second career as a social worker whose client case load includes patients with schizophrenia. He indicated that his father showed no signs of psychiatric disorder and was mentally healthy. As a father himself, Steven had actually read Elaine Mazlish's books on child rearing and loved them. He was also familiar with Bob Mazlish's laundry business, having grown up in Brooklyn. As an only child, Steven had desperately wanted to have siblings. He had no idea that his father had had a brief relationship with another woman before marrying Steven's mother, or that he had half-siblings who were twins. He recalled his father as having been a "loving and attentive parent," which was comforting news to Liz.[24]

KATHY JO

Kathy met her new parents less than one week after her mother relinquished her for adoption. Bob and Elaine Mazlish first visited their new, four-month-old daughter in her temporary foster home on August 11, 1952. They spent time that day and the next playing with her and getting to know her. Kathy seemed happy and relaxed with her new parents. When they arrived the following day, on August 13, it was to take her home, although the final adoption papers weren't signed until October 27, 1953, over one year later. There is typically a trial period between receiving a child and becoming the child's legal parent; until the adoption is finalized, the agency retains legal rights over the child. The agency also uses this time to make home visits to assess the child's well-being and allow parents to decide if they are happy with how the child fits into their new home.

Kathy may have been an easy baby in foster care, but this changed during her early months in the Mazlish home. She was difficult to care for, hard to handle, and a high-maintenance baby overall. She also suffered from coeliac disease, a digestive condition in which the small intestine cannot absorb certain nutrients.[25] Symptoms such as bloating and abdominal pain are common and usually appear by eight to twelve months of age. The ingestion of gluten-free foods is required, but such foods were less commercially available in the 1950s than they are today. Because there is a trial period, Kathy's maternal grandmother urged her daughter Elaine to give up the baby, but that didn't happen.[26] Elaine and Bob chose to keep her, believing that their love and resources would ultimately foster her health and well-being. *They believed that nurture would prove more powerful than nature.* They also imagined that LWS might have chosen them to raise a potentially problematic child because they were such reliable and responsible people.

Regardless of any intentions imagined or otherwise, LWS had not told Elaine and Bob that Kathy's biological mother had a history of serious psychiatric disorder. And they were not told that Kathy had a twin sister Betsy—living just twenty miles away in Brooklyn and later forty-five miles away in West Orange, New Jersey—whose adoptive parents might be experiencing similar struggles.

BETSY CAREN

As the second-born twin, Betsy was at greater physical risk during delivery than her twin sister, Kathy. Vaginally delivered second-born twins are more likely to experience respiratory distress, neonatal trauma, and infection than first-born twins. Unfortunately, there is no available information about Betsy's early health. However, the brief three-minute interval between the two births was in her favor, given that shorter intervals are associated with more desirable outcomes.[27]

Betsy grew up in Brooklyn and West Orange, but her last residence, once she left home, was in the lower Manhattan meatpacking district of New York City.[28] This area is now considered upscale, but in the mid- to late 1970s Betsy would have experienced a rundown, gritty neighborhood.[29] Rents would have been considerably lower in those days, possibly an attractive feature for a young woman just starting her career. Moreover, the bohemian lifestyle of nearby Greenwich Village appealed to Betsy who enjoyed hearing jazz, learning philosophy, and writing poems.[30] Betsy had an artistic bent, as did her birth parents and her twin sister who were variously drawn to music, art, and literature. Kathy wrote poems that she contributed regularly to a poetry magazine run by a friend.[31]

Like the Mazlishs, Betsy's parents, Seymour and Edie, would not have been told of their daughter's family history of mental disorder, nor that she had a twin sister adopted by a different family nearby. Whether Betsy was a difficult child is unknown, although she showed confusion and "mind drifting" at times and was occasionally troubled. She had a tense relationship with her mother, Edie, who was very controlling. Betsy was also described as "different" and "unusual."[32] Whether these behaviors were evidence of a more serious mental condition is uncertain, but she apparently developed serious psychopathological symptoms over the years. Still, Betsy attended college at the New School for Social Research, in New York, with a double major in English and psychology.[33] Individuals who knew her did not think she had completed her undergraduate degree. Still, they described her as very bright, even brilliant, and considerably more articulate and intellectual than Kathy.[34]

Betsy was interested in finding her biological parents, a desire that ultimately led to the discovery of her twin sister.

KATHY: GROWING UP

The teenage years were hard for Kathy and had an extremely disruptive effect on her parents and younger siblings. At her core, she was a sweet, giving, and loving child, but her appearance and behaviors were odd, and children mocked and taunted her. They called her names, such as "witch," because of her prominent nose, and "gummy," because her large gums were quite visible when she spoke. With these features, and her thin arms and legs, she hardly conformed to even the average image of her peers. Boys and girls picked on her, and her friends were from the less popular crowds. According to Liz, Kathy's presence brought an "irrational element" to the home atmosphere.[35] Elaine's relationship with each of her daughters differed greatly—Elaine was often in conflict with Kathy during her growing up years, less so with Liz who tried to be better behaved.[36] Still, Bob and Elaine stayed highly focused on helping Kathy cope and, hopefully, overcome her physical and emotional difficulties. At age thirteen, when Kathy complained that she felt unattractive, Elaine agreed to rhinoplasty to smooth her nose and blepharoplasty to remove dark areas under her eyes. It was unusual for a young teenager to undergo these procedures, but exceptions were made in her case.[37]

Elaine and Bob arranged private psychotherapy for Kathy when she was five years old, sessions that continued throughout her childhood and adolescence. In 1965, when Kathy was thirteen, Elaine joined her friend and future co-author, Adele, in attending parenting sessions organized by the late Dr. Haim Ginott, a psychotherapist, parent educator, and author dedicated to helping children develop self-confidence. "If you want your children to improve, let them overhear the nice things you say about them to others."[38] These experiences led to Elaine's books that have made such a positive difference in parents' and children's lives.

There is a moment in time that speaks to Kathy's humanity and integrity. It involved a well-liked boy in her elementary school class who could not tie his shoes. One day his lace became loose, so he asked Kathy to tie it for him. No one else was around. The boy asked Kathy to do him the favor of keeping her help a secret which she did—he never heard about the incident from his classmates. Over fifty years later, he was still moved by what she had done— he sought out Liz to tell her that and to express his admiration and gratitude toward Kathy. "It was a great act of kindness that even all these years later, I treasure," he said.

Kathy enrolled at Webster College in St. Louis, Missouri, as a music major. She played both piano and guitar and was a talented singer—gifts she most likely inherited from her birth father who was a professional musician and played in dance bands. However, after one year she decided to attend a more prestigious institution and transferred to Washington University as a sophomore. Like her twin sister Betsy, she declared a double major in English and psychology.[39] However, Kathy's mental challenges were escalating, and she was diagnosed with schizophrenia at age twenty while in college. The Mazlishs continued to support her emotionally and financially. They placed enduring value on loyalty to Kathy and confidentiality regarding her mental condition. Not even their closest friends knew very much.

Washington University was a positive experience for Kathy in some ways. It was there that she met Bruce Mayo, an international student from Germany, who became her tutor for a German class. Their relationship transitioned into a friendship, then a romance, and eventually they moved in together before heading to the Boston area. Once there, Kathy worked at various odd jobs, some at psychiatric treatment centers, while receiving outpatient psychotherapy. The following summer, 1974, Bruce received a scholarship and returned to Konstanz, Germany, for several years. During that time, Kathy found a new boyfriend. She maintained that relationship for a while even after Bruce returned to Boston in about 1977. Bruce stayed in Boston until 1984, living with Kathy some of the time. However, life with Kathy proved very difficult for Bruce during those years as he found himself transitioning from friend to "live-in therapist." Kathy slept throughout the day, could not hold a job, and showed paranoid behaviors. Only later did Bruce learn that Kathy had developed serious symptoms of schizophrenia and had possibly attempted suicide by drug overdose. He left the United States in 1984 for professional reasons but had "serious qualms" about leaving Kathy behind. Elaine, always watching out for her daughter, arranged for Kathy to have a private psychotherapist who enrolled her in the Massachusetts mental health system.[40]

As of 1974, Kathy and Bruce were no longer romantically involved, but they remained very close friends. "I still loved the person Kathy had been," Bruce told me.[41] Even after Bruce returned to Germany, began dating his future wife in 1998 and married her in 2006, Bruce was the "next biggest thing" in Kathy's life.[42]

SEARCHING FOR FAMILY

The Adoptees' Liberty Movement Association (ALMA) is the "oldest, most comprehensive and successful registry of its kind." Founded in 1971 by adoptee Florence Fisher, ALMA assists adopted individuals wishing to find their birth parents and other biological relatives.[43] Fisher remains famous for her book *The Search for Anna Fisher*, the best-selling true story of her search for her own birth family.[44]

There is a letter sent by Kathy to Bruce that is not dated, but was most likely written in late 1982 or 1983.[45] Kathy wrote that she had called ALMA and spoken to two people who knew Betsy. One person was Fisher, who labeled the twins' separation by LWS a "monstrous thing." The other person was Karl Zimmer, who provided advice to adoptees searching for family members. There was also a file at ALMA that contained letters and postcards from Betsy and Kathy to Florence Fisher. This file also contained a form filled out by Betsy in 1981 or 1982, when she sought assistance from the association in locating her biological parents. At the time, Betsy didn't know she had a twin.

When I called Fisher in December 2019, she was in the process of packing her belongings to move from her Brooklyn, New York, apartment. As part of her relocation process, she had been transferring files from ALMA to her home and deliberating over which ones to keep. I contacted her because of her correspondence with Kathy, described in the letter Kathy had sent to Bruce. Fisher knew why I was calling because I had told her associate at ALMA about my interest in the "Mazlish twin." I was excited to talk with Fisher to learn what she knew about the case. I was unprepared for her regret, frustration, sorrow, and self-blame—only a few days earlier she had held the file in her hand, mulled over the value of keeping it, then placed it in the trash.

At age ninety-one, Fisher still had a sharp mind and a good memory for past details. Over the next forty-five minutes, she mentally reviewed the contents of that crucial file, focusing not on Kathy, whom she had never met, but on memories of Betsy, whom she had met. In 1981 or 1982, Betsy had visited Fisher's office unannounced and they spoke for about an hour. Florence liked her. She recalled a "slender, not-too tall girl with dark hair who didn't seem to care a great deal about how she was dressed." Betsy was unemployed at the time, and Florence described her as looking very unhappy. In fact, Betsy may have attempted suicide on one occasion by taking an overdose of pills, but was supposedly saved by her boyfriend who brought her to the hospital in time.[46] Whether the overdose was accidental or intentional, and when it occurred are unknown. Betsy completed the paperwork required for finding family, but never returned to ALMA. However, Betsy took Karl Zimmer's advice to search for her birth records in the New York Public Library.

Flipping through the library's holdings Betsy found her biological mother's last name—Crain—and her own first given name—Renee. It was her random glance at the adjacent record that proved life-changing—it was for a female named "Ruth Crain" born in the same Staten Island hospital, to the same mother, on the same day. No doubt, this was her twin sister. With the help of a private investigator, Betsy located Kathy's parents and phoned Elaine Mazlish, claiming to be an old friend of Kathy's. Elaine gave Betsy her daughter's telephone number in Boston, and Betsy called her immediately.

What is it like to answer the phone and hear someone say, "Kathy Mazlish—I am your twin sister, Betsy," especially when one's mental health is fragile? Without speaking, Kathy hung up the phone two times, not sure what to make of this information. In between these calls, she spoke with Bruce who encouraged her to ask the caller why she thought Kathy was her twin. Kathy suffered from schizophrenia and paranoia at the time, but her condition may not have fully accounted for her response. Learning that one is a twin is an extraordinary event, information that significantly revises personal history and identity. It is even more shocking when the news is delivered by a stranger.[47] Perhaps Betsy knew that, having experienced it herself. Betsy persisted and on the third call convinced Kathy that what she said about being her twin was true.

Kathy spoke about the call with her therapist who thought her news of a twin sister had to be another hallucination. Her friend Bruce didn't think so and agreed to be with her at the twins' first meeting in Boston one week later, along with a producer from CBS's television magazine *60 Minutes*. Betsy's mother Edie had been friendly with Mike Wallace, a correspondent for the show. Edie had apparently contacted Wallace about her daughter's discovery of her twin and the twins' early separation. At this time, in late summer and early fall of 1982, Wallace was fully committed to exposing LWS's policy of placing twins apart, as well as the study that covertly tracked them; he and his team were still involved with producing Tim and Ilene's story. Betsy and Kathy promised to add another vital dimension to a television program about LWS's twin adoption practices that would be heart-rending, revealing, and controversial. Whether they were identical or fraternal twins would never be resolved.

TWIN TYPE

Twin type is never definitively determined by merely comparing common-alities in selected behavioral traits, because both identical and fraternal twins can match or differ, but some physical traits can be informative. As I indicated, either DNA testing or a standard physical resemblance questionnaire is required.[48] Kathy's sister Liz was told by their mother that Kathy and Betsy were fraternal twins and while she believed that for many years, Liz has begun to question that assignment. Not only is the source of Elaine's information uncertain, but some relatives believed they were identical because of what Betsy had told them. Bruce, who had met both twins, believes they were identical, based on their appearance, but few people had seen them together.[49]

My inspection of infant photographs reveals marked similarities in the twins' facial structure from the nose up, but less so around the mouth. In later years, both twins underwent different types of cosmetic surgery, altering their appearance somewhat. However, both twins showed some sharpness in their facial features, as did their birth mother; this description was included in the letter Kathy had received from Spence-Chapin. It is not possible to know their twin type without comparing their DNA.

I learned early in my career that the judgment of someone who does *not* know both twins well can be *more accurate* than the judgment of someone who does, because the latter are more sensitive to subtle differences between them. This may explain why more identical twins are misdiagnosed as fraternal twins than the other way around.[50] Interestingly, Liz had never met Betsy, a situation I will explore later on. Given the foregoing, I view Kathy and Betsy's twin type as undecided. Because these twins were separated in 1952, eight years before the twin study began, attention to twin type by LWS was probably given less weight or was disregarded by staff when placing the babies.

REUNION

In late 1981 or early 1982, Betsy and Kathy met for the first time at the Copley Plaza Hotel in downtown Boston. Their reunion was witnessed by Kathy's friend Bruce and *60 Minutes* producer, the late Madeline Amgott.[51] Bruce's being there was a precondition set by Kathy that both Betsy and Amgott had to accept. "I felt that she wanted me there for protection," Bruce told me.[52] "I can't say what frightened her, but her feelings definitely went from bad to good at the meeting." Neither set of parents was there, but we can only speculate as to why that was so. Perhaps *60 Minutes* allowed the twins a little privacy during their first precious moments together, or worried that the families' presence would distort the amazing story they hoped to capture. Bruce recalls no discussion about inviting the twins' mothers and fathers, either by CBS or by the twins.

In his mind's eye, Bruce recalled the four of them sitting around a table, the twins directly opposite him and Amgott to his left. Kathy and Betsy studied each other intensely as newly reunited twins do, trying to gauge their similarities and differences. Bruce thought they looked very much alike, suggesting that they could conceivably be identical twins. According to his description,

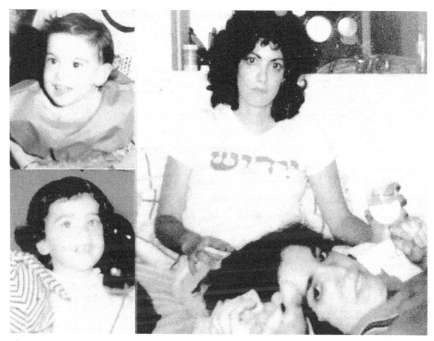

Figure 5.1.   Reunited twins Betsy (top) and Kathy, as toddlers and at age twenty-nine. Their twin type remains uncertain. Courtesy of Liz Mazlish.

the twins' faces were clearly as alike—perhaps more alike—than those of most fraternal twin sisters.

The twins had the same curvature of the spine (scoliosis) which they apparently inherited from their birth father who was diagnosed with the condition as a teenager.[53] They also had the same voice quality, although Bruce detected differences in their accents, probably reflecting Betsy's Brooklyn-New Jersey and Kathy's Long Island upbringings. Accents, unlike voice quality which has a partial genetic component,[54] start becoming acquired in early infancy from hearing the language spoken in one's social environment.[55] Regardless, Kathy's mother, Elaine, could not tell the twins apart when they spoke on the telephone.[56]

Both twins suffered from serious psychiatric conditions most likely transmitted from their maternal side of the family. Results from fourteen studies show that the similarity rate for schizophrenia converges on 48 percent for identical twins and 17 percent for fraternal twins, indicating genetic effects.[57] The same pattern emerges for bipolar disorder, with figures of 55 percent for identical twins and 7 percent for fraternal twins.[58]

For forty-five minutes, the twins answered Amgott's questions, most likely about their adoption and reunion, their families, and other significant events in their separate lives. Producers can be business-like, but Amgott was both empathic and professional.[59] Wallace called Kathy's mother's co-author, Adele, for information about Kathy's growing up years, but Adele declined due to privacy considerations. And Adele had never met Betsy.

In the days following their reunion Kathy expressed a mix of emotions. According to Bruce, she was initially shaken and frightened. It was "like she'd seen a ghost," wondering how she and Betsy could possibly have been put into different homes. She felt some anger toward LWS for their separation, but seemed to accept it. But as the weeks went by, her apprehension was replaced by great joy. The twins met several times in New York City and spoke regularly by telephone. Photographs show them together in Betsy's apartment.[60] Liz understood the twins' evolving relationship as one of "love, bonding, and completion."[61] Such sentiments are not unusual, having been expressed by other newly reunited twins, but they are not unique to twins. They characterize the experiences of many adoptees who finally recognize a physical and behavioral likeness in someone else.[62]

Kathy's parents, Bob and Elaine, were angry and felt "doubly duped" upon learning the hidden truths about their daughter's background.[63] Not only was Kathy a twin, but her troubling behaviors and psychiatric disorder suddenly made sense in light of her biological mother's mental health history. Her parents also felt some relief that they did not bear responsibility for Kathy's illness. At the same time, they were delighted that she had found her twin. They regretted the lost opportunity to adopt them both, an offer that was never made to either family. Elaine and her husband had the love and resources to raise two children at the same time. And for them it was a matter of what their moral compass told them was right, and that was raising the twins together.

60 MINUTES

Betsy eventually returned to Boston with Madeline Amgott, who came to conduct additional interviews and obtain the signed release forms required for television tapings. The program was progressing on schedule, which is why no one expected it to come to a sudden halt. The twins' tapes were never edited, becoming what are known as outtakes—recordings that are never aired. There are competing explanations for why production ceased. According to Bruce, Kathy changed her mind about appearing on television and refused to sign the release form. The twins engaged in several heated arguments over this, during which Betsy tried to convince Kathy to cooperate. Kathy's refusal to give signed consent would have been only a partial accounting of what happened.

Interviewees sometimes have second thoughts about publicity, but Kathy reveled in the media attention[64] and most likely would have reconsidered and taken part.

The second explanation for why *60 Minutes* failed to move forward came from Liz who had heard her family's side of the story, but it is only speculation. When the twins were in New York for their taped interviews, Mike Wallace asked Betsy: "How do you feel knowing that your twin sister was born with a silver spoon in her mouth?" This may sound like a safe query, but co-twin differences in social stature can be sensitive. The same question or situation may appear harmless to one person and toxic to another. At that time, Betsy was also experiencing difficulties with her boyfriend, which may have increased her sensitivity to stress. Soon after her interview with Wallace, on September 2, 1982, Betsy died, allegedly from suicide. The cause of her death has not been fully confirmed, but suicide seems most likely.[65]

Suicidal tendencies are complex behaviors that have been associated with genetic factors, mental disorder, impaired impulse control, and depression.[66] Betsy did have a genetic predisposition toward depression. Her alleged suicide, if proven, would have been her second attempt, apparently due to a drug overdose as before. A suicide note was never found. Karl Zimmer from ALMA, who had met Betsy, was certain that such a note existed, but the basis of his belief is uncertain.[67] Betsy's death was devastating to Kathy, who requested psychiatric hospitalization after Betsy died; her therapist reported evidence of hallucinations. How Kathy received the news is uncertain, but it may have come from Betsy's mother, Edie; Kathy and Edie had spent some time together in the days following Betsy's death. Bruce recalled his shock at coming home from work to find Kathy idling on his porch with one of their mutual friends. Kathy told him what had happened and that she could not be alone that night, or even live alone after that. The two eventually moved back in together. Kathy also entered day treatment at the Somerville Mental Health Clinic, in Somerville, Massachusetts, at the end of 1982. According to Bruce, "Possibly Betsy's loss was the straw that broke the camel's back."[68]

What is certain is that Betsy's death prevented *60 Minutes* from going forward. According to a March 1983 LWS memo, Mike Wallace had heard there was a "suicide" of a "30-year-old female twin."[69] The timing of the memo is interesting, given that Betsy's death had occurred six months prior. Decisions about the nature and direction of television programs can be unpredictable; scheduled programming may change at any moment due to unforeseen events. As it happened, production did not stop right away because there was one more person Wallace wanted to talk to: Florence Fisher, the founder of ALMA who had met Betsy in the past year or so. Fisher, who was vacationing in Rome, received an invitation from Wallace to interview for an upcoming segment on adoption and twins. She had been away for the first two months of a six-month stay, but she returned to New York City immediately. Mike Wallace and *60 Minutes* were too important for her to turn down.[70]

Florence entered the studio exhausted from her long flight. Aside from the camera crew, no one else was present, allowing her to answer Wallace's questions directly. Betsy had already died when the interview took place, but Florence, who had seen Betsy within the last year, wasn't told until the session had ended. When she heard of Betsy's death from one of Wallace's colleagues, she broke down in tears. As Wallace turned to leave, Florence overheard someone tell him that if the show was aired there would be a lawsuit. The threat may have come from a member of Betsy's family.[71] Edie Leon, still grief-stricken, did not wish to discuss her loss when contacted in 2013 by filmmaker Lori Shinseki.[72]

Kathy had spoken by telephone to Shinseki, who had considered including Kathy in her film *The Twinning Reaction*. However, Shinseki ultimately decided against it—she felt that inviting Kathy for an interview would be exploitative of Kathy's mental illness.[73] Another difficulty was that Kathy had asked Shinseki for fifty dollars which, aside from expenses, is never given for documentary film participation to avoid bias or the appearance of bias.

AFTERMATH

Betsy remained a constant presence in Kathy's life, occasionally appearing in her dreams. Kathy also acquired a pet cat and named the cat "Betsy," giving her some comfort.[74] Kathy also did something she considered to be "special"—she planted a tree in Israel in honor of her twin sister.[75] And Kathy recalled a "beautiful day" when she and Betsy walked down New York's Park Avenue and saw a horse break free from a carriage and run unrestrainedly down the street. "I felt like that horse—very free and triumphant."[76] Betsy was "the biggest thing in my life."

Liz never met Betsy. Liz recalled that Kathy had referred to her twin as "my sister," keeping Betsy close and not wishing to share her with her younger siblings. Liz believes that Kathy felt threatened by others when it came to her twin—Betsy belonged to Kathy, and no one was going to interfere with that relationship. In fact, Kathy and Liz rarely visited with one another, although both sisters were living in the Boston area. Liz had moved to Boston from Minneapolis in 1983 and stayed there until 2014, several years before Kathy was diagnosed with leukemia. There was even a time when Kathy lived in Arlington, about eight blocks away from Liz's office. Kathy's intensifying psychiatric illness over decades kept them apart. During this time, when Kathy was in her mid-thirties, she changed her name to Katherine.[77] To honor her preference, I will use the name Katherine for the rest of this chapter; when Liz accidentally called her sister "Kathy," she was corrected.

Liz and Katherine met by chance one day in Arlington in 2009. That day, Liz had finished reading *Identical Strangers*, a book written by the LWS twins Elyse Schein and Paula Bernstein, who found each other after a thirty-five-year separation.[78] The book prompted Liz to think about her sister and Betsy who had been apart nearly as long. Suddenly, that same day, Liz saw Katherine, sitting outside a Starbucks coffee shop, eating popcorn and drinking coffee. Katherine said "hi" in a casual tone as if they had been in touch all along. The sisters started to talk, and Katherine spoke about Betsy to Liz as though Betsy were still alive—in fact, for the rest of her life she believed that Betsy had not died. Katherine invited Liz to come to her apartment. Liz asked her sister if she had photographs of her twin—Katherine did and showed them to her.

When Liz and Katherine arrived at the apartment, one of the first things Katherine said was that she had read *Identical Strangers*, and showed Liz where she had placed it on her bookshelf. Then, while sitting on a sofa, Katherine reached for an album that contained photographs taken of Katherine with Betsy during the time they knew each other. "I was very touched," Liz recalled. "There were the two of them together and I could finally see what Betsy looked like." There was more. In the center of Katherine's kitchen table was a framed photograph from 1968, of Liz, age ten, and their brother John, age eight, dancing together at their grandparents' fiftieth wedding anniversary party. There was nothing else on the table. "I broke down and cried. It was moving to see how important we were to her," Liz told me. She remembered the cards and gifts that Kathy sent to her when Liz was away at summer camp. Sometime later, Liz told John about the photograph—its prominence was a part of Katherine that Liz and John hadn't realized, a glimpse of what meant something to their sister. John fondly recalled that "Kath" had once bought him a Beatles album and was "totally in on a Christmas caper—we replaced the fake white tree with a real one while mom and dad slept."[79]

Liz shared many of these thoughts with me when I visited her in northern California, in October 2019. As she was leafing through a picture album, she suddenly cried out, "Oh my God! These are the pictures Katherine was showing me that day."

LAST DAYS AND BEYOND

Katherine was diagnosed with leukemia in 2017 and was treated in a Boston hospital. Liz visited her frequently and the two grew closer; John made a trip to Boston from New York to see his sister. These meetings filled Liz and John with regrets over the lost opportunities they might have had to truly be sisters and brother. During this time, Katherine experienced periods of lucidity while undergoing psychiatric care. Her longtime friend, Bruce, flew to Boston to be with her in the hospital, but he arrived a day late—Katherine passed away on February 1, 2018.[80] Liz organized and conducted a memorial service in Boston, immediately across from the medical complex so that Katherine's family, friends, doctors, nurses, and social workers could attend. The memorial was a moving ceremony that included ritual, photos, flowers, music, singing, and a sharing circle, followed by a dinner. The people who treated her said that they loved her—they recalled her clever wit and giving spirit. Liz also arranged Katherine's funeral service in Great Neck, Long Island, that allowed time for memories of her sister to be expressed. Liz still keeps Katherine's last voice messages on her cellphone.[81]

We can never know how Katherine and Betsy would have fared had they been raised together. Judging by their closely evolving relationship, it is likely that Katherine and Betsy would have benefited from the support they could have shared, especially during the early years before their mental disorders became severe. "I still think happiness was something I could give [Betsy] without [drugs]," Katherine wrote to Bruce.[82] In fact, the suicide rate of twins is below that of non-twins, a finding explained by the special social bonds that bind twins together.[83] It is also possible that, as a full sister, Betsy might have provided life-saving cells for treating her sister's leukemia had she lived—LWS never anticipated that separating twins might deny them these medical benefits.[84] We will never know the answers to these questions because Katherine and Betsy never had a chance.

Over the years, Liz has tried unsuccessfully to obtain the outtakes from her sister's interview with *60 Minutes*. Several high-level executives at CBS explained to me that such materials are entirely inaccessible to the public if they are not aired. I appreciate the policy adhered to by CBS, but I persisted in my quest nonetheless. When the documentary film *Mike Wallace Was Here* was released in October 2019, its director Avi Belkin had access to "decades of never-before-seen footage and interviews from the *60 Minutes* vault."[85] In response to my query as to whether Belkin had viewed these materials, a representative from Delirio Films—the company that produced the documentary—replied that neither Avi nor Delirio had any knowledge of these stories or related footage at CBS News. I wonder—did Belkin see something, but overlook its significance? It is curious that the vault was unsealed for a film-maker, but perhaps the twins' outtakes were stored elsewhere. In fact, I would not have known about them if not for Liz. It is possible that the CBS staff I contacted initially believed I was referring not to the 1982 *60 Minutes* tapings of Kathy and Betsy, and Tim and Ilene, but to a second LWS exposé attempt in the late 1990s. That episode, which focused on the separated LWS triplets, was led by Walt Bogdanich, now an investigative reporter for the *New York Times*. That story comes in chapter 10.

Despite my failed efforts to acquire the *60 Minutes* tapes, I have learned what I believe is the *complete chronology* of the reactions and responses by Viola Bernard, Peter Neubauer, and LWS administrators to the tapings of the two twin pairs, Tim and Ilene, and Kathy and Betsy. This information had been placed in a medium-sized file tucked into one of Viola Bernard's 382 boxes, maintained by the Columbia University archives.[86] Reading through each page, some marked "Confidential," I was astonished that this material was not kept secret. These events are the focus of the next chapter.

· *6* ·

60 Minutes

Media Inquiry

$\mathcal{O}$n Friday, May 15, 1981, television producer Madeline Amgott telephoned Dr. Viola Bernard, requesting an interview on "children's rights" for CBS News. Dr. Bernard's secretary told Amgott that Bernard was leaving for an appointment and would return the call. The secretary later phoned Amgott to say that Bernard would be out for the day and gone for the weekend. Could Bernard call her on Monday? In response to the secretary's further questioning, Amgott explained that CBS was preparing a program on twins adopted apart and wanted an "official opinion" on this practice from Dr. Bernard. Bernard knew that twin study director Dr. Peter Neubauer had also been contacted by CBS and would be meeting with Amgott to discuss this issue. Bernard's secretary told this to Amgott, explained that Bernard's schedule was "terribly tight" in the coming weeks, and assured her that Neubauer could speak for both. "To this [Amgott] said, 'Oh really' and seemed quite satisfied."[1]

May 1981 was the start of CBS's continuing investigations into Louise Wise Services' (LWS's) twin adoption policies, and the LWS-Child Development Center (CDC) study that quietly tracked the twins. Led by *60 Minutes* correspondent Mike Wallace, the material was to be presented alongside interviews with several separated twin sets. Wallace was persistent in his efforts to persuade Bernard, Neubauer, and Barbara Miller, head of LWS post-adoption services, to be interviewed. They resisted. These opposing campaigns went on for nearly two years. Walter Cronkite, *CBS Evening News* anchor, and Dan Rather, *60 Minutes* correspondent and *CBS Evening News* anchor after Cronkite, were also interested. Neither side was willing to concede.

Bernard and her colleagues were clearly worried. A number of issues were extremely troubling to them, such as the twins' and families' reactions to learning about the separation and study from the media, and concern that

91

other adoptees might start wondering if they had a twin. I discovered details about *60 Minutes'* attempts to present this story to the public that have never been disclosed publicly.

This saga began with the May 15, 1981, interview of Justine Wise Polier, former LWS president and then board member, for Cronkite's summer special, *Children in the World Today*.[2] Her questions came from CBS's medical correspondent Dr. Holly Atkinson.[3] What transpired during that interview worried Bernard. The conversation began as a discussion about "children's rights" of which Polier was knowledgeable, then detoured into LWS's twins' adoption policy and the twin study, with which Polier was less familiar. Polier was surprised that the interview, which took place in her home, was taped and believed that CBS had purposely planned the pivot in advance. Bernard learned about this interview when she phoned LWS Executive Director Morton Rogers to tell him about Amgott's call.

In her May 20 memo to investigators Neubauer and Christa Balzert, and Director Rogers, Bernard wrote that Polier was "quite unprepared for these questions, and indeed had no reason for being intimately conversant with the situation, about which she was, of course, in general, familiar." Bernard also complained that Amgott's initial phone call did not specifically reference Cronkite's program and that "her first call to my office did not reveal her true interest any more than was the case with Judge Polier." Bernard also noted that "you Peter . . . have connections which you may be able to use to straighten out things with CBS." Ultimately, Cronkite, with no apparent pressure from Neubauer, decided that the material on children's rights was not scientific enough for his program and turned the material and crew over to Wallace.[4] Perhaps Neubauer did not capitalize on his connections or Bernard overestimated his influence.

Polier served as president of LWS's Board of Directors from 1946 through at least 1981.[5] During this time the board had endorsed, then formally approved, separating twins, and the study had been ongoing for over ten years. At the time of her 1981 interview, Polier was an active LWS board member and honorary president of the agency. None of her personal or professional papers, archived at Radcliffe Institute's Schlesinger Library in Cambridge, Massachusetts, reference LWS's twin adoption practice, the twin study, or her CBS experience.[6] Her association with the twin study is evident from documents archived with Viola Bernard's papers at Columbia University.

Following Polier's interview, a series of memos, mailings, and telephone calls passed between the Wallace team and Viola Bernard, and among the LWS administrators/associates, CDC researchers, Jewish Board of Family and Children's Services (JBFCS) officers and Bernard's close colleagues/friends.

The writers and recipients of some or all of Bernard's communications about the "CBS Affair" are listed in the following:[7]

LWS Administrators/Associates

Morton Rogers (executive director)
Justine W. Polier (honorary president; board member)
Barbara Miller (post-adoption services)
Stephen Tulin (attorney)
Sheldon Fogelman (president)
E. Gerald Dabbs (psychiatrist)
John Steinfirst (staff planning committee)
Helen Tucker (executive committee)
Florence (Brown) Kreech (former executive director)

CDC Researchers

Peter Neubauer
Christa Balzert

JBFCS Officers

Saul Z. Cohen (president)
Jerome Goldsmith (chief executive officer)

Colleagues/Friends

Phyllis

A transcript of Bernard's conversation with Polier, following Polier's CBS interview, was appended to Bernard's May 20 memo, and marked "Confidential." She cited two errors on Polier's part.[8] The first was her failure to distinguish between LWS's "service policy" of placing twins in separate homes and the CDC's research project resulting from that policy. LWS recognized the opportunity for exploring nature-nurture questions and "undertook a collaboration with a research agency," but Bernard stressed that the two bodies were distinct. Polier's second mistake was saying that placing twins together twenty years earlier was "too difficult." According to Bernard, "It was no harder than many of the other efforts we made to place kids with special characteristics, including sibling groups. In fact, the demand for babies was so great that adoptive parents would have accepted infant twins"; elsewhere, she noted that while it was hard to place siblings together, this was not so for twins.[9] Bernard reiterated that twins who had formed a relationship with one another stayed together. However, as I indicated earlier, reared-together twins placed by LWS have never come forward.

Polier couldn't recall if she asked every biological mother if she knew that her twins would be placed apart, or if she had volunteered the information—but Polier recalled saying that the mothers were not told. She said the thinking was different twenty years ago and that researchers thought that studying reared-apart twins would reveal a lot about nature and nurture. When Dr. Atkinson asked her if separating the twins had been a mistake, Polier said no. "You couldn't make judgments of that kind, except in the context of when things were done. I did not feel it was a mistake then." But Polier added that, in 1981, such decisions "would present different problems," such as rights to "privacy," "information," "counsel," and "informed consent," concepts that were "not part of one's thinking [twenty years ago]." Polier was uncertain if the study was still continuing—it had stopped in 1980—and if there were plans for publishing the findings—she thought so.

Bernard also noted in her memo that "over twenty years ago," in the late 1950s and early 1960s, LWS had discussed the twin separation policy with other adoption agencies. Their executives were "impressed" by the supporting literature and favored implementation, but their boards disagreed "because of the prevailing feeling that twinship was beautiful."

Along with the transcript, Bernard sent a copy of her "1978 note on service policy" to Rogers, Miller, Polier, Tulin, and Fogelman.[10] These individuals were on the "laundry list of who got what in the big mailing of the 'CBS affair.'"[11] The 1978 note was not in Bernard's archive, but a different document referenced a 1977 revision.[12] This change in policy was apparently in response to new developments in the adoption field, such as the increased number of adoptee searches: "twins, like other siblings, would be placed together unless such placement was contraindicated for exceptional casework reasons."[13]

COMMUNICATIONS AND MEETINGS

A June 12, 1981, letter was sent to CBS by Jack Solomon, attorney for the newly reunited identical triplets, Bob, Dave, and Eddy. The triplets had been separated by LWS in 1961 at age six months, but met by chance in 1980 at age nineteen years. The letter, which outlined Solomon's concerns about the triplets' appearance on Cronkite's program *Universe*, was sent to the attention of Walter Cronkite—Personal; Bill Leonard—CBS president; and Charles

Osgood [news anchor].[14] By then, the three young men had been filmed by CBS, but Solomon was adamant that no further interviewing or filming take place by anyone else without his permission. He was upset that CBS had told Dr. Bouchard that Solomon had agreed to filmed sessions of the triplets when they came to Minnesota for the study—he had given no such consent. Solomon also complained that the CBS crew had damaged his Venetian blinds and demanded that the crew return to repair them.

Two months later, on July 30, 1981, Solomon notified the CDC that his clients would appear on Cronkite's show slated for August 13.[15] This decision was confirmed by Madeline Amgott in a call from Peter Neubauer. Amgott explained that LWS and CDC would not be mentioned in the program because the focus would be on the triplets and the Minnesota Study of Twins Reared Apart. The program actually aired over a year later, on August 31, 1982; I will return to that later.[16] But in July and August 1981, Bernard was left wondering what Wallace and *60 Minutes* were planning.[17] Then, on October 21, 1981, a CDC secretary called her to say that Wallace wanted to set up a meeting.[18] It was scheduled for October 26.

Representing CBS were Wallace, Amgott, and Atkinson, and representing LWS-CDC were Bernard, Neubauer, Cohen, Fogelman, and Rogers.[19] Bernard, who had not intended to take notes, produced a three-page memo on the meeting that she circulated to her colleagues. She wrote that Wallace was interested in how and why twins were separated, and if this practice had stopped. He said that reunited twins would be interviewed about the experience of finding each other, but only with their consent and that of their parents. His team had already identified some pairs. Wallace intended to obtain the views of individuals opposing the separation of twins, such as Dr. Thomas J. Bouchard Jr., director of the Minnesota study.

Bernard seemed concerned that ethical issues would be discussed, but she was uncertain if they would come up. Wallace did say that ethics was one topic among many that he hoped LWS and the CDC would address. However, Bernard believed that Wallace's chief interests were the twins' reactions to their separation and reunion. She urged her colleagues to "consult their notes and memories," because this was "an extremely important matter." In the meeting, Amgott had also raised the ethics of separating twins and "what happens now," but Amgott's remarks were "unfortunately interrupted," leaving Bernard in the dark. Neubauer objected to questioning the twins on the grounds that their answers would be "unscientific." He also worried about how the show might affect the twins and their families, and if all LWS adoptees might start wondering if they had a twin. In response, Wallace became "rather heatedly defensive," claiming that his program was reviewed for accuracy. And, as if to calm their concerns, Wallace noted that the British psychologist Sir Cyril Burt had appeared on *60 Minutes* and had spoken freely about his own controversial reared-apart twin research.[20]

Wallace ducked a question about whether twins had already been interviewed.[21] He mentioned twins who wished to participate, but would not take part because the parents of one twin refused. Bernard was left wondering which pair this was, speculation that continued beyond the meeting for nearly a year. She thought it "sound[ed] like C1 and C2." I discovered that the twins were not C1 and C2; both twins and C1's mother told me that the Wallace team never contacted them. I will say more about this pair later.

This was not the first meeting between CBS and Bernard et al., although minutes from any previous meetings were absent from the file. We know this because someone mentioned Wallace's "accusation that we had been playing God," made at an earlier session. When questioned about this by Wallace at the October 26 meeting, Bernard said that this role was "inevitable" in the adoption field. Her response was applauded by Wallace as an example of why she and her colleagues should cooperate. Years later, Neubauer denied saying that "we were 'playing God'"—a remark that was, in fact, attributed to the "psychiatrist involved in the study"—and accused the media of making this statement.[22] But regardless of what the group decided, Wallace intended to do the program with or without them. According to Amgott, Wallace was not the only reporter to have this story, but he wanted to air it before anyone else.

A similar, albeit more succinct, memo of the October 26 meeting was prepared by Saul Cohen, president of JBFCS, and circulated to LWS-CDC colleagues, and to Dr. Jerome Goldsmith of the Jewish Board.[23] Cohen noted that, "It is quite clear that a quarrel will be developed as to whether the separation was done for research. An attempt will clearly be made to pursue that line and to inject the ethical question into the situation on the premise that the twins were used as 'guinea pigs.'"

Sheldon Fogelman, an attorney, currently heads the Sheldon Fogelman Agency, Inc., representing authors and illustrators of children's books.[24] We talked for several hours over lunch at Benjamin Prime, located on New York's east side. I arrived first and was escorted to his preferred table away from the crowd. Fogelman's recollections of events preceding the October 26 meeting and the meeting itself align with Bernard's, but with some additions and exceptions.[25] Fogelman joined the LWS board in 1974 or 1975 and was president from June 1981 or before, serving in that capacity until 1985 or 1986. He maintained his board membership before retiring from LWS in 1989.[26] Both the twin separation policy and twin study had begun and ended prior to his service, at least informally. He did not know about either one until the publicity surrounding the identical triplets' reunion in 1980 became widespread. "I spoke to Vi [Viola] and I asked what had happened. And then she told me why she did it and why she thought it was a good idea. And she said it was only two years and we stopped it. I asked her why. She said 'I don't remember.' I didn't press her, and I never found out."

Fogelman claimed that Wallace "planted" himself in front of the LWS building and tried to get comments from staff members.[27]

> He was being very intrusive, so it was decided to sit down and figure out what we were going to do about this. We thought about all the things that were good or bad about talking to him. There was hardly anything good about talking to him because he was not interested in the facts, he was interested in a crusade. He was only interested in one side of it.

The group decided to meet with Wallace and designated Fogelman as their primary spokesman. "I only came in when the fire started and I had to deal with the explosion."[28]

Fogelman, neither a psychologist nor a psychiatrist, based his assertions on what his professional colleagues believed.[29] "It was felt by both Peter and Viola, particularly, that [the program] would be very, very detrimental to [the twins'] development," most of whom were teenagers at the time. Fogelman argued that the damage would extend to other LWS adoptees and to adoptees around the country who might start wondering if they had a twin. He also recalled that Wallace posed some "silly" questions, such as if they thought it was fascinating to separate twins. "I said, not at all, it's terrible [that twins would learn this on *60 Minutes*]." The meeting lasted a long time. "And [Wallace] said to me, 'well, don't you think you're playing God?' And I said, the adoption process is playing God. Don't you think? You're making a decision as to where a child should go—to be brought up by people they don't know. Playing God. Anyway, he didn't respond to that at all." This discussion over "playing God" differs somewhat from Bernard's account.

Fogelman added that "people try to do good things in life, but sometimes seemingly good deeds can be offensive. Viola Bernard was one of those people who tried to do something good. And it probably wasn't."

LWS was not the only agency that interested *60 Minutes*.[30] About two weeks later, a telephone message in Bernard's handwriting revealed that Wallace and Amgott were "in the neighborhood," interviewing staff at Spence-Chapin, an adoption agency just blocks away from LWS. Wallace restated his desire for their cooperation. "I'll be damned," someone said to Fogelman.

THE END OF THE BEGINNING

On November 16, 1981, approximately three weeks after the October 26 meeting, JBFCS President Saul Cohen and LWS President Sheldon Fogelman co-authored a letter to Mike Wallace, stating that LWS and CDC would not be participating in the program.[31] A copy of the letter was sent to Madeline Amgott. However, the story was far from finished. Anxious to know when the *60 Minutes* segment might air, Bernard and Neubauer had a secretary impersonate an "interested viewer" and call CBS to inquire about a program on identical twins.[32] The "viewer" learned that a date had not been set and while production was progressing—*60 Minutes* was actively investigating other pairs, as I indicated in chapters 4 and 5—it was uncertain if the show would actually air. Bernard found this news "encouraging" and "helpful," reasoning that if the program was completed and families were not forewarned, then the uncertainty surrounding its showing offered an excuse for not telling them.

The next communication from Bernard to her colleagues was dated April 28, 1982, a half year later.[33] It is possible that sensitive documents created during that time were removed from her open files and embargoed until 2021. However, this seems unlikely because I found several papers marked confidential that *were* available for public viewing. Meanwhile, Bernard's April 28 memo summarized a telephone call from Madeline Amgott to an unnamed female psychoanalytic colleague of Bernard's referred to as "Dr. X," that occurred ten days earlier. Amgott had "complained" to Dr. X that Bernard and Neubauer "were refusing to discuss their research findings with Wallace and herself." Amgott had also asked Dr. X if she thought that "separated twins would miss each other." Dr. X replied that she "wouldn't expect them to miss each other a lot more than the separations between siblings that she thought were rather frequent." Bernard concluded that the program might or might not air, "but it may, and is rather disquieting." She thought Dr. X might try to discover a projected air date.

The next memo, dated August 6, 1982, summarized a telephone message from Barbara Miller in post-adoption services to Viola Bernard, taken by "Kelly." The message concerned *60 Minutes*' contacts with fraternal twins, Tim and Ilene, separated by LWS as babies in 1947. Recall that the twins were reunited in 1982, at age thirty-five. CBS had told the families about the twin study, but Miller assured them they had not been involved in any research. As I explained in chapter 4, Ilene ultimately refused to be recorded on camera, so these twins were to be dropped from the program. Still, Tim's wife Susan promised that *60 Minutes* would be "villifying" LWS at a later date. Miller was quite "excited" about this news and wanted to speak to Bernard immediately, but Bernard was out of town. Bernard did call in for messages that day, but she chose not to get involved at the time.[34] When she saw the original message, she scribbled a question at the top: "@what age placed?"[35] Several days later, Miller sent a more detailed memo about this situation to Bernard and Rogers.[36]

The August 6 telephone message also indicated that *60 Minutes* knew about a set of separated twins of which LWS was unaware. This seems odd because LWS would know which twins they had separated. Alternatively, these twins may have been placed apart privately or by another agency, but then they would not have been directly relevant to the LWS exposé. The identity of these twins worried Bernard. Meanwhile, on August 31, 1982, Cronkite aired a half-hour program about twin studies on *Universe*, a 1980–1982 series concerned with timely scientific topics. After days of searching, I tracked down the four-page transcript of "Twins" from the University of Rochester in upstate New York. A package of seven microfiche films arrived, an outdated medium that requires considerable patience, dexterity, and hand-eye coordination to use. The library at my institution maintains one rarely used machine for reading these materials. The segment I was searching for did not appear until I got to the final film.[37] However, a few weeks later I remembered having worked with Sari Aviv who produces programs for *CBS Sunday Morning*. Sari helped create a DVD of Cronkite's show, which she made available to me. Seeing the matched behaviors of the separated identical twins and triplets was more persuasive evidence of genetic influence than the lines in the transcript.[38] The producer, Madeline Amgott, was correct—neither LWS nor the CDC was mentioned.

"Twins" featured Cronkite; CBS News anchor Charles Osgood; reared-apart twin researcher Dr. Thomas J. Bouchard Jr.; Harvard University geneticist Richard Lewontin; talk show host Phil Donahue; University of Minnesota psychologist Dr. David Lykken; Princeton University sociology professor Dr. Howard Taylor; several male and female twin pairs; and the LWS-separated identical triplets who had met at age nineteen. Cronkite and Osgood defined the program's theme, namely how much of who we are is explained by heredity and how much by environment. Cronkite explained that Bouchard's study aimed to answer that question, but noted that some scientists question the validity of his study. Observations by one of the triplets captured what Bouchard's data had been saying, despite their separate rearing, "we've all learned extraordinarily similar things, and we've all done extraordinarily similar things, and we've all formed into extraordinarily similar people." Two reared-apart female twins said little except that they had been married four and five times. Lykken, a Minnesota colleague of Bouchard's, commented on some other separated female twins who independently wore seven rings on their fingers: "Wearing seven rings might result from the confluence of a group of independent traits that are genetically determined, like a woman who has good-looking hands with long fingers is more likely to adorn those hands." Donahue chimed in with references to twins who married women with the same name. Bouchard lacked a definitive explanation for this observation, but noted that some twins chose the same name for their children. Lewontin and Taylor criticized the methods and goals of reared-apart twin research, claiming that participating twins are self-selected, and the results say nothing about how we can change behavior. I have challenged their remarks and others in detail and found them wanting.[39]

Osgood closed the program by saying that the nature–nurture debate will not be settled on television, and that disentangling genetic and environmental influences might reveal little compared to how we "learn and change. . . . Still, there is a fascination in finding likeness where we are used to finding difference and using twins as a mirror for ourselves." "Twins" was seen by Bernard who called it "inconsequential" and "superficial."[40]

CONTINUING COMMUNICATIONS
AND RELATED HAPPENINGS

The next communication from Mike Wallace was a September 14, 1982, letter to LWS Executive Director Morton Rogers.[41] It was sent nearly one year after LWS-CDC declined to participate in the program. Wallace said that *60 Minutes* had recorded interviews with twins over the age of twenty-one. He said that each twin had met separately with Barbara Miller and were upset that they hadn't received help in finding their biological family or each other. Furthermore, Miller had not told either twin about her meeting with the other twin. Wallace wished to interview Miller to explore these issues further. And he wanted Bernard to explain her twin separation policy and the "twinning reaction," referenced in her 1963 *Encyclopedia of Mental Health* article.[42]

Over the next two days, September 15 and 16, Bernard drafted a five-page memo to Neubauer, Balzert, Rogers, and Miller in advance of a meeting to be planned for the following week.[43] She focused on identifying which pair of twins Wallace had interviewed: "we might extract this information as a basis for considering the request, as far as Wallace knows, even though we plan to decline." Bernard could think of only two pairs, Tim and Ilene and the pair labeled "C1 and C2." She decided that Tim and Ilene were the more likely candidates because Ilene had never sought assistance from Miller—but both twins Wallace mentioned *had* met with Miller, so perhaps Bernard misread Wallace's letter. Furthermore, according to Miller's memo of August 6, 1982,

Tim and Ilene were to be dropped from the program because Ilene refused to be filmed.

Bernard did not rule out the possible participation of C1 and C2. She noted that one of the mothers had been "openly hostile" and that the other parents "understandably deplore[d] the whole twinship situation . . . so if they are the pair for 'Sixty Minutes,' the agency and I may well take a beating." However, C1 and C2 had *never* been interviewed by *60 Minutes* at that time and had *never* been contacted by the media or interviewed for television; one twin had been filmed by a freelance artist, but he had no plans to use it.[44] Bernard wondered if Wallace had found a pair she was unaware of, "but I doubt it." In fact, Wallace *had* found such a pair, separated by LWS in 1952—it was Kathy and Betsy. Details about the twins' meetings with Miller may not apply to Kathy and Betsy, but they appear to be the only other twins he interviewed. Perhaps Bernard had forgotten about this pair.

Fogelman replied to Wallace's September 14 letter, but Bernard was motivated to respond on her own.[45] In fact, she was "troubled" that she hadn't received a copy of Fogelman's letter. Two drafts of her response contend that her encyclopedia article was *not* an agency document, and that she prefers sending copies of her publications to the media in lieu of sitting for interviews. She also noted that her encyclopedia article, which did reflect LWS practices, had been reprinted three times. In the end, neither draft was sent to Wallace because Polier, Fogelman, and Neubauer disliked it and there was no time for them to meet on this particular issue.[46] However, a session to discuss the handling of the "aftermath of the Wallace program, if indeed it goes on the air, which seems likely," occurred soon after that. What happened at the meeting, which included Bernard, Neubauer, Balzert, and Miller, was summarized by Bernard in a September 29 memo.[47]

A resolution wasn't reached, but Bernard proposed two courses of action. The first was to recommend a formal revision of LWS's twin placement policy at the next board meeting. She supported this plan by noting that in the late 1950s, a review of the professional literature by the director, staff, and consultant—herself—provided justification for placing twins apart.[48] The benefits of this practice were the separate development of each twins' identity and the lessening of parental caretaking burdens. However, she stressed that placements were made on an individualized basis. Bernard framed the proposed revision as a "shift in practice in the last years," rather than a "reversal of policy"—although the word "reversal" appears in the title of her second draft. She explained that the purpose of her statement was to formalize what LWS had been practicing since the last pair had been separated in the late 1960s, and to stay current with trends toward greater openness in the adoption field.[49] However, despite her emphasis on "individualized" placement considerations,

LWS considered it "psychologically safer" to conceal the twinship so as not to undermine its benefits; there did not appear to be exceptions. The statement was finalized following suggestions from Rogers, Fogelman, and Polier.

Bernard's second recommendation was to prepare a "post-*Sixty Minutes* handout" about the revised policy for the press/media, the professional community, and adoptees, adoptive parents, and birth parents, in the event that *60 Minutes* should air.[50] She clearly noted that such a handout was *not* a response to media pressures.[51]

A meeting of the board took place on October 6, 1982. Minutes from the meeting, in which "The Adoption Policy of Louise Wise Services" was fifth on the agenda, appears to have been distributed to all six officers and eleven members who voted on Bernard's proposal.[52] The minutes state that there was much discussion, and that the policy that had actually been in place over the past fifteen years (1967–1982) was approved: like siblings, twins would be adopted together, barring unusual circumstances.[53] The revised policy statement was read, not given, to the membership. In a memo to Rogers, Fogelman, and Polier, Bernard said, "I now understand and agree that the minutes of this part of the meeting need to be prepared with care and should be the only written record of this agenda item."

Bernard identified two errors in the report of the minutes, jotted down in the margins of her copy. First, it was not true that several board and staff members had been contacted by Wallace for interviews. "No one on the board except myself and I'm the staff." It was also not true that LWS was no longer active in research. "I am active in research still, but no need for board discussion." Bernard missed the inconsistency between the first year that the revised policy was in place—1967—and the separation of identical twins in 1969.[54] The twins, Paula Bernstein and Elyse Schein, were initially in the study but were dropped early on, due to their marked weight difference. Neubauer also felt that because one twin had been adopted four months before her sister, who stayed in foster care, their different rearing circumstances would have prevented valid developmental comparisons.[55]

Weeks passed and the airing of *60 Minutes* hung in the balance. On October 27, 1982, Bernard wrote to Dorothy Krugman, a research assistant who observed the young twins in foster care and in their separate adoptive homes.[56] Bernard noted that agency executives, with whom they had met "way back," were impressed by the LWS-CDC twin study data. Nevertheless, the executives could not convince their agencies to place twins apart. Bernard claimed that due to the "media blitz" surrounding the triplets' 1980 reunion, the agencies told reporters that they never separated twins. But recall that in her 1981 reference to Polier's CBS interview errors, Bernard noted that the other agency boards *did not* agree to separate twins because twinship was considered "beautiful."[57] Still, she asked Krugman for a list of adoption agencies that had been separating twins and the criteria for their separation. I found a page of notes, handwritten by Bernard, in the archived file just behind this letter.[58] It is hard to decipher completely, but Bernard was trying to determine which of four twin pairs had been placed before and after the policy had been formalized. There is also reference to other New York area adoption and foster agencies that may have placed twins apart: Leake & Watts, Wyndham, and Gould, which had nation-wide branches, including Illinois. Gould's Illinois branch may have some significance, as I will explain later.

Penciled into the margins of her October 27 letter to Krugman, Bernard had written, "Evidences of CBS activity including bringing in CDC: (1) Seeking Peter and my photograph /p Col. Psychoan. Center (2) Checking on Peter's [National Institute for Mental Health] consultancy /p Stanley Greenspan."[59]

That same day, on October 27, Bernard sent a letter to Fogelman, complaining that a Mrs. Jackson, executive secretary at the Columbia Psychoanalytic Center, notified her that CBS had requested photographs of Bernard and Neubauer. Jackson was unaware of the *60 Minutes* situation, but advised CBS to contact Bernard directly. The request was "deceptive," Bernard wrote, because CBS told Jackson they had contacted her because they couldn't reach Bernard. Bernard said she had been taking calls all day and was covered by a service when she was out, so she *was* available. "Clearly, whoever it was knew I wouldn't give it to them." She alerted Neubauer, Balzert, Miller, and Rogers, noting that despite their absence from the television program, CBS would "drag us in as fully as possible." She also hoped CBS would not discover photographs held at another Columbia Medical Center location: "for all I know, Peter, she [Miller] and I may get photographed as we emerge from our respective domiciles."[60]

The prominent child psychiatrist Dr. Stanley Greenspan directed the Clinical Infant Development Program at the National Institute of Mental Health during the 1970s.[61] CBS's interest in contacting him may have been linked to Neubauer's National Institute of Child Health and Human Development grant that had funded the twin study in 1965. Greenspan and Neubauer were also allied as founding members of Zero to Three, the organization dedicated to promoting infant and toddler well-being, launched in 1977.[62]

FURTHER DEVELOPMENTS

The next development was an undated, handwritten letter sent to Bernard by her friend "Phyllis." The letter was probably sent in late November 1982 because Bernard replied on December 8.[63] Phyllis suggested that Bernard recruit clinical psychologist Harold Michael Smith to intervene with CBS on Bernard's behalf. Smith admired Bernard, and Mike Wallace had consulted with him over the years. Phyllis sensed that "Wallace really hasn't heard the other side or if he has he hasn't listened . . . the problems inherent are abundantly clear—people will be hurt. At least it might change the tone of the approach." However, both Bernard and Neubauer concurred that this approach risked "widening the situation." But Bernard agreed that hiring a "top-notch P.R. guy informed and ready for immediate action" would be important.

While the idea of a public relations consultant was under consideration, an additional CBS inquiry was ongoing in February 1983.[64] Neubauer learned that Richard Cohen, producer for Dan Rather's *Evening News* since 1981,[65] was looking into the twin study and LWS's separate placement of twins. Cohen was occasionally tapped to work on stories that did not make it into *60 Minutes* and recalled that Wallace was really "pissed" about having to pass on this one. Cohen reviewed the research materials Wallace gave him and found it all "horrifying at first." An unidentified individual Cohen had contacted did not wish to discuss the matter. He also brought the case to Dr. Willard Gaylin, an ethics specialist at the Hastings Center.[66] Gaylin discouraged him from pursuing the story, on the basis that informed consent procedures were not in place at that time.[67] I contacted Gaylin, now in his nineties, for his current thoughts about the policy and study, and will summarize his views in a later chapter. Still, no information about an air date or whether the program would be broadcast in the morning or evening was available.

The February 7, 1983, memo that referenced Cohen included an additional recipient, child and adolescent psychiatrist Dr. E. Gerald Dabbs, a protégé of Bernard's.[68] Dabbs called Bernard a "vital link between the board and the agency's mental health services."[69] Beginning in 1984, Dabbs headed a psychiatric team at LWS that included Dr. Dorothy Krugman who had been closely involved with the twin study; however, Dabbs does not recall any discussions with Krugman about the twin research. Dabbs, a member of the LWS Benefit Committee,[70] did not mention his association with Bernard and LWS in a professional oral life history interview; Dabbs was supposedly very protective of Bernard. He described her as "private and extraordinary—a wonderful person, really. She was also a spokesperson for people who were neglected, deprived or rejected." They never really had a conversation about the twin separations.[71]

Dabbs described a case to me in which the birth mother of opposite-sex twins separated by LWS had suddenly appeared at the home of the female twin. Once their daughter's twinship was revealed, her parents sought additional information from the agency. Barbara Miller in post-adoption services contacted the male twin's family to prepare them for a possible visit from their son's birth mother—the boy's parents had not told him he was adopted, and his parents had not been told he was a twin. Dabbs said that the twins were "young"—teenagers at the time—and believes this incident occurred in the early 1990s. Therefore, these twins were probably separated in the early to late 1970s.[72]

Ten days after Bernard's February memo, Miller sent Bernard a newspaper advertisement seeking adoptees, birth parents, and adoptive parents for an unpaid interview. The address given was 175 5th Avenue, that of the famous Flatiron Building.[73] At the bottom of the page Miller scribbled, "Couldn't help wondering whether CBS News is casting a wide net."[74]

Two other new developments occurred during the weeks that followed and were summarized by Bernard in March 1983.[75] Neubauer had been told confidentially that someone (who Wallace's team goes to for information about twins) had been approached to discuss the topic, not for *60 Minutes*, but with CBS News. The twin expert was referred to as a "she," so it was not Harold Michael Smith. Next, Neubauer had attended a social gathering where he had "picked up from a high CBS official" that Wallace was "debating" over whether to air the twin program. There was no discussion on this point between Neubauer and the CBS guest.

In that same memo, Bernard turned to events under the heading, "About Today." Her friend, presumably Phyllis, had learned that her "psychologist friend," presumably Smith, had talked to Wallace about the program and thought it would air soon. Phyllis then decided to speak to Wallace directly and recapped the conversation for Bernard who wrote, "He [Wallace] said there had been the suicide of a 30-year-old female twin who had been placed by LWS, that the topic was dynamite. . . . The big news was that '60 Minutes' would probably not do the show but that Dan Rather was very interested in doing so on his *Evening News*." These communications aligned with Neubauer's information, and with the inquiry made by Richard Cohen who worked for Rather at the time. However, the date of Bernard's memo is March 1983, six months after Betsy allegedly took her own life. As I indicated in chapter 5, pressure from Betsy's family to silence the show was probably the critical factor in Wallace's decision to halt production. However, the timing of both Wallace's decision and Rather's interest are uncertain—recall that Wallace interviewed Florence Fisher *after* he knew of Betsy's death.

When I interviewed Fogelman in October 2019, I had asked him what he thought had ultimately persuaded Wallace to stop the story.[76] "We haven't got the vaguest idea . . . we all have our own impressions. And my impression was that it was the arguments I had presented to him with the assistance of Vi and Peter." Fogelman's arguments may have carried weight, but Betsy's alleged suicide and her family's wishes appeared to carry much more.

EXPLANATORY HANDOUT

Bernard wanted to consider Phyllis's suggestion that LWS-CDC take a proactive stance. This would involve preparing a statement about LWS and the twin study to be published in the *New York Times* in advance of a possible CBS program. Both she and Neubauer had contacts at the *Times*. This strategy differed from their initial plan of providing a "reactive explanatory 'handout'" to journalists, professionals, and families. Bernard favored the reactive approach because it would benefit adoptive parents who still did not know they had raised a separated twin who had been in a study. The group ultimately chose their initial plan.

Bernard's thirteen-page draft of a March 22, 1983, handout was delivered to colleagues by her personally, or by messenger in advance of a meeting to be held that night.[77] The recipients were Neubauer, Polier, Fogelman, Miller, Rogers, Balzert, Dabbs, then retired LWS executive director Florence Kreech, and an unnamed "Public-Relations Consultant" whose materials would be forwarded by Fogelman. All copies were labeled, "CONFIDENTIAL: NOT FOR PUBLICATION OR CIRCULATION."[78] A condensed three and a half-page statement, "Re: CBS News program attacking LWS/CDC," dated April 11, was distributed to the group on April 13, given their objections to the longer version.[79] The shorter statement was also forwarded to John Steinfirst of LWS's Staff Planning Committee and Helen Tucker of LWS's Executive Committee. In her cover letter, Bernard expressed the hope that a public relations representative would be identified shortly.[80] One was—in early May, Fogelman notified Bernard that he had forwarded "a pamphlet and several articles about you and your work" to Sunny Bierman at the public relations firm of Ruder Finn & Rotman.[81] No mention was made of the explanatory statements, but it is likely that he forwarded them at the same time or on another occasion. The firm was co-founded by Bill Ruder, father-in-law of Polier's granddaughter Debra Bradley Ruder.[82]

The key points in Bernard's long and short statements are summarized in the following. I have used the same headings that appear in her long statement, but have added the label "Introduction" to her opening paragraph.

Introduction

- At issue is the separate placement of a few twins and a study that tracked their development. The policy and study antedated changes in adoption practices and research regulations.
- A prompt response to the airing of the program is required, given the impact of CBS television.

Reasons We Stayed Off the Program

- The tone of the program is adversarial. The format of a news magazine and the allotted time of a few minutes are inappropriate for scientific discussion.
- CBS would edit the interviews, thereby manipulating the content. Opportunities to review the final version are denied.
- New developments in adoption make the intended benefits of twin separation "more problematic."
- Preserving confidentiality of clients is central to professional ethics. We would violate this responsibility were we to comment on the twin sisters CBS interviewed.

About the Agencies

- Viola W. Bernard and Peter Neubauer provided the history of the LWS twin adoption policy that CBS "condemns."
- Since the 1940s, LWS, based on interdisciplinary research, recognized the importance of placing siblings in the same home, regardless of the extra effort.

Adoption of Twins

- Twins births are rare, and twins relinquished for adoption are even rarer. CBS News might give the false impression that many twin adoptees were separated from one another.
- Based on the 1950s professional literature, there were clear advantages to placing twins apart. This applied to twins under six months of age who had not developed a twinning reaction.

- Twins were placed in families that had an older adoptive sibling so they would not be raised alone.
- Most twins are raised together by their biological parents. "The obvious advantages of being part of their own family since birth are of overriding value." However, because being an adoptee and being a twin pose additional problems, it is "desirable to improve on nature [by separating twins]."

Withholding Fact of Twinship (LWS)

- Birth mothers, when available, were told about their twins' separation and accepted it.
- The literature reported that "awareness of twinship influences development, even if reared apart."
- Lack of knowledge about twinship would free adoptive families from "emotionally charged attitudes and myths" surrounding twins, especially identical twins.
- Board members of other adoption agencies opposed the idea of separating twins, despite endorsement by their executives. Journalists use that opposition to support their own criticisms.

CDC Study: Origins and Goals

- Once the twin separation policy was in place, a pair of identical twins was referred to LWS. At this time, Bernard made "another recommendation," which resulted in setting up the LWS-CDC twin study collaboration.
- Study goals were to derive information that would inform future adoptions, and to better understand nature-nurture interactions.

Withholding Fact of Twinship (CDC)

- CBS News failed to make the distinction between LWS—adoption service—and the CDC—research center.
- Twins were not separated after 1967.
- If twins met by chance as adults the parent-child relationship and each twin's identity would have been established. Disclosing this

information to them at this time—in the 1980s—could be "unpredict-able" and "more damaging than helpful."
- Bernard had placed explanatory notes about the twinship in each twin's file in the event that they requested information about their biological background and neither Bernard, nor Miller, were available.

Post-Adoptive Changes and Services

- In 1977, in response to trends toward greater openness in adoption, LWS agreed to contact the biological relatives of adult adoptees in search of family. If the biological relatives and adoptive parents agreed to the reunion, then LWS would act as facilitator.
- The separated twins may find one another more easily now, increasing the "rate and range of psychological complications."
- Regarding CBS's "accusatory focus," the twins and their adoptive parents have expressed both positive and negative reactions to the twins' separate placement that was concealed from them.

LWS/CDC Study as of 1983

- Without a formal plan, LWS stopped placing twins apart ten to fifteen years ago: 1968–1973.
- Given that Bernard had initiated the twin separation policy in 1959, she now "felt a responsibility" to recommend formalizing the revised policy that had been in place since 1968: twins, like ordinary siblings, would be placed together, barring exceptional circumstances. Board members voted to approve this revision on October 6, 1982.

A page with Bernard's handwritten notes from communications with Neubauer, Polier, and Miller is dated March 23, 1983, a day after she forwarded the explanatory statement. Issues raised were the appropriate time to inform twins of their twinship and separation, current informed consent procedures, and the timing of the alleged suicide by the LWS twin adoptee.[83]

Bernard's abbreviated statement, composed on April 11, 1983, stressed the following points:

- The number of separated twins represented a "tiny fraction" of the children placed by LWS.

- In the 1940s and 1950s, families' reluctance to adopt two babies simultaneously was a factor in LWS's decision to place twins apart.
- The last pair of twins was separated in 1967.

A letter from Florence Kreech acknowledged receipt of the materials. The first page indicated she was "delighted" to receive them. The rest of her letter was missing from Bernard's archived file.[84]

It is unclear exactly when CBS dropped the LWS-CDC program entirely. However, Bernard's concern and focus on how the media presents news to the public continued. She saved several newspaper articles on the topic, published in May and June 1983.[85] One article described various lawsuits brought against *60 Minutes* by an army colonel, a physician, and a CBS News producer for misrepresentation, inaccuracy, and broadcast rights, respectively.[86] Two notable lawsuits, pending in 1983, were filed by General William Westmoreland over the content of a CBS documentary, and by Colonel Anthony Herbert over the content of a *60 Minutes* segment.[87] These legal battles may have put pressure on Wallace to avoid others. The article also referenced "many other cases" in which the program was accused of "ambush journalism," the surprise filming of individuals who had previously declined to be interviewed. CBS's Don Hewitt, along with Wallace, had made this method famous, but Wallace later expressed misgivings. A variation of that technique involves letting people believe they will be interviewed about one topic, but are questioned about another, often prosecutorial topic, once the cameras are rolling. In the margin next to that paragraph, Bernard had scribbled "example: JWP [Justine Wise Polier]."

Public interest in LWS's policies and the LWS-CDC twin study never disappeared. In 2006, *60 Minutes* approached another set of separately placed LWS twins for a program. In 2019, Shinseki's film *The Twinning Reaction* was featured on ABC's news magazine *20/20*, and Wardle's *Three Identical Strangers* aired on CNN. Professional conferences and public lectures on the topic have taken place around the United States because of those two films.[88] I will address these developments in the chapters to come.

TRIBUTE TO MADELINE AMGOTT

My introduction to the late CBS television producer Madeline Amgott came from *New York Times* staff writer, Stephanie Saul, when I interviewed her in New York City in June 2019. Saul and I had met years before, in September 1997, when she interviewed me for an article she was researching on the separated identical triplets and their discovery that they were subjects in a hidden study. I still have my scribbled notes from our telephone contacts in May and June before our first meeting took place—in one note I had recorded Saul's research plan as "Christa Balzert, research assistant, next step" and "Susan Farber."[89] She had also told me that LWS staffers and adoptees did not wish to talk. It was at our 2019 meeting that Saul identified Amgott as the producer of a 1980s *60 Minutes* segment about the LWS practices and CDC twin study—a program that never aired.

Amgott passed away in 2014, but I have learned that the children of key figures often have a lot to tell.[90] I contacted Amgott's son Seth who works in public relations and politics in Washington, DC. Seth recalled how much producing the twins' piece had meant to his mother and how very involved she became with Betsy Leon, the twin who allegedly took her own life. Amgott was "deeply frustrated" when production stopped—it was her "great unfinished thing, a great disappointment, the only program she produced that never aired." Seth explained that Amgott was "motivated to tell stories that were difficult, about powerful people who were misbehaving and hurting others in the process. And as much as she loved telling stories she hated not telling this one. She was part of the storied CBS News team—Roger Ailes, Harry Reasoner, Walter Cronkite, Don Hewitt, Mike Wallace—a pioneer when it came to women working in high profile media." Amgott's first job as a journalist was in San Diego, thanks to Eleanor Roosevelt who wanted women covering her weekly press conferences. According to her son, had she lived she would have "loved" the #MeToo movement.

I contacted several of Amgott's former colleagues. None was familiar with her failed *60 Minutes* piece, perhaps because it was painful for Amgott to bring it up. Everyone spoke glowingly of her: "brilliant, creative, unflappable, classy and cool." In a moving tribute following her death, a friend wrote, "she showed straightforward opinionatedness rooted in a sense of justice and right and wrong that never became calloused."[91] I regret missing the chance to have met Madeline Amgott and hearing her recollections and impressions of what happened at CBS.

• 7 •

Dancing Solo

Anne and Susan

$\mathcal{B}$y December 2019, I knew the identities of three of the four twin pairs and the one triplet set whose data are stored in Peter Neubauer's archives at Yale University. As I explained in chapter 3, I speculated that the "missing" set might be a pair of seven- or eight-year-old male twins who met by chance because of their identical looks. A research assistant at the Child Development Center (CDC) who did not work on the study and Dr. Bernard had talked about these two boys, one raised in New York and the other raised in New Jersey. As they described it—the former assistant to me and Bernard to author Lawrence Wright—the New York family had visited a New Jersey family that lived next door to the New Jersey twin. It was then that the New York twin's mother and the New Jersey neighbor became aware of the striking resemblance between the two children. Questions about the children's birth date and adoption details led them to the same conclusion: *the two children had to be identical twins*. "We knew at that point what had happened," one mother told me.[1] Their astounding realization was later confirmed by Dr. Bernard, who informed the other twin's family.

In fact, that is *not* exactly how it happened. I know, because I spoke to both twins and to one adoptive mother and can tell their story for the first time.[2] I learned about these twins, Susan Engel and Anne Adler, from Becky Read, the award-winning producer of *Three Identical Strangers*. "There are some other twins I should ask you about," she texted to me as I mulled over the identity of my "missing pair."[3] Susan and Anne had been put in touch with Read and director Tim Wardle by Susan's friend Susan Golomb, a New York literary agent, after their film was released in 2018.[4] The twins turned out to be the pair I was seeking, and both were happy to speak with me. Of course, they are females, not males as I had originally thought, and the New Jersey incident

113

The Twins, Their Family Members, and Friends*

Anne

Anne (Feinberg) Adler Susan's reared–apart twin
Donna ("Donnie") Feinberg Anne's adoptive mother
Bob Feinberg Anne's adoptive father
Mark Feinberg Anne's older adoptive brother
Mr. and Mrs. Fleishaker family friends
Bruce Fleishaker Anne's childhood playmate
Amy (Fleishaker) Tubbs Anne's childhood playmate
Barry Kostrinsky Anne's childhood friend, steady date, and current partner
Ann Rubin teenage friend

Susan

Susan (Birnbaum) Engel Anne's reared–apart twin
Martha Birnbaum Susan's adoptive mother
James Birnbaum Susan's adoptive father
Peter Birnbaum Susan's older adoptive brother
Heather Rockwell Susan's best friend in high school
Susan Golomb Susan's long-time friend

---

* Some names have been altered in the interest of privacy.

happened when they were six or seven, not seven or eight. Moreover, the events leading to Susan and Anne's reunion were far more complex and drawn out than either the former assistant or Bernard had revealed.

Susan and Anne were no longer studied once the truth about their twin-ship was exposed. Nevertheless, the data gathered on them up until that time are with Peter Neubauer's other twin study records at Yale that are unavailable for viewing until 2065. Their file, located in volumes 1-2, is housed in box 23.[5] As such, these twins were not dropped from the study entirely. Their names are not associated with the data, nor do their names appear in any of the archival material I examined. However, messages exchanged between Viola Bernard and Barbara Miller at Louise Wise Services (LWS) refer to specific child numbers that match those in the archive, clearly identifying them as these twins.[6]

SUSAN AND ANNE

Susan and Anne were born on September 13, 1960, and placed apart by LWS in March 1961, at six months of age. Anne, a breech delivery, was born first, at 11:11 a.m. and Susan followed at 11:17 a.m.[7] They are the first pair of LWS-separated twins studied by Neubauer and his colleagues. The twins grew up about sixteen miles apart: Susan in Tenafly, New Jersey, and Anne in Westchester County, New York. Neither twin knows which one was adopted first, but they stayed together in foster care during their first six months of life—they were photographed side by side as infant twins in a picture Bernard gave to Susan and Anne years later.[8]

Susan has a brother, Peter, whom her parents, James and Martha Birnbaum, had adopted from LWS four years before they had adopted Susan. James, now deceased, was a mathematical engineer and an instructor at Bronx Community College until his retirement. Martha, now ninety-two, was a sixth-grade schoolteacher, specializing in reading, English, and social studies. She was also a gifted musician, having received a scholarship to the Manhattan School of Music at age sixteen, and performed as a singer alongside the legendary American songwriter Buddy Kaye. Susan's brother Peter earned a degree in communications, worked for years in computer sales, and is now retired.[9]

Anne's parents, Bob and Donna ("Donnie") Feinberg, now deceased, had also adopted their son Mark from LWS; he is two years older than their daughter. Mark was just five weeks old when the Feinbergs brought him home. Bob was a financial planner, and Donnie taught children with learning disabilities. In her later years, Donnie was a docent at the Jewish Museum and a volunteer at White Plains Hospital in New York. Mark is a law school graduate.

Both Susan and Anne were talented and passionate dancers. Susan started jazz dancing at age fifteen with aspirations to turn professional. She also sang, played in musical bands, and wrote songs. Anne had been dancing competitively since she was five years old and had spent summers training with different dance programs. She had trained with the Jacobs Pillow Dance Festival in 1976, the summer before she met her twin sister. Anne had also majored in dance at college. The twins' shared dance interest is loosely connected to their discovery of each other and their first meeting at age seventeen. However, their parents discovered their children's twinship years before, because of the chance encounter that happened in New Jersey in 1965 or 1966. Once this happened, both sets of parents were warned by LWS to keep this news quiet. The twins could not know—Bernard said it would be far too damaging.[10] Here is how it all really began.

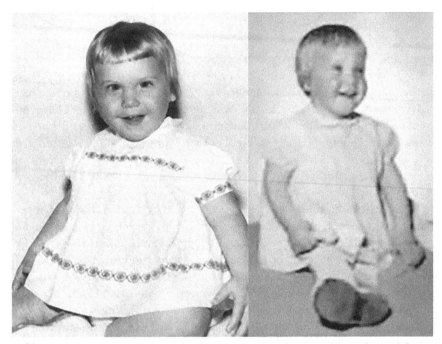

Figure 7.1.   Reared-apart identical twins, Anne (L) and Susan (R), at about eighteen months of age. Their faces and expressions are closely matched. Courtesy of the twins.

TWIN SIGHTINGS

What seemed like a simple lunch invitation set off a chain of revelations, followed by deceptions and uncertainties that the twins and their families faced over the next decade. When Susan was six or seven years old, her family was invited to lunch by her mother's college friend who had just purchased a home in Paramus, New Jersey. Another family—Marvin and Martha Fleishaker and their two children, also LWS adoptees—were invited. But once the group gathered, Susan became extremely uncomfortable because the Fleishaker children, seven-year-old Bruce and eleven-year-old Amy, kept staring at her. She was nervous, unable to eat, and insisted that she never wanted to go back. It turned out that the Fleishakers lived three doors away from Susan's twin sister Anne, and Bruce and Amy were her playmates. Both youngsters were amazed and perplexed by the striking resemblance between their friend Anne and this new girl Susan. "What is Anne doing here?" Amy asked her mother.[11]

Anne recalls, "I vividly remember Bruce saying to me 'today we met a girl that looked just like you, that talked like you and that acted like you.'"

Bruce's mother, Mrs. Fleishaker, telephoned LWS to relay what had happened, leaving Viola Bernard no choice but to invite each set of parents to meet with her separately. After that, Mrs. Fleishaker became a "go-between," delivering and comparing information between the two mothers who had not yet spoken. Because the twins could not meet, she had to make certain that their families would not enroll the twins in the same dance camp or dance class, or allow their paths to cross in any way.

I spoke with Bruce Fleishaker, now fifty-nine and a corporate controller for Nippon Paint in Tenafly, New Jersey. Bruce recalled details from his first encounter with Susan. Clearly, he was stunned at how much Susan looked like Anne, whom he had known since kindergarten. "We [my sister and I] even called her Anne, but she said her name was Susan. We went through the day like this." Amy recalls being "whisked away" before lunch was served, once her mother and Susan's mother saw the similarities between the two girls.[12] In fact, Bruce said that he and his sister were kept away from the house in Paramus, given the risk of seeing Susan again—because as Bruce and Amy grew older it would have been easier for them to connect Susan and Anne as twins. I wonder—what if the Fleishaker children had invited their friend Anne to come with them to that "ordinary" lunch?

Still, there were near misses. When Bruce turned thirteen, Anne, Anne's parents, and Susan's parents, but not Susan, were guests at Bruce's bar mitzvah. Bruce was too preoccupied with reciting his prayers properly to notice if the twins' parents talked to one another or if Susan's parents got a good glimpse of Anne.[13] It is likely that Susan's mother, Martha Birnbaum, who was told to stay silent about the twinship, made certain that her daughter did not attend. But as the twins approached adolescence, strangers, as well as people who knew one twin, were puzzled by seeing the other one.

According to Bernard and Neubauer, keeping separated twins from meeting was essential to the integrity of their twin study. They made efforts to prevent chance encounters even when twins were young. Susan was modeling at the age of three, had secured an agent, and was chosen to appear on the cover of a magazine. "But LWS got in the way—they were afraid that the other family might recognize my picture," Susan recalled. Susan's mother Martha was ambivalent about the photo shoot, so when the day arrived, Martha left the choice to her young daughter. Susan preferred to play with her friends, after which the modeling agency dropped her as a client.[14]

Following their shocking experience in New Jersey, Martha and James immediately went to see Bernard at her Nyack, New York, estate. They had to learn how and why the twins had been placed apart. "My husband and I met many times with Dr. Bernard, we were so very upset. We were hysterical about it. And we were *furious* that they had lied to us . . . but we were not able to tell Susan that she had a sister. We couldn't tell Susan she had a sister if she couldn't meet her sister. You know what I mean? So that was a horrible thing for us."

I asked Martha what Dr. Bernard had advised at that meeting—what did she say about bringing the twins together? "She didn't have any answer—she told us nothing about her philosophy behind her decision to separate twins. She did not help us at all. No. But we went and met with her many times. We were so very upset about this thing."[15] As I indicated, Anne, who had met with Bernard as an adult, said Bernard believed that a meeting between the young twins would be damaging—that is, in fact, what Bernard had told her family. I also wondered how Bernard explained the twins' separation to Martha and her husband. "She [Dr. Bernard] said, 'Well, we were doing a study and it just so happens that this thing happened. You know, and there's nothing we can do about that now.'" Martha countered to Bernard, "Those [twin] studies have been done over the years and I could have told you the results."

Martha never met Peter Neubauer, but she spoke with him by telephone when Susan and Anne were in their early twenties. "I was just so furious about everything that happened and the lie. He was convincing me that what they were doing was a good study. He said that we're learning a lot. He had no remorse—and he's a Holocaust survivor!"

Bernard felt "obligated" to tell Anne's parents who were equally horrified by the news, never having known that their daughter was part of a twin pair.[16] Like Susan's father and mother, once Bob and Donnie learned the truth, they considered bringing a lawsuit against LWS; however, Donnie worried about how doing so might affect her son, whom she wanted to protect. "They [my parents] said they would have taken both twins. They didn't have a lot of money then—my dad was just starting out. But they said they would have taken two," Anne said.[17] In fact, LWS had wanted Anne and Susan to be placed far apart, one in New York and the other in the Midwest. "But the agency did not have enough money to pay a tester to fly out there," Anne explained.[18] Bob and Donnie ended their participation in the study once the truth was known; of course, the researchers would not have allowed them to take part regardless. Donnie, a former psychology major at Wheaton College, in Norton, Massachusetts, quickly figured out that the "child development study" was really a study of separated twins.

Ten years passed, during which both sets of parents kept their silence. Anne and Susan finally learned about each other when they turned seventeen—it took another ordinary, but life-changing event to bring them together. Until that time, each twin was mistaken for the other several times and did not know why. Their parents couldn't help them.

GROWING UP APART: SUSAN

James and Martha Birnbaum were eager to have a family, but after two miscarriages and an ectopic pregnancy, they decided to adopt.[19] They chose LWS because Martha's research convinced her that LWS was "the place to go" for a Jewish baby. They received their son, Peter, in 1956, but the agency knew that they wanted a second child. Unlike the other parents who raised lone twins, Martha was not surprised when LWS notified her that a baby was available, as she and her husband were in frequent contact with the agency. However, receiving the second baby was contingent upon her participation in a "child development study" in which Susan was already enrolled. "They said the study would start soon and people would come to our home periodically. I said 'OK'—I thought it would help me as a mom," Martha said.

Martha was later told that her daughter Susan and Susan's twin sister had shared a crib in foster care. She believes that Susan was adopted first, leaving Anne on her own. Interestingly, the concept of twinship first came up when Susan was three years old. The little girl stood in the back seat of her family's car, leaned over, and said she wished she were a twin. "It came out of the blue," Martha said. Martha thinks the comment was inspired by Susan's early memory of her being together with Anne during their first half year of life. Other LWS parents of twins I have interviewed, as well as parents who have lost one twin during pregnancy or shortly thereafter, have raised similar notions. They point to their single twin's craving for physical comfort and/or interest in twins. However, reduced oxygen tension in fetal blood, plus the pregnanolone and prostaglandin D2 provided by the placenta, keep fetuses sedated.[20] The tactile sensations twins experience before birth might be recalled at some level, but that has not been demonstrated conclusively, so cannot be linked to being a twin.[21] It is also known that newborn infants can distinguish between self and non-self touch, and that they express emotions and show signs of shared feelings.[22] However, most children's memories are of people, places, and events they experience at three years of age and beyond.[23] Thus, despite sharing a womb and her first six months with a twin sister, Susan had no inkling that she was part of a pair. Neither did Anne, nor did other separated twins from LWS and those in the Minnesota Study of Twins Reared Apart.[24]

Susan does not recall the testing she completed at a very young age, but she does recall being tested when she was six or seven. "There were so many IQ tests." She liked the attention she received from the two or three researchers who periodically came to her home, and she enjoyed being filmed. Martha is uncertain if the same investigative team came each time, but said that the researchers never interviewed her or her son Peter.[25] The twin study researchers did, however, speak with some parents and all of them recorded their observations of how each mother interacted with her own twin child.[26] Of course, the mothers had no way of knowing that the researchers might be mentally comparing how well each identical twin rode a bicycle, how often their parents indulged them, or how much each house needed cleaning.

Over the years, Susan and Anne's striking resemblance perplexed the people who knew one of them and encountered the other. In a truly curious twist, they might have met several years after the New Jersey episode because the twins' families were unknowingly connected. When she was ten years old, Susan and her family went to a family gathering in the Catskill Mountains, located in southeastern New York State. Anne's former school mate, fifth-grade "steady boyfriend," and current partner, Barry Kostrinsky, and his older brother Ira were there because their grandfather is Susan's mother's cousin. Barry recalled, "A girl catches my eye. I swear it is Anne, I stared at her for 30 minutes, but I was too shy to talk to her. I watched so long that this is stronger in my memory than most things. I was hypnotized—it was not just her looks, but the way she spoke, the way she moved, the little things, they were all the same. But I knew it wasn't Anne." The next time Barry saw the real Anne he announced, "I met a girl who looks just like you—you have a twin sister."[27] I asked Barry if his parents noticed the resemblance, but they hadn't. He is convinced that "kids are more perceptive than adults."

Similar things were also happening in Teaneck, New Jersey, where Susan lived. When Susan was in high school, she attended a concert where people came up to her and said, "We saw a girl who looks just like you."[28] Susan decided that everyone has a double.

GROWING UP APART: ANNE

In March 1961, Anne's parents received a telephone call from LWS saying that a baby girl was available for adoption. The Feinbergs had already adopted a child from LWS after Donnie was unable to conceive. The agency generally allowed just one child per family, but staff members knew that the couple wanted another child. This second adoption process proceeded quickly. The agency told Bob and Donnie that their daughter was part of a child development study, and they accepted that as part of the arrangement. The agency also said that Anne was a good baby who slept through the night, but the Feinbergs' experience was the opposite. Anne "screamed" every night, showing "separation anxiety" at nine months of age. For months, she was unable to sleep anywhere except in her own home, and a doctor had to be consulted.[29] Eventually, her distress subsided.

Why did LWS keep Anne and Susan together for six months? Anne claims it was because her biological mother could not decide if she wanted to raise or relinquish her two newborns. There is no federal law to this effect, but most states give women six months to reach the best decision.[30] Anne believes that her screaming episodes resulted from sharing a womb with Susan for nine months and sharing a foster home for six. "This is the tragedy, this is the mistake they made, keeping us together [if they intended to place us apart]," Anne said. As I explained, it is impossible to assess the extent and/or level of infant twins' awareness of one another. But according to Bernard, twins who showed signs of twin-to-twin interaction would not be parted.

Anne remembers the twin study sessions when testers would come to her home to make movies and administer lots of tests. Unlike Susan, Anne didn't enjoy them. "It was horrible—I had test anxiety, and I was shy and insecure. I didn't like them watching me. I was very self-conscious. You know, I didn't know if I was doing something wrong. But I think I enjoyed the films—I probably wanted to put on a show. I was dancing by then." Of course, the testing was suspended when Anne was six or seven, once the news of her twinship was uncovered. Interestingly, Anne's friends, Amy and Bruce, knew Anne was being tested and sometimes wondered why no one came to study them. After all, they were LWS adoptees, too.[31]

Because the separated LWS twins grew up in the New York area, it was not surprising to learn that Anne lived near Robert Shafran, one of the reared-apart identical triplets. Robert was just one school grade below her, and many of her friends knew him. Anne joked that, "They [the twin study team] probably tested me and then went to test him."[32]

As I indicated, the resemblance between Anne and Susan was apparent to people besides her friends Barry and Ira. Anne hadn't told her mother that her two friends had discovered her "look-alike" at a party in the Catskills. Perhaps she was too young at the time and just thought it was funny. But such incidents happened again. When Anne was in the tenth grade, she attended an Alvin Ailey dance performance. "These girls came up to me and said, 'Oh my goodness, you look like Susan Birnbaum! Were you adopted?' I said 'no' and walked away." Anne did tell her mother about this particular incident, but Donnie simply remarked that "everyone has a twin."[33] Of course, not everyone has a twin, but Anne had one and her mother knew it.

REUNION

Ordinary events can have life-changing outcomes. I have worked with separated twins whose reunions were the upshot of returning a t-shirt, planning a barbeque, or attending a convention.[34] Like the New Jersey luncheon, the event that actually joined Anne and Susan for the first time—a friends' get-together—was not out of the ordinary.

Anne had spent the summer of 1977 in Boston as a participant in the American Dance Festival at Connecticut College in New London, Connecticut. By September 5, she was home in Westchester County, just one week shy of her seventeenth birthday. "I was at my friend Ann Rubins's house. Ann and I were both in a dance company together. There was another girl there named Heather whom I did not know. Heather looked at me and said, 'My goodness, you look just like my best friend Susan!'" Heather instantly began posing the questions that no one who was previously struck by Susan and Anne's likeness had thought to ask. Heather's words were familiar to me when I asked her to repeat them forty-two years later—I have heard them from others who were curious enough to figure out why someone they knew and someone they did not know looked so much alike:[35]

H: "Were you adopted?"

A: "Yes."

H: "Were you born on September 13?"

A: "Yes."

Anne started to cry. Heather insisted that Anne call Susan right away, but first Heather wanted to inspect Anne's ears because Susan's right ear lobe has a distinctive feature—the top part curls down slightly. Anne had it, too. "So, I call her [Susan] up. I say, 'Hi Susan, my name is Anne and I'm here at my friend Ann's house. And her friend Heather is here—you know, Heather Rockwell. And she says we look exactly alike, that we're twins. Were you born September 13?' And she said, 'Yes.' I said, 'Were you from the Louise Wise adoption agency?' She said, 'Yes.'" Both of them were astounded. They arranged to meet the following day, at New York City's Plaza Hotel on 5th Avenue and 59th Street.[36]

As it turned out, Susan and Anne could easily have met during the previous summer, in 1976. Anne, her friend Ann, and Heather Rockwell's older sister had danced together at Jacob's Pillow, a dance center in the Berkshire Mountains of Massachusetts. However—for some reason that no one can figure out—Heather's older sister didn't see the resemblance between Anne and her sister's friend Susan. Her blind spot still puzzles Heather a great deal. "My sister knew Susan very well since Susan was always at our house. Maybe my sister was just into her own thing that summer."[37]

Heather and her older sister had been heading to Maine when they stopped at Ann's house. En route to Maine, they visited Boston and according to Heather, they "randomly ran into Peter Birnbaum, Susan's older brother," who was studying at Boston University. Heather was excited to tell him that Susan had met someone who was most likely her identical twin, but she was unprepared for his response. "Peter didn't seem happy about this. His face showed it. As an adoptee himself, maybe he felt bad not knowing anything about his own biological family," she wondered.

September 6, 1977, was Labor Day. Susan brought a friend and Anne brought two friends along for the occasion, one of them Ann. Inviting a family member or friend when twins meet for the first time is not uncommon because some twins are unsure about how the reunion will go. As adoptees, they are excited at the prospect of meeting not just a biological relative, but a twin—a relationship that carries some caché—but twins may also feel apprehensive. Some twins have worried that the other person wants a favor, has staged the situation as a joke, or might even harm them. One of the switched-at-birth Colombian twins I worked with insisted that his twin meet him at the lively Lourdes Plaza, in Bogotá, because a police station was set up on the premises.[38]

The Plaza Hotel is situated off 5th Avenue, set back from a small square, but the twins found each other despite the crowds. They studied each other momentarily, then laughed. They looked exactly alike except for their hairstyles—Anne's hair was short, and Susan's was pulled back into a long ponytail—but their gestures and mannerisms were near perfect matches. Their friends could see it, too. The five young women sat on the steps of the hotel, talked, and smoked cigarettes. "What else do teenagers do?" Susan recalled with a laugh.

Susan and Anne described their reunion as "shocking," "exhilarating," and "wild." A week later they ate their first birthday cake together when they turned seventeen. First Anne visited Susan's house, then Susan visited Anne's home. Bruce Fleishaker remembered coming out of his house one day and seeing Anne and Susan walking down the street together. "I felt a stunned silence. They looked exactly the same, except that Anne's hair was shorter then."[39] Bruce also mentioned Anne's habit of grabbing the charm of her necklace and moving it back and forth when she felt nervous—Susan did that, too. Both twins introduced their newly found sister to their friends and soon everyone at their schools knew. Susan's close friend, Susan Golomb, remembered the day that Susan called to say that she had found her twin sister and was bringing her to Golomb's home. "It was shocking—who suddenly has a twin?" Susan asked.[40] She was struck by the twins' similar head tilt and voice inflection. "It was wild!" Anne's high school class included six sets of identical twins and forty-two years later she could recite the names of almost all of them. "They all feel for me," she said.

I was fortunate to find Anne's friend, Ann, in whose house Anne's likeness to Susan was finally more than a fluke. Ann, now a pediatrician on the East Coast, had been out of touch with Anne for a long time, but she remembered the phone call and the reunion "as if it were yesterday." Ann explained,

> "This was not an event I could bury. I thought about it a lot over the years, worrying how Anne and Susan were doing. We were teenagers, so innocent, we had no idea what we were doing. None of us told our parents about the phone call or that we were meeting in New York City. It was weird and crazy and exciting, and we didn't think about the repercussions, the impact it could have on their lives. And yet, at the same time, deep in my soul I felt a weight because maybe their meeting wasn't a good thing. When we got to the hotel, they [Anne and Susan] looked at each other, hugged and cried. And maybe I was crying, too. They looked incredibly alike."[41]

Soon after Susan and Anne met, neither Neubauer nor Bernard asked them, "Would you mind coming in for some testing?" However, they had something else in mind. "We ended up going to Greenwich Village and meeting with a psychologist. People in glass houses shouldn't throw stones," Susan said. The location of these data, why they were collected, if they were analyzed, and, if so, where they were published, are unknown.

FAMILY MATTERS

Toward the end of the film *Three Identical Strangers*, Brenda Galland, one of the triplets' wives, astutely observed that when twins and triplets are separated it affects not just them, but their entire families. Susan and Anne's meeting was *not* a joyful experience for everyone who was close to them. Susan confirmed that her brother Peter was upset, as observed by her friend Heather when she met him in Boston. "It made him think about his own adoption and not knowing where he's from. And it made him wonder whether he's got a twin or a brother or a sister," Susan confessed.[42] Martha sometimes wondered if the mental health of Peter's biological parents concerned him.[43]

Viola Bernard believed that the chances of twins meeting were slim in infancy and toddlerhood, but would increase as they grew older. "In such an eventuality, the early parent-child relationships and formative years so critical to the development of individuality would have already been experienced by the child thus serving, to the extent, the purposes of the twin's growth as an individual."[44] Bernard's reasoning was untested until some twins inadvertently met. Despite Susan and Anne's elation on September 6, each twin experienced some difficult moments that Bernard had not envisioned. Recall that Susan had started jazz dancing at age fifteen, whereas Anne had been dancing since she was five. Susan reflected,

> "And that was her [Anne's] identity as a teenager, and it completely devastated me. I was always a singer and I played in bands, so I started focusing my energy into that. So, I was able to come to terms with it and do something else. I felt like because everybody has an identity at that age with a hobby or something—and she [Anne] was going to be a professional dancer—I felt like it wasn't my sole ambition anymore and it was not something we could have shared. There was competition there; I hadn't been doing it [dancing] as long as she had."

As much as Anne loved to dance, she left Adelphi University's dance program in her sophomore year. "It was really the post-traumatic stress of meeting my sister and finding out everything," Anne explained. "It was a difficult time in my life. I had met Susan in the beginning of my senior year [in high school]. I was depressed. She called me and I found out that she was not doing so well. My dad was very upset when I left Adelphi." Anne continued, "[The whole twin situation] really disrupted my education—it changed the trajectory of my career. I was very talented in dance and had high ambitions for professional companies and everything, and it thwarted my career."

Bernard assumed that if twins reunited accidentally, they and/or their parents would contact LWS or the CDC for an explanation. In such cases, the staff would explain the agency's policy regarding twins that was in effect at the time. It is likely that Bernard followed through with this plan when she spoke with Susan and Anne's parents, but I wanted Susan's mother's take on Bernard's justification. "Bullshit," Martha replied. Bernard also believed that it would be "more damaging than helpful" to offer unsolicited information to families who were unaware of their child's twinship.[45] Her hand was forced when it came to Susan and Anne.

The teenage twins' revelation and reunion were especially painful for Susan's parents, who had been hiding her twinship for so many years. "Keeping the truth from Susan was an absolute nightmare," Martha recalled. "It was so terrible; you have no idea." Martha and her husband saw Bernard from time to time at her estate and would tell her they were ready to disclose the truth to their daughter—but Bernard insisted that they refrain from doing so. Then, on September 6, Susan called her mother on the phone when she returned from the Plaza Hotel, having just met Anne. "Could I be a twin?" she asked. Martha recalled her response at the time. "I didn't intend to tell it to her on the phone, but I had no way of saying no. It killed me." Martha explained to her daughter that she couldn't tell her the truth until Anne knew, and Susan understood that.

Anne's parents also kept silent about their daughter being a twin. Like the Birnbaums, they were unprepared for Anne's news when she returned from her friend Ann's home after talking with Susan on the phone. "I think I have an identical twin sister," she announced. Bob and Donnie said nothing that evening. The next day, when Anne returned from her meeting with Susan, her parents sat her down and said, "We have something to tell you." They proceeded to explain that they had known all along that she was a twin and that they had planned to tell her before she went to college. But they had been told to keep it a secret. Anne became very emotional as she spoke about this, even after forty-two years. "My whole world shattered. This was very, very traumatic. My parents knew about this and I didn't know. The trust just sort of fell out from underneath me and just talking about it [now] is very upsetting. . . . I understood intellectually why they couldn't tell me, they were told by the psychiatrist [Bernard], but emotionally it was pretty difficult. My parents had known about the situation for so many years, but they were inno-cent—they didn't have any idea when they adopted me that I was a twin."

Holding the two sets of parents hostage to a secret truth introduced a destructive element into both twins' homes. Apparently, Bernard and Neu-bauer never fully considered the possible far-reaching consequences of their difficult request, probably because they believed chance meetings of young twins seemed so unlikely. But Susan and Anne's situation was different—they didn't know they were twins, but their mothers and fathers *did* know and had to bury that knowledge for years. The twins' parents stayed distant from one another as they tried to manage the situation. Occasionally, Susan's mother Martha visited the Jewish Museum where Anne's mother Donnie was a docent. The two mothers talked with each other, but never discussed their shared concerns.[46]

POST-REUNION: INSIGHTS AND CHALLENGES

After their initial meeting at the Plaza Hotel, Susan and Anne discovered a number of similarities and only a few differences between them. The most obvious difference is that Susan is right-handed and Anne is left-handed. This mirror-imaging effect and others, such as opposite hair whorls—which Susan and Anne also have—are found among 25 percent of identical twin pairs. The reasons behind these reversals are speculative, including developmental disturbances and unusual embryological events associated with identical twinning; delayed division of the fertilized egg had been raised as an explanation, but is now considered less likely. Environmental factors, such as sleeping posture and smoking, have also been linked to opposite-handedness in twins. Anne's adoptive mother Donnie and brother Mark are left-handed, so she wondered if she might have environmentally acquired this trait from them. However, studies show that a child's hand preference is unrelated to the handedness of his or her adoptive parents, but is related to that of the biological parents, favoring a role for genetic factors.[47]

The twins are both five feet, two inches tall and have the same physique, although Anne is slightly slimmer, due to her constant physical activity. Both twins have the same blonde hair and "outy" belly buttons. Their preferred foods include Italian dishes and anything with chocolate. Their musical tastes also align. Today, neither twin endorses the reasoning behind Bernard's belief that twins are better off apart, although they accepted it when they first heard it as teenagers. According to Anne, "I think it was horrible. . . . I was just talking to Susan on the phone tonight and we always say how horrible it is that we were so deprived of a sister and being a twin, especially being adopted which is hard enough. I also said that we don't know the difference. We've only experienced, you know, being separated and not growing up together." Like Anne's parents, Susan believes that her parents would have taken both twins if they had only known.

Neither Susan nor Anne was serious about academics, in contrast with their parents and brothers, who variously earned college and professional degrees. But both twins loved to dance and had hoped to build their careers around dancing. Even though they grew up apart, their resemblance in these areas can be partly explained by their shared genes—numerous twin studies have demonstrated genetic influence on educational attainment, physical abilities, and vocational interests.[48] However, careers based on the twins' shared dance passion did not happen.

Susan had auditioned for a place in the theater department at Adelphi University in Garden City, New York, but failed to make the final cut. "Anne was already there in the dance department and it was humiliating for me." So Susan decided to take a year off from school. During that time, she enrolled in a course at New York's Fashion Institute of Technology and worked at a boutique, but she felt a lack of direction. The following year, she enrolled in Glassboro State College in Glassboro, New Jersey, taking liberal arts classes, but eventually left because of ups and downs in her life. She finally settled on Marymount Manhattan College in New York City, but she didn't complete her degree.

Susan met several times with Dr. Bernard in the early 1980s, after having met her sister. They discussed Susan's feelings about the meeting and what it meant to be together again. Bernard offered to meet with Susan anytime and said to call. Anne also began visiting Bernard at about this time, as I will explain, although the twins never saw her together. Meanwhile, in 1979 the twins' biological mother had written to LWS, saying she was willing to reconnect with her twin daughters if they were willing to see her. By then, both twins had received non-identifying information about their biological family from Dr. Bernard. Susan met her mother first, in April 1980, a reunion facilitated by Barbara Miller in LWS's post-adoption services.[49] Their biological mother flew from her home on the West Coast to meet Susan at the adoption agency in New York. Since then, Susan has visited with both of her biological parents—who never married, but did marry other people—and is "good friends with both of them." She learned that their mother was nineteen years old and a high school graduate when she delivered her twins. Because an unwed mother brought shame upon her family, her mother's parents flew her to New York, putting her in the care of an aunt and uncle who brought her to LWS. According to Susan, their mother knew that her twins would be separated. "I think they told her that by doing this, they would satisfy two couples who couldn't have children. And they convinced her that it was a good thing to do. And what does she know?"

Susan married in 1995 at age thirty-four, became a mother at age thirty-eight, and divorced at age fifty-four after a twenty-year marriage. She is now a clerk in an immigration court, doing work that is "pretty interesting." Susan's son, now twenty-one, has dealt with his own behavioral difficulties and withdrew from college for a while. Her former husband, whom she met in the United States, was from Germany. He was both an engineer and a talented cook. Susan kept her married name.

After Anne left Adelphi University, she instructed and trained people in fitness for a number of years. "I love this stuff . . . it's like a natural antidepressant." But Anne still felt depressed at times. Her mood upset her father, who demanded that Anne meet with Dr. Bernard, pro bono, on a weekly basis. During these sessions, Bernard gave Anne some information about her biological parents—it seems that the twins' mother also experienced periods of ups and downs. Bernard also told Anne that she couldn't really treat her like a patient. "She was seeing me because it was sort of like [according to my father], either you see Anne or we will sue you, or something." When I asked

Anne for the photograph she had received from Bernard, showing the twins as infants, she said she had misplaced it. Susan had, too. Anne's last meeting with Bernard was in April 1981. Bernard declined an invitation to her wedding in 1985, but she sent a gift.

Anne met her biological mother in October 1980 at the LWS agency, a reunion also facilitated by Miller.[50] The two of them have become very close. It turned out that Anne shares interests with her biological grandparents whom she met in 1984—her grandmother was a massage therapist, and her biological grandfather was a chiropractor. The couple had left Sweden for California, where they started a wellness center. And the twins' biological father was a pre-medical student before changing his focus to marriage and family psychotherapy. Anne has always been concerned with topics related to the body, science, and medicine. In 2002, she earned her certification as a massage therapist. The twins have several half-siblings whom they have met, related to them through their father. Their biological mother does not have other living children; after having her twins she delivered a baby boy who was stillborn, due to Rh blood factor incompatibility.[51]

Anne has married twice and divorced twice. Her first marriage at age twenty-four was to a man of Italian descent. This early relationship was a source of jealousy to Susan who was single—the kind of within-pair tension that LWS's twin separation practice was intended to avoid. Anne's second marriage at age thirty-nine was to a German citizen living in the United States—an engineer and a good cook. The fact that Susan had also married and divorced a German engineer with a flair for food is one of many similarities that some people attribute to coincidence, but there is more to it than that. People choose their significant others largely on the basis of similarities to themselves, not differences, the previously noted phenomenon called *assortative mating*. For example, spouses tend to match on age and ethnicity, but they show greater resemblance on behavioral traits, like educational level and values, than on physical traits, like height and weight.[52] However, my Minnesota colleagues reported a curious finding, namely that the spouses of identical twins are *not* more alike across seventy-four mainly psychological measures than the spouses of fraternal twins. They concluded that romantic infatuation explains people's partner choice and that this process is essentially random. Moreover, few of the non-twin spouses said they were romantically attracted to their spouse's identical twin—just 13 percent of the males expressed interest in their wife's twin sister.[53] In contrast, more recent work has found that the spouses of identical twins *are* more alike than those of fraternal twins, although not in all ways.[54]

Perhaps the different inventories used in these studies explain their different outcomes. But a more significant question is: *how similar are the spouses of identical reared-apart twins?* The Minnesota Study of Twins Reared Apart found just modest spouse resemblance for dietary preferences[55] and whether individuals are "morning people" or "evening people."[56] However, no one has fully investigated this interesting issue. I suspect that identical reared-apart twins' spouses may be more similar than those of reared-together twins. That is because the pool of potential mates is broader, allowing greater freedom of choice—if identical twins reared together *do* like the same person, then one twin needs to back away. However, this may be what occurred in Anne and Susan's case—Anne married seven years after the twins first met. Furthermore, the husbands and wives of reared-apart twins might feel attracted to their spouse's twin whom they would be meeting for the first time—when twins are reared together the potential brothers- and sisters-in-law become familiar figures, thereby dampening romantic attraction.

Anne kept her German last name to avoid the difficulties of changing her legal documents. She is currently partnered with her former fifth-grade sweetheart, Barry Kostrinsky, and has no children. Kostrinsky is the founder of Havensbx and Haven Arts, an art gallery in the South Bronx, and the father of thirty-two-year-old male-female twins. Anne now lives outside New York City where she administers massage full time and teaches fitness classes several times each week. It's work that she loves, possibly because it has a dance component to it. "Us dancers never get over it," she said.

LATER YEARS: LOOKING BACK AND LOOKING AHEAD

Not long after they had met, Anne and Susan visited Dr. Neubauer at his apartment. Anne remembers his accent and his interest in having them tested once again. Susan told me about another time she had called Neubauer on the telephone. She did so after the publication of Lawrence Wright's 1995 twins article in the *New Yorker* magazine that briefly mentioned the LWS-CDC twin study on the first page.[57] Susan yelled at him and then he hung up the phone. "None of us likes him," she said. Susan had another reason for her interest in Wright's article. The article describes a pair of separated identical twins, Amy and Beth—Susan thinks that she is Amy, and Anne is Beth, although Anne is less certain of this. The twins in both pairs had (have) blonde hair, oval faces, and slightly snub noses, but Susan and Anne's eyes are green, whereas Amy and Beth's are blue-gray. Susan sees some parallels in the family dynamics, but Anne does not—and whereas Susan and Anne each had one older sibling, Beth had two.[58] I also questioned the twins about a different identical pair, Shauna and Ellen, mentioned in Neubauer's 1990 book.[59] Here, he described a culinary quirk unique to the twins: From an early age, both twins showed an extreme fondness for cinnamon and *had* to have it sprinkled on whatever they ate. One twin's mother stressed what a good eater her child was, while the other twin's mother despaired of her daughter's unusual taste. Neither Susan nor Anne recalled a particular fondness for cinnamon.

It is possible that Amy and Beth are a "composite pair," showing an amalgam of traits that the researchers observed across the different sets. "I know that I'm Amy, but the descriptions of the families are not accurate," Susan told me.[60] A presentation like this would have had the benefit of sharing interesting observations with colleagues, while concealing the twins' identities. In fact, I discovered the *real* LWS pair in which both girls showed an unusual food preference—it was for all things spicy. One twin even drank salad dressing from the bottle.[61] However, the twins in this other pair both preferred ketchup, not cinnamon; perhaps substituting cinnamon for ketchup in the professional literature was done to mask the twins' identity. I did confirm a childhood passion for ketchup with a female twin in a different pair who poured it on meat and chicken to add flavor and moisture.[62] In the next chapter, I will describe another separated identical female pair with some features that match those of Amy and Beth. And later in this book I will describe identical male twins, separated by LWS, who shared an intense distaste for condiments of any kind.

I wondered if Susan and Anne had seen the film *Three Identical Strangers*, and they had. "I believed it. I lived it. You know, we had the same story," Susan said. Anne had a similar response but expressed it differently. "I thought it was old hat—been there, done that." Susan's mother Martha also sat through the film. "I was so hysterical when I went to see that. Hysterical crying. My heart was broken. My neighbor came with me and if she hadn't embraced me and I had gone alone they would have found me there in the morning. I just couldn't move. . . . I was feeling sick about it."

Three Identical Strangers raised the possibility of parent-to-child transmission of mental disturbance in some cases. Martha told me she had "read" that some children placed by LWS had been born in mental hospitals. A 1962 letter to Bernard from Dr. David E. Sobel, at Columbia University's College of Physicians and Surgeons, outlined his assessments of children born to two schizophrenic parents. He referenced data, albeit "scanty," from geneticists showing that two out of three such children will develop the disorder. However, Sobel wondered if certain key features of these children, such as unusual variations in sensitivity and excitability, if handled appropriately, might make the difference between sickness and health. Two of the five children Sobel was interested in had been placed by LWS. In the margins of the letter, Bernard had scribbled, "Mrs. F has seen family and they didn't want to see Sobel. She spoke of him as following children born in mental hospital."[63] A colleague's

1963 letter to Bernard expressed the concern and lack of consensus among LWS staff about informing adoptive parents if there was mental illness in a child's biological background. "Our practice [based on Child Welfare league standards] is to share it only when a child is born in a mental hospital . . . some workers question whether we have a 'moral obligation' to share such a history even if the mother was not in a mental hospital when the child was born."[64]

Bernard's 1964 summary of a staff adoption meeting continued this theme. She stressed that the agency's goal was "not to find the correct or objective way to tell [parents], but rather an attempt to identify significant matters and to assess the relative importance of these variables, such as future welfare of children." She continued,

> "Relative to examination of experience is the CDC study of the develop-
> ment of twins in whose background there is a good deal of psychopathol-
> ogy. Both children now 3 years old are doing extremely well in adoptive
> homes. . . . The weight of environmental and experiential factors lead us to
> pay more attention to choice of parents, more evaluation in the supervisory
> period, more help to adoptive parents, more attention to and observation
> of children."[65]

The three-year-old twins Bernard refers to are not identified but appear to have been in the study. Perhaps the "down" periods experienced by Susan and Anne, and some other LWS twins whose biological parents showed such tendencies, would have been mitigated had their parents been told and been prepared for them—or if the twins had grown up together.

Susan and Anne were the first pair of twins to meet each other, in 1977, so it is curious that they were not in the public eye. In approximately 1981, four years after their reunion, Susan was filmed once by freelance filmmaker Jan Peterson, but nothing was done with that footage. In stark contrast, the identical male triplets, who met in 1980, became instant national and international media stars with celebrity that stuck. As I described in chapter 6, Bernard and her colleagues speculated over which twins were interviewed by Mike Wallace for the *60 Minutes* program on the LWS-CDC twin study. As they debated the identity of the possible pair, Bernard noted that the time sequence "might give a clue to at least the girls' current feelings against the Agency, if sufficiently fomented as well by [*Sixty Minutes* producer] Ms. Amgott." Of course, the twins in question were *not* Susan and Anne, but Kathy and Betsy. Susan, Anne, and Martha independently confirmed that their only contact from *60 Minutes* was in 2006, and came from the late noted television journalist Ed Bradley. Bradley's interest may have been kindled by an inquiry from Susan's friend, Jill Butterman, daughter of Arthur Bloom who created the famous *60 Minutes* ticking clock that precedes each televised segment.[66] However, the twins' program did not progress beyond the initial stage because of Bradley's untimely death from leukemia in November of that year.[67]

Susan was working with attorney Jason D. Turken of Turken & Heath, LLP, in Armonk, New York, to retrieve her records from Yale University. Their last communication had been just before the December 2019 holidays. She often wonders why the process is moving so slowly. Then, on February 17, 2020, Susan received an email message from Turken's law firm informing her that the Jewish Board had turned matters over to attorney Mark Barnes of Ropes & Gray LLP in Boston, Massachusetts. Barnes was copied on the message, and his telephone number was provided. Susan asked me, "Am I getting the run around?" In fact, I had been told by another twin that Barnes was now assisting several of the sets. Then, in June 2021, I learned that Susan was no longer seeking her records. In contrast, Anne has been generally uninterested in obtaining her data. "What are [the records] going to tell me?" she asked. "I was just a kid." However, any difference in opinion on this matter has not interfered with the twins' evolving relationship—in fact, Anne has recently shown some interest in seeing her data. Now in their late fifties, Susan and Anne enjoy a loving association with one another. The two-hour drive between them, coupled with Anne's Saturday work schedule, limits their times together, but they talk by telephone and text each other daily.

Anne's partner Barry said it was "wild" to meet Susan when he and Anne got together ten years ago. He is intrigued by the fact that both twins had married engineers from Germany. "There's no connection point like they went to a German engineer party together." In this respect, Anne and Susan's marital choices suggest that choosing a mate is not the same for reared-apart and reared-together twins, as I proposed earlier. Watching these twins has convinced Barry that genes play key roles in shaping our personalities and mannerisms—"the 'micro-things' that make a person a person." He is as fascinated with the twins' similarities as he was when he first saw Susan in the Catskills as a child. He sees slight differences in appearance and behavior, but the similarities are overwhelming. He regrets not having followed up an event that happened in August 2019, when he and Anne visited Anne's late mother at Westchester Medical Hospital. A nurse approached them to say that a woman who looked just liked Anne was working in the hospital cafeteria. Barry and Anne were preoccupied with Anne's mother's health at the time, but Barry means to go back there some day. "Could they be triplets?" he wonders.[68] Once you encounter a reared-apart twin as Barry did in the fifth grade, seeing or hearing about the near identity of two people assumes new meaning.

Barry calls the twins' relationship "bittersweet"—they enjoy each other a lot, but they grew up apart, so there are gaps that can't be filled. The twins will never know what it would have been like to have shared their lives as most twins do. "We are very close now," Susan told me. "When her [Anne's] mother was dying last year, I drove down and spent every weekend with her." Anne said, "I love her."

Identical, but Not the Same

Melanie and Ellen

$\mathcal{E}$xtraordinary things sometimes happen in ordinary places. I made this point in the previous chapter, but my list grows longer with each reared-apart twin pair I have come to know. The International House of Pancakes, familiar to most people as IHOP, is such a place. The bright blue roof, brown upholstered booths, and blueberry pancakes look virtually the same across the nearly two thousand current locations of this popular eatery.[1] Each year, IHOP serves millions of diners and employs thousands of waiters and hosts to serve them. That is why the chance pairing of a curious customer and a young hostess in a Brooklyn IHOP is so stunning—the accidental joining of these two people ended up changing the course of many lives. Because of that meeting, twenty-three-year-olds Ellen Carbone and Melanie Mertzel learned that they each had an identical twin sister living nearby. And they and their families eventually discovered the real purpose of the Louise Wise Services (LWS)-Child Development Center (CDC) researchers' regular visits to their homes.

MY FRIEND WANTED PANCAKES

Arlene Lippel, Ellen's "Aunt Arlene," has retired to Florida, but she lived for many years in the southern Brooklyn neighborhood of Sheepshead Bay. I talked to her twice, once on a stormy afternoon from a car while I was visiting her twin niece Ellen in Lyndhurst, New Jersey, and several weeks later from my home in sunny California. Arlene was thrilled to relive the events leading to her discovery that her niece Ellen is an identical twin.[2] Knowing that her story would be part of a book and read by many people energized her.

The Twins, Their Family Members, and Friends

Melanie

Melanie Mertzel Ellen's reared-apart twin
Alice Mertzel Melanie's adoptive mother
Bert Mertzel Melanie's adoptive father
Jeff Mertzel Melanie's older unrelated brother
Nancy Mertzel Melanie's older adoptive sister
Devon Mertzel Melanie's son

Ellen

Ellen (Lieber) Carbone Melanie's reared-apart twin
Thelma Lieber Ellen's adoptive mother
Sol Lieber Ellen's adoptive father
Alan Lieber Ellen's older adoptive brother
Carl Carbone Ellen's husband
Fiona, Ivy, and Bella Ellen's daughters
Arlene Lippel Ellen's aunt
Molly Rothberg Ellen's grandmother

Most importantly, Arlene feels gratified that she was not dissuaded by skeptical family members from pursuing what she believed was not mere coincidence. When I asked Arlene for her address so I could eventually mail her a copy of this book, she said, "I am really happy you are doing this." And she is proud that her sons think of her as a detective.

In the fall of 1989, Arlene was entertaining an out-of-town friend who expressed a penchant for pancakes.[3] Arlene wasn't thrilled with this idea because the only IHOP was in the Flatbush area of Brooklyn, an inconvenient trip from Sheepshead Bay. Moreover, it was the weekend, and she knew that the restaurant would be crowded. Still, Arlene agreed to go, and the two friends waited patiently in the long line as it inched forward. As they got closer to the front, Arlene heard a familiar voice, then caught sight of the hostess—she was stunned. "As we were escorted to our seats I grabbed my chest and asked my friend, 'What is my niece doing here? She lives in New Jersey.' Then the girl spoke and I said 'Oh, my God, she sounds exactly like Ellen!' I grabbed my chest again." Arlene knew that Ellen had been adopted, so perhaps this IHOP hostess was a sister, maybe even a twin sister. But her suspicions needed to be confirmed. When Melanie came by her table, Arlene asked her if she had been adopted. Melanie said "no," not wishing to reveal her personal details to someone she didn't know.

When their food came Arlene said she "kinda left it," but she really didn't. She could not stop staring at the hostess, and watched as a young man, most likely a boyfriend, approached the young woman and kissed her on the cheek. Arlene admitted, "I could see that I made her uncomfortable because I kept staring at her." Later that night, once her friend had left, Arlene thought a lot about her niece's look-alike and what she should do. She telephoned her youngest son who told her she was "crazy" and that she was imagining the whole thing. Then she called her eldest son who sounded interested and said he would go back with her to IHOP to investigate if he weren't living three hundred miles away in Buffalo, New York. Afraid to upset her sister-in-law, Ellen's mother Thelma, Arlene called Ellen's father, Sol. "He also said I was crazy and hung up the phone." At this point Arlene called Thelma who simply said, "Oh, my God! I wish I could have adopted them both!"

Thelma, her husband Sol, daughter Ellen, and son Alan lived in Old Bridge, New Jersey. Traveling to Brooklyn required some effort, and the ambiguity surrounding Ellen's look-alike was unsettled and unsettling. There was no reason to ask Thelma to come to Brooklyn at this point, but Arlene was excited and eager to know more. She was curious, but also cautious. She decided to invite Ellen's grandmother, Molly Rothberg, to go back to the IHOP with her the following week "to prove to myself that I am not crazy."[4] When the two arrived at the restaurant "Molly saw Melanie [the hostess] and she just leaned against the wall [in shock]." Then Arlene spotted the boyfriend. She asked the young man (Paul) to step outside to speak with her privately and said, "I know you will think I am crazy, but I don't want to hurt anyone. Now I am going to ask you a question—do you know if [your girlfriend] was adopted? He stiffened, and truthfully, I'm not sure if he said 'yes' or 'no.'" I showed him a picture of Ellen I had brought with me and I said, 'She looks just like your girlfriend, but she's my niece. He said 'Nah, I think you're mistaken.'" Arlene decided that that was the end of it, but there was more.

Arlene continued, "Someone came and took us to our table. We ordered and finished eating. We asked for our check, but we were told that there was no check. So, we put a tip on the table." According to Melanie, before Arlene and Molly left, Arlene gave Ellen's phone number to her and suggested that she give her niece a call. Not surprisingly since so many years have passed, Arlene remembers these events somewhat differently. She recalls giving her own phone number to Melanie's boyfriend Paul in case Melanie wanted more information.

When Arlene got home, she immediately called her son in Buffalo to tell him what had happened. While he was interested before, he was now persuaded that his mother had a "real imagination."[5] Arlene recalled that twenty minutes later the telephone rang. "It was the hostess, the one who looked exactly like my niece Ellen. She said her name was Melanie. We talked a little bit—she told me her parents were out of town. She asked me a few questions about the adoption agency, but whatever I could tell her she knew already. And that was the end of the conversation."

What Arlene didn't know was that after her first visit to IHOP, Melanie had asked her mother, Alice Mertzel, if she could have a twin.[6] Alice, who was also working in the restaurant, denied it—she had never been told that her daughter was a twin and was angry that a stranger had asked Melanie if she had been adopted. "What if you hadn't known you were adopted? That woman didn't know you!" Alice's remarks seemed to settle the situation, and Melanie forgot all about it. But after Arlene came back to the restaurant a second time the situation gained significance. Paul had seen the picture of Ellen and was confused because he believed it was Melanie. He also knew that Melanie was adopted. "He thought the girl in the picture was me and that I was mad at him," Melanie recalled. "My parents were away, but I decided to call Ellen on the phone that night." Melanie does not recall speaking to Arlene before calling Ellen.

BECOMING TWINS

Events unfolded differently for Ellen, the twin in New Jersey. It was left to Thelma to call Ellen and tell her daughter that a chance look-alike at a pancake restaurant was most likely her identical twin. Ellen was shocked, not just because there was never any reason to suspect it, but because she had had an imaginary twin as a child. "I would mow the lawn with her and talk to her. But she didn't have a name." Ellen's best friend from preschool through fifth grade was named Melanie. People who knew them called them "the Bobbsey twins," after the popular series by Laura Lee Hope.[7,8] "Mel and El" even dressed alike when they first met. But this other person, also named Melanie, could be her *real* twin sister.

Speaking by phone for the first time, the two discovered an impressive list of common characteristics, typical of other separated identical twins.[9] Both were about five feet, one inch tall, had the same curly blonde hair, and gained weight easily. Their food preferences were, and still are, "95% alike." One of their dietary differences is that Melanie thinks mushrooms are "gross," whereas Ellen likes them. Another difference is that Ellen avoids seafood, whereas Melanie makes an exception for shrimp. Years later, assuming that her sister would eat shrimp Melanie served that as an entrée at a dinner she prepared, but Ellen avoided seafood of every kind.

They had their tonsils removed at the same time and sport matching dimples, although Melanie's is on the right side of her face and Ellen's is on the left. And like 25 percent of identical pairs, Melanie is left-handed and Ellen is right-handed.[10] Their voice qualities are alike, enough to have made Ellen's Aunt Arlene take notice when she first encountered Melanie at the IHOP. However, the twins were quickly aware of their different accents that reflected Ellen's northern New Jersey rearing and Melanie's Brooklyn background.

The twins realized that they had both been tested by researchers who visited their respective homes until they turned twelve.[11] However, an unusual difference was that Ellen had an older brother, whereas Melanie had an older brother *and* an older sister. Even though LWS carefully crafted matching family structures for the separated twins, Melanie's parents would learn that a family with two older siblings had been intentionally chosen by the adoption staff. The twins set a date to meet for dinner at Ellen's apartment and decided to bring their boyfriends.

While these developments were taking place, Melanie's parents were vacationing in Florida and had no idea of what was happening back home. Melanie knew she had to tell her parents, but she was struggling to come up with the right words. Just before they returned, Melanie poured herself several glasses of wine, then confided to her mother and father that she had spoken to a woman who looked just like her, had the same birthday, and had been adopted from LWS—and was most likely her twin sister.[12] Shocked, Bertram (Bert) and Alice Mertzel immediately scheduled an appointment with the agency. Ellen's parents, Sol and Thelma Lieber, who had heard the news from Ellen's Aunt Arlene, also met with an LWS staff member to understand exactly what had transpired twenty-three years before. Ellen was too angry to go with them.[13]

MELANIE'S FAMILY

Alice and Bert Mertzel raised their three children in Brooklyn, New York.[14] Alice was a first-grade schoolteacher before leaving that job to run the IHOP restaurant that her husband Bert owned in Queens. When Melanie was old enough, she ran the restaurant with her mother. But during Melanie's first year of life, Bert stayed home with his young daughter and was largely responsible for her care. He eventually acquired the Brooklyn restaurant and one additional IHOP restaurant in Queens, New York, when Melanie was still very young. The Mertzels later owned property in the Corinthian Building, an imposing apartment structure in midtown Manhattan.

The couple had always wanted a family, but after Alice's first pregnancy ended in miscarriage, they decide to adopt. They adopted their oldest child,

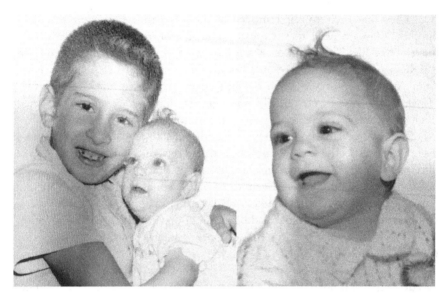

Figure 8.1.   Separated identical twin Ellen with her older brother Alan (L); and Ellen's twin sister Melanie (R). The infants' facial features are nearly identical, as is the tuft of hair on the top of each small head. Courtesy of the twins.

Jeffrey, in 1959, through a private arrangement. Then, after a second miscarriage, the Mertzels contacted LWS and adopted their second child, Nancy, in 1963. "We told LWS that we wanted a third child, but they said that was not their policy, because too many families wanted babies. But then they called us and we met many times with a social worker before we took Melanie home," Alice told me. Melanie was two and a half months old when her new mother and father picked her up from the agency; she had supposedly been in the care of a foster family until then. Alice learned that her daughter's biological parents were young and unable to care for a newborn baby. Alice wasn't told that Melanie was a twin.

I asked Alice to think back to the day at the IHOP when Melanie was first spotted by Ellen's Aunt Arlene.

> It was the weekend, and Melanie was complaining that one of the customers was staring at her and making her nervous and upset. I told Melanie to let me know when she [the customer] comes in again and I will speak to her. Then Bert and I went away to Florida for a few days and we came home late. We saw that the light was still on and Melanie was awake. I asked her what she was still doing up and she said she wanted to talk to us. We looked each other in the eye and I went into her room, just the two of us, and we sat down. I thought either she's pregnant, or since she was engaged at the time she wanted to do something with the wedding—never,

of course, dreaming [that Melanie would tell me she was a twin]. She started off by saying, "I want you to know that I am grateful that you are my parents. I never would have wanted any other parents, but the two of you." Then she said, "If I was a twin, what would you have done?" I said, of course, I would have taken the two of you. And then she proceeded to say, "Remember that lady at the IHOP, etc., etc." Melanie was quite excited [in a positive way] at the time.[15]

We were thrown—completely thrown and, of course, after thinking about it we were very angry. [The testers] came to our house under false pretenses and gave us some kind of story. I wanted badly to have a third child. LWS said the only reason they were giving us a third child was: Would we be willing to be part of a study? And the study was about the third child in an adoptive family. I had a B.A. degree in Psychology and a Master's degree in Teaching, so I was ecstatic—I was into testing and loved all this. When they came I would ask the testers what the results were, but they said there weren't any or something like that. But needless to say, we were in shock. [Alice recalled that their anger didn't actually set in for a few days.] Bert and I discussed it, but we didn't tell Melanie how angry we were. We were deceived by the agency—they had put us through the wringer. We had gone to a lot of meetings [at LWS] and met with the person who was handling it [the adoption], but they were dishonest. The whole thing smacks of Nazi Germany. I was very disturbed that our only Jewish agency would do something so terrible—separate twins. I was hurting. I was hurting for her [Melanie] and I was hurting for us.[16]

Alice and Melanie went to the agency with questions; Bert was working full-time so could not attend. Alice wanted proof—"she didn't believe it at first," Melanie recalled. Alice said that the LWS social worker with whom they met was very evasive. She confirmed that Melanie was a twin, but did not discuss the study at all. By the time they left, Alice was very disappointed. Of all the meetings she has attended, she remembered fewer details about this one because of her intense anger. "What they did to those kids was wrong. What is the best way to describe it? It was like Mengele." Ultimately, it was a *New York Times* article on twins that alerted Alice to the LWS-CDC twin study in which her daughter had taken part.[17]

Melanie's parents did not want to turn their daughter's twinship into something "too big," but Melanie was excited, and they didn't want to dampen her spirits. Now in her mid-eighties, Alice says that she would have loved to have spoken with Ellen's mother Thelma, to compare notes on how their daughters developed over the years.[18] But the initial situation was a tense time for her family, and the Mertzels wished to keep their professional and personal lives private. It was like a family secret, and she wanted to be protective.[19] Melanie's sister Nancy said that, at that time, her mother gave LWS "a kind of pass," suggesting that the twin separation policy might have been for the best—she acceded to the experts in the field.[20] Nancy is skeptical of what LWS practiced and believes that placing twins apart is "terrible." Nancy has her own issues with LWS regarding obtaining information about her own birth family that she did not wish to discuss with me. She was also very upset by the suicidal loss of a non-twin LWS adoptee, Michael Juman, that received considerable public attention.[21]

The meeting of the two mothers never happened, but Alice eventually met another adoptive mother who could completely understand her anger and outrage. In the late 1980s or early 1990s, Alice and Bert sold their Brooklyn home and moved to an apartment in Manhattan. Their building was conveniently located one block away from the Apartment Dweller, a large hardware store.[22] Alice went there often to buy new furnishings and noticed a picture of the LWS separated triplets pinned to the wall. "I questioned the woman running the store," Alice said. She turned out to be the mother of one of the identical triplets, separated by LWS and involved in the CDC twin study. In fact, she was David Kellman's mother. Mrs. Kellman and Alice became friendly. "We liked each other so we used to chat a lot. We didn't really discuss the study, but focused on what had happened to our kids." Years later, Alice watched the 2018 film *Three Identical Strangers* that tracked the lives of the triplet brothers. "I cried," she said.[23]

Alice now lives on her own in Monroe Township, New Jersey. Her husband, Bert, passed away in December 2018. Alice's daughter Nancy Mertzel is an attorney in New York City. She is divorced and has a fourteen-year-old son and a twelve-year-old daughter. Alice's son Jeffrey did not finish high school and has held a variety of jobs, among them owner of a bagel store in Staten Island financed by his parents. I wondered if a meeting between Alice and Thelma might be arranged, but Ellen and her brother Alan decided against it, perhaps because of the travel logistics and Thelma's poor health. Interestingly, but perhaps because the Mertzels prized their privacy, the two couples never met even after Melanie's parents left Manhattan in about 2010 for New Jersey and moved into a housing complex across the street from the Liebers. When Bert passed away in December 2018, Alice relocated to a different development.

ELLEN'S FAMILY

Sol and Thelma Lieber raised their two children in Old Bridge, New Jersey, a small town in Middlesex County.[24] Their home was in a small private development considered to be the richest part of the town. The Liebers have a biological son, Alan, who is six and a half years older than Ellen and was conceived with some difficulty after Thelma underwent reproductive assistance. A year later and still in her late twenties, Thelma tried to become pregnant again, but that was not to be. After some discussion about adoption, Sol went along with his wife who proposed adoption. "Whatever you want!" he declared. They decided to adopt a child—a boy or a girl, it didn't matter—and chose LWS because the agency provided Jewish babies to Jewish couples. After contacting LWS they waited a year before a baby girl became available. "I was so thrilled, my heart was thumping," Thelma recalled happily, as she became a mother again at age thirty-four. Ellen was three months old, "a perfect age," when they picked her up, either at a foster home or at LWS. Thelma also described Ellen as "scrawny, but all babies are scrawny." They had her examined by a pediatrician when she was four or five months old and was assured that their daughter was "fine." Thelma believes that Ellen was treated well during her first three months of life.

Sol passed away in July 2017. Ellen says she is unsure of how her father reacted to discovering she was a twin, partly because she was not living at home at the time. But she knew he would have gladly taken two babies—after all, they had an extra bedroom.[25] It was left to Thelma to share details about her family and her feelings about suddenly discovering that her daughter was a twin. I met her in October 2019 at her assisted living facility in River Vale, New Jersey. Photographs of Thelma, her husband, and her two children decorate the walls of her room. One especially sweet picture shows Ellen as an infant cuddling up to her big brother whose arms are wrapped protectively around her. I had seen a nearly identical image in Melanie's collection two days before, down to the small tuft of blonde hair that stood up straight from the top of her small head.

Thelma, now in her eighties, spoke candidly.[26] Like Melanie's mother, Thelma is bitter about the agency's decision to hide the truth about Ellen's adoption and the reason why people came to their home to administer tests and make films of her daughter. Unlike the other twins' parents, she and her husband were *never* told that Ellen was in a child development study. Instead, she was told that in order to adopt Ellen she would have to participate in a study of how a biological child and an adopted child got along. Thelma and Sol also assumed that the visitors came every so often to make sure that they were being good parents. She recalled telling the researchers how Ellen was doing in school and how easily she made friends, but she never spoke about herself unless asked.

Thelma was outraged that the twins were reared apart and vowed that she would have welcomed two babies into her home. "How do you split two children apart?" she asked as if she still could not believe what the agency had done—even fifty-three years later. "That is foreign to me, that bothered me a lot. I would have taken them both. Then I realized that it wasn't easy to get babies at that time, so they [LWS] wanted to help two different families. That's what I thought." Thelma admitted that she only surmised the purpose behind LWS's twin separation policy and did not know for sure.

Once she and Sol had cause to believe that Ellen was a twin, they went to LWS to find out if it was true. The staff member they met with confirmed that Ellen was a twin, but maintained silence about the study. Thelma continued, "When I learned that Melanie's family had adopted two other children, I became angry. Why didn't they give me Melanie *and* Ellen?" It took years for Thelma to realize that Ellen was in a study centered around the nature-nurture debate, something she learned from Ellen who had learned about the study in 2007 from *Identical Strangers*, the book by the LWS-separated twins Elyse Schein and Paula Bernstein.[27] However, Thelma was less concerned with the study than in how she performed as a parent. And throughout our interview she kept repeating, "Why didn't they give me two?"[28]

Thelma had less to say about how her husband had reacted to the news, emphasizing that he was a kind man who was delighted to play with his young daughter. But according to Arlene, Sol was very upset and couldn't handle it when he first heard what had happened. Recall that he hung up the phone the first time she called him.

Thelma was initially "very interested" in meeting Ellen's twin Melanie, to see how they compared. "I wanted to know if she was as good as Ellen as a person." When Melanie visited their home shortly after the twins had reunited, Thelma thought they didn't look exactly alike, probably because "they were all grown up." But like her sister-in-law Arlene, she could not get over how similar they sounded. The two sets of parents never met, although Thelma was "dying" to meet Alice and Bert, Melanie's mother and father. But as Alice had explained, she and her husband did not wish to make a "big thing" of the twinship and wanted to protect their privacy. However, when the twins were in their early forties and had children, Melanie and Ellen visited each other's families at two Passover seders. And in 2005, Melanie joined Ellen's family on a cruise to Bermuda.

Looking back, Thelma admitted that Ellen was not an easy child to raise.[29] She was very different from her son Alan, who did whatever he was told. "I was very upset—what am I doing wrong? Ellen had her likes and dislikes and gave me a hard time. I did the same things for both children, but children are different." When Ellen turned seventeen, it was as if "a cloud opened up over her and she became a good person." Thelma also explained that her son was "very smart," and Ellen felt that she was expected to be the same way, but Thelma denies this. "I just wanted Ellen to know that she was capable of doing more than she did. Then all of a sudden she was getting good marks in school."

Thelma understood that children come into the world with different genetically influenced predispositions, requiring parents to adjust their practices to nurture the interests and talents of each one.[30] The effects of different parenting strategies on children remain controversial among developmental psychologists. This topic was the focus of a lively 2019 debate, "Parenting Is Overrated," an event in which I took part and a motion I supported.[31] However, I would have substituted the word *misunderstood* for *overrated* because parenting is extremely important, just not in the way many people think it is.

After an hour or so Thelma had to leave her room at her residential facility for a medical appointment. I asked her if she had any last remarks. "All I can say is they never should have been separated! There's something in them [the twins] that I never learned, but I read about. Ellen told me little things. They are almost the same person—there is something there that makes them part of the same DNA. I swear to God, I believe in that DNA. . . . I am really sorry to this day that they were not brought up together." She turned to Ellen and said, "I feel that somehow something was taken away from you—and Melanie."[32]

Either Arlene did not express or did not sense how enraged and embittered Thelma had become by what LWS had hidden from her and Sol. Thelma was happy that Ellen had reunited with a close biological relative. But her feelings seemed to have changed over the years, as she witnessed the effects of Ellen's lost twinship on her daughter, and her own missed opportunity to become a multiple birth mother.

REUNION

Melanie and Ellen met each other for the first time when they were twenty-three. Melanie and her boyfriend drove to Ellen's apartment in Hoboken, New Jersey, where Ellen lived with her boyfriend. "Right before she came over, I threw up. It was nerves," Ellen confessed. The two had talked on the phone quite a bit before meeting, but seeing Melanie in person was a more daunting prospect. And there was little time to prepare for this moment because the reunion had been arranged quickly, within a week or two of Arlene's discovery.[33]

Melanie and her date arrived. When Ellen opened the door, the sisters looked at each other and began to laugh. Their laughs sounded the same to them, just as they did over the phone. The two couples drove together to Ellen's favorite restaurant in Hoboken to have dinner. Melanie recalled, "We

Figure 8.2.   Melanie (L) and Ellen (R) meet for the first time at Ellen's apartment at age twenty-three. Courtesy of the twins.

had to stop on the way because Ellen had to go to the bathroom. I was like, that's ridiculous! Both of us go to the bathroom a lot. We have the same bladder—small. Ellen should never have had a drink before we got in the car." Melanie and Ellen also found that they both enjoyed drinking and smoking— vodka and rum; Marlboro and Marlboro Menthol.[34] Over the years, they have switched places with respect to who drinks more and who smokes more, a tendency seen among many twin pairs with respect to such habits.[35] Melanie now smokes more than Ellen, although Melanie had quit in March 2020 and Ellen had stopped smoking when she was pregnant with her first child.[36] It was pointed out to them that how they hold a cigarette and the way they inhale are the same, behaviors neither had noticed. Their gait and gesture are also alike. However, their most distinctive physical feature is a long tongue—a reunion photo shows them displaying their striking appendages that are truly outstanding in length.

At some point during dinner, the twins left the table, headed for the bathroom, and began comparing their bodies. "We actually lifted our shirts and compared our boobs," Ellen said. They were especially curious to see if any of their physical features showed mirror-imaging because, by then, they knew that they were opposite-handed. Melanie, the left-handed twin, had a longer left arm and Ellen, the right-handed twin, had a longer right arm. "Everything seemed to be mirror-imaged," Ellen recalled. They also found some differences, explaining why Ellen described them as "opposite, but alike"—Ellen dyed her hair and her blue contact lenses hid her natural green eyes that matched Melanie's. Both twins liked to dress casually, but Ellen chose what would then have been a "hippier" style of dress, whereas Melanie's style was more conventional and upscale. Melanie explained that her clothes in those days reflected her mother's tastes, whereas her own tended toward jeans and t-shirts.

The twins' search for similarities and reversals is typical of what most reunited twins immediately do. Mark and Jerry—both firefighters from different New Jersey towns—were awed by their same bald heads, big belt buckles, and pinky fingers placed beneath cans of Budweiser beer. Standing before a mirror in the men's room of Jerry's firehouse where they first met, they stripped to the waist to discover that the tracks and swirls of their dark chest hair meandered the same way across their chests and shoulders. Sharon and Debbie learned that they could both roll their eyes upward to hide the pupils, a trick they enjoyed doing. Identical triplets Jim, Trent, and Tracy were mesmerized by the matching clefts in their chins.[37]

After dinner, the twins and their boyfriends returned to Ellen's apartment. The two young men, Paul and Stephen, were alike in appearance, both slim with dark hair, features that may have also drawn Arlene's attention to the IHOP hostess. Ellen and her boyfriend had been guests at Arlene's son's wedding the year before, so perhaps Arlene thought she was seeing the same couple again. The second time the twins met was a dinner at Melanie's apartment in Manhattan. Their third meeting was a dinner at Ellen's apartment and according to Melanie, "hers [Ellen's] was fabulous."[38] Interestingly, neither boyfriend was particularly enthused or mystified by the twins' similarities, thinking the situation was just "weird." Ellen commented that, "It was not their story," yet most people find reunions between reared-apart twins to be among the most remarkable and memorable of events.

Melanie explained that when she and Ellen first met, they did not have hard evidence that they were twins, as their parents had not yet confronted LWS. "But we *knew*," she said. As part of that "hard evidence," Melanie cited the photograph of Ellen that Arlene had given to Melanie's boyfriend Paul. "When I saw that picture—Oh, my God!" Melanie recalled.

I have worked with other separated twins who celebrated their relationship before having confirmatory birth documents or matching DNA tests in hand. South Korean–born twins, Samantha (Sam) Futerman and Anaïs Bordier, discovered their identical twinship when they were twenty-five.[39] Samantha, an actress adopted by a New Jersey couple, had created an online video that was viewed by a friend in England; Anaïs, an art student in London, had been adopted by a French couple. Anaïs's friend was struck by the identical faces and physiques of Anaïs and the young woman in the video. When the two got in touch via Facebook, they found that their birthdays, laughs, and health histories were all in sync. Still, I cautioned Samantha about early celebrations and raising funds for a documentary film until a DNA test had been completed. I hoped to spare her the disappointment of a mother I had worked with whose adopted Chinese daughter had a close look-alike who ultimately proved to be unrelated.[40] But Sam and Anaïs's excitement could not be contained and quickly culminated in a family get-together in London. Happily, several days into their visit, I informed them via Skype that the genetic tests I had arranged confirmed their conviction: they are identical twins. Sam, all smiles, dropped her glass of red wine.[41]

The age at which twins meet affects the way their relationship goes, but timing is not everything and its importance varies across pairs. Melanie and Ellen were still young when they met at age twenty-three, but they were "past the party scene." Because of that, Melanie regrets that she and Ellen missed out on the fun they might have had together if they had met sooner. This may partly explain why these twins did not become close until they had children.[42] In contrast, one of the switched-at-birth Colombian twins I studied, William, believed that meeting his identical brother at age twenty-five was "perfect."[43] He explained that by then each twin was mature enough to handle the shock, young enough to forge meaningful relationships with the others, and old enough not to be returned to his biological parents. However, what does unite virtually all reared-apart twins is the dramatic revision of their lives once their twinship is discovered, and the wish to have grown up together.

MELANIE

Melanie Cara Mertzel was born on May 25, 1966, at Misericordia Hospital, in the Bronx, New York.[44] She was delivered at 11:22 p.m., seven minutes behind her identical twin sister Ellen who arrived at 11:15 p.m.[45] The number on Melanie's birth certificate is one digit higher than that of her twin, corresponding to the order of their birth. Melanie's birth document does not indicate that she was a twin, but her multiple birth status was confirmed by LWS. Her adoption was finalized on November 22, 1967, about fifteen months after her parents, Bert and Alice, brought her home. Bert's "usual occupation" and "kind of business" were listed as "executive" and "restaurant," whereas Alice's were "housewife" and "own home." Melanie's first residence was a house at 2610 Avenue I, in the Midwood section of Brooklyn, New York; a year later, the family moved to a house on Avenue M. A handwritten, five-digit number appears on the upper left corner of the certificate, but its significance is uncertain; Ellen's document does not have such a number. Melanie's original birth report was filed on June 1, 1966, while the second one that she provided to me was filed through the Borough Registrar. The name on her original birth certificate, given to her by her biological mother, was Ellen.

Melanie began elementary school at Packer Collegiate Institute, a private school in Brooklyn. She left Packer at age eleven to enter the local public school, largely because her mother wanted her to have neighborhood friends. However, the quality of the school was unsatisfactory, and Melanie had many friends close by, so she was enrolled in the Brooklyn Friends private school.[46] Over the years, Melanie sensed that her "other half was missing" and admitted that she never liked being alone. Growing up, she had always wanted a twin and was surprised to find that her friends did not share this desire. She was intrigued by the twins she had met at summer camp and would find herself watching them. As I explained, prenatal knowledge of twinship does not exist—however, it is not uncommon for adoptees to feel an "inner emptiness,"[47] and to think about biological relatives who might resemble them. Some older, but still wonderful, articles associate twinship with "sameness, familiarity and security" and link fantasies of having a twin to having someone who "shares everything of importance."[48]

Melanie enjoyed the mental ability tests and other inventories she completed as part of the twin study that she and her family didn't know about. "I loved it," she said. "The focus was on me, I got the attention and they played with me—after all, I was the third child."[49] However, these sessions were a source of jealousy for Melanie's older sister Nancy, also an LWS adoptee. "I demanded that [the researchers] pay attention to me, so they gave me busy work to keep me quiet," Nancy recalled.[50] Drs. Neubauer and Bernard did not foresee that other children in the family might feel neglected because no one came to study them, but Melanie's mother Alice did think about that. After Melanie and Ellen reunited, Alice worried that Melanie might grow closer to her newly discovered twin sister Ellen than to Nancy. Nancy thought about this, too—"Is Melanie going to see Ellen as her 'real sister'? Will Ellen replace me?" Nancy admitted that her fears were not borne out and believes that she and Melanie enjoy a good relationship to this day. Melanie's family's concerns may partly explain why the twins were not always in touch and did not become close until their mid-thirties.

After graduating from high school, Melanie enrolled in the College of Boca Raton, in Boca Raton, Florida, majoring in liberal arts. She didn't care for school and "hated" being away from her friends and boyfriend, so she left college at the end of her first semester. She had no idea that an identical twin sister whose existence was unknown to her had also left college early. Melanie returned to New York City and took a job as a bank teller for a year, then became a secretary for a Manhattan curtain company the following year. After that, she was a hostess at her father's Brooklyn IHOP, eventually becoming manager.

Looking back, Melanie believes that if she and Ellen had grown up together their college experience would have been different. "We would have had each other," she explained. Melanie was never a "school person," but she thought that they would have had fun as a pair and possibly finished school together. It has generally been hard for her to meet people, although she has become more outgoing lately—but together the twins could have been "powerful" in a college setting. She regrets that "that is something we will never know."

Melanie lives in a two-bedroom apartment in the Oakland Gardens area of Queens, New York. She works as a secretary in the general pediatric department at Long Island's Northwell Medical Center, a job she has held since 2014, but has been employed at the hospital for the past fifteen years. She has never married, but has a twenty-year-old son, Devon, who lives at home, attends college and works part-time. In a way Melanie has four children, because Ellen's three daughters—her nieces—have the same genetic relationship to her as they do to her mother. In fact, when identical twins have children, these cousins become "half-siblings" because they have one genetically identical parent.[51]

ELLEN

Ellen Sue Lieber's adoption by Sol and Thelma Lieber was finalized on October 25, 1967. The legal details were handled by the New York law firm of Pross, Halpern, Lefevre, Raphael & Alter.[52] The October date on the letter from attorney Albert A. Raphael Jr. places Ellen's final adoption about one month before Melanie's. The reason for the difference is unknown, but it could reflect each twin's time of receipt and/or various legal actions. Ellen's first residence was at 26 Jasmine Road, in Old Bridge, New Jersey, where she lived with her parents and older brother Alan. It was also where she would periodically take tests administered by the twin study researchers. The twins joke that Ellen exited the womb first when she "kicked off Melanie's head."[53]

Both twins are eager to learn who cared for them before they were adopted and to know if they were kept together or apart. Thelma said Ellen was three months old when she received her from LWS, but her actual age appears to be four months. An LWS-issued document that lists new parents' obligations and responsibilities, such as not instituting formal adoption procedures without LWS's consent, is dated September 20, 1966, four months after Ellen was born. Inexplicably, the date of birth on this document is given as May 20 when, in fact, the twins were born on May 25. The Liebers' signatures were not on the page I examined, but it was signed by an LWS witness.[54]

A second letter from attorney Raphael to the Liebers, also dated October 25, described a change in adoption law, such that the last name of the child is omitted from the portion of the papers signed by his or her new parents. However, the certified copy of the Order of Adoption, sent by the law firm to LWS, would include the child's original last name. A new birth certificate would be sent to the Liebers several weeks later.

Thelma was excited by the scheduled home visits from the LWS-CDC researchers and took pleasure in serving them lunch. The visits occurred every three months when Ellen was young, then tapered off to every six months until they took place just once each year. Ellen disliked the testing she had to endure and pleaded with her mother to put a stop to it. The test sessions finally ended for Ellen in 1978, when she was about twelve, but her mother did not effect this change. By 1980, the study was terminated by Bernard and Neubauer. The years 1978 to 1980 coincide with the formal end of LWS's twin separation policy,[55] widespread attention to human informed consent procedures,[56] and headline news announcing the chance meeting of the identical triplets.[57] In a 1993 interview with Lawrence Wright, Neubauer claimed that the study had ended because it "became too expensive." When asked about his primary source of funding, he replied, "Oh, some private family foundation and once in a while we got money from Washington."[58] And when pressed about whether "some sort of political reaction" was responsible for ending the study, Neubauer denied it.[59]

On September 21, 1978, Thelma received a letter from project director Dr. Christa Balzert, requesting her signature on an enclosed "consent and release form for our files." Thelma signed the form on September 30 and returned it as indicated. Interestingly, a form from Melanie's parents was recorded as having been signed on January 22, 1969, the only one of five signed forms that does not have a 1978 date; four parents did not return a form.[60] Melanie does not have a copy of this document, but she pointed

Child Development Center, Inc., Consent and Release Form

Child Development Center

120 West 57th Street
New York 19, New York

Consent and Release

In order to facilitate effective study and treatment by the Child Development Center, Inc., and to further its educational and research program, I hereby consent to the use of any material relating to the study and history of my child or children (ward or wards) in any oral or written presentation prepared, released or published by Child Development Center, Inc., either independently or in conjunction with any scientific publication, so long as no names are used.

I hereby release Child Development Center, Inc., its officers, employees, successors and assigns, from any and all liability or damages relating in any way to the use of such study and history material.

Dated: _____

_____
Parent or Guardian

Witnesses:

_____

Address: _____

_____

mlw
1-1-66
31a(ab)

Figure 8.3. Consent and Release Form. Viola W. Bernard Papers, Columbia University Heath Sciences Library.

out that, "the consent was a lie because they [my parents] thought the study was to see how a third child adapted in a home, and Ellen's parents signed thinking the study was to see how a biological and adopted child interacted in a household."[61] The consent form, reproduced in Figure 8.3, states that the aim of the project was to "facilitate effective study and treatment by the Child Development Center, Inc., and to further its educational and research program."[62] Interestingly, the lower left corner indicates that the form was prepared in 1966, twelve years before it was sent to the families but six years after the study began. I will say more about informed consent issues later in the book.

Ellen attended James A. McDivitt elementary school, Carl Sandburg middle school, and Cedar Ridge high school, all local public schools. She went to overnight camp during the summer, but "hated" it. Like Melanie, she says she is shy and does not make friends easily. Ellen lived at home while going to one of several campuses of Middlesex County College in New Jersey, majoring in business management. But like her twin sister, whom she did not know existed, she disliked college and withdrew after one semester at age eighteen. Looking back, she concurs with Melanie that both twins would have stayed in college had they been raised together, allowing them to draw support from one another. After leaving college, Ellen held a variety of different jobs. For the next ten years she worked in an office and in 1994, at age twenty-seven, met her future husband, Carl Carbone. They were married soon after that.[63]

Ellen stopped working at age thirty after delivering her first child, a daughter named Fiona, and became a stay-at-home mother for the next fourteen years. She had a second daughter, Ivy, three years later and a third daughter, Bella, three years after that. When Bella turned four, Ellen took a job babysitting for children at a gymnasium while their parents worked out. When the gym closed, she became a school crossing guard and then an ambulance courier. Ellen now serves as a unit representative in a hospital where she responds to patients' requests for various services. Her husband, Carl, is part owner of Carl Carbone Plumbing and Heating, in Lyndhurst, New Jersey. He is also a licensed building inspector, but now teaches plumbing to high school and adult education students full time. The couple lives in Lyndhurst with their three children, in a spacious home with a swimming pool.

My interviews with Ellen took place at her New Jersey home, her mother's New Jersey residence, and a Greek restaurant she had chosen for dinner. The setting felt familiar because when I had met Melanie two days earlier, we began our interview at a Greek restaurant she had selected in advance before we relocated to her apartment. Both twins are great fans of Middle Eastern cuisine, explaining their independently matched choices.

TOGETHER AGAIN

Every identical twin pair has a singular "culture" or way of doing things. During their times together, Melanie and Ellen have discovered new behaviors that they share, but sometimes express differently. Both twins are "savers" and "cleaners." Ellen is adept at clipping coupons and using them to her advantage when she goes food shopping. Melanie is less proficient in managing coupons, but she visits different supermarkets to find the lowest price and purchases sale items even when she doesn't need them. Both twins also keep their homes extremely clean, wash their hands carefully after handling raw meat, and dislike using public restrooms. And both twins try to follow healthy diets. Melanie was slimmer than her twin when they met and still is, a difference she explains by her focus on low-calorie foods like vegetables and Ellen's preference for nutritious, but higher-calorie items like natural peanut butter. Given their dietary differences, their health histories show some striking detours. Ellen has no blood pressure or cholesterol problems, but Melanie does.[64] Melanie's more frequent smoking may be implicated in her lower body weight, higher cholesterol level, and earlier menopause.[65]

Like most siblings, even twins, Melanie and Ellen have had tense times, good times, and great times together. Early on, the situation was complicated because Melanie's parents did not wish the discovery of their daughter's twinship to be exposed. A turning point in the twins' relationship was the delivery of Ellen's second daughter, which occurred three and a half months before the delivery of Melanie's son. Ellen's husband Carl called Melanie at that point, and the twins spent a weekend together, becoming close as they shared childcare and apple picking. Some "back and forth periods" followed, but they have been close sisters for the most part. Ellen recalled that her father was unhappy when she and Melanie were out of touch because he was close to his own family.

I believe it is harder for some reunited twins to negotiate differences because they lack shared family relationships and experiences. Without a past, it may be easier to walk away from a newly discovered twin than from a twin you were raised with, because the outcome of an argument is less certain. Most reared-together twins know that things will return to normal once a disagreement has passed—and they understand when their differences have actually been put to rest. Ellen's husband Carl has been instrumental in reconnecting the twins on several occasions. He was prompted to do so when Ellen cried because she missed Melanie. Melanie always responded positively, believing that a twin is someone you want to know for your whole life. An event that brought them solidly together was the 2007 book *Identical Strangers*, referenced earlier.[66] Melanie's sister Nancy discovered the book and gave it to

Melanie. "That is when I realized we were guinea pigs," Melanie confessed, "although we sort of suspected it. I called Ellen to tell her about it." *Identical Strangers* delves into more detail about the study and the investigators than Lawrence Wright's 1995 *New Yorker* magazine article.[67] It is likely that Alice saw the article sometime after it appeared, because Melanie did not know about the study until she read Schein and Bernstein's book.

Both Ellen and Melanie were outraged to learn that they were part of a twin study under false pretenses, even though Melanie enjoyed the sessions and Ellen did not. In a great ironic twist, in 2019 both twins completed an IQ test and a personality inventory that Melanie asked me to arrange and Ellen agreed to. As before, Melanie showed enthusiasm about participating, while Ellen was somewhat uneasy. I explained the findings to both twins, and they were each happy to have me share their results with their sister. Twins generally enjoy research because they learn a lot about themselves and know that they further scientific knowledge by doing so. If LWS had placed Melanie and Ellen together, they would have still been valued research participants. With their consent and that of their parents, similarities and differences in behavioral and physical traits could have been compared between the twins, with each parent, with unrelated siblings in the home, and with those of other identical and fraternal pairs. The psychological literature includes few studies of twins adopted together, so such research would have been welcome.

PAST, PRESENT, AND BEYOND

My experience is that reunited twins enjoy dressing alike on occasion and/or pulling pranks as if making up for their lost time together. Ellen and Melanie are exemplary in this regard. They are also on a quest to readjust their adult lives in light of discovering an identical twin. According to Melanie, "I wish someone would start a support group. This is all so crazy—no one, not even us twins understand the complexity."

RECREATION

Melanie sent me a photo taken on October 5, 2019, in which she and Ellen were part of a Zombie Walk. Zombie Walks are gatherings of people who put on zombie-appropriate attire, then parade around city streets in an orderly fashion.[68] Both twins decorated their face and neck with dark wounds and fake blood, and wore torn clothes with images of protruding organs. This event was a foreshadowing of the twins' Halloween party plans.[69] Ellen explained that they had bought matching shirts in black and white to mimic "Salt and Pepper." Ellen also said that Melanie had sent her some inspirational photographs, among them the "Shining Twins." The Shining Twins, or Grady Girls, were characters in the 1980 horror film, *The Shining,* based on the 1977 novel by Stephen King. These twins wore distinctive light blue lacey dresses with long pink ribbons. "When Melanie sent me the pictures I thought, oh, we could have done that as kids—we could have gotten those little dresses." Ellen's husband Carl interrupted her thoughts. "Sisters don't always get along, and you don't know what your childhood would have been like," to which Ellen countered, "Twins are different."

RESEMBLANCE: AMY AND BETH?

In the previous chapter, I raised the possibility that certain features of Anne and Susan are part of a fictitious composite reared-apart pair, created by the researchers and labeled "Amy and Beth." This pair is described in several sources.[70] "Amy and Beth" each had a brother nearly seven years their senior. Amy's brother was the biological son of her adoptive parents, whereas Beth's brother was an adoptee; Beth also had an adopted sister who was three years older. Both twins were blonde and fair-skinned with blue-gray eyes. Amy was right-handed, and Beth was left-handed. Both twins were adopted by families in New York, and both twins' mothers stayed home to raise their children. Beth's mother dyed her hair to match her daughter's in an effort to emphasize their similarity.

There are parallels and divergences between "Amy and Beth" and Ellen and Melanie. Like Amy, Ellen has a brother who is nearly seven years older and is the biological child of her adoptive parents. Like Beth, Melanie has a brother who is about seven years older *and* a sister who is three years older; she is the only twin in the study with two older siblings. Like "Amy and Beth," Ellen was the first-born twin and is right-handed, and Melanie was the second-born twin and is left-handed. However, unlike "Amy and Beth," both twins were *not* raised in New York—Melanie grew up in Brooklyn, whereas Ellen grew up in New Jersey. Melanie and Ellen were both blonde as infants, but they have hazel-colored eyes. Ellen's mother stayed at home until Ellen was thirteen, but Melanie's mother taught school and later managed one of the family's IHOP restaurants; recall that Melanie's father was largely responsible for her care during her first year. Melanie's mother Alice added "highlights" and "streaks" to her hair before Melanie came home, but never changed her hair color to match her daughter's. In fact, the resemblance between mother and daughter was apparent, causing Alice to say that "her children were conceived for her."[71] Details about "Amy and Beth's" complex intra-family dynamics are provided, but are difficult to judge with reference to those of Melanie and Ellen. As I suggested before, a fictitious pair would have the advantage of reporting observations without compromising confidentiality.

A 1986 article describing "Amy and Beth" by Neubauer's colleague Samuel Abrams is not cited in the notes or suggested bibliography of Neubauer's 1990 book on nature and nurture. In fact, "Amy and Beth" are not mentioned.[72]

MY LIFE, YOUR LIFE, OUR LIVES

Twins raised apart and reunited are in the unique position of seeing a life they might have lived.[73] In contrast, non-twins can only imagine what life might have been like had they lived in a small town or a big city, married their high school steady or college sweetheart, or studied medicine rather than law. Melanie senses that both she and Ellen are somewhat jealous of certain slices

Figure 8.4. Ellen (L) and Melanie (R) at Hunter College, following the Intelligence Squared Debate, "Parenting Is Overrated," held October 29, 2019. Courtesy of the twins.

of each other's lives. Melanie envies Ellen's marriage, and the fact that Ellen has three children and didn't have to work when her girls were small. However, Melanie also feels that Ellen covets Melanie's independence and ability to do things on her own. What each twin is seeing is an alternate version of themselves—how they might have turned out if some circumstances had been different.

Despite their work schedules and the inconvenience of driving between New Jersey and Queens, the twins stay in touch by telephone and by text, not every day, but many days. It was wonderful for me to see them together on October 29, 2019, just several days after I had met each one separately for the first time. They came to Manhattan to attend the debate, "Parenting Is Overrated," in which I participated, and stood arm in arm as I took their photo. Melanie says she reserves the term "sister" for Nancy and "twin" for Ellen. Ellen calls Melanie "sister," but Ellen only has an older brother.

COMMENTS AND SCRIBBLES

Everyone I interviewed either said or wrote something memorable. The twins' unplanned statements revealed thoughts and ideas that truly touched the core of the extraordinary situation in which they, their friends, and their family members found themselves. Among Ellen's collection of papers and documents was a crumpled sheet of paper torn from a three- by five-inch notepad. Scribbled hastily and messily across the page were these lines: "I didn't choose this life, they chose it for me. They messed w/Nature and although I was nurtured something was always missing." Melanie's spoken words echoed these sentiments: "The person I should have been closest to I did not know."

· 9 ·

Parallel Paths

Howard and Doug

$\mathcal{H}$oward Burack and Douglas (Doug) Rausch were born in New York City on March 12, 1963.[1] They were six months old when they began living parallel lives apart, a fate that was sealed by the Louise Wise Services (LWS) when Doug was adopted on September 18, 1963, one week ahead of his brother. They wouldn't meet again for another thirty-six and a half years, but when they did their brotherly bond was immediate, a connection that has delighted both twins. But there is a dim side to their newly found happiness. The twins are severely pained as they mourn the years that were stolen from their twin relationship during childhood, adolescence, and adulthood. They were separated "by design." Howard reflected, "If that didn't happen maybe the hard spots in life wouldn't have been so hard."[2] Both Howard and Doug still become upset when talking about the decision to place them apart. Neither twin is bitter or angry—any such feelings were probably tempered by the fact that both had loving mothers and fathers, raised families of their own, and are pursuing jobs they enjoy. But they feel that a terrible injustice was done to them, their parents, and other twins at the hands of Drs. Viola Bernard and Peter Neubauer—an injustice that was beyond horrific. No one has apologized.

Doug and Howard have known each other for a little over twenty years. When I contacted them during the writing of this book, they respectfully declined to participate.[3] Howard explained that the brothers were focused on obtaining their records from the Yale University archives and wanted to avoid possible exploitation by some scientists and journalists. Nevertheless, both twins knew me from the past and applauded my efforts. I followed their suggestion. I have a brief history with Doug and Howard that dates back to the Twins Days Festival of August 2000, held in Twinsburg, Ohio.

159

TWINS DAYS FESTIVAL: TWINSBURG, OHIO

Twinsburg, Ohio, located in northeastern Ohio, is home to the largest annual gathering of twins in the world—the Twins Days Festival.[4] This event really began with the identical twins Aaron and Moses Wilcox, born in 1771. The Wilcox twins purchased property in this area, then known as Millsville.[5] In 1821, they donated six acres of land for a public square and twenty dollars for a school, contingent upon city commissioners renaming the town in their honor. The commissioners complied and Millsville became Twinsburg in 1823. Over a century and a half later, in 1976, citizens set aside a special day to recognize all twins as part of the US bicentennial. Dedication of the Wilcox Monument on the public square also took place on that day. Every year since, hundreds if not thousands of twins have traveled to Twinsburg in early August to celebrate the uniqueness of twins and the heritage of the town.[6]

I met Howard and his wife Diane at the 2000 Twins Days Festival. They drove to Twinsburg from their home in New Albany, Ohio, about one hundred miles away. Doug and his wife Ronni did not make the trip from Natick, Massachusetts, but I spoke to Doug by telephone a few days before that and several times subsequently. By then, Howard and Doug had known each other for just two months, having reunited at John Glenn International Airport in Columbus, Ohio, on Memorial Day 2000. Howard had known he was a twin for about two years, while Doug had heard news the year that they met. The twins reconnected because of a compassionate act by a dying woman.

The Twins, Their Family Members, and Friends

Howard
Howard Burack Doug's reared-apart twin
Diane Burack Howard's wife

Doug
Doug Rausch Howard's reared-apart twin
Helen Rausch Doug's adoptive mother
George Rausch Doug's adoptive father
Ronni Rausch Doug's wife

Others
Lawrence (Larry) Perlman assistant who tested Doug and Howard
Barry Coburn attorney for Doug and Howard

A LETTER AND TWO PHONE CALLS

Howard Burack had always known he was adopted.[7] In 1998, he wrote to LWS to request background and medical information about his biological family. Once he submitted the required paperwork he waited, unprepared for what followed. He received a call from an LWS staff member that "floored" him— Howard had an identical twin brother. But it would be a while until they would meet because his brother's identity remained confidential under New York State law. However, he was told that if his twin asked the agency for information and agreed to have his name released, then the two could meet. As it was, Howard had no way to find his brother, but the thought of having a twin consumed him daily for two years. He found himself searching for faces that matched his own, even asking people if they knew someone who looked like him.

Doug Rausch also knew that he had been adopted. In 2000, Doug contacted LWS in search of medical information.[8] The agency was in the process of closing down, finally doing so in 2004, so it was fortunate that he made the contact when he did. Then, one day while out driving his car, Doug received a call from a woman working at LWS. She told him she was dying of cancer. Doug recalled, "She goes, 'I'm not supposed to do this. I can get in a lot of trouble, but I'm going to do it anyway.' So, I appreciate that. She said, 'Well I have some news for you. You have an identical twin brother.' And I was like, I literally almost drove off the road. It's not something you ever expect to hear." Filmmaker Lori Shinseki observed, "She [the LWS staff member] couldn't go to her grave without letting some of these kids know that they had an identical twin."[9]

I do not know if the woman notified other twins, perhaps those that have never gone public, but Doug and Howard were finally reunited because this woman kindly bent the rules. She has not been identified, most likely because by informing Doug as she did, she sidestepped the agency's procedure. If only someone had done so thirty-seven years earlier, the twins would have grown up together—both sets of parents would have welcomed twins into their home. As it was, they were as surprised as their sons to learn that Doug and Howard were separated twins and part of a secret study. The four parents were also bitter and angry. Doug's mother, Helen Rausch, called it Nazi science.[10]

DOUG'S FAMILY

Helen and George Rausch of Westbury, Long Island, were eager to have a family.[11] When Helen, a homemaker, had difficulty conceiving, the couple turned to LWS for assistance. The couple adopted their daughter Debbie in 1960, but hoped for another child. Three years later they were thrilled when LWS offered them six-month-old Douglas. They were advised that staff members would come to their home periodically to monitor Doug as part of a study. Doug's father George, a former business executive, recalls some coercion on the part of LWS—if the couple didn't consent to the visits then they couldn't adopt the baby. However, the Rauschs agreed with this arrangement. According to Helen, "They made it sound like this was to everybody's benefit to see how smart this kid is, because I don't know him. Here, we're adopting a child we don't know. We don't know his background, but it never dawned on me why they're coming back so many times."

According to Helen, Doug was a happy child who joined his older sister Debbie in the playroom their parents had constructed for them in the basement of their home. But one day Doug was no longer playful.[12] He insisted that nothing was wrong, but he was unhappy, angered easily, and wrangled with his classmates. His father George sensed that his son was missing something—but what?[13] Meanwhile, Doug remembers a team of researchers coming to his home to give him a lot of different tests, watch him ride his bike, and make films of him doing different activities. He said it was "kind of fun" for a while, but he eventually felt bored. That's when he would ask, "Can I go now?"[14] He also recalled that his mother "freaked out" whenever the researchers came to their home because she was afraid they might take him away. The team stopped coming in 1975 when Doug was twelve.

HOWARD'S FAMILY

Howard Burack was raised in "a nice, upper-middle-class family in a nice, suburban area north of New York City, in Rockland County." He had a "normal childhood, normal whatever, and great parents." Little did the Buracks know that their son had an identical twin brother who had been adopted into a similar home. Howard's father, like Doug's, was a business executive, and his mother was a housewife. Howard also had an adopted sister who was three years older than he was. And what Doug's father sensed about his young son, Howard expressed more openly as an adult. "[You] feel like you're missing something, just don't know it was. You can't touch it. You can't feel it. Something was there."[15]

Howard recalls the testing that took place periodically during his childhood and adolescence. Aside from psychological tests, he answered questions, drew pictures, and looked at inkblots.[16] Howard described himself as a shy child who wasn't comfortable with the testing situation, actually calling it "horrifying." The visits were also stressful occasions for his family because they worried his parents. Howard said that the researchers' visits ended when he was eleven or twelve because he didn't want to participate.

Howard and Doug both value their privacy. This may be especially true of Howard as he never mentions his parents or sister by name.

THEIR FIRST SIX MONTHS

Doug and Howard were kept together in foster care for the first six months of their lives. Notes made by LWS staff members reveal that as early as four months of age, the twins were observed interacting with one another in foster care.[17]

> "Usually, Howard initiated contact with his twin, with Douglas then re-sponding. This would involve them both in the twinning interaction. . . . We see the twins pending adoption into separate homes as additional potential complications for separation-individuation. . . . For Douglas and Howard, who were shifted from hospital to one foster home, then to another, then back to the first foster home in the first half year prior to their separate adoption, the co-twin may have been the most stable human object in their environment."

These comments oppose Dr. Bernard's assertion that twins would not be separated if they developed the "twinning reaction," what she considered to be an attachment between the two twins. Twin infants appear to be ahead of non-twins in responding to another infant as a social being, partly because their close proximity offers numerous opportunities for interaction. Recall that Dr. T. Berry Brazelton found that a four-month-old identical twin noticed her sister's absence when her twin was taken from their room. (When she heard her twin's voice she stopped moving or feeding.) Brazelton's observations advanced the social timeline for twins to three or four months of age, placing twins two to three months ahead of singletons in this respect.[18]

Both Howard and Doug believe that being separated from one another explains the sadness, loneliness, and depression they experienced as children.[19] That is possible, but we cannot know for certain. As I explained earlier, adoptees may sense that something is missing from their lives, a feeling that may be linked to their lack of resemblance between themselves and their rearing family and/or their feelings of rejection by their birth parents. It is also true that some discontented non-adoptees—people raised by their biological parents—search for an intangible "something" that they believe would put their lives back on track. It is very hard to make a firm connection between an infant event and a childhood outcome because so many experiences happen in between. But permanently removing "the most stable human object" in Doug and Howard's environment is a decision that is difficult to understand. Perhaps the unusual infant behaviors the twins displayed after their separate adoptions, such as body rocking and head banging that I describe later, signaled a need for the physical presence and comfort of the baby that lay beside him. These behaviors may have replaced the concepts they were too young to convey or understand.

THE TWIN STUDY

Researchers visited Howard at home, just as they visited Doug, keeping the between-twin intervals small to better track their development in tandem. One chart with the heading "Dates of Current Visit" indicated that Doug was studied at fifteen months, seven days, and Howard was studied at fifteen months, twenty-eight days, although the visits began soon after their six-month separation and continued for over a decade. Notes also reveal that, after their adoption, both twins showed declines in motor dexterity and engaged in body rocking. They began to walk when they were thirteen months old, one month later than the average child, but well within the nine- to seventeen-month range during which 90 percent of infants achieve that behavior.[20] One twin showed greater coordination in walking and crawling than his brother, but that is not unusual—identical twins sometimes switch developmental places, so the other twin might have been more advanced at a later date. It was also noted that the baby who showed longer bouts of body rocking also displayed head banging until age two.

Body rocking and head banging are stereotypical behaviors—that is behaviors that are repetitive and rhythmical, such as swaying, rubbing, and banging.[21] Psychologists are divided over whether such actions are signs of normal or abnormal development. Stereotypical behaviors may persist because they are interesting to a child, or they may reflect reduced contact with a caregiver and/or placement in physically restricted settings. Psychologist Susan Farber, a former Child Development Center (CDC) staff member, hypothesized that one twin's head banging "was more a frustration discharge rather than organic. It was also suggested that it could be a component of a temper tantrum."[22]

Dr. Farber's interpretation of the twin's behavior was made in February 1976, about the time that Doug and Howard's testing stopped. When I read the comment to her over the telephone, she could not recall having made it and suggested that it must have come from analyzing "written material."[23] She explained that she had never observed these twins. Farber believed she had heard about Doug and Howard at a meeting, most likely one of the CDC's case conferences that she said she did attend. She could not recall names, but that is not surprising as over forty years had elapsed. Farber knew that twins had been separated, but said she never worked with the adoption agency and was not employed at the CDC when the study began. As part of her research with reared-apart twins many years ago, she did have contact of "various forms" with twins separated at some point in their lives—one set in the study and others from the literature outside of it—but she does not recall names or details.

Farber authored a 1977 paper showing that girls display greater interest and conflict surrounding adoption than boys.[24] I found an early version of this paper in Dr. Bernard's files, one that Farber had presented at the 1976 American Psychoanalytic Association meeting.[25] The study periodically studied nine adoptees, four females and five males, from birth to adolescence, as well as twelve of their mostly adopted siblings. The study children were matched so that the girls had older brothers and the boys had older sisters. The children's parents were told that LWS was interested in tracking child development. Several of Farber's colleagues were acknowledged in the conference paper for their assistance and comments—P. Neubauer, V. Bernard, S. Abrams, C. Balzert, V. Wolsk, S. Kofman, and Ms. Lynn Kelly—but not in the final publication.[26] Twins are not mentioned in either version, but the CDC conducted adoption research on topics that did not necessarily include twins.[27] I will return to this interesting study in the next chapter.

Farber also authored the 1981 book *Identical Twins Reared Apart*, a compendium of findings from studies of separated twins.[28] In that book, Farber estimated that more than twenty reared-apart twin pairs resided in the New York metropolitan area;[29] however, the LWS-CDC twin study isn't mentioned. After her book was published, she left twin studies to relocate to Boise, Idaho, as a clinical psychologist.[30]

As the 1970s drew to a close, there was growing attention to informed consent issues by behavioral and health professionals. The National Research Act of 1974 led to the formation of the National Commission for the Protection of Human Subjects of Biomedical and Behavioral Research. The commission went on to publish the Belmont Report in 1976, outlining principles and guidelines for the ethical treatment of human subjects.[31] These developments did not escape Bernard's notice. As stated earlier, in a 1976 letter to LWS Executive Director Florence (Brown) Kreech, she wrote, "We are still being very careful about the research and do not wish to share information about it, especially in these days of informed consent concerns."[32]

In 1978, the twins' mothers received letters from twin study staff requesting their signatures on informed consent letters. Neither Doug's nor Howard's mother returned the form. In response to that request, Doug's father George Rausch sent a detailed letter to Dr. Vivian Wolsk, a member of the research team who had gathered data on Doug.[33] George began by noting that the letter had been sent to his wife, Helen. He continued to say that the couple supported the use of the information if it enhanced our understanding of children, but he objected to the way the document was worded. He reminded Wolsk that a great deal of material had been gathered during his son's research visits, including manually recorded information, still photographs, films, and live audio recordings of Doug and his parents, both individually and together. He therefore felt compelled to request a revised document that would provide "ironclad assurance and guarantee that identifying information will NOT become part of '. . . any oral or written presentation prepared, released or published . . . either independently or in conjunction with any scientific publication.'" George indicated his willingness to sign a form that was approved by his personal legal counsel. It appears that a revised form was not prepared, or if so was not acceptable to him.

The late 1970s was also the time when LWS formally acknowledged their changed policy regarding the separation of twins. The last pair of twins had been placed apart in 1969, but Bernard indicated that the policy had actually been applied earlier. It was recommended that twins be kept together, barring unusual circumstances.[34] Developments in adoption, such as more frequent searches by adoptees and greater openness by biological parents, forced the issue.

Doug and Howard joined the list of reunited LWS twins when they met in 2000. They were not the last pair to finally meet.

REUNION

Monday, May 29, 2000, was Memorial Day. Howard Burack and his wife, Diane, waited nervously at the airport in Columbus, Ohio, for the arrival of America West flight 314 from Boston.[35] On the plane were Howard's twin brother, Doug, and Doug's wife, Ronni. Doug was nervous, too, even though the twins had spoken by phone, exchanged pictures, and felt like familiar friends. The plane landed at 12:24 p.m. Captured on film, the twin brothers finally stood face to face, their first moments together a combination of staring, laughing, and hand shaking. Doug stood two to three inches taller, carried an additional twenty pounds and wore eyeglasses, but the resemblance between them was unmistakable and they knew it. Like many other twins meeting for the first time, Doug and Howard could not look at each other for too long.

Seeing oneself mirrored so perfectly in another for the first time is like staring into the sun—the desire to look is irresistible, but the intensity becomes overwhelming. The twins are also shown seated side by side, enjoying their first beer together. But the occasion called for more; Howard's wife Diane announced that champagne was chilling at home. Doug and Ronni stayed at Howard's home for the next few days and "after one or two days, it felt very familiar. I felt like I knew [Howard] better than most people."

According to Doug, Howard and he were friends from the start, becoming aware that they had lived, and were living, parallel lives.[36] They married the same year, in 1992, and had children the same year. Both chose wives with Type-A personalities, meaning that Ronni and Diane are competitive and hard-working; both also like to run. Doug concluded that he and Howard must be attracted to similar women. Both twins are hockey coaches and have sports-minded children—Howard's son and Doug's daughter both played hockey and wore the number two on their jersey.[37] Both twins carry their wallet in a front pocket. They also pursue similar lines of work—Doug is a residential home contractor and Howard is in commercial real estate. As Doug explained to me, "we both fell into what we are doing." Most intriguing, perhaps, is that neither twin uses condiments of any kind, including mustard, ketchup, and salad dressing. As Ronni noted, "[Doug] has no use for them."[38]

Most of the twins' similarities make sense within the larger twin research context. Scores of studies show that occupational choices and work values are partly influenced by our genes.[39] As such, it is unlikely that the twins simply "fell into" their jobs. It is more likely that their common genetically based interests and abilities predisposed them toward certain occupations and away from others. Of course, the actual job they held when they met might have been affected by knowing the right person, or being at a certain place at the right time. Studies also show physical and behavioral similarities between the children of identical twins, who are as closely related genetically as half-siblings; the two sets of cousins have one genetically identical parent.[40] Athletic abilities and interests are also partly influenced by genetic factors.[41] However, it would be a mistake to assume that the twins' hockey-playing children are simply mimicking their fathers—that is because parents pass on genes, as well as environments, to their children. A more accurate interpretation is that their children inherited physical abilities that underlie good sports performance and the environment facilitated their expression.

The twins' distaste for condiments is consistent with twin research showing genetic influence on dietary preferences.[42] Doug and Howard are the first identical set I have encountered who have shown this particular food aversion. The positive side of this unusual similarity is that it prompts researchers to think creatively about what features of mustard or ketchup—the texture, the smell, the aftertaste—the twins' dislike. And as I explained in chapter 7, twin studies are mixed on whether identical twins select similar spouses. It would be interesting to know if Doug and/or Howard could imagine themselves married to their sister-in-law, or if Ronni and/or Diane could envision being married to their spouse's twin. Further research on twins' mate selection would bring new insights to our understanding of why people pick the partners that they do.

A number of parties followed Doug and Howard's reunion. One large get-together took place at Doug's home in Natick, Massachusetts, where the twins celebrated their first birthday together. And in an odd twist that occurred in late 2018 or early 2019, Howard's daughter attended an Ohio State University fraternity event with the son of another separated LWS twin, Michele Mordkoff, whom I will introduce later. The two students were fixed up for the occasion by friends.[43]

LOOKING FOR ANSWERS

There are questions that still need answers: Why were Doug and Howard raised apart? Why were they studied? Can they get access to their data?

In 2000, after meeting his twin, Doug wanted to find Dr. Neubauer and retrieve his records; he spoke to Neubauer by telephone. Neubauer denied having done anything wrong and, instead, proposed that Doug visit him in New York for an interview. "The conversation didn't end well, let's put it that way," Doug said. In 2011, the twins wrote to the Jewish Board of Family and Children's Services (JBFCS) in New York City, requesting their records. They knew that their material was archived at Yale University until 2065 and could only be given to them with the JBFCS's approval. Their request was turned down. In fact, the twins received a letter stating that they were *not* in the study. Whether the JBFCS's reply was an oversight or an effort to avoid a difficult situation is unknown.

Doug and Howard eventually gained access to some of their material, thanks to the efforts of Washington, DC, attorney Barry Coburn. I spoke to Coburn in October 2019, over lunch at the House of Foong Lin in Bethesda, Maryland. Coburn became involved with the twins' case in 2010 or 2011, during the early production of Shinseki's film.[44] Before he could approach the JBFCS and Yale University, he needed proof that the twins had been in the study; recall that the JBFCS denied that Doug and Howard had been participants. Fortunately, a former research assistant on the twin study, Dr. Larry Perlman, had kept his notes on visits he had made to Doug and Howard's homes, beginning in 1968. Data were released to the twins, based on this material, but I found other supportive evidence.[45] A note in Bernard's file reads: "Krugman Neubauer/ (1) Mrs. Rauch twins." It is dated Saturday, July 13, so it could have been written in 1968 or 1974 when Doug was in the study; July 13 falls on a Saturday in both those years.

Perlman, now a clinical psychologist in Ann Arbor, Michigan, had been hired by the CDC to analyze data. As a New York University graduate student, he had hoped to use some of the twins' material for his doctoral dissertation. However, the CDC's lack of guidance and the disorganized manner in which the data were processed persuaded him to leave after one year. Saving his material was a prescient act on his part because it was the proof needed to show the JBFCS that Doug and Howard were part of the twin study—and it eventually allowed the twins access to their records.

Coburn worked with Jason Turken, the attorney formerly representing the JBFCS, to facilitate the release of Doug and Howard's documents in 2013. The twins received only a portion of their data, some of it redacted because full disclosure requires signatures from each person whose name appears on any document. Coburn does not know the precise steps taken between the lawyers' discussion with the JBFCS and Yale archivists, and the release of information to the twins. He opined that the JBFCS should honor the twins' requests by way of an apology. Coburn appeared in Shinseki's film, *The Twinning Reaction*, and posed the critical question, "Who owns the data?"

Perlman also appeared in the film, in several riveting scenes in which he meets Doug and Howard at his Michigan home for the first time in over forty years.[46] The small boys were now grown men whose lives were never intended to cross—but the twins did meet and deserve answers to countless questions. Perlman reviewed some of the test records made when the twins were six and explained how the study visits were organized. These details, while important, are less concerning than what the twins said in response. Their lives were manipulated, and they and their families had been lied to. They were "lab rats." The fact that the twins' papers have been sealed and are hard to obtain brings elements of mystery and uncertainty to the situation. What is being hidden?

Perlman admitted that he had not previously considered the damage done to all the twins and their parents. In a set of related papers about the twin study we authored in 2005, he wrote, "As for the ethics of the research, I do not recall a single discussion of whether or not it was inappropriate to conceal the knowledge of twinship from the families."[47] Seated before Doug and Howard and hearing their words, Perlman confessed, "It was a piece I had not thought through. It made me sad—it was an injustice to all the twins."

TOGETHER AGAIN

Doug and Howard are together again, united in their quest to acquire all of their study records and other materials. Shinseki's film shows them seated on a sofa in Doug's home, inserting a disk into Doug's laptop computer to examine the findings.[48] Doug's wife Ronni looks on anxiously, her hand over her mouth. A bit of hilarity lightened the mood momentarily when both twins laughed out loud, realizing that they both loved the same film—*Rollerball*. Returning to the computer screen, they learned that they had been together for about six months, then adopted separately one week apart. They read about their decline in motor dexterity and display of stereotypical behaviors as infants. They also saw that their records had been reviewed by the researchers in 1985 and 1986; a 1987 document is titled "First Draft."[49] Howard commented, "People sitting around dissecting your life!" Doug agreed. "It's just wrong. What they did was really, really wrong. The more stuff I read, the more wrong it seems and the more upsetting it gets. . . . It's upsetting to know that these people were able to affect our lives in ways that I don't even understand."

Neither twin is interested in publicity, having turned down an opportunity to appear in a *60 Minutes–Australia* program that aired in August in 2020.[50] However, they did agree to appear in Lori Shinseki's documentary film. In the film, Helen Rausch, Doug's mother, seemed to be speaking for all the families.[51] "They [LWS and the CDC] didn't give a damn," she said angrily. Howard reiterated what virtually all the twins have told me.[52] "They stole our childhood. I would not trade my life for anything, but you can't get that back." His voice trembled.

"Three Versions of the Very Same Song"

Identical Triplets

"[The reunited triplets] were ubiquitous in our world. Everyone everywhere knew who they were."[1]

$\int$o recalled Farrell Hirsch, chief executive officer of the Cultural Center in Fullerton, California. Hirsch stages plays, arranges concerts, and organizes educational events for the hundreds of patrons who frequent this popular venue. Now in his fifties, Hirsch grew up in the largely Jewish, but well-integrated community of Merrick, Long Island, a city that borders Queens, New York. I met him at Fullerton's Rotary Club in July 2019, where I delivered a lunchtime talk about my latest research on separated twins. Hirsch paced by the podium at the end of the session, eager to get my attention. We spoke for several minutes that day, but for nearly an hour a week later as he shared "forty years of fuzzy memories."

"YOU COULDN'T GET AWAY FROM THEM"

It was the early 1980s. "You couldn't get away from them," Hirsch told me. By "them" he meant the nineteen-year-old reared-apart identical triplets, Robert (Bob) Shafran, Edward (Eddy) Galland, and David (Dave) Kellman, whose chance reunion sparked media frenzies across the globe. Their story was captured in the 2018 award-winning documentary film, *Three Identical Strangers*. In a brilliant reenactment of events that happened in September 1980, we meet Bob on his first day at Sullivan County Community College in Loch Sheldrake, New York. The college's current enrollment includes just 843 full-time and 743 part-time students.[2] The college town, located one hundred

171

The Triplets, Their Families, and Friends

Bob
Robert (Bob) Shafran Dave and Eddy's reared-apart triplet
Alice Shafran Bob's stepmother
Elsa Shafran Bob's late adoptive mother
Dr. Mortimer Shafran Bob's father

Dave
David (Dave) Kellman Bob and Eddy's reared-apart triplet
Claire Kellman Dave's adoptive mother
Richard ("Bubula") Kellman Dave's adoptive father

Eddy
Edward (Eddy) Galland Bob and Dave's reared-apart triplet
Annette Galland Eddy's adoptive mother
Elliott Galland Eddy's adoptive father
Michael Domnitz Eddy's friend – reunited Eddy and Bob

Observers, Onlookers, and Others
Farrell Hirsch triplets' contemporary
Howard Schneider assistant managing editor, *Newsday*
Dr. Thomas J. Bouchard Jr. director, Minnesota Study of Twins Reared Apart
Pauline Bouchard Dr. Bouchard's spouse
Elizabeth (Liz) Bouchard Penning the Bouchards' daughter
Dr. Leonard L. Heston physician, Minnesota Study of Twins Reared Apart
Kevin Haroian researcher, Minnesota Study of Twins Reared Apart

miles northwest of New York City, has just over one thousand residents. The chance of running into an old friend probably ranges between slim and none. Nonetheless, Bob found himself kissed, hugged, and high-fived by fellow students he had never seen, all of whom called him "Eddy" and wondered why he had returned after leaving at the end of the fall 1979 semester.

Bob's experience was mind-boggling until one of Eddy's close friends, Michael Domnitz, started asking him the right questions: "Are you adopted?" "When was your birthday?" Responses: "Yes." "July 12, 1961." It was the same for Eddy. The two ran to a phone booth and got Eddy on the phone. "What adoption agency did your parents use?" they asked. Eddy put down the receiver, called to his mother, then reported back. "Louise Wise Services (LWS)," he said—the same for Bob. It was enough to convince Mike that something extraordinary was starting to take shape—could he have found Eddy's identical twin? Bob and Mike, now bonded by a common purpose, got into Bob's car and raced through the night to Eddy's New Hyde Park home, only slowing down to collect a speeding ticket from a state trooper. The two arrived outside Eddy's house at about 11:00 p.m. When Eddy opened the door, both he and Bob just stared at their identical other. Nothing else mattered. "It was just Eddy and me," Bob recalled. "Choreographed, but unrehearsed."[3]

The registrar at Sullivan County Community College could not disclose the reason for Eddy's leaving the college after a single semester, understandably citing student privacy issues. Bob's explanation for attending the school was to start life anew after an entanglement with the law that was later pronounced "minimal."[4]

The meeting of Bob and Eddy was not the end of this story, but the first in a series of life-changing events that would bring great jubilation, sudden fame, painful revelations, and ultimate heartbreak. Just days later, the "twins" became triplets when David Kellman's friends came across a *New York Post* article announcing the reunion of nineteen-year-old twins.[5] Dave, a student at Queens College, was born on July 12, 1961, and adopted from LWS—*just like Bob and Eddy*. Dave studied the photograph of the two that appeared alongside the article. The physical likeness between himself and the two young men was extraordinary, especially their curly locks, large hands, and athletic bodies. Once he was convinced that he was one of their brothers, Dave called Eddy on the phone, but ended up speaking to Eddy's mother. He told her he thought he was the "third one." "They're coming out of the woodwork!" she declared. On September 18, 1980, they knew that they were triplets.[6]

Things moved swiftly after that. Dave met Eddy first, then finally got Bob on the phone. They compared the things that matter to nineteen-year-olds—music, food, sports, women. According to Dave, "It's all the same, just like it was with us [Dave and Bob]."[7] As Dave's Aunt Hedy observed, the first time the three brothers were all together they rolled around on the floor together like puppies.[8] They bonded instantly, becoming nearly inseparable. Eddy felt that they "fit together from the very beginning." Dave recalled feeling "ecstatic shock."[9] Bob found that they finished each other's sentences, making it easy to have an argument because you knew what the other guy was thinking. But while they were enjoying life as a threesome, their outraged parents went en masse to LWS demanding answers, accompanied by an attorney.[10] The agency administrators told them that the separate rearing of identical twins and triplets helps children develop as individuals and avoid sibling rivalries. They added that finding a single family for three babies was difficult. David's father insisted that he and his wife would have taken all three.

The three couples left the meeting with little confidence in what they were told, and it seems they were correct. Recall Bernard's statement that "the demand for babies was so great that adoptive parents would have accepted infant twins."[11] Furthermore, nothing was said to the parents about the study and the involvement of other families. Based on notes from meetings with Bernard, Neubauer, and others, the *60 Minutes* producers were clearly aware of the research.[12] However, as I noted in chapter 6, the program's attempts to discuss the topic on air and make it widely known had been halted. The families tried to bring legal action against LWS for separating the twins, following them, and concealing information. Initial interest in their case soured because the attorneys they contacted did not wish to hurt their current and prospective clients' chances of adopting children from LWS.[13]

A critical commentary of *Three Identical Strangers* indicated that "this is the study which *presumably* separated the triplets [emphasis my own]."[14] A look at the relationship between LWS and the Child Development Center (CDC) regarding the twin separation policy and twin study is presented in the final chapter. The adoption agency never denied having separated the triplets, and board members discussed the triplets' unexpected reunion at their meetings, once under Agenda E. The Return of the Triplets: "As a continuing report on what is happening with the triplets who were adopted through us by three different sets of parents."[15]

It would be another fifteen years until the triplets and their families understood the comprehensiveness of the study, and why their sons were tested, filmed, and photographed. Until that happened, the brothers basked in their newfound fame, even while Eddy, the most gregarious of the three, uttered brief words of concern: "I don't know if this will turn out to be great or terrible."[16] It was great for a long time.

INDIVISIBLE BY THREE

Bob, Dave, and Eddy appeared in dozens of newspapers, magazines, and talk shows across the country and around the world—the *New York Times*, *New York Post*, *Good Housekeeping*, *United Press International*, the *Today Show*, and *Nightline*, to name a few.[17] The first newspaper to break the story was Long

Island's *Newsday*.[18] Then assistant managing editor Howard Schneider received a call from Eddy's friend Michael Domnitz, alerting Schneider to "the most interesting, amazing, special story" of his journalistic career. He was skeptical at first—at the time, the noted advice columnist and identical twin Ann Landers had been receiving crank letters from college students—so Schneider had a writer flown to the Catskills to actually see Eddy and Bob side by side. The writer called back to say it was true. "You are not going to believe this!" he told his boss. Within a day or two, Dave had seen *Newsday*'s story and the picture of his two brothers reprinted in the *New York Post*. Schneider thinks that Dave called *Newsday* to say he was the third, leading to extensive coverage of the three young men. The atmosphere at the newspaper was "just amazing because there were so many twists and turns."[19]

"We felt like we owned the story," Schneider recalled. He added that it was a great example of why journalistic truth is provisional. Things can change dramatically over time, as this story did.

The triplets quickly became well known among local crowds. For Farrell Hirsch, the presence of the three brothers was up close and personal. Hirsch and several of his buddies were aspiring comedians, circulating throughout Long Island's stand-up comedy clubs on open-mic nights. Anxious to get their careers going, they would stand on stage and perform for free. But Hirsch and company couldn't compete with the triplets' oversized hairdos, playful personalities, and irresistible smiles that outshone the other entertainers—Alice Shafran, Bob's stepmother, said that if anyone had an Afro, the triplets had bigger ones.[20] Bob, Dave, and Eddy were paid to perform, not a lot, but enough to cause resentment among Hirsch and his crowd. "They exploited their fame, but they didn't have to do anything to exploit it," he said. "They were also exploited by the clubs because they attracted crowds. And they partied way too much—I never heard a hint of them saying no to anything." The triplets also frequented New York's trendy nightclubs, such as Studio 54, the Copacabana, and the Limelight.[21] The celebrity photographer Annie Leibovitz took them to the Peppermint Lounge and the Mudd Club.[22]

As we spoke, Hirsch continued to withdraw from his memory bank, his initially "fuzzy memories" becoming increasingly clear. "We had all seen the *Newsday* article about their reunion.[23] But then we would sit around watching TV and there they would be—on *Phil Donahue* and *Jenny Jones*—they were everywhere." But in a sober tone, Hirsch confessed that, as a young man in the 1980s, he and his friends "really didn't care about the other guy's story. We resented [the triplets] in a way that made sense then. I have no memory of hearing about their separation or the experiments they were in—and even if I did, I probably wouldn't have thought it through."

As the years went by, interest in the triplets persisted. Their celebrity was likened to that of the Marx Brothers—they were doing their shtick.[24] They scored a small part in the 1985 film *Desperately Seeking Susan*. The three brothers eventually moved in together, worked at Famous Sammy's Roumanian Steakhouse, earned international marketing degrees, and in 1988 opened Triplets Old New York Restaurant in New York's SoHo district of lower Manhattan.[25] The establishment was enormously successful, earning over one million dollars during its first year of operation. The place was lively, the food was delicious, and the triplets were charming—I know because I ate there one night in 1986 or 1987. Joining me was the set of reunited identical twin firemen from New Jersey, Mark Newman and Gerald (Jerry) Levey, mentioned earlier, who met by chance in 1985 at age thirty-one.[26] Mark and Jerry were famous for placing a pinky finger under a glass of beer, wearing big belt buckles, carrying large key rings, and ordering steak exceedingly rare. Their similarities intrigued scientists and fascinated the public. Their fame might have been greater, but the triplets were stiff competition.

Most people of a certain age recall where they were, or what they were doing, when John F. Kennedy was assassinated, when the Beatles played their first American hit, and when terrorists attacked the World Trade Towers. For those of us who study twins, we also know how we first heard about the triplets and their remarkable meeting.

TWIN STUDIES: CHICAGO AND MINNESOTA

I remember when I learned that Bob and Eddy had met one another. I was a graduate student at the University of Chicago, working on a twin study for my doctoral dissertation. But in mid-September 1980, I was at my parents' home in Riverdale, New York, enjoying a few free days before the fall quarter began. I planned to sleep late on that particular day, but my mother woke me up early to tell me that identical twins had just met for the first time because one was confused for the other at a community college. I got up immediately and devoured the story that she handed me, printed in the *New York Times*.[27] Several days later, the scene repeated, except that the "twins" were now triplets. It was beyond extraordinary. The news spread quickly, challenging minds over why they were separated in the first place and why they were so alike. I was certain that the triplets would come to Minneapolis to participate in the Minnesota Study of Twins Reared Apart (MISTRA). I hoped to become associated with that project as a postdoctoral fellow after earning my PhD degree.

Figure 10.1. The reared-apart identical triplets (L to R): Eddy Galland, David Kellman, and Robert Shafran, taken during their participation in the Minnesota Study of Twins Reared Apart at the University of Minnesota, in June 1981. The triplets turned twenty years of age one month later. Photo by Dr. Thomas J. Bouchard, Jr.

The MISTRA, launched in March 1979 by professor of psychology Thomas J. Bouchard Jr., had been in progress for one and a half years when the triplets reunited.[28] In December 1980, the three young men spent several days with Bouchard and his wife Pauline in a New York City hotel, completing inventories and interviews. Bouchard had previously met with two of the families to explain his study and answer any questions.[29] The triplets also came to Minneapolis in June 1981 for medical and psychological tests. On both occasions, lunches and dinners were opportunities for socializing with staff and members of Bouchard's family.

The date of the triplets' New York and Minnesota assessments is important—they took place nine months after their reunion, *and almost fifteen years before they and their families understood the full scope of their involvement, and that of other twins, in the LWS-CDC twin study.* Correspondence between Bouchard and the triplets' attorney Jack Solomon shows that two of the triplets' families agreed to letting their sons participate in the MISTRA, but one father raised questions about the testing that was done by the CDC.[30] The nature of his questions was not specified, but his concerns were apparently satisfied to the extent that his son did take part in the Minnesota study. Solomon also requested certain conditions, such as keeping the study scientific and respecting the parents' privacy, but he enthusiastically supported their participation.

Following the success of *Three Identical Strangers* in 2018, the triplets declined most invitations for interviews and appearances to focus exclusively on personal projects of their own. I respect their decision. The triplets' Minneapolis study days predated my association with the MISTRA by a little over a year. Still, I learned a lot about them from my Minnesota colleagues. And I met all three brothers in 1986, staying in touch mostly with Bob. I can share observations and perspectives that have not appeared elsewhere.

DISCOVERIES

It was fall 1982 when I arrived at the University of Minnesota as a postdoctoral fellow. By then, the MISTRA had gained considerable stature, drawing attention from national and international scholars, students, and journalists. But during my early weeks in Minnesota, I was hearing about an older twin study, orchestrated by Drs. Viola Bernard and Peter Neubauer, that was getting attention from *60 Minutes*' reporter Mike Wallace. As I explained in the preface and in chapter 6, *60 Minutes* was producing a program about the inner workings of the agency and the critical implications of the study. Ultimately, the planned television special was cancelled. I became intrigued by that investigation because its methods and design were far beyond the mainstream of twin research as I knew it, and because so few of my colleagues had heard about this work. Some of my current colleagues learned about the study only recently by watching the 2017 or 2018 documentary films, or by catching ABC's *20/20* program that aired in March 2018.[31] I was surprised by their lack of awareness, although I had been researching the study in earnest. Samuel (Sam) Abrams, one of the three main investigators of the LWS-CDC twin study, provided answers.

In a mid-1990s interview with author Lawrence Wright, Abrams indicated that the LWS–CDC study was never intended to be widely known but was targeted to psychological professionals. "It would be terrible if misunderstandings arriving from a wider dissemination of this data would hurt anybody. And that's always a principal thing we worry about." However, researchers, especially those publishing case reports, carefully conceal identifying features of their participants in the interest of confidentiality. The psychoanalytic literature is replete with such examples, among them the identical twins "Amy and Beth" that the CDC researchers referenced occasionally when describing their observations. Abrams's 1986 article presents considerable details about these twins, although neither Bernard nor features of the adoption agency are mentioned.[32] Moreover, a proposal to publish a comprehensive treatment of the findings in book form, to be authored by Neubauer, Abrams, and Balzert, was approved by Yale University in 1987;[33] I will say more about their final contract and related documents in a later chapter. For now, it is hard to reconcile their professed concern over participant identity with serious efforts toward book publication.

Abrams also alleged that the Danish Professor Niels Juel-Nielsen published his own reared-apart twin research in English, not in Danish, to protect the twins' privacy.[34] "He knew that [his study] would have a limited readership." I believe it is more likely that Juel-Nielsen published his book in English, rather than in Danish, *because he wanted his findings to be known and discussed.* English is a universal language, spoken and read around the world, especially by academics. In fact, 86 percent of Danish citizens speak English and 44 percent use English often, so the study information would have been accessible in Denmark in any case.[35] Furthermore, Juel-Nielsen presented his reared-apart twin findings in a number of international journals and at conferences, including the First International Congress of Human Genetics.[36] I posed this issue to Professor Bouchard who said that Abrams's interpretation of Juel-Nielsen's language choice "verges on the absurd."[37] However, Juel-Nielsen did protect his twins by giving them false names and omitting their photographs.

The connection between the LWS–CDC study and the reared-apart triplets was detected in the mid-1990s by Lawrence Wright who lives and works in Austin, Texas. In the 2018 film *Three Identical Strangers*, Wright recalled that he had stumbled upon an "obscure [1986] scientific article" while researching nature-nurture studies for a *New Yorker* magazine article. The article's author was Sam Abrams. Wright was "shocked and intrigued" to discover that the source of the separated twins was a single adoption agency. As I indicated, the name of the agency was not mentioned in Abrams's article, but the agency *was* mentioned in hundreds of newspaper and magazine articles about the triplets. "It's a very restricted literature," Abrams told Wright, referring to what had been written about the study. Wright countered that the work had been referenced in books, so it was "not that obscure." Strangely, Wright was correct in calling Abrams's article both "obscure" and "not that obscure." Abrams's study appeared in the *Psychoanalytic Study of the Child*, a journal that is read only by the minority of psychoanalytically oriented clinicians and researchers. Even within the field of psychoanalysis, the number of child psychoanalysts is small, relative to those focusing on adults. The modest readership of the journal is reflected in its low SCImago journal rank or SJR factor score of just 0.3, based on 2000–2017 data.[38]

Wright could not determine how many twin pairs were involved, but he did bring a more comprehensive and accurate picture of the twin study to the triplets' attention.[39] Dave said the news hit him like a "tidal wave." Bob allowed that there were clues—at a young age, people came to his home, usually a young man and a young woman, to measure his intelligence, test his hand-eye coordination, and ask for his interpretation of amorphous ink blots. His brothers had similar recollections. Dave talked about being filmed when he played on slides and swings, and Eddy recalled questions that made him feel frustrated. Despite these memories, Bob admitted that they never really recognized "this stuff" until it was in newsprint. Wright's *New Yorker* magazine piece was published in 1995, followed by his book and Stephanie Saul's *Newsday* exposé, both in 1997.[40] The breadth and depth of the twin study was starting to be understood.

GOING SEPARATE WAYS

In the spring of 1961 Dave's mother, Claire Kellman, informed LWS that she wanted to adopt a baby boy. She and her husband Richard already had a daughter, Sandy, whom they had adopted from LWS three years earlier. They were told that the wait for a baby would be long but, surprisingly, a male infant became available just six weeks later.[41] The Kellmans welcomed six-month-old David into their home, but were unaware that he had just been separated from his two identical brothers. Bob was adopted at about the same time by Dr. Mortimer Shafran and his wife Elsa; however, Eddy's arrival in the Gallands' home may not have happened until he was eight months old.[42] It is possible that Eddy was placed with a different family at five or six months before his parents, Elliott and Annette Galland, received him a few months later.[43] I will explain my reasons for suggesting this after describing where the triplets were raised and who raised them.

The adoptive parents were all in their early thirties when they adopted their sons, except for David's mother who was in her late twenties.[44] However, the three families differed quite a bit in background, education, and rearing practices.[45] The Shafrans lived in the upscale town of Scarsdale in Westchester County, about ten miles north of New York City. Bob's father, Mortimer was a physician, and his late mother Elsa was an attorney, both of whom held higher professional degrees. Bob's father was away a lot, but he was very devoted to his son.

The Kellmans lived in Howard Beach, New York, a blue-collar neighborhood in the southwestern section of Queens, New York. They were from an immigrant family that had fled Europe for the United States during the Holocaust. David's father, Richard, owned a hardware store in Manhattan and his mother, Claire, assisted in the store. Both of David's parents had finished high school. David's father was known to the triplets as "Bubala," a Yiddish term typically reserved for children, but applied to anyone considered to be a darling and close to the heart.[46] He doted on Dave, and after the triplets met he announced that he had "three sons."

The Gallands' home was in New Hyde Park, in Nassau County, Long Island, a middle-class village about six miles southeast of New York City.[47] Eddy's father, Elliott, taught shop in a local high school and his mother, Annette, was a homemaker. Eddy's father had completed a Master's degree in Industrial Arts, and his mother had finished one year of college. Eddy's father called himself a "strict disciplinarian," perhaps explaining why Eddy's wife Brenda admitted that Eddy did not feel he belonged in that family.

Why do I suspect that Eddy did not join the Gallands until he was eight months old? In chapter 9, I referenced a paper by Dr. Susan Farber that discussed sex differences in ideas about adoption.[48] The study sample included nine adopted children and twelve of their siblings who came from nine different families. According to the article, the nine core adoptees "have been followed intensively from birth through latency and sometimes into adolescence." While it is possible that these children were part of some other studies conducted by LWS and CDC, none of the children in the other studies was as closely followed from birth to the teenage years as were the separated twins. Neubauer also indicated that lack of funding was partly responsible for terminating the twin study by 1980, so it is unlikely that another group of adoptees was so closely tracked. The article continued, "All but two of the siblings are adopted themselves, the exceptions being one female's older brother and one male's younger sister . . . the study children were matched so that the females had older brothers and the males had older sisters, though subsequent births and adoptions altered this slightly. . . . All of the females were adopted at three months, and all but one of the males at five or six months. The exception was 'Male Z' who was placed in his eventual home at eight months, subsequent to an unsuccessful placement two months earlier. This also is the child whose family withdrew from the study when he was five."

I believe that the nine core adopted children comprise three of the LWS separated identical twin pairs—two female and one male—and the separated identical triplets. Consistent with the data in Table 1 of the original article, all three triplets had a sister who was three years older. Table 1 also indicates that one male child also had a brother who was seven years younger, and another male child also had a sister who was one year younger. I confirmed the presence of these younger siblings in Bob and Eddy's homes, respectively, as did a family photo of the Gallands. Once I obtained the siblings' names, I conducted an internet search and confirmed that their ages aligned with those given in the table. In the article, Eddy's sister is identified as the biological child of his adoptive parents, information I could not verify.

Additional evidence that the paper describes the separated twins and triplets is a detailed outline of the proposed book about the project. The outline summarizes various data for several twin pairs, but includes only two of the children who were most likely the triplets. It is noted that the data on these two children were gathered until at least the eighth year of the study. This makes it likely that Eddy is "Male Z," the child who left the study at age five—he is the only male who had a younger sister and is the only one of the triplets whose parents did not return a consent form to the researchers in 1978.[49] In fact, it is more than likely. Christa Balzert, one of the three main twin study researchers, gave an exclusive interview in which she said, "Originally, there were four sets of twins and one set of triplets. One set of twins dropped out early, *and so did one of the triplets*" [italics are mine].[50] The twins, Susan and Anne, whom I described in chapter 7, left the study when they were six or seven years old, once their twinship was discovered. Furthermore, Anne's brother is two years older than she and all the female twins in Farber's study had a brother who is at least three years older.

Recall that adoptive parents were able to relinquish a baby if they felt that the infant showed a poor fit with their family. This may have happened in Eddy's case. If Eddy had indeed been part of another family when he was six to eight months old, the Gallands would probably not have been told of his previous placement. Long-time LWS President and Board Member Justine Wise Polier believed that adoptive parents should be told only what is necessary.[51]

The Table 1 data also match with what is known about Ellen and Melanie, and Doug and Howard, as well as Sharon and Lisa, whose story comes later. This information has been reproduced in Table 10.1. However, the consistency of these data with what is known about the separated twins and

Table 10.1. Study Child and Siblings: Age and Sex

Study Child	Sister	Brother
Female:		
A		+6
B	+3	+7
C		+4
D		+3
Male:		
V	+3	
W	+3	
X	+3	-7
Y	+3	
Z	+3, -1*	

>+ Years older
- Years younger
*Adoptive parents' biological child

A: Ellen, B: Melanie, C: Lisa, D: Sharon
V, W: Howard or Doug, X: Bob, Y: Dave, Z: Eddy

Table 10.1 adapted from Table 1 in Farber (1977).

Note: Both Howard and Doug were raised with an older sister. When Howard was in his twenties, he acquired a younger brother and a younger sister when his father remarried. He did not grow up with his younger siblings, explaining why they are not included in the table. See https://www.legacy.com/obituaries/dispatch/obituary.aspx?n=alvin-l-burack&pid=175159160&fhid=8669.

their siblings does *not* prove that they are the subjects of this study. It only suggests that they might be.

Over forty years have passed since the publication of Farber's paper. It is possible that, if the paper *did* include the twins and their siblings, Farber could not recall the source of her data. It is also possible that she analyzed the sex difference material and other information without full knowledge of the background of the adopted children in her sample. This research practice is often used to reduce the possibility of biased assessment, due to raters' knowledge of hypotheses, subject characteristics, or other factors.[52] Abrams and Neubauer credited her for "data collection and assistance in organization of the illustrations" in their 1976 paper related to the study, but she may have been "blind" to the nature of that data.[53] Farber is also listed as an attendee at a 1975 adoption study meeting, along with Drs. Abrams, Balzert, Naubauer, Wolsk, and several others; Dr. Bernard was "absent." The subject of the meeting was "Revision of Outline and C-7 [Child 7] Films 4-8 and 4-11."[54] She did have contact with one of the separated twins in the study, as she indicated and as I will describe in chapter 11.

"THREE VERSIONS OF THE SAME SONG"

On October 2, 1989, ABC's popular news magazine *Nightline*[55] featured the triplets, MISTRA director Dr. Thomas J. Bouchard Jr., and Harvard University geneticist Dr. Paul Billings.[56] The program, hosted that night by Forrest Sawyer, explored the MISTRA's 1988 findings that personality traits have a partial genetic basis, and the more provocative message that shared home environments do not make family members alike.[57] It was an opportunity to consider why the triplets' abilities, personalities, and interests were so similar, despite being raised in different families. During the conversation, Dave repeated the phrase that Bouchard often used to describe the triplets: They were like "three versions of the very same song." I asked Bouchard to clarify the meaning behind his words.

Bouchard explained, "Different artists play the same song, but you can identify the artist because each one has a unique style in qualities like tone and speed. This also tells you why different orchestras sound different even while you recognize that the music is the same. My analogy conveys the idea that there is both a fundamental similarity and a uniqueness to each individual triplet."[58] Elsewhere, Bouchard noted that our twin and triplet data could be understood at two levels, one based on anecdotal evidence and self-reports, and the other based on measured behaviors and physical traits.[59] He explained that similarities in the anecdotal/self-report kind were so great as to "overwhelm" the twins. In the triplets' case, they would include their outgoing personalities, sports interests, food choices, fear of needles, and taste in women, all of which astounded them because they matched so strongly.

The triplets' objectively measured traits, such as weight, height, and IQ, while extremely close, showed slight differences. In Minnesota, their weights differed by two to seven pounds. Two of the triplets were identical in height, while the third triplet was one half-inch shorter. Bob and Dave had completed one year of college, whereas Eddy had earned a high school degree. Nevertheless, the largest IQ score difference among the three pairs of two was just two points, consistent with genetic effects.[60] The triplets' hand preference scores varied somewhat—Bob is left-handed, and Dave and Eddy are both right-handed, a difference seen among 25 percent of identical twins.[61] Left- or right-hand bias may be evident as early as six months of age, developing further and stabilizing during early childhood.[62] Unseen films[63] of Bob as a youngster, made by researchers during home visits and retrieved from the Yale archive, show him drawing designs, sorting pictures, and building a block tower, mostly using his left hand.

Nightline focused on our finding that home environments show little relation to personality traits, such as traditionalism, harm avoidance, and well-being. Thus, personality similarities among family members come from their shared DNA, whereas differences come from events family members experience individually. I think of children as bringing up their parents, rather than the other way around. Children's individual genetically based proclivities largely shape how parents treat them, explaining why siblings raised together end up being so different. Bob put it beautifully by saying that "our parents are very different, but we are very much the same—in ways that have no bearing on the influence from our parents." Bob listed the triplets' gregarious personalities, wrestling histories, hyperkinetic tendencies, outspoken manners, and book reading as examples of behavior that all three shared that were not related to how they were raised.

As the triplets grew older together, people close to them saw personality differences.[64] Dave's friend Ellen said that Bob had "raw intelligence," Eddy was "mushy," and Dave was "the best of the three." Dave's friend Alan claimed that Eddy got the most out of the threesome when they were together. Eddy's wife Brenda said that Eddy especially wanted the three to have a beautiful life as one big family; in fact, Eddy had moved his family several times so he could be close to David.[65] The triplets also knew that they were not carbon copies. Dave observed that Eddy more than the others was the "driving force" in the search for their biological mother—but then Bob pushed Dave to help find her and Dave went along with it.[66] In 1985, the triplets and Dave's friend, Alan Luchs, found her name at the New York Public Library which, at the time, held vital statistics records from the Department of Health. Bob and Dave positively acknowledged her decision to keep a low profile as their public personas soared. Each triplet has had varied communications and relations with their biological mother over the years.[67]

It seems that the triplets' differences emerged more clearly when they were together than apart, at least in their later years. Older twin studies showed that identical twins raised together are less alike in some personality traits than those raised apart because they can express themselves freely, unaffected by the social presence of their co-twin.[68] Such findings have not been replicated by more recent studies, perhaps because of different inventories, but anecdotally the pattern seems to hold.

THE MISTRA: RECOLLECTIONS

"If a woman under twenty-five came in contact with them, they all pounced on her." This was Pauline Bouchard's first quick response when I asked for her memories of Bob, Dave, and Eddy.[69] As I explained, Pauline was with her husband, the MISTRA director Thomas J. Bouchard Jr., in New York, to help him administer inventories to the triplets prior to their Minnesota visit. They were great womanizers, she recalled. In the hotel elevator, she and several other riders watched as the triplets jockeyed for the closest position next to a young female. Pauline also described a "physical energy" about them that was "visceral and overwhelming." When they were alone they quieted down, becoming "individual, but not that different"—but when they got together "it was like having six people in the room, not three." All of them were "cheerful and happy and leaned on each other—they were phenomenal, and very, very special." Pauline also found that the triplets were "extremely animated in how they approached a conversation, one more so than the others—they would lean in toward the other, laughing, talking, and waving their hands with jerky movements." She reflected, "Were they like this, or were they still learning to interact with each other?"

I asked Professor Bouchard to remind me how he found the triplets and what he remembered most about them. He usually heard about newly reunited sets from several sources. This time it was a call from an interested individual in New York State, a slew of newspaper articles from colleagues, and correspondence with the triplets' attorney, Jack Solomon. Bouchard's first meeting with the triplets was in Denver, to tape the *Phil Donahue Show*, shortly before their New York City assessment. Bouchard recalled the constant stares of onlookers whenever the group emerged from the hotel. And, like his wife, he didn't miss the triplets' laser-like attention to any young woman who passed. Bouchard also spoke of an incident in Minnesota in which one of the triplets nearly fainted from fear, but he couldn't remember what had provoked it. I reminded him that all three were terrified of the needles used in the allergy testing lab, so it might have been that.

Other Minnesota researchers had their own memories. Psychiatrist Leonard Heston, who administered psychiatric and medical interviews, described the triplets as "notably energetic, personally engaging, and highly verbal."[70] Heston added that, "Three at one time kept one's head constantly turning. I've never experienced anything quite like the three of them at once, not even a room full of children. But taken one at a time, they were tractable and focused." Heston's sketch of possible scenarios by which a single fertilized egg, or zygote, divides to yield three identical offspring was tucked into the triplets' assessment schedule. In one scenario, the zygote splits into two, followed by division of one of the products to yield three. Another possibility is that the zygote divides and both products divide again to produce identical quadruplets, one of which does not survive. Some sources have alleged that Bob, Dave, and Eddy were originally such a quartet.[71] However, the biological evidence to support this claim, such as the prenatal detection of four fetuses or the delivery of four newborns, has never been cited or produced.

Kevin Haroian, from Dr. David Lykken's psychophysiology lab, recorded the triplets' brain waves, gave them computer-administered ability tests, and took their photographs and fingerprints.[72] Haroian described the three as "affable, gregarious and having a great time together." They were easy to test, probably because he saw only one triplet at a time when each was more reserved. But his most "vivid memory" involved graduate student Francie Gabbay, who escorted the triplets from one test setting to another. "They hoisted her high on their shoulders and carried her across campus. She got all the machoism they had."

On March 26, 2020, Bouchard's daughter, Elizabeth (Liz), also shared a behind-the-scenes perspective on Bob, Dave, and Eddy.[73] In June 1981, Liz was a nineteen-year-old student who had finished her freshman year at the University of Wisconsin. Home for the summer, she was available for dinners with the triplets at Rudolph's Bar-B-Que and at her family's home in Wayzata, Minnesota. They were "super-enamored of having found one another," Liz told me. "They were very giddy, excited and bright, and the reunion added something to their lives. They reveled in it all." Liz added that while they conversed with everyone at the table, they were clearly grouped together. "Nothing would get between them," she said.

The next day, I received an email message from Liz who had found a journal she had kept back then. I have reproduced her reflections on the triplets, made in real time:

Monday June 22, 1981
"Met the Triplets for dinner tonight. I'm in love with 3 guys from New York.

They're great guys. David on my left kept his arm around me, fed me onion rings and the cherry from his Zombie. Eddie on my right fed me his cherry and kept his hand on my leg. I winked at Bobby.

I had such a great time and they wanted me to go out with them tonight too, but Daddy said NO. Later he said it was because they were really tired and he hoped they would get to bed earlier."

Friday June 26, 1981
"Wednesday [June 24 presumably] was a super nice day so I stayed in the sun, mowed the lawn. . . . The triplets were here for dinner around 7:30. Daddy wanted to take pictures first, so we ran around the front yard, then to the dock. Dinner was very good and we had fun. Mark [my brother] liked them too. After dinner, we showed them Mark's room, then I gave them a ride home. . . . They were such great guys. They all said if I ever went to New York, I could stay with them."

In 1985, Bouchard received funding for the "Twin Film," a twenty-eight-minute documentary proposed to us by Minneapolis-based director Ken Greer and identical twin co-producers Jill Siegel-Greer and Judy Siegel-Freeman.[74] The film was intended to showcase the MISTRA research, explore the lives of several separated sets, and examine twinship as a phenomenon. The first time I met Bob, Dave, and Eddy was on November 11, 1986, when we visited them to talk to them about the project. The setting was their shared bachelor-style apartment, famous for the local liquor stores' generous deliveries.[75] The triplets behaved exactly as the press had presented them—warm, outgoing, and dazzled by each other. Unfortunately, the high cost of filming prevented completion of the "Twin Film," although clips that did not include the triplets were shown on *Nightline* and at the 1987 International Twins Association convention in Oklahoma City.[76]

LWS AND THE CDC: THE TRIPLETS' REUNION AND *60 MINUTES* REDUX

"It's possible that they got the triplets to go along but no mention was made of triplets."[77]

Viola Bernard's comment is from her notes made after a 1981 meeting with Mike Wallace of *60 Minutes*. Her words, sent to her colleagues who were at the meeting, show her concern over which twins Wallace planned to interview. She was worried even though three months earlier, producer Madeline Amgott had told Neubauer that while the triplets would be on the program, the focus would be the MISTRA, and LWS and the CDC would not be mentioned.[78] Of course, the *60 Minutes* exposé never came to pass, as I explained in chapter 6. It is also worth noting that the triplets were *not* the first identical LWS-separated multiples to reunite, but they *were* the first to draw widespread interest. Susan and Anne's parents learned of their daughters' separation in 1966, but Bernard advised them to keep silent. Susan and Anne finally met in 1977, three years before the triplets and also because of an unusual chance encounter that would have fascinated people everywhere. However, no publicity surrounded their reunion, probably because one of the families preferred privacy, whereas the media's attention to the triplets, their adoption circumstances, and their evolving relations was overwhelming. LWS and the CDC tried to control it.

- A May 1982 LWS board meeting included an item, "Return of the Triplets," on its agenda: "As a *continuing* [italics are mine] report on

what is happening with the triplets who were adopted through us by three sets of parents and discovered each other while at college, it seems that apparently their story is going to be the basis for a two-hour motion picture for television. Also, they may star in their own weekly television series."[79]
- Four pressing issues that LWS and the CDC listed: 1. Separation of twins and triplets, 2. Secrecy of placements, 3. Secrecy of CDC subjects—assistance if they meet, 4. Ethical issues of the study.[80]
- In 1983, following her retirement, Bernard informed LWS President Sheldon Fogelman that she would like to be involved as a consultant in "ongoing matters with regard to the twins and triplets and relationships with CDC and others about these."[81]

It was prescient of Bernard and colleagues to consider the issues raised by their discussions with *60 Minutes*. First, in 1997, Stephanie Saul published her riveting piece about the triplets and the LWS-CDC twin study in *Newsday*.[82] It was shocking to read that researchers went from home to home, tracking the behaviors of the separated twins and triplets without their parents' knowledge. Experts weighed in as well. Bouchard said that separating twins "does not feel right to me." Adoption specialist Florence Fisher called the twin separations "criminal." The National Institute of Mental Health, which had partly funded the study in 1965, said it could not comment until the project's records were reviewed. Colleagues and I have tried many times, and in many ways, to obtain these records, but they have never been found, as I explained earlier—paper copies were kept in pre-digital days so the original proposal and records may have been destroyed to free up cabinet space. Another possibility is that these materials are under seal at the Yale archives. LWS was also funded by Jewish philanthropies that could potentially have copies or similar documents; the United Jewish Federation of New York listed the six branches of the former Jewish Board of Guardians, the Jewish Board of Family and Children's Services, the Louise Wise Child Adoption Center, and LWS among their affiliated agencies.[83]

Saul's article touched on another tragic event—the suicide of triplet Eddy Galland on June 16, 1995, at age thirty-three. Eddy shot himself. Bob said that losing Eddy was probably the greatest loss of his lifetime. Dave had to run a party at the triplets' restaurant the next day, the "toughest thing" he ever did.[84]

Suicide is a complex behavior that reflects a genetic tendency that may be rooted in impulsivity, combined with events that trigger that tendency.[85] *Three Identical Strangers* leaves the impression that Eddy's death was largely linked to his feeling like a poor fit in his family—the film's director Tim Wardle characterized the father-son relationship as "very dysfunctional."[86] Recall that his father, Elliott Galland, was strict with his children, a practice that probably cut against Eddy's fun-loving, carefree grain. Still, Elliott loved his son and felt he had acted in his son's best interest. On July 12, 2018—the day that would have been Eddy's fifty-seventh birthday—Elliott sat in the audience at the *Today Show* to see his son's two brothers, Bob and Dave, interviewed about their lives and the making of *Three Identical Strangers*.[87] Eddy's wife Brenda believes that Eddy was never at peace with not having his brothers with him during childhood—he was "devastated and traumatized" by this loss.[88] These life events probably played some part in Eddy's death by suicide. I also believe there is a deeper story here.

All three triplets experienced psychiatric problems between fifteen and seventeen years of age, and all three showed behavioral problems before then. As a youngster, Bob was prone to temper tantrums, head banging, and holding his breath until he blacked out.[89] The triplets possibly inherited a predisposition toward behavioral disorder from their biological mother who may have had some psychopathology. The precise nature of her mental complaints is unknown, although when the triplets met her, they found that she drank fairly heavily.[90] Alcohol consumption is not a definitive indication of mental illness, but it can be a sign. They learned that their mother was young and single when she delivered her babies at Hillside Hospital in Glen Oaks;[91] Hillside Hospital, now Zucker-Hillside, was always a psychiatric facility.[92] Perhaps Eddy was more vulnerable than his brothers to behavioral "highs" and "lows," due to events before and/or after birth. Lower birth weight and obstetrical complications have been implicated in some cases of identical twins with bipolar disorder whose co-twins are unaffected, but the evidence is inconsistent.[93] In addition, we lack information about the triplets' birth histories. Epigenetic changes, or changes in gene expression, have also shown co-twin differences, and some changes have been linked to bipolar disorder.[94] Brain structures can also differ between identical twins in which only one twin is affected.[95]

Two events—the death of Dave's father "Bubala" who had held the triplets so tightly together, and the departure of Bob from the restaurant to become a lawyer—may have conspired to set off Eddy's behavior. As Bob so thoughtfully and soberly asked, "Why Eddy? Why not me?" Dave suggested that the strong foundation his own parents had provided may have protected him from some adversities.[96] There are no definitive answers to such questions.

Second, *60 Minutes* made another attempt to produce a segment about the triplets. This effort was led by Walter (Walt) Bogdanich, now an investigative reporter for the *New York Times* and married to journalist Stephanie Saul. I met with them both in 2019 at the *Times'* building where they both work.[97] Walt, previously at CBS, believed that Saul's piece was "good for print, but better for TV." In 1999, he brought Wallace to the triplets' restaurant and introduced him to one or both of the brothers. "We were lining it all up, then one day Mike comes in and says I am not doing it." There was no explanation, but Walt didn't need one. "Louise Wise is very influential—lots of connections, and Mike is susceptible to that—Mike [was] a great correspondent to work with. I enjoyed most of my experience working with him—and depending on the story he was fearless about getting the truth, but he was susceptible in certain circumstances to the influence of his powerful friends." Wallace had been embroiled in previous lawsuits in the early 1980s, as I indicated in chapter 6. And according to the *Sun Sentinel*, in 1995, Wallace and CBS Executive Producer Don Hewitt "all caved" when they chose not to air a segment on the tobacco industry's whistle blower Jeffrey Wigand.[98] Pressure from industry executives appears to have persuaded Wallace to drop the segment. Similar outside influences may have been behind the collapse of the triplets' program. It is also likely that Wallace and *60 Minutes* wished to avoid further legal entanglements.

Walt did produce a *60 Minutes* segment called "Secrets and Lies," which documented the tragic story of Michael Juman, a young man adopted from LWS.[99] The program aired in 1998. Juman had a history of mental illness on both sides of his biological family, information that was never disclosed to his adoptive parents.[100] He was diagnosed with schizophrenia and took his own life at age twenty-nine after several attempts. A lawsuit was brought against LWS in a landmark legal case, and the family prevailed. Journalist Lisa Belkin authored an in-depth article about the Jumans, originally intended as the *New York Times* magazine's lead story. Belkin explained that her article did not make the cover because of *60 Minutes'* extensive coverage.[101]

AFTERMATH

Dave said the study made him feel like a "lab rat." Bob called it "Nazi shit."[102] The triplets know that their purposeful separation and secret scrutiny had disastrous effects on every member of their families. Eddy's wife, Brenda, called it fraud. Bob's stepmother, Alice Shafran, asked why the study was never published, a question I will address later. Everyone lost Eddy. If the three had been raised together, his brothers' love and support may have saved him.

Some people have claimed that analogies to "lab rats" and "Nazi science" are overblown, whereas others have said they are justified—of course, everyone deserves an opinion. But perhaps it is time to step into the shoes that Bob, Dave, and Eddy wore.

Figure 10.2.   Triplets Robert Shafran (L) and David Kellman (R), at my New York City book party, celebrating the publication of *Accidental Brothers*, June 15, 2018. Photo by Dr. Nancy L. Segal.

The last time I saw Bob and Dave was in June 2018. I hosted a party in New York City to celebrate the publication of my book, *Accidental Brothers*.[103] Bob came with his wife Ilene and Dave came with a friend who was part of an opposite-sex twin pair. It was wonderful to see them. They were no longer the unrestrained, outspoken teenagers of the early 1980s, but their faces, smiles, and warmth were familiar. True to form, Bob and Dave lifted me up for a photo and put me down only when they were ready.

In 2018, Farrell Hirsch sat through a showing of *Three Identical Strangers*. The film gave him insights he never expected, making him rethink his views about the triplets and the lives they led. "To have been purposely separated and to have had your life manipulated!—as twenty-year-olds, we didn't see their suffering. Maybe we saw the results, but we didn't recognize them. Today I feel sorry and embarrassed [for that]."

Hirsch is the father of an adopted daughter. He knows that she is not a twin because the child's biological mother had lived at his home during her pregnancy. Of course, Bob, Dave, and Eddy's parents never even considered that the baby they brought home from LWS was a twin—or a triplet. They were only told that their sons would be taking tests and answering questions from researchers who would visit their homes from time to time. Nothing seemed amiss.

THE MOST AMAZING STORY (ALMOST) NEVER TOLD

In 2003 or 2004, I asked Bob if he would agree to my writing a book about the triplets' lives. Other people had wanted to do this, but none had succeeded. We talked for a bit, but it was clear that the strong editorial control Bob insisted on maintaining would interfere with my writing, so I abandoned the project. Before I hung up the phone, I told him that the triplets' life history would be the most amazing story never told. Now that they have been part of two documentary films with a biopic on the way, a great many of their life events have been revealed. And remember what Eddy said when it all began—"I don't know if this will turn out to be great or terrible." It was both.

• *11* •

Twinless Again

Sharon Morello

"They took [my twin] away from me twice."[1]

$\mathcal{S}$haron Morello of Pompton Plains, New Jersey, thought of herself as a daughter, sister, wife, and mother. But one relationship was missing. On February 10, 2015, Sharon received a telephone call from her adoptive mother, Vivian Bregman, with news that was "shocking, emotional, mind-blowing and confusing—it was so surreal it was real."[2] Vivian had learned that Sharon, whom she had raised for forty-eight years, had an identical twin sister. The news brought anger, uncertainty, and many hard questions. "Who separated us?" "Why were we separated?" "Does my sister know?" Sharon needed answers. Alternatively, could what her mother told her have been a scam? Sharon confessed that she slammed down the phone after receiving this call from her mother.[3]

This story began in 2015 when Lori Shinseki, director of *The Twinning Reaction*, was searching for twins, researchers, and anyone who might have knowledge of Louise Wise Services' (LWS's) separate adoptions and the twin study that followed. Looking through documents that the Jewish Board of Family and Children's Services had agreed to release to twins she had interviewed for her film, Shinseki identified Dr. Janet David. David, now a psychologist at New York's Institute for Contemporary Psychotherapy, had worked at Neubauer's Child Development Center (CDC) in the late 1960s.[4] The records showed that David had tested identical twins in their separate homes in 1967. Shinseki contacted Dr. David to learn more about her role in the study. Over their dinner together, Shinseki discovered something more: David had also tested a twin in a New Jersey family—the adopted daughter of her college roommate—however, she couldn't recall the name. But later that evening, David's memory of her old friend returned and she called Shinseki right away. David's friend was Vivian Bregman.

195

The Twins' Families and More

Sharon's Family
Sharon Morello Lisa's reared-apart twin
Vivian Bregman Sharon's mother
Myron (Mickey) Bregman Sharon's father
Jonathan Bregman Sharon's brother
Scott Morello Sharon's husband
Nicholas Morello Sharon's elder son
Joshua Morello Sharon's younger son

Lisa's Family*
Lisa Banks Sharon's reared-apart twin
Max Sharon's adoptive brother
Larry Banks Lisa's husband

Observers, Onlookers, and Others
Mrs. Raffio Sharon and Lisa's foster mother
Janet David twin study researcher
Pamela Slaton investigative genealogist
Sara Sharon and Lisa's birth mother*
Rose Wagschal twin study researcher
Dr. Levi twin study researcher
Dr. Vivian Wolsk twin study researcher

---

* Names have been altered in the interest of privacy.

In a televised interview broadcast in 2018, David explained that she had been an administrative assistant at the CDC and was asked to do a number of home studies "like yours [Sharon's] and a couple of others."[5] In a 2015 email message to Sharon's mother, David wrote, "I only visited you once which means I saw the other twin once—as I was subbing for another research assistant."[6] A "Face Sheet" completed by the twin study researchers shows that David was actually at the Bregman home on seven occasions, between August 1966 and March 1968, but there may have been as many as nine such visits—a handwritten note on the Face Sheet indicates that films were made in May and June of 1967, but the researchers' names are not listed.[7] David's resumé lists her positions and experience, but does not include the CDC. The years 1967 to 1978 are also unaccounted for.[8] Although some people do not include predoctoral research activities in their professional biography, this represents a large gap of unexplained time.

In a remarkable occurrence of chance encounters, it turned out that August 1966 was not the first time that Janet David met Vivian Bregman. The two women had known each other in the 1950s, as college roommates, during one semester at Brandeis University, in Waltham, Massachusetts.[9] They did not meet again until David's first visit to the Bregman home when Sharon was nearly three months old. They were friendly during those home sessions, but David left a lot unsaid. She never disclosed to Vivian that she had observed Sharon five times prior to the home visits, between April and July 1966. During those months, Sharon was in foster care, sleeping in a shared crib with her twin sister.[10] Over forty years later, Dr. David still knew how to find the Bregman family, letting Shinseki deliver the real facts about Sharon's birth and placement. Later, I will return to a significant event that occurred several years after this astounding revelation.

MISSIONS IN LIFE

Following her mother's phone call, Sharon became fixated on finding hard evidence that she was a twin and on meeting her sister. In her own words, she became "obsessed" with this dual mission that nearly consumed her over the next two months. Her husband Scott said she was "hell-bent" on it. I learned that Sharon is incredibly organized, having filled ten notebooks with every name, place, date, phone call, email, and document related to her quest. On February 13, when news of her twinship was just three days old, Sharon contacted Spence-Chapin, the adoption agency that had acquired LWS's records. She was advised to register with the New York State Adoption Information Registry to obtain non-identifying data and medical material.[11] She did this. Meanwhile, Sharon read through *Identical Strangers* by LWS-separated twins Elyse Schein and Paula Bernstein, who had found their original names in the vital record collection at the New York Public Library.[12]

On February 26—just two weeks after her mother called to tell Sharon she was a twin—Sharon and Scott, who is a heating, ventilation, and air conditioning technician at New Jersey's Morristown Medical Center, headed to the library in mid-town Manhattan. Their goal was to match Sharon's birthday, first given name and initial—Danielle G, as entered on her birth certificate—with that of her twin. They searched from 11:00 a.m. to 12:45 p.m., assuming that twins' entries would appear together by identification numbers arranged in chronological order. Their plan wasn't working. Once they realized that the data were organized by year, and then alphabetically by name, they found what they were looking for. At 1:13 p.m., Sharon saw her twin's original name—Denise—and their shared last name—Greene—for the first time. It was listed seven lines under hers. Their four-digit birth certificate numbers were identical except for the last digit—7 and

8. And the four digits of the first number that appeared (for Danielle G) matched the number on the birth certificate Sharon had at home, further proof that she had identified herself and her twin. Fortunately, their birth mother had chosen first names that were similar, or the twins might have been listed pages apart.

"I didn't believe it until I saw it in the New York Public Library," Sharon said. "I mean I kind of did, but I didn't until I looked at that book to see my name, and then hers." The library did not allow visitors to photograph their records, but Sharon left with a quick snapshot. It was that important. "I could not let go of that book," she said.[13]

In late February and early March 2015, Vivian Bregman and Janet David spoke once by telephone and exchanged several email messages. Vivian reflected, "the more I thought about it the more I realized you must know more about the twin study than what you have told me. After all, you were testing the twins, which means that you must know more about the other twin than we do." David replied, "We did see both twins. I left the study around 1967–1978 so I don't have—or remember specifics. I only visited you once."[14] Note that I reproduced David's message verbatim. If she left the twin study in 1967–1968, then the 1967–1978 date indicated in the email message is a typographical error. It is also conceivable that David continued to work at the CDC from 1967 to 1978, but assessed other twins during that eleven-year period; 1967 is the last year that she was at Sharon's home.

On March 23, 2015, Sharon received a telephone call from Spence-Chapin with news that was nearly as unsettling as her mother's February phone call. *Sharon was not a twin after all!* An agency staff member had been asked to read a prepared narrative to Sharon as evidence of this latest discovery. But as Sharon listened, she realized that the details did not fit her family's circumstances—even her date of birth was wrong. She was certain that the narrative could not be hers, especially because she had found her name and her twin's name in the library records. Nevertheless, Sharon, her mother, and her father were in turmoil. The following day, a Spence-Chapin administrator called Sharon to apologize and to admit that the information read to her was from someone else's file. Later that evening, Sharon received a second call from Spence-Chapin, this time to confirm that she *was* a twin. She received a letter and the correct newborn narrative from the agency a week later and was told the narrative had been placed in both twins' files.

BEGINNINGS

There is a picture in Sharon's photo album showing a woman holding newborn identical twin girls with the caption, "Your first picture. You are on

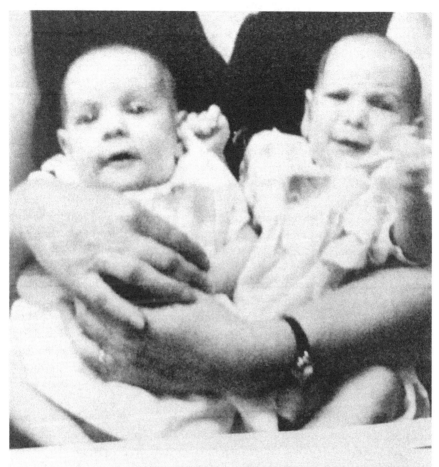

Woman holding you
social worker who lied and separated you

Figure 11.1. Identical twins, Lisa Banks (L) and Sharon Morello (R). The twins' birth mother wrote the caption under the photo. However, social workers did not decide to separate the twins—that was the policy of LWS. Courtesy of Sharon Morello.

right." A second picture is much like the first, but the caption reads, "Woman holding you—social worker who lied and separated you." There is also a picture of just one baby. "I didn't see you for this photo. Sent to me right before adoption. I never saw you again. Sad is not a strong enough word." The words under each photo were written by Sharon's birth mother, Sara, who sent them to Sharon.

Sharon found her birth mother in May 2016, over a year after learning she was a twin. There is some suggestion that Sara had looked for her twins but never found them. Sharon and Sara have spoken by telephone but have never met; later, I will say more about why this was the case. I asked Sharon about the second picture showing the social worker whom her birth mother had accused of lying. Sara had been led to believe that the twins would be adopted together. She had signed the papers for relinquishing her daughters, then phoned LWS a week later to see how they were doing. She was heartbroken to learn that they would be separated.[15]

"Your birth mother showed a considerable amount of warmth and sensitivity towards you and sister after you were born. She requested that you be in her room rather than in the nursery so you would get extra attention. . . . Your birth mother visited with you and your sister two times after birth."[16]

Twenty-year-old Sara had been referred to LWS by a psychologist she was seeing during her pregnancy. Her first appointment was in October 1965 when she was four months pregnant. She was five feet tall with a slight build, straight black hair, brown eyes, and a light medium, freckled complexion. After earning her high school degree, Sara worked for an insurance company and an attorney, before completing one year of college. Her first serious boyfriend was the twins' birth father whom she met at college; he was a sophomore who was twenty-one years old when the twins were born. He stood five feet, nine inches tall, with a slight build, blond hair, and blue eyes. Sara loved him, but felt he was somewhat immature and irresponsible; he didn't feel ready for marriage when his mother suggested it. Both birth parents were Caucasian and Jewish.

In June 1965 Sara suspected that she was pregnant, but she waited several months before contacting LWS for assistance. The agency arranged for Sara to be admitted to Lakeview, their maternity shelter, on November 15, 1965, where she remained until the birth of her twins on March 14, 1966, at thirty-nine weeks.[17] Sharon was born first at 7:28 a.m., and her twin sister followed at 7:41 a.m. The pregnancy was uneventful, except for Sara's preeclampsia[18] and Sharon's low forceps delivery.[19] Sharon's birth weight was four pounds, thirteen ounces, and her birth length was eighteen and three-quarter inches. The average birth weight of female twins born at thirty-five weeks is a little over five pounds, so Sharon's weight was considered satisfactory; still, she was small for a twin born at thirty-nine weeks. She required an incubator, but oxygen was not needed. Her overall health was good as reflected in her Apgar score of nine.[20]

Some early physical descriptions of Sharon and her twin sister match closely, as expected for identical twins.[21] Both newborns had curly hair, blue eyes, an upturned nose, a pretty mouth, a red mark on the eyelid and nape of the neck, and well-proportioned bodies. However, Sharon was somewhat smaller, her face was thinner, her almond-shaped eyes differed from her sister's round ones, and her hair was light brown, whereas her sister's hair was described as reddish brown. Interestingly, identical twins may show greater average differences in birth weight than do fraternal twins, given their unique prenatal circumstances which may include mutual circulation and shared placentation.[22] In fact, Sharon's birth weight was 86 percent that of her sister's. However identical twins' weights generally converge over time—on June 13, 1966, when the twins were in foster care, Sharon's weight increased to 97 percent of her sister's weight.[23]

Some of their early differences, such as weight and hair color, probably faded over time—observers often exaggerate identical twins' slight differences in order to tell them apart. Anecdotally, some people believe that one identical twin always has a thinner face, but there is no scientific evidence to support this claim.[24] Sharon's face appeared thinner, but she was also the lower birth weight twin.

The twins left the hospital on March 22 to be cared for by "Mrs. Raffio" in her boarding home.[25] Mrs. Raffio was the mother of three sons and described as intelligent and warm. During their three-month stay in the boarding home, the twins were visited regularly by an LWS social worker who monitored their development. A placement summary shows that Sharon was observed seven times, between March 24 and May 24, 1966, by "S. Schneer," presumably the social worker from LWS. She was also observed twice, on June 14 and July 8, 1966, by "IR." Notes on Sharon's feeding and sleeping behaviors form the bases of these reports.[26] Presumably, all LWS adoptees, not just twins, would have undergone similar observations. Some early descriptions in the twins' Spence-Chapin narrative appear to be those made by Schneer—such as having an internal "alarm clock" that awakened her for feedings, while other characteristics—"less active and vigorous" than her twin—may have come from other sources. Schneer's document lists the final date of surrender by the birth mother as May 6, 1966, as does the Spence-Chapin report.

Sharon was also visited by Janet David from the CDC. David was not a social worker, but an administrative assistant who contributed to the study. David completed her five research visits on days that the LWS social worker was not present. David was accompanied by a Dr. Levi on four of these five visits, during which time they observed and filmed Sharon's behaviors—perhaps it was David and/or Levi who had detected differences in the twins' activity and vigor. Consistent with the Spence-Chapin narrative Sharon received, the first paragraph of Schneer's document states that Danielle Greene was admitted to her foster home on March 22.[27] It also states that Danielle was referred by a person (name redacted) of "JGS"—the Jewish Board of Guardians.[28] The director of the JGS's CDC was Dr. Peter Neubauer.[29] Sharon would remain in foster care for a three-month period until she was adopted. Her sister left a week earlier to join her new family.[30]

THE BREGMANS

Vivian and Myron (Mickey) Bregman of Wayne, New Jersey, were married in December 1957. They were well educated, had good jobs, and were financially comfortable. Vivian, a college graduate, had dreams of becoming a veterinarian. When she was advised that "girls do not become vets," she chose professional dog training as her profession. Mickey earned a bachelor's of science degree at the University of Oklahoma where he developed a passion for horseback riding. He became an electrical engineer and president of Rexon, an engineering, manufacturing, and development company.[31] Vivian and Mickey were eager to start a family, but after three years of marriage and miscarriages, they decided to adopt a baby. Vivian's mother urged her to go to LWS in order to adopt a Jewish baby. The Bregmans took her advice and in early 1963 the couple received their blond, blue-eyed son Jonathan when he was just one month old. Jonathan had been cared for in a foster home after his birth.

On January 23, 1965, when Jonathan was two years old, Vivian and Mickey sent a letter to LWS indicating their interest in adopting a second child—a baby girl. They received a reply ten days later from senior caseworker Dorothy Scherl, explaining that priority was granted to couples adopting for the first time and to couples whose oldest child was three years old. Still, Scherl offered to add the Bregmans to her list of interested parents. In early December, Scherl contacted the couple again to say that their request would be considered upon receipt of the application form and fee, although the agency's placement priorities were unchanged. Six months passed. Then, in the summer 1966 Vivian and Mickey were elated when a three-month-old female infant became available.

The couple arrived early on July 7, 1966, for their first meeting with their new daughter. When she was brought in, they instantly held her, cuddled her, and played with her. They took her home the next day. Their son, three-year-old Jonathan, brought gifts for his new sister—a teething ring and a plush puppy. "They [your parents] had no doubts about you [Sharon] being their child."[32] Some non-identifying information was provided to the Bregmans when they adopted their baby. And they had already agreed to have researchers visit their home for the "child development study" in which Sharon was enrolled—they understood that the purpose of the study was to see how much the child resembles his or her adoptive parents. As Vivian said, if adopting a baby was contingent upon learning to fly, she would have done so.[33] An "Arrival" announcement for "Sharon Alissa" is proudly displayed in the family's photo album.

Thinking back, Vivian admitted to being "suspicious" that Sharon's birth weight was under five pounds. She actually wondered if Sharon might have been a twin whose birth weights are typically low; however, the thought was fleeting and one she didn't take seriously. She mentioned this to no one.[34] About ten years before Vivian learned the truth about her daughter, she happened to pick up *Identical Strangers*, the same book that Sharon had read once the discovery was revealed. She noted that the LWS twins who had written the book had been separated in the 1960s as had Sharon, so could Sharon be a twin? Again, Vivian quickly dismissed this possibility. "It was a stupid thought, and there were so many babies adopted from LWS," she said.

Once Sharon was in her new home, her family received "routine post-placement supervisory visits" on August 5, September 20, and November 15, 1966, followed by an office visit on January 6, 1967. The first home visit was originally scheduled for August 2, but Sharon's brother developed the mumps, so it was delayed. None of these dates are times that the researchers were present, with the exception of August 5, the day that David and Levi first visited the Bregman home. Perhaps the researchers *did* conduct the first home visit; the "Home Visit" dates of November 29, 1966, and January 13, 1967, by the social worker do not match those on the twin study Face Sheet or the Spence-Chapin narrative. This suggests that the Bregmans had both regular visits by a social worker *and* regular visits by the researchers. It is also worth noting that Sharon was not adopted until she was three months old, whereas her brother was adopted at one month. All the identical twins and triplets in the study were adopted when they were between two and a half to six months of age, probably to have time to observe them together in their foster homes and/ or to coordinate their separate placements. As I indicated, the twins' families were chosen because they had successfully raised a child approximately three years older than the twin. With one exception, each twin's older sibling was of the opposite sex; Melanie, whom I described in chapter 8, had a sister older by three years and a brother older by six years. Some co-twins were placed in families with different incomes and social status, such as the triplets portrayed in *Three Identical Strangers*; Sharon later discovered that she and her twin were another such pair. This decision would have given an informed glimpse of how different environments affect the expression of identical genes; my book on identical Colombian twins switched at birth illustrates this concept quite clearly.[35] However, Bernard denied that such placements were intentionally arranged—"The people who were making the placements, the social workers, didn't know anything about these factors. . . . We didn't place the twins for research purposes."[36] But Bernard also acknowledged that "it was no accident that they all had siblings." She explained that families who had successfully raised a child were chosen; having an older sibling guarded against the difficulties of a twin being an only child.[37] All older siblings were three to four years older.

LWS was a private, non-profit social welfare agency. The New York Federation of Jewish Philanthropies and New York City Department of Welfare provided 80 percent of their support, with the remainder covered by client fees. Client fees were determined on a scale commensurate with each family's combined income during the year preceding the adoption, plus a twenty-dollar application cost.[38] In 1966 when the Bregmans adopted Sharon, fees ranged between two hundred dollars for incomes under forty-five hundred dollars, and the maximum amount of eighteen hundred dollars for incomes of six thousand dollars and above. The Bregmans paid eighteen hundred dollars according to the agency's set schedule: one-half, or nine hundred dollars, on July 15, following child placement; one-quarter, or $450, on October 1, three months after placement; and one-quarter on January 6, six months after placement. The 1966 fee of eighteen hundred dollars would be equivalent to $14,545.70 in 2020.[39]

Sharon's legal adoption occurred on April 19, 1967, in the Surrogate's Court of New York County. She grew up like most children in the middle-class New Jersey suburbs, except for not knowing that she had an identical twin and that she was part of a secret study.

DAUGHTER, SISTER, WIFE, MOTHER

Sharon knew from a very young age that she had been adopted. As a child, her mother often read *The Chosen Baby* to her, a beloved children's book about adoption.[40] Vivian knew that hiding such news from children can upset then when they do find out, so she tried to be open and honest with her son and daughter. Vivian had collected several children's books on the topic, including *The Adopted Family*,[41] but Sharon insisted that *The Chosen Baby* was "hers."

Family photographs show Sharon as a smiling baby, a young girl in pigtails, a ballerina wearing a tutu, a rider high on a horse, and a dutiful daughter seated next to her mom. As a child, Sharon attended the local elementary and middle schools until the sixth or seventh grade. She remained in the LWS-CDC twin study during these years, until 1978 when she turned twelve. Records show that Janet David's last visit with the Bregmans was in March 1968. The last home visitation sheets I inspected, dated January 1970 to June 1973, listed other investigators, among them Dr. Esther Gottstein, Mrs. Blanca Masor, Dr. Susan Farber, and Dr. Vivian Wolsk. In June 1973, Rose Wagschal, who had made visits to the Bregmans' home, sent a letter to Sharon's mother informing her that she would no longer be making these visits and named one of the aforementioned researchers as her replacement.[42] It is possible that some or all of these researchers did not study Sharon's identical twin sister, Lisa. That is because Dr. Esther R. Gottstein (now Goshen-Gottstein), the clinical psychologist whom I introduced in chapter 2, recalls visiting only one twin in three separated identical pairs.[43] However, I previously noted that some assistants, such as Dr. Larry Perlman, had studied both twins.

Sharon attended kindergarten through the ninth grade at her local elementary and middle schools until she was fifteen years old. The following year she enrolled in a private boarding school in Vershire, Vermont.[44] Sharon was attracted to the school because of its equestrian program, although she didn't take full advantage of it while she was there—typical teenage turmoils were probably why.[45] She left the school several years later and earned her high school degree back home in New Jersey. After a brief stint in cosmetology, she worked as a bank teller and at various other jobs. She married her husband Scott on April 26, 1991, and was the manager of her brother's liquor store for

Figure 11.2. Sharon's family (L). Front row (L to R): Sharon's parents Mickey and Vivian Bregman; Sharon Morello. Back row (L to R): Sharon's sons Nicholas and Joshua; Sharon's husband Scott Morello. Courtesy of Sharon Morello. Individual photo of Sharon Morello (R). Photo by Scott Morello.

about a year. She gave birth to her two sons, Nicholas in 1993 and Joshua in 1995, and stayed home to raise them. Between 2000 and 2006, when her boys were older, Sharon performed various volunteer duties at a local elementary school and was involved in home childcare until 2010. Five years later, she was formally hired as an aide for school lunches and transportation, working solely as a lunch aide after 2015. In 2018, she became a para aide at a local elementary school where she assists in activities with autistic children—it's a job that means a great deal to her. Vivian called her daughter "a wonderful young lady."

At the start of this chapter, I wrote that Sharon thinks of herself as a daughter, sister, wife, and mother. Being an identical twin was not something that had crossed her mind. But once she knew it was true, she thought of little else except meeting her twin. The timing seemed significant because Sharon had undergone breast cancer surgery just a few months before her twinship was known, so perhaps her sister needed her help.[46] For this reason, she disclosed her medical history to Spence-Chapin to persuade them to work quickly on her behalf, and on behalf of her twin. Having weathered the emotional challenges of cancer diagnosis and treatment, Sharon was confident in her ability speak up and demand answers.

MEETING LISA: BEGINNINGS AND ENDINGS

At Sharon's request, Spence-Chapin contacted her sister on April 22, 2015, to break the silence about her being a twin. A week later Sharon received a letter from the agency saying that her twin sister Lisa agreed to meet with her. The next step was for both women to complete what Sharon called a "twins' application."[47] Sharon returned the form to Spence-Chapin on May 1, for forwarding to the New York State Registry in Albany. By May 4, the registry had received the forms and their mutual consent to have their names released to one another. On May 19, Sharon found Lisa on Facebook, and Lisa replied immediately. Elated, Sharon sent an email message to attorneys Barry Coburn and Kara Allen at Coburn & Greenbaum LLC, and social worker Dana Stallard and legal manager Jackie Delacy at Spence-Chapin, announcing, "Now I can totally focus on my health and my new friendship with my sister."[48] The twins spoke for the first time on May 20. Sharon described Lisa as "floored"— by then, her sister had known the truth about their twinship for only a few weeks, whereas Sharon had had three months to try to adapt.

I tried contacting Lisa and her husband by email, but received no replies. I did not expect to. Lisa declined Lori Shinseki's invitation to appear in *The Twinning Reaction*, and according to Sharon, Lisa prefers staying away from the media. In deference to her wishes, my references to Lisa and her family members use assumed names. Sadly, the twins are no longer in touch after a fantastic first meeting and some good times after that. Still, the days leading up to their first meeting on June 7 were difficult for Sharon because Lisa's brother Max, an attorney, insisted that the women undergo DNA analysis to prove that they were identical twins. Max is four years older than his sister and an adoptee, although not from LWS. He sent Sharon a kit for the DNA testing which she had agreed to do. Nevertheless, the twins and their husbands managed to meet before the results were available.

The two couples met at a neutral location, choosing a scenic overlook about halfway between their two homes, along Route 80 in New Jersey.[49] Scott and Sharon arrived first. Scott described how things unfolded. "When [Lisa and her husband Larry] got out of the car, the twins hugged each other—it was real." After chatting together for about a half hour, they decided to have lunch at a nearby restaurant. Sharon and Lisa sat on one side of the table, and the two husbands sat on the other side. "It was wild," Scott recalled. "They carried on like they had always known each other. It was 'twin overload.'" According to Sharon, "It was wonderful—from day one it was like we knew each other. We clicked totally. We had lived parallel lives." Both twins had two children—Sharon had two boys, and Lisa had a boy and a girl—and both twins had named their sons "Joshua," just because they liked that name. Similarity in child-naming is one that my colleagues and I observed among several reunited identical pairs in Minnesota. The famous "Jim twins"—Jim Lewis and Jim Springer who launched the study in 1979—had named their sons James Alan and James Allan. A British pair, Dorothy and Bridget, known for wearing seven rings, three bracelets, and a watch, had named their sons Richard Andrew and Andrew Richard, and their daughters Catherine Louise and Karen Louise.[50] Such matches are challenging to explain. Perhaps each twin associates a certain name with status or prestige, likes the sound of the name, or believes in preserving names across generations. It is conceivable that these tendencies, which could lead identical twins to independently choose similar names for their children, have a partial genetic basis. I do not recall studying reared-apart fraternal twins whose sons and daughters had matching names.

Sharon and Lisa are the same height, four feet, eleven inches tall, and about the same weight. Both twins have freckles, as did their biological mother, although Sharon has a more generous sprinkling. Freckle count is influenced by genetic factors, being more similar in identical twins than fraternal twins, and is more common in people with lighter than darker complexions.[51] Both twins were working or had worked in school settings. When they met, Lisa was doing the bookkeeping for Larry's business, as Sharon had done previously at her brother's liquor store. Both twins loved dogs and rode or had wanted to ride horses. Among their greatest fears they named snakes, spiders, and heights.

When they ordered lunch, the twins had a chance to discuss their food preferences and most of them matched—eggplant parmesan, spaghetti, and salads are their favorites. They disagree on veal, which Sharon loves and her sister loathes. When the twins started eating, an obvious difference between them was that Sharon is left-handed and Lisa is right-handed. All three identical female sets and the male triplets in the twin study had a left-handed member. The twins in the one male set also appear to be opposite-handed.

Scott continued, "I was not so much struck with their similarities, but with how well they got along. They were so in sync, moving their heads back and forth in a complementary way without thinking about it, just enjoying each other."[52] Scott got along well with Lisa's husband. The meeting lasted for two hours.

On June 9, two days after they first met, Sharon and Lisa received the DNA test results. The finding confirmed what LWS had told them, that they were identical twins with over 99.99 percent probability.[53]

The next time the twins met was at Lisa's home, together with their families. After that, Lisa and her family visited Sharon's home for the day. Their children, the "genetic half-siblings," liked one another enormously. Sharon's mother Vivian saw greater physical differences than similarities between the twins, but some resulted from cosmetic intervention—Lisa had permed her naturally straight hair, and Sharon had had rhinoplasty because of a broken nose. But Vivian recognized a "family type" that was common to both twins. Vivian shared Sharon's disappointment that Lisa did not wish to go public with their story. Both mother and daughter believe it should be told—Sharon has now made it her story.

Sharon and Lisa enjoyed being twins for about a year. They had agreed to find their birth mother together, but Lisa found her first and on her own. This revelation fed a mutual lack of trust, causing their seemingly close but fragile relationship to crumble. Such conflicts have cascading effects, a situation I will touch on again. The twins have now been estranged for over two years. As Sharon's husband said, "Sharon is a straightforward person, Lisa is more reserved. Sharon's motto is: 'I should not have to work for a relationship—it works or it does not work.'"[54] The twins' hard moments echo what transpired among the triplets when Bob walked away from the reared-apart triplets' joint business venture. Recall that in 1988, the three brothers launched Triplets Roumanian Steakhouse, their lively establishment in lower Manhattan. Clashing ideas about running the restaurant led Bob to leave after several years and enroll in Brooklyn Law School; he was admitted to the New York State Bar in 1998.[55]

Relationships between separated twins occasionally fall apart, even when they start off well. It was heartwarming to watch identical twins Mark

Newman and Jerry Levey became instant friends as they completed the week-long assortment of tests at the University of Minnesota. Reunited at age thirty-one, both were dedicated to volunteer fire fighting, a calling to which they brought shared understanding and respect. Their fondness for drinking Bud-weiser beer, going fishing, and hanging out with friends at Luigi's Tavern in southern New Jersey drew them closely together, even while they kept their separate lives. Mark once said that being with Jerry "was like being with me." But when Jerry got married in 2002, at age forty-eight, the twins' relationship unraveled. Mark believed that Jerry's new wife, Susan, was too controlling and was coming between them. Jerry didn't agree, but said that Mark had to do what he had to do.[56] Opportunities to resolve differences that reared-together twins and siblings experience during their shared childhood had been denied in the case of the triplets, the firemen, and now Sharon and Lisa. Sharon and Lisa remain identical strangers despite their instant rapport.

Most reared-apart twins I have worked with have gotten along well, enjoying their common interests and the in-laws, nieces, and nephews they never dreamed about. However, reunited identical twins generally express greater social closeness and feelings of familiarity than reunited fraternal twins, possibly due to their perceptions of similarity.[57] The few pairs whose members have parted ways still say they are grateful for the chance to have met and to have learned more about their lives. And while it rarely happens, some reared-together twins cannot settle their differences and decide to end their relationship—perhaps these twins have behaviors or beliefs that get in the way. Being apart can ease their conflicts, but it does not ease their loss.

Sharon thinks that all the separated twins have difficulty trusting others.[58] She senses depression and sadness among the separated twins she has known and wonders if things would have been different had they been raised together. Sharon's parents say she was a clingy child, but Sharon says she never felt that something was missing. "But did I know something deep inside?" she wonders.[59]

There is more to the broken bond between Sharon and her sister, possibly dooming them from the start. Sharon was placed with a financially affluent family. Her large home was located in a desirable New Jersey suburb, and her parents treated her adoption proudly and openly. Lisa was raised in a financially less comfortable family. She had grown up in a Bronx apartment with parents who took a dim view of adoption, keeping it largely in the background. Whereas most twins were tested and observed by the researchers at home, Lisa was brought to the CDC for this purpose. Perhaps her home was too small or too crowded to enable effective assessment; however, the twins' different testing venues would have compromised the comparability of the findings. Sharon senses that her more advantageous background aroused jealousy in her sister, even though Sharon knows she is not to blame—she had no control over where they were placed.[60]

With the help of investigative genealogist Pamela Slaton, Sharon located her birth mother, Sara, in July 2016.[61] Sara had lived about fifteen miles from Sharon's childhood home in Wayne, New Jersey, and had attended college about ten miles away. Birth mother and daughter might have passed each other on the street any number of times without knowing. Sharon was shocked to learn that Lisa had located Sara on her own two months earlier, in May 2016, and had met. More upsetting, Sharon was aware that her birth mother had turned against her, but for reasons she could not comprehend. They were only in touch by email and telephone and not until September 2016. Later, she wondered if the infant photos that she received from Sara were sent out of guilt. Regardless, Sharon sensed growing distance and secrecy on Lisa's part. According to Sharon's husband Scott, "Things got weird after that."[62]

In the 1950s and 1960s, LWS did not sufficiently consider the negative effects of the twins' separate rearing on their relationships, were they to meet. Bernard's 1983 response to *60 Minutes'* planned program on twins states that LWS initially reasoned that "the early parent-child relationships and formative years so critical to the development of individuality would already have been experienced by the child thus serving, to that extent, the purposes of the twin's growth as an individual."[63] In her opinion, withholding twinship information from families would be less damaging than disclosure. This assertion was supported by recognizing that, "[The twins'] psychological status as of then was unknown to CDC staff. . . . This made the impact all the more unpredictable of intruding on these adolescents with such emotionally complicating information." Media exposure most likely made Bernard and colleagues admit that the separations had consequences. And the media was interested.

HOME VISITS REVISITED

After *60 Minutes'* aborted attempts to produce a program in the early 1980s—with twins Tim and Ilene, and Kathy and Betsy—and the late 1990s with the identical triplets, ABC's *20/20* aired segments of Shinseki's film *The Twinning Reaction* in March 2018.[64] A week before it aired, Sharon's father Mickey sent an email message to family and friends urging them to watch.[65] The subject line was "A Tale of Two Sisters." Mickey wrote, "Some 50 years ago we adopted a daughter from the Louise Wise Agency. She came with the proviso that she was in a psychological study. . . . We thought it was cool that our daughter came with a built-in psychologist and readily agreed." Mickey explained how Shinseki had found researcher Janet David who "spilled the beans" about the Bregmans. "After getting whatever the journalist had, we embarked on the difficult journey against the forces of bureaucracy and the law and verified that our daughter was a twin. . . . The *20/20* episode is the tale of this unethical study."

The *20/20* program included an extraordinary clip that was not in *The Twinning Reaction*. Producers brought Sharon, her mother, and Janet David together again after fifty years. The last time they were together, David had recorded clinical impressions of Sharon and her mother.

The meeting was filmed in a conference room in midtown Manhattan.[66] Dr. David sat alone, waiting for the others to arrive. She appeared uncomfortable, looking about and running her hands up and down her legs. Sharon arrived with her mother and with Pamela Slaton, the woman who had found her birth mother, Sara. Slaton's husband and a camera crew were also there. After a quick handshake Sharon said, "My first question is why you never called even when the study was over, to say there's a twin out there, if you ever want to find her." David explained that she had left the study shortly after meeting the family and "had nothing to do with anything." She was a new graduate student, "low on the totem pole," and did not influence policy—she had no authority and no clout. Then Vivian spoke up. "But you *knew* that she was a twin and you never mentioned it!" David responded that this was the way the study was set up, that the families didn't know that they had a twin. Vivian countered, "You know it is something I would have *really* liked to know." David nodded. Vivian pointed toward Sharon. "And so would she."

The film clip lasted for one minute and thirty-nine seconds, leaving me curious about what did not air and what people thought about the encounter.[67] "One of the guys—maybe from the camera crew, said he wanted to slug [Dr. David]," Sharon told me. She credited David for coming, but complained that David just sat there as if nothing was at stake. "She had no heart. She was just a body. There was no remorse, never an apology to my mom," Sharon said. "It was a rough day." At the end, everyone just left. "I still can't get over it," Sharon confessed. Vivian recalled watching David walk down the driveway when she arrived for the first home visit—and the moment David suddenly remembered that she knew her. Vivian still speaks bitterly and angrily about her college roommate's silence.[68]

I reached out to Dr. David several times, by letter and by email. I wanted to hear her side of the story, but she never returned the contact.

OPENING THE ARCHIVES

"The data belong to me."

Sharon is represented by the same attorneys from Hunton Andrews Kurth LLP as are several other LWS twins. Like them, Sharon is furious and frustrated by the time it is taking to obtain her materials that still remain sealed in the Yale University archives. As I have indicated elsewhere, Yale can only release these records upon approval from the Jewish Board of Family and Children's Services.

On November 17, 2015, Sharon received a portion of her records—seven hundred pages, much of it heavily redacted because she wasn't told that prior consent is required from anyone whose name appears on a given page. A great deal of her data, including photographs and films, have not been released and will stay restricted until 2065. Meanwhile, Sharon obtained consent from her parents and brother in this final attempt to receive her remaining materials. She will not have access to everything because getting consent from her twin sister is not possible, due to their estrangement.

Sharon shared a great deal of the material she had received from Yale's archives, and I examined it carefully. I wanted to know the kinds of tests, interviews, and activities that were completed by the twins and their families. Out of respect for her privacy, I will reveal none of Sharon's personal data.

Visits to the Bregman household—and presumably the other twins' homes—consisted of psychological tests, parent interviews, child observation, child filming, and clinical impressions of twins and family members.[69] Psychological tests of intelligence were the Cattell Infant Intelligence Scale, Merrill-Palmer Scales, and Stanford-Binet.[70] Other abilities and behaviors were assessed by the Einstein-Piaget Scales,[71] Bender Visual Motor Gestalt Test,[72] Human Figure Drawing Test,[73] Children's Apperception Test (CAT),[74] Three Wishes Tasks, Sentence Completion Test,[75] and Rorschach Inkblot Test.[76] A psychological test component took place at most visits, although the actual tests administered varied with the child's age. Sharon's chronological age, mental age, and IQ were regularly reported, supplemented by a summary highlighting her intellectual strengths and weaknesses.[77] Clinical impressions, such as Sharon's Freudian stage of development, based on behaviors such as her observed dependence, frustration, obstinance, and anxiety, were routinely made. A "dream report" was included in the November 1972 home visit when Sharon was six and a half years old. Similar to some other siblings, Sharon's older brother Jonathan wondered why he wasn't tested.

Scattered within the archived pages are observations and characterizations of Sharon and her family. Their mannerisms, what they wore, the condition of their home, and even the weather were subjects of interest to the research team. Sharon was labeled "Miss Worrywart," a name she found annoying and unnecessary.[78] The Bregmans' home was described as "messy," angering Vivian quite a bit. "I had two children, a boy and a girl. I was running a *Star Trek*'s store ten minutes from here and training dogs, so the house was a little messy—and frankly, everybody I know who had babies has a messy house." Vivian also told me that before she received her son Jonathan, an LWS staff member, "Ms. Fisher," came to inspect her home. Ms. Fisher apparently disliked the Bregmans' large German shepherd that eagerly licked the bare toes of her sandaled feet. Vivian was about to joke that "the dog is just tasting you," but didn't for fear of saying the wrong thing and not getting the baby.

Sharon's materials from Yale University's archives included a March 8, 1966, letter from Dr. Peter Neubauer to Dr. S. B. Gusberg, director of obstetrics and gynecology at Mt. Sinai Hospital.[79] Sharon and her twin sister were born at Mt. Sinai six days later. Neubauer's first purpose was to "reacquaint" Dr. Gusberg with "the outlines of our twin research, jointly sponsored by our Agency [the Jewish Board of Guardians—CDC], the Louise Wise Services, and the Columbia University Division of Community Psychiatry."[80] Neubauer enclosed a copy of 1963 correspondence between Gusberg's office and Dr. Bernard. The second purpose of his letter was to request delivery room information and blood samples that, Neubauer understood, were routinely gathered in Gusberg's department. Neubauer's letter was sent "in the hope that we can get this information along with the twins' blood samples." Routine analyses, such as the test for phenylketonuria that is done for all newborns, were most likely performed at Mt. Sinai on the twins' blood—results from this test appear on Sharon's hospital chart. It is possible that other, non-standard tests were done at the request of the twin researchers, either at Mt. Sinai or at Columbia University. Such tests, such as establishing each pairs' twin type as identical or fraternal, would have been done using the blood samples that Neubauer requested.[81]

I found another request for medical information in Sharon's archived files. This 1971 letter is from researcher Rose Wagschal, written when Sharon was five and a half years old. Wagschal had made a number of visits to the Bregmans' home as part of the twin study. Her letter asked Sharon's family physician to provide Sharon's "entire medical record." Wagschal wanted office visits, home visits, illnesses, hospitalizations, growth charts, family histories, and any other developmental information. Sharon assumes that her doctor complied with this request. In contrast, Sharon's efforts to obtain her own study materials have met with resistance, but now appear to be moving forward, albeit very slowly. In 2065, anyone can know her name and access her confidential data. She and several other twins are convinced that something is being hidden from them. But Sharon is less interested in what that possible secret might be than in obtaining what she believes is her personal property.

FOREWORD AND FILE NOTE

In April 2020, I ordered *The Adopted Family*, a two-part children's book that Vivian Bregman had read to Sharon and Jonathan when they were small.[82] The book was written to describe adoption in simple, understandable terms and to help parents through the process of explaining adoption to their children. The two-page foreword compliments the authors—themselves adoptive parents and adoptees—for helping to minimize anxieties associated with adoption and strengthen possibilities for healthy family relationships. It was written by Dr. Viola Bernard. Bernard lauds the balance between the guidelines offered to parents and the freedom they were given to apply this advice according to their individual circumstances. The main value of the book, as Bernard saw it, was in "how the parents use it with the child." When *The Adopted Family* was published in 1951, LWS had separated one pair of twins (Tim and Ilene) and would separate another pair the following year (Kathy and Betsy). The parents of these twins, the Bregmans, and at least sixteen other couples might have used the book differently had they understood their situation.

In the event that one separated twin learned about a twin brother or sister, Bernard said she would feel compelled to tell the truth to the other twin.[83] Recall the case of Anne and Susan in which Susan's family inadvertently discovered their daughter's twin, Anne, when she was six or seven—Bernard did tell Anne's parents, but advised both couples to conceal the truth from their children. They did so until the twins met by chance just before their seventeenth birthday. When two of the separated triplets, Bob and Eddy, met in September 1980, several days passed until the third triplet, Dave, came forward. In the days before and after the time of the second reunion, LWS did not approach the families. The wave of media surrounding those two meetings could not have escaped their notice.

As I indicated earlier, in 1978, Dr. Bernard inserted an explanatory note into each twins' case record. She did so because she realized that, in the future when she and the LWS staff were gone, any inquiries would need to be addressed in an informed and helpful way.[84] In the note, Bernard described the rationale for why the twins were separated—fostering each child's individuality, especially for identical twins because of the "'mystique'" surrounding their connectedness, and easing early parenting burdens, presumably imposed by raising twins of either type. She explained that these advantages would be denied if families were informed of their child's twinship. Thus, it was considered "psychologically safer" for parents to be free of this knowledge, thus enabling LWS to make the best placements possible. As I explained, Bernard said her reasoning was grounded in the child development literature of the late 1950s. She also indicated that the twins' birth parents understood the reasons for the separation and agreed to it. She concluded by stating that "many changes" had affected adoption practices since LWS's policy of separating twins began, necessitating rethinking about twins' placement in the days to come.

Bernard reiterated that twins who were socially attached to one another were not separated. Again, where are these reared-together twins, and why has a single intact pair never been found?

Bernard's note was provided only to the identical twins in the study, not to twins from the four or five fraternal pairs who were ostensibly parted for the same reasons. The basis for this decision is unknown. Other uncertainties in her document are redactions in the first and last sentences. In both cases, reference is made to the joint twin study by LWS and the _____. The blank would logically be filled in by "Dr. Peter Neubauer," the "Child Development Center," and/or the "Jewish Board of Guardians," whose participation was always clear. The omission brings another element of secrecy to the collaboration, intentional or not.

I asked Sharon if Bernard's note brought comfort or consolation to her or to her family. She said that reading it only made her feel worse, especially because her parents who were so desperate to have children would have loved raising twins. "They took advantage of the kids and the people who wanted them," she said. And as Sharon stated regretfully—and angrily—at the start of this chapter, "They took her away from me twice."

Unpublished or Unavailable?

In Search of the Findings

> "Many investigations have been made into the development of twins who have been separated during their lifetime; very few can be found in which the separation occurred at birth." –Peter Neubauer, 1973[1]

The twins and their families still wonder why the findings from the study have not been published, why the records were sealed, and why the twins have had so much difficulty acquiring them. Many scholars, including twin researchers who constantly comb the scientific twin-related literature, are either unaware of the study, first read about it in papers published in 2005,[2] or learned of it from the 2017 and 2018 documentary films. In this chapter, I will survey the publications produced by the twin research team. I will also replay the uncertainties and worries that arose with regard to publishing a book about the study, and the decisions and actions that occurred along the way.

It is also important to ask why Yale University, located seventy miles outside of New York City in New Haven, Connecticut, became the sanctuary for Neubauer's twin study collection. The Jewish Board of Family and Children's Services' (JBFCS's) Child Development Center (CDC), the New York Psychoanalytic Society and Institute, and the Psychoanalytic Centers at New York University and Columbia University would have been more logical and convenient choices. Neubauer directed the CDC from 1951 to 1985, was a former trainee and active member of the New York Psychoanalytic Society and Institute, was a clinical professor at New York University's Institute for Psychoanalytic Education,[3] and was a lecturer and chairman emeritus at Columbia University's Psychoanalytic Center for Training and Research.[4] Another obvious choice would have been Zero to Three, a Washington, DC-based organization dedicated to promoting infant and toddler well-being;

Neubauer was a founding member of Zero to Three.[5] Neubauer was neither a Yale University alumnus nor faculty member, but he had several Yale colleagues and was senior editor of a Yale University Press journal, *The Psychoanalytic Study of the Child.*[6] I will look into this issue, and the question of why the files were sealed at all, more closely in chapters that follow.

Thanks to the two documentary films, *The Twinning Reaction* and *Three Identical Strangers*, many people now know about the hidden study that gathered information on separated twins and triplets in the 1960s and 1970s. They also know that the materials of the head researcher, Dr. Peter Neubauer, were placed in Yale University's archives, to remain sealed until 2065. The twin study files of Neubauer's collaborator, Dr. Viola Bernard, are sheltered at Columbia University's archives, closed to the public until January 1, 2021; however, some files may stay closed indefinitely.[7] It was also possible that Bernard's twin study materials would remain sealed until 2065 in order to coincide with Neubauer's release date. That is because Columbia University's literary executor who received the material had assumed that Neubauer's papers were to remain closed until 2021.[8] When I spoke with him in 2019, Stephen E. Novak, head of Archives and Special Collections at Columbia's Health Sciences Library, planned to review Bernard's papers in fall 2020 and forward his recommendation to the university's legal counsel.[9] The files were made available in January. However, since Bernard's files have been opened, a faculty member of Columbia University's psychiatry department has objected that twin study participants can be identified. Thus, researchers are required to "de-identify" their notes and publications.[10]

In my examination of Bernard's files in October 2019, I did not find any twin study publications bearing her name as author or co-author. It is unlikely that such materials would be considered confidential and inappropriate for public viewing.

DISSEMINATING THE DATA

A total of four publications, variously referencing a "systematic longitudinal study," the "study of identical twins reared apart in *prospect*," "intensive observations of separated twins," and a "prospective study of twins reared apart" have appeared in the professional literature.[11] The four publications—three articles and a book—are cited in an exclusive 2020 interview with former Louise Wise Services (LWS)-CDC twin study researcher Dr. Christa Balzert, conducted by Neubauer's former friend and colleague, Dr. Lois Oppenheim.[12] These four sources, plus a 1996 chapter in an edited Austrian volume[13] and several conference presentations,[14] were cited to show that "definitive" findings from the twin study were reported in scholarly works. Neubauer's statement at the start of this chapter comes from a source that predates the four publications, but there was no reference to the LWS-CDC twin study that had been ongoing for thirteen years.

The three articles were published in 1976, 1986, and 1994, and the book, *Nature's Thumbprint*, appeared in 1990. The articles were variously authored by Samuel Abrams and Peter Neubauer, individually and jointly, and the book was co-authored by Neubauer and his son Alexander, a professional writer. All four publications were informed by psychoanalytic perspectives and draw upon detailed case study material as is characteristic of psychoanalytic studies. In their book, Neubauer and Neubauer used information from the LWS-CDC study and excerpted material from previous reared-apart twin investigations. The previous investigations consisted of individual case reports, as well as three book-length treatments that combined quantitative findings and detailed life histories from the American, British, and Danish studies conducted between 1937 and 1980. Aside from some general findings, material from the Minnesota Study of Twins Reared Apart, launched in 1979, was not included despite extensive reporting in scientific journals and the media. In some cases, Neubauer and Neubauer did not provide the original reference for the early work, and in other cases they cited secondary sources, such as Susan Farber's book on separated identical twins.[15] However, scholars familiar with these early studies will recognize some or most of them. Several anecdotes appear to be from the LWS-CDC study because they refer to separated infant twins, but they are not cited. One such anecdote describes identical twins "Shauna and Ellen," who both demanded that their mothers sprinkle cinnamon on whatever they ate.[16]

I have always appreciated the meticulous reporting of events, influences, signs, and symptoms that characterize psychoanalytic analyses. Peering deeply into the life of another individual is a fascinating and informative experience that quantitatively oriented psychologists rarely enjoy. One of my favorite papers was by the late psychiatrist and analyst Dr. George L. Engel, who published a riveting analysis of his reactions to losing his identical twin brother.[17] Just as compelling are details of the LWS twins' developmental parallels that appear in the different publications and are considered with respect to each twins' unique rearing experiences. A pair labeled "Amy and Beth," whom I mentioned in earlier chapters, showed some remarkable similarities despite their different upbringing. Amy's separation-individuation problems were tied to her mother's difficulty with hostility and negativistic behavior, and her insensitivity to Amy's need for closeness. Beth's separation-individuation problems were linked to her mother's inability to recognize and accept her differences and limitations.[18]

The investigators concluded that our genetic blueprint, or dispositional organization, largely guides human behavioral and physical maturation, but are subject to environmental contingencies. This is not a novel finding, but one that runs through every previous reared-apart twin study. However, because the LWS-CDC study followed separated identical twins in real time since birth, albeit a tiny number, the evidence of genetic effects is striking. This appears to have stunned the psychoanalytic researchers for whom early experiences play a major role in developmental outcomes.

None of the publications identify the source of the infant twins, other than to mention an "adoption agency." Dr. Bernard's rationale for separating the twins is not explained, and she is mentioned only in the 1976 paper as a "consultant." The Neubauers' 1990 book omits the 1976 and 1986 papers from the notes section and from the selected bibliography. Finally, few details are given about the number of participating pairs and research methods in any of the papers; in fact, this number is still debated among people familiar with the project. An exception is a footnote in Abrams and Neubauer's 1976 paper that lists the cognitive tests administered to two adopted boys that they studied: the Cattell Infant Intelligence Scale, the Stanford-Binet, and the Wechsler Intelligence Scale for Children. Also indicated in the footnote is that additional measures, including projective tests, were given to the children beginning at age three years. The specific projective tests are not listed in the footnote, but the boys' performance on the Rorschach, Thematic Apperception Test, and Human Figure Drawing Test are described in the text. Instruments and procedures are usually provided in a methods section of an empirical scientific paper, but that is a format that psychoanalytic journals do not follow.

The 1994 paper, also by Abrams and Neubauer, states that although four pairs of twins were studied, information would be presented for just two. Why the data were not reported for all four pairs is unexplained, although the two selected pairs were identified as the most and least alike. The identical reared-apart triplets I discussed in chapter 10 were not included in the description of the subject sample. By 1994, the triplets who had met in 1980 had received considerable media attention. Concern for their privacy may have prompted the authors to omit them from the paper—had their data been reported the triplets could have easily been identified. Another possibility is that limited information was available for one of the triplets. In chapter 10, I offered evidence that one of the triplets had left the study early, based on my reading of a paper by Susan Farber;[19] later, I will provide further support for that supposition. Lastly, the investigators may have hoped to avoid the negative fallout that could have ensued from writing about the three brothers. The triplets and their families were still furious about the separation and the secret study.

Failure to describe their subjects in full was evident, but not obvious, in Abrams and Neubauer's 1976 publication. There is also a puzzling feature of that paper that deserves a closer look.

MATCHED SAMPLINGS OR TWINS?

Abrams and Neubauer's 1976 paper explored individual differences in animate and inanimate orientation, that is, the tendency to relate more to people or to things. The authors focused on two boys, Alan and Benjamin, described as "matched samplings." Alan and Benjamin were chosen for the report because of the vast quantity of data gathered on them as subjects in a study of children "destined for adoption." The boys were first studied while they were in foster care, at ages four and a half months and five and a half months. They continued to be studied in their separate adoptive homes, periodically but at the same time, until at least six years of age. The authors *do not* mention that the boys are twins which I fully expected, because that paper is cited in Oppenheim's interview as one of four publications reporting twin study findings. A word search within that paper identified the term "twin" sixteen times—twelve times in the introduction and four times in the reference list, but never in relation to Alan and Benjamin.

Are Alan and Benjamin a pair of separated twins? I believe that they are. It is hard to find two children so well matched in age and time of placement. And were other "matched samplings" among the children that were studied—that is, other twins in the LWS-CDC study?[20] The many cognitive and projective tests given, and the coordinated tracking of the children over time, are consistent with what is known about how the twin study proceeded, as I described in chapter 11. *However, without this prior knowledge, readers might not suspect that Alan and Benjamin were identical twins.* If the boys were twins, this vital feature of their background required reporting, since such knowledge could affect readers' interpretations of the findings.

Perhaps Dr. Oppenheim, a professional and personal associate of Neubauer's, knew things beyond the 1976 publication, one being that the boys were indeed twins. After all, she cited this paper as proof that the twin study researchers published their findings. "I had access to material that was virtually unknown to exist by anyone other than the source of that access, the Project Director of the study [Balzert]." But perhaps Oppenheim's privileged access was not needed in this case—Abrams and Neubauer's 1994 paper, written eighteen years later, presented data for *two pairs of separated identical twins*—one of them "Barry and Ben." Some findings in the two papers overlap, in that Alan (Barry) was more task-oriented and Ben was more person-oriented, so they may have been the same pair. And according to my research, there was only one other separated identical male set in the study aside from the triplets. However, because the two papers differ in the behaviors they are reporting, it cannot be known with complete certainty that Alan and Benjamin are also Barry and Ben.

Abrams's 1986 paper described an identical twin pair, "Amy and Beth," whereas the 1994 paper described "Abby and Amy." Are they the same two girls? Beth in the first paper and Amy in the later paper are described as clingy and stubborn. Amy in the first paper and Abby in the later paper were close to their mothers, but not clingy. In both papers, each twin engaged in nail biting, thumb sucking, and the use of a blanket to relieve tension. Still, the different directions taken by these two papers make data alignment challenging. It is likely, but not certain, that the children in both papers are the same. I thought that some answers to these questions might come from an overseas source.

READERS AND LISTENERS

The 1996 book chapter, "Genetik und Psychotherapie," co-written in German by Neubauer and Balzert, was part of a Festschrift honoring the Austrian neurologist and psychoanalyst, Dr. Harald Leupold-Löwenthal. Having witnessed the Nazi atrocities in his country, Leupold-Löwenthal focused on resurrecting psychoanalytic studies, even convincing Anna Freud, who was Jewish, to return to Austria from England.[21] He was co-founder of Vienna's Sigmund Freud Society and its president from 1976 to 1999. Neubauer and Balzert's Festschrift paper was probably inaccessible to most psychologists trained in the United States who did not read German. Neubauer and Balzert also co-presented the paper, translated as "Genetics and Psychotherapy" at an American Academy of Psychoanalysis meeting,[22] but conference talks reach limited audiences. The Festschrift's publisher, Mag. Sylvia Zwettler-Otte, kindly sent me a copy of the paper, saying she was pleased that the conference volume is still of interest.[23]

I reviewed a translated copy of "Genetik und Psychotherapie." The chapter summarizes previous reared-apart twin research, explains the advantages of the authors' prospective study of separated twins, and provides a general outline of the study's design: tracking twins' development from shortly after birth until twelve years of age by means of films, psychological tests, interviews with family members, and observations made several times a year in twins' homes and twice a year when they were older. The authors presented findings for two pairs of *twins*, "Amy and Abby," and "Barry and Ben." The term "matched samplings" did not appear in papers other than the 1976 report.

Some information presented in the 1996 chapter also appears in the earlier papers. "Abby and Amy" are "Amy and Beth" in Abrams's 1976 paper. In both reports, both twins engaged in nail biting and thumb sucking. "Barry and Ben" are still "Barry and Ben" in Abrams and Neubauer's 1994 paper. In both sources, Barry lacks self-confidence—"He described himself as a monkey which gets fed rather than a lion which bites"—and Ben needed his mother close by in new situations.[24] And as in the 1994 paper, the 1996 chapter revisited findings for the most similar and most dissimilar pairs. It is not uncommon for scholars to rework older papers for publication in different books and journals, noting that some findings have been published previously. Neubauer and Bazert did not cite the earlier sources.

The measured dissemination of the twin study findings may have been purposeful. Bernard had concerns about their twin study becoming widely known. She opposed sharing information about the work, especially in the late 1970s when informed consent issues were pressing.[25] Abrams and Neubauer published for professional audiences, but the journals they chose, such as *The Psychoanalytic Study of the Child* and *The Psychoanalytic Quarterly*, were read mostly by psychoanalysts, not by the broader psychological community.[26] According to a colleague, Abrams spoke openly about the twin study to his clinical psychiatry classes at New York University, but one of Abrams's former students could neither confirm nor deny this. However, Abrams did discuss the study with his colleagues at study groups.[27] The Neubauers' 1990 book, *Nature's Thumbprint*, was more accessible to behavioral science researchers, but as I said, some names and details were omitted.

The LWS-CDC twin study materials would have engaged the growing number of behavior geneticists and twin researchers at that time, whose newly established organizations, journals, and conventions would have been ideal outlets for the findings.[28] Three of the landmark studies of reared-apart twins were ongoing just as the LWS-CDC study was in progress, offering opportunities for collaboration.[29] But that was not possible because the twin separations and the study's methods created controversies outside the small circle of LWS and CDC personnel, their colleagues, and some adoption agencies. Neubauer did, however, consult with Professor Niels Juel-Nielsen who directed a reared-apart twin investigation in Denmark from 1954 to 1959, with a follow-up study completed by 1979. The date and substance of that consultation are unknown, but according to Neubauer, Juel-Nielsen both understood the uniqueness of the LWS-CDC study and had suggested in his book that such a study would make a valuable research contribution.[30] In his 1965 and updated 1980 publications, Juel-Nielsen stated that, "The ideal material would be one in which monozygotic [identical] twins were separated at birth, put into foster or adoptive homes and brought up without knowledge of each other's existence."[31] Juel-Nielsen did not say that such twins should be followed periodically over time without their parent's knowledge. (He also did not suggest that twins should be deliberately divided.) Regardless, his comment is understandable because most twins in his study had met briefly in childhood or had known they had a twin. These were factors beyond control and could have affected the findings. However, the Minnesota Study of Twins Reared Apart did include some identical twins who met for the first time as adults, unaware that they had a twin sibling, just what Juel-Nielsen had called for.[32] Neither Dr. Juel-Nielsen's colleagues or his family had copies of correspondence between Juel-Nielsen and Neubauer. Correspondence between Neubauer and the late Dr. Irving I. Gottesman, who had authored an introduction to Juel-Nielsen's study (that followed Neubauer's enthusiastic foreword in that volume—calling the work "a model of research methodology"), was also unavailable.

Guarding the study's methods and findings, and selectively channeling how and where the findings were presented, were paramount. So, what drove the researchers' desires to publish and present the papers that they did, risking uncomfortable consequences? Lawrence Wright's interviews convey Neubauer's conviction that the study was seminal in the history of reared-apart twin research, because it addressed nature-nurture questions in a unique way. No one had ever prospectively studied separated newborn twins. Neubauer's belief in the power of the study, one he shared with his colleagues, may have overridden any publishing concerns. Even before the project ended in 1980, the idea of writing a book about the twin children was taking shape. The rarity of the data and its anticipated impact on the field might have made the project irresistible. But challenges, mostly related to human subject issues, loomed large.

GRAPPLING WITH HUMAN SUBJECT ISSUES: ADVICE AND CONSENT

The years 1974 and 1976 were pivotal for bringing informed consent issues to the fore in behavioral and medical science research. Recall that these years saw passage of the National Research Act and the Belmont Report that outlined mandatory principles and guidelines for protecting the rights of human subjects.[33] It is unclear when Bernard first experienced unease over parental consent issues, but she expressed them in a 1978 letter to twin study researcher Christa Balzert.[34] "We could find nothing about Dorothy Krugman [observer and research assistant] and/or the caseworker with respect to explaining the project to the prospective adoptive parents and obtaining their signed consent." Krugman had understood that caseworkers explained the project and sought parents' cooperation during home visits, *before* the agency decided if the child would be placed permanently with a particular family. This understanding applied to the triplets and to one other pair of twins. LWS Executive Director Florence Kreech recalled that consent took place verbally though the case worker, but Bernard said she had wanted this process done differently, as she said she had stated in an earlier memo. I do not have access to this memo, so I cannot know what Bernard had specified.

A consent form with a creation date of January 1, 1966, was returned by some families twelve years later, in 1978, except for one curiously dated 1969. Recall that in 1978, upon receiving the 1966 form from Dr. Vivian Wolsk, one of the fathers had requested a revised form that would provide "ironclad assurance" of privacy. As of June 1986, he had not given his consent, nor had his twin son's family, greatly upsetting Bernard;[35] whether he had received a revised form is unknown. By 1966, the project had already been tracking the development of two pairs of twins and the triplets. Perhaps the consent forms weren't issued earlier due to an oversight, but were mailed to the families in 1978, in response to growing pressure.[36] It seems strange that a consent form was composed in 1966, given that the group's 1980s' conversations referenced the absence of consent procedures in the field, in general, as absolving them from being delinquent when it came to consent.

There is a gap of several years, 1979 to 1983, during which I did not identify documents related to informed consent concerns, records that could be sealed in Bernard's archives. However, letters, memos, and minutes from 1984 onward show that such discussions were ongoing. Simultaneously, efforts were underway to convert the twin study material into a format suitable for book publication.

FURTHER DEVELOPMENTS

On October 10, 1984, Lynn Kelly of the CDC informed Bernard that Neubauer and Balzert had edited materials for "Child-5" and "Child-6" on September 18 and 19, but said that no meeting had taken place. She added that they had worked on "definitions" on October 9 and promised to send them to Bernard upon completion. Kelly also noted that there would be no minutes of this meeting.[37] Meanwhile, concerns over informed consent persisted.

An adoption study meeting on the topic "Publication/Legal Issues" took place on October 2, 1984. The three main investigators, Samuel Abrams, Peter Neubauer, and Christa Balzert, were present, as was Professor Bertram

J. Black of the JBFCS. Bernard was absent but added her comments to the minutes. Neubauer raised legal questions for which Bernard had urged discussion with knowledgeable individuals in Washington, DC. Neubauer worried that the twins would say they were deprived of their twinship and were misled about the study. The "agency's" concern was that publicity would be regarded as detrimental—here Bernard had penciled in, "which agency? CDC or LWS?" The group was not concerned about the public recognizing the twins in published documents—however, as I indicated, the triplets had enjoyed considerable public attention by then, making them easy to identify. The group *was* worried about the twins recognizing themselves, but Black implied that this would be an onerous task. It would require reading the report and distinguishing between information that applied and did not apply to the individual. Black suggested that the "worst" that could happen would be charges by the twins that their twinship had been concealed. He concluded, "Yet it was not part of the study to inform each of the other," next to which Bernard had penciled in "good point."

The consensus of the group was that the participants should *not* be told that they were separated twins. They reasoned that no harm was done to them since they and their families were aware of the kind of data being collected. Instead, harm would have come from divulging their twinship early on, as it would have disrupted family bonding.

The conversation of that meeting then turned somewhat abruptly to publication plans. Balzert announced that a Dr. Kofman had volunteered to write up edited versions of material that she and Neubauer had been working on. Neubauer outlined the different chapters and content areas. Methodology would be described by Balzert, supplemented by tables and charts. Detailed presentation of data gathered on two twin pairs—"C-5/C-6 and C-3/C-4"—would come next, followed by a general description of data from other pairs and a discussion of the findings. The book would close with a statement covering questions, answers, and future directions. Recall that as of 1986, signed consents had not been returned by both sets of parents of one pair.

A 1984 interoffice memo from Professor Black, sent to Peter Neubauer and five other staff members, concerned how publishing the twin study would legally affect the LWS and CDC. The memo was dated October 9, just one day before Kelly had communicated with Bernard.[38] Black, who had consulted several National Institute of Mental Health (NIMH) officials, had learned that there was "no set policy" regarding informed consent for publishing when data were gathered before consent forms were required and before institutional review boards (IRBs) monitored human research. He described a Columbia University study of children at high risk for schizophrenia and other psychiatric disorders, who had been studied at that time. The investigator of that study, Dr. Niki Erlenmeyer-Kimling of Columbia University, had been advised to seek the assistance of the university's newly established review board. The board suggested that she modify the wording to protect the participants, and publication of the study followed. Neubauer was advised to confer with Erlenmeyer-Kimling in order to take appropriate steps; Bernard did so, as I will explain later.[39]

Black also conferred with the US Children's Bureau, whose adoption division had dealt previously with cases involving twins and siblings—although Black does not state if the bureau's prior dealings had involved research or practice. The Bureau's advice was that the agency (LWS) should organize a meeting of the twins to explain their earlier placement practices. Black added that the study need not be mentioned and that no one he spoke with suggested that Neubauer, the CDC, and/or JBFCS were legally responsible for the adoption process or for withholding the fact of twinship.

Several words in Black's memo had been "whited out" and the word "agency" added. A second page displays the retyped memo, with the suggestion to hold a meeting deleted. In the revised version, Bernard has penciled in "& LWS" next to the section in which doubt was cast on the investigators' legal responsibility.

Bernard circulated a January 30, 1985, memo to LWS Executive Director Morton Rogers, Peter Neubauer, and attorneys Roger E. Sher and Stephen W. Tulin.[40] Her purpose was to convene a meeting of authors and administrators regarding publication of a monograph reporting findings from the twin study. Bernard explained that informed consent procedures were not in place when the study began in 1960. Therefore, the signed forms that had been received were "not as complete as current requirements would necessitate," because families were unaware that their adopted child was a twin. Earlier, she had agreed with Black that informing families was not part of the study.

A follow-up memo sent February 20, 1985, explained Erlenmeyer-Kimling's experience in greater detail.[41] A young man who had been in foster care wanted access to his materials, but he was denied. He sent Erlenmeyer-Kimling an angry letter with copies to the NIMH and other relevant parties. Once Erlenmeyer-Kimling met him and allayed his fears about becoming sick, he dropped his charges. It also turned out that that study began in the early 1970s, just after Columbia University's review board had been established—and that while informed consents had been obtained, they did not meet the required standards. Erlenmeyer-Kimling was advised not to recontact the families to obtain updated consent to avoid upsetting them. She was also advised to omit the name of the hospital where the work took place.

Erlenmeyer-Kimling told Bernard that when her project began, NIMH had consulted William ("Bill") Curran at Harvard University who was conversant on health, medicine, and patients' rights.[42]

These memos eventuated in a March 7, 1985, meeting of the CDC's internal review board. The meeting was attended by six members and seven investigators/guests.[43] Two projects were discussed, the first being "The Development of Identical Twins Reared Apart: A Longitudinal Study." Dr. Bruce Grellong, former chief psychologist at the JBFCS, was one of two chairpersons present. Grellong announced that the group's compliance agreement with the Office of Protection from Research Risks, Department of Health and Human Services, M-1351, had been approved.[44] Neubauer then outlined the approach that the researchers planned to take for publication. Steps toward disguising the identity of the participants would be taken, but could not be assured, given the level of detail to be presented. The board members recommended that the publication (1) include an explicit statement to the effect that efforts were made to protect individual identification, and (2) not provide an explanation for why twins were separated—because this was initiated by LWS, not by Neubauer.

The last paragraph of the minutes underlined the unique contribution that the study would make to the developmental literature, especially twin studies. The other chairperson, attorney William Nimkin, concurred, yet urged that the issues under consideration be examined further. Nimkin also noted that the IRB's current guidelines did not cover risks to individuals who were interviewed and observed unless identification placed them at risk for criminal liability or employability. Professor Black added that informing subjects prior to publication would violate adoption regulations. As a final task, the board voted to approve publication. The minutes from this meeting may have been the first formal document in which "twins reared apart" was used in the book's working title. However, as I followed the unfolding of events that term was placed in jeopardy.

On March 14, 1985, Professor Black sent another interoffice memo to Peter Neubauer.[45] The memo mentioned Howard D. Davidson, an attorney at the National Legal Research Center for Child Advocacy and Protection. Davidson, who had been consulted by Black's contact at the US Department of Health and Human Services, favored publication and agreed that the adoption agency need not inform the subjects of their twinship. Black added that even if some twins recognized themselves in the text, infringement of the laws at that time did not come with penalties—the only negative outcome might be "increased embarrassment" for the agency. Black's take on the topic may have assuaged some fears, at least in part, enabling publication plans to proceed.

CONSENT AND LIABILITY

Concerns over informed consent issues and agency liabilities still festered in 1986. An adoption study meeting, convened on April 15, 1986, was attended by Abrams, Balzert, Neubauer, and Bernard.[46] Issues under discussion were insurance coverage in the event that a lawsuit was filed by the twins and their families, the lack of disclosure regarding subjects' twinship, and various other publication risks. Abrams worried that Yale University Press would not offer legal protection; the press had only seen an outline of the book at this point. Abrams also felt that the question of violation of human rights was of greatest concern. Neubauer suggested that Yale might share liability if the JBFCS offered partial financial protection. Bernard wondered if LWS would cover post-adoption worker Barbara Miller and Executive Director Morton Rogers if they were named in a suit. Bernard also called for a meeting with LWS once the written description of the twin sample was decided. And she planned to confer with LWS attorney Stephen Tulin, who insisted that participant identification be made "impossible."

The group revisited a question they had grappled with before: Should the book be published in another country? "It would make it less likely that anyone would pay attention, yet it may not conceal the liability."[47] Another option for "reduction of risk" was proposed: removing the words "twins reared apart" from the title.

Three weeks later, in May 1986, Bernard composed a more detailed memo for Neubauer, Abrams, and Balzert, to follow up on issues raised in April.[48] Attorney Stephen Tulin confirmed that the risk of a lawsuit would be considerably reduced if twins were not recognized by readers. However, he believed that a suit would be "expected" if twins and family members saw themselves in the material. "[T]here is a definite risk; I just can't quantify it," he said. Tulin requested copies of the signed consent forms that were received, but which Bernard had not found time to locate; she asked Balzert to look for them. Regarding insurance, Bernard determined that she, as well as Abrams and Neubauer, were protected through their professional organizations. In addition, LWS and CDC were covered by the Jewish Federation and could offer insurance to everyone if needed.[49]

Summer was approaching. In June 1986, Bernard sent a "PERSONAL AND CONFIDENTIAL" letter to Tulin, with a copy to Neubauer.[50] She explained that the book would focus on just two twin pairs, and at Tulin's request she enclosed a signed release form from one of the parents, dated 1978. Bernard was concerned that forms had not been returned by the parents of the male twins whom they planned to write about, and wondered why this situation had not been addressed. In closing, she said she hoped for another "C.D.C.-L.W.S. meeting fairly soon."

In July, Bernard sent Neubauer a letter that listed the titles of three publications authored by Dr. Erlenmeyer-Kimling, who studied development in children born to schizophrenic parents, parents with other psychiatric disorders, and parents without mental illness.[51] She had only single copies of these papers in her possession, so she provided Neubauer with just the titles. Next to the list she penciled in "dates?" She had indicated the titles and authors, but not the journals and time of publication, but they were easy to find.[52] The three papers were published between 1984 and 1987. They reported elevated levels of psychopathology in the children born to schizophrenic parents, followed by children whose parents had other psychiatric diagnoses or no psychiatric difficulties. Some references cited in the texts refer to relevant studies ongoing in the 1950s and 1960s.[53] Interestingly, Bernard wrote, "I think we should be clear as to where [Erlenmeyer-Kimling's papers] are being kept, once you've looked them over, i.e., your office, mine or at CDC."

Bernard also enclosed a copy of her February 20, 1985, publication memo, which I discussed earlier, and a copy of an April 13, 1983, letter about twins from attorney Stephen Tulin to LWS Executive Director Morton Rogers, which I have not seen. In reference to Tulin's letter, Bernard intended to discuss "this topic"—presumably publication or consent—with Barbara Miller that weekend. Bernard recalled "a rather tense meeting between me, Mort [Rogers], Barbara and, I think, Shelly [Fogelman, LWS Past President]." She also encouraged following up Tulin's earlier suggestion to consult with Harvard University professor William Curran about legal issues related to publication. Both Bernard and Neubauer were in touch with him, but she took the lead.

In preparing an information packet for Curran, some old memos were retrieved and revised. Professor Black's 1984 memo had a handwritten note from Bernard at the top. Bernard's note is dated November 3, 1986, and read "corrected re LWS mention . . . for inclusion in [Peter Neubauer's] letter to Curran." Bernard also added a note to Black's 1985 memo that read, "For enclosure to Curran—corrected as of 11/3/86 re LWS mention by mistake." Again, some words were deleted and replaced by "the agency." Bernard composed a two-page letter to Curran dated October 10, 1986, with a copy to Neubauer; that letter was apparently sent to him that day.[54] She also sent a copy to Tulin on October 31. At the top of the page, she had written "In Legal Medicine"—Curran, who died in 1996, was a professor of legal medicine and a pioneer in the development of health law.[55] The letter was mailed on October 10.

Bernard's letter expressed her difficulty reaching Curran by telephone, summarized her professional background, and described her prospective study with Neubauer that she said began before informed consent procedures and IRBs had been established.[56] She mentioned that the study had been federally funded, but could not recall if the source was the NIMH or the National Institute of Child Health and Human Development. Bernard then described the legal consulting that the group had engaged in regarding publication— Black's discussions with Washington, DC officials and her own meeting with Erlenmeyer-Kimling. She hoped to be in contact with Curran shortly because Neubauer was leaving for London.

Bernard compiled a list of materials that she mailed to Curran on November 3. The packet included a four-page overview of the history of LWS's twin separation policy, the origins and goals of the twin study, and post-adoptive changes and services.[57] The original 1983 document from which this overview was taken had a note from Bernard written across the top: "This was in preparation for Curran—omit 'LWS' throughout and substitute 'ad. [adoption] agency' or whatever non-identifying designation." The packet also included an outline of legal questions.

Two key questions were of interest to the investigators.[58] The first question was whether it was suitable for an adoption agency to separate twins. "This is not one to which we assign a good deal of significance, for siblings have been traditionally placed in different homes and we consider the twins to fall into this category." Elsewhere, Bernard stated that it was in siblings' interests to be placed together, and that couples who had already adopted a child were eligible to adopt siblings.[59] Moreover, research on sibling placement policies shows that in the 1960s siblings were sometimes placed in the same foster home, and that this arrangement was generally successful.[60]

The second question related to legalities. From a legal standpoint, would it have been judicious to tell the twins and their families about the twinship years ago? The investigators considered this second question to be "more significant" than the first. They worried that informing the twins during adolescence might have been upsetting during this sensitive developmental time. However, now that they were adults, would it be advisable to tell them? A related concern was the best interests of those involved—knowledge of twinship might complicate the lives of the twins, their families, and the twins' biological parents. Perhaps it was best to leave well enough alone, rather than disturb the lives of "40 or so individuals."[61] Lastly, publication in light of inadequate and missing consent forms was worrisome—if just one form was missing, then publication might be prevented. A concluding statement stressed the absence of any "misgivings," "negative reactions," and "ethical questions" from the CDC's IRB and the NIMH's reviewing committee regarding the twin study.

Other materials forwarded to Curran were a blank consent form; a signed consent form; a list of consent forms received and outstanding for Child-3 to Child-11; Bertram Black's October 9, 1984, and March 14, 1985, memos to Neubauer; and the recommendations of the CDC's IRB.[62] Items sent to Neubauer, but not to Curran, included an addendum to the outline of legal questions and Bernard's October 10 letter to Curran that Neubauer had already received.[63] The addendum referenced the outline of legal questions, which stated that refusal by even one parent or twin might preclude publication. However, in the addendum Bernard explained that this statement referred only to the four families of the two twin pairs to be highlighted in the book. She asserted that information from the other twins and families could be included in statistical tables. However, Bernard did not feel that this statement posed serious consequences, because it was proceeded by the phrase "as we understand it."

A cover letter, dated November 3, 1986, and signed by Neubauer and Bernard, was included with the packet.[64] By then, Neubauer and Curran had spoken by phone. The letter referenced Curran's interest in reviewing the project and meeting with Bernard and Neubauer in New York. Meanwhile, another letter passed between Bernard and Neubauer.[65] Dated November 5, Bernard's letter drew Neubauer's attention to the list of enclosures. She explained that she had omitted the minutes from the CDC's March 7 IRB meeting because of "brackets and crossouts," and because the whole document was not what Neubauer had intended. A "cleaned up, excerpted" memo from Black was sent instead. Bernard also reminded him that both of Black's memos had mentioned LWS by name, despite their efforts to remove it from the historical overview. Therefore, Bernard's office redid the memos, substituting "the agency" for LWS.

A postscript to Bernard's letter recounts her very recent meeting with attorney Stephen Tulin. Their meeting seems to have concerned the publishing consequences if a twin or parent failed to provide consent. Bernard did not offer details, but it seems she was referring to Tulin's suggestion that "improve[d] our situation a bit"—namely, that the phrase "as we understand it" would mitigate concerns. Bernard told Neubauer she would summarize this matter separately, most likely explaining the addendum.

In their November 3 letter, Neubauer and Bernard informed Curran that Yale University Press had agreed to publish their work. The proposal was approved, and contract negotiations were underway.

• *13* •

Yale University Press

The Book That Never Was

$\mathcal{T}$here is a nine-page book proposal in one of Bernard's archived files. By July 1985, Neubauer, Abrams, and Balzert, with Bernard's assistance, had crafted a plan for a volume titled, *Identical Twins Reared Apart: A Longitudinal Study*.[1] The header reads "Proposal to Yale University Press"; whether the group approached other publishers is unlikely, but unknown. The submission date was not indicated, but correspondence between Bernard and Neubauer shows that they sent it to Yale sometime after June 1986. The proposal was organized into seven sections:

1. History
2. The Uniqueness of the Study
3. The Study's Limitation: The Number of Subjects
4. Developmental Approach
5. Data and Findings
6. Protection of Subjects
7. The Proposed Volume

Section 7, "The Proposed Volume," would include the

I. Introduction
II. Literature Review
III. Methodology
IV. Data
V. Findings
VI. Implications

Bernard's edits were penciled into the 1985 document and detailed in a 1986 letter to Neubauer.[2] It seems unusual that nearly a year went by between Bernard's first review and her explanatory letter, except that rounds of revisions and publication discussions probably delayed things. Bernard began her letter with the hope that her questions were not "nitpicking." She objected to the opening sentence that read, "Twenty-five years ago an adoption agency instituted a practice of separating twins who were being placed for adoption." Bernard reminded Neubauer that Louise Wise Services (LWS) had placed twins both apart *and* together, at different times, and according to different criteria. Bernard was also bothered by the use of the word "ethical" in three different places: In two instances, she preferred stating that "clinical" considerations, not ethical ones, explained why parents and children had not been told of the twinship or the study. She called attention to a passage stating that periodic reviews of the study by the National Institute of Mental Health, state and city officials, and the boards of the agencies involved were done to "insure that ethical principles would continue to prevail," then decided that the wording was acceptable. However, Bernard agreed that "ethical" was used appropriately in the statement that "None of the reviewing groups ever concluded that the research was in violation of any ethical principles or legal statutes."

In December 1986, Neubauer, Abrams, and Balzert were offered a contract with Yale University Press (YUP) for a volume tentatively titled, *Identical Twins Reared Apart: A Longitudinal Study*.[3] The contract, or letter of agreement, required the signatures of the three co-authors, Neubauer, Abrams, and Balzert, and the YUP Director John G. Ryden. At that time, YUP was also publishing *The Psychoanalytic Study of the Child*, the journal edited by Neubauer, Abrams, and some of Neubauer's Yale colleagues. It seemed like a natural choice for the twin study researchers.

The targeted date for delivery of the manuscript was June 1, 1987. However, the 1986 contract was superseded by a revised contract dated July 8, 1987, that specified a delivery date of January 1, 1988.[4] Contracts between authors and publishers typically undergo several rounds of negotiation. Comparing the 1986 and 1987 contracts reveals some differences. The later document included several italicized additions and adjustments:[5] If publishing rights were violated, then the authors would reimburse the press for money they would be legally liable to pay, *except that the authors' liabilities would be limited by their earnings on the book*; the publisher's right to sell other versions of the book or allow use of the material *would be subject to the authors' approval*; the authors would not publish a similar version of the book *intended for the same audience*; the authors would receive 10 percent of the US list price *on the first thirty-five hundred copies*, fewer than the original five thousand copies.

In the midst of finalizing the contract, Neubauer was trying to arrange a meeting with William Curran, the Harvard University professor with expertise in legal matters surrounding medical research and informed consent. In a December 1986 letter, he wrote, "As I mentioned to you [Curran], your consultation is most urgent and timely before we sign a contract with Yale University Press."[6] A meeting on January 18 or 19, 1987, was possible when Curran planned to be in New York, although Neubauer would not be returning from London until January 18. He suggested that Curran contact Bernard, who received a copy of the letter. At the top of her copy she wrote, "1/18/87 Never heard from him—Told Peter this." Neubauer sent another letter to Curran on April 9, noting that they had been out of touch for a while and apologizing "if I seem to be a nuisance."[7] Neubauer expressed his interest in coming to Boston with Bernard for a meeting, or arranging a meeting in New York when Curran might be in town. He offered to cover Curran's travel expenses. "Your expertise, as you can see, is quite important to us." I found no additional correspondence on this topic—whether or not a meeting took place is unknown.

The contract gave the authors just six months to produce a 115,000-word document with tables and figures. Clearly, a substantial portion of the writing and preparation had been ongoing; recall Kelly's 1984 memo regarding work on the twins' materials and definitions. In February 1987, Bernard sent a letter and copies of Abram's 1986 paper to Justine Polier, Morton Rogers, Stephen Tulin, and Barbara Miller as "an instance of pre-publication from the project," not as a sample, as the book would be targeted toward a broader audience.[8] But Bernard had reservations about Abrams's article, which she communicated to him in May 1986.

Abrams had suggested that the article might be a model for the monograph, but Bernard saw "risky issues."[9] Abrams said that the twins had been separated due to "clinical considerations," a statement Bernard wanted to qualify—because the nature of the infant twins' relationship affected the placement decisions. She also wanted "clinical reasons" to replace "ethical reasons" to justify why parents were not told about the twinship. And she wanted to say that "separation was discussed, explained and approved" by the biological mothers. Regarding the "extraordinary research opportunity" that Abrams highlighted in his article, Bernard noted that the adoption agency's lack of resources mandated collaboration with a well-prepared team. She also encouraged Abrams to include data from hospital records related to the pregnancies, placentae, and blood tests.

Bernard sent a briefer letter to Abrams in March 1987, also written with the planned book in mind.[10] Here, she explained the important difference between a baby's time of placement and legal adoption, a distinction she believed Abrams failed to make in his paper. A waiting period between these two events protects the child, should the new home situation prove unsatisfactory. Bernard urged Abrams to bring this point to the attention of Neubauer and Balzert, adding that the twins' records contained this information if needed.

In April 1987, while YUP was preparing a revised contract, Bernard circulated additional book-related materials to Polier, Rogers, Tulin, and Miller, with copies to authors Neubauer, Abrams, and Balzert. This time the enclosures consisted of data and discussion of three topics—affect, cognition, and object interactions or relationships—about one set of twins. She did this to provide her four colleagues with a sense of the writing style. Each enclosure had been reviewed or revised by the three authors. These documents were not available in Bernard's public archives; however, I discovered a book outline that listed seven chapters in greater detail than did the 1985 proposal. I have reproduced the main features here because they become important later on.

    I. Ego
        A. Apparatus
            1. Cognition
            2. Motor Funct.[ioning]
            3. Perceptual Proclivities
        B. Affect
    II. Core Matrix
    III. Physical Illness
    IV. Psychopathology
    V. Phase Organization
    VI. Human Interaction
    VII.Environment

    Bernard noted that further review of the enclosures would be completed to guard against participant identification. She hoped to meet everyone soon for further discussion. In June 1987, Bernard did meet with the members and trustees of her Tappanz Foundation to approve a twenty-five hundred dollar grant to the Child Development Center (CDC) for the "Child Development Center Project."[11] Awards of thirty-five hundred dollars, three thousand dollars, and twenty-five hundred dollars had been made to the CDC in 1983, 1984, and 1985, respectively. An award was not issued in 1986 because Neubauer said that the only expense that year was the secretary's salary for maintaining the study records. However, in 1987, the CDC's financial difficulties necessitated securing support from other sources—the Tappanz Foundation and contributions from Neubauer and Balzert. Data processing continued.

YALE UNIVERSITY PRESS II:
MOVING FORWARD, BUT HOW FAR?

On July 10, 1987, Neubauer forwarded a copy of the revised contract, dated July 8, 1987, to Bernard.[12] Neubauer also showed it to LWS Past President Sheldon Fogelman. Recall that Fogelman ran a publishing company and was savvy when it came to clients' rights and liabilities.[13] Neubauer summarized the recommendations he had gleaned from talking to Fogelman: It would be advisable to allocate movie rights to the publisher; the issue of reduced royalties should be addressed, especially if the book were read in schools and book clubs; the authors should have the right to review translations; digests and abridgments should be subject to the authors' approval; the authors should have the right to seek other publishers if Yale discontinued publication. Fogelman also asked if including the LWS or CDC in the dedication and acknowledgments would increase the chance of recognition by participants. He also offered to read the final manuscript as a check against further liability, such as coverage and identity. Neubauer did not indicate the recipients of this summary, but it was certainly sent to Bernard as it was part of her archived collection.

Tucked into the archives is a twenty-one-page draft of the book's first chapter. Its structure corresponds to the detailed outline displayed previously, except that the chapter title read, "FINDINGS I: The Individual Children," and "I. Ego" is a section of that chapter, rather than a chapter on its own. Readers are informed that the first part of section I, "1. Cognition (memory and language)," was based on intelligence tests, developmental scales, clinical evaluation, and parent and teacher reports. Tables and figures would display highly detailed information for each child, such as IQ scores over the first ten years of life, and graphic representations of each pairs' cognitive performance over time. The tables were not appended to the chapter, with the exception of graphs depicting one pair's scores on the Cattell, Stanford-Binet, and Wechsler Intelligence Scale for Children intelligence tests; I have reproduced these graphs in Figures 13.1 and 13.2.

The authors correctly realized that this form of presentation gives readers "a quick impression of continuities and changes in each child's mental functioning." Of course, such graphs can be composed for any child—but the

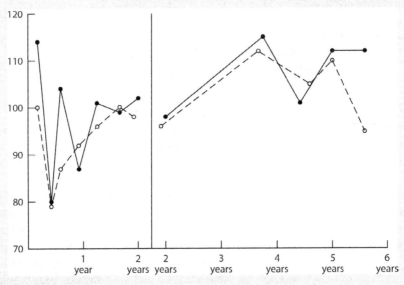

IQ Scores for a Pair of Separated Identical Twins

Cattell Infant Intelligence Scale *(left)*   Stanford-Binet Intelligence Scale *(right)*

Identical twins generally show more coordinated patterns of intellectual development as they age. Note the greater profile similarity of the IQ scores obtained during childhood (Stanford-Binet) than during infancy (Cattell).

Figure 13.1. IQ scores for separated identical twins during infancy and early childhood. Viola W. Bernard Papers, Columbia University Heath Sciences Library.

significance of these particular graphs is that they involve identical co-twins, thus lending a genetic perspective to mental performance. Identical twins typically show coordinated patterns of mental performance that can be partly explained by their shared genes. In contrast, developmental changes seen for non-twin children are often incorrectly attributed to environmental events. The late Ronald S. Wilson, who ran the well-known Louisville Twin Study, called identical twins' mental parallels "spurts and lags."[14] Spurts are periods of intellectual growth or change, whereas lags are periods of stability or decline. The Louisville Twin Study lasted from 1959 to 2003.[15]

The section on cognition includes descriptive accounts of mental performance for six children. Recall that one pair of twins was dropped from the study once their twinship became known to their families; however, it is uncertain why these summaries are missing for two other twins who participated throughout. Information for one other child is completely missing from

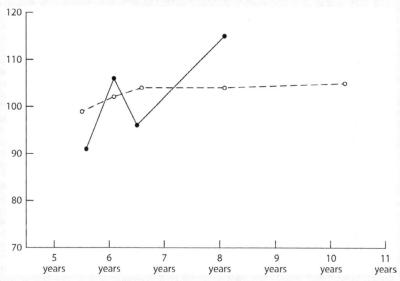

IQ Scores for a Pair of Separated Identical Twins

Wechsler Intelligence Scale for Children (WISC)

In contrast with the Stanford–Binet results, the same twins show a different pattern of intellectual development from 5.5 to 8.0 years of age—in fact, they change places at each timepoint. Reasons for the discrepancy are uncertain, but could reflect examiner characteristics, age differences, and/or test conditions. It is unfortunate that data were missing for both twins at age 9.0 and for one twin at age 10.5 years. Research comparing nontwins performance on these two tests yielded mixed findings with regard to how much the scores differ at different ages. See Glen A. Holland, "A Comparison of the WISC and Stanford-Binet IQs of Normal Children," *Journal of Consulting Psychology* 17, no. 2 (1953): 147–52. Note: An older study is cited here because the original WISC, administered to the separated twins, has undergone considerable revision and updating.

Figure 13.2.   IQ scores for separated identical twins during early and later childhood. Viola W. Bernard Papers, Columbia University Heath Sciences Library.

this chapter. I believe that this child is one of the triplets whose parents ended their study participation early.

The cognitive descriptions, and those in the other two areas—"motor functioning" and "sensory-perceptual"—are summaries based on quantitative findings. As indicated in an early outline, data were complete for one of the pairs and for "partial duplicates." In order to offer a sense of the material that was to be presented, I have reproduced some of the descriptions without indicating to which twin they refer. Note that each "x" replaces the child's actual identification number (C-1 to C-11), and that C-x represents different children throughout. I have also concealed the sex of each child, which was revealed in the actual descriptions.

- In the early years, C-x's investment in intellectual activity is normative. However, from age four on involvement and attention span diminish. C-x gives evidence of good ability for abstract thinking. However, throughout the years they show little innovative strategies, and tasks requiring new learning or integration of diverse elements tend to cause anxiety and withdrawal.
- Expressive language is considered low average in the first two years after which C-x moves into the above average to superior range. C-x's verbal interactions often have an egocentric quality; C-x's responses are personalized. In school C-x has occasional transient problems. C-x has some problems working neatly, and there are occasional complaints about C-x's "daydreaming." No serious problems are reported.
- In school C-x is considered a slow learner. Spelling and math are C-x's best subjects. There are difficulties in reading comprehension and in understanding assignments.

The next section of the chapter, labeled "2. Motor Functioning," was based on direct observation and visual-motor items from standard ability tests. Motor functions can be organized into skills classified as *gross* or *fine*. *Gross motor skills*, such as walking and standing, require whole body movements and large muscles. *Fine motor skills*, such as using a scissors or opening a lunch box, involve the use of smaller muscles.[16] Summaries of motor functions were provided for seven children. The areas of interest were development (gross and fine), skill (gross and fine), involvement (gross and fine), coordination (gross and fine), visual-motor coordination, handedness, relative interest in gross and fine, activity repertoire (gross and fine), integration with other functions, pleasure in motor functioning (gross and fine), emotionally related issues, structurally related issues, family-related issues, and noteworthy features.[17] The consensus of four to five child development experts determined the evaluations. Some motor functioning measures were judged on a five-point scale, ranging from low to high. Sample descriptions are as follows:

- C-x shows less involvement as well as achievement in fine motor activities than with gross. Overall, C-x's achievements in fine motor skills are judged as low average to average; only at age two is it, transiently, regarded as above the norm.

- A characteristic pattern when C-x learns to walk: C-x starts out very cautiously and slowly to the point where C-x seems to fall behind. Then C-x's skill improves to the extent that at twenty-three months C-x's walking is "beautiful." Right-hand dominance is established by 3-11 [three years, eleven months] for C-x.
- The establishing of dominance is noteworthy with C-x. Although left-hand dominance occurs in the third year, up through the fifth year attempts are made by C-x's family to encourage the use of the right, and in fact, the right is used for some tasks at least well into the seventh year. Foot and eye dominance remain unclear and variable over the ten years.

The last part of section 1 is "3. Sensory-Perceptual Apparatus." This material, available for eight children, was based on descriptions from family members and film recordings. Information from these two sources was rated on a five-point scale with respect to general responsivity, general activation, specific responsivity (visual, auditory, tactile, gustatory, olfactory, kinesthetic, pain), special sensitivities, preferred modality, integration of modalities, and other noteworthy features. Some sample summaries follow:

- During the second year, C-x begins thumb sucking. C-x is also strongly attracted to their blanket, sleeping on top of the silky coverlet while sucking their thumb. By three and a half years, the association between thumb sucking and their blanket is so strong that if C-x goes near something silky, C-x will put their thumb into their mouth.
- C-x's sensitivity to acoustical stimulation is consistently high. A strong sensitivity to light is noted periodically. The importance of touch and kinesthetic sensations increases from the end of the first year on both in the active and in the passive form (touching and being touched).
- Except for this preference for gentle tactile stimulation, C-x gradually moves toward a preference for strong stimulation in most sensory areas: visual—color preferences (reds and purples); auditory—loud sounds and music; gustatory—spicy foods (ketchup); and kinesthetic— intense total body movement (gymnastics).

Based on extensive research, I have determined the names of the twins and triplets that link to the twin study identification numbers, C-1 to C-11. At the time of this writing, I have forwarded descriptions to several of the twins—I always ask them first and assure them I will not share the material with their twin unless they agree. One twin wrote back, "I just read it, they nailed it with the thumb sucking and silky thing." This twin's response makes some of the group's publication concerns real, because recognizing oneself from the text *is* possible. Moreover, anyone who knew of this twin's early behaviors might have recognized this twin, too.

Identical Twins Reared Apart: A Longitudinal Study was moving forward, but it came to a halt. There is no such title in the succession of books reporting findings from reared-apart twin investigations. Had Neubauer's volume been completed, it would have been the fourth, following the Chicago study in 1937, the British study in 1962, and the Danish study in 1965. The fourth position in the "series" is now held by the Minnesota Study of Twins Reared Apart in 2012.[18]

UNFINISHED AND UNPUBLISHED

Contracts were to be signed and returned to YUP, after which a "fully executed copy" would be sent to each author. A copy of the signed document was not in Bernard's public files. Its absence suggests, but does not prove, that the form was never signed; it may be sealed in the archives at Columbia University and/or Yale University. However, the book was never published. I suspect that the authors did not sign—there would have been consequences for breaking the contract, especially if the two thousand dollar advance against future royalties had been issued upon signing; the balance of two thousand dollars would have been issued upon YUP's acceptance of a complete and final manuscript. In January 2020, I consulted John G. Ryden, the director emeritus of YUP, about whether the authors had signed the contract.[19] He did not know. He was with YUP from 1979 until he retired in early 2003. If the authors had signed and returned the contract, he would have co-signed it.

Ryden had just a vague recollection of Neubauer's proposal, despite his professed interest in the topic—he is an identical twin who, sadly, lost his brother several years ago. He was also unaware that Neubauer's papers had been placed in a sealed archive and had not heard of either documentary film. He explained YUP's publication process. Editors (called acquisition editors at most presses) evaluate proposals submitted to the press. These are sent to outside scholars for review and, if positive, are submitted to the publications committee (of which the director is a member). If approved, an advance contract is issued. When proposals result in completed manuscripts, they are subsequently sent to outside readers, and if their reports are favorable, they are submitted to the publications committee to be accepted and approved for publication.

Ryden's recollection of the proposed book grew clearer as we spoke, but he could not recall why it was never published, or if it were ever written. Had it been unpublished, it was unlikely to have been rejected for failing to meet the press's standards, which would have been "rare and memorable." At the same time, Ryden said it was not unusual for books to hit dead ends or take years to complete—he mentioned a manuscript that took forty-five years for delivery. Sometimes editors contact authors when deadlines are not met, but that isn't required. Ryden suspected that there is no official record for books that aren't delivered. "It just doesn't happen." My own literary agent Carol Mann, founder and director of the Carol Mann Agency in New York City, outlined several scenarios: Unsigned contracts are not binding. Sometimes authors change their minds about publishing. If a publisher finds a manuscript to be actionable, or requested changes are not made, the publisher may cancel the agreement. Ryden believed that the editor most likely to have worked with the twin study proposal was Ms. Gladys Topkis, who died in 2009. He suggested that I contact YUP senior executive editor, Ms. Jean E. Thomson Black. Ryden added that YUP editorial files were periodically deposited in Sterling Library.

Subsequent research revealed that Ms. Topkis was a senior editor of books in sociology, psychology, and psychoanalysis. When she left YUP in 1998, she was honored with a symposium featuring original papers by internationally known psychoanalysts.[20] In January 2020, I contacted Ms. Thomson Black by email to learn the name of the assigned editor; why the book was never published; if the book/proposal had been vetted by legal counsel prior to acceptance; if correspondence, reviews, or related documents were available at YUP; and if any material was stored in the YUP's archives.[21] Ms. Thomson Black was extremely helpful and continued to be throughout our communications. She agreed that Ms. Topkis was the editor most likely assigned to the project, and she proved to be right. Ms. Thomson Black cautioned that relevant files were probably long gone from the press offices, and she was uncertain if they would have been archived. Ms. Thomson Black did say that if a scanned contract file was located it might say something about why the project was cancelled.

Two weeks later, Ms. Thomson Black's assistant had located a scanned file and a letter from Ms. Topkis to Neubauer. Ms. Thomson Black also said that Ms. Topkis's "editor's file" might be in the library's basement, but her assistant did not have time to find it—even after I offered to send a gift card. However, Ms. Thomson Black was unclear on YUP's policy of releasing these documents, so she suggested I write a formal letter that she would share with the press. Several days later, my request was rejected on the basis that contract files are confidential, and I was not a party to the contract. This denial struck me as another instance of the secrecy surrounding the many sides of the LWS-CDC twin study. However, I managed to learn that Ms.

Topkis's letter did not say why the book was not published, although I was not given its contents.

Ms. Thomson Black had attended the 1998 symposium marking Ms. Topkis's retirement from YUP, but the proceedings were not published, and she no longer had the list of presenters. However, Ms. Topkis had a daughter Maggie, founder of the New York–based publishing house Felony & Mayhem, who had spoken at the gathering.[22] Unfortunately, Maggie doubted that her mother's files had been preserved. She agreed to search for the conference program, but she was unable to find it.[23]

A former YUP staff member, with no knowledge of Neubauer's submission, offered several possible explanations that match the experiences of some of my colleagues. One or both external reviewers might have raised objections to the completed manuscript; authors can gain access to these confidential documents only if reviewers agree. The book's editor may have suggested modifications or additions to which the authors did not consent. The manuscript might have been forwarded to YUP's legal department where potential difficulties with the content were identified. I believe it is also possible that the confidentiality and legal concerns expressed by Neubauer and his co-authors could have prompted them to withdraw their work and/or may have contributed to a decision by YUP to not publish it.

The range of possible explanations does not stop there. It is well known that YUP books are mostly aimed at academic and professional audiences, although the press does publish books with broad appeal. Perhaps Neubauer chose to redo his book with a popular slant—even after a contract was offered—and brought it to a publisher that reaches a wider readership. However, given the authors' care to conceal details about the twin study in previous papers and to even consider publishing the book in another country, this seems unlikely. At the time, YUP was one of the leading publishing houses for books in psychology and psychiatry, an attractive feature for any author. Thus, it was likely that Neubauer favored publishing his work with Yale. I found no evidence that the proposal had been sent to other academic publishers, either at the same time or at a later date.

The former staff member concluded that there may or may not be a story around the Neubauer case. Having learned about the study only by watching *Three Identical Strangers*, this person found it amazing and upsetting. I was advised to contact John Donatich, current director of the YUP, who might offer some knowledge or insights. It was a good idea.

I did not hear back directly from Donatich, but he forwarded my message to a member of YUP's Acquisitions Department. I was informed that the contract *had* been signed. I also learned that Neubauer's book contract had been terminated in 1996, consistent with Ms. Topkis's letter to Neubauer that I referenced previously.[24] The letter did not say why this action was taken or who initiated it. I have not determined if the authors received the two thousand dollar advance and, if so, whether they returned it to YUP. I followed up with a request to review these documents and/or to at least find answers as to these questions. Again, I was told that the files were confidential, and because I was not a party to the contract file the materials could not be made available.[25]

The contract termination occurred six years after the 1990 publication of *Nature's Thumbprint* and nine years after the contract with YUP had been signed. This means that the group had two contracts active simultaneously—one with YUP and the other with Addison-Wesley—but there does not appear to be a conflict of interest because the books were quite different in content and scope. The fact that the YUP contract was in place until 1996 raises the possibility that Neubauer thought about returning to the YUP book at a later date. In his mid-1990s interview with Lawrence Wright he said he planned to publish the findings in a year and a half.[26]

For now, there is no answer to the question of why *Identical Twins Reared Apart: A Longitudinal Study* was unpublished. But two years later, in 1990, Neubauer and son published their book *Nature's Thumbprint: The New Genetics of Personality*.[27] Recall that this book was one of the four sources Oppenheim cited to show that the twin study researchers published their findings. The publisher of the 1990 book was the Boston-based press Addison-Wesley. But the story did not end there. Twenty years later, in 2019, a twin study manuscript suddenly surfaced. Few people have seen it, but Lois Oppenheim has.

"BOOK DICTATION AND DRAFT"

Dr. Lois Oppenheim is professor and chair of Modern Languages and Literature at Montclair State University in Montclair, New Jersey. One of her six areas of specialization is psychoanalysis and the literary/visual arts. I contacted her in April 2019 when I learned that she was researching an article about the LWS-CDC twin study. We corresponded by telephone and email between April 2019 and April 2020. We also met briefly, and unexpectedly, in New York City, in October 2019, when she attended an Intelligence Squared debate on parenting in which I was a participant.

An article, co-authored with Neubauer's former colleague Dr. Leon Hoffman, appeared in the *Journal of the American Medical Association* in July 2019. It is the first source to cite an unpublished manuscript by Neubauer, Abrams, and Balzert. "Finally, little known is that Neubauer and his team drafted a nearly 200-page report entitled, 'Becoming Mind: Identical Twins Reared Apart,' which described the study methods and findings, but struggled with the question of how to author and publish a manuscript that, if sufficiently clinically detailed for research purposes, might compromise the families' confidentiality."[28] Oppenheim also cited this manuscript in her 2020 interview with Balzert, as evidence of the researchers' serious intent to publish the findings. "And then there is this: An approximately 200-page manuscript . . . remains an unpublished, incomplete draft."[29] The contents of Neubauer's collection at Yale's archives lists a "Book Dictation and Draft," but the link is inactive and will be until 2065.[30] Perhaps this document includes the sample chapter I described earlier—or perhaps it is the nearly two hundred-page manuscript, "Becoming Mind."

I asked Oppenheim about the manuscript in a July 2019 telephone interview. She was unable to tell me how she knew about it, but assured me that when my book (that is, this book) was finished I would know more. I assumed that the document was at Yale, but she said she couldn't answer that. I asked if she had read it, but she could say nothing. However, Oppenheim did say that she understood my questions and would be concerned if I had not asked them. It has been over two years since that conversation took place. I do not know more about the nearly two hundred-page manuscript, but I do know more about *Nature's Thumbprint*.

Yale University acquired Neubauer's twin study records in 1990. The timing of that event closely followed the 1988 delivery date specified in the 1987 YUP book contract and coincided with the publication of the Neubauers' book *Nature's Thumbprint*. It also predated Bernard's 1998 death by eight years and Neubauer's 2008 death by eighteen years. Speculation crafts any number of explanations for why Yale received the materials when they did. Perhaps the researchers could not resolve the vexing legal issues posed by possible participant recognition and preferred to place the materials in secure surroundings. Or maybe they feared future contacts and criticism from the press. However, Neubauer's desire to publish did not diminish. With the help of literary agent Pamela Bernstein, a book proposal was submitted to the Addison-Wesley Publishing Company in New York City. The proposal evolved out of a series of conversations among Neubauer, his son and co-author Alexander (Sandy), and Pamela Bernstein.[31] The proposed book would examine the origins of personality through observations of separated twins and parent-child interactions, and was intended for a general commercial trade audience. Both genetic and Freudian perspectives would inform the findings.

Bernstein and I have a history. I met her in January 1979 when her seven-year-old twins, Josh and Andy, took part in my doctoral study of cooperation and competition in young twins. At that time, she was employed as a literary agent at the William Morris Agency, before establishing her own business in 1993.[32] Bernstein also has a history with Neubauer. She sought his expertise in 1980 to assess her twin sons, and the two became closely acquainted. She admired his son Sandy, calling him a "great writer." Neubauer asked her to be his literary agent, and she enthusiastically agreed—he acknowledged her "loyalty and professionalism" when his book was published.

Bernstein recalls hearing Neubauer tell two of his "twin stories," which have remained vivid in her mind. In the first story, reared-apart identical twins both craved a solitary existence, but one twin ended up as a monk and the other a convict. These Japanese twins, Kazuo and Takau, are from a 1941 case report—both twins also had a history of stammering and suffering from tuberculosis.[33] In the second pair, young female twins insisted on having "ketchup" or "tomato sauce" with their meals, a habit that charmed one mother and annoyed the other. This anecdote has been recounted before, but with cinnamon instead of ketchup. I noted that the sources for these two stories, which appear in *Nature's Thumbprint*, were not cited.

Pam Bernstein only learned about the twin study and Neubauer's role in 2018 when she watched *Three Identical Strangers*. Bernstein admitted that she was shocked by the revelations in the film.

I asked Bernstein about Neubauer's proposal submission process.[34] She explained that she would have submitted it to ten or twelve publishers and negotiated the best arrangement. This strategy is still practiced today for general audience books that typically require an agent—books designed for professional audiences usually go to academic publishers and agents may not be necessary. Bernstein does not recall which publishers reviewed Neubauer's proposal or how many offers were made. She was unaware that a different proposal by Neubauer, Abrams, and Balzert had been accepted by YUP just prior to her involvement with the more general work. "I would have known if he had signed with Yale University Press—I did a lot of books with them. But contracts are not binding if they are not signed." (It had been signed.) Bernstein no longer has the proposal she submitted to Addison-Wesley.

The Neubauers' editor for *Nature's Thumbprint* was Jane Isay.[35] Ms. Isay began her career at YUP in 1964, creating their lists in psychiatry, psychology, and child development.[36] She worked with many well-known psychoanalysts, including Neubauer's colleague Anna Freud and psychoanalyst Alice Miller, whom she discovered some years later.[37] Ms. Isay was also well known to the members of the Yale Child Study Center with which her former husband, psychoanalyst Richard Isay, was associated. Ms. Isay moved to Basic Books in 1979, so she had left YUP when *Identical Twins Reared Apart: A Longitudinal Study* was under consideration in the mid-1980s.[38] After holding editorial positions in several publishing houses, she joined Addison-Wesley in 1984. In May 2020, I spoke with Jane Isay about her work with *Nature's Thumbprint* and about her friend and client, Peter Neubauer.[39] Based on my reading of the YUP proposal, the outline, the sample chapter, and *Nature's Thumbprint*, the latter is a very different book from what the authors had proposed to Yale.

Ms. Isay greatly admired Neubauer as a scholar as she recalled his considerable depth of knowledge.[40] To Neubauer's credit, when Ms. Isay's former husband came out publicly as a gay man, Neubauer remained one of the few supportive persons in the New York psychoanalytic community.[41] And "when Peter discussed the nature-nurture controversy, he knew more than anyone else alive." It is, therefore, not surprising that as Addison-Wesley's editorial director, Ms. Isay was very pleased to have received the proposal for what became *Nature's Thumbprint* and, as with all submissions, sent it to Addison-Wesley's editorial committee for approval. Upon completion of the manuscript, she thought of the title which she considers brilliant. She had no knowledge of Neubauer's previously proposed book project with YUP.

Unlike most of Neubauer's other associates whom I contacted, Jane Isay said that Neubauer spoke often and excitedly about his twin study. He also talked about twins being separated, but the basis of their separation was not explained. I expressed my surprise that Neubauer had been open about the project with her. As I indicated earlier, the researchers were careful as to who had knowledge of their findings—and Neubauer remained guarded in his 1993 interviews with Lawrence Wright. Ms. Isay jokingly asked whether the work was a "dirty secret" or a "help to humanity," but she clearly endorsed the latter. It seemed to her that Neubauer and his colleagues were doing wonderful things for the twins and their families.

Ms. Isay's understanding was that the data gathered during the twelve-year longitudinal study of each pair would be "grist for the book," which she felt would become the definitive work on nature-nurture questions.[42] But Neubauer was not fully forthcoming. After signing the contract, he informed her that he could not use his own data because he did not have written permission from the families to do so. Thus, ethical challenges were raised—it is unknown, but conceivable that these issues contributed to the authors' ending their relationship with YUP. Neubauer suggested that he use examples from other reared-apart twin studies in place of his own, and Ms. Isay reluctantly agreed. She regards the absence of Neubauer's data as a weakness of the book, and the reason why it lacked the impact it had once promised. "The book was good enough, but it was not first rate."

YALE UNIVERSITY ARCHIVES:
DECISIONS AND CONDITIONS

Until I reach the last chapter, my discussions of where the data are stored will be limited to information given by the individuals who control the archived material or have worked with it. I will reserve my own take on these topics and others, such as why Neubauer and Bernard's records were sealed, until the end.

The Neubauer collection names the "Jewish Board of Family and Children's Services (New York, N.Y.). Child Development Center" as the "Creator." The Yale University library catalog records a "gift" from the Jewish Board of Family and Children's Services (JBFCS), acquired by Yale in 1990.[43] As I suggested in chapter 12, Yale seemed a less likely choice to receive the twin study material than some other institutions, but someone made that decision. It is reasonable to suppose that Neubauer made that choice, but the JBFCS is named as the creator. I asked Christine Weideman, Yale's director of manuscripts and archives, if the records had been placed by Neubauer or the Jewish Board. She indicated that it was the Jewish Board, as shown in the finding aid, the document showing detailed information about the contents of an archival collection. I then wrote to a former administrator at the JBFCS, asking specifically who chose Yale as the depository. The reply was, "As we have stated before, no one presently involved with the Jewish Board has any knowledge of how or why the decision was made. We have tried to find the answer, but have not been successful." Next, I turned to Dr. Lois Oppenheim, who said, "I really don't know the answer to your question. Neither does his son, whom I asked (and hence the delayed reply to your email). Peter was involved with Yale insofar as they were publishing the *Psychoanalytic Study of the Child* of which he was co-editor at the time. Also, he worked closely with Dr. Albert J. Solnit,[44] so that may well have had something—or much—to do with it. But that is only speculation on my part."[45] Somebody must know. As someone close to Neubauer once told me, the situation is complicated, and some people do not want to talk.[46]

Even though the materials were sealed as of 1990, Neubauer and son published their book in that year, Neubauer and Abrams published their paper on object-orientedness in 1994, and Neubauer and Balzert published their chapter in 1996. Perhaps copies of some records, even the "book draft and dictation," were retained by the investigators so they could prepare these publications. After all, in 1993, Neubauer told Lawrence Wright that the researchers planned to publish their findings in a year and a half—by then the materials would have been sealed for about five years.

When the JBFCS donated the twin study data to Yale in 1990, Yale agreed not to release the data to the public for seventy-five years. By 2065, the youngest twins would be ninety-nine years old if they were to survive to that age. But most likely none of the twins would have ever seen their personal data, whereas anyone else who wanted to would have access. In a later chapter, I will address questions of institutional responsibility in accepting and managing highly restricted collections. However, I wanted to know how common it is to place such extended delays on the availability of archival material. I asked Columbia University's head archivist, Stephen E. Novak, who was present when Bernard's records were given to Columbia, some with restrictions. Commenting on Neubauer's materials, Novak said that Columbia would never have accepted such a large collection that would stay closed for so long. "I think what happened at Yale was that they accepted this material without really knowing what was in it. That's called *appraisal.* And unfortunately, it's not always very easy to do appraisal when you are kind of confronted with someone wanting to give you [material] that may be inaccessible. . . . Somehow, something went wrong because I can't imagine they really wanted a collection of that size closed for more than half a century."

A Yale University archivist had a different view regarding archival closure. This individual felt that seventy-five years was not necessarily a long time. I was told of collections that are closed for one hundred years, plus an additional twenty-five years, possibly to assure that the owner or donor is deceased at the time of release in order to protect identity.[47]

Recall that I had asked Novak if Bernard's files would be opened in 2021, as specified in the deed of gift. "That was the intention of the donor, the executor, and a deed of gift is a legal document," he explained. As I indicated in chapter 12, the files were opened on schedule despite the pandemic, but not without some concerns.

Novak also explained the important difference between *closed* and *restricted* materials—*closed* collections are unavailable until the specified interval has expired, whereas *restricted* collections may be opened under certain circumstances and with certain requirements agreeable to the donor. However, even when closed collections are finally opened, there may be some limits imposed by the Health Insurance Portability and Accountability Act and/or Family Educational Rights and Privacy Act.[48] When I tried to obtain Neubauer's correspondence stored in Professor Donald J. Cohen's archives at Yale, restricted for thirty-five years, a request with the Office of the Secretary was filed on my behalf. The request was denied. Prior to filing, I was cautioned that rejection was likely, because of the sensitivity of the material—it contained the names of donors and their donations.[49]

"OMG, YES I WOULD LOVE TO SEE THEM"

Most of us learn about our infancy and early childhood from the stories told to us by the people who raised us. Baby books, photographs, and films often supplement these tales, and hospital cards with our birth weight, birth length, and Apgar scores are sometimes available. All this information is given freely. However, the circumstances of the twin study participants were drastically different because nearly every aspect of their being was scrutinized and recorded—and concealed.

The process of unsealing the records is decided by the JBFCS in New York City. Yale University must abide by the 2065 date, but the JBFCS, as the creator, can make changes. I was told by a representative of the Jewish Board that, as of May 2020, every interested twin and the triplets had received portions of their materials, some of it with redactions. As I explained before, in early 2020 the JBFCS hired an attorney, as well as a psychologist, to work with the twins and the twins' attorneys toward the further unsealing of their documents. The twins are understandably frustrated by the delays, which they do not understand.

The final segment of the 2018 film *Three Identical Strangers* informs viewers that, as a result of the film, ten thousand pages of records were released to the triplets, although much of the material was heavily redacted.[50] Also as a result of the film, the JBFCS's president, Alice Tisch, issued letters of apology to the twins and triplets: "We realize that our efforts have fallen short and that we can and should do more . . . we feel we must reach out, acknowledge our past error, and set a new moral course for the future."[51] ABC's *20/20* program, "Secret Siblings," invited LWS adoptees who suspect they are twins to contact Spence-Chapin, the agency holding LWS's records.[52]

In July 2018, Megyn Kelly, then host of NBC's *Megyn Kelly Today*, interviewed triplets Robert Shafran and David Kellman, and author Lawrence Wright. The network had reached out to the JBFCS, whose spokesperson indicated that the board is contacting all twins and the triplets involved in the study. The board also stated that it neither condones, nor supports, Dr. Neubauer. Still, the JBFCS has yet to tell their story in full. Their board members know that I want to hear from them, and that I am not the only one. Before this book went to print would have been the perfect time.

The researchers constantly worried that public exposure of the study might cause the hundreds of other LWS adoptees to wonder if they had a twin. This happened to Justin Goldberg, a resident of Los Angeles, California, whose story comes next.

• *14* •

Not Just a Doppelgänger?

Justin Goldberg

"I saw this guy that looked exactly like my dad. The resemblance was remarkable—they were absolutely identical! I almost said 'dad' because they were so much alike."[1]

*T*hroughout 2017, I met periodically with journalist Erika Hayasaki to discuss the ways that twin studies enhance our understanding of behavior, health, and the new discoveries in epigenetics. Hayasaki, also a mother of identical twins, was writing an article on the current status of twin research for *The Atlantic Monthly*.[2] As November approached, Erika sent me a link to a story in *Deadline*[3] (a source for entertainment news) that gave life to a concern that had nagged at the Louise Wise Services (LWS)-Child Development Center (CDC) research team for years: Would professional and public attention to the separated twins and their long-term study cause other LWS adoptees to ask if they had a twin?

SIGHTINGS

My first involvement with this story was in November 2017, but the main event happened several months before. It began when Charlotte Goldberg, the teenage daughter of then fifty-one-year-old entertainment executive Justin Goldberg, encountered an extraordinary look-alike. It happened at Marconda's Puritan Poultry, a popular eatery in Los Angeles's Farmers Market. Charlotte spotted someone who so closely resembled her father that she wondered what her dad was doing at the market. But she knew that whoever this person was, he was *not* her father. Instinctively, Charlotte grabbed for

The "Twins," Their Family Members, and Friends

Justin

Justin Goldberg possible reared-apart twin
Rema Goldberg Justin's adoptive mother
Jay Goldberg Justin's adoptive father
Toni-Ann Goldberg Justin's former wife
Grace Goldberg Justin's oldest daughter
Charlotte Goldberg Justin's youngest daughter
Jack Goldberg Justin's son and youngest child

Julie

Julia Goldberg Maniha Justin's younger adoptive sister
Rema Goldberg Julie's adoptive mother
Jay Goldberg Julie's adoptive father

Others

Christina Fitzgibbons investigative genealogist and Justin's friend

her phone and filmed the "double" as he waited by the outdoor counter and checked his cell phone.

When Justin, Charlotte's real father, viewed the clip, he was stunned by the physical likeness between himself and this stranger. Their narrow faces, prominent noses, and angular jaws looked identical in profile. Not only that, Justin watched as this other man reached into his pocket and pulled out his phone in a strangely familiar way. He could hear his daughter's friends in the background shouting, "Oh my God, that's so weird!" Justin wondered: Could this doppelgänger be his identical twin, separated from him at birth? His sister Julie saw a "definite similarity" between them, but thought that the look-alike seemed younger.[4] Only Justin's wife Toni-Ann remained skeptical—but she is a skeptical sort.[5]

Justin was born on April 12, 1966, in New York City, and relinquished for adoption as a newborn. His parents, Jay and Regina ("Rema") Goldberg, adopted him through LWS when he was two months old.[6] By 1966, the LWS-CDC twin study had been under way for six or seven years, and twins were still being separated. But at this point in the story, Justin had no idea that the adoption agency had been placing twins apart and documenting their subsequent development. It was not until he began reading about LWS, searching for clues to his past, that he unexpectedly found articles about the twins' and triplets' separate adoptions, the secret study, and Neubauer's sealed records.[7]

Justin was stunned—the thought that he might have an identical twin was life-changing. He was determined to discover the truth about his birth, but he was still puzzling over a curious encounter that had happened the week before.[8] The incident involved his younger sister, Julie, who had been adopted from LWS at four months of age, in early 1970. Shortly before his daughter's sighting, Justin and his eleven-year-old son Jack were walking through their Larchmont Village neighborhood. They noticed a woman who bore an uncanny resemblance to Justin's sister Julie. According to Justin, "She was *identical* to my sister, but I wasn't sure of the age factor . . . it was extraordinary because [my sister's] features are distinctive, not typical . . . but I knew it couldn't be her because we had just spoken on the phone."[9] Justin's son Jack concurred, stating unequivocally that the woman looked "exactly like my aunt."

Father and son angled toward the woman for a closer look before Justin pulled out his GoPro camera and set it at high resolution. He made a short film of Julie's look-alike and sent it to their mother. Before viewing the clip, Rema was dismissive, claiming that there are probably a hundred people who look alike.[10] But Rema saw "something similar" between the two, although the look-alike came across as an "older, wilder version" of her daughter. She was less impressed with the similarity between Justin and his look-alike, saying she could not see a front view of his double. But she was intrigued by the complete story of Charlotte's discovery that Justin had told in his posted video. Rema also said that LWS never told her that Justin was a twin—but of course, if Justin *were* a twin they would have kept this hidden for purposes of the study.

The thought that LWS would place two unrelated singleton twins in the same home is incredible, but conceivable. If Justin had a twin and they were a fraternal pair, this could explain why he was not placed in a family with an older sibling. Recall that all LWS-separated identical twins had an older sibling, whereas fraternal twins—who were not in the study—were sometimes the first adopted child in their family. If Justin's sister Julie were an identical twin, then it would have been important to place her in a family with a sibling approximately three years older—the same age difference between Julie and Justin.[11] The Goldbergs do not recall anyone coming to their home to test their children—so if Julie had a twin she and her sister might have been fraternal twins as well. A small proportion of fraternal twins look remarkably alike and can fool investigators based upon physical inspection alone.[12] If this hypothetical case were proven true, an extraordinary, but logical question follows: Could a twin of Justin's and a twin of Julie's been raised together by a different family? Justin and Julie had independently thought about this too, thinking they might be "an experimental pair."[13]

SEARCHING FOR FAMILY AND SEEING DOUBLE

Rema admitted that when Justin was young, she might have quietly worried if he had shown a desire to find his birth parents.[14] Perhaps he would have abandoned his adoptive family in favor of biological kin. But she admitted that this fear subsided as Justin grew older. Rema was actually more intrigued with why Justin felt that he had a twin and why he was looking for one. Justin's father, Jay, was surprised and "distressed" at the sight of his son's look-alike.[15] He strongly believes that adoptive families must sever ties with the biological family. "I want him for my own," he insisted. Jay praised Justin's warm heart and creative bent—"so different from mine." Unlike the other parents I spoke with, Jay claims he would not have accepted twins had LWS made the offer, explaining that twins tend to compete with one another. At this point in our telephone conversation, Rema overheard her husband's remarks and commented in the background, prompting Jay to say, "Rema disagrees with me. What am I saying that is wrong?"

Despite his curiosity, Justin didn't speak to his sister's look-alike when he saw her, worried that he would disrupt her day and possibly her life. He showed the video to the stylists at a nearby hair salon who said they knew her, but he stopped there.[16] The wisdom of approaching a stranger suspected of being someone's twin is understandably hard to decide. Doing so risks exposing family secrets and impairing family relationships. Some parents hide their child's adoption for purposes of privacy, and some parents fear intrusion by their child's biological family. Justin's parents spoke openly about adoption to their son and daughter, telling them they had to adopt because they were "allergic" to each other—suggesting to their children that together they could not create a baby like other couples. Rema was twenty-eight and her husband Jay was thirty-three when they adopted Justin. Rema was very eager to become a mother and would "probably" have taken twins if they had been available.

When nine-year-old Justin mentioned his adoption to his maternal grandmother, he was reprimanded for "making it up."[17] Justin thinks his grandparents were too preoccupied to pay attention to what was happening in his family. He added that in the early and mid-1960s his father, an attorney, prosecuted cases in Indiana, Pennsylvania, and Buffalo, before returning to New York. Justin's grandparents may have assumed that his mother was pregnant during that time. It might have been easier to let them think that; however, Rema believes that Justin's grandmother—her own mother—knew that Justin was adopted and was perplexed by her son's recollection.[18]

On the positive side, speaking up after seeing someone's look-alike might lead to a unique and meaningful sibship. Two of the separated identical pairs I have written about—Anne and Susan, and Melanie and Ellen—and the triplets—Robert, David, and Eddy—might never have known one another if someone hadn't voiced their suspicions. None of the twins or triplets regrets having met, but they all grieve over having been apart. This is also true of the reunited twin participants in the Minnesota study. Identical twins Carole and Sylvia met because Sylvia's Australian friend "recognized" Carole during a visit to Carole's tiny British town and said something.[19] Fraternal twins Kerrie and Amy were brought together by a young man who was certain that they were sisters. Even though they were not identical twins, their physical similarities were so striking that Kerrie was often mistaken for Amy by people she didn't know.[20]

We can only speculate over what might have happened if Justin had spoken to Julie's double. This woman may have felt the same curiosity and excitement that Justin would soon experience at the prospect of having a twin. In the weeks and months that followed, Justin spotted his sister's look-alike from time to time as she walked through his neighborhood, and he studied her intensely. Beyond their matching faces he saw matching mannerisms, especially the way they handled a phone, touched their hair, and displayed solitary speech. The thought that his sister Julie could be related to this woman still haunts Justin.

Julie has viewed the video and had her DNA tested, but has "mixed emotions" when it comes to finding her biological kin.[21] Her reluctance is partly linked to uncertainty over whether her birth family is interested in finding her, but she is open to the idea. Julie also feels strongly that the parents, brother, aunts, uncles, and cousins she grew up with *are* her family. Still, she is impressed with the physical resemblance between herself and the woman in the video, allowing that they could be fraternal twins—the woman in the video looks older—or more distant relatives. Julie had some interest in knowing her biological family when she was a teenager and young adult. Twice when she was in her twenties, she bumped shoulders with a woman in New York City who looked "exactly" like her but was about twenty years older. Julie wondered if the woman might be her birth mother and began asking questions about her adoption. However, when she learned that LWS had not disclosed adoptees' medical and mental health information to adoptive parents, Julie's interest turned to fear, thinking that perhaps she had been born in a psychiatric facility. Her interest waned further when she delivered her son,

Zachary, at age thirty-five. "It was cool to meet my first biological relative and to see our physical similarities—just as Justin had described when he encountered the woman who looked like me." Julie also has a daughter named Zoe.

LOOKING FOR MR. LOOK-ALIKE

Justin's chance meeting with his sister's look-alike was fresh in his mind when he saw his own double on his daughter's phone. The possibility of having a twin inspired him to create an online video about his possible connection to the LWS-CDC twin study and to be interviewed for the online news site *Deadline* by an interested reporter. Justin's video is riveting—one viewer commented that it was "better than *SYFY*," NBCUniversal's station that features science fiction, fantasy, paranormal, and superhero programming.[22] Social media exposure promised to increase the chance that Justin might connect with his look-alike. I had another idea.

In late 2017, Lori Shinseki, director of *The Twinning Reaction*, was working with ABC producer Eric Strauss for a *20/20* program about her film.[23] It occurred to me that if Justin were included in the piece, it would significantly expand the range of people who might know his double and help them connect. It was also possible that the person he was searching for might see it. I contacted Bruce Haring, the author of the *Deadline* article, and explained my

Figure 14.1. Justin Goldberg (L) was searching for his look-alike at the time this photo was taken. The middle panel shows Justin's look-alike, as captured by his daughter Charlotte (top), and the real Justin assuming the same position using his cell phone (bottom). Justin and his sister Julie are pictured to the right (R). Photo of Justin Goldberg by Dr. Nancy L. Segal; other photos are courtesy of Justin Goldberg.

interest in the story.[24] Haring was intrigued and forwarded my note to Justin. "Expect to hear from him," he wrote, and I did. Justin was eager to know more.

By then, Shinseki had completed her film and put me in touch with Eric Strauss at ABC. The timing of Justin's possible discovery was ideal for *20/20*. Strauss was thrilled by the opportunity to include an LWS adoptee searching for a possible twin. Strauss arranged for a crew to record an interview with Justin at his Los Angeles home and for me to be there to bring a research perspective to the program. Justin was excited to see us and dazzled by the detour his life was taking. He spoke openly about his adoption, his parents, his family, and his career.

FROM NEW YORK TO LOS ANGELES

Justin was raised in Tarrytown, a village on the east bank of the Hudson River, outside New York City. It was a "wonderful place" to grow up. Justin played by the stream in his backyard and skated on ponds in the winter. Partly because "half the kids in the neighborhood were adopted," he never felt different from his friends or disturbed by his circumstances. It was also important that his father, Jay Goldberg, and his mother, Rema, were open about his adoption and didn't treat it like anything embarrassing or shameful. Justin pronounced them "great parents," unwavering in their love and support of himself and his sister.

When Justin was growing up, it was not unusual for him to find his father on the phone with high-profile politicians, industrialists, entertainers, and even members of the mafia. Jay Goldberg was a prominent attorney, who served as acting US Attorney for Indiana's Northern District and Special Counselor to the US Department of Justice in Washington, DC. He is famous for assisting James B. Donovan whose efforts allowed the transfer of Russian spy Rudolph Abel for Francis Gary Powers, portrayed in the film *Bridge of Spies*.[25] Jay Goldberg also represented Donald Trump in his divorce proceedings.[26] He is the author of the 2018 book *The Courtroom Is My Theater*, in which he describes his legal experiences with the first Jewish Miss America Bess Myerson, country music legend Willie Nelson, business mogul Armand Hammer, and organized crime figure Meyer Lansky, among others.[27] Justin's mother, Rema, began her career as a teacher before earning a Master's degree in Counseling and becoming a career counselor. She was also involved in jury selection for her husband, leading to full-time work as a jury consultant. And Rema paints portraits, landscapes, and still lifes. [28]

Despite the devotion and warmth that Justin knew as a child, he sensed that he was not really where he was supposed to be. He craved the California deserts that he saw in pictures, but his family preferred to keep him close. His parents even hid his acceptance letter from the University of Southern California, but he managed to enroll there regardless. Justin described himself as a "weed who had to grow through whatever crack in the sidewalk appeared," explaining that he needed to adapt to whatever situation presented itself. He believes that this feeling came from the behavioral differences he observed between himself and his parents. As a young boy, Justin liked to swim, fix cars, and go fishing, interests he didn't share with his family. His father tried to involve him in baseball, but Justin didn't like competitive sports—he was more interested in the concession stands when his father took him to games.[29] And "from day one" he was dying to ride a motorcycle, a desire that went far outside his parents' lifestyle. His father "nudged him toward a law degree," but Justin knew that would never happen.[30] "It was hard to make that orchestra go into tune," he said. I understood Justin to mean that his interests and talents could not be changed or channeled in certain directions. Justin also knows that some children raised by their biological families do not feel a close fit, but that may not be what's most important. "You gotta ask yourself: What is family and what is love?"

After graduating from the University of Southern California in 1988, Justin entered Los Angeles's lively entertainment scene.[31] He began his career as creative manager at Sony/ATV—Artists and Repertorie at their Santa Monica, California, location, working with clients in music publishing and international projects. He eventually became a senior director at Sony, responsible for signing and helping to develop artistic talent. Justin returned to New York City in 1996 as a project director for the Trump Organization, working in building remodeling for the next two years. At that time, digital music was just starting, and Justin presented Trump with a plan for a digital music company. Trump was uncertain, not understanding how an online venture would work—possibly like a fax machine? For some reason, Trump was fascinated by Justin's adoption and raised the topic from time to time.

Beginning in 2012, Justin held various executive level positions in the Los Angeles area, including Red Light Management, Measurement Arts Management, and SyncLab. Since 2017, Justin has been a freelance producer at Justin Goldberg Creative Management. He is interested in working with new writers, artists, entertainment properties, and technology companies to promote projects with lasting impact.[32] Justin is married and has three children—Grace, Charlotte, and Jack, ranging in age from thirteen to nineteen. He has no regrets about the life he has led and, aside from one exceptional circumstance, was never curious about his biological family. Charlotte's tape changed that.

TWIN TRACKING

Until 2018, Justin knew virtually nothing about his biological mother, but correctly assumed that she was young and unwed when she delivered him. The only two pieces of information he had were his original first name—Michael—and his mother's last name, as indicated on a birth document.[33] Because of his happy childhood, he didn't want to upset his parents by searching for her. However, in 2014, it suddenly hit Justin that there was a woman out there who gave him up and might think about him every day. "She has no idea of me!" he thought. At the time he was driving to the Coachella Valley Music and Arts Festival near Palm Springs, California. It was a dark, rainy night, and the thought forced him to pull over to the side of the road, dangerously crammed in between two eighteen-wheelers. "It was a dramatic movie moment," he recalled. The experience persuaded him to post a note on an online adoption site, but nothing came of it.

Justin remarked that the physical similarities among his family members have changed over the years, but were "uncanny" at times. His sister Julie said that she and Justin have a number of characteristics in common. Brother and sister have similar hair, dimples, and blue eyes that change color depending on the context.[34] Because of that, people seeing them together never questioned their relatedness or membership in the family.

Despite the warmth and security Justin knew, he admitted that he has always scanned faces when entering theaters, arenas, and other public places, though he can't explain why. Perhaps as an adoptee, this behavior reflects a desire to see someone whom he resembles more closely than his parents and sister.[35] On a scale of one to one hundred, Justin judged his resemblance to the man in the video as "98." Given that high rating and knowing how quickly social media spreads, Justin was puzzled that his look-alike hadn't surfaced. In contrast, he was contacted for the interview with *Deadline* just five minutes after posting his video, and *20/20* called him three weeks later. Events beyond our control can derail such searches, as happened to two separated twin sets we studied at the University of Minnesota.[36]

Both sets were from Great Britain and had benefited from 1975 legislation allowing adoptees to apply for a copy of their original birth certificate.[37] The twins in one pair were born on October 31 and November 1, dates that straddled midnight and the following day. This difference in timing delayed their reunion indefinitely, as the twin in search was hunting for someone with the same birthday. A twin in the other pair was told he was not a twin at all when he began searching for his birth family. It turned out that a clerk in the records office had inadvertently placed her thumb over the time of birth, information recorded on the birth certificates of all British twins. The twins' reunion was delayed until this oversight was corrected. Fortunately, Justin had an old friend who could help him.

MAKING SENSE OF THINGS: BIRTH MOTHERS, MOTORCYCLES, AND POCKET KNIVES

Christina Bryan Fitzgibbons is a San Francisco–based genetic and investigative genealogist. Her Hoodie Project offers professional consultation for biological family searches and paternity verification.[38] She has known Justin since the early 1990s when she was interning for a record company in northern California and he was working for Sony Music. After twenty years of being out of touch, coincidentally Christina called Justin just after Charlotte's 2017 sighting at the Los Angeles Farmers Market. She wanted him to produce a video for one of her clients. They talked for hours about his possible twinship and, as a friend and a genealogical professional, Christina was happy to help. She advised Justin to submit a DNA sample for genetic analysis, which he did. Christina and I discussed Justin's case then, and again in 2020.[39]

Justin began by calling the Jewish Board of Family and Children's Services to find out if he was a twin. A staff member he spoke with was initially dismissive. She said he had no connection to the Neubauer study, and that she had no authority regarding the adoption records. She later called him back, was "nicer" this time, and advised him to submit a request to the Spence-Chapin agency that was managing the LWS records. Christina was in the room when these calls took place.

I reviewed the letter sent to Justin by Spence-Chapin in February 2018, detailing Justin's birth history, biological family background, and adoption.[40] He weighed six pounds, seven and a half ounces at birth, and he was nineteen and a half inches long. He stayed in foster care from the age of one week until the time of adoption. His adoptive parents, Rema and Jay, first met him on June 15, 1966, and took him home two days later. They were "rapturous"—Rema was so "tender" with her new son, and Jay showed "extreme excitement." Subsequent home visits by LWS social workers showed that Justin's extended family provided a "royal" welcome.

Christina was more intrigued by the behavioral descriptions of Justin's birth mother. It appeared that Justin had made many of the same choices that his birth mother had made, even though they had never known one another. She later learned that both had left New York for the more laidback lifestyle of California. Both are free-spirited, adventurous, and socially conscious. Christina now leans toward the nature side of the nature-nurture equation, as the similarities she saw suggested genetic effects. "It explained a lot about him in an amazing way—wow!" Justin shared several more pieces of information with me that had made his "mouth drop."

Justin's birth mother rode a motorcycle! Of course, growing up, Justin had despaired at being deprived of riding a motorcycle, finally owning one as an adult. Reading that in the letter, "I burst into tears, I was so overwhelmed with emotion. This never-completed item in my history fell into a logical place." Christina had also tracked down the name of Feldmesser, linked to Justin's DNA report. Feldmesser is the name of the Austrian pocketknife that Justin obsessed over as a six-year-old child and still carries today. Even Justin's children were shocked by this discovery. The DNA findings also suggested that Justin and his adoptive mother Rema could be distant cousins. His biological mother and adoptive mother were from the same New York City area and the Jewish families living there were in close contact. Rema also believes this is possible.

Christina indicated that the Spence-Chapin letter contained information about Justin's family that was not conveyed to his adoptive parents.[41] She believes that Rema and Jay were lied to, although Justin feels they were just not informed about certain things. For example, Justin's birth mother had experienced depression about two years before giving birth at age nineteen. Christina felt that this information should have been conveyed to Justin's parents. At the time, adoption agencies strictly controlled the release of birth parents' health histories, although this question was debated by LWS staff members. In addition, Justin had developed a whooping cough as a young infant. "This was a revelation!" he said. Rema recalled that Justin's symptoms, which developed a week after he came home, were "scary."[42] She finally found a doctor in the Bronx who recognized his condition and cured it over the next month. It is possible that, prior to his adoption, Justin wasn't well, and she and her husband were not told. Rema was also disturbed to later discover that Justin had not received the standard infant inoculations. She said that LWS told her nothing about Justin, except that his birth mother was young and single. She was shocked to later learn that LWS, held in high esteem by Jewish families, received some babies from women confined to psychiatric institutions, either before or after delivery.

The Spence-Chapin letter also revealed that Justin's birth father was not Jewish, causing Justin to wrestle with what it means to be of the Jewish faith.[43] "That was another revelation!" And he learned that his birth mother had experienced some depressive episodes. "It would have been nice if my adoptive parents had been told about this. I might have benefited."

Christina described a posting by a male adoptee from New York City, born on the same day as Justin, that seemed significant. He lives in Santa Monica, California, just fourteen miles to the west of Los Angeles. However, his birth certificate number does not immediately precede or follow Justin's, as would be the case with twins, and whether he was adopted through LWS is unknown. Families can adopt children from other states when agencies cooperate, and Christina knows that LWS has been part of such arrangements. Recall that LWS had considered placing one identical twin in the Midwest, but the cost of tracking her development was prohibitive.

Christina has made progress on Julie's file. Julie has shown little interest in finding her biological family and is unmoved at the thought of having an identical twin. However, Julie's interest in the situation could change. Christina's research shows that Julie is most likely not a twin. That is because the birth index does not show a second child with a consecutive birth certificate number. Moreover, no other infant sharing her date of birth had the same last name. Meanwhile, Christina was able to locate Justin's birth mother—I will call her Joan—although the two have not met. Their reunion was purposely postponed at the request of a production company that wanted to capture it live for a program they were planning.

A LOVELY CONVERSATION

Justin spoke to his birth mother in the spring of 2019. Justin began the process by first calling one of his birth mother's acquaintances, acting under Christina's guidance. Christina had advised Justin to proceed carefully. Sometimes, an acquaintance or other intermediary is used to alert the birth mother that an adopted away child may call, in order to prepare her for the surprise. However, Joan was annoyed that Justin did not phone her first and took it upon herself to contact him. It is possible that, acting on his own without Christina's suggestions, Justin would have contacted Joan first—he is assertive by nature, a tendency he appears to share with his birth mother. Justin also explained that he was not emotionally invested in Joan's reaction, but approached the situation as if he was doing her a favor by letting her know who he was. "I am fifty-four and have been through a lot. I had no information about her for years, so this wasn't so pivotal for my sense of self-worth." It turned out that they had a lovely conversation that lasted for two hours.

Justin learned that he is the first of six children, fathered by two or three of his mother's different partners. Joan was seventeen and single when she delivered him, and not well positioned to raise a child successfully.[44] She had told the agency that she was unsure as to who Justin's father was because she was involved in two relationships when he was conceived. One of her partners was Irish Catholic, a musician, and a "ski bum" with reddish hair and blue eyes. Justin is certain that this man is his birth father because of his own tastes in music and non-competitive sports. Joan claims that Justin's father is still alive—recall that she had told LWS she wasn't sure who his father was—and years later she seemed reluctant to provide much information about him. Neither of Justin's potential fathers had been told of the pregnancy. Most importantly, Joan said that she delivered just one baby on June 16, 1966, confirming that Justin is not a twin.

THE WAY IT IS

In the immediate aftermath of posting his video, Justin received dozens of tips about his look-alike. Once he raced off to a restaurant in the area after a phone called alerted him that his double was there. By the time Justin arrived, the person had left, so he headed home. On the way, he stopped for coffee in Melrose, a trendy shopping and dining district in Los Angeles. This time *he* was the person confused for somebody else. A car pulled over and the driver shouted, "Hi, Buddy!" to which Justin said, "Do you know me?" "You're here all the time," the driver said, then decided, "Well, maybe it's not you." Justin showed him his video and "the guy was blown away."[45]

When this story began, Justin could have been an identical twin, a fraternal twin or a close-in-age brother, but it now appears that he has a chance look-alike. At first, Justin was "swept away" with the possibility of being an identical twin, but he is not really disappointed. In fact, he is somewhat relieved, because of some worrisome questions: Would his twin have been a more successful version of himself? Would he have measured up to his twin? These questions are understandable and can foster resentment if one twin's opportunities seem more favorable than the other's. Recall from chapter 11 that Sharon Morello's twin sister felt embittered, knowing that Sharon had been raised in a wealthier household. Still, Justin said it would have been fascinating . . . but chance look-alikes draw lots of attention.

Some look-alikes are extremely striking in their degree of physical resemblance, to the point of mimicking identical twins. Explaining this phenomenon is challenging, but perhaps different gene combinations can yield the same face and physique—like different recipes for the same treat. These curious pairs captured the interest of Canadian photographer François Brunelle, whose "I'm Not a Look-Alike!" gallery of photos fascinates everyone who sees them.[46] Some people expect that people who look alike will also behave alike, but I have compared the personality traits of Brunelle's participants and it is just not so. I have used this finding to counter the criticism that identical twins have matched personalities because their matched appearance triggers similar treatment by others. I believe, instead, that identical twins' similar personalities evoke similar responses from those around them.[47]

There are popular websites allowing people to search for their double, not just in the population, but in works of art.[48] This trend may reflect the universal human tendency to seek others who share observed characteristics. My doctoral thesis advisor, Dr. Daniel G. Freedman, suggested that recognizing common features may foster a "sense of 'we' between ourselves and our fellow tribesmen. Recognition of this sense triggers a series of emotions whose net effect is tribal unity and the increased chance for altruism."[49] However, I also found that most unrelated look-alikes *do not* form close relationships once their initial excitement at seeing one another wears off. That is because social attraction is based more on perceptions of behavioral similarity than physical similarity and, as I discovered, look-alikes do not share personality traits.[50]

Having a look-alike brings moments of surprise or amusement to most people. But having a double assumes profound significance for LWS adoptees born in the 1960s because of the twins' separate placements and the study that followed. Even without having a look-alike, just seeing *Three Identical Strangers* or *The Twinning Reaction* caused some LWS adoptees and their parents to wonder if they had a twin or had raised one; I will describe such a case in a later chapter. Justin and Julie do not have twins, but their experience exemplified the researchers' fear that adoptees might start asking questions.

Having examined LWS's policies and the LWS-CDC twin study as a possible participant, Justin was shocked. "How could it have happened?" he wants to know. Justin is mystified by the fact that the researchers who visited the twins' homes kept the twinship a secret. "They were not high-level CIA agents, but none of them folded!" He wants to believe that Dr. Neubauer's intentions were altruistic, "but that's just wishful thinking."

When I met Justin in December 2017, he was in the midst of considering the next step in his career. He has received offers from production companies to tell his story, and one was moving forward until the coronavirus pandemic crippled California and the rest of the nation in early 2020. It turned out that ABC's program on *The Twinning Reaction* did not include Justin's story. This was partly because the production company, hoping for twin and mother-son reunions, wanted exclusive rights to the story.[51] Justin now hopes to meet his birth mother in the near future. When they last spoke on the telephone, they both agreed that each has been holding back somewhat.

Justin is still curious about his identical other. He has been to Marconda's Puritan Poultry many times, hoping his look-alike would show up, but he never has. And no one at the restaurant recognizes him from the video, so he was probably a one-time customer. Justin wonders—would they share personality traits? odd behaviors? life events? His company, Justin Goldberg Creative Management, is focused on developing innovative projects for television audiences. Always thinking creatively, Justin affirmed, "If I find him I would make him part of the show."

• *15* •

Artists from Afar

Paula and Elyse

$\mathscr{I}$n the epilogue to her co-authored book *Identical Strangers*, Paula Bernstein wrote, "When I was younger, I believed that blood connections were insignificant. But that changed after I met Elyse. I initially resisted the pull of our bond, but it is now impossible to deny."[1] She added, "Although we don't always fit together neatly, we are missing pieces to the same puzzle."[2] I sensed a dubious tone in her statement, perhaps an attempt to smooth over the tensions and doubts that followed the twins' glorious reunion. But when *Identical Strangers* was released in 2007 and for the next several years, Paula Bernstein and Elyse Schein were busy promoting their book about separation and loss, identity and individuality, reunion and reconciliation. They beamed at one another in photo shoots and television appearances.

Both Paula and Elyse declined to be interviewed for this book when I contacted them in April 2020, a decade after I last saw them. Both twins wished me well. I will say more about their decisions at the conclusion of the chapter. The material here has been drawn mostly from their well-researched book *Identical Strangers* and the media opportunities in which they participated over the years.

MEETING THE TWINS

My first introduction to Paula and Elyse was in June 2004, about two months after the twins first met. Paula had contacted the University of Minnesota for information about reared-apart twins and the project director, Thomas J. Bouchard Jr., advised her to call me. The Minnesota twin study had ended by then, and I had been a psychology professor in California for thirteen years. I

The Twins, Their Family Members, and Friends

Paula

Paula Bernstein Elyse's reared-apart twin
Marilyn Bernstein Paula's adoptive mother
Bernie Bernstein Paula's adoptive father
Anthony (Avo) Orkin Paula's husband

Elyse

Elyse Schein Paula's reared-apart twin
Linda Schein Elyse's adoptive mother
Martin Schein Elyse's adoptive father

Others

Katherine Boros director of Postadoption Services, Louise Wise Services

was still following cases of reared-apart twins and was interested in knowing more about Paula and Elyse. Paula wanted to know if I was able to locate other twins who had been separated by Louise Wise Services (LWS). We arranged to meet during my next visit to the East Coast.

I met Paula alone in New York City in February 2005 at the Café Un Deux Trois, near Times Square. Paula later referred to the restaurant as a "cavernous bistro."[3] I showed her an article I had written about LWS and the twin study and one by Dr. Larry Perlman who had been one of Neubauer's research assistants. Paula and I also discussed the horrific experiments conducted on twins by Dr. Josef Mengele in the Auschwitz-Birkenau concentration camp in Poland. Paula thought that an "apt" comparison could be made between the LWS-Child Development Center study and Mengele's experiments. As a Jewish twin, Paula knows she would have been a valued subject at the Auschwitz-Birkenau concentration camp in Oświęcim, Poland.

Two months earlier, in December 2004, Larry Perlman and I had met with Dr. Neubauer in his New York City apartment. I showed Paula a photograph taken on that day, in which I am standing next to him. In her book, Paula stated that I showed her the picture "proudly," but that was not the case. I had the picture taken to document the meeting, something I was taught to do as a postdoctoral fellow in Minnesota. I thought Paula would be interested in seeing it.

Perlman later sent Paula information from his observation of the twins when they were twenty-eight days old and in foster care. Their foster mother, Mrs. McGowan, had observed some apparent differences in the twins' weight and facial features. She had also detected differences in their activity and sleeping patterns that were not obvious to Perlman. Mrs. McGowan was very fond of the twins and favored Paula, the more active of the two, but she felt guilty for preferring one twin over the other. Elyse was not pleased when she read this part of the report. She noted the series of separations she had endured thus far—separation from her birth mother, foster mother, and adoptive mother. Then she discovered that her sister was the preferred twin.

Once their book *Identical Strangers* was published in 2007, Paula and Elyse cycled through countless talk shows, newspaper articles, and magazine stories telling their extraordinary story. They hired agents and designed websites. The twins were popular among the media because they were so lively, entertaining, and informative. However, watching them together during their joint interviews, I detected a restrained tension on the part of the twin who was not speaking at the time. Elyse tended to do more of the talking, perhaps because she had done the searching, so it seemed natural to begin the interviews with her.

The last time I saw Paula and Elyse was on February 4, 2010, in the green room of the Martha Stewart Show. Dressed in matching black sweaters and wearing round framed eyeglasses, they looked more alike than I had ever seen them. The program that day, titled "The Twins Show," opened with identical twin chefs Fabrizio and Nicola Carro from Miami Beach, Florida, who prepared a savory Italian tomato sauce on the set. It ended with a stand-up routine by comedian Jeffrey Ross. In between these segments, I spoke with Martha about how twin studies offer insights into human developmental processes. But the audience was spellbound by Paula and Elyse, separated at birth because the Columbia University psychiatrist, Dr. Viola Bernard, believed that twins fared better that way.

These identical twins unexpectedly discovered each other when they were thirty-five. Adding to their interest are their similar faces—both twins have brown eyes, upturned noses, and broad foreheads. More impressive are their matched gestures and mannerisms, even to someone like me who is accustomed to seeing such similarities. Both twins move their hands and bodies a lot when speaking, drawing attention to the points they are making. They are both right-handed.

IN THE BEGINNING

Paula and Elyse were born on October 9, 1968, at New York's Staten Island Hospital. They were placed together in foster care until Paula, the firstborn twin, was adopted when she was five months old. She weighed just ten pounds at the time. The pediatrician who examined her suspected that Paula's foster family had boiled her formula for too long a time, stripping it of any nutritional value. Hearing that, her adoptive parents, Marilyn and Bernie Bernstein, saw to it that Paula was a well-fed child. Elyse, the second-born twin, was adopted at six months of age according to a letter she received from LWS in 2004. However, this information was incorrect. Elyse later learned that her parents, Linda and Martin Schein, didn't adopt her until she was nine months old—she had been in foster care four months longer than her twin sister.

Paula and Elyse were dropped from the twin study because of the difference in their early rearing and a marked discrepancy in their weight. This decision by the researchers explains the confusion over how many twins were in the study—eleven or thirteen. My research shows that there were originally thirteen children who comprised five sets of twins and one set of triplets. Once Paula and Elyse were eliminated, the number reduced to eleven. Recall that Susan and Anne were removed from the study when they were six or seven years old, after their parents accidentally discovered that they were twins. However, the information collected from Susan and Anne to that point appears to have been archived and, in fact, attorneys had been working with one of the twins to retrieve her materials from Yale. The finding aid, an index to the archived twin study records, shows material for Child-1 through Child-11, filed under the categories "Home Visits," "Raw Data," "Analyzed Data," and "Developmental Sequences." It is unclear if the small amount of data most likely gathered on Paula and Elyse was sealed along with Neubauer's other papers. It is conceivable that their materials were included under "Adoption Issues" or "Intra-Twin Comparisons," a matter that will not be settled until 2065 when Neubauer's files are opened.

It is worth noting that omitting Paula and Elyse from the twin study because of their observed differences was poor science. The study's aim was to compare developmental trends in identical twins reared in different homes. Therefore, removing a pair because their early life histories differed in some ways removed a potentially informative data source. In particular, it left open the question of how similar the twins might become despite their different body weights and dates of adoption. Similarly, some critics of the Minnesota study have argued that twins who spent time together prior to participating had matching IQ scores and food preferences because of their social contact. However, we found that twins' time together was unrelated to their resemblance across most traits, demonstrating genetic effects. This would not have been known if twins had been omitted from the study based on their degree of contact.

ARTISTS FROM AFAR

Elyse and Paula grew up in the New York area about ninety miles apart, Elyse in Suffolk County and Paula in Westchester County. Because they were initially part of the study, both twins had been placed in families with brothers who were three years older. Their brothers, Jay Schein and Steven Bernstein, had also been adopted from LWS.

As a child, Elyse relished listening to her parents as they "lovingly recounted" the story of how she became part of their family. Sadly, her adoptive mother passed away from spinal cancer when Elyse was just six years old. Five years later, her adoptive father remarried and moved the family to Oklahoma. The situation at home grew increasingly tense over the years as Elyse's interests and inclinations clashed with those of her father and stepmother, Toni. She increasingly embraced the avant-garde lifestyle of film artists living abroad, while rejecting the "uber-consumerism" she saw in her home. Adding to the difficulties, Elyse's older brother Jay suffered from schizophrenia. Jay fathered a son named Tyler to whom Elyse became close until Tyler began abusing drugs as a teenager.

After graduating from the State University of New York at Stony Brook, Elyse moved to Paris. She changed her first name from Stacie to Elyse—Elyse was her middle name—as part of her plan to embark upon a new life. Elyse also studied for three years at Prague's Film and Television School for the Performing Arts. Her acclaimed short film, *Je Voie Le Bonheur* (*I Steal Happiness*), was shown at the 1996 Telluride Film Festival in Telluride, Colorado. Elyse has also worked as an English teacher, photographer, and translator. At times, she experienced bouts of depression, assuming these episodes were linked to trauma surrounding the early loss of her mother and the mental illness affecting her brother. When this happened, Elyse would tell friends that she felt as if she had lost a twin.

Paula grew up in a warm loving home, always comfortable knowing she was adopted. Like Elyse, she often asked her mother to repeat the story of her earliest days in her new home, and their worries over her fragile health. As a child and teenager, Paula was an overachiever whose artistic talents were starting to show. She was the editor of her high school newspaper, the class secretary, and a yearbook photographer. Paula was also hard on herself and sensitive to criticism. As a nineteen-year-old college student, she grew depressed, prompting her to telephone old friends and engage in binge eating. Wondering if she shared these traits with her birth mother, she wrote to LWS for information. Paula learned that her mother was a single Jewish woman who had given birth to her at age twenty-eight. She also learned that her mother had attended a prestigious university, but had dropped out and begun working in an office. Paula suspected that there was a deeper story behind what LWS chose to reveal.

Paula went on to graduate from Wellesley College in Wellesley, Massachusetts, then earned a Master's degree in Film Studies at New York University. She became a successful freelance writer, contributing articles to the *New York Observer, Redbook, Fortune,* and *Filmmaker Magazine.* In 2018, she directed and produced *Sole Doctor,* a short documentary film set in a shoe repair store that was shown at several film festivals across the United States. Paula is married and has two daughters that she and her husband had been raising in Brooklyn, New York, before moving to the West Coast. Prior to that, Paula had lived a "bohemian life" in New York's Greenwich Village, frequenting film screenings and hosting "raucous" parties—just like an identical twin sister she didn't know she had.

BECOMING TWINS

Elyse found out first. It was fall 2002 and Elyse was living in Paris, working as a receptionist for a French venture capital firm. This was not a job she relished given her professional background in film, but she needed a salary. One afternoon with time on her hands, she searched the internet for adoption websites thinking they might eventually lead to her birth parents. After filing a form with the New York State Registry, she waited six months before learning that the registry had contacted LWS and asked them to send her non-identifying information. The registry informed her that her birth mother was American and twenty-eight years old at the time of her delivery. It took another six months for a letter to arrive from LWS. The news was stunning, but Elyse was jubilant—she was the younger of twin girls! She phoned a close friend and over beer shared the details and also disclosed the fact that her birth mother had suffered from mixed-type schizophrenia—currently called schizoaffective disorder—a condition marked by psychotic episodes and mood instability.[4]

Elyse phoned her father in Oklahoma to tell him the news. Aside from the shock of learning that that his thirty-three-year-old daughter was a twin, Martin Schein was angry that LWS had separated twins and hidden this practice from the adoptive parents. Like the other mothers and fathers, Schein felt betrayed by LWS, whose work he had so highly respected. He insisted that he and his wife would have taken both twins had they been available. Father and daughter decided that Elyse would come home and together they would visit New York to find her missing twin. Elyse arrived in New York two months later, after completing qualifying examinations for teaching French.

Once there, Elyse learned from an LWS staff member, Katherine Boros, that her twin sister was living in Brooklyn.

In April 2004, Paula and her husband Anthony (Avo) Orkin had left their East Village residence and were moving into an apartment in Brooklyn's Park Slope neighborhood. Paula was home with their two-year-old daughter Jesse when the call came. It was Katherine Boros, the LWS director of postadoption services, who had spoken to Elyse. Without any introduction or warning, Boros announced to Paula that she had a twin sister who was searching for her. It felt like a "slab of cement" had landed on her chest. She did not feel the euphoria that had initially overtaken her sister. Instead, her mind raced—she wondered what her adoptive parents had known, feared the loss of her happy life, and questioned who she might have become if raised by Elyse's family. A few hours later, Paula decided to call Boros with questions, but she inadvertently dialed Elyse's number that she had been given.

Paula was unprepared for what followed in that conversation. The twins' voices were the same, they had engaged in binge eating during depression, were allergic to sulfa drugs, and had begun menstruating at age thirteen. Both twins were also passionate about film, and Elyse had even considered studying at New York University where Paula had received her master's degree. The twins agreed to meet two days later at the Café Mogador, a Moroccan restaurant in Manhattan's East Village. In the aftermath of the call, Elyse was eager for the two of them to become close, whereas Paula was relieved that she perceived personality differences between them.

Paula and Elyse's first in-person conversation at the café is riveting and is best appreciated by reading the original telling of this event in their book, *Identical Strangers*. For now, it is enough to know that their meeting, which began during the day, lasted for hours into the night. They discovered many more shared tastes and preferences, some of them rare, which speak strongly to genetic influences. For example, most people love the 1961 film *West Side Story* because it brings love, longing, despair, and sacrifice to the big screen in a genuine and entertaining way. Therefore, if reunited identical twins both named *West Side Story* as their favorite film, their resemblance would not be noteworthy. In contrast, fewer people would name the 1987 romantic fantasy *Wings of Desire* as a favorite film, but Paula and Elyse both chose it when comparing their cinematic preferences. The twins also discovered that they had sucked the same two fingers when young, saved their *Alice in Wonderland* dolls in decanters,[5] and currently typed out words while thinking. The relative rarity of these behaviors makes these resemblances remarkable.

Specific genes for choosing films, fingers, and phrases do not exist. However, many genes acting together may underlie our temperamental, physiological, and cognitive traits.[6] These traits, in concert with the environment, may end up as various idiosyncratic behaviors and habits. Identical twins have the same genes, so perhaps it is not terribly surprising that even their unusual behaviors are alike. The Minnesota researchers encountered many such examples among the reunited identical twins—reading books from back to front, leaving love letters around the house, hooking pinky fingers under cans of beer. These similarities were rarely observed among the reunited fraternal twins.

Paula and Elyse left one another at midnight after sharing a hug. They planned to see each other several days later when Elyse and her father would come to Park Slope to meet Paula's family. Reflecting on meeting her newly found twin, Elyse felt "giddy" and celebrated the event with her family on Long Island. Paula experienced a range of emotions—some giddiness, but happy to return to her husband and child, and relieved that she and Elyse had not grown up together. An essay Paula wrote in 2000, just four years before discovering her twin, offers insight into her response. Titled, "Why I Don't Want to Find My Birth Mother," Paula took strong exception to claims that adoptees can only feel fulfilled after reuniting with biological kin. She insisted that her adoptive family *is* her family, and that she felt well-adjusted, enjoying close friends and a romantic relationship. She was grateful that her birth mother had given her up, hoping for a better life for her daughter.

Paula's essay was written without the idea of an identical twin sister in mind. While meeting Elyse challenged her views on the meaning of genetic connections and family ties, it did not change them completely. "There was an immediate intimacy that was misleading," she said.[7] The twins' warm beginning did not forecast what lay ahead.

ROCKY ROAD

Paula and Elyse sometimes came up in my conversations with other LWS twins I spoke with for this book. Some twins had had prior contact with Paula and Elyse, but now there was some suggestion that the two were no longer in touch. When reading *Identical Strangers*, it is easy to overlook the times that the twins faced difficulties in their relationship, given their instant rapport and strong feelings for one another. There was a time when Elyse left for Paris, and while Paula thought about her sister, she didn't miss her. When the twins eventually met up in Paris there was tension between them and a greater focus on their differences than on their similarities.[8] Elsewhere, Paula joked that writing the book together "saved us a fortune in therapy." She also noted that, "We both led lives we loved and didn't want to leave that. I felt very possessive of the life I've led."[9] They have also said that they love each other.[10]

I do not know for certain if Paula and Elyse are estranged from one another, but signs point to it. At the start of this chapter, I noted that neither twin wished to be interviewed for this book. Random House, the publisher of *Identical Strangers*, boasts that the book was featured in the "hit documentary, *Three Identical Strangers*." Only a brief televised clip of the twins appears in the movie.

The twins' words probably explain why I failed to hear back from one of Paula's relatives whom I had met on a flight from Chicago to New York City in April 2018—the woman's aunt is Paula's first cousin. I also understand why the twins' agent, once enthusiastic about talking to me, suddenly changed his mind. I wrote to him in May 2020 to request Elyse's email address, which he gladly provided. I also asked him if we could talk, and he enthusiastically agreed. Several days later, he asked for information about my project and when he received it, he wrote that he was no longer interested in talking. The twins' decision to avoid media attention seems to have been made recently. They took part in a 2016 radio interview with NPR—their strong connection is evident throughout the program, but at the end Elyse wondered where their relationship would go.[11] In August 2018, she referred a *Reader's Digest* editor to her publicist at Random House, who provided photos of both twins. Their pictures are included in the article about separated twins that was published online.[12]

The twins' lives have changed. In 2016, Elyse became a counselor at the Open Path Psychotherapy Collective in Oklahoma City, Oklahoma.[13] She now holds licensed professional counselor and national certified counselor degrees from Southeastern Oklahoma State University. Her personal narrative states that, "With warmth and humor, I will help you work on finding meaning in your life; accepting yourself for who you are, and creating the life you want." Elyse also specializes in sexuality, LGBTQIA, and gender identity issues. There is no mention of her sister, her twinship, her book, or her media appearances. Adoption/foster care issues is listed as one of her fourteen areas of expertise. Elyse is still single and likes to travel.

Paula has continued to work in journalism and film, but now lives in Portland, Oregon, about two thousand miles from Elyse's home in Oklahoma City. Her website lists her as a writer, filmmaker, author, content creator, reporter, non-fiction storyteller, editor, and social media strategist.[14] She is writing a book, *Love Is All Around*, in the genre of mind, body, spirit/self-help/motivational, and inspirational—the same area as Elyse's new profession.

To a knowing eye, Paula's website seems as sanitized as her sister's, with all evidence of twinship removed, except for her co-authorship of *Identical Strangers*. None of her many media appearances are indicated. Her 2000 essay in *Redbook* on why she didn't want to find her birth mother is missing from the "Articles" list.

Most identical twins raised together celebrate their mutual love, trust, and unconditional acceptance. Having established a bond built on years of experiences, understandings, and memories, they can negotiate differences and disagreements within the safety of their relationship. These opportunities were denied to the LWS twins. Despite the affection that Paula and Elyse felt for one another, the difficulties they faced further challenge Dr. Bernard's assumption that twins are better off apart until they establish separate and secure identities. At one point in their story, Paula wondered if the two would have been friends if they hadn't met as twins. Perhaps. Elyse replied that both twins might have been more open with each other if they had met in their twenties.[15] Maybe. Unfortunately, they cannot know the answers to these questions and many others.

· *16* ·

Opportunities Lost

Paula and Marjorie

"My twins—I used to call them 'my twins.' . . . They were not supposed to be separated." –Hedda Schacter Abbott, birth mother of Paula and Marjorie[1]

$\mathcal{O}$n November 4, 1960, nineteen-year-old Hedda Schacter of Ellenville, New York, delivered a pair of fraternal twin girls. Single and pregnant, she contacted Louise Wise Services (LWS) in her fourth month and lived in their Staten Island residence for unwed mothers from her sixth month until they

Figure 16.1. Infant fraternal twins Marjorie (L) and Paula (R) before being separated. Courtesy of Hedda Schacter Abbott.

279

were born. Hedda said that her baby girls were "beautiful." She named them Jamie Kim and Diane Lori. They were healthy, with birth weights of about five pounds each, just under the average for female twins born at thirty-five weeks.[2] Knowing she couldn't raise the twins on her own, Hedda decided to give them up for adoption so they could enjoy a better life. But it "broke my heart." She told me several times that doing so was the "hardest thing she had done in her entire life." Hedda stayed with her father after leaving the care of LWS, sobbing for hours in the bathroom.[3]

Hedda, whose married name is Abbott, has lived in Las Vegas, Nevada, since 1966. Her brief marriage in 1967 ended in divorce the following year. Hedda is a retired bookkeeper but works part-time managing accounts for a local restaurant. She has been physically unwell at times and is currently coping with the 2018 suicide of her son, Jacob Hafter, at age forty-two.[4] Jacob, the twins' half-brother, was sixteen years younger. He was a Las Vegas attorney whose controversial legal career ended in suspension.[5]

Hedda spoke with me by telephone in 2019 and 2020. She had refused to sign papers relinquishing the twins for adoption until she was given a picture of her daughters and assurance that they would be placed together. She did receive a photograph of the infant twins, showing them at three months of age and still together in foster care. However, Hedda had no idea that her twins had been adopted separately until one of them, Paula, unexpectedly contacted her after nearly forty years. Hedda was stunned—when she received her daughter's first email message "it was a dream come true—I lost it." But

The Twins, Their Family Members, and Friends

Marjorie

Marjorie Silverman Paula's reared-apart twin
Celia Silverman Marjorie's Adoptive mother
Samuel (Sam) Silverman Marjorie's adoptive father
Leo Silverman Marjorie's older adoptive brother
Hedda Schacter Abbott Marjorie's birth mother

Paula

Paula Sherman Marjorie's reared-apart twin
Dorothy Schulman Paula's adoptive mother
Meyer ("Mike") Schulman Paula's adoptive father
Adam Sherman Paula's husband
Dylan Sherman Paula's son
Hedda Schacter Abbott Paula's birth mother

Hedda was livid to learn that her twin girls had been raised apart. She believes that her own mother, embarrassed by her daughter's pregnancy, had had something to do with the twins' separate placement. Again, she insisted that she had signed papers stating that the two infants were to stay together. Sadly, the twins never met, despite Paula's success in finding both her birth mother and the Silverman family who had raised her sister.

ADOPTED APART

Celia Silverman and her husband Samuel (Sam) were eager to start a family.[6] They adopted their son Leo from LWS in 1957 when he was four months old. Leo was "a smiley baby, just unbelievable," Celia recalled fondly. Leo reached out naturally to the couple's family and friends who delighted in his warmth and playfulness. Wanting to have a little girl, the Silvermans contacted LWS again and adopted five-month-old Marjorie (Margie or Marge) four years later. Celia and Sam were financially secure—Celia was a nursing instructor and Sam was a builder. They lived in a comfortable house in the New York City suburb of East Rockaway. "We had plenty of money and I always wanted four kids," she said.

Early on, Celia observed that her two children were on "opposite ends of the spectrum." Leo was lively and joyful, whereas Marge was quiet and glum. Leo walked at an early age, whereas Marge took her first steps much later. But Celia accepted these differences between her children, knowing that no two are alike. What Celia did not know was that her daughter had a fraternal twin sister with whom she had shared a crib for her first three months. She would later learn that Marge's twin sister, Paula, had been adopted about two months earlier, leaving Marge alone.

Celia and Sam preferred adopting through an agency, rather than privately, to avoid worrying over whether their child's birth parents might intervene at a later date. Their decision to use LWS was prudent in that respect, but not in another. Celia said that when the Silvermans picked up their children, Sam told LWS on both occasions that they would love to adopt twins. They would have also adopted triplets. It was the early 1960s, and the agency was placing twins apart.

The Schulmans, who lived in the Little Neck neighborhood of Queens, New York, adopted Paula from LWS when she was three months old. Her father Meyer ("Mike") was an accountant, and her mother Dorothy was a schoolteacher and artist; both are deceased. Paula's older brother Alan is a veterinarian who lives and works in southern California. Her husband Adam insisted that his in-laws would have adopted both twins if given the chance—"absolutely."[7]

It is impossible to know for certain why Paula was adopted first.[8] Paula believes it is because she was thriving at the time, edging out Marge who had been doing better initially. It is not uncommon for twins to change developmental places early on—identical twins are more likely to go back and forth, whereas fraternal twins tend to maintain their respective ranks.[9] Regardless, Paula's parents did not purposely choose the more robust baby because they had no inkling that Paula was a fraternal twin.

Marge's older brother Leo recalled that his younger sister cried a lot during the weeks and months after she came home. He wonders if Marge sensed something missing from her world, perhaps the presence and feel of another small being. "The body remembers," he remarked. Marge's mother, Celia, voiced similar thoughts, as have some parents who claim that a surviving twin child often craves excessive physical contact.[10] Decades later, Paula often expressed that she had—and continued to have—an intuitive and physical feeling of someone missing. Later, she was certain that this feeling was explained by having been separated from her twin.[11] *Production memory*—the ability to detect the absence of something familiar—generally does not emerge until infants turn six months of age. However, as I discussed in chapter 9, a twin may notice the absence of his or her co-twin as early as three to four months of age, probably due to their close physical proximity.[12]

SEPARATE LIVES

Both Paula and Marge had been placed in homes with brothers who are four years older, both LWS adoptees.[13] Unlike the separated identical twins who were purposely placed with older siblings, few of the other separated fraternal twins I know of had older brothers or sisters. That is because fraternal twins were not part of the study. Interestingly, when Paula first learned she was a twin she was told that she and her sister were identical.[14] Perhaps she and Marjorie looked enough alike at birth to keep the researchers guessing until the twin type results were available. In that case, it would have been pragmatic for LWS to find two families with same-aged older siblings whom they had also placed, just in case the twins proved to be identical. This seems likely since Paula and Marjorie appear to be just the second set of twins born once the study began and gathering cases would have been important—Susan and Anne described in chapter 7 were born two months earlier, in September 1960. Of course, it is also possible that placing the twins in similarly structured families was coincidental.

Paula and Marjorie grew up just fifteen miles apart from one another. They may have passed by their sister's family members and friends, but because they did not look exactly alike, they were unlikely to have been confused. Mistaken identity sometimes brings identical twins together as I described in chapter 14, but rarely reunites twins who are fraternal. Several of Marjorie's relatives who met Paula felt that the twins looked a lot alike, but their different personalities and lifestyles may have limited the entry of each twin into her sister's world as they were growing up. However, based on her general resemblance to her twin sister and their similar voices, Paula was approached several times by women who thought they knew her. Once she discovered she had a missing twin, Paula understood the reasons for the mistaken identity. In one encounter, Paula was finally able to name Marjorie to a woman who knew her sister years ago at summer camp.[15]

MARJORIE

Marjorie and her brother Leo felt "cared for and loved in a way" by their parents. However, Leo believes that Paula and Marjorie led very different lives from each other because of the "emotional fracturing" in his home and the emotional nurturing in Paula's.[16] Some harsh verbal exchanges took place as he and his sister were growing up. Celia admitted to having a temper, especially during Marge's first five years of life. Leo coped with the situation by staying active and outside the house, whereas Marge had a difficult time from an early age because of who she was as a person. Leo and Marge felt ambivalent about their childhood and had many conversations together about the atmosphere at home. Leo also acknowledged that there were good moments.[17] Celia recalled some pleasant family times, such as a trip to California, a Caribbean cruise, and a visit to Old Sturbridge Village in Worcester County, Massachusetts.[18]

One of Marjorie's uncles, a photographer, sensed that something was not quite right with his niece when he took her picture at age two.[19] As Marjorie grew older, her appearance troubled her greatly.[20] She complained that she was tall and thin, her nose seemed large, her ears protruded, and she had acne. She persuaded her parents to let her undergo cosmetic surgery to improve her features. However, Marge's younger cousin Martin said she was "beautiful," but didn't take care of herself. He never recalled seeing her in a dress or wearing makeup. Martin also detected a "rebellious streak" in Marge, recalling the time she got him drunk when he turned eighteen and introduced him to the *Rocky Horror Picture Show*.[21]

When I asked Celia to describe Marjorie, she said "serious," "quiet," and "withdrawn," tendencies she noticed as early as age six. "Something was amiss," Celia commented. Marge had a few friends and was basically a "loner." She occasionally showed sadistic behaviors, hurting her pet dog Liza and tossing darts at her therapist. However, she took good care of a pet bird named Albert. Leo spoke of the "unusual-looking characteristics" with which Marge presented herself, in particular her isolation and lack of response. Her cousin Janet, who is five years older, said it was hard to get close to Marge because "she lived in a world of her own." George Silverman, also Marge's first cousin and older by seven years, remembered her as "distant and unconnected—and she never looked happy in pictures."[22] A seven-year age difference, especially between opposite-sex cousins, is considerable during childhood and adolescence. But as regular weekend visitors to Marge's home, George, as well as Janet, were well positioned to observe their younger cousin. George also wondered if Marge struggled with gender identity.

Janet recalled that Marge had an acoustic guitar, but she played the music and sang the songs alone in her room. She was a talented piano player and took part in childhood recitals, "but she was not a performer."[23] Marge was also an equestrian who engaged in dressage, a form of riding done in competition and exhibition. Her father drove her to the riding track before school started so she could practice; eventually, she got her own car—a green Gremlin. When Marge was in high school, she worked as a hot walker at the Belmont Racetrack—a helper who hand walks sweaty horses after their workouts. These are solitary activities.

According to Leo, Marge was very smart and quite capable with her hands—able to take things apart and figure out how they worked. Celia, recognizing her daughter's talent in crafting objects and making repairs, asked the Lynbrook Middle School grade advisor, then the principal, and finally the superintendent to enroll Marge in shop class. She was told that female students are only eligible for classes in home economics.[24] "Do you mean to tell me that if Marjorie had a penis, she could take shop?" she asked. They sensed that a lawsuit might be pending, so Marjorie became the first female student at the high school to take shop. Bright as she was, Marjorie didn't take schoolwork seriously, earning mostly C and D grades.

Celia and Sam were concerned and decided that psychotherapy would help Marge weather the adolescent and teenage years.[25] Therapy sessions began when Marge was eleven but ended after her first suicide attempt at age seventeen. Marjorie didn't wish to continue with the same therapist, so her parents found her a different one. Factors that possibly precipitated her attempt were tensions at home over Marjorie's wish to delay her high school graduation.[26] A teacher at the high school discovered her lying unconscious in a staircase after having ingested a high dosage of over-the-counter medication. A school administrator called Celia at work to tell her. Celia was working in White Plains at the time and recalled taking the Hutchinson Parkway home. The "Hutch" is a windy stretch of road that requires close attention while driving—Celia chose that route because it prevented her from "driving like a lunatic." Marge was hospitalized after that and, despite receiving medication, she was still depressed. Other suicide attempts followed.

After graduating from high school, Marge took classes at Nassau Community College and worked part-time at an aviary whose owner imported tropical birds. Never having left the United States, this job took Marge across the world to Guyana in South America and Tanzania in east Africa. While there, she "wheeled and dealed," trading currency on the black market. Leo said she could do this successfully because she was smart but said that Marge's real talents emerged once she discovered computer programming. She held several programming jobs but was fired because of a demeaning note she wrote about her last boss. Marge was also interested in target practice and owned a rifle. She liked guns and enjoyed going to the firing range.

PAULA

"Paula was an absolute gem in my film," said Lori Shinseki, director of *The Twinning Reaction*. "There was something special about her—she was easy to deal with, deep, and insightful." Viewers also have that impression when they see and listen to her. What they don't know is that Paula's husband was sitting off camera, supporting his wife during the interview. Being part of the film was a difficult decision because Paula had made disturbing discoveries during her attempts to find family. And despite being a private person, she felt driven to have her story told for the benefit of the twins and everyone who knows them. Once Paula started speaking, she was "great." Her husband and sons called her the "gem of our family."

In the film, Paula described her adoptive parents as "the most nurturing people ever." Her adoptive mother said that if she were to take a lie detector test to determine if she were Paula's birth mother, she would pass easily. It was a happy childhood but infused with lots of sadness. Paula often pouted and ran away from home "about twenty times." She also had temper tantrums.

The film captures a picture of Paula as a young child with her big brother's arm draped warmly around her.[27] The Schulman's family photo album includes other scenes of Paula and her family members interacting playfully. I also found online pictures of Paula, taken at Benjamin N. Cardozo High School's thirtieth reunion, class of 1978.[28] She appears radiant with long dark hair, wearing a multi-colored halter-style blouse over dark slacks. In one scene Paula is surrounded by several former classmates who are focused attentively on what she is saying. In another frame she is standing next to a female friend, beaming at the camera. In yet another, Paula is standing alone, in an exaggerated pose for the camera with her arms held out far from her waist. She is walking toward the podium to accept the award for the student who "Changed the Least Since High School."[29] Marjorie's brother Leo said that in this photograph Paula looked the most like Marge.

High school reunion photos, posted on Flickr by "funkyken78," led me to some of Paula's classmates. I chose several who were seated or standing next to Paula, thinking she would be most likely to congregate with those she was closest to. Classmates remember her as "smart, sharp and in the upper echelon of her class." They also spoke of her strong athleticism, especially her high ranking as a tennis player in her Long Island tennis club that earned her trophies. But more than anything, those who knew Paula acknowledged her kindness and generosity. High school yearbook editor Jeff Noreman recalled that when his wife passed away in 2014, Paula arrived at his home with food, plates, and a gift card. "She told me that I had enough to think about." Paula was also among the first to sit shiva with Jeff's family.[30]

After leaving high school, Paula attended her first two years of college at the State University of New York at New Paltz, concentrating in mathematics and fine arts. She later transferred to Queens College in New York City where she earned a Bachelor of Arts degree in Fine Arts. According to her husband Adam Sherman, a banker involved in project finance and municipal finance, "Paula was super smart with a photographic memory." Paula had also been admitted to law school, but preferred a career in artistic design, hoping to become a fashion designer. With this goal in mind, Paula went on to earn a fine arts certificate from New York City's Fashion Institute of Technology.

After meeting her future husband through mutual friends at New York City's now defunct discotheque Interferon, Paula married Adam in October 1983. The couple had four sons, Michael in 1985, Franklin in 1987, Alec in 1991, and Dylan in 1993.[31] They settled in the upscale town of Old Westbury, New York, and became active members of their local synagogue. Paula was an involved volunteer, serving as chair of the synagogue's educational board. She was also a full-time mother who drove her sons to school to enjoy extra time with them. "She was our everything," Paula's son Dylan told me. "And she was our best friend. She was genuinely excited for us even when it came to the smallest things that made us excited—and she empathized with us about things that, frankly, somebody else wouldn't necessarily care about."[32]

The Shermans' home became a meeting place for the neighborhood children to gather. Some of them confided their concerns to Paula who had the

Figure 16.2. Paula's family, on the occasion of her eldest son's bar mitzvah, October 1998. Front row (L to R): Sons Michael, Dylan, Alec, and Franklin. Back row (L to R): Paula's husband, Adam, and Paula. Paula was nearly thirty-eight years old at the time. Courtesy of Adam S. Sherman.

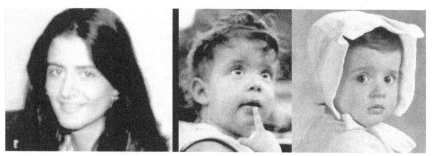

Figure 16.3. Marjorie (L) at age twenty-four years. Paula (middle) and Marjorie (R) as toddlers. Marjorie's photos courtesy of Celia Silverman; Paula's photos courtesy of Paula's family and film director Lori Shinseki.

knack of putting people at ease. Years later, she became a certified life coach—she had been performing informally as one with her sons and their friends.

Other classmates and friends highlighted her selflessness and loyalty, displayed in her devotion to her husband and children. Paula also supported a number of charitable causes, efforts for which she never sought attention or reward. Paula's best friend insisted that "she was the jewel of everything."[33] Her husband recalled her smile that lit up a room. "She was a really kind good-natured person—and so bubbly."

DISCOVERY

In 1999, Paula responded to surprise correspondence from LWS, indicating that she could access her medical records for information about her biological family. As a way of helping her sons plan families of their own someday, Paula submitted her inquiry in 1999, five years before the agency closed. LWS then invited her by telephone to visit the agency to collect her records and speak to an administrator. She was accompanied by her husband Adam, who waited outside the agency, double-parked in Manhattan traffic. Paula was expected to return in just a few minutes, but Adam waited for half an hour. When she got into the car "she was in complete shock—she couldn't speak." Paula had been told that she had an identical twin sister from whom she had been separated at several months of age. LWS refused to divulge further information and handed her a folder with medical information. Paula was thirty-nine years old at the time.[34]

Like many adopted children, Paula had always been curious about her beginnings. Once she discovered that she had a twin, she dove into a search for her sister in her usual well-planned way. This particular period in her life followed the illness and eventual passing of both her mother and father whom she didn't wish to burden with difficult questions or hurt feelings about her birth parents and her adoption. Paula learned everything she could about searching for biological relatives. She accessed multiple databases and, more than once, visited the New York Public Library to look for her name among the female babies born in November 1960 in the greater New York City area.[35] "Paula was excited, and I was excited for her," Adam recalled.

FINDING FAMILY

Paula began by scanning the "S"s of the 1960 birth file.[36] This made sense at first because her adoptive family's name was Schulman. But babies given up for adoption are listed by the last name of their birth mother. Paula also had her birth certificate number, which she found under the "S"s, listed as the child of Hedda Schacter. But Paula made a second discovery—she saw the name of another baby girl born on the same day and to the same mother, with a birth certificate number just one digit away from hers.

Thus, on her own, Paula confirmed that she had a twin sister. But as I noted earlier, Paula was incorrectly told that she and her sister were identical. She decided to search online to find her twin and hired a private investigator to help her.

Celia's 6:30 p.m. patient was waiting for her when the call came through. It was the LWS staff person who had spoken with Paula. She asked, "Is Marjorie Silverman there?" Startled, Celia replied, "No, who's calling?" The staff member stated her name and said, "her twin sister is looking for her." Celia recalled, "After I picked myself up off the floor the person asked, 'would it be alright for me to give your number to the twin?' I said yes." Paula received a call from LWS shortly after that, telling her that Celia had agreed to be contacted. But sadly, by then Paula had learned some difficult news from the private investigator: her twin sister, Marjorie, had been deceased for eleven years. Paula was absolutely devastated. Her extraordinary excitement had ended in extraordinary sadness. Paula also felt anger toward LWS for separating her from Marjorie and for separating the other pairs. "It was a very hard time in both of our lives," Adam admitted.[37]

Paula learned that her twin sister Marjorie had died by suicide on June 30, 1988, when she was twenty-seven years old.[38] (Thus, Celia's shock when LWS called looking for Marjorie is understandable.) Marjorie's therapist called Celia to say that her daughter had been cancelling appointments and quitting her jobs. Celia called Marjorie's apartment, but there was no answer. Marge had been living alone in an apartment in Astoria, Queens, near New York's LaGuardia Airport. Then she phoned Marjorie's neighbor and asked if Marjorie's car was outside. It was—but there were no lights on in the apartment. Celia called the police, who went to investigate. They called her back with some dreaded news. Celia and her son Leo raced to the apartment. Marjorie had shot herself with a new gun that Celia hadn't known about. They noticed that Marge had put out food and water for her pet cat. Leo identified the body. Celia said that "you never get over the guilt."[39]

Celia remembered another piece of the conversation she had had with the LWS staff member. "When I blurted out to her that Marjorie had killed herself, she said that a lot of them did that. . . . I don't know if she meant the LWS group [separated twins or all adoptees]." She might well have meant the separated twins. There were three suicides among the twenty-one separated

individual twins—Betsy in 1982, Marjorie in 1988, and Eddy in 1995—
amounting to 14.3 percent. In 1999, the suicide rate for females between
twenty-five and forty-four years of age was 0.0055 percent, and for males was
0.02 percent.[40] The relatively high 14.3 percent finding for the twins is probably linked, in part, to genetic predispositions the twins inherited from their
biological families. In addition, the number of LWS twins is very small, so the
rate is probably not representative. Findings are mixed with respect to whether
adoptees are at higher risk for suicide than non-adoptees.[41]

In 1978, when the twins turned eighteen, their birth mother, Hedda Abbott,
joined a registry that helps family members find each other. She waited for
twenty years until Paula found her.

IT FINALLY HAPPENED

Having found her birth mother through the registry in 1999, Paula traveled
to Hedda's Las Vegas home to meet her.[42] Hedda was thrilled, hoping for
a long time that this reunion would happen. She was never secretive about
having had twins. Their first reunion at the Venetian Hotel and Casino in
Las Vegas began in awkward silence that was quickly replaced by continuous
conversation. Paula's husband sat by quietly, providing the support that Paula
needed.[43] The meeting was a good one—Hedda was happy to learn that Paula
had been raised in a good home, "better than I could have provided." But she
was shocked and angry—"the whole nine yards"—to learn that the twins had
been separated against her wishes. She was saddened to hear about Marjorie's
death, but said she did not feel its full impact until she saw Marjorie's picture.
    Paula and Hedda met several times over the next few years. In 2000,
Hedda and her son Jacob went to New York for Paula's son Franklin's bar
mitzvah, the Jewish coming of age ritual, where Hedda met Marjorie's family
for the first time. Paula returned to Las Vegas in 2010 to celebrate Hedda's
seventieth birthday, and in 2015 for Hedda's grandson Gabriel's bar mitzvah.
Gabriel was one of Paula's two newly acquired nephews, both of whom
adored her, as did her two newly acquired nieces. This time Paula didn't spend
time with her birth mother because things between them were not going well.
Hedda had said something to upset Paula, then tried to make things right.
Paula said they would get together "next time," but they never did.

Paula met her sister's mother Celia shortly after her first visit with Hedda, at
Celia's Long Island home. "It was very emotional," Celia recalled tearfully.
"We both cried. I didn't know what to make of it." She said that while Paula

and Marjorie looked very similar, they were clearly not identical twins, despite what LWS had said to Paula. "It broke my heart," she told me, recalling how much she and her husband had wanted twins and how often they had asked LWS for them.

Paula and Celia met again soon after that, at a local diner. Joining them was Celia's niece from Vermont, coincidentally named Paula. Not only that, Celia's maiden name and her niece's last name—Shulman—are the same as Paula's maiden name—Schulman—but spelled differently. Adding further to the confusion, Paula's married name was Sherman. It also turned out that Paula and her family lived in Old Westbury, New York, a mile and a half from Marjorie's brother Leo, who lived in Westbury.

Living twins are constant reminders of twins who are deceased.[44] Their presence is particularly painful on holidays, especially birthdays, when two people, not one, should be acknowledged. Living twins also become other people's connection to the deceased twin because of their common features and shared experiences. These events are not limited to twins who grew up together. Some reared-apart twins in the Minnesota study who lost their brothers and sisters experienced profound grief after the loss, even though they had known each other briefly. In a poignant scene in the film *The Twinning Reaction*, Paula visits the New Montefiore Cemetery in Babylon, New York, where Marjorie is buried.[45] She expressed "an overwhelming desire to lie down on this spot." Later, Paula asked Celia if she could plant a yew bush on her sister's grave. "I needed something on there," she said.[46] Paula's mother and father are buried in the same cemetery.

Paula sat shiva with Marjorie's family when Marjorie's grandmother passed away, later in 1999. According to Leo, "Paula was quite the mensch."[47]

There was a gathering that Celia had arranged at her home to give more of her relatives a chance to meet Paula. Marjorie's brother Leo "was all over the place" when he learned that his late sister had a twin.[48] He felt an immediate connection to Paula—later, they met for walks and talked on the phone several times. Paula admitted to Leo that she sometimes felt as if something had been missing in her life. Paula's husband Adam understood this—he said that Paula may have felt the presence of her sister when they shared a crib together as infants. "It was a physical feeling she couldn't articulate before learning she was a twin," Adam recalled.[49]

Leo sensed that Paula was the person his sister could have become if she had been emotionally healthy. He was not the only one who felt this way. Marjorie's cousin Janet recalled, "When she [Paula] came to the door I was crying. I am crying now—she looked like what Margie would have been like if she'd been happier."[50] Janet was also impressed by how much Paula and Marjorie resembled one another. "When I met Paula, I thought she was Margie." Both twins were tall, but there was a two-inch difference between them—Paula measured five feet, six and a half inches, and Marjorie was five feet, eight and a half inches. Being tall ran in their family—the twins' birth mother Hedda was five feet, seven inches tall when she delivered them, and their birth father was between five feet, eight inches, and six feet.[51] Paula and Marjorie also had similar coloring and body builds.[52] It is likely that Janet responded to the twins' general family resemblance because their individual features were not the same.

Marjorie's cousin Janet, a clinical social worker, commented on Paula's fragility. She believes that Paula and the other twins were traumatized by learning why they were separated and having to piece together the different parts of their lives. She suspects that Paula was completely devastated by this knowledge and by the realization that she would never meet Margie because Margie had ended her life. Thinking back to the support Paula needed as she told her story on film, Janet appears to have been right.

In spring 2000, the members of the three families—the twins' birth family and their two adoptive families—convened on Long Island to celebrate the bar mitzvah of Paula's son Franklin. It is the only time that Celia met Hedda. The two mothers hugged and cried. According to Hedda, Celia couldn't say Marjorie's name for several years after her death, although this may have been true only with people outside the immediate family—Leo recalls many conversations with his mother about Marjorie's death. Hedda and Celia have stayed in touch by exchanging messages with each other from time to time. Paula's parents are deceased, but Celia became friendly with Paula's four sons. When Paula's second youngest boy Alec showed an interest in birds, Celia invited him to visit a bird feeding station. However, seeing Paula became too painful.[53]

At the bar mitzvah, Leo stayed "laser focused" on Hedda, trying to see if she looked like his sister. He didn't think so, but he did see similarities between Hedda and Paula, especially in their profiles. Adam had never met Marjorie, but he had seen her face and figure in photographs. Like Marjorie's cousin Janet, Adam saw varying degrees of family resemblance in the overall appearance, complexion, and body type of the three women, but he would have never thought that Paula and Marjorie were identical twins.[54]

Leo didn't maintain ties with anyone in Paula's family, except Paula. During one of their conversations, he discovered another odd occurrence: Paula's close friends at the time were named Marjorie and Ellen—her twin sister's name was Marjorie Ellen.

FAST FORWARD

Thirty-two years had passed since Marjorie's death when I spoke to Celia in the summers of 2019 and 2020. "You never get over it," she said. Celia had seen the 2017 documentary film *The Twinning Reaction* in which she appears, although her face is hidden. She explained that she didn't go completely public because she is known to many of her patients and students in the area and preferred not having to answer their inevitable questions. Celia had not seen the 2018 documentary film *Three Identical Strangers*—a friend invited her to see it, but she declined.

Celia believes that each child enters the world as a "genetic package" that the environment modifies to a degree.[55] She believes this because she watched her two children display drastically different personalities when they were just a few months old. Still, Celia believes that events in the first five years of a child's life can leave a lasting impact on how they turn out. Given that, she wondered if Marjorie might have been spared had she and Paula grown up together. "She would have had a sister. They would have shared secrets that sisters share." Paula also believed that her strength could have helped her sister through difficult times.[56] However, Celia questioned whether the twins' different personalities might have posed a problem. "Paula was a little more outgoing than Marge—but maybe Marge would have been more outgoing— it was the trauma of being separated that way. Bingo! You're now picked up and moved to another environment."

We talked about the LWS-Child Development Center twin study even though Marjorie and Paula had not been part of it. "It was a monstrous experiment," Celia insisted. "I see a parallel between the study of the triplets and Nazi science. It's hard to believe that, you know, somebody like Neubauer who had to flee Austria for his own survival could do something like this." She concluded, "If God gives you twins, you keep them together because God gave you twins. You don't mess with nature."

LEGACY

The story of Paula and Marjorie had a dubious start and an unhappy ending. Perhaps Paula's presence alongside her sister would have protected Marjorie from her sadness and loneliness, and ultimate demise. A close friend of Paula's said that Paula could "handle anything."[57] Even though the twins had never met, Marjorie became an important part of Paula's identity and a part of her family's life. Two pictures of Marjorie were on view in the Shermans' home.

And Marjorie's name carried a great deal of weight even though Paula and her family never knew her.[58]

We can never know for sure what the outcome would have been had the twins grown up together, but research is suggestive. Twins have lower suicide rates than non-twins, attributed to their close companionship and deep understanding.[59] The three LWS twins who took their own lives had never fully developed the unique support system that twinship offers. They also had genetic predispositions toward mental difficulties, triggered by life events in their respective environments.

On May 25, 2015, Paula suffered a brain aneurysm, a weak spot in the brain that fills with blood.[60] Paula passed away in her sleep at the age of fifty-four years—she was twice as old as Marjorie when Marjorie ended her life at age twenty-seven. She is buried in the same cemetery as her parents and sister. Two families grieved for the twin daughter they raised and the one they did not. Paula's four sons, still shaken by the loss of their mother, found it too painful to share their thoughts when I first approached them—until Paula's youngest son Dylan later felt compelled to add to his mother's story. And once again, a birth mother mourned the loss of her twin girls, one whom she knew briefly and one whom she never knew at all—she would later struggle with the suicidal loss of her son.

Marjorie's cousin, George Silverman, adopted a son in December 1995 who is now twenty-four. George was "horrified" that LWS had not revealed the twinship to the family. "To not say that there is another child is criminal. You never get the whole story [on a child you adopt], but if I had learned that my son was a twin, I would have adopted them both. There would have been hurdles, but you just do it."[61]

LWS did not anticipate the possibility that one twin might be incapacitated or even deceased when their twinship was discovered. Marjorie took her own life never imagining that she had a twin sister. Paula could only know Marjorie through the family her sister grew up with. Celia hoped to develop a relationship with Paula, but she couldn't because it became too painful. And Leo lost his only connection to his younger sister when Paula passed away so suddenly. Also affected are countless children, cousins, grandparents, uncles, aunts, nieces, nephews, and friends, each in their own way. Many people who attended Paula's funeral told her family that they thought of Paula as their best friend.[62]

There were no good-byes. There can be no closure.

• 17 •

Fraternal, Almost Identical

Michele and Allison

"Today is August 10, 2018, but I feel as if it's my birthday—because I'm meeting my sister for the first time."[1]

$\mathcal{O}$n October 5, 2018, I received an email message from my brother-in-law, attorney Mark Silverschotz, with the subject line: "New Twins Video from *The Atlantic.*"[2] I was puzzled. *Three Identical Strangers*, Tim Wardle's documentary, about reunited identical triplets and the secret study in which they had unknowingly participated, had been playing in theaters since June. Moreover, the link to the video and accompanying text contained the phrase "two-identical-strangers," confusing me further—*Identical Strangers* is the 2007 memoir authored by separated twins whose story I told in chapter 15.[3] I wondered momentarily if the twins, Paula and Elyse, both being filmmakers, had collaborated on a short film about their lives—however, that seemed unlikely since they are no longer accepting interviews. When I clicked on the link, what unfolded was a story of fraternal twins, separated as infants by Louise Wise Services (LWS), who had just discovered each other because one of them had watched the trailer to Wardle's full-length film. The director of the short video was Wardle.

I have watched the 7:52-minute video clip many times since it first appeared and have reread the narrative posted with it. The emotional elements that the events convey—exhilaration and anxiety, self-reflection and regret—do not diminish with each viewing. The story it tells is another living example of the researchers' fear that public awareness of their study might prompt some adoptees to wonder if they have a twin, especially if they were born in the 1960s. Such awareness led Justin Goldberg to search for a twin after his

The Twins, Their Family Members, and Friends

Michele

Michele Wolk Mordkoff Allison's reared-apart twin
Iris Wolk Michele's adoptive mother
Allan Wolk Michele's adoptive father
Glenn Wolk Michele's younger brother, closest in age
Brian Wolk Michele's youngest brother
Josh Mordkoff Michele's oldest son
Andrew Mordkoff Michele's youngest son

Allison

Allison Kanter Michele's reared-apart twin
Florence Rodnon Allison's adoptive mother
Herbert Rodnon Allison's adoptive father
Stewart (Stewie) Rodnon Herbert's identical twin brother
Lori Kritzer Allison's older adoptive sister
Mark Kanter Allison's husband
Jeremy Kanter Allison's oldest son
Kyle Kanter Allison's youngest son
Callie Kanter Allison's daughter and youngest child

Others

Lisa Belkin journalist

daughter discovered his look-alike, as I discussed in an earlier chapter. And at the end of this book, I will further explore the roots of the researchers' fear of exposure. However, Wardle offers a different take on the question of how LWS adoptees and others might think about a possible twin, either their own or someone else's. Wardle was "thrilled that *Three Identical Strangers* could have such a positive legacy, helping to reunite twins after decades apart."[4] And the quotation at the start of this chapter reflects one twin's excited anticipation of adding a celebrated relationship to her life.

This story is about Michele and Allison, fraternal twins who are very much alike and whose lives became closely entwined in a short time. It will warm hearts, but also break them.

FINDING FRATERNALS: FACEBOOK, DNA, AND DILIGENCE

I am not a frequent Facebook user, but it has sometimes been a valuable resource for reconnecting me with twins and families I have worked with in the past. Facebook led me to Michele and Allison whom I messaged, texted, emailed, spoke to, and met with between October 2018 and March 2021. My conversations with each twin, and my viewing of Wardle's video, showcase the critical timing and complex interplay of events preceding the twins' remarkable reunion.

Michele called it "divine intervention" on an ordinary workday.[5] On June 25 or 26, 2018, fifty-four-year-old Michele Mordkoff, a fifth-grade schoolteacher, was on her way to class at the elementary school in Wayne, New Jersey. She was on her cell phone when "up popped a movie called *Three Identical Strangers*." It seized Michele's attention because, like the triplets in the film, Michele was born in the 1960s and her parents had adopted her from LWS. "I had a sick feeling," she recalled. "I thought there might be something more to this." The feeling "drove" her to submit a DNA sample to 23andMe, a service that connects biological relatives and provides personal health information, based on analyses of individuals' genetic background.

A day or two later, Michele contacted journalist Lisa Belkin who had authored the *New York Times* magazine article on the suicide of LWS adoptee Michael Juman.[6] As I discussed in chapter 10, Michael's birth parents had suffered from severe psychotic disorders, information that the agency never disclosed to his adoptive family. Michele told Belkin that she was "horrified" by what LWS had done.[7] Belkin tried to assure Michele that she was not mentally disturbed and she was not a twin. But when they reconnected during the second week of August, Michele told Belkin she was correct on the first try, but not on the second. A lot had happened.

Genealogical companies can only find genetic connections between biological relatives if two or more people submit their DNA samples. Both Michele and Allison had submitted their samples to Ancestry.com, although Michele had initially used 23andMe; had Michele started with Ancestry.com she would have found Allison sooner. As of 2008 Ancestry.com and 23andMe forged a partnership to improve the quality of genetic information provided to their clients.[8] Such data sharing helps expand family trees, providing new insights into their clients' background, identity, and health. However, reuniting relatives requires that both individuals submit saliva samples to the same service. Interestingly, the twins' motivations for submitting their DNA samples were different.

Allison had always known she was adopted, but she was never really inspired to search for her birth family.[9] Just once, in 2006, after talking with a friend about the topic, she searched online for LWS and Spence-Chapin, the agency that had taken over LWS's records two years before. Allison read through the website and decided against moving forward. She admitted, "I was nervous. I didn't want to open a Pandora's box." Besides, Allison had "great parents" who adored her and an older sister, also adopted from LWS, with whom she enjoyed a close and loving relationship. Her feelings about searching for her birth family stayed the same, but Allison's son Kyle had a different idea.

In 2017, Kyle presented Allison with a DNA test kit from Ancestry.com as a Hanukkah gift. "I didn't want to do it, but he was bugging me," she recalled.[10] She submitted a sample, worrying that she did not produce enough saliva because the solution "bubbled." Allison explained to me that she did this to satisfy her son, but also for fun, thinking she might discover where her birth parents came from. Her results were available in January 2018, but she never examined the site. She admitted that she did not have full knowledge of where the results could lead—of course, at that time Michele hadn't sent in her sample to Ancestry.com.

Just two months later, in March 2018, ABC's television news magazine *20/20* broadcast excerpts from Lori Shinseki's film *The Twinning Reaction*.[11] Also included were interviews with special significance for Allison and her family. Allison's older sister, Lori Kritzer, had seen the show and urged Allison to watch it, which she later did online.[12] "I was in shock," Allison admitted. "I called Lori and she asked me, 'What if I am a twin? What if you are a twin?' I had heart palpitations when I got off the phone." Allison's parents were stunned, but they were certain there was "no way" that what they witnessed on *20/20* related to their daughters. Allison quickly dismissed the possibility of being a separated twin, as "The odds would be like finding a grain of sand in the Sahara Desert." Moreover, Allison hadn't been studied like the twins and triplets in *20/20*. She never jotted down the telephone number for the Jewish Board of Family and Children's Services that appeared at the end of the program, inviting concerned adoptees to contact them. In fact, Allison forgot all about the program until one of her family members went to the movies.

A week before Michele received her DNA results, Allison's in-laws, Bruce and Marlene Kanter, had seen *Three Identical Strangers*.[13] When they returned home, Bruce called Allison and asked, "Where were you adopted from?" Allison answered quickly, "LWS—and [the triplets' story] is not mine!" But on August 4, "it was my life," she said, still somewhat stunned by her new reality. Allison recalled that when the truth came out her in-laws could hardly believe it. Allison eventually saw *Three Identical Strangers*—"about one hundred times"—the first time on a plane en route to meeting Michele. "The film was fascinating and sickening."

THEIR FIRST FIVE MONTHS

Michele and Allison were born on May 12, 1964, at Staten Island Hospital where many LWS mothers delivered their babies.[14] Their birth mother was seventeen years old at the time. Her pregnancy lasted for thirty weeks, five weeks less than the average twin pregnancy of thirty-five weeks and nearly nine weeks less than the average singleton pregnancy.[15] After five and a half hours of labor Allison emerged first, followed by Michele ten minutes later. Despite their early delivery, the twins' birth weights were favorable—Allison weighed five pounds, eight and a half ounces, and Michele weighed six pounds, seven and a half ounces. Both twins' birth weights exceeded the average of five pounds, two and three-quarter ounces for female twins born at thirty-five weeks, based on current standards.[16] At seventeen inches, Allison was one inch shorter than Michele.

"It's a mystery to me that they 'knew' from the minute we were born that we were not identical," Allison said.[17] According to information the twins received from Spence-Chapin, there were two placentae, explaining the doctors' conclusion that Michele and Allison were a fraternal pair. The presence of two placentae was confirmed by the twins' birth mother whom they eventually met and are getting to know slowly and privately. However, the presence of two placentae does not prove fraternal twinning because one-third of identical twins, as well as all fraternal twins, have separate placentae.[18] Even today, not all medical professionals are aware of this fact, but such misunderstandings were probably more prevalent among doctors in the 1960s. Recall that Dr. Neubauer questioned whether the separated identical triplets were truly identical because two placentae had been delivered.[19]

It is very likely that the doctors who delivered Allison and Michele decided that they were fraternal based on the number of placentae. They may have also been persuaded by the twins' different eye color, known to be a highly heritable trait[20]—Allison's eyes are dark hazel mixed with green and brown, and Michele's eyes are a blue-hazel blend. Furthermore, baby pictures show Allison's darker hair and complexion, and Michele's fairer hair and skin tone. Regardless, the twins stayed together for a week, leaving enough time for their blood groups to be analyzed and compared if requested by the twin study staff—at that time extensive blood typing was used to classify twins as identical or fraternal. If their blood groups didn't match across the entire series, this would have been scientific proof of their fraternal twinship. Whether blood typing was done in their case, as it was apparently done for the other LWS twins, is another mystery.

Doctors humorously described the newborn twins as "noisy with strong cries" who showed a lot of arm and leg movement.[21] They were in good health when discharged from the hospital, marking the end of their week-long life together as twins. The babies were sent to separate foster homes arranged by LWS until suitable adoptive families were found. Michele was sent to a second foster family after six weeks when her first family left for vacation. According to Michele, after the delivery their birth mother consented to the separation, but LWS never gave her a choice—her only options were to keep both twins or to place them apart. She received no explanation as to why they would be separated, only that no families would agree to take twins. Was there a reason?

Earlier in the book, I indicated that Viola Bernard knew that it was possible to find families willing to raise twins. Furthermore, a number of adoptive mothers I interviewed—Celia Silverman, Alice Mertzel, Thelma Lieber— would have gladly taken two children. Richard ("Bubula") Kellman, father of one of the triplets, would have raised three. Therefore, it is not true that families were unwilling to adopt twins, as some believe. "Did they even try to keep us together?" Allison wondered. Perhaps Bernard's beliefs that development proceeded more smoothly for singletons than for twins, or that raising one baby was easier than raising two, were the deciding factors, but we cannot be sure. Neither Michele nor Allison can comprehend why LWS divided

Figure 17.1   Fraternal twins, Allison Kanter (L) and Michele Mordkoff (R), as young girls growing up apart. Courtesy of the twins.

them because fraternal twins were never studied. "We were just separated," Michele said, and sighed.

ADOPTING ALLISON

Allison was adopted by Herbert and Florence Rodnon, a couple living in Wantagh, Long Island, twenty-six miles outside New York City. Her birth announcement was inscribed with two dates—the day she was born (May 12, 1964) and the day she arrived at the Rodnons' home (October 16, 1964). Herbert was a certified public accountant, and Florence was a bookkeeper for real estate companies. The couple married in their early twenties. After trying unsuccessfully for ten years to have a child, they adopted their older daughter Lori from LWS. Three years later, they adopted Allison. They had no idea that Allison's twin sister had been adopted the week before by a Bronx, New York, couple and was living just a forty-five-minute drive away.

Documents from Spence-Chapin describe Allison as a bright baby who was sweet, gentle, feminine, relaxed, active, and well-coordinated. Her new home with the Rodnons was a seven-room dwelling with a basement and playroom. The couple actually bought their suburban home just because they wanted to adopt a second daughter. LWS social workers had visited their Brooklyn apartment, studied their finances, and insisted that the couple could afford to buy a private house. According to Allison, her parents were told that if they had a home, they could have a baby.

LWS also knew that Herbert Rodnon had an identical twin brother, Stewart, and that Herbert and Florence had asked only for girls.[22] Allison thinks her father might have been thrilled to adopt twin daughters. According to Allison, the LWS narrative that Michele received in 2018 from Spence-Chapin showed that the agency was very careful about where they placed twins. "They described my parents to a tee—their personality and their looks—and they knew my dad was an identical twin. When I read that I just lost it, thinking that they could even imagine splitting up twins and giving one to a twin."

I spoke to Allison several times by telephone before meeting her on January 26, 2019, at a restaurant near Amtrak's Union Station in Los Angeles. I had met Michele six weeks earlier during a trip to New York, so I could compare them up close. To my twin researcher's eye, some differences in their facial features and coloring were unquestionably those of fraternal twins, but Allison and Michele looked very much alike. They remind us that fraternal twins and non-twin siblings, both of whom share 50 percent of their genes, on average, vary in resemblance due to their degree of genetic overlap. I "met" Allison again in June 2020, on a Zoom video call, when the coronavirus pandemic prevented us both from traveling.

Allison's family lived in Long Island until Allison was four and a half, then left the East Coast for Westwood, California, when her father was offered a new job.[23] They resided in Westwood until Allison was six, before relocating northwest to Tarzana, California. Given the three thousand-mile distance between them, it is not surprising that the twins were never mistaken for anyone else—except on one occasion. Michele was vacationing on a New Jersey beach when a stranger approached her and said, "I know you!" Michele "freaked out."[24]

CALIFORNIA DREAMIN'

Allison had a happy childhood, raised by parents who loved her completely.[25] She always had a close relationship with her sister Lori and surrounded herself with lots of friends. Still, she thought of herself as shy, staying closely attached to her mother until she turned ten and became "boy crazy." Having a social life was a high priority for her. Allison liked being in "any school play" and performing in dance recitals. A lifelong regret is not having been chosen for the cheerleading team at William H. Taft High School in Woodland Hills, California.

Allison also described herself as a "well-behaved child, trying not to cause friction in the home—my parents had their own friction," she confessed. Allison assumed that her desire to "always do the right thing" was motivated by these home experiences. That assumption would later change.

Upon graduating in 1986 from California State University, Northridge, with a Bachelor's degree in Journalism, Allison embarked on a variety of careers. After a brief period in advertising, she worked for the toy company Applause and for the Disney stores in product development and consultation. On September 11, 1993, Allison married Mark Kanter, owner of Commercial Realty Consultants, Inc., whom she met at the popular Mid Valley Athletic Club, in Reseda, California. In between jobs, Allison gave birth to her three children—Jeremy, now twenty-four; Kyle, now twenty-one; and Callie, now nineteen. She is passionate about the people closest to her, evident by the rows of family and friend photos framing the walls of her study.

In 2008, Allison developed Tempt Jewelry in Calabasas, California, with partner Tracy Dekel, who is now the sole owner.[26] Since then, she has worked part-time in her husband's realty office. Allison and her family live in Calabasas, but often vacation in their second home in California's Palm Desert.

When Allison's first son Jeremy was born, she realized that he was the first biological relative she ever knew. "He looks like parts of us [my husband and me combined]."[27] The excitement she felt at that time returned when she delivered her second and third children. Allison explained, "I was always fascinated, not so much with genetics, but with people looking like their parents and siblings. Growing up, Michele didn't seem to have the same questions I did. People would meet my parents and say, 'Well you don't look like your mom or your dad, and you don't look like your sister.' And I would just make up something like, 'I've got this from my dad, or I've got this from that one.' I was always somebody who looked at people and their kids—and, to this day, I still look at parents and their kids to see who looks like them." Allison's fascination reminded me of Justin Goldberg's habit of scanning faces in crowds. Perhaps this tendency is common among adoptees who do not resemble the family members they are raised with.

Allison has a nephew, Ryan, who attended my developmental psychology class at California State University, Fullerton, probably in 2010. I lecture a lot about twins in that class, and often reference the LWS-Child Development Center study. However, twin studies would not have had special significance for Ryan, because in 2010 he didn't know his aunt was a twin—nor did his aunt. It also happened that Allison had attended junior high school in California with Michele's friend Constance, who now lives in New Jersey. Allison had even invited Constance to her sixteenth birthday party.[28]

Allison's 2013 Twitter page lists her as a "Jewelry designer, wife, mom of three beautiful kids."[29] That was in September 2013. Five years later she would meet a twin sister she never dreamed she had.

MICHELE: "SHE IS OURS"

Michele was the first child to arrive in her family, adopted at five months of age by Iris and Allan Wolk.[30] After failing to conceive after six or seven years of marriage, the Wolks decided to adopt a baby; by then, both husband and wife were in their late twenties. They turned to LWS as the preeminent adoption agency for Jewish children. Once approved, the couple waited thirteen months before Iris contacted the agency to see when a baby would be available. The staff member said she was "just about to call them" to pick up their baby the following day. They would have taken twins if they had known.[31]

Iris and Allan lived in a low-rent apartment complex in the Parkchester neighborhood of the Bronx. Their combined income was limited, but they benefited from LWS's sliding fee scale tailored to couples' financial circumstances. Iris worked as a secretary in the social service department of the nearby

Jacobi Hospital, but she left her job once Michele arrived. She returned to school several years later, earning both a Bachelor of Arts degree and a Master's degree in Social Work. During these years, Allan had a flexible schedule that allowed him to care for Michele while his wife was in class.

Iris calls herself an "academic widow." Her husband Allan, having earned a Bachelor of Arts degree in Political Science, earned a Master's degree during their first year of marriage, also in Political Science. He then taught at the junior high school level for five years before entering New York University's doctoral program. After graduating with a PhD, he ascended the academic ladder, becoming a political science professor at Bronx Community College for the next thirty-two years. Upon retiring, Allan completed a law degree and went into practice. Now in his eighties, he is still practicing law.

While the Wolks waited for a baby, a social worker periodically visited their home and they visited LWS. "[The social worker] was lovely," Iris recalled. "She was so attentive to us. She seemed to like us so much and I felt very close to her."[32] But years later, having learned that LWS had been secretly separating twins, Iris felt deceived. "I can't believe she didn't tell me Michele was a twin, but I guess that would have meant her job. We would have probably taken twins. We wanted a baby so much." Allan agreed, but wondered if LWS would have given twins to a couple living in a one-bedroom apartment. As it turned out, Iris and Allan added two more children to their family. When Michele was a year old, the family was in the process of moving to a larger apartment when Iris conceived her son Glenn. She had been feeling nervous about the move and consulted her physician who prescribed tranquilizers. Iris is certain that the combined effects of already having a baby and feeling less pressure were the keys to her surprise pregnancy. Glenn and Michele are just nineteen months apart in age. When Michele turned two, the Wolks relocated to New City, a hamlet of Rockland County, located within the New York metropolitan area. Iris conceived her second son Brian eight years later.

The Wolks never doubted that Michele "is ours." Their baby was "so adorable, so smart and so delicious," feelings that never wavered as they raised their little girl.

NEW YORK TO NEW JERSEY

I first met Michele on December 11, 2018, at Mediterraneo, a Middle Eastern restaurant in Ridgewood, New Jersey. I was in New York City at the time to comment on *Three Identical Strangers* that CNN would be airing prior to the film, hosted by Dr. Sanjay Gupta. Michele and Allison were also being interviewed for the program. Michele and I met again on June 6, 2019, at

New York's Hourglass Tavern and on October 26, 2019, at her Wayne, New Jersey, home. I also saw her briefly on October 29 when she attended a debate on parenting in which I participated, held at Hunter College in Manhattan.[33]

Having worked with many reared-apart twins, I am used to hearing about the remarkable co-occurrences and unusual incidents in their separate lives. These events happen more often to identical twins than to fraternal twins, most likely because of their greater genetic relatedness. Many seemingly rare similarities between reared-apart identical twins make sense because they are partly grounded in the twins' shared genes—such as experiencing severe headaches, reading books by the same author, or yearning to become an actor. Other matches are more mesmerizing because they are harder, if not impossible, to explain—finding a stone with your twin's initials years before knowing you have a twin, marrying twice to women with the same first name, and liking to sneeze loudly in elevators. Michele shared some curious childhood memories with me.

Growing up, Michele had a favorite doll she had named Allison. None of her friends had that name and she can't recall where or when she first heard it. "The doll was a replica of me, chubby-faced with light eyes and white blonde hair," she said. Moreover, Michele's parents didn't give her a middle name, so at ten years of age she was determined to go to court to get one. She wanted to be known as "Michele Allison Wolk." Michele never officially changed her name, but she practiced writing "Michele Allison Wolk" as if making it permanent.

"Want to hear something weird?" Michele asked me.[34] Since discovering Allison, Michele has been in touch with other LWS separated twins, including Howard Burack, whom I wrote about in chapter 9. "Howard texted that his daughter is running around town with my son," she told me. Michele's son Andrew escorted Howard's daughter Olivia to a dance at Ohio State University in Columbus, where both were students. It was October 2019 when Andrew needed a date for his Alpha Epsilon Pi fraternity "dress-up" night. A friend of his put them in touch thinking they would make a "perfect" match since both are easy-going and fun-loving. Andrew hoped to dazzle Olivia with the "amazing story" of his mother's twin. When he finished, she replied, "The same thing happened to my dad!" Andrew called it the "craziest coincidence." Aside from the small odds of them attending the same university, Ohio State's enrollment includes over sixty thousand students, so the chance of them meeting was especially slim.[35] Andrew and Olivia have remained friends. It also turned out that Michele and Howard had both grown up in Rockland County, New York.

It is probably not coincidental that both Michele and her father were attorneys and educators who changed careers along the way, albeit in reverse order. They have no genes in common by descent, but Michele's abilities and interests aligned with those of her father's and flourished in the supportive home environment her parents created. Interestingly, neither of Michele's younger brothers—the biological children of her parents—became an attorney or a professor like their father, or a social worker like their mother. Glenn is a graphic designer in New York City, and Brian is a clothes designer and interior decorator in Los Angeles. Their father has some artistically talented relatives who are biologically related to Glenn and Brian.[36] Genes explain both similarities and differences among biological family members.[37]

Michele was a good student with lots of friends. Beginning in middle school she admitted to being "boy crazy," just like the twin sister she didn't know she had. However, her social life didn't hamper her academic achievements. After graduating from Clarkstown High School North in 1982, Michele earned a Bachelor of Arts degree in Criminal Justice from the State University of New York at Albany. Three years later, in 1989, she graduated from Emory University's Law School in Atlanta and began a career at Fred Murphy Associates in Goshen, New York. On October 14, 1990, Michele married Allan Mordkoff, an attorney whom she had met in law school.[38] She continued as an attorney for fifteen years in the firm of Maloof Liebowitz before practicing law on her own for several years. She divorced in 2012 and four years later became engaged to be married for a second time.

By 2004, Michele was the mother of two boys under ten years of age and wanted to think through her next career move.[39] While still practicing law, she earned a Post-Baccalaureate degree in Elementary Education at William Patterson University in Wayne, New Jersey. With her new degree she began teaching math to fifth-grade students in the Wayne School District, a job that she has loved for over fifteen years. Then, in 2020, Michele completed a two-year Master's degree in Educational Leadership through the American College of Education, with the aim of becoming a school principal. However, focusing on her newly found twin, niece, nephews, and brother-in-law, as well as her two sons, parents, and fiancé, may delay this occupational goal. In fact, Michele's interest in family began nearly thirty years before when she contemplated becoming a mother.

Adoptees considering parenthood often wonder about medical predispositions they might transmit to their children.[40] That is what motivated Michele to contact LWS in 1992 for information about her birth family—she was twenty-eight years old, newly married, and thinking about having children. Her request was for non-identifying information only. The letter she received said nothing about Michele being a twin, information that she claims would not have compromised her birth parents in any way. "[LWS] had an opportunity to make good, but they didn't. They could have told me over twenty years ago that I had a twin sister." I saw tears in her eyes as she said this. Michele explained that LWS could have contacted both twins and obtained their consent to be put in touch. In fact, as I indicated in an earlier chapter, Sheldon Fogelman, former LWS president, had helped put together a similar plan for reuniting the agency's adoptees with their birth parents.[41]

"I could have had Allison and her family in my life all this time, but they stole from me. Allison and I never shut that door at all, they shut it for us," Michele said sadly. Again, there were tears in her eyes.

COMPLEXITIES AND COMMITMENT

Locating biological relatives is difficult and delicate, but Michele has perseverance and a smart legal mind. She also has informed and caring friends, some of them adoptees who had found their birth families. Michele calls them her "search angels."

Michele's first action after seeing the trailer to *Three Identical Strangers* was to contact Spence-Chapin to see if they could forward her birth information.[42] An indifferent staff member advised Michele to submit a formal request and to expect to wait up to three months for a reply.[43] Feeling put off, but with a goal in mind, Michele submitted the application. Meanwhile, she had dinner with one of her "angels" and several old friends during a trip to Delray Beach, Florida, on July 18, 2018. By then, Michele had mailed her first DNA sample to 23andMe and had met several of her biological family members living in Florida. But the conversation that night centered on Michele's possible twinship. Her friends were excited, but Michele was guarded. One of them advised her to send a second DNA sample, this time to Ancestry.com, which had recently acquired the New York Public Library's birth records. Their online database covered births from 1949 to 1965, and Michele had been born in 1964. The next day, Michele's "angel" returned to New York, checked the records, and delivered some extraordinary news.

Michele recalled, "My friend phoned me the next day and said that only seven baby girls had been born on Staten Island on May 12, 1964.[44] Then she told me to sit down. *She said that there are listings for two newborn girls who had the same birth mother's last name and no first name.* When I heard that I saw the whole kitchen start spinning around me." Then Michele called her son Andrew and had him read the last four numbers of her birth certificate—the numbers were an exact match with one of the two unnamed babies. Michele's friend also informed her that the only children sometimes listed without first names are adoptees.

Being a twin was starting to seem likely, but Michele stayed cautious—in fact, she admitted to being in denial. She wondered if she had been listed twice by mistake—except that the last four digits of the only other newborn without a name were just one number away from hers. Despite her doubts, Michele was committed to finding the truth.

Her next step was to phone the New York State Birth Registry, hoping for clarification about birth certificate notation. She explained to me that *four* numbers were listed in the birth registry and, while they matched the last four digits on her birth certificate, the birth document contained *nine* numbers. Michele wanted to know exactly how newborns are recorded. "Does that [matching numbers] mean that's me?" she asked. The person on the other end promised to find out, but she could not reach him a second time. Michele called the registry again, but "got shut out immediately." She also phoned the surrogate courts of New York County and Staten Island, but without success. Even Spence-Chapin couldn't tell her. Then a "search angel," one with legal credentials, flapped her wings.

The angel explained the significance of the nine-digit number appearing on Michele's birth certificate. The first three digits are the area code of the babies' birthplace, the next two digits are the babies' year of birth, and the last string of digits is a unique number corresponding to each newborns' sequential filing. That explains why twins' last four birth certificate numbers are consecutive.[45] The angel also confirmed that Michele *was* the person listed in the registry whose four digits matched the final four numbers on her birth certificate. And she reiterated that twins' numbers are likely to appear in numerical order. Regardless, Michele remained skeptical, partly because she could hardly believe that anyone would separate twins—and because the letter she had received from LWS in 1992, an agency she trusted, hadn't said she was a twin. That was about to change.

Several weeks after sending her application to Spence-Chapin, Michele received a response. The letter began by saying something like, "You are correct, you are a twin!" Michele believes there was an exclamation point at the end of the sentence. "It made me angry," she said. "It was a very uncomfortable way of putting it after all the damage LWS had done." Michele also noted that except for the first line, Spence-Chapin's letter was identical to the one she had received from LWS in 1992.

CONNECTING

There are three main characters in the finale to the search that had begun over a month prior—Michele, Allison, and Allison's son Kyle. There were some tears along the way as each of them spoke to me, reliving a memorable summer night.[46]

On August 1, 2018, Michele was driving to her parents' summer retreat on the New Jersey shore.[47] On the way there, a text message from Ancestry .com appeared, indicating that her DNA test results would be available shortly. The report showed up three days later, on Saturday, August 4, while her family was relaxing on the beach. Michele and her parents rushed back to the house and gathered around the computer. Scanning the results, Michele learned that her DNA profile linked her to an "immediate family member," which is defined as a parent, child, spouse, or sibling. This individual was identified by the initials "A.K."[48] Because biological relatedness is expressed as a probability, rather than a certainty, the nature of Michele's relationship to "A.K." was not specified.[49]

Toward late afternoon, Michele spoke with her friends who had conducted their own family searches. They gave her a better understanding of how genetic relatedness works, specifically the significance of centimorgans. Centimorgans (cM) are units that express how much DNA, and how much DNA segment lengths, are shared between relatives.[50] The average cM number for full siblings and fraternal twins is 2,613 with a minimum–maximum interval spanning 1,613 and 3,488. Michele and Allison's cM number is 2,317, which is close to the average and well within the given range.

It was a long day's journey into night. Having initials rather than a full name might have hindered Michele's efforts, but "Kyle Kanter" was listed as the account manager.[51] Kyle was key to finding "A.K." Kyle turned out to be her twin sister's son, although she didn't realize that at the time. The dinner hour approached as Michele continued searching through Facebook, trying furiously to find Kyle. Her search continued at Xina, a local restaurant that serves "the best sushi," although Michele ate little that night. Michele asked her father if he remembered that she had named her doll Allison and had wanted to change her name to "Michele Allison Wolk." He said that he did. Michele believes that seeing the initials "A.K." triggered these childhood memories that she hadn't thought about in years. "They just came up from my brain," she said.

It was then, the moment after her memories returned, that Michele found Kyle on Facebook. Then she discovered Callie, her twin sister's daughter and Michele's niece. She searched through Callie's photos, stopping at a picture of Allison Rodnon Kanter—"A.K."—leaning against her husband, Mark. "I saw myself in her face. And then I saw her birthday—May 12, 1964—the same as mine. That's when I lost my footing and fell to the floor."

Michele's friends stayed in touch with her over the next several hours, running names through databases to confirm that she had the right contacts. Allison and her family lived in Calabasas, California.[52] Michele wanted to contact Kyle first—Ancestry.com had also matched Kyle with Michele because he was Michele's biological nephew, although not an immediate family member. Michele worried about "freaking him out" with the news that she was his mother's twin. It was close to midnight, but she couldn't rest.

Michele sent Kyle a Facebook message saying that Ancestry.com had matched her with his mother. When he replied with some interest, she "upped" the conversation. "I think I am your mother's twin," she said and explained that she was adopted from New York and had the birth certificate numbers. Kyle was stunned. He thought the situation was "crazy" and wouldn't lead to anything. It was late and he was at a friend's house, but he called his mother and told her to get her birth certificate. He also said that there was someone who thought she was Allison's twin. Allison's first reaction was that she was being scammed—when she was nineteen, she had lost her wallet and someone had tried to assume her identity. It took six years before the credit card frauds were resolved. But Kyle told her that this contact had come from Ancestry.com.

Allison retrieved her birth certificate from the safe. She confirmed that her four-digit birth certificate number matched Michele's except for the last digit that was one number lower, telling them that Allison was the firstborn twin. The twins texted each other late into the night and early morning. Allison was in complete shock, disbelieving that so much time had gone by without her knowing this critical fact about her birth. This new revelation was especially astounding to Allison because, unlike Michele, she hadn't done the searching and was completely unprepared. "If I hadn't seen the *20/20* program I would have fainted."

Michele and Allison spoke again by telephone the next day. Their timing was perfect. They would meet six days later when, by chance, Allison and her husband would be in New York City. And fortunately, Michele's planned cruise had been scheduled for the following week. Lisa Belkin, the journalist whom Michele had contacted after seeing *Three Identical Strangers*, put the twins in touch with the film's director, Tim Wardle. Wardle captured the twins' meeting, their first in fifty-four years.

Every twin reunion is unique, but each one combines exhilaration and wonder, self-reflection and regret, as I said earlier. Allison entered the room of New York's Kimberly Hotel, where Michele was waiting. The twins hugged each other, held on, then stepped back and stared.[53] There was a familiarity about them, rooted in the connection that had evolved over the course of their phone calls and texts. Michele acknowledged that it was not important for them to look alike but confessed that their unexpected resemblance made being twins "so much more real—and also more hurtful." They had the same arms, the same "little girl hands," and similar facial contours. They both admitted to talking fast and talking a lot. And both twins appreciate art, while acknowledging their inability to create it. Both twins also admired each other's outfit—casual, stylish, and well-matched to their comparable body types.

Allison experienced their meeting as "an out of body experience."[54] Almost immediately she gently rubbed Michele's arm, a gesture that appeared so natural and easy it seemed to go unnoticed by both; although Allison later said that touching her sister was "amazing—she exists!" Allison questioned what might have happened if LWS had "swapped" their families, keeping her in New York and sending Michele to California. "How do you do this to people?" she asked in disbelief. Neither twin could answer that query, but they exchanged glances as if tacitly acknowledging that arbitrary decisions can have major consequences. Even if Allison's placement with an identical twin father had been purposeful as both twins suspect, why did LWS choose Allison and not Michele to be raised by a twin? Somewhat jokingly, Michele complained that she and Allison had been deprived of being "the twins" in high school. "We were screwed out of twin popularity," she said.[55]

BECOMING TWINS

"Except for the birth of my children, it was the most amazing day of my life." Michele and Allison ended their first meeting with happiness and relief, captured in sentiments that they expressed independently. They looked forward to private time to get to know one another, and they have made this happen. Despite the distance between them, they spend weekends together when they can, along with their families. They are exceptional in this respect. A study of adult twins found that the attachment security and relationship satisfaction of fraternal twins, but not identical twins, depended on their frequency of in-person contact.[56] But Michele and Allison do not let distance come between them. They also telephone and text one another almost daily. When I visited Michele at her home in October 2019, her phone lit up with a greeting from Allison. "Hope you have a great day!" Allison wrote. This seemed unexpected to me, but customary to Michele. Their intimacy has come easily. And both families have embraced both newly discovered twins.

Michele's parents, Allan and Iris, are delighted that their daughter has a twin sister. They immediately warmed up to Allison and her family, whom they found "lovable and lovely," and Allison has called Michele's parents

Figure 17.2   Reunited fraternal twins, Allison Kanter (L) and Michele Mordkoff (R). This is the twins' favorite picture taken of them together again. Courtesy of the twins.

"amazing." Michele had an opportunity to meet Allison's mother, Florence, who showed her the same warmth and affection. "My mom loved Michele," Allison told me. "They had an instant connection."[57] Sadly, Florence passed away in September 2019. Michele came to California for the memorial service and had been there before when Florence was sick. Allison was concerned about the travel and expense involved. "She loves me—it was so unbelievable that she was here," she said.

Because of the timing, Allison's father, Herbert, never had a chance to meet Michele. Herbert passed away at age ninety-one, just six weeks before Michele and Allison came together. The day of his death—June 25, 2018—was either the same day or the day before Michele watched the movie trailer that changed both of their lives. Allison believes that, as an identical twin, Herbert would have loved meeting Michele and sharing his twin stories with the two of them. Curiously, both Allison and her father would have had twins living in New Jersey. In October 2006, Herbert lost his twin brother Stewart (Stewie) to Parkinson's disease; Stewie had been an English professor at Rutgers University in New Brunswick, New Jersey. Allison didn't recall her father speaking much about his twin until Stewie passed away. "He just broke down," she said. "And he felt guilty. It was heartbreaking—I never realized how hard it was for him." The day I heard that story from Allison was Herbert and Stewie's birthday.

Curiously, genealogy lacks terms for a child's newly acquired sibling. Like the triplets' father who embraced all three boys as his own, Allan considers Allison his daughter, although fatherly feelings vary across the LWS twins' families. Iris thinks of Allison as Michele's twin sister, but not as her daughter, explaining that, "I took care of Michele and diapered her." Many parents of other reared-apart twins, especially the young separated Chinese pairs I have studied, are experiencing similar quandaries—what is their relationship to their child's twin? As Iris suggested, the parent-child bond evolves from the love and care a parent dispenses over time. Whether Iris defines Allison as "her daughter" doesn't really matter—what matters is that Iris adores Allison, and she and Allan have welcomed her into their family. Interestingly, the members of the twins' nuclear families are easily becoming "aunts," "uncles," "nieces," "nephews," and "cousins." Perhaps because such relatives often live apart, their coming together does not seem unusual.

Most reared-apart twins' relationships flourish, but they occasionally fail. Among the few that have failed, I have observed that the twins' initial high, based on their instant rapport and perceived similarities, is all-consuming, omitting time for building a strong foundation between them. Michele and Allison are not like that—from the start, they wisely "took it slow, step by step." Initially, they saw the three thousand-mile distance between their homes as a plus, because it let them maintain their usual personal and professional lives. Now that they have connected on so many levels, the distance between them is challenging, because they are loving the process of becoming twins. Nothing feels forced. "If we lived in the same city we would get together every day," Allison said.[58] And while being identical would have been "cool," both twins are happy to be fraternal because their twin type kept them from being secretly studied by the LWS-Child Development Center researchers.[59] They and their parents avoided the regular visits to their home for testing and observation that many of the twins found uncomfortable.

Michele is thrilled to have a sister. "Sometimes when I talk to Allison, I feel like I am talking to myself. She kind of sees things from a perspective I would see—I love when she calls me for advice." Allison didn't cry when the twins first met, but "now I cry all the time when I see her." Allison's daughter Callie said she has never seen her mother so happy.[60] And I have rarely seen reunited fraternal twins so closely aligned and attuned to one another. Research shows that identical twins, both reared-apart and reared-together, develop closer social bonds than their fraternal counterparts, but there are exceptional pairs; Michele and Allison are among them.

It is worth noting that both twins came from loving childhood homes, never feeling as if something was missing. Still, Allison now feels "complete, because there is someone who gets me completely." Michele feels the same way. "When I talk to myself, I talk to her." Michele wondered if she and Allison were loved even more than biological children because their parents tried so hard to get them.[61] Perhaps their security and confidence let them accept their twin as an addition to their life, rather than as a replacement.

I was concerned about the twins when I joined Michele's Zoom-based birthday party on May 12, 2020. I wondered—Where was Allison? Did they have a falling out? I raised this possibility gingerly with Allison when we spoke later that month. "That will never happen with us!" she insisted. Allison explained that she had joined the party when it began but left early for a birthday party of her own.

THE TWO MAYORS

Friends have independently called them the "Mayor of Calabasas" (Allison) and the "Mayor of Wayne" (Michele). These labels come from the twins' shared interest in people, their loyalty to friends, and their ability to lead. They are both worriers, but they bring a positive perspective to most situations—even to their separation as newborns. Allison feels some anger, more than she did at first, about having grown up apart. She calls it the "cloud covering" that sometimes intrudes. While she and Michele were not followed systematically like the identical pairs, she believes that the twin study was done to boost the researchers' reputations, not for the good of others. But Allison is happy knowing that she and Michele will have the rest of their lives together. That is her goal—to spend as much time together as possible. "We are so lucky because of how well we do get along and it's almost like we didn't skip a beat in some ways."

Michele agrees. She also feels occasional "pangs" thinking about why she and Allison could not have been together all along. "But we are so fortunate to have it now—we do not let this overshadow our lives." There is another fork in her road. As an attorney Michelle is also focused on addressing the injustice that was done to her and the other LWS twins. She wants to see someone take responsibility, which does not mean they would be admitting to culpability or liability—because the people who can bring the twins together and release their records did not decide to separate them and did not study them. She wants her file, not a letter. And she is uninterested in a lawsuit—"how do you attach monetary value to the loss of your sister?" she asks. When Michele contacted the Jewish Board of Family and Children's Services for information and guidance, as advised in *20/20*'s exposé, she received no assistance.

Michele and Allison allow us to see the twin bond ripen in real time. Allison spoke of the ease and naturalness of being with Michele. The two shared a hotel bed in New York City when they were there to film for CNN. "It would have been odd *not* to have done that!" she said. Other reunited twins have felt the same way when it comes to physical closeness.[62] At one point I wondered if Michele and Allison would have been drawn to each other if they had met socially, assuming they had not been twins. "I would have picked her out of a million people to be friends with," Michelle said.

Allison and Michele use the word "we" a lot. It's a very twin thing to do.

ENDNOTE

Sitting with me in the noisy Hourglass Tavern in midtown Manhattan, Michele spoke for both twins. "We always wanted to be part of our adopted families. But when you open the 'proverbial door' to meet your birth family it's a little scary. It's like being pulled into a vortex. You know who you are. You know who your mom and dad are. Now all of a sudden, it's confusing, a little scary and somewhat of a betrayal. But the relationship that you have with a sister that is similarly adopted like you are is very different. It's twofold—one part is knowing your sister or brother—the other part is knowing who you are. *I think being a twin is an identity of birth.*"

I highlighted Michele's last line because it reinforces Dr. Bernard's underestimate of how much discovering one's twin as an adult affects identity and selfhood. Both Allison and Michele had to rethink the people that they were and their relations with others. Other people also viewed them in a new way. Being a twin revised Michele's sense of herself, as she expressed earlier. Her sons Andrew, now twenty-three, and Josh, now twenty-five, were with her the day she met her sister. "The word *twin* is just a whole new word and a whole other thing," Andrew reflected. "It does make [my mother] a different person a little bit, in the best way possible—it's a different back story to her life. She is one in a million."[63] Josh, who is very protective of his mother, commented that, "The most beautiful part is that they were always sisters, but now they have a real relationship."[64] Both Andrew and Josh love "hanging out with Aunt Ali," and Jeremy, Kyle, and Callie love their "Aunt Michele."[65] And the two cousins who have met—Andrew and Kyle—interacted in ways that felt natural, "like we've known each other for a long time."[66] Their connection may be partly rooted in what Michele says are their "very similar personalities." Michele's parents, Allan and Iris, think of her twinship as a new beginning. However, Iris may be a little jealous of Michele's relationship with Allison. Her husband commented that mother and daughter would call each other daily, but now Michele has become harder to reach.[67]

Allison went through similar transformations. For a long time, she woke up mornings, reminding herself that she is a twin. She still finds it hard to think that she and Michele are part of the plot behind *Three Identical Strangers*. "It's our story, but without the science part [because we weren't studied]," she said. This explains why Allison finds her separation from Michele so hard to comprehend and accept. "There was no motivation behind it. They were just keeping protocol."

When the truth was known, the first person Allison thought about was her sister Lori. Allison had a "gut feeling" that she and Michele would become close. She worried that Lori would feel rejected seeing how much she was enjoying her twinship with Michele. However, Lori, also an adoptee, found her half-sister a year after Michele found Allison and is becoming involved in that relationship. Allison is now more content, knowing that she and Lori have their own "biological connections."

Allison's perspectives on human nature have changed. She has acquired greater appreciation for how genes shape our personalities and predilections. Earlier, I wrote that Allison believed her good childhood behavior came from her need to avoid family friction. Then she discovered that Michele behaved the same way even though Michele was raised by different parents. Now Allison attributes their shared behaviors to their "wiring." She still thinks about how things would have been if their home situations had been switched. "Our lives would have been all the same and all different," she decided, adding, "I might not have met my husband."

In 2019, Michele was diagnosed with cancer, an illness that demands considerable care and attention. Allison was with her in New Jersey during one of her bouts. "I couldn't sleep for more than an hour, I was so upset," she told me. She started to cry, then expressed relief that Michele was doing so well.[68] "We deserve this time together as sisters."

Michele and Allison decided to go public with their story.[69] As Michele explained, "This is our way to gain closure. And to share our happiness." The twins are also at work on a memoir and both are curious to see where it will take them. For now, they are enjoying their relationship and caring for each other as newly minted twin sisters. There is also a playfulness about them, as though they are trying to recreate their lost childhood—not uncommon among reunited twins. But thoughts of their stolen years still sting. As Michele said, "a broken arm heals, but a broken heart does not."

POSTSCRIPT #1

Late in the day of June 1, 2021, I received a text message from Sharon Morello, the twin whose story I told in chapter 11. Michele (Morkoff) Fraenkel passed away earlier that day, at age fifty-seven, having known her twin sister Allison for less than three years. Michele had remarried only recently, on July 21, 2020, to her longtime fiancé Ian Fraenkel, owner and president of the IJF Creative Group. Michele was a kind, compassionate, and brilliant woman with a keen sense of justice. I am grateful for our many hours of conversation and for her thoughtful and insightful contributions to this book. Michele will be missed greatly by everyone who knew her.

POSTSCRIPT #2

The Memories page of the funeral service chosen by Michele's family includes many moving tributes to a beloved friend, teacher, colleague. There is also a heartfelt and heartbreaking entry from Michele and Allison's birth mother. She described Michele as a "brilliant and loving person . . . an exceptional human being." She added, "I was so happy I had the chance to meet my daughters after 55 years." Not all the twins' birth mothers had that special privilege.

POSTSCRIPT #3

On June 19, 2021, Michele's family held a service to honor her memory. Michele's twin sister Allison shared several memories and reflections. Everyone laughed hearing about the twins' Passover strawberry shortcake that collapsed when they removed it from the oven. But Allison's stories of her sister's compassion and understanding brought tears and smiles.

· *18* ·

Letters of Protest

Oscars and Emmys

$\mathcal{T}$im Wardle's documentary film *Three Identical Strangers* was considered an early contender for an Oscar.[1] A pre-Oscar nomination viewing of the film took place on December 4, 2018.[2] This event, held at the Public Hotel on Chrystie Street in Manhattan's lower east side, was intended to showcase the film and, hopefully, attract attention and support from voting members. Michele Mordkoff, one of the recently reunited Louise Wise Services (LWS) twins filmed by Wardle, had been invited to attend. A dinner at Famous Sammy's Roumanian Steakhouse followed. Seated at the table with Michele and her son Josh were Bob Shafran, one of the separated triplets, and his wife Ilene; the Shafrans' daughter Elyssa; the Shafrans' son Brandon and his girlfriend; Bob's best friend and his wife; and film director Tim Wardle. The triplets had worked at Sammy's between 1982 and 1986, prior to starting a restaurant of their own.[3]

It was a special night. The restaurant attempted to recreate the atmosphere of the 1980s days when the triplets had worked there. The staff hired their piano player from that time, served vodka frozen into giant ice blocks, brought out old-fashioned oversized bottles of seltzer, and provided milk, seltzer, and Fox's U-bet syrup for mixing old-fashioned egg creams. Pictures of the triplets were displayed along the walls. Sammy's served their classic menu of bread, chopped liver, steak, and chicken schnitzel. A video clip taken that night shows Bob mixing an egg cream, stirring the contents together without spilling a drop, just as in days past. The dinner guests enjoyed his vivid accounts of the jokes and pranks that he and his two brothers had inflicted on their fellow employees. But from Josh's perspective, Bob didn't seem to be completely happy in a place where such familiar surroundings recalled both the heady days of becoming triplets and the tragic suicidal loss of his brother

Eddy in 1995. I suspect that Bob wrestled with similarly opposing emotions when he watched the film earlier.

SHORTLISTED—BUT SHORTCHANGED?

I listened to Michele's detailed account of the December 2018 film event when we met at New York City's Hourglass Tavern in October 2019.

> I sat on the side of the room with the people who were going to be voting. I looked around at my son, Josh. And I looked around the room and tears were flowing from the audience. As I sat in the room afterwards, I was listening to people that had much more objectivity than I do. I just don't understand why the film didn't go farther than it did. There were other great things that won, but not moving on to that next place [nomination]. . . . I'm still wondering how these things happen without being influenced by people who didn't want the film to be that popular.

That's when I told Michele about the letter.

A "Letter of Protest—*Three Identical Strangers*" was circulated among mostly psychological professionals, including colleagues of Dr. Lois Oppenheim at Montclair State University who led this effort. Recall that Dr. Oppenheim had known Dr. Peter Neubauer for many years. She had authored an interview with one of the three key twin study researchers, Dr. Christa Balzert, and co-authored a review of *Three Identical Strangers* for the *Journal of the American Medical Association* (*JAMA*). I discussed both of these publications in previous chapters. I learned about the protest letter in an April 2019 telephone conversation with Dr. Oppenheim.[4]

In January 2019, a protest letter with fifty-two signatories was sent to the American Academy of Motion Picture Arts and Sciences, headquartered in Beverly Hills, California.[5] The letter was also sent by email to CNN in Atlanta, Georgia, the station that would air the film on January 27, 2019. Discussions led by CNN's medical reporter, Dr. Sanjay Gupta, that included various experts and reunited twins, were recorded to supplement the viewing. The letter was posted on Facebook, on January 25, 2019.[6] The Academy was scheduled to present the annual Oscar awards to winners on February 24, 2019, in an internationally televised ceremony. These dates are made publicly available.[7]

Oppenheim promised to send me a copy of the letter and she did, commenting that it was "not the focus of her life." While we were still on the phone, I asked her about the timing of the letter. She couldn't recall the date it was written or the date it was sent, but she was "certain that it was sent before the final announcement" of the Oscar nominations. On February 5, she had told someone that the letter had been sent on or about Thursday January 24, before the film's CNN airdate, adding that it would have been sent to the Motion Picture Academy earlier that week. Oppenheim also said that on January 20, someone had asked to see the letter and she said it would be sent to the Academy the next day, and to CNN after that. She also said that the letter was seen by "hundreds of people," all of whom wished to sign it. When I received the letter, I noticed that it had no date.

The process of choosing Oscar contenders begins the year before the awards are decided. On December 17, 2018, the Motion Picture Academy released the ninety-first shortlist for films under consideration for award nominations in nine categories.[8] *Three Identical Strangers* was one of fifteen documentary feature films that had advanced to this semi-final level. The voting date for choosing the final five 2019 nominations in each film category was announced on April 23, 2019. Voting for nominated films opened on Monday, January 7, 2019, and closed one week later, on Monday, January 14. The five nominated films in each category were announced on Tuesday, January 22; *Three Identical Strangers* was not among the final five.[9] If the protest letter had been received by the academy after January 14, it would not have affected the outcome. If the film had been nominated, it is unlikely that the nomination would have been affected. Since the award process first began in 1929, only eight nominated films have been removed from consideration, mostly due to violation of rules regarding authorship, adaptation, or promotion. Only one Oscar winner was forced to relinquish the coveted statuette after the ceremony, once the Academy learned that the film had been released earlier than allowed; it was a documentary film.[10] These offenses most likely come to the attention of the Academy's governing board in a variety of ways. No doubt, the Academy receives scores of complaints about controversial films as the award season approaches.

I was still curious about the letter's timing because of Oppenheim's uncertainty over when it was sent. Two months later, in June 2019, I spoke with Oppenheim's colleague, Dr. Leon Hoffman, the lead author of their co-written film review in *JAMA*. Hoffman co-directs the Pacella Parent Child Center of the New York Psychoanalytic Society and Institute.[11] He knew Dr. Neubauer "mostly around meetings—I was not with him, quote, unquote, as a friend. . . . I was not a close friend of his at all." Hoffman was a signatory on the letter.

According to Hoffman, an editor from *JAMA* had contacted him prior to the Academy Awards nomination announcement to request a review. If the film had been nominated, the journal would have published their review "much sooner" than when it appeared in July 2019. Hoffman also had "no idea" of how Oppenheim had handled the logistics of the protest letter in terms of the Motion Picture Academy or CNN. However, the film was not nominated "so the whole thing became moot," Hoffman said.

In the course of writing this chapter, I contacted the Motion Picture Academy. The Academy would not comment as to whether or not the letter had been received.[12]

WHAT THE LETTER SAID

I have reprinted the letter of protest in full to provide greater awareness and understanding of the controversies that erupted around the release of *Three Identical Strangers*. An annotated list of the fifty-two signatories follows the text of the letter, but appears later in the chapter. I attempted to contact every person who signed it.

LETTER OF PROTEST: *THREE IDENTICAL STRANGERS*

We feel compelled to speak out about the so-called documentary *Three Identical Strangers*, a film that ignores crucial information, omits context, and unfairly vilifies people in its attempt at dramatization. By skewing its story in the way and to the degree it does, the film unfortunately closes off any meaningful discussion about the history of the research in question and the people involved.

In a glaring omission, there is no mention in the film of the role of Dr. Viola Bernard, who singly created the policy that led to the separation of the adopted triplets. As chief psychiatric consultant to the Louise Wise adoption agency in the late 1950s, Bernard advised the agency to separate identical twins and one set of triplets for adoption, given her belief (as she expressed in a recently uncovered memo) that by doing so, "early mothering would be less burdened and divided and the child's developing individuality would be facilitated." Louise Wise Services was not alone in this practice among agencies, as reported by *Slate*, although the practice has long since been abandoned. Nevertheless, Bernard's name, words, and role are completely ignored by the film, with the misleading inference left to viewers that it was Dr. Peter Neubauer who separated the twins and triplets for the purposes of secret research. By creating this story, the film creates a villain for its purposes, and worse: Post-premiere publicity even allowed for morning talk shows to describe Neubauer as participating in a "Nazi-like" experiment. Such a misleading accusation, especially against a Jewish refugee from Austria during WWII, is inexcusable; yet the allegation has been allowed to stand and the film continues to be rewarded.

According to Dr. Lawrence M. Perlman, a clinical psychologist and first-hand witness to the study as a researcher, his own appearance in the film was also dramatically cherry-picked, omitting insights into the study's origins and other pertinent details on which he and others have written in critical scientific papers. About the question of informed consent, for instance, Perlman writes that existing state and agency adoption laws in the early 1960s ensured that adoptive parents "were guaranteed that they would not know anything about the family background of their infants, including the possible existence of biological siblings," and, he adds, "it was the obligation of the research team to preserve this confidentiality." Also, as Perlman notes, along with researchers' single-day, once-a-year visits to the homes of the children, therapeutic guidance was offered if needed. The film neither describes this environment nor mentions that the study began long before codification of the rules of informed consent, not in place until the late 1970s. Dr. Leon Hoffman, co-director of the Pacella Research Center, rightly observes in *Psychology Today* that the film "retrofits todays values onto the past . . . hammering home the fantasy that Neubauer and colleagues should have known better."

Regarding the film's accusation of secrecy, it should be noted that numerous researchers were involved in the study over 15 years and that it had funding by the National Institute of Mental Health after review. Also, Peter Neubauer spoke openly about the twin study and even published a book on its conclusions for the public—*Nature's Thumbprint: The New Genetics of Personality* (New York, Columbia University Press, 1996). The film ignores the book's existence, though it significantly helped broaden our understanding of the role of genetics in the interaction between nature and nurture.

Instead, the film leaves the impression that he and other researchers acted with a cavalier disregard for the impact of their work on the lives of the children they were studying. Never mind that Dr. Neubauer played a crucial role in the emerging fields of child psychiatry and psychoanalysis, as the *New York Times* wrote in his obituary, helping to inaugurate groups such as the Academy of Child Psychiatry, the National Center for Clinical Infant Programs (in Washington, D.C., now called Zero to Three), and the International Association of Child and Adolescent Psychiatry and Allied Professions, for which he served as Secretary-General. As Clinical Professor of Psychiatry at New York University and Lecturer at Columbia University, he spoke out against television violence and wrote meaningfully on single-parent families and children reared in collectives. Not only was he highly esteemed in his profession, he was known for his deep commitment to children. He and other professionals were the ones who helped create an environment of guidance and care for children in this country.

How unfortunate that *Three Identical Strangers* passes for truth so much that is inaccurate and misses out on a unique opportunity to reassess changing ethical norms in a serious way. A documentary concerned less with drama and more with fact would have been most worthwhile.

In this chapter, I speak to one point with which I agree before identifying content in the letter that is factually incorrect—much of which was included in 2018 and 2019 blogs by Hoffman and Oppenheim, both published in *Psychology Today* magazine.[13] As I indicated earlier, my personal views, thoughts, and commentaries regarding the LWS twin separations, researchers, and investigation will appear in the final chapters.

Point 1. Dr. Viola W. Bernard's role in separating twins was omitted from the film. As I explained in previous chapters, Bernard, the psychiatric consultant for LWS, believed that purposefully separating newborn twins benefited their psychological growth and avoided parental overburdening. However, it should be noted that Bernard separated fraternal twins as well as identical twins and a set of identical triplets, although fraternal pairs were not included in the study. Several known pairs of separated fraternal twins and a pair of undetermined type have been described in this book.

Error 1. The statement that other adoption agencies have separated twins, as reported by Slate*, is misleading.* The *Slate* citation was not provided in the letter, but I was able to locate it.[14] Adoption staff in agencies across the country have sometimes separated twins when prospective parents could not afford to raise two babies.[15] In the 1950s through 1970s, some agencies separated twins for financial reasons, acquiring two family fees rather than a single one. These agencies neglected to consider the twins' best interests. However, there is no evidence that agencies other than LWS separated twins because they believed that growing up apart enhanced twins' individual development.[16]

Dr. Neubauer tried to convince Catholic Charities in New York to separate twins, but their staff refused to do so.[17] Other adoption agencies in the New York area did not agree to cooperate with LWS's proposal to place twins apart, as I documented previously in this book. When I visited Dr Neubauer in 2004, he informed me that he and the other twin study researchers were "there from the birth." I will return to Dr. Neubauer's role in the twin separation policy in the final chapter.

Error 2. The researchers assessed the twins more frequently and regularly than single-day visits once each year. The single-day visits are credited to researcher Dr. Larry Perlman but lack formal citation. To the contrary, Perlman noted that twins were assessed "every 3 months for the first year, every 6 months for the next 2 years, and annually thereafter." Reference to chapter 9 of this book shows that during her first year of life, identical twin Sharon Morello was observed five times in foster care and eight times in her adoptive home, with several visits each year in subsequent years. Morello's data come from the Yale University archival records that were released to her. Another informative source on this issue is a 1996 chapter, co-authored by Peter Neubauer and Christa Balzert. They explain that "The investigation included films, psychological tests, interviews with family members and documented observation periods several times a year during infancy and twice a year when the children were older."[18] Oppenheim cited this source in her 2020 interview with Balzert.[19]

    Error 3. Neither Neubauer, nor his book Nature's Thumbprint, *provided open discussion of the LWS-Child Development Center (CDC) twin study.* The book failed to mention Dr. Viola Bernard or her contribution to the research—an omission that Oppenheim raised against *Three Identical Strangers* in the protest letter; see *Error 1.* As I indicated in chapter 13, the researchers' lack of informed parental consent prevented publication of LWS-CDC twin study data in *Nature's Thumbprint,* with the exception of several anecdotal accounts. According to Neubauer's book editor Jane Isay, Neubauer used information from extant reared-apart twin studies to make his points. In addition, as I noted previously, he often included this material without citation. And as I documented in previous chapters, Viola Bernard, Samuel Abrams, and colleagues attempted to limit dissemination of their findings. Some individuals who signed the letter, including Neubauer's colleagues and associates, first learned of the LWS-CDC twin study upon seeing the film *Three Identical Strangers.* Also recall that during discussions of book publication, the researchers considered the possibility of publishing the book in another country. Finally, a former social work intern at LWS was stunned to learn about the twin separations, which she discovered from watching the film.[20]

    Note. The original version of Nature's Thumbprint *by Neubauer and Neubauer was published by Addison-Wesley in 1990. A second printing was published in 1996 by Columbia University Press (Morningside edition).*[21]

    Error 4. Many researchers were involved in the twin study project that occurred over fifteen years. The study was ongoing for at least seventeen years. The first twin assessments occurred in 1961 and the last most likely occurred in 1978, when one of the youngest twins turned twelve.[22] Also recall that the archived twin study records are listed as circa 1960–1980.

The letter of protest raises legal and moral issues that I will address in the next chapter. Among them are informed consent, project funding, academic integrity, and professional responsibility.

SIGNATORIES

The letter of protest was signed by twenty-five psychiatrists, seventeen clinical psychologists, two educational practioners, three authors, three filmmakers, and two artists. I interviewed and/or received email commentary from twenty-one of the fifty-one signatories I contacted, or 41 percent. Five individuals declined to be interviewed or to send an email commentary; twenty-three individuals did not reply; one individual requested email correspondence following my letter, but did not reply to that message; and one individual agreed to an interview, but later declined upon learning that her colleagues had been interviewed, saying there was nothing more to add. One individual was ill when I tried to obtain contact information and is now deceased, explaining why I contacted fifty-one rather than fifty-two individuals. Interviewees were variously invited by email, letter, and/or telephone—only one letter was returned, but I reached that individual by email. Three individuals who signed the letter had completed interviews with me, but later decided to withdraw their names from the book; I have omitted them from the list below.

- Karen A. Abrams, MD, child and adolescent psychiatrist
- Henry Bachrach, PhD, clinical professor of psychiatry (retired), New York Medical College
- Anna Balas, MD, distinguished fellow, American Psychiatric Association; faculty, New York Psychoanalytic Society and Institute
- Christa Balzert, PhD, fellow of the International Psychoanalytic Association
- H. Scott Barshack, MD, psychiatrist, Marin General Hospital
- Francis Baudry, MD, faculty, New York Psychoanalytic Society and Institute
- Antonio Beltramini, MD, faculty, New York Psychoanalytic Society and Institute
- Harold Blum, MD, president, Psychoanalytic Research and Development Fund; faculty, Institute for Psychoanalytic Education affiliated with New York University School of Medicine
- Patrick V. Brown, MFA
- Irene Cairo, MD, faculty, New York Psychoanalytic Society and Institute; faculty, Contemporary Freudian Society
- Anna Chapman, MD, president, Neuropsychoanalysis Foundation
- Stan Coen, MD, clinical professor of psychiatry, College of Physicians & Surgeons, Columbia University; faculty, Columbia University Psychoanalytic Center

- Jonathan Cohen, PhD, incoming co-president, International Observatory for School Climate and Violence Prevention; president emeritus, National School Climate Center
- Maxine Gann, PhD, developmental and clinical psychologist, psychoanalyst
- Carol Gilligan, PhD, university professor, New York University
- Karen Gilmore, MD, clinical professor of psychiatry, Columbia University School of Medicine
- Ellen Glass, MD, psychiatrist, psychoanalyst
- Maida Greenberg, EdD, faculty, Pine Psychoanalytic Center
- Philip Herschenfeld, MD, faculty, New York Psychoanalytic Society and Institute
- Leon Hoffman, MD, co-director, Pacella Research Center; faculty, New York Psychoanalytic Society and Institute
- Bob Holof, Bob Holof Productions
- Ruth Imber, PhD, faculty, William Alanson White Institute
- Theodore Jacobs, MD, faculty, New York Psychoanalytic Society and Institute; past president, Association for Child Psychoanalysis
- Navah C. Kaplan, PhD, faculty, New York Psychoanalytic Society and Institute
- Susan Kolod, PhD, chair, Committee on Public Information, American Psychoanalytic Association
- J. Ronald Lally, EdD, co-director, Center for Child and Family Studies, WestEd; founding member, National Center for Clinical Infant Programs
- Christian Maetzner, MD, associate dean of education for child analysis, New York Psychoanalytic Society and Institute
- Gail Marks, artist
- Edith McNutt, MD, faculty, New York Psychoanalytic Society and Institute
- Marina Mirkin, MD, faculty, Institute for Psychoanalytic Education affiliated with New York University School of Medicine
- Ira Moses, PhD, ABPP, faculty, William Alanson White Psychoanalytic Institute
- Patricia Nachman, PhD, faculty, New York Psychoanalytic Society and Institute; faculty, Mount Sinai School of Medicine
- Alexander Neubauer, author
- Henry Nunberg, LLB, MD, faculty, New York Psychoanalytic Society and Institute; clinical assistant professor psychiatry emeritus, Weill Cornell Medical College

- Wendy Olesker, MD, faculty, New York University Postdoctoral Program in Psychoanalysis and Psychotherapy
- Lois Oppenheim, PhD, university distinguished scholar, Montclair State University
- Daniel Orlievsky, director, Postgraduate Psychology Program, Argentine Catholic University
- Sarah Paul, MD, faculty, New York Psychoanalytic Society and Institute
- Jeree H. Pawl, PhD, former clinical professor, Department of Psychiatry, University of California at San Francisco; former director, Infant-Parent Program, San Francisco General Hospital
- Mervyn M. Peskin, MD, clinical associate professor of psychiatry, Weill Cornell Medical College; Faculty, New York Psychoanalytic Society and Institute
- Ann Pleshette Murphy, author; former parenting correspondent, *Good Morning America*
- David Pollens, PhD, clinical director of the treatment center, Director for Clinical Services, New York Psychoanalytic Society and Institute
- Michele Press, MD, clinical assistant professor of psychiatry, New York University Langone Medical Center; president, New York Psychoanalytic Society and Institute
- Arnold Richards, MD, publisher, ipbooks.net
- Albert Sax, MD, faculty, New York Psychoanalytic Society and Institute
- Theodore Shapiro, MD, professor of psychiatry, Weill Cornell Medicine; director, Sackler Infant Psychiatry Program
- Mark Solms, PhD, director, science department, American Psychoanalytic Association
- Serena Wieder, PhD, clinical director, Profectum Foundation
- Ben Wolf, cinematographer

THE DEFENSE

Several common and partly overlapping themes emerged from the interviews and commentaries regarding the impetus to sign the letter. Everyone who responded is represented to avoid selective reporting; however, names are not linked to the statements to prevent repercussion from colleagues or the media.[23] Their remarks and reflections are stated in the following without assessment of their significance or veracity, which I will discuss in the final chapter.[24] Passages without quotation marks are based on extensive handwritten notes, rather than tape-recorded interviews or email correspondence, when individuals were interviewed by telephone and did not wish to be recorded.

I have organized the responses into four broad categories. *Category 1* includes statements reflecting individuals' high regard for Dr. Neubauer. *Category 2* provides comments questioning the veracity of *Three Identical Strangers* as a documentary film. *Category 3* lists descriptions of signatories' knowledge of the twin study, and *Category 4* includes criticisms of the twin separation policy and twin study that were provided by some signatories even while they defended the researchers.

Category 1. Dr. Peter Neubauer was a highly admired, respected, and revered scholar, and/or close personal friend. He did not decide to separate the twins, but he studied them given the opportunity to do so.

"I signed the letter because I found Peter Neubauer to be an honorable person who was devoted to his patients and had the highest ethical standards. Given those qualities, he would not knowingly have done anything that would injure children under his care or whose placement with adopted parents he supervised. Perhaps mistakes and misjudgments were made, but I felt that to condemn Dr. Neubauer and paint him as callous and self-serving was wrong."

I knew Peter Neubauer from our involvement in the psychoanalytic community. I have known him a long time and have the highest regard for him—he was congenial, intelligent, and good-humored. The twin study never came up in conversation, and it was not supported by this fund.

This puts me in an awkward position. It would not be appropriate for me to comment on the film because I cannot be objective—I have my own personal feelings, tinged by the longstanding closeness we shared.

I signed the letter because I felt he was being maligned and disparaged. His motives were not malicious. I did not know it was sent to the Motion Picture Academy or to CNN. If I had known, I do not know if it would have made a difference—hard to say.

"I guess he did not design [the study], but he entered as a practitioner. And one can kind of imagine that you might have had the notion that this seems like a terrible idea, but it certainly wasn't his to create. It was twenty some years later that I think he became involved in working on this study that they did on their children."

"I did not know Dr. Neubauer personally. His reputation as a caring doctor and his work with children were widely known and highly respected among parents and educators when I was raising my son."

"These films were so upsetting to me because they did not have anything to do with reality. I mean they just had nothing to do with who [Neubauer] was—he was the most kind-hearted human being and so to see how distorted things were in the film, that is what got me so involved. I just wanted to defend him, it was such a gross distortion. I do not know—there is not really much I can say—I just knew him as an incredibly kind human being."

Peter told a story about two boy twins that they were studying who were both very neat about arranging their clothes. Peter asked one of the boys why he did that, and the boy said that his parents were that way. When he asked the other boy the same question, the child said he did that because his parents were messy. I don't recall hearing about any of the scientific details of the study. Peter was quite attractive and quite intelligent. The film was upsetting because it made him out to be something he wasn't.

"I mean, to me, what was just unconscionable was that they made it seem, you know—if it's true and my understanding from a lot of different people is that it was Viola Bernard, not Peter, who originally made the decision to separate the twins and triplets for the purpose of the research. Even if Peter had more, you know, a say in that, then, you know, I think or the people who knew Peter think or you uncover something that I don't know about, the idea of portraying him as [a] kind of Mengele, you know, researcher doing research for, you know, a sort of almost capricious reason is so completely a misrepresentation of what he was about in terms of his commitment to children and his sensitivity to children and his advocacy for children."

Category 2. Dr. Neubauer's defenders criticized Three Identical Strangers *for sensationalism and lack of objectivity, transforming a documentary film into a dramatization that vilified Neubauer. The appropriateness of applying modern ethical standards to the LWS-CDC study of the 1960s and 1970s was also questioned.*

"I actually found the film a quite fascinating demonstration of epigenetic variation. Where it went overboard was the retroactive application of current ethical standards to what I felt was a well-intended effort to solve the nature/nurture controversy. Furthermore, might one argue that had all three [triplets] been adopted by one set of parents their individual outcomes may have been worse?"

The film suffered from oversimplification and lack of objectivity. A particular point of view was being promoted, so the film lacked balance.

"The main reason I signed the petition, or the letter, is because I think that the accusation that is against Peter Neubauer is based on a model for human subjects that wasn't established until the mid-1970s, you know with the IRBs [Institutional Review Boards]. From everything I understand, Peter Neubauer was a completely ethical person, and nobody ever had any question about his ethics."

"I don't even remember signing any letter any time. Maybe I did. I thought [the film] was sleek. I thought it was slippery. I thought it was contrived and made to look like, 'Wouldn't that be fun to get somebody in a whole lot of trouble for this?'"

"There's a paper by Neubauer and I think it's in that, a one-parent child paper where he quotes Anna Freud about, what's the term? An accident of nature, a serendipitous situation that is found, like for example, the one-parent child, where they found families where a parent had died. It was not a clinical or formal study and I think that's what this [twin study] was—that they found that the agency made this decision so they were going to study it, you know it's like an accident of nature—and that was not at all clear in the movie. The main theme was that they did this in order to experiment on twins. And the families—I think that's the biggest critique. . . . [Film director Tim Wardle] could have presented a pros and cons kind of picture, he should not do just a one-sided exposé."

"There's no actual publication as far as I could find—is there a place where [Viola Bernard] says why twins should not be in the same home?"

"I think that [the 2017 documentary film, *The Twinning Reaction*] seemed a little bit more balanced. It did not get so much splash, it was not so melodramatic as the triplets movie. . . . I think that blaming everything, that all [the triplets'] problems, what really struck me about it, about the triplets movie, it put everything on Neubauer. There was something very ethically problematic about that movie."

"The movie was absolutely an unfair portrayal of Neubauer. I don't think it took into account the way adoptions were handled back in that era. It's a totally different situation for people seeking to adopt or to give up children for adoption. It was a very different way of handling things, and it didn't take into account any of those variables. The fact that adoptions were supposed to be totally private. I think another thing that I thought of is that, you know, they stressed the high degree of mental illness in the people they filmed. And, you know, in that era, a great many of the people given up for adoption were what we call high risk. You know, they were given up for adoption because they were the children of people who were so impaired that they couldn't deal with an unwanted pregnancy."

"Well, the real reason I signed the protest letter was I felt that the movie for whatever, you know—obviously, issues around ethics in this area are, you know, complicated and [decided] by many different things and what standards are at one period of time are not standards at another time. . . . I felt that the movie took a very unbalance, unnuanced and—what's the word?—you know, sort of a hype story."

"I was unaware of the twin study until I saw the film *Three Identical Strangers.* Peter Neubauer was faulted and maligned, but he did not separate the twins— Dr. Viola Bernard did that."

Category 3. A number of signatories were unaware of the LWS-CDC twin study until they saw the film—two had never seen it. Some individuals acquired a modicum of familiarity with the film's contents from readings and conversations, mostly after viewing. Pressure from peers or loyalty to colleagues explain why some individuals signed the letter.

"I am embarrassed to say that I have not seen the film. I mean, I don't really feel like I am in a position to judge. I felt strongly that there was some misrepresentation going on. But you know, again, it was a little bit not with full knowledge. So, I would say that is something to keep in mind. But I think I was joining with other people because of my loyalty to them. . . . But there were a lot of people at the institute who felt he was being unfairly characterized. So that was, I mean, I have to say, I didn't know I'd be taken to task, but I felt I wanted to be part of that support group to help [Neubauer's] memory."

"I did not know Dr. Neubauer. I signed the letter after reading different takes on why the children were separated to be raised apart. I agreed the movie had taken a negative position about the events. To be honest, I no longer remember the details of the movie and the controversy. I took a position based on the information I was given from psychoanalysts whose work with children has made them leaders in the field."

"I knew Peter Neubauer only very slightly and was not involved with the Jewish Board of Guardians or in any of his projects. I thought of [Dr. Neubauer] as an honest person who had the best interests of children at heart and was not self-serving. But I do not know what went into the decision to separate the triplets or what policies were followed at the time. I would like to be of help, but I did not know enough to be really informative or helpful."

"It's true that I signed the letter but did so principally out of an intuitive support for the points being made in the authors' comments. While I have seen the documentary in question, I have almost no familiarity with the actual study."

"I am afraid my signature does not mean I have special knowledge or interest in the twin topic."

The twin study never came up in conversation and I do not how it was supported financially. I was unaware of the study until I saw [*Three Identical Strangers*] at a movie theater while vacationing at my summer house in 2018. I had heard of the film through word of mouth. "I was shocked by it and struck by it." This was the first I knew about [the twin study]. Standards were different then—there was no IRB and information on adoptive children could not be revealed to their adoptive parents. I am not surprised that [Neubauer] did not mention the study. Since seeing the movie, I did some reading and Neubauer just took advantage of agency policy [regarding twin separations]. I have to read more about how LWS arrived at that policy.

We never discussed the LWS-CDC twin study, but we may have discussed the importance of genetics and environment in a general sense. I first learned of the study from an article in the *Psychoanalytic Study of the Child*, by Sam Abrams, maybe 1986. I have my own issues with the study.

It was a different time, and we are more aware of the complex ethical issues today. There was no IRB back then.

Maybe Peter was silent about the study because he worried that others might use his research or publish similar findings ahead of his.

"I had never known about the study until the movie, but I guess that people who studied at what was called Downstate—[New York University] and had Sam Abrams in classes that he was quite open about [the study] but I hadn't known about it at all."

"Well, I just heard about the movie and I then heard about it from Lois. And I watched it and, you know, signed the letter that she crafted. . . . I don't really know the study."

"I have just seen the film, that's all, and talked to Lois about it and felt that they were not fair to just you know—the elements of these things were all done with a great deal of emphasis on privacy. . . . You know, it's like it's so horrible that these kids didn't know they had siblings. I think this was well-intentioned. It was not malevolent."

"I didn't [see the other film, *The Twinning Reaction*]. I just saw this one, and I'm a friend of Lois, so I signed her letter. That's all it is. And I'm not a child psychiatrist, so it's not an area that I know. . . . [Lois] organized the letter. I'm just a tremendous fan of Lois, I wanted to support her, that's all."

"I think that [Neubauer] was depicted unfairly. Now, of course, I don't know, being outside of it. I don't know all the details. So, you know, I can't—but all I know is that I didn't feel like it was a balanced take on it. . . . That [seeing the film] was a first look. That was a first indication I had of that—the controversy around the whole thing."

"I signed that letter in support of my friend and collaborator Dr. Lois Oppenheim. . . . Typically I do my research before putting my name to a petition or letter. . . . This time, however, I had not seen the film at the time of signing. Still haven't. A mistake, I know. I have a great deal of respect for Lois. She is extremely knowledgeable in a number of disciplines, so I trust her implicitly and signed without doing my homework."

"I don't even remember signing any letter any time. Maybe I did."

Category 4. Criticisms of twin separation and research policies and practices were indicated. Interspersed among the various comments were criticisms of separating twins, concealing twinship, restricting the twins' records, and other matters.

"I thought that [concealing twinship from the parents] was suspect. There was nothing that I heard that was a good rationale for keeping the records closed—it seemed odd since the parents requested them."

"If it's an adoptive parent and the agency believes that the parents and the babies would be better off having more one-to-one attention, then I could see the rationale for doing that. From what I understand about twins and the unusual relationship that they have with one another, and how important and supportive their relationships can be on the whole, you know, private language they develop. It seems like a shame to me, especially with a child who's being adopted to be separated from their twin or their triplet."

Neubauer was too concerned with his study. There was deception. Any kind of survey given without consent poses a problem.

"My impression was [Neubauer] wasn't paying attention to that variable [the high risk of mental illness among adoptees]."

"These things were all done with a great deal of emphasis on privacy. It's horrible that these kids didn't know they had siblings. I think it was well-intentioned, it was not malevolent. . . . I don't know how much Neubauer was thinking about the impact [of] being recurrently observed and felt—and that's part of these kids' early experience. Does that have something to do? I didn't much care for the twins [the two triplets in the film]. I thought they were publicity seekers. But I wondered if the process of the research had somewhat conditioned that in them, you know? But, I mean, those are just my idle speculations."

"I feel bad for everybody. I mean, you know, too bad for the kids who were separated and bad for Peter's children, you know. So, it's just a terrible, terrible situation."

"Peter was not a 'Jewish Mengele.' If you put it on some kind of a scale of morality, what Mengele did and compare it with Peter did—but they are both wrong. I mean, there's no question about it."

"You know, what was done to [the twins] was unconscionable. I am not defending what was, you know, as you know better than I do. You know, it's not unusual practice the separation of siblings and twins. I think that that will be a really interesting part of your book, Nancy, because I think that the whole issue of what are the ethical standards now versus then, and what can be done now to compensate for what was done then? It's really important, not just for twin research, but for all sorts of research."

"I can identify with the children and with their feelings. Just all the anger and the rage were what I didn't understand."

"I know he was a caring man and for all intents and purposes, you know, a very, very good man. But, you know, people have blind spots and maybe that weighed in here, you know, because of his interest in the topic and his real, you know, kind of intellectual curiosity. Did it allow him to put aside, you know, maybe he did feel uncomfortable about it in any way? I don't know. I wasn't close enough to him to know that. . . . I remember him mentioning [the twin study] a couple of times in passing. And at some point, he said the results were very dramatic and that they were like not going to be revealed for a long period of time, something like that."

A number of individuals who signed the protest letter commented on various legal and moral issues raised by the twin study, some expressed earlier. These issues have attracted the attention of leading scholars in medicine, law, bioethics, and related disciplines. I will address these concerns in the next two chapters. However, I also attempted to determine what transpired at CNN when the station received Oppenheim's letter. And another protest letter against *Three Identical Strangers* was circulated through the Television Academy whose members decide which films earn Emmys. I will examine that letter, as well. Both of these letters raise issues that are important, although it appears unlikely that their content affected the award decisions. At the same time, films that win awards attract large audiences, so lost accolades mean lost opportunities to educate and inform.

CNN

Shortly after learning that Oppenheim's letter has been sent to CNN, I called a producer at the station's New York City office. She had been enormously helpful and friendly to me in December 2018 when I was in the studio to record an interview with the station's medical expert, Dr. Sanjay Gupta, for CNN's airing of *Three Identical Strangers*. I was surprisingly rebuffed when I raised the question of the protest letter with my contact. Following that, I tried contacting CNN's Atlanta, Georgia, headquarters, then sent a message directly to Dr. Gupta, indicating that I wanted to talk with him. I did not hear back, then turned my attention to earlier chapters, knowing that this part of the book would be written later. In September 2019, I wrote to Dr. Gupta again and attached a copy of the letter that had been sent to CNN. He was unaware of it and offered to forward copies to the appropriate individuals. I declined his offer, hoping to learn more about what had transpired on my own, but was unsuccessful. I contacted him again in July 2020, but I suspect—and understand—that his obligations regarding the coronavirus pandemic took precedent over this letter. Finally, in July and again in August 2020, I reached out to a high-ranking CNN communications officer, both directly and through an assistant, but received no response.

EMMYS

The second protest letter was intended to call attention to what were considered to be errors in *Three Identical Strangers*. The letter was written by a journalist, filmmaker, and Emmy award-winner, one of the signatories of Oppenheim's original protest letter. It was sent directly to Dan Birman, who serves on the Board of Governors for the Television Academy representing the Documentary programming group. The letter raised many of the same objections expressed in Oppenheim's letter. The letter is reproduced in the following, exactly as it was written, but with some bracketed information included for clarity and/or confidentiality.[25, 26]

> Dear Dan,
>
> As a TV Emmy winning producer, I understand the struggle to make a responsible film with a strong point of view that requires tough choices—what to leave in, what to take out, and the ethical questions that present themselves.
>
> That is why I am writing to protest the TV Academy considering, *Three Identical Strangers* for an Emmy. At best *Strangers* is poor journalism, at worst it is a deliberate attempt to create a more dramatic film by casting Dr. Peter Neubauer as a villain, a Mengele like villain, as one reviewer said. This is both inaccurate and unethical.
>
> I knew Dr. Neubauer, as he was a close friend of my wife's family. But I like to think that even if I hadn't known him I would be writing this letter to protest some of the facts and omissions of fact in this film.
>
> There is no question that separating twins/triplets at birth is immoral. But the filmmaker owes it to his audience to provide the context for the practice, especially since it was almost sixty years ago, and practices in the mental health field have changed.
>
> It was not Neubauer who was responsible for separating twins/triplets at birth. It was the Louise Wise Adoption Agency.
>
> That policy was promulgated by psychiatrist Dr. Viola Barnard, who was chief consultant to the Louise Wise Agency in the 1950s. She believed that separating twins/triplets was in the best interests of the children and parents—adoptive and biological.
>
> The Neubauer study followed and observed the children hoping to add valuable information to the nature/nurture debate.

The study was never secret as the documentary claimed. Neubauer mentioned his study to us, without revealing any confidences. The National Institute of Mental Health knew about and *approved* the study.

The film makes the case that Neubauer was covering up the study. This is not true. He intended to publish the whole study but was deterred by confidentiality requirements in adoption agencies and adoption *law* at the time. i.e. The guarantee of confidentiality to the biological parents including the existence of biological siblings.

Both Dr. Lawrence Perlman, the young researcher for the CDC interviewed for the film and [an assistant] who worked in the same office as Neubauer but had nothing to do with the study disavowed the veracity of the film's claims. The former saying the filmmakers had "cherry-picked" his interview to paint an incomplete and damning picture of Neubauer. (Psychology Today August 20, 2018). While that is a common claim of interviewees who feel embarrassed by what they've said, given the films other inaccuracies I'd check the transcript of the interview.

[The assistant] claimed that what she knew was all hearsay. (JAMA July 2, 2019). And when first contacted by the filmmakers told them "I really did not know anything about the study and would be of no use to them."

Maybe most damning is the fact that Mathew Jacobs in reviewing the film, notes that the two living brothers were *paid* for their life rights. (Huffington Post, June 26, 2018). I have not checked with Mathews about what else he knows of the filmmakers financial arrangement with the brothers, but it is worth noting.

Thanks for reading this Dan. I know it's late but hope you can share this with other members of the Committee.

As with the previous letter, I have identified information that is factually incorrect. The legal and moral issues that the letter raises will be considered in the remainder of the book.

Error 1. Findings from the study were not disseminated widely, as I indicated previously and in earlier chapters. The work was discussed only among a close group of psychoanalytic colleagues, and the few publications hid many details about methodological aspects of the study and its participants. Describing entertaining anecdotes to friends is not equivalent to publication in scientific journals and presentation at national conferences. Furthermore, many of Neubauer's professional colleagues were unaware of the study until the film was released. Samuel Abrams, Christa Balzert, two key investigators, in addition to Viola Bernard, were not mentioned in *Nature's Thumbprint.* All of Neubauer's materials and some of Bernard's records were placed under seal.

Error 2. Confidentiality requirements in adoption agencies and adoption law at the time did not prevent the researchers from publishing their planned book. Instead, failure to obtain informed consent from the families was the decisive roadblock. The researchers were also concerned about possible legal charges against them for failing to inform families of their child's twinship, the purpose of the study, and the chance that the twins might identify themselves in the data.

EMMY NOMINATIONS

The 2019 Emmy nominations voting began online on June 10 and ended on June 24. Nominations were announced on July 16, 2019.[27] *Three Identical Strangers* was nominated for an Emmy award in three categories.[28] Tim Wardle received a nomination for Outstanding Directing for a Documentary/Nonfiction Program: CNN, CNN Films, RAW in association with channel 4 films. Michael Harte ACE Editor, RAW, was nominated for Outstanding Picture Editing for a Nonfiction Program: CNN, CNN Films. And producer Becky Read was nominated for Exceptional Merit in Documentary Filmmaking. The final round of voting began on August 15 and ended on August 29. The awards were announced on ABC in a televised ceremony held on September 22, 2019. *Three Identical Strangers* did not win an Emmy in any category; however, Tim Wardle and the film have received top awards in other international film competitions and festivals, such as the Sundance Film Festival and the Directors Guild of America.[29]

INSIDE THE EMMYS

I spoke with the author of the letter in November 2019, a month after the Emmys had been awarded. He told me he had received a note from Birman acknowledging receipt of his letter, but saying there was nothing he could do and that he would pass the letter on. "Obviously nothing happened. I don't know whether he did [passed it on] or not." The writer believes that he sent the letter to Birman after the nominations were decided, but he cannot be sure; he indicated in the letter that his timing was "late." The copy he sent to me was not dated. He did not wish to be identified.

I spoke with Birman who referred me to Maury McIntyre, president and chief operating officer of the Television Academy. After several unanswered emails, I spoke with Jim Yeager, whose firm Breakwhitelight was managing the academy's publicity. We spoke in mid-December 2019. Yeager assured me that, "The complaint had no bearing on the competition. The Emmy is awarded to recognize the quality and professionalism of the work, regardless of the point of view of the content."[30] Yeager promised to look up the date that the letter was received, but despite several requests on my part I did not hear back.

I wonder what the letter writers' underlying motives actually were if their letters were sent and received after the award nomination deadlines. Perhaps their aim was to hurt future sales, although by then *Three Identical Strangers* was enormously popular. If their intent had been to discourage moviegoers, then an opinion piece in a major newspaper would have been the preferred route. However, it is also possible that their efforts increased viewership to some degree, especially because Oppenheim's letter was posted on Facebook. Word of mouth is also a powerful means for promoting or deflecting interest in a film. Dr. Daniel Wikler, Harvard University professor of population ethics and population health, has challenged aspects of the film, yet finds it entertaining and recommends it to many people. He also cautions viewers to think carefully about how the material is presented and what they can learn from that.[31] Findings from my interview with Dr. Wikler are presented in the next chapter.

Elsewhere in this book I have referenced a debate, "Parenting Is Overestimated," held in New York City in October 2019, by IQ2, or Intelligence Squared. One of the signatories of Oppenheim's protest letter and I took opposing positions on stage. Our exchanges during the debate, immediately afterward and since then, have been congenial and respectful. But an incident happened at the end of the event that involved one of my opponents, as well as a separated twin pair and an adoptee of LWS who were in attendance as my guests. Later, I will revisit that incident and what it means for the twins, the twins' attempts to secure their records, the researchers who studied them, and the colleagues who knew them.

· *19* ·

Professional Standards

Codes of Conduct, Legalities, and Moralities

"Law and ethics are not always running along the same course."[1]

*W*hat is legal is not always moral. Acceptable procedures in one generation may be deplorable practices in another generation. Venerated people can commit egregious acts that go unchallenged because they have status and power. Throughout the previous eighteen chapters, the twin separation policy, the Louise Wise Services (LWS)-Child Development Center (CDC) twin study, and the plight of the reared-apart twins and their families have raised concerns that warrant serious legal and ethical discussion and investigation. Some specialists in law and bioethics have undertaken this critical task, but their analyses have been limited to scholarly journals and professional conferences. Despite the passage of sixty years since the first twins were studied, the issues raised by Drs. Bernard, Neubauer, Abrams, Balzert, and their associates continue unabated. The researchers, their decisions, their actions, and the consequences of their actions deserve public attention. The twins and their families are still around, and they are still hurting.

What I consider to be the most pressing legal and moral considerations surrounding the adoption practices, twin study, and their aftermath are presented in this chapter. However, other important questions and concerns were raised by the study and some will be listed at the end. In this discussion I will refer to the judgments and conclusions of attorneys, ethicists, psychologists, and physicians whose backgrounds bring diverse perspectives and opinions to these topics. Several individuals are among the psychoanalysts and psychiatrists who knew one or more of the major contributors to the twin study. Material presented at conferences and other professional gatherings of interdisciplinary scholars will be included. Given its relevance for this discussion, I will also

341

describe events behind the closure of the Viola W. Bernard Foundation, based on interviews with its former board members.

I have organized the controversial topics raised by the LWS-CDC twin study into three categories: legalities, framework for research, and moralities. My aim is to present different sides to these issues, voiced by attorneys, ethicists, psychologists, and physicians. I will include my own judgments in this chapter and in the chapter that follows. I will begin with the legal considerations.

LEGALITIES: WAS THE TWIN STUDY LEGAL?

Consideration 1. Twins were studied without disclosing the true purpose of the study to their adoptive parents.

In the 1920s, "anonymity and secrecy" were normative in adoption, intended to advance the best interests of the child, the adoptive family, and the birth parents. This view persisted. By the early 1950s, most states had passed laws making court adoption records and birth records confidential to protect the birth parents' identity. However, over the next several decades, public attitudes began to favor openness in adoption as more adoptees sought connection with their birth parents and adoptive families requested more information about prospective adopted children.[2] This led to the passage of New York's 1983 law requiring adoption agencies to provide medical information to prospective adoptive parents and adult adoptees. This information included psychological factors that might affect the child's health.[3]

By the early to mid-1980s, the importance of knowing an adoptive child's background was widespread, as evidenced in a landmark case. In 1986, adoptive parents in Ohio were awarded damages for intentional misrepresentation of their adoptive child's history.[4] Had Bernard and Neubauer been aware of this development—as they probably were, given Bernard's adoption consultancy—they should have given serious thought to the difficulties of keeping the twinship quiet when the youngest twins turned twenty. Another 1980s' misstep was not telling twins or their adoptive families about the psychopathology that was evident in some of the birth parents. After all, the twins were starting to marry and needed to make informed family planning decisions. It was also in the mid-1980s that the LWS-CDC researchers were weighing the pros and cons of publishing a book with their findings. An American Bar Association attorney recommended withholding the fact of twinship because he said that adoption law at the time prevented such disclosures.[5] Bernard, Neubauer, and their colleagues concurred.

The twin study researchers were guilty of a double deception. The twins' adoptive parents were not told that their son or daughter was enrolled in a twin study, but in a child development study. Of course, disclosing the true nature of the study would have exposed the initial deception, because this would have revealed that their child was an identical twin or triplet. These non-disclosures were *not* illegal in the 1960s. At that time, laws were not in place that required adoption agencies to share a child's background information with prospective parents. However, in 2018 and beyond, some of Neubauer's supportive colleagues, such as Dr. Arnie Richards, were troubled by the lack of disclosure.[6]

It is worth nothing that by 1929 all states had passed adoption laws, and most states made the best interest of the child the standard for adoption.[7] Certainly, the meaning of "best interest" varied across children and involved some measure of subjectivity. In the twins' case, Bernard reasoned that enhancing identity development and reducing parental overburdening were in everyone's best interest. However, being a twin—either identical or fraternal—is a key component of one's medical background because it provides clues to disease susceptibility and other developmental events.[8] While a law allowing disclosure of medical information to adoptees was in effect by 1983, the fact that twinship was not specified may have signaled to the researchers that not disclosing it was within their legal right. And as I indicated in an earlier chapter, the researchers agreed that "informing each [twin] of the other" was not part of the study. Interestingly, a member of the adoption study meeting claimed that "both the adoptive parents and child were aware of what we were gathering."[9] We know they were not.

Consideration 2. Siblings have a legal right to be raised together.

New York State law requiring minor siblings and half-siblings to be placed together when relinquished for adoption was not in effect until 1981, shortly after the LWS-CDC study ended. However, the court's appreciation for the significance of sibling relationships was evident in the 1960s, 1970s, and 1980s.[10] Courts were reluctant to separate siblings when their parents divorced. The US Supreme Court had not addressed directly whether siblings have constitutional rights to stay in contact with each other, but Supreme Court decisions on other issues implicitly supported such a right. In addition, based on the concept of intimate association—a close and familiar personal relationship like marriage—it was asserted that siblings' rights to associate with one other might be protected by the associational rights guaranteed by the First Amendment.[11] It was also noted that parents typically pass away before their children, underlining the importance of the longer-lasting sibling bond.

These concepts are captured in the following statement, written in the mid-1980s as the researchers decided against disclosing the twin separations.

> Surely, nothing can equal or replace either the emotional and biological bonds which exist between siblings, or the memories of trials and tribulations endured together, brotherly or sisterly quarrels and reconciliations, and the sharing of secrets, fears and dreams. To be able to establish and nurture such a relationship is, without question, a natural, inalienable right which is bestowed upon one merely by virtue of birth into the same family.[12]

This quotation is from a 1985 case, cited in a historical review of legal developments in sibling adoption. Two conjectures elsewhere in that review are problematic. The difficulty of placing siblings together in adoptive homes or foster care was assumed. It is conceivable that sibling's different birth dates and consequent age differences could complicate their common placement, but not necessarily prevent it. However, twins do not differ in this regard and we know that several, if not all, of the LWS parents would have adopted both twins. It was also suggested that separation might not be so detrimental if siblings are unaware of each other's existence. To the contrary, discovering their twin later in life, especially the circumstances surrounding the separation, was painful and traumatic to the LWS twins and their families.

We also know that the newborn LWS twins were kept together for up to six months. It is not possible to definitively assess the immediate and long-term effects of their separation, although we know that some infant twins and triplets displayed atypical behaviors such as screaming and head-banging when they entered their adoptive homes. The effects of separation on young infants are hard to assess given their pre-verbal status and immature memory capacity. Recall that a four-month-old identical twin clearly reacted to the absence of her sister. Parent reports on the behaviors of young surviving twins suggest cravings for physical comfort and contact—although these behaviors cannot be definitely due to the missing twin. And many non-twin adoptees sense something missing in their lives, possibly associated with the lack of behavioral and physical resemblance to their rearing family. Still, we cannot and should not dismiss the effects of the twins' separations from one another.

Twin separations caused by accidental switching at birth, followed by chance discovery, have also been harrowing for twins and their families.[13] Some twins and parents have reacted more severely than others. A subset of twins in the Minnesota Study of Twins Reared Apart did not meet diagnostic criteria for psychiatric disorders or for antisocial personality, but they showed slightly elevated levels of alcohol or drug abuse/dependence and antisocial personality.[14] However, these tendencies could have been genetically transmitted to them from their birth parents, rather than caused by their early separation from their twin. We know that a number of the birth parents of the LWS twins had been treated for psychiatric disorders.

As I indicated in chapter 13, any violation of legal statutes by the researchers was never indicated by twin study reviewers. It is true that Bernard and Neubauer did nothing illegal, but that does not justify or excuse their actions. The 1981 law requiring agencies to place siblings together came about to correct problematic situations that existed during the time that the twins were being separated. Surely, Dr. Bernard and her LWS associates kept abreast of laws, developments, and trends in adoption. They would have known that the sanctity of the family was never at issue in a legal sense. However, issues regarding adoptive siblings' placement and association were still evolving at that time and twins, in particular, were never specifically referenced. Furthermore, agencies retained the right to separate siblings when circumstances indicated that it was in the siblings' best interests; thus, they had a legal justification. Given the foregoing, it is of interest that Bernard's files include a 1964 telephone memo from LWS's public relations office stating that, "I told him most agencies place twins together and it is only recently that we have done otherwise."[15]

Practices that were not illegal at one time may be illegal at a later time, and professional standards change. It is important to briefly review events leading to a "Code of Conduct" and a "Code of Ethics" for individuals conducting research with human subjects. Then we can address the question of whether the LWS-CDC study met professional standards.

Code of Ethics and Code of Conduct

A Code of Ethics sets forth the attributes of the members of a profession, organization, association, or company that distinguish acceptable from unacceptable behaviors and practices. Ethical principles established by the American Psychological Association (APA) include competence, integrity, professional and scientific responsibility, respect for people's rights and dignity, concern for others' welfare, and social responsibility. As stated in the association's official protocol, these principles are intended to "guide and inspire psychologists toward the very highest ethical ideals of the profession." A Code of Conduct sets forth the rules, regulations, and standards that ensure ethical behaviors and practice in research. For example, explaining the risks and benefits of engaging in research and securing informed consent from subjects, prior to their participation, is a requirement that would satisfy concern for rights, dignity, welfare, and professional responsibility.[16] The first version of the APA's ethical principles was published in 1953, prior to the start of the LWS-CDC collaboration.[17]

It is often assumed that human subjects' protections began at Nuremberg with the "Doctors Trial" of 1945 and 1946. Over the course of eight months, twenty-three doctors stood trial for crimes against humanity and for conducting horrific medical experiments on concentration camp inmates and prisoners of war.[18] An outcome of the trial was the Nuremberg Code of 1947, a document that outlined ethical principles for conducting human research and upon which subsequent professional codes of conduct are based. The importance of informed and voluntary consent was emphasized.[19] However, public and professional concern for the rights and welfare of research subjects began much earlier, in 1898, with the controversial studies of Dr. Albert Neisser at the University of Breslau, in what was then Prussia.

Neisser was interested in syphilis prevention, particularly the responses to injections of serum from infected patients into patients with other medical conditions.[20] These injected patients predictably acquired the disease; however, because most of them were prostitutes, Neisser argued that they contracted the disease because of their livelihood. Physicians aware of this experiment supported Neisser, with the exception of German psychiatrist Dr. Albert Moll. In his writings, Moll called attention to the importance of informed consent and presented a legal framework for doctor-patient relationships.

Eventually, Neisser was fined by the Royal Disciplinary Court for not obtaining the consent of his subjects. Pressures toward governmental actions that would require informed consent in research prevailed. In 1900, Prussia's minister for religious, educational, and medical affairs authorized medical directors to make certain that patients understood the risks and benefits of non-therapeutic interventions. Prussia was the first country to do so; however, this directive was not legally binding.

In 1931, following criticism of human experimentation, Germany's Reich government issued a set of guidelines for ethical practice, which emphasized informed consent. Ironically, these guidelines were in place during the medical experiments performed by the Nazi doctors in concentration camps.[21] As I indicated, the Nuremberg Code of 1947 evolved out of the process of putting these doctors on trial. Although the Nuremberg Code was not studied in a sustained way until the early 1970s, national and international guidelines for human experimentation were substantially broadened between 1945 and 1965.[22]

In 1953, the Clinical Center of the National Institutes of Health issued a patient handbook, with the indication that "The welfare of the patient takes precedence over every other consideration."[23] Statements issued by the World Medical Association in 1954 and the General Assembly of the United Nations in 1958 emphasized scientific and moral aspects of experimentation, among them informed consent.[24] The Declaration of Helsinki in 1964, announced by the World Medical Organization, listed ethical principles for medical research and medical care involving human subjects.[25] The next critical development was the National Research Act of 1974 that required prior approval of human subjects' research by an Institutional Review Board (IRB).[26] IRBs are committees that evaluate proposed projects for degree of risk, informed consent, confidentiality, and other standards. The Belmont Report of 1976, based on the work of the National Commission, specified three ethical principles intended to guide human studies, namely respect for persons, beneficence, and justice. The Belmont Report serves as the ethical framework for current research, but its principles and guidelines are not legally binding.[27] Unanticipated research challenges, such as access to experimental drugs and the unique features of certain populations, may warrant some revisions of the original report.[28]

Human subjects research is conducted by individuals from many different professional bodies, including universities, laboratories, clinics, organizations, foundations, and companies. Each entity has its own IRB, which decides the merits of projects based on their research promise and adherence to ethical principles and standards. Each IRB operates with its own forms and focus, but it must comply with the regulations set forth by the Department of Health and Human Services Office for Human Research Protections.[29] The fact that IRBs function internally means that researchers and committee members are from the same institution, an arrangement that could jeopardize objective review in some cases.

It is also worth mentioning the Hippocratic Oath, a pledge whose content and wording have evolved since written by Hippocrates in the fifth century BC. The original oath includes pledges to avoid patient suffering and falsehood, statements that no longer appear; the modern version of 1964 mentions warmth, sympathy, and understanding. The actual phrase "do no harm," while not in the original version, appeared hundreds of years later, but was clearly implied in prior renderings. The Hippocratic Oath is recited by all new physicians.[30]

FRAMEWORK FOR RESEARCH: DID THE LWS–CDC TWIN STUDY MEET PROFESSIONAL STANDARDS?

Consideration 1. IRBs were not in place when the LWS-CDC twin study started.

It has been argued that the absence of IRBs exonerated the researchers from failing to obtain informed consent from the twins' adoptive parents. Two staunch supporters of the twin project, Drs. Lois Oppenheim and Leon Hoffman, concluded that "the study was ethically defensible by the standards of its time—principles of informed consent and the development of institutional review boards lay in the future." Some other friends and colleagues of Neubauer's have concurred.[31] Oppenheim, in her letter of protest discussed in chapter 18, further commented that the film *Three Identical Strangers* "retrofits today's values onto the past."[32] These views embody what I call "the culture of the times explanation"—the belief that past activities or actions cannot be condemned because laws were not in place to prevent them.

Dr. Mark Mercurio, director of the Bioethics Program at Yale University's School of Medicine, explained that behaviors such as violating people's privacy are inappropriate on the part of researchers *because* they are wrong. Just because laws do not make them illegal does not justify carrying out such activities. "Looking back, I wouldn't say that because you were within the rules it was okay to me. There's something deeper than just following the rules."[33] Dr. Jonathan Moreno labeled this issue *retrospective moral judgment*, that is, assessing past behaviors in light of present standards.[34] He suggests that current investigators can see the implications and effects of past research that former investigators could not see, hopefully leading to moral progress. However, it is troubling that two esteemed psychiatrists—Bernard and Neubauer—could not see that separating the twins would have dire consequences. Perhaps they could not predict the full array of effects, but the ensuing anger and sadness of the twins and their families would seem clear. I believe that the pain and suffering of the twins and their families, and the reasons behind it, explain why the two documentary films about the study have stunned so many viewers and scholars. I will say more about this later in the chapter.

In the late 1970s or 1980s, the Jewish Board of Guardians, now the Jewish Board of Family and Children's Services (JBFCS), established an IRB to examine the twin study and other projects conducted by its CDC. Neubauer's IRB membership (and presence at their meetings) likely compromised the committee's ability to assess the twin study objectively and dispassionately. At a 1985 meeting, the IRB determined that, for the purpose of Neubauer's proposed book, he did not need to describe the clinical considerations leading to the twins' separation. This decision was based on the premise that Neubauer was not responsible for their placement.[35] I believe that Neubauer's participation in the twin study made him complicit in the twins' separation, another topic I will revisit later in this chapter. Interestingly, at the 1985 meeting, William Nimkin, chair of the Jewish Board of Guardians' IRB, said that the IRB's current guidelines "really excludes this kind of publication from its rules."[36]

Consideration 2. Consent forms were distributed to parents in 1978, although the study began in 1960.

"The Nuremburg Code of 1947 set forth basic principles such as: 'the voluntary consent of the human subject is absolutely essential' which requires a capacity to consent, freedom from coercion, and comprehension of the risks and benefits involved."[37] This statement by Dr. William Spivak was a comment on Drs. Leon Hoffman and Lois Oppenheim's assertion that informed consent procedures were not in place when the twin study began. I spoke with Dr. Spivak, a clinical professor of pediatrics and pediatric gastroenterologist at Cornell University's Medical School in New York City, after reading his words. "It's just hard for me to understand how researchers who were alive and mature during that particular time wouldn't know about the decisions that were made by the Nuremberg Court of Justice. It must have been so open in the newspapers that I just can't fathom how one would say we didn't know about this. I mean, it was hot."[38] Other bioethicists have drawn similar conclusions.[39]

Of course, human experimentation guidelines were somewhat "unsettled" until the late 1970s despite the Nuremberg Code.[40] In other words, human protection guidelines were not uniformly integrated into experimentation in the United States until the early 1980s. And the Nuremberg Code did not specify the manner in which consent was made, such as verbal agreement or signed document.[41] But as I indicated, laws do not need to be enacted in order for acts to be judged as appropriate or inappropriate. Spivak noted that even without reference to Nuremberg, one would wish to protect people for their own good. "Protecting the identity of the subjects with knowledge of the severe psychological harm that this could cause the subject is just poor ethics and, ultimately, lousy research that cannot be justified now, fifty years ago, nor two thousand years ago (remember—'first do no harm')."

Although adoption of the separated twins was contingent upon research participation, periodic home study visits seemed a small price for parents to pay for a newborn baby. One of Neubauer's champions believes the parents' upset at discovering the true purpose of the study has no basis. "The parents agreed without protest to cooperate."[42] Elsewhere, she wrote that, "Ideally, [Neubauer] should not have been secretive concerning his study and should have given a clear statement of goals to the adoption agency and to the parents." But why wouldn't the parent cooperate? These mothers and fathers were eager to have children, and they trusted LWS completely. They did not have all the facts.

Harvard University professor of population ethics, Dr. Daniel Wikler, believes that if the twins had been placed according to the practices followed before the study began, there would at most be a "status harm" or a "dignitary harm."[43] This means that a twin would not be worse off because their life's path was dictated by the research, but rather that consent had not been obtained. However, I would not dismiss LWS's practices for placing twins too swiftly. Recall that the identical twins' parents were selected specifically because they were successfully raising an older adopted child. I wonder—if some of the chosen couples had declined to take part in the study, would the twins have been placed with willing families who were less desirable? Some twins were raised by parents who were less affluent than their co-twin's parents. This difference in financial status between Sharon and Lisa's families caused friction between them once they met. It also could be argued that the couples who were chosen improved the rearing circumstances of some twins, but that is not the point—the point is that the twins' lives were manipulated in ways that served the interests of the investigators.

Informed consent cannot be obtained retroactively, as this would violate the stipulation that participants be informed about the nature and risks of the research at the outset. Pressured by attention to consent issues in human studies in the late 1970s, twin study staff mailed consent forms to the twins' parents in 1978. "By 1975 or 1976, [the researchers] understood that they were in deep legal trouble."[44] As I indicated in an earlier chapter, only a few parents returned them, and one father challenged the wording. This evidence contradicts Oppenheim's claim that the parents received and signed the required consent documents,[45] and contradicts her own defense of the study based on the absence of consent procedures at that time. One has only to examine Bernard's archives to know that consent forms were not distributed or received in a timely manner. Despite that, in outlining their planned book, the research team chose to include comparative data from a pair of twins whose parents had not provided consent.[46] As it was, findings from various twin pairs were used in the few publications resulting from the study, albeit with details disguised to protect their privacy. Yet some twins I interviewed have recognized themselves in some case descriptions.

Records show that the study began while the newborn twins were in foster care, awaiting placement in adoptive homes. During this time, LWS, as their legal guardian, provided consent for their participation, appropriate according to law. However, their doing so raises concerns about connections between the twin separations and the twin study—efforts to locate adopted away identical twins were evident once the study began.[47] Ethicists Adam M. Kelmenson, M.S., and Dr. Ilene Wilets note that, "Based on this clear conflict of interest, it is more accurate to say that consent was not absent but immoral."[48] In other words, LWS had a vested interest in the study that appears to have overridden what would have been best for the twins.

A related issue concerns the current recommendation that an "assent" form be signed by a child participant aged seven to twelve years.[49] This form is completed in addition to the informed consent provided by their parents. Assent procedures were not in place when the LWS-CDC study was underway but have become important—at least one twin was pressured by a researcher to remain in the study. Of course, applying such pressure was inappropriate regardless of whether the practice had been established. Other LWS-CDC practices, such as withholding information about mental illness in the twins' birth families, also warrant examination with respect to their moral integrity.

"An experiment is ethical or not at its inception; it does not become ethical post-hoc—ends do not justify means. There is no ethical distinction between ends and means."[50]

MORALITIES: WAS THE TWIN SEPARATION POLICY MORAL OR IMMORAL?

Consideration 1. Newborn twins were purposefully placed in separate adoptive homes, based on the purported beliefs of psychiatrist and LWS consultant Dr. Viola Bernard, that this served the twins' best interests.

Dr. Bernard claimed that separating newborn twins would optimize their identity development and increase their parental attention. Twins were sometimes placed apart without the knowledge and/or against the wishes of their birth mother. Dr. Willard Gaylin is a retired professor of psychiatry and co-founder of the Hastings Center for Bioethics Research. Gaylin spoke of the "arrogance" that would allow manipulating other individuals in order to enhance human knowledge in a way that would justify such manipulation.[51] He felt that if he were to label the twin separations and study "immoral," it would only enhance interest in the topic. Gaylin actually felt that discussion of the LWS-CDC study lent it more significance than it deserves. I understand his position, but believe that current and future researchers need to understand it to prevent such activities from recurring.

Several ethicists and others with whom I spoke asked: Was separating the twins really in the children's best interest?[52] It may help to think about the purposeful taking of a newborn from its mother and falsely informing her that the child had died. Such practices have occurred in Argentina (1970s), with the dictatorship's seizure of countless children that were given to other families; in Israel (1950s), with the stealing of Sephardic infants from mothers to satisfy childless Ashkenazy couples; and in Tennessee (1924–1950) with the removal of newborns from poor couples for purchase by wealthy couples.[53] These practices horrify us, given the inviolability of the mother-infant bond, and we would call them immoral.

The taking of a newborn twin from their co-twin is also unimaginable, because it severs a natural bond that runs deep and lasts a lifetime. Few people have thought of the twin relationship in quite this way, although Washington, DC, attorney Barry Coburn likened separating twins to dividing a happily married couple.[54] Other exceptions are the two recent documentary films that have focused attention on these bereft twins. Like the unfortunate mothers in Argentina, Israel, and Tennessee, the twins did not choose to give each other up. Furthermore, there were attempts by LWS and Dr. Neubauer to encourage cooperation from other adoption agencies in separating newborn twins. Recall that when I met him in 2005, Neubauer said he had contacted Sister Bernard at Catholic Charities in New York, hoping to see if the agency was willing to separate other sets; whether he told the sister about the study is unknown. The sister declined at first, explaining that twins have been put together naturally and should not be divided. Neubauer countered that mothers and children are also put together naturally, yet can be separated by adoption. He also asked Sister Bernard if the bond between a mother and child is any less holy. Neubauer recalled that the sister eventually agreed to help him, but she never provided the promised pairs. What Neubauer failed to see is that the mother-child separation (but not the twin separation) was a matter of necessity—a choice made by the mother due to her personal circumstances—whereas the twins' separation was intentionally decided by the investigators.[55] We can call the twins' purposeful separate placements and the hidden study immoral.

It is also clear that the LWS agency tried to recruit the cooperation of other adoption agencies in placing twins apart. Bernard's role in that process is not completely clear, but she was involved. In a 1965 letter to Bernard, LWS's Executive Director Florence Brown congratulated Bernard on securing continued funding for the LWS-CDC study. Then she wrote, "I do hope that the other agencies will participate so that the sample can be large enough. I do know that you are going to be speaking to the Case Committee at Inwood House and also know that you are aware that the public Westchester agency will not be able to participate."[56]

A related issue raised by Dr. Spivak is one that I had thought about in 2005 after my 2004 meeting with Dr. Neubauer. If Viola Bernard truly believed that separating twins was in the twins' best interest, then why didn't she advocate this position more widely? Playing devil's advocate for the moment: Wouldn't separating twins at birth benefit *all* twins with respect to their identity development, not just those given up for adoption? I discussed this idea with my colleague Dr. Thomas J. Bouchard Jr., who agreed that the logic held.

Had Bernard presented her views to the members of national and local child development organizations and parenting groups, they may have given her theory serious consideration. Of course, mother-infant bonding would make it extremely difficult to encourage a biological mother to relinquish one or both of her twins—but it can be argued that parents make sacrifices for their children all the time. This argument could be used to persuade a new mother to find different homes for her twin infants. Interestingly, the author of the letter to the Television Academy stated that, "[Viola Bernard] believed that separating twins/triplets was in the best interests of the children and parents—adoptive *and* biological [italics are mine]." Whether or not he heard her voice these views is unknown; elsewhere, Bernard did not refer specifically to biological children.

A "softer" version of Bernard's theory might have involved persuading parents to place their twins in different schools, play groups, and summer camps, maximizing their time apart. Recall that when Susan and Anne's twinship was discovered accidentally, Bernard advised their parents to keep the girls apart and to keep their relationship concealed. However, these practices were harrowing and heartbreaking for their parents, as they would be for all families. Moreover, such restrictions would be resisted by twins living in the same home, most of whom enjoy spending time together. It remains significant that Bernard never published her theory in scholarly journals, nor did she seek support from child development associations. She never presented her ideas at professional conferences, nor did she promote her views at parenting groups. Bernard did reject invitations to discuss the study on national television, forfeiting opportunities to share her ideas with large audiences. And she worried when she thought the collaboration was becoming too widely known.[57]

Consideration 2. The investigators did not inform the twins' parents that their adoptive child was a twin.

Even prior to the film releases, studies have shown that identical twins enjoy the closest of human social relationships.[58] These twins are the lucky few for whom love, acceptance, and understanding come so easily. Furthermore, the unique medical advantages of twinship are undermined when twins are raised apart. A telling example from the LWS-CDC twin study, cited in chapter 2, concerns healthy separated identical female twins who developed spontaneous convulsions. One twin's doctor treated the condition as an infection or allergic reaction to food, whereas the other twin's doctor had the child examined for lesions linked to a suspected brain disorder. The episodes lasted for several months, then disappeared ostensibly on their own. As I indicated earlier, in their book *Nature's Thumbprint*, Neubauer and son write that, "If each pediatrician had known that his patient's convulsions were shared by an identical twin, they each might have approached the condition differently, with a strong suspicion of genetic influence."[59] The pediatricians could not know the twin status of their patients because the twins' parents were never told. The researchers did not disclose the twinship at this point—doing so would have destroyed the premise of the study. Thus, the health of these twins was seriously compromised, and there may have been other such incidents. This issue caused great concern among the physicians and bioethicists with whom I spoke.[60] According to Yale University bioethicist Dr. Stephen Latham, "That seems unethical to me."[61]

Dr. Thomas Mack is a professor of preventive medicine and director of the International Twin Study and California Twin Program at the University of Southern California. He stressed the importance of physicians' obtaining family background information when taking their patients' medical histories. Given a genetic basis for many disorders, knowledge of identical and fraternal twinship is critical. "[A diagnosis] that is missed and goes untreated (when there is a specific treatment) would be at least a major embarrassment, if not a tragedy if the clinician ignored a family history."[62] Identical co-twins are also ideal donors and recipients when it comes to blood and organs, barring infection.[63] The LWS twins were deprived of these medical benefits during infancy, childhood, and into their adult years. This consideration never arose during the researchers' discussions of whether to proceed with book publication, which largely focused on the researchers' personal liabilities in the event of a lawsuit.[64]

Consideration 3. Separating the twins and studying them is tantamount to "Nazi science."

"I was very shocked that a Jewish agency was engaged in this so shortly after the [the Second World] War."[65]

"It is strangely and disturbingly ironic that an Austrian Jew who had fled the Nazis should develop and run a study with a Jewish adoption agency that involved almost Nazi style abuse of Jewish twins."[66]

"It was a Nazi operation in modern day Manhattan."[67]

Parallels between the LWS-CDC twin study and "Nazi science" have been drawn by some twins, their families, scholars, and viewers.[68] Is this a fair analogy? It is first important to know what is meant by "Nazi science." During the Holocaust, experiments were conducted to improve the survival of military personnel, test drugs and treatments, and advance Nazi ideology regarding the superiority of the German population over others.

Medical experiments at the Auschwitz-Birkenau concentration camp were performed on Jews, Romani, and individuals with various genetic anomalies. Dr. Josef Mengele, known as the "Angel of Death," carried out horrific medical experiments and procedures on hundreds of twin pairs between 1943 and 1945. These experiments were conducted without the consent of the subjects and with no regard for their suffering or survival.[69] "As [Mengele] no doubt saw it, no one in history had access to the raw material that stood before him or had been so liberated from the restraints that tamed ambition and limited scientific progress."[70]

There are a few parallels between Mengele's experiments and the LWS-CDC twin study. Informed consent was lacking. The twins' psychological well-being was neglected. The investigators tampered with the twins' lives. The experiments betrayed a lack of respect for the twins' humanity. However, there are major points of departure between the two. The Auschwitz twins were taken from their families and housed in overcrowded, disease-ridden barracks. They feared for their lives. In contrast, the LWS twins were adopted by loving parents in homes that were safe and secure. They were not physically harmed in any way.

It is easy to label the LWS-CDC study "Nazi science," but given the important differences I would argue otherwise, as would several ethicists I interviewed.[71] At the same time, I believe that the twins, families, and others who acknowledge the equivalence of the LWS-CDC twin study and Nazi science have reasons for doing so that cannot be discounted. Whether the twin study fulfills a formal definition of Nazi science matters less than how we think about the twins, their separation, and the study, and how the separation and study are perceived by the twins who went through it. Had I been one of the twins, I might call it Nazi science as well.

Three Identical Strangers director Tim Wardle was criticized for not challenging the two surviving triplets who spoke of "Nazi shit." I believe Wardle, as a documentary filmmaker, was correct in letting his subjects speak freely. Suppose the triplets had denied any similarities to Nazi science, or failed to raise them, should Wardle have pointed out the parallels I have listed? Probably not. Would these same critics have accused Wardle of staying silent on this question? Unlikely.

Summation

In this discussion I have focused on considerations of legal concerns, professional standards, and ethical issues raised by scholars and members of the general public familiar with the LWS-CDC twin study. There is also the question of the obligations and regulations of libraries and other facilities that accept and restrict archival materials. However, the dialogue does not end here. The topics raised require further debate, given that a great deal is still unresolved. Questions regarding the publication of research results from questionable studies and the examples set for future researchers are of paramount importance. Publishing the twin data might signal to others that it is possible to get away with obtaining information in inacceptable ways. In 1986, attorney Stephen Tulin, LWS legal consultant and son of former LWS president Justine Wise Polier, said that New York State civil rights law forbids using subjects in publications without full informed consent and prior agreement, even if identifying information is hidden. This remains a timely topic of considerable interest.

Decisions by principal investigators are often modeled by those they work with. Requiring assistants to maintain silence about the twin status of the children they studied might encourage deceptive approaches by their research protégés. Some assistants spoke with me reluctantly and expressed discomfort over their participation. One assistant denied taking part in the study, although her name appeared repeatedly on records released to one of the twins by Yale University (with the permission of the JBFCS). Graduate students and young staff rarely question their esteemed mentors for fear of jeopardizing their future careers—one of Neubauer's former graduate student assistants, who wished to remain anonymous, said that that was the case. "I would say I accepted the party line. I looked at it as a job, but there was something disconcerting about it."[72] Her husband is aware of her involvement in the study, but she has not disclosed this to her children. She also has a granddaughter who joined her family through an open adoption. "I just felt mortified. I think we all feel that, however minor our role, if we participated in something that now seems so abhorrent to us it just doesn't feel good." In contrast, after the triplets' reunion, one of the mothers asked an LWS psychologist how she could have carried out such research. "How could I resist?" the psychologist replied.[73]

It is worth peering into the personalities and dispositions of the study's two main contributors with this in mind. Henry K. Beecher, the late Harvard University anesthesiologist and medical ethicist, stated that, "A far more dependable safeguard than consent is the presence of a truly responsible investigator."[74]

A VEXING QUESTION: WHAT SHOULD WE THINK
OF VIOLA BERNARD AND PETER NEUBAUER?

The scholarly credentials and humanitarian activities of Drs. Bernard and Neubauer are not in dispute. Their contributions and accomplishments in psychiatry and psychoanalysis have been referenced throughout earlier chapters of this book. The vexing question is: What prompted these prominent professionals, dedicated to improving people's lives, to separate the twins and study them covertly? What they did was not a snap decision or momentary lapse in judgment, but a well thought out process that unfolded continuously over many years. Warning signs were ignored—the upset that ensued when Susan and Anne's parents discovered their young daughters' twinship did not derail the research plans that Bernard and Neubauer had put in place. Why not? Who were these investigators really?

DR. VIOLA W. BERNARD

I had the pleasure of speaking with Viola Bernard's niece, Joan Wofford, and two of her great-nieces, Jennifer (Jen) and Martha. All three women had been board members of the Viola W. Bernard Foundation until it closed in 2016. Joan Wofford was the daughter of Bernard's older sister, Diana.

Joan described her Aunt Viola ("Aunt Vi") as "commanding, knowledgeable and committed," someone who gave selflessly to numerous social causes. Bernard helped underprivileged minority children, supported Holocaust survivors, fought against racism, and promoted world peace.[75] As an example of Bernard's generosity, her niece Jen highlighted her aunt's weekly mentoring of Margaret Morgan Lawrence, the only African American student in Columbia University's medical school class of 1940. Lawrence eventually became the first African American psychoanalyst.[76] Bernard's benevolence extended to the patients she treated, particularly those who could not afford her fees.[77] Jen underlined Bernard's thoughtfulness by describing a patient Bernard had treated who was a cross-dresser. The patient finally gave up his clothes, but Bernard kept them in her attic in case he ever wanted them. Jen also mentioned the singers Harry Belafonte and Pete Seeger as the more well known among Bernard's admirers. Bernard was "inspiring, but a tough cookie," she said.

Dr. Trudy Festinger is professor emeritus at New York University's Silver School of Social Work. Her mother, Judge Justine Polier, was the former LWS president and a close friend of Viola Bernard's. Festinger recalled that

Bernard "could be very tough and very loving. It was a mixture of all sorts of things. She was very well-spoken and could be a lot of fun."[78] Festinger had been trying to find a "wonderful portrait" of her grandmother, Louise Wise, with Justine Polier looking up at her, that had hung in LWS's boardroom. Festinger had no idea if her mother knew about the twin study. Polier did know, based on correspondence with Bernard over her CBS interview I described earlier. Festinger's daughter is Boston-based writer and editor Debra Bradley Ruder, referenced in chapter 2. Ruder does not recall seeing twin-related materials in the collection of papers that Polier donated to Radcliffe's Institute for Advanced Study.[79] The correspondence and other documents I received from the institute's Schlesinger Library did not mention the twin study. The absence of such materials was confirmed by a library staff member.[80]

A frequent visitor to Bernard's New York apartment parties was Peter Neubauer, whom Jen labeled a "guru in psychiatry—he was so wise and kind and knowledgeable."[81] Joan commented that Bernard and Neubauer were so close it was impossible to tell whose idea it was to study the separated twins. "Both were terribly excited by the possibilities of the collaboration."[82] Bernard also maintained a close friendship with Justine Wise Polier, who took over LWS after the death of her mother, who founded the agency. Their relationship was personal as well as professional—a 1981 letter to Bernard from Polier was signed "Love, Justine."[83]

Bernard was popular among her friends and colleagues for the lively get-togethers she hosted at her summer home in Nyack, New York. She drove to Nyack in a red convertible, a vehicle she operated "probably longer than she should have."[84] She was adventurous with a love of outdoor sports.[85] One of Bernard's close friends of twenty-five years was child psychoanalyst Dora Hartmann, wife of psychoanalyst Heinz Hartmann and mother of psychiatrist Lawrence Hartmann. Viola and Dora played tennis and climbed mountains together. Lawrence, the younger Hartmann and former president of the American Psychiatric Association, liked and respected Bernard. They were occasional tennis partners and while they discussed their work the twin study never came up. Hartmann remembers her as "enthusiastic, forceful and exuberant. . . . Some found her a bit intimidating. She was capable of being a bully, such as when she was a school consultant and wanted things done her way." Neubauer's article "Hartmann's Vision" extolled Heinz Hartmann's work on identical twins.[86]

Getting to Nyack meant crossing the Tappan Zee Bridge that connected Rockland and Westchester Counties. Tappanz was the name of Bernard's private foundation that supported her philanthropic concerns and some of her research. She chose that name to keep her donations private, but after her death her relatives changed its name to the Viola W. Bernard Foundation to honor her memory. They also wanted transparency.[87]

Bernard's great-niece Martha saw her aunt as a "role model for female leadership, someone who was easy to look up to and who was fun to be around as a young child." Martha said that they had a certain affinity for one another. She recalled a memorable tenth birthday when Bernard took her on a tour of New York City's five boroughs, all in one day. Bernard wanted her niece to experience diverse people and places, such as the Harlem neighborhood and a Jewish delicatessen. They traveled across the city by public bus.

Martha recalled that both Bernard and Neubauer related well to small children. "They would listen to us, then ask us hard questions that we had to think about." Bernard placed all her great-nieces under "intense scrutiny— you could feel that you were under a microscope. . . . You couldn't just give her non-answers. You had to really think about what she was asking you and answer the questions."[88] A curious twist to this story is that Bernard's niece Joan gave birth to identical twins Jen and her sister Carrie, whom I did not interview. Her twin great-nieces were born in 1968, eight years into the twin study. At the time, Bernard provided Joan with information about distinguishing identical from fraternal twins, based on the number of placentae. Half-jokingly, I asked Joan if Bernard tried to persuade her to give one twin away. "No," she said and laughed. "I wasn't part of the study. I was just her niece."

Jen was at her Great-Aunt Vi's funeral when Bernard passed away in 1998. She knew that Bernard did not talk about her work, keeping it mostly private. Therefore, Jen was stunned to discover about thirty people at the funeral whom she did not know, but who spoke of Bernard as a great personal friend who did so much for their families. Of course, Bernard did speak about her professional work in social and community psychiatry at conferences and in several lengthy life history interviews, although she did not mention the twin placement practices and twin study.[89] On her resume, she lists herself as "Collaborator, Longitudinal Study of Adopted Children" with a start date of 1962, two years after the twin separations were underway.[90] But Bernard was involved—her advocacy of separating twins while she was an LWS consultant has left a lasting stain on an agency that performed important services.

A moving tribute to Dr. Bernard's memory by Dr. Lawrence Hartmann tells the story of a small boy who was afraid to talk until Bernard took him rowing in Central Park. "Viola W. Bernard, M.D., was a moral compass for psychiatry for most of her long and distinguished life."[91]

DR. PETER B. NEUBAUER

There are two stories about Peter Neubauer, told to me by one of his colleagues, that add insight into the doctor, scholar, and friend.[92] The first story concerns Neubauer's "capacity for 'gentle humor'" and his "reflective capacity for human foibles," both on display at a Fourth of July fireworks in New York City's Central Park. "Peter would laugh at all the hoopla and exaggerate the responses of people seeing the show. He commented on it in a caring way, not in a disparaging way, aware of our investment in the spectacle." The second story draws upon Neubauer's subjection to antisemitism as a young Austrian. Forced to relocate to Switzerland to finish his medical studies, he was acutely aware that social forces can hurt and persecute certain groups. Neubauer's colleague speculated that this experience gave rise to a "secretive side" that made Neubauer cautious about speaking publicly. "In other words, watch your step, and watch what you say."

These two stories impressed me, even as I acknowledge that single life events may not faithfully reflect a person's characteristic values and beliefs. Yet, across the many interviews I conducted with colleagues, friends, twins, and Dr. Neubauer himself, in addition to Neubauer's published articles, Bernard's archival materials, and other sources, several common themes make these stories resonate.

The Fourth of July story aligns with "arrogance" and "narcissism," terms that several colleagues used in reference to Neubauer, even while they stressed his knowledge and brilliance. These qualities could have fueled Neubauer's beliefs that concealing the twinship and studying the twins were acceptable practices. Perhaps he reasoned that the twins were the children of single unwed mothers, not the children of married, well-to-do women, so manipulating their lives in the service of science could be justified—their lives would be manipulated regardless, as LWS would have to find them homes. If Neubauer was truly as caring about families and children as most of his friends and colleagues claimed, I wonder why he did not persuade Dr. Bernard and LWS to stop the twin separation policy, or at least refuse to study the twins—either action would have sent a strong message and with his prominence he would have most likely succeeded. Neubauer, himself the victim of antisemitism, should have thought much more carefully about how he treated others.[93]

When I visited Neubauer in 2004, he expressed no remorse for what he had done. When he met the separated twins Paula and Elyse a year or so later, he remarked that adoption agencies did not try to keep siblings together, so he wondered why twins should be managed differently.[94]

Neubauer's reasoning typifies the quotation I used at the start of this chapter—"law and ethics are not always running along the same course." Just because a law did not require agencies to keep siblings together did not mean that separating them was right. As I indicated, Neubauer assumed no responsibility for the twins' separation at LWS, even while he encouraged another adoption agency to place twins apart. Neubauer was widowed as a young father with two small boys. If he had had to make special arrangements for his children, would he have placed them apart?

Dr. Dorothy Krugman, a developmental psychologist associated with the twin study, told me that the twin study research meetings were "like a Broadway show."[95] Neubauer's colleague Sam Abrams concurred, stating in his 1986 paper that, "It would be difficult to convey adequately the feelings generated in those conferences. Frequently dominated by excitement, they were often invaded by disbelief, occasionally by wonder."[96] The researchers did not expect to find the vast number of behavioral similarities they were observing between the separated twins. Given the foregoing, I am struck by how few of Neubauer's colleagues and how few of mine knew about the study. Perhaps Neubauer's "secretive side" described in the second story offers some explanation. Krugman recalled that LWS "knew from day one that they were doing something [separating twins and studying them] that was not quite right." She claims to have been present when Dr. Bernard proposed the idea, and it was "controversial—it was not a slam dunk." Krugman suggested that the researchers tried to "mask" the study under the name of another investigation.[97] Perhaps Dr. Neubauer eventually sensed that concealing the twinship from the parents and studying the twins covertly were not quite right. If he did have reservations, they were not expressed, and they were not enough to dissuade him.

Neubauer seemed to watch what he said and did when it came to the LWS-CDC twin study. The LWS agency and other details of the study are absent from his writings. These details are also missing from a lengthy 1977 life history interview, in which he discussed CDC activities and the genetic approach to understanding separation and individuation from birth to age three.[98] Dr. Susan Sherkow, director of the Sherkow Center for Child Development and Autism Spectrum Disorder in New York City, had no association with the LWS-CDC twin study. She explained that the psychoanalytic literature of the time pointed to the idea that if you were placed in a crib with someone who looked exactly like you, that person would become your primary object to some extent.[99] Thus, the value of twinship was debatable in some professional circles. Sherkow could not name the studies that supported this idea because she believed they had not been done. She cited the

Minnesota Study of Twins Reared Apart as the first study to publish statistical information about separated twins. Actually, the Minnesota Study was the fourth such investigation. The key point is that as a psychoanalytic psychiatrist, Neubauer would have sensed that separating twins after several months together in foster care could have dire effects.

Despite his close working relationship and years of friendship with Dr. Bernard, the many testimonies written after her death in 1998 did not bear Neubauer's name. He did attend a memorial for family and friends held at Bernard's home, seeming "surprisingly and awkwardly stuffy at that informal event."[100] When he passed away in 2008, his colleagues remembered him fondly. "We regret the passing of Peter B. Neubauer, M.D. who was always there with his warmth, brilliance and creative contributions to the Freud Archives."[101] Harry Belafonte, who was one of his patients, wrote, "I came not only to trust Peter, but to regard him as in a sense my best friend—a man I loved dearly, whose passing, when it came in 2008, left me truly devastated."[102]

HOW SHALL WE JUDGE THEM?

"A man [person] is not just one thing." This line, spoken in the 2019 film *The Last Black Man in San Francisco*, captures the complexity of Drs. Bernard and Neubauer as psychiatric professionals and as human beings. They were brilliant and benevolent according to many individuals I interviewed, although some people alluded to Bernard's stubbornness and unhelpfulness, and Neubauer's closemindedness and narcissism. When it came to the twins, I believe they were both continually blinded by scientific ambition and eventually consumed by potential lawsuits. They bypassed the twins' best interests by keeping them together in foster care, then placing them apart. Some people have wondered why the twins were fostered together if the intention was to place them in different homes. Neubauer's expressed interest in separation and individuation probably explains why.[103] Even after the triplets' reunion revealed the separations and the study, Bernard and Neubauer decided it was best not to disclose the twinship to the other twins and their parents. They said it was to protect the twins.

Bernard's theory that twins' identity development is optimized when they are raised apart was based on a tiny series of unrepresentative case studies. However, Bernard never cited relevant research in her writings—she only referred vaguely to the developmental literature of the time. It is also curious that Bernard took an interest in twin development at the time that she did. None of her earlier work covered twin studies or genetic effects on behavior. LWS, presumably with her counsel, separated two twin pairs in 1947 and

1952—Tim and Ilene, and Kathy and Betsy—eight years and thirteen years before the twin study began in 1960. Perhaps these twins were placed apart to satisfy four childless couples rather than two, but the reasons are unknown. It is likely that Kathy's parents would have adopted both twins.

Former LWS President Sheldon Fogelman told me about a 1950s to 1960s program offered by LWS to help young mothers complete their education.[104] Women were given assistance with housing, finances, and childcare while they attended school. The program was not designed for women relinquishing their babies for adoption, but it could have helped some of the twins' mothers. Giving up Paula and Marjorie was very painful for Hedda Schacter Abbott, but Hedda did so in order to give her daughters a better life.

According to playwright, director, and LWS adoptee Suzanne Bachner, who has researched the twin study, "It's not like a million adoption agencies were crowding at the door to be part of it [separating twins and studying them]. They got turned down a lot before LWS finally said, OK, we'll do it, you know, or we'll allow it. So, the culture of the times argument really doesn't work because they actually knew that they were doing something inappropriate and unethical, and those kinds of behaviors and actions prove that."[105]

It is also questionable as to whether Neubauer truly believed Bernard's theory. When asked this by the separated twins Paula and Elyse in 2005 or 2006, Neubauer said Bernard would not have suggested such an idea today.[106] Pressed further by the twins, Neubauer said Bernard felt that twins do not get enough attention from their parents. When they asked him again if he believed in her theory he refused to answer, saying he had had nothing to do with separating the twins. They repeated the question, and this time he said that if he thought Bernard's theory was wrong, he would not have been involved. Elsewhere, journalist Lawrence Wright wrote that Neubauer did not counsel LWS to separate twins but was in favor of it.[107] *But why exactly did Neubauer favor separating the twins?* There is no answer to this question in the interviews Wright conducted. However, Neubauer did not display enthusiasm or certainty when questioned by Paula and Elyse—he never definitively endorsed or disputed Bernard's views.

According to Nottingham Trent University associate professor of health law and ethics Austen Garwood-Gowers, Neubauer was colluding with rather than challenging the twins' separation from which he benefited career wise. As such, he provided LWS with a reason not to revisit the policy.[108] Professor and ethicist Dr. Daniel Wikler believes that if Neubauer truly endorsed Bernard's theory then we can say that he conducted the study in good faith.[109] However, as Paula and Elyse clearly showed, Neubauer sidestepped questions about his thoughts on her theory, never providing a clear answer. Whether or not Dr. Neubauer endorsed the rationale for the twin separation policy, his studying the twins indicated tacit endorsement of their separation. He is complicit.

Professor and physician Dr. Mark Mercurio believes that people should be judged on the entirety of their life's work.[110] He reasons that most of us have done good things, but we have also made some serious mistakes along the way. Thus, it would be wrong to base our judgments solely on a person's troublesome actions. "It's more nuanced than that," he said. I agree with Mercurio, but to a point. I believe that the basis of the mistakes, the consequences, attempts to rectify them, and how much the hurt parties and others can tolerate the decisions and outcomes are critical factors in passing judgment on a person's professional legacy.

Mercurio also made the point that how we personalize a situation bears on the perspective we bring with us and, ultimately, on how we judge a person. Having studied twin relationships for many years, I am acutely aware of the closeness, happiness, and intimacy that identical twins uniquely enjoy growing up together. This level of connection extends to most reunited identical twins, whose genetically based behavioral similarities seem largely responsible for drawing them closely together. The bond between fraternal twins is more variable because of their behavioral differences, but virtually every separated fraternal twin I have studied was delighted to have met their twin sibling and most have gotten along well; recall Allison and Michele's story in chapter 17. It seems counterintuitive, but I have also shown that most separated twins—identical and fraternal—feel closer to their newly found twin than to the unrelated siblings they were raised with since childhood.[111]

Mercurio felt that my being a twin was "fascinating" because of the viewpoint I could bring to my assessments of Bernard and Neubauer. As a fraternal twin from a Jewish family and a developmental psychologist, I cannot condone the LWS twin separation policy, nor the study that took place. The late Dr. Isidor Bernstein, an identical twin, was closely connected with the New York Psychoanalytic Society and Institute from the late 1940s until 2000. His daughter Jessica believes he knew Peter Neubauer professionally, but she does not know if her father had been aware of the LWS-CDC twin study. "It's hard for me to imagine that he would have been comfortable with that research, given how close he was with his twin brother."[112]

As I indicated earlier, the study was not the result of a quick decision, but of careful planning, allowing time to anticipate the potential pitfalls that are obvious, not just in hindsight. Bernard was too quick to dismiss what she called the "twin mystique," the quality of twinship that kept other agencies from placing twins apart, and that has a basis in fact.[113] I expected more of

Bernard and Neubauer's professional colleagues to concur with me. But few of their colleagues knew much about the study or that it had even taken place. Perhaps their personal loyalties, unfamiliarity with the work, lack of twins in their own social sphere, and/or "the culture of the times argument" explain their support.

Some individuals have mixed feelings about the study, such as Dr. Lawrence Hartmann. Hartmann knew and respected Dr. Bernard, but he had no knowledge of the twin study until recently. He claimed that most people today would be against doing the study, including Bernard, but fifty years ago "good people would have considered it a good opportunity." On this point, I side with Mercurio's earlier comment that, "There's something deeper than just following the rules." Hartmann added that current ethics would argue against concealing the twinship, but that the solidity and validity of the study would be reduced if the twins knew of one another and knew they were being compared.[114] Hartmann's last point is challenged by the scores of highly informative twin studies in which twins take part, knowing that their co-twin is also being studied.[115]

Even those who say that they understand the twins' sadness and rage believe that Bernard and Neubauer should not be judged harshly. Some even feel they should be congratulated for undertaking such a novel and promising study—one person suggested that the twins might have been "flattered" to have participated. But do these colleagues and friends really understand what the twins have been experiencing? Throughout this book, I have tried to be a voice for the twins, but there is another voice that needs to be heard. She speaks not only for the twins, but for many adoptees.

Constance Krauss is not a twin, but she is a 1960s LWS adoptee who brings a deeply personal perspective to the twin separations and twin study.[116] "Let's talk about what somebody feels like on a daily basis, what it's like to wake up and not know who you are. You know that you're missing a part, but you don't know what you're missing. Do [Bernard and Neubauer] think that what they did was okay on any level?" Krauss raised this challenge at the October 2019 Intelligence Squared debate on parenting. Along with one of the separated twins, she confronted one of the speakers on stage who had known Neubauer; another pair of separated twins appeared to have done so, too.

CLOSING COMMENT

I began this chapter by stating that what is legal is not always moral. Drs. Bernard and Neubauer did not break any rules in a legal sense, but they violated many tenets in a moral sense. Professional standards evolved in the 1970s because earlier research practices failed to acknowledge investigator responsibilities and participant sensibilities. The absence of laws and guidelines does not make past wrongs right, nor does it prevent us from judging former activities with fresh vision. We need to "historicize, but not minimize"—explanations are not justifications.[117] If that were the case, we would not prosecute Nazi criminals whose horrific deeds were the norm in concentration camps, we would not penalize powerful males for sexual harassment in workplaces that tolerated such behavior, and we would not criticize politicians for impersonating African Americans—wearing "blackface" makeup—at social events they attended before holding office. I reject "the culture of the times" justification for these individuals and for the twin study investigators. I understand a "culture of the times" explanation for what Bernard and Neubauer did, but I do not accept it as a justification—not every person acts on whims and impulses that are allowable, but not acceptable.

Not everyone will agree with me, including most of Neubauer's colleagues. Of course, mitigating factors affect our judgments. Most of Neubauer's colleagues knew little about the study and had a hard time reconciling the unfeeling twin researcher with the caring child analyst they knew so well. Twins and parents of twins may view the twin separations and twin study more harshly than those who do not have twins in their lives. There are many lessons to be learned. One is that a study is ethical from the beginning—it does not become ethical post hoc by producing valuable data.[118] The LWS-CDC study is delinquent on both counts. It is immoral to conduct some research projects just because you can.

· 20 ·

Over or Unfinished?

Continuing Controversies

$\mathcal{T}$hroughout the writing of this book, I have tried to report the facts as I found them, saving my opinions for the last two chapters to allow readers to draw their own conclusions. It is now time for me to reflect further on what I have learned. Some issues and questions will sound familiar as I have touched on them previously—but new information from the countless interviews I have conducted will add depth and meaning to that material. I will also discuss events surrounding the twins' separation and the study collaboration that have occurred since Neubauer's death in 2008—the rise and fall of the Viola W. Bernard Foundation, academic attention to the twin study, potential use of the data, media interest in the twins, and lessons learned.

DR. VIOLA BERNARD'S TWIN SEPARATION THEORY

There is not now, nor was there in the 1950s and 1960s, psychological literature to support the claim that placing twins apart optimized their identity development and reduced parental overburdening. In fact, Hoffman and Oppenheim noted that the benefits of separating twins at birth was "a premise that has no single identifiable historical source but was characteristic of the era's thinking."[1] Not every psychologist embraced that view. Dr. Susan Sherkow, whom I cited earlier, earned her medical degree in 1969, completed a pediatric internship in 1969 and 1970, and has performed psychological services since the early 1970s. She was active in the child development field when the twin study was underway. "I don't buy the argument that it's too hard to take care of twins. I don't know that it creates a less favorable upbringing for twins to be twins instead of solo. And I know you know this is unmeasurable

367

from a psychoanalytic perspective."[2] Adoption specialist Dr. Joyce M. Pavao, whom I referenced in chapter 7, also takes exception. In 1980, former Louise Wise Services (LWS)-Child Development Center (CDC) twin study assistant, Dr. Esther R. Goshen-Gottstein, observed the mothering of a small sample of Israeli twins, triplets, and quadruplets.[3] Despite some initial concerns, the "mothers of twins came to relate warmly to their infants in a relatively short time." The higher order multiple birth mothers experienced some early difficulties, but eventually resolved them. Signs of insecure attachment were not seen when the infants turned one year of age, except in the case of one quadruplet who showed autistic traits.[4] The idea of rearing the babies apart was never raised by anyone.

The five studies upon which Bernard's twin separation theory was ostensibly based were not cited by Bernard or by her colleagues in the 1960s or 1970s—in fact, they were not referenced until Sam Abrams's 1986 paper appeared.[5] I closely reviewed these five studies to see if their content and conclusions did, in fact, support the opinions and policies of Dr. Bernard and the LWS. After all, purposefully placing twins apart to assure their separate identities was a radical idea, a "paradigm shift"[6] in the management of twins' special developmental circumstances. It was a drastic departure from customary interventions, such as enrolling twins in different school classes, encouraging twins to play with different friends, and/or arranging for twins to spend periods of time alone with each parent, that did not damage twins' evolving relations. Every paper, except for one that summarizes material from some of the others, is a highly detailed psychoanalytic case study of one to three pairs, some fraternal as well as identical. These particular pairs had experienced psychological difficulties that the authors specifically attributed to their twinship. Such twins attract the attention of psychological and psychiatric professionals because they present interesting, as well as atypical, outcomes and behaviors. They are unlikely to represent the situation of twins in general.

The only evidence that Bernard was previously aware of some of this work is a typed passage from Dorothy Burlingham's 1952 case studies of three reared-together pairs, tucked into an archival folder.[7] Bernard highlighted the line: "[Twins] will be helped in this adjustment [relationship to their parents and each other] neither by the forcible breaking up of the twin relationship through outside influence, nor by the withdrawal of their parents which leaves them exclusively dependent on each other for the fulfillment of their emotional needs." Burlingham suggested that parents' sensitivity to their twins' differences would help mothers and fathers make informed rearing choices for their children. This passage does not support Bernard's theory—it undercuts it.

According to a former research assistant, the research team did not consult the twin literature beyond the psychoanalytic studies.[8] There was mention of the previous reared-apart twin studies in the various documents I reviewed. However, most references criticized the retrospective nature of the earlier work.

Bernard also wanted to avoid parental overburdening yet placing a newborn twin in a family with a sibling several years older would seem to do the opposite, especially given the children's different developmental status. The unique challenges of twinship were recognized in the 1960s—twin relationship issues, family financial concerns—but there were fewer studies on the mothering of multiples from which Bernard could form her views. Again, no one suggested that the panacea was raising twins apart.[9] The National Mothers of Twins Club, with state and local branches, was established in 1960 to "promote the special aspects of child development which related specifically to multiple birth children." Renamed Multiples of America, it continues to provide advice forums, clothing exchanges, and other supportive services.[10] The International Council of Multiple Birth Organizations, established in 1980, performs similar functions and meets biennially with the International Society for Twin Studies.[11] I have addressed these groups often and can attest to the happiness and satisfaction that many parents experience from raising twins, and the support that these parents provide to one another.

Raising two or more near-in-age children is welcomed by some families. Separated LWS twin Michele Mordkoff grew up with her adoptive parents' biological son who was born when Michele was not yet two years old. Michele recalls her mother saying that the time spent raising two small children of similar age were the best years of her life.[12] The over 150 families in my study of virtual twins—same-age unrelated children raised together from birth—revel in the closeness and companionship between their two children.[13] Contrary to what Bernard claimed, separation did not protect some LWS twins from competitive, jealous, and/or hostile tendencies toward one another when they met as adults.

If the researchers had been that confident that separation would benefit the twins if they met, why would she have been against informing them of their twinship when book plans were being discussed? The claim was that such disclosure would be "unpredictable" and "more damaging than helpful." Furthermore, "there were no legal requirements to tell them that they had a twin."[14] Who was being protected? James Shields, who authored the 1962 study of reared-apart British twins, observed, "In most of the cases where the twins knew of each other's existence from an early age, they appear to have accepted the situation and the reasons given for it."[15] My prospective study of reared-apart Chinese twins, who are aware of their twinship and meet occasionally, suggests that serious child and family difficulties are infrequent.[16] However, these twins were not separated because of one psychiatrist's theory and they are not being covertly studied—they were separated indirectly because of China's

One-Child Policy (1979–2015). Of course, many of the twins express sadness and regret when leaving their co-twin after a family get-together.[17]

When I saw *Three Identical Strangers*, I wondered why there was no mention of Viola Bernard's contribution. Perhaps that was because a document showing that Bernard's claims about the benefits of separating twins, issued prior to the study or coinciding with its start date, had not been located. However, there are publicly available materials in her archive that are revelatory. In 1963, Bernard wrote that the study "provides a natural laboratory situation for studying certain questions with respect to the nature-nurture issue and of family dynamic interactions in relation to personality development."[18] This statement does not fully resolve the question of timing because, by 1963, the study would have been underway for several years—Anne and Susan were born in September 1960 and separated by the age of five months. However, there are memos, written in 1978 and in 1982, stating that the twin separation policy was implemented in the late 1950s.[19] A formal statement from LWS affirming 1950s approval of the twin separation policy may be among her restricted materials.

I also reviewed Lawrence Wright's interview with Bernard, looking for a definitive answer, but there was none. She stated, "This was a collaboration in which the Child Development Center did the research, and the child adoption service did the clinical work. And, uh, I don't know if I can emphasize that enough, because that's the whole issue. . . . Research was an opportunity, it seemed, to make an additional contribution about child development because they [the twins] happened to have been born that way—I don't know if I am making myself clear."[20]

I am reminded of Pirandello's 1921 play, *Six Characters in Search of an Author*[21]—did Bernard construct and promote her theory to justify separating twins in order to allow the study to take place? Prior to the research I conducted for this book, I had been led to believe that Bernard's twin separation theory was in place before Neubauer put forth the idea for the study. Now I am not so sure. In fact, in the film *Three Identical Strangers*, one of Neubauer's former assistants said he had expressed interest in studying separated twins before the study got started.

BERNARD VERSUS NEUBAUER: WHOSE IDEA WAS IT?

There are conflicting opinions over whose idea it was to longitudinally track infant twins separated at birth. The generally accepted view is that the LWS twin separation policy was in place by 1959, and that Neubauer capitalized on an existing structure. Of course, Neubauer's fervor at the prospect of studying the separated twins probably reinforced this practice, whether or not he felt that it benefited the twins. As I said, I had always believed that the policy came first until one of the twins suggested otherwise—*perhaps Bernard's policy evolved to justify separating twins for the study.*[22] One of Neubauer's colleagues admitted that Neubauer, intent upon having things his way, could have searched for justification for separating twins, "but we will never know."[23]

Dr. Lois Oppenheim remains convinced that Bernard's policy preceded the study.[24] Regarding Bernard's policy, Oppenheim said, "as you know better than I, that [the belief that separate rearing was in twins' best interests] was the thinking at the time."[25] As justification for the policy decades later, the *Journal of the American Medical Association* (*JAMA*) article cited a 1997 paper indicating that twins receive fewer verbal exchanges with their parents and fewer expressions of affection than non-twins.[26] Although not indicated in *JAMA*, this study was limited to male children whose reduction in verbal skills, relative to females, is well known. And as I indicated, parents and educators have been—and are—well aware of twins' unique developmental circumstances and have suggested ways to manage them. No well-respected researcher or clinician has ever suggested raising twins apart. I have also been encouraged by several recent twin studies showing that membership in a multi-party social arrangement facilitates twins' language skills via taking turns, monitoring interactions, mobilizing responses, and timing replies.[27] Of course, this work requires replication using larger samples. It is also worth noting that recent work from Denmark and the Netherlands shows that twins do not score below non-twins on tests of general intelligence, as older studies had shown.[28]

In their *JAMA* paper, Hoffman and Oppenheim cited a 2005 paper I wrote about the LWS-CDC twin study, but they did not fully cite the original studies I referenced.[29] I presented findings from the few studies of adoptive sibling placement that were available in the 1970s and 1980s. More social workers favored common placement of brothers and sisters (49 percent) than separate placement (35 percent), whereas foster parents were more evenly divided (27 percent and 25 percent). More social workers favored keeping siblings together than placing them apart, but Hoffman and Oppenheim used these data to suggest otherwise. They also failed to include other work I cited, indicating that investigators generally agreed that adoptive siblings should remain together, a policy that the Child Welfare League had endorsed in 1989. Finally, it is worth noting that Neubauer's close colleague, Dr. Leon Yarrow, whom I referenced in chapter 3, stated in his 1965 paper that most twins are kept together in foster care and adoptive homes.

I explored the origins of the idea for the twin study with Bernard's niece, Joan Wofford, who knew Bernard well. Wofford recalled that "When [Bernard] and Peter came up with the idea of doing [the study], they were so excited about this capacity to do a genuine nature-nurture study and invested a huge amount of time and energy into the formulation of it—[Bernard was] into her work with Louise Wise Services as a consultant to help with it, with the placement of adopted children." I asked Wofford directly if she knew who proposed the idea for the study. "No, but those two were so close, you know, it'd be hard to pull that apart."[30] Her comment also contradicts Drs. Hoffman and Oppenheim's assertion that "Bernard had no substantive connection to Neubauer or the Child Development Center."[31]

In a statement to CBS News, Bernard wrote that once the twin separation policy was decided, a pair of identical twins was referred to LWS. She indicated that at that time, she made "another recommendation," resulting in the LWS-CDC twin study collaboration. The precise nature of Bernard's "recommendation" was not specified, adding to the uncertainty over whose idea it was to launch the twin study. She noted that Dr. Neubauer and the CDC had already developed a methodology for following adoptees' development over time.[32] However, efforts to locate identical twins for adoption were made once the study began.[33]

In his 1993 interview, Lawrence Wright asked Dr. Neubauer how the study had come about. "I tell you, I would rather not speak about it," he replied. He added that he would discuss the study's origin when the data were published in a year, or a year and a half from then, in 1994 or 1995.[34] In 1990, Neubauer's book *Nature's Thumbprint* had gone to print without his twin data because consent forms had not been signed by the twins' parents.

HOW MANY TWINS WERE SEPARATED?

The number of separated twins has been a matter of debate, but there are actually two numbers of interest. The first is the number of pairs that were *separated and studied*, and the second is the number of pairs that were *separated but not studied*. We know that four identical twin pairs and one identical triplet set were studied, for a total of eleven children. This information is revealed in the finding aid, the document that lists the contents of Neubauer's twin study collection at Yale University's archives.[35] A fifth pair of identical twins, Paula and Elyse, had been separated, but were dropped from the study early on when it was decided that their different adoption ages would have compromised the findings. The number of studied twin individuals—eleven—also appears in the researchers' book proposal submitted to Yale University Press.[36]

I have provided the life histories for four twin pairs that were separated, but not studied—three fraternal and one of undetermined type. Recall that Dr. E. Gerald Dabbs, Bernard's associate, mentioned an opposite-sex twin pair separated by LWS in the 1970s. The last pair of twins was supposedly separated in 1967, except in cases involving developmental or severe medical discrepancies; however, Elyse and Paula were born in 1969.[37] There may have been others who have never learned the truth. Fraternal twins, especially the members of opposite-sex pairs, do not look as much alike as identical twins, so the chance of them discovering their twinship due to mistaken identity is slim. Confusion by others led to the meetings of the identical twins Susan and Anne, and Melanie and Ellen, and the first two identical triplets, Robert and Eddy. In contrast, the separated fraternal twins learned of one another because they were told by LWS, discovered a twin from the New York Public Library's records, or were matched through a DNA database because they met the genetic criteria for being an immediate family member.

In a 1993 interview, Wright asked Bernard, "How many such twins are there?" This question is somewhat vague because, as I indicated, twins were either separated and studied or just separated. At first Bernard answered that there were eight such pairs—then she thought that there might have been six. She added that these separated pairs were identical "because that was the point."[38] Bernard never mentioned the fraternal twins that LWS had placed apart. However, she was close to ninety years old at the time, so her memory may have dimmed.

Adding together the four identical sets and the identical triplet set *that were studied*, and one identical set, the four known sets of fraternal twins, the undecided twin pair, and the opposite-sex pair referenced by Dabbs *that were not studied* yields a total of twenty-three children. However, it is possible that some separated fraternal twins are still unknown to one another. LWS did not notify all twins of their background, although some staff members did so, as in the case of identical twins Doug and Howard, and Paula and Marjorie.[39] However, in 1992, LWS fraternal twin Michele Mordkoff left the LWS agency knowing her family history, but not knowing that she had a twin sister. Spence-Chapin, the agency that has managed the LWS records since 2004, does not volunteer twinship information. Adoptees seeking their family background data must submit an application and only then is the twinship revealed if it is detected.

There are other reasons to suspect that LWS separated additional fraternal twin pairs. The natural fraternal twinning rate is twice that of identical twinning.[40] This difference would have been in place when the LWS-CDC study was getting started because contraceptive pills did not receive federal approval for birth control until 1960,[41] too soon for some of the twin mothers to have taken advantage of it. While reproductive interventions may have reduced fraternal twin conceptions somewhat in the years that followed, it is unlikely that they would have affected the young pregnant mothers of twins assisted by LWS. That is because legal restrictions for unmarried women under age twenty-one blocked their ability to consent to using the pill; these restrictions were lifted gradually in the late 1960s and early 1970s on a state-by-state basis.[42] In addition, a British study found a higher frequency of sexual activity among women who conceived fraternal twins, especially single women.[43] Therefore, it is likely that more fraternal twins were managed by LWS. In a letter to Viola Bernard, Executive Director Florence Brown mentioned a new twin referral, then wrote, "We have enough twins!" This letter was written in 1961, when the study had been ongoing for just one year.[44]

It is critical to know how many fraternal twin pairs were placed apart by LWS. It is also possible that some separated identical twins were dropped from the study and are unaware of their twinship. These twins would still be young enough to benefit from knowing their health histories and knowing each another. Bernard insisted that twins who developed the "twinning reaction"—mutual awareness of one another—would not be parted. But recall that not a single reared-together set has come forward.

STUDY AIMS: THE DEVELOPMENT OF ADOPTED CHILDREN, THE NATURE-NURTURE DEBATE, OR THE ROOTS OF MENTAL ILLNESS?

There have been disagreements over the true purpose of the LWS-CDC twin study. Few people dispute the idea that the study was designed primarily to determine if and how different parenting styles affected a child's behavior and health. Comparing the developmental outcomes of genetically identical twins raised in different homes was the researchers' way to answer this question. The project was presented to the twins' parents as a developmental study of adopted children, which it was—but labeling the study as such disguised its true purpose. Of course, hiding the purpose of the study was done intentionally to conceal the children's twinship.

Whether the study also aimed at uncovering the roots of mental illness is less certain. I believe that that was not an initial goal—however, some separated pairs were born to mothers and fathers suffering from mental disorders. Recall that the triplets were born in a psychiatric facility. Thus, there were opportunities to determine if sensitive parenting could overcome potentially inherited child difficulties. LWS also accepted abandoned Jewish babies born at Mt. Sinai Hospital in New York. Myra Kahn, a former nursing student at Mt. Sinai in the late 1950s or early 1960s, explained that Jewish babies left in the nursery, then brought to the pediatric wing, would be placed in adoptive homes by LWS. Catholic Charities arranged the placement of non-Jewish babies. Myra could not say why the infants were left, nor could she provide information about the health of their mothers—but abandoning a newborn after birth is atypical behavior. A Facebook page whose members are largely LWS adoptees or family members have raised several concerns, among them the agency's withholding of information about birth parents' mental health from the adoptive families.[45]

Hereditary transmission of schizophrenia and other forms of psycho-pathology was recognized years before the LWS-CDC began.[46] However, the pathway from parent to child was unclear, given that not all siblings were at equal risk. The Galvin family, the subject of the 2020 book *Hidden Valley Road*, included twelve children, born between 1945 and 1955, six of whom became schizophrenic as they neared adulthood.[47] In the 1960s, many psychologists and psychiatrists believed that schizophrenia and other serious mental disorders did not have a hereditary basis, but some did. At that time, a growing number of twin and adoption studies were reporting genetic influences on psychopathology.[48] Bernard and Neubauer would have had access to the latest professional literature on the subject but appeared to ignore it—this is curious because Neubauer was interested in genetic influ-ences on behavior. At the time, adoption agencies did not disclose biologi-cal background information to the children's adoptive families—still, LWS staff members debated how much to tell a prospective adoptive family. In my view, hiding this information from adoptive parents, just to test an idea about parenting, was unconscionable. Parents of disturbed children were wracked with guilt. Other children in the family were burdened. Family harmony was disrupted.

WHERE WERE THE COLLEAGUES?

The film *Three Identical Strangers* was faulted for failing to seek comments and advice from Dr. Neubauer's colleagues. It is possible that such assistance was sought, but that the individuals who were contacted declined. I had such experiences, especially when I attempted to interview the signatories of the letter of protest—some people did not reply, claimed to know very little, or agreed to speak if they could do so anonymously. I am grateful to Neubauer's friends and colleagues who were willing to share their thoughts, either in interviews, email messages, or publications.

There was indication that the film would have gained credibility and balance with input from informed individuals at the New York Psychoanalytic Society and Institute or at the Columbia University School of Medicine.[49] The names of several individuals who were suggested to me replied that their contacts with Dr. Neubauer were too limited for them to be helpful, or that they had nothing to add. Ironically, many people I contacted learned about the twin study *from the film*.

I would like to know what the silent colleagues could have told me about the twin separations, the twin study, and Drs. Neubauer and Bernard. Perhaps their insights would have affected my conclusions and perspectives in meaningful ways. Because they remained quiet, they cannot take exception to what has been presented.

CONCEALMENT

Journalist Lisa Belkin commented that Bernard and Neubauer convinced themselves that they were conducting great research. "They persuaded themselves that what they were doing was okay. But they didn't brag about it—they knew it had to be hidden."[50] There were attempts to minimize the study. Upon reviewing her initial draft to CBS News when Mike Wallace requested an interview for *60 Minutes*, Bernard changed the phrase "some twins" to "a few twins." Bernard and her colleagues eventually declined to appear on the program for reasons I provided in chapter 6. One of their concerns was that CBS might manipulate the content, giving the impression that LWS had separated many twin adoptees, not just "a few." Did Bernard believe that "a few twins" suggests a smaller number than "some twins"? My experience working with the media is that producers focus on facts and enjoy working cooperatively with interviewees. However, I do know colleagues who have been disappointed.

There are several explanations for why the twin study progressed quietly, why the study was never published, and why the data were concealed. I believe that Bernard and Neubauer were carried away by conducting an experiment that was ideal in theory, but immoral in practice. I agree with Belkin that the researchers' general reluctance to discuss their work outside LWS board meetings, CDC research sessions, and select academic circles betrayed their sense that separating twins and deceiving families was not right. But they were undeterred.

When informed consent issues came to the fore in the late 1970s, preventing them from publishing freely, the researchers focused on their personal legal liabilities should the twin study participants be recognized. They resolved not to inform the twins, a decision they claimed was taken to protect the twins, but who were they protecting? Revealing the truth to the twins and their families at that time would have been uncomfortable, but it would have been the right thing to do. Even when the triplets met by chance in 1980, leading to Lawrence Wright's investigation and exposure of the study, the members of other separated sets weren't told that they were twins.

The few reports and book Neubauer published between 1976 and 1996 masked many details of the study. One, especially, appeared to be a twin analysis disguised as an adoption study. In 1993 interviews with Wright, Neubauer claimed that Abrams's 1986 paper was written for a "professional audience with limited readership," and his son Alexander added that "no one is reading these things anyway and it would not get out to the public very much." When Abrams was asked why there were not more publications, he replied:

> "Well I think it's the process of fulfilling the data and putting it together and all of us are always involved in that, considering how best to do it and how to organize it, and what we've done instead is to select topics that seem to be useful topics that seem to employ some of the information we have, some of the theories we have developed, and as you see from these two papers and from Dr. Neubauer's work, as well, our principal interest has been to promote the value of recognizing the usefulness of the developmental process, both for our understanding of human behavior and also for the therapy—utilizing its therapeutic applications for patients."[51]

This was not an answer to Wright's question.

There was discussion of book publishing outside the United States. Given the enthusiastic spirit with which the study began, one would expect Bernard and Neubauer to want to disseminate their findings as widely as possible. Just the opposite was true—their actions appeared to limit publication and to avoid controversy at all costs.

Neubauer's colleague, Dr. Lois Oppenheim, cited an unpublished, unseen manuscript as evidence of the team's scholarly reporting of findings.[52] There is an entry in Neubauer's archives titled "Book dictation and draft," but they are inaccessible to the public. It is possible that Oppenheim was referring to these particular materials in her article and/or has a personal copy of the manuscript for examination, but at present we do not know. If one of my students informed me that they had completed a project, but would not allow me to review it, I could not assign that student a grade.

Lawrence Wright suggested that the researchers' observations of unexpected behavioral similarities between the separated twins, which supported genetic influences on development, were partly responsible for their failure to produce a comprehensive report. Wright explained that such findings would have undermined Neubauer's work with its environmental focus.[53] I do not agree—Neubauer and his colleagues were surprised by the findings, but they were also excited by them. Neubauer was ahead of his psychoanalytic colleagues (as well as many psychologists at that time) in terms of his interest in how genes interact with experience to yield particular outcomes.

Behavioral genetics, while still controversial, entered the mainstream of psychology in 1980, just as the LWS-CDC study was ending. Twin and adoption studies are key methodologies of this discipline. The Minnesota Study of Twins Reared Apart was just getting started and the International Society for Twin Studies held its third congress in Jerusalem, Israel. Neubauer and Bernard had receptive audiences for their work, but they stayed away.

It is striking that in several life history interviews, both Bernard and Neubauer cite many of their influential colleagues, yet they do not mention each other. I did find one exception. In a 1985 conversation with psychoanalyst Dr. Nellie Thompson, Bernard named Neubauer as one of her still closest colleagues and friends. Thompson then asked her for recollections of the people she had mentioned. Bernard described consulting activities with social work agencies that she and Neubauer had done together in the 1940s and 1950s.[54]

THE VIOLA W. BERNARD FOUNDATION: CROSS CURRENTS

In his 1986 paper, Abrams named Bernard's Tappanz Foundation as a source of LWS-CDC twin study support. However, former Tappanz and Viola W. Bernard Foundation (VWBF) board member and attorney, Stephen Wise Tulin, disputed this. When I mentioned Abrams's citation to Tulin, he said that, "Abrams can say what he likes, but it doesn't make it so."[55] Tulin later sent me a letter stating that as Secretary-Treasurer for forty years, "all grants by it [Tappanz Foundation] passed through me. There were none to LWS or anyone else for the Twin Study, although I believe there were occasional grants to that agency for other purposes."[56]

Eric Brettschneider assumed the presidency of the VWBF in 2011. He noted that any financial contribution to the twin study from the VWBF was uncertain, even while Bernard's involvement in the research was clear. However, there is evidence to the contrary concerning the Tappanz Foundation's contributions to the study. A 1987 memo, "Child Development Center Project," from Bernard to the members and trustees referenced awards of twenty-five hundred to thirty-five hundred dollars made to the CDC between 1983 and 1985. Bernard's 1987 request was for approval of twenty-five hundred dollars to the CDC to support clerical assistance for the project. "With

[Stephen Tulin's] OK we can proceed to do so," she stated. Perhaps Tulin did not approve this request, or the funds were drawn from other sources.

Both Drs. Neubauer and Balzert intended to contribute additional funds for clerical assistance. Plans to revisit the securing of an additional grant would be discussed at the next foundation meeting.[57] Given the foregoing, Abrams appears to have correctly cited Bernard's Tappanz Foundation as a source of twin study support.

Following Bernard's 1998 death, existing board members, including her niece Joan Wofford, continued the work of Dr. Bernard's philanthropic Tappanz Foundation. They changed the name to the VWBF to lend it transparency and to honor her work. Several years later, Dr. Bernard's great-niece, Carrie, was invited to join the board, and several years later her great-niece Jen was invited to replace Carrie on the board. As of October 2009, its members variously included the late Dr. Perry Ottenberg, Eric Brettschneider, Cary Koplin, Stephen Wise Tulin, Joan Wofford, Jennifer Wofford, Carrie Wofford, Tim Ross, and Marta Siberio.[58] Dr. Peter Neubauer was a board member and VWBF president until his 2008 death. Brettschneider had been recommended for the VWBF board by Gretchen Buchenholz, founder of the Association to Benefit Children, who later became a member.

According to Joan Wofford, the VWBF closed in 2016 because the world was changing. She explained that the board had accomplished its goals, dispensing funds in ways that Bernard would have liked. Former VWBF board member and president, Eric Brettschneider, tells a different story. Brettschneider was then chief of staff and assistant commissioner at the New York State Office of Children & Family Services, headquartered in Rensselaer, New York, a position he held from 2010 to 2014. The mission of this office is to promote the safety, permanency, and well-being of children, families, and communities.[59]

Brettschneider had no knowledge of the twin separations or the LWS-CDC twin study until fellow board member Marta Siberio, who joined in 2010, forwarded relevant material she had found online. Brettschneider explained that the material did not connect the VWBF to the twin policy and twin study per se, but it did connect Viola Bernard and Peter Neubauer to the separations and the study. Despite Brettschneider's association with Neubauer through the VWBF, there was no discussion of this topic between them. Brettschneider only recalls that Neubauer had formerly been part of the Jewish Board of Guardians (JBG)—Brettschneider had been a childcare worker at the JBG when he began his career. By the time he learned of Neubauer's connection to the twin study, Neubauer was deceased.

Upon learning more of the history of the LWS twins, Brettschneider understood that the twins and their families had been part of an experiment of which they did not have full knowledge. "I didn't have any sense—or I was told over and over again by the older board members that we had nothing to do with the research. Then I learned that Bernard's Tappanz Foundation [the former VWBF] might have helped finance the original research. I also under-stood that it [the study] was never finished and that everything was sealed." The critical issue for Brettschneider was the twins' separation. He stated that his proudest professional efforts had been his efforts against the separation of siblings in child welfare and foster care when he had been employed by the city and state of New York in the 1980s. "I had fought to work on that," he said. He was also interested in knowing how many foster care siblings had been separated, and in knowing how subjects are treated in research.

Brettschneider repeated that it wasn't clear that the VWBF was involved in the twin study. But the more he read, he learned that there were people who thought it was a good idea to separate twins to relieve parenting burdens or allow faster placement.

> I wanted to write about that, and I wanted to announce that we were giving money to do policy research and program work around improving the way siblings are managed, in a way that preserves their relationships. If siblings had been separated, we wanted to enable visitation and to be sure that everything humanly possible had been done to keep them together. We also wanted to acknowledge from a restorative standpoint that it was wrong for the twin separations and study to have occurred. We were taking a restorative approach since we were not involved in the actual research at that time.

Brettschneider drafted a statement to be placed on the VWBF's website to acknowledge Bernard's involvement in the twins' separate placement and subsequent study.

When Brettschneider had proposed this idea to another board member, the reaction was very favorable. But there was dissension among the members at their next meeting. It was decided to take a vote and Brettschneider lost, albeit narrowly. He announced his resignation and those opposed to his state-ment said that if he resigned as president, the VWBF would shut down. He resigned. At that point the question of how to distribute the funds was raised. "We fought over that until we reached some kind of compromise. Some money went to Columbia, some went to Yale. But I saw to it that some went to more grassroots progressive child welfare organizations."

In spring 2016, the VWBF made an endowed gift of $2.35 million to Yale University's Child Study Center, to establish the Viola W. Bernard Fund for Innovation in Mental Health Care.[60] The fund provides a fellowship in social justice and health care equity for mental health professional trainees, awards a prize for innovation in child mental health care delivery to a mental health professional working in partnership with a professional from another discipline, and funds an annual lecture series addressing social justice and health care equity topics.

Cary Koplin, VWBF's financial advisor and treasurer, applauded the work of the VWBF and its decision to select Yale University and Columbia University as the primary recipients of funding when the foundation closed. Koplin, who had seen *Three Identical Strangers*, said he had no comment on the film.[61] Columbia University received $1.1 million for the Dr. Viola W. Bernard Endowment, with emphasis on the needs and special problems of children who, due to poverty or other reasons, suffer from being part of underserved or disadvantaged communities. The following final grants were also awarded to the following organizations:[62]

- Association to Benefit Children: $250,000
- Center for Family Representation: $90,000
- Citizens Committee for Children: $180,000
- Howard Center in Vermont: $90,000
- Jewish Board of Family and Children's Services: $180,000

Brettschneider was pleased with how the funds had been allocated. "We ended up doing some good things with that money. I [was] delighted to be a part of that." I asked him if anyone on the board had considered establishing a fund on behalf of the twins, as an attempt at some form of compensation. He said that this idea was never raised at meetings because the controversies surrounding the twin study were raised first. He added that if a twin contacted the VWBF, the board members wouldn't respond other than to refer people to the JBFCS or to Columbia.

Once the foundation closed, Brettschneider forwarded copies of VWBF documents for placement in Viola Bernard's archives. Stephen E. Novak, Columbia University archivist, noted that some records belonging to Bernard were discovered in 2016, several years after the death of Bernard's assistant, Dr. Kathleen L. Kelly. He never learned the complete story of how they surfaced, but they were found in the building where Kelly had once had her business. One of the boxes had the address of the VWBF and their staff were contacted to obtain it. The VWBF, in turn, delivered the box to Columbia. Most of the material was disposable, such as stationery, and the records were unrelated to the twin study.[63]

I asked Brettschneider if he had had contact with the Jewish Board of Family and Children's Services (JBFCS).[64] He had. Not long before the VWBF closed, Brettschneider received a call from then JBFCS Chief Executive Officer David Rivel. The call concerned discussions Rivel was having with his board about the research and the files. Brettschneider recalled that Rivel "wasn't sharing much," other than wanting to know if Brettschneider would be open to supporting access to the data. Brettschneider answered that he was open to that, not knowing at the time that he probably couldn't make much progress with the Jewish Board. Then the case was suddenly dropped—Rivel was going to call him back but didn't.[65]

Brettschneider believed it is important to know who on the JBFCS board was driving the discussion. Based on his brief conversation with Rivel, Brettschneider said that Rivel sounded like somebody who favored openness. "Something happened before [Rivel] got involved and something happened after he got involved." We both understood that Rivel could not act alone and could not violate the trust of the board.

ARCHIVING DATA: WHO OWNS THE RIGHTS TO THE TWIN STUDY MATERIALS?

Consideration 1. The twins are attempting to acquire the data that were gathered on them, despite the fact that the twin study materials archived at Yale University are restricted until 2065. Who should have access?

In 1990, eighteen years before Peter Neubauer's death, the JBFCS donated his twin study materials to the Yale University archives.[66] These records are unavailable for public review until 2065. The JBFCS does not know who made the decision to leave the materials to Yale, although it is likely that the decision was made by Neubauer. Researchers can request access to the files, but more importantly, the twins are trying to retrieve their materials. It is a formidable task. Yale University lacks the authority to release these records. Their archivists must defer all requests to the JBFCS, whose title appears on the deed of gift as the collections' donor.

Attorneys Sima Kazmir and Patrick L. Robson, of New York's Hunton Andrews Kurth law firm, are working pro bono on the twins' behalf to secure their records. They took over this task in 2015 from attorneys Barry Coburn of Coburn and Greenbaum, PLLC, and Tim Heaphy, formerly of Hunton Andrews Kurth's Washington, DC, office.[67] The lawyers' efforts are ongoing.

As I indicated in chapter 7, attorney Jason Turken's earlier association with the JBFCS and the work of his firm on behalf of the twins ended in December 2019. Turken declined my July 2020 request to discuss the matter, citing law firm policy. The JBFCS replaced Turken with attorneys Mark Barnes and David Peloquin from Boston's Ropes & Gray law firm. Their specializations variously include legal issues pertaining to human subjects' research, research misconduct, and data privacy.[68] One of the attorneys I contacted would not discuss the confidential process by which twins can acquire their records but underlined the JBFCS's commitment to assisting the twins.

Prior to receiving their records, the JBFCS now requires twins to meet with a professor of psychiatry who will review each file to decide if information hurtful to the twins should be withheld.[69] This strikes me as demeaning to the twins who are now adults and capable of making their own decisions. My requests to the psychiatrist for an interview in order to understand his role in the process went unanswered. (I have not named the psychiatrist to protect the twins' best interests.) As I indicated earlier, I released short research summaries of twins I discovered in Bernard's collection which were of interest to those who received them. Each twin was first asked if they wished to have them. With their consent, I then sent the summaries only to that individual unless I was advised that their twin brother or sister should also receive them. I did this because I believed it was clearly the right thing to do. It wasn't a hard choice.

Researchers can request permission from the JBFCS to review the twin-related documents and data. In late 2019 and early 2020, I sent a second request to the JBFCS to inspect materials for one twin pair with names redacted. I explained that I wanted to learn the range of tests, inventories, and other activities administered to the twins. I was told that my requests had not been forgotten and that the board would be meeting again in January 2020 to take up the question. As the time drew closer, I learned that records would be shared only with the people involved in the study, and that this process would be in place indefinitely. "Thus far, we have only shared records with the people involved in the study. We are not prepared to share documents, in any form, without the consent of each and every person involved, a process which will be in place for some time into the future." It is unclear if researchers or other outside individuals could acquire the material if both twins and their families agreed. It is probably unlikely.

WHO OWNS THE TWINS' RECORDS AND WHO SHOULD GAIN ACCESS?

In March 2020, I attended a discussion of issues raised by the documentary film *Three Identical Strangers*, hosted by Yale University's bioethics program. Shortly after I returned to California, I heard from Yale that my request for file RU 910 was not approved by the Office of the Secretary at Yale University. This file is *not* part of Neubauer's closed collection, but was donated by Neubauer's Yale University colleague, the late Donald J. Cohen. I learned that the reasons for rejection are never given and the decision cannot be appealed.[70]

The foregoing events raise hard questions that lawyers and ethicists are attempting to address. Who owns the twin data? Should universities accept records that include human subject information? Should universities make exception to the release of such data on a case-by-case basis? Who should decide if requests for the release of materials can be granted? Are there data that might assist the twins and their families? Why is virtually every phase of the twins' process shrouded in secrecy?

The twins cannot easily gain access to their own materials. Attorney Barry Coburn believes that the phrase "own materials" is key—who owns these records? In the absence of consent, he questioned whether the interests of Viola Bernard's estate or those of an educational institution supersede an individual's own best interests. Given that the principal investigators are deceased, Coburn feels it is time to take a hard look at the situation and make amends. Others concur.[71] Bioethicists Robert Klitzman and Adam Kelmenson, whose request to the Jewish Board of Family and Children's Services to access the records was denied, argue that more harm could occur from not releasing the data than releasing it. "The researchers and agencies involved have refused to provide participants with information that may be helpful to these subjects' personal health and well-being." And the need for students and scholars to learn from this episode in twin studies was underlined by New York University bioethicist Dr. Arthur Caplan and others.

Even some of Neubauer's supporters have questioned the secrecy and deception surrounding the study and the decision to seal the records at Yale University for so many years. Dr. Susan Kolod felt that there was no good rationale for doing so.[72] The ethicists I spoke with also expressed their views. Caplan called the decision "a little unkosher." Given that the materials are so restricted, Kelmenson and his colleague Ilene Wilets wonder if Neubauer's unpublished book manuscript was actually read by Dr. Lois Oppenheim, who brought our attention to it.[73] When I questioned Oppenheim about the whereabouts of this manuscript, her response was vague and non-committal, as indicated in chapter 13.

Ethicists Stephen Latham and Mark Mercurio were among several individuals consulted by the Yale University Library regarding the disposition of Neubauer's collection. The meeting was called following the 2018 release of *Three Identical Strangers*. According to Latham, "I certainly got the impression that no one at Yale knew that there were any human subjects' study records in the records that they were getting." He continued.

> "Basically, we sort of said that there were pretty compelling reasons to release individual study subjects' records to them, because possibly for medical reasons and also just because we thought it was the right thing for the study subjects to understand what had been gathered about them. Mercurio and I agreed with that and said that to the library staff. I don't know whether anything came of that in terms of internal Yale policy discussions and so on, because eventually the Jewish Board decided to release the records anyway."

Of course, the JBFCS's record release has been slow and painful.[74] Part of the problem is that the JBFCS, as well as Columbia University and Yale University, are watching out for their own potential civil liability.[75]

Some of Viola Bernard's twin study files were archived at Columbia University, not to be opened until 2021. Dr. Kathleen L. Kelly, Bernard's longtime assistant, believed that 2021 was the year also chosen for the release of Peter Neubauer's files at Yale University. Columbia University archivist Stephen E. Novak now regrets not having confirmed this information with Yale University, but Kelly was certain of the date. Novak noted that Yale never contacted him about the handling of Bernard's papers. He also wonders if perhaps 2021 *was* the original opening date for Neubauer's collection, but upon closer inspection of the materials it was decided to change it to 2065.[76] Meanwhile, in 2065 anyone who has an interest can learn every detail about the twins and the twin study by visiting Yale.

OPENING THE ARCHIVES: REDUX

A former JBFCS staff person has dutifully forwarded my requests to the board to obtain limited access to the files. In spring 2020, I was informed that I could contact one of the officers, if necessary. When I asked him if we could set up a time for a telephone chat, he replied that the JBFCS could not cooperate with me this year, but I should try again in 2021. That was not really my question. When NBC news contacted the Jewish Board in 2018, a spokesperson said that the JBFCS neither condones nor supports Dr. Neubauer, and that they are reaching out to the twins and triplets.[77] What assurance is there? Is the JBFCS in touch with the fraternal twins who were separated but not studied? Perhaps the JBFCS does not realize that the difficult controversies would subside considerably if the records were provided to the twins along with an apology. The mysteries and delays are worrisome to the twins. Is uncomfortable information hidden in the files?

MOVIES, MEETINGS, AND MEDIA

In 2013 when director Lori Shinseki decided to create her 2017 documentary film *The Twinning Reaction*, she mentioned the project to her colleague, filmmaker Jon Alpert. Alpert, in turn, discussed the premise of the film with his nephew Dr. Michael Alpert, then a student at the School of Medicine at Yale University. The younger Alpert was unaware of LWS, the LWS-CDC twin study, and Neubauer's concealed collection on his campus —and he was both intrigued and incensed. "My uncle put me in touch with Lori in the hopes that we could try and get some kind of awareness or take some kind of steps forward with Yale University's School of Medicine around these archives."[78]

Michael Alpert organized a "Yale Ethics Meeting Re: Neubauer-Bernard Twin Study," held on July 25, 2013. In attendance were a member of Yale's legal counsel, medical school deans, Yale University bioethicists, and others. He prepared a handout with a timeline highlighting key events, beginning with Neubauer's appointment as director of the Jewish Board of Family and Children's Services (JBFCS) in 1951 (actually the Jewish Board of Guardians until 1978), and ending with the opening of the archives in 2065. The group discussed many of the same legal and moral issues I raised in the previous chapter. They also asked, "In a tort, do they have a property right?" They noted that there is case law regarding medical research on donated physical specimens, adding that it is "unclear whether this precedent applies to psychological 'donations.'" I believe this question should be revisited, but not just in terms of the twins' psychological data—blood samples were taken from the infant twins to determine their twin type as identical or fraternal. The researchers also took the twins' fingerprints and footprints.[79] Do the twins have property rights to these materials that were obtained for non-medical reasons?

The last page of Michael Alpert's handout listed several individuals to contact, including William Massa, the head of Yale's Collection Development, Manuscripts and Archives, and Barry Coburn, an attorney working on behalf of separated twins Doug and Howard. (Massa has since retired and New York City attorneys are now working on behalf of the twins.) The legal team representing the JBFCS refused to communicate with him or with anyone else from Yale.

Dr. Michael Alpert is now a psychiatrist working in Boston, Massachusetts, committed to examining social justice issues within his field. He strongly advocates educating future physicians in the ethics of medical practice and research. The meeting he convened in 2013 was an important, albeit small step toward informing a select group of Yale University colleagues about the twin separations and the study behind the concealed archive on their campus. The next important steps were made by Lori Shinseki, director of the 2017 film *The Twinning Reaction,* and Tim Wardle, director of the 2018 film *Three Identical Strangers.* Both Shinseki and Wardle were highly motivated to make their films after discovering the story of the separated triplets. Shinseki hoped to give voice to the separated twins and their families who were unwitting participants in the LWS-CDC twin study.[80] Wardle hoped to make a film about a life history that was "truly special."[81] These two documentary filmmakers took giant steps.

Scores of movie reviews appeared once the films were seen at theaters and film festivals, watched on television, streamed on computers, and discussed at schools, synagogues, and other venues. I have referenced a number of these reviews throughout the book, but the one published by William McCormack in the *Yale Daily News* in 2018 was particularly impressive. It was also one of the few articles, if not the first, to provide the correct year that Neubauer's files were scheduled to be opened—2065, not 2066. The article covered the background of the study, Dr. Alpert's 2013 meeting at Yale, and the twins' ongoing struggle to obtain their sealed records.[82] It also described Yale's concerns that releasing documents before the 2065 date agreed to in the contract would lead to a lawsuit. The consequent worry that other scholars would hesitate to donate their materials to Yale was also indicated. As I have noted, release of the records is controlled by the JBFCS, but tensions surrounding the restriction on the twins' data underline the serious consideration that libraries and other institutions must take when accepting archival collections.

Given the professionalism of the article, I had assumed that McCormack was a senior member of the writing pool, an administrator, or possibly a faculty contributor. I spoke with him by telephone in 2019, then arranged to meet him when I visited Yale later that year. I was shocked to discover that McCormack was just a sophomore—slim, blond, and boyish—and had authored the article as a freshman. In the summer 2018, after watching *Three Identical Strangers,* he was "fascinated, concerned and intrigued." Dropping by the newspaper's open house, McCormack saw the story posted on the list of assignments and immediately seized it. Thirteen months later, he learned that his article had received over sixty thousand page views, making it one of the most highly read *Yale Daily News* stories of the 2018/2019 school year.[83]

A number of professional meetings have brought lawyers, ethicists, physicians, psychologists, and students together to review the origins and outcomes of the LWS-CDC twin study, and to make suggestions for rectitude and justice. On March 29, 2019, I participated in "The Twinning Reaction: Science and Deception," held at the University of Virginia Law School in Charlottesville. The idea for the meeting came from law professor Paul B. Stephan, a Yale University alumnus, who had seen *Three Identical Strangers*. Stephan was troubled that his alma mater held the twins' documents under seal and hoped to help the twins' retrieve them. Many conference details were worked out during Stephan's morning runs with my University of Virginia colleague, psychiatrist Andy Thomson, who was also concerned. Shinseki's film, *The Twinning Reaction*, was shown at that event, and Shinseki herself was a speaker. I also attended "A Viewing and Discussion of the Film *Three Identical Strangers*," held at Yale University on March 2, 2020. Dr. Mark Mercurio, director of Yale's biomedical ethics program whom I interviewed for this book, had seen *Three Identical Strangers*. He believed it was vital to arrange a viewing and discussion for members of Yale's bioethics and pediatric ethics program, medical school, and community at large.

These sessions took place because one individual was deeply moved and extremely troubled by what had happened to the twins, enough to secure the efforts of concerned colleagues. Other such conferences and media events have occurred across the United States and beyond, and some are scheduled, evidence that interest in the twins and the twin study is high. In August 2020, *60 Minutes–Australia* aired *Three Identical Strangers*, with an additional segment featuring several commentators and a pair of separated twins.[84] A virtual discussion hosted by Harvard University, in March 2021, drew nearly 200 attendees.[85] In May 2021, I was the keynote speaker at "Twins: Multiple Perspectives on Multiples," a conference recognizing the fiftieth anniversary of the founding of the Los Angeles Institute and Society for Psychoanalytic Studies. Organized by Dr. Linda Sobelman, this day and a half event featured a showing of *Three Identical Strangers* and a discussion by twin researchers and panelists with diverse backgrounds and perspectives, myself included. Prior to the COVID-19 outbreak, Lori Shinseki was asked to discuss *The Twinning Reaction* at the annual meeting of the American Academy of Psychiatry and the Law. It is likely that other such meetings have occurred and will occur at other venues. I would like to see the separated twins fill these slots at future meetings. Some twins' words have filled the pages of the chapters of my book, and it is gratifying for me that they have finally been given a voice. They deserve a wide forum.

Universal interest in the LWS separated twins remains high, a phenomenon that has a dual explanation. Identical twins, by virtue of their matched behavioral and physical traits, highlight the effects of shared genes, while preserving the uniqueness of all individuals. Of course, identical twins are not exactly alike, due to environmental influences before and after birth, but they are more alike than any other pair of people. Observing them interact so easily and effortlessly with one another suggests a social intimacy that many find attractive, some find forbidding, but that everyone finds intriguing. More importantly perhaps, severing this bond cuts at the heart of our reverence for family connection. The idea that newborn twins were deliberately adopted apart, never knowing one another, feels cruel and unnatural. Separating them was not in their best interests as one psychiatrist had claimed. Thus, I believe that this tragic episode in twin studies, while over, is unfinished.

LESSONS: WHAT DO WE TAKE AWAY?

"The law said, 'Okay.' Ethics asked, 'Are you out of your minds?'"[86]

Virtually everyone I interviewed believed that present and future scholars can become better professionals and better human beings by taking a critical look at the LWS-CDC twin study. It is instructive to see how researchers performed in the time and place that they did. Dr. Mark Mercurio expressed it best—it is not enough to say that you were behaving in ways that were consistent with legal standards just because rules at the time did not apply to your situation, or relevant rules had not been enacted. Certain behaviors are wrong if, for example, they violate privacy or confidentiality. Dr. Robert Klitzman and Adam Kelmenson have argued that "Such historical examples remain critical, highlighting ongoing needs for vigilance and self-scrutiny." Ethicist Arthur Caplan argued that the purpose of preserving papers is to allow libraries to maximize learning and scholarship. "Negotiating deals to keep materials sealed for significant periods of time makes no sense."[87]

If the records were to be released, should the data be analyzed and the findings published? Publishing the data might satisfy those twins and families who feel that their ordeal served no useful purpose in the end. However, doing so would send the wrong message to some zealous researchers that one can escape criticism for unethical practice if the data proved interesting or meaningful. It could also be argued that if data gathered by unacceptable means could save a life then it may be used, but with qualification. Regarding the LWS-CDC study, I predict that nothing novel, illuminating, or lifesaving could be derived from that dataset. Present methods for studying twins and adoptees are far more sophisticated, and sample sizes are far larger than the eleven children followed by Neubauer and Bernard. At best, we might find confirmation of what we already know—that genetic influences are far more pervasive than people have believed.

SHOULD WE STUDY SEPARATED TWINS? AND A LAST WORD

A former CDC associate admonished the Minnesota Study of Twins Reared Apart staff for inviting separated twins to the university to be studied at the same time. She suggested that the twins may have been more alike if they had been studied apart as individuals, unaffected by the presence of their co-twin. I explained that bringing the twins together was partly an incentive for study participation—some twins lived far from one another and some twins had never met. It would have been cruel and callous to keep them apart for purposes of the study. It is also unlikely that testing the twins at different times would have significantly altered the results. Of course, during daytime assessments, the twins were separated as much as possible to avoid any possibility or appearance of bias, but they enjoyed each other's company during their lunch breaks with the staff and during their free evenings. They understood the importance of not exchanging answers or information until both twins had completed a certain test or activity. They were also eager to discover the origins of their abilities, personalities, and health, information that comparison with their co-twin could uniquely provide.

We should continue to study separated twins, both identical and fraternal, with the full consent of the twins and their families. Reared-apart twins remain valued participants in the quest to understand how genes and environments mingle to yield the behavioral and physical traits that make up every one of us. But there are important differences between the LWS-CDC collaboration and the other reared-apart twin studies, one in particular: Bernard and Neubauer purposely placed and kept twins apart—everyone else intentionally brought (or brings) twins together.

The LWS-CDC twin study has taught us many lessons. It remains a great example of how not to do research.

Notes

PREFACE

1. William McCormack, "Records From Controversial Twin Study Sealed at Yale Until 2065." *Yale Daily News*, October 1, 2018, https://yaledailynews.com/blog/2018/10/01/records-from-controversial-twin-study-sealed-at-yale-until-2065/. The data are actually sealed until 2065.

2. Leon Hoffman and Lois Oppenheim, "*Three Identical Strangers and The Twinning Reaction*—Clarifying History and Lessons for Today from Peter Neubauer's Twin Study." *Journal of the American Medical Association* 322, no. 1 (July 2019): 10–12.

3. Jeremy Pearce, "Peter B. Neubauer, 94, Noted Child Psychiatrist, Is Dead." *New York Times*, March 3, 2008, B7.

4. Peter B. Neubauer, "Playing: Technical Implications." *The Many Meanings of Play* (New Haven, CT: Yale University Press, 1993).

5. Gabrielle Kardon, "Life in Triplicate." *Science* 359, no. 6381 (March 2018): 1222.

6. Jewish Board of Family and Children's Services, "Adoption Study Records of the Child Development Center." *Yale University Archives*, call no. MS 1585 (circa 1960–1980), https://archives.yale.edu/repositories/12/resources/3434?stylename=yul.ead2002.xhtml.xsl&pid=mssa:ms.1585&query=adler&clear-stylesheet-cache=yes&hlon=yes&big=&adv=&filter=&hitPageStart=1&sortFields=&view=all. The 66 boxes take up 69 linear feet. https://archives.yale.edu/repositories/12/resources/3434/collection_organization.

7. Multiple sources including attorneys, twins, and family members, 2019, 2020.

8. Nancy L. Segal, *Born Together—Reared Apart: The Landmark Minnesota Twin Study* (Cambridge, MA: Harvard University Press, 2012); Nancy L. Segal and Yesika S. Montoya, *Accidental Brothers: The Story of Twins Exchanged at Birth and the Power of Nature and Nurture* (New York: St. Martin's Press, 2018); Nancy L. Segal,

"Reared-Apart Chinese Twins: Chance Discovery." *Twin Research and Human Genetics* 20, no. 2 (2017): 180–85.

9. Robert Plomin, *Blueprint: How DNA Makes Us Who We Are* (Cambridge, MA: MIT Press, 2018).

CHAPTER 1

1. William E. Blatz et al., *Collected Studies on the Dionne Quintuplets* (Toronto: University of Toronto Press, 1937).

2. Nancy L. Segal, "Holocaust Twins: Their Special Bond." *Psychology Today* (August 1985): 52–58.

3. Juliet Butler, *The Less You Know the Sounder You Sleep* (London: HarperCollins, 2018).

4. John Money and Anke A. Ehrhardt, *Man & Woman, Boy & Girl* (Baltimore: The Johns Hopkins University Press, 1972).

5. Milton Diamond and H. Keith Sigmundson, "Sex Reassignment at Birth: Long-Term Reviews and Clinical Implications." *Archives of Pediatric and Adolescent and Medicine* 151, no. 3 (March 1997): 298–304.

6. Nancy L. Segal, "Commentary: More Thoughts on the Child Development Center Twin Study." *Twin Research and Human Genetics* 8, no. 3 (2005): 276–81.

7. Francis Galton, "The History of Twins, as a Criterion of the Relative Powers of Nature and Nurture." *Fraser's Magazine* 12, no. 71 (1875): 566–76.

8. Nancy L. Segal, *Twin Mythconceptions: False Beliefs, Fables, and Facts About Twins* (New York: Elsevier, 2017).

9. Jeffrey P. Baker, "Autism in 1959: Joey the Mechanical Boy." *Pediatrics* 125, no. 6 (2010): 1101–03.

10. Michelle L. Esterberg and Michael T. Compton, "Causes of Schizophrenia Reported by Family Members of Urban African American Hospitalized Patients with Schizophrenia." *Comprehensive Psychiatry* 47, no. 3 (2006): 221–26.

11. Nancy L. Segal, *Born Together—Reared Apart: The Landmark Minnesota Twin Study* (Cambridge, MA: Harvard University Press, 2012).

12. Pam Jarvis, "Born to Play: The Biocultural Roots of Rough and Tumble Play and Its Impact Upon Young Children's Learning and Development." *Play and Learning in the Early Years* (2010): 61–77.

13. David C. Geary, "Evolution and Developmental Sex Differences." *Current Directions in Psychological Science* 8, no. 4 (1999): 115–20.

14. Segal, *Born Together—Reared Apart.*

15. Alexander Thomas, Stella Chess, and Herbert G. Birch, *Temperament and Behavior Disorders in Children* (New York: New York University Press, 1968). According to Dr. Chess, Bernard "treated me like her protégé, but I wasn't."

Chess also recalled that Bernard thought of herself as a "psychiatric busybody." Stella Chess, interview with Nancy L. Segal, 2005; also see footnote 6.

16. Alexander Thomas, Stella Chess, and Herbert G. Birch, "The Origin of Personality." *Scientific American* 227, no. 2 (1970): 102–09.

17. Most identical twins are not strictly genetically identical, due to epigenetic and other prenatal and postnatal events, as well as pretwinning and/or postzygotic mutations. Helen C. McNamara, Stefan C. Kane, Jeffrey M. Craig, Roger V. Short, and Mark P. Umstad, "A Review of the Mechanisms and Evidence for Typical and Atypical Twinning." *American Journal of Obstetrics and Gynecology* 214, no. 2 (2016): 172–91; Hakon Jonsson, Erna Magnusdottir, Hannes P. Eggertsson, Olafur A. Stefansson, Gudny A. Arnadottir, Ogmundur Eiriksson, Florian Zink, et al., "Differences Between Germline Genomes of Monozygotic Twins." *Nature Genetics* 53, no. 1 (2021): 27–34.

18. Segal, *Twin Mythconceptions*.

19. Valerie S. Knopik, Jenae M. Neiderhiser, John C. DeFries, and Robert Plomin, *Behavioral Genetics* (New York: Macmillan Higher Education, 2017).

20. Tina J. C. Polderman, Beben Benyamin, Christiaan A. De Leeuw, Patrick F. Sullivan, Arjen Van Bochoven, Peter M. Visscher, and Danielle Posthuma, "Meta-Analysis of the Heritability of Human Traits Based on Fifty Years of Twin Studies." *Nature Genetics* 47, no. 7 (2015): 702–09.

21. Joyce A. Martin, Brady E. Hamilton, Michele J. K. Osterman, Anne K. Driscoll, and Patrick Drake, "Births: Final Data for 2017." *National Vital Statistics Reports* 67, no. 8 (November 7, 2018): 1–50.

22. Segal, *Twin Mythconceptions*; Joyce A. Martin, Brady E. Hamilton, Michelle J. K. Osterman, and Anne K. Driscoll, "Births: Final Data for 2019." *National Vital Statistics Reports* 70, no. 2 (2021): 1–51.

23. Segal, *Twin Mythconceptions*.

24. Joyce A. Martin and Michelle J. K. Osterman, "Is Twin Childbearing on the Decline? Twin Births in the United States, 2014–2018." *NCHS Data Brief* no. 351 (October 2019).

25. Sarah Guy, "One Embryo as Good as Two for IVF Success," *IVF. Net*, November 4, 2009, http://ivf.net/ivf/one-embryo-as-good-as-two-for-ivf-success-o4568.html.

26. Horatio N. Newman, Frank N. Freeman, and Karl J. Holzinger, *Twins: A Study of Heredity and Environment* (Chicago: University of Chicago Press, 1937).

27. Niels Juel-Nielsen, *Individual and Environment: A Psychiatric-Psychological Investigation of Monozygotic Twins Reared Apart* (Copenhagen: Munksgaard, 1965).

28. Juel-Nielsen, *Individual and Environment*.

29. James Shields, *Monozygotic Twins: Brought Up Apart and Together* (London: Oxford University Press, 1962).

30. Nancy L. Pedersen, L. Friberg, B. Floderus-Myrhed, G. E. McClearn, and R. Plomin, "Swedish Early Separated Twins: Identification and Characterization." *Acta Geneticae Medicae et Gemellologiae: Twin Research* 33, no. 2 (1984):

243–250; Nancy L. Pedersen, Robert Plomin, John R. Nesselroade, and Gerald E. McClearn, "A Quantitative Genetic Analysis of Cognitive Abilities During the Second Half of the Life Span." *Psychological Science* 3, no. 6 (1992): 346–53.

31. Segal, *Born Together—Reared Apart.*

32. Segal, *Born Together—Reared Apart.*

33. Peter M. Visscher, Naomi R. Wray, Qian Zhang, Pamela Sklar, Mark I. McCarthy, Matthew A. Brown, and Jian Yang, "10 Years of GWAS Discovery: Biology, Function, and Translation." *The American Journal of Human Genetics* 101, no. 1 (2017): 5–22.

34. Nancy L. Segal, "Cooperation, Competition, and Altruism Within Twin Sets: A Reappraisal." *Ethology and Sociobiology* 5, no. 3 (1984): 163–77.

35. Nancy L. Segal, *Indivisible by Two: Lives of Extraordinary Twins* (Cambridge, MA: Harvard University Press, 2005); Denise Grady, "Surgeons Transplant Testicle From One Identical Twin to the Other." *Independent*, December 8, 2019, https://www.independent.co.uk/news/health/testicle-transplant-identical-twin-brother-serbia-a9237771.html.

36. Nancy L. Segal, Scott L. Hershberger, and Sara Arad, "Meeting One's Twin: Perceived Social Closeness and Familiarity." *Evolutionary Psychology* 1, no. 1 (2003): 70–95.

37. Segal, *Born Together—Reared Apart.*

38. Robert F. Krueger, Kristian E. Markon, and Thomas J. Bouchard Jr., "The Extended Genotype: The Heritability of Personality Accounts for the Heritability of Recalled Family Environments in Twins Reared Apart." *Journal of Personality* 71, no. 5 (2003): 809–33.

39. Lawrence Wright, "Double Mystery." *The New Yorker*, August 7, 1995, 45–62.

40. Segal, *Indivisible By Two.*

41. Joyce M. Pavao, interview with Nancy L. Segal, 2019.

42. Segal, *Born Together—Reared Apart.*

43. Nancy L. Segal and Yesika S. Montoya, *Accidental Brothers: The Story of Twins Exchanged at Birth and the Power of Nature and Nurture* (New York: St. Martin's Press, 2018).

44. Segal, *Indivisible By Two.*

45. Nancy L. Segal, Francisca J. Niculae, Erika N. Becker, and Emmy Y. Shih, "Reared-Apart/Reared-Together Chinese Twins and Virtual Twins: Evolving Research Program and General Intelligence Findings." *Journal of Experimental Child Psychology* 207 (2021): article 105106, https://www.sciencedirect.com/science/article/abs/pii/S0022096521000230.

46. Nancy L. Segal, "Co-Twin Control Studies: Natural Events, Experimental Interventions and Rare Happenings." *Twin Research and Human Genetics* 22, no. 4 (2019): 272–76.

47. Segal and Montoya, *Accidental Brothers.*

48. Segal, *Born Together—Reared Apart.*

49. Twins Days, Inc., *Twins Days Festival*, https://twinsdays.org/.

50. Nancy L. Segal, "Art for Twins: Yorùbá Artists and Their Statues/Twin Research Studies." *Twin Research and Human Genetics* 17, no. 3 (2014): 215–21.

51. EuroNews, "Double Vision? 50 Pairs of Twins Gather for Parade in Crimea," https://www.euronews.com/2019/05/27/double-vision-50-pairs-of-twins-gather-for-parade-in-crimea.

52. Nancy L. Segal, "Centenary Celebration for Scottish Missionary Mary Slessor: A Lasting Legacy for Twins/Twin Research." *Twin Research and Human Genetics* 18, no. 3 (2015): 328–33.

53. Ellen A. Stewart, *Exploring Twins: Towards a Social Analysis of Twinship* (New York: Palgrave Macmillan, 2000) 5454.

54. Christiaan Monden, Gilles Pison, and Jeroen Smits, "Twin Peaks: More Twinning in Humans Than Ever Before." *Human Reproduction* 36, no. 6 (2021): 1666–73. Twinning rates in the modern world have been increasing since the 1980s, largely due to assisted reproductive technologies.

55. Segal, *Born Together—Reared Apart*.

CHAPTER 2

1. Groesbeck Walsh and Robert M. Pool, "Shakespeare's Knowledge of Twins and Twinning." *Southern Medicine and Surgery* 102, no. C11 (1940): 173–76.

2. David Langerkrantz, *The Girl Who Takes an Eye for an Eye* (New York: Vintage Books, 2017).

3. Findings from the MISTRA were published by me in book form with the title, *Born Together—Reared Apart: The Landmark Minnesota Twin Study* (Cambridge, MA: Harvard University Press, 2012).

4. Joe Rooks-Rapport, "Notable American Jewish Women: A Computer Aided Study in Collective Biography." Rabbinic thesis, Hebrew Union College (1984), cited in Joe Rooks-Rapport, "Louise Waterman Wise." *Jewish Women: A Comprehensive Historical Encyclopedia (Jewish Women's Archive)*, February 27, 2009, https://jwa.org/encyclopedia/article/wise-louise-waterman.

5. Board of Directors, LWS, "Minutes," October 6, 1982. Viola W. Bernard Archives, Columbia University; staff member, Schlesinger Library, Justine W. Polier archives.

6. A recent account of a Louise Wise Services adoption case noted that the agency participated in the national Indian Adoption Project, which took Native American children away from their families for placement with Caucasian parents. Gabrielle Glaser, *American Baby: A Mother, a Child, and the Shadow History of Adoption* (New York: Viking, 2021).

7. Ellen Herman, *Kinship by Design: A History of Adoption in the Modern United States* (Chicago: University of Chicago Press, 2008); also see Ellen Herman,

"Matter of Vardinakis, 1936." The Adoption History Project (160 Misc. Reports New York 13-17), https://pages.uoregon.edu/adoption/archive/MatterofVardinakis.htm; Ellen Herman, "The Difference Difference Makes: Justine Wise Polier and Religious Matching in Twentieth-Century Child Adoption." *Religion and American Culture* 10, no. 1 (2000): 57–98.

8. Debra Bradly Ruder, interview with Nancy L. Segal, 2019; Stacey Dresner, "Hadassah Presents Play About Judge Justine Wise Polier." *MA Jewish Ledger*, April 18, 2013, https://www.wmassjewishledger.com/2013/04/hadassah-presents-play-about-judge-justine-wise-polier/. *The Grain of the Wood* was written by playwright Ellen W. Kaplan.

9. Sara B. Edlin, *The Unmarried Mother in Our Society: A Frank and Constructive Approach to an Age-Old Problem* (New York: Farrar, Straus and Young, 1954); "Home for Jewish Mothers and Babies." *New York Times*, April 10, 1911, 6; also see https://adoption.com/forums/thread/100900/louise-wise-1964/; https://www.ancestry.com/boards/thread.aspx?mv=flat&m=1254&p=localities.northam.usa.states.newyork.counties.richmond.

10. Viola W. Bernard, "Louise Wise Services-Directors Profile," Columbia University Archives and Special Collections. An apparent "to-do" list of Bernard's, dated Monday, July 22, includes the entry: "Mt. Sinai/twins." It appears to be from the year 1963, given the month and day. An arrangement with Mt. Sinai Hospital is also indicated in an archival document, reporting minutes from an LWS Board meeting, April 3, 1957.

11. Viola W. Bernard, "Louise Wise Services-Directors Profile," July 18, 1986, Columbia University Archives and Special Collections.

12. John Patrick Schutz, "Revisiting a True Nyack Character—Dr. Pierre Bernard," https://athomeinnyack.wordpress.com/. The Clarkstown Country Club was "part yoga center, part ashram, part entertainment venue." It was also the site of the "Free Love" movement.

13. Ellen Herman, "Viola Wertheim Bernard (1907-1998)," *The Adoption History Project*, February 24, 2012, https://pages.uoregon.edu/adoption/people/bernard.htm.

14. Viola W. Bernard, "Louise Wise Services-Directors Profile," July 18, 1986, Columbia University Archives and Special Collections.

15. Viola W. Bernard, "Resignation Letter." Columbia University Archives and Special Collections (June 3, 1981).

16. Viola W. Bernard, "Adoption," *Encyclopedia of Mental Health* 1: 70–108; Viola W. Bernard, interview with Lawrence Wright, 1993; Samuel Abrams, "Disposition and the Environment." *The Psychoanalytic Study of the Child* 41, no. 1 (1986): 41–60; Leon Hoffman and Lois Oppenheim, "*Three Identical Strangers and The Twinning Reaction*—Clarifying History and Lessons for Today From Peter Neubauer's Twins Study." *Journal of the American Medical Association* 322 no. 1 (2019): 10–12.

17. "Doing it Better: The Twin Study, NYC – 1960s." *San Diego Community Newspaper Group*, October 16, 2015, http://www.sdnews.com/view/full_story/26913001/article-DOING-IT-BETTER--The-Twin-Study--NYC---1960s; Tim Wardle, *Three Identical Strangers* (film) (Raw: United Kingdom, 2018).

18. Columbia University Archives and Special Collections, "The Papers of Viola W. Bernard, M.D." Memo, September 29, 1982, Child Development Center—Twin Study (Twins Reared Apart).

19. Columbia University Archives and Special Collections, "The Papers of Viola W. Bernard, M.D." 17.6: Artifacts and Ephemera. The COVID-19 pandemic prevented my access to these materials in 2021.

20. Columbia University Archives and Special Collections, "The Papers of Viola W. Bernard, M.D." *Child Development Center—Twin Study* (Donor Agreement Form) Accession No. 00.10.13. This document states that the material "shall be closed until January 1, 2021." This date was intended to correspond closely with the date on which related records contributed by Peter B. Neubauer, MD, to Yale University will no longer be closed. It appears that there was a miscommunication between the various parties, given that the Neubauer records are sealed until 2065.

21. Susan J., interview with Nancy L. Segal, 2012, 2018, 2019; Viola W. Bernard Archives, Columbia University.

22. Liz Mazlish, interview with Nancy L. Segal, 2019. Their twin type is uncertain.

23. Viola W. Bernard Archives, Columbia University.

24. Viola W. Bernard, *Encyclopedia of Mental Health* 1. Also see Adam M. Kelmenson and Ilene Wilets, "Historical Practice of Separating Twins at Birth." *Journal of the American Medical Association* 322, no. 18 (2019): 1827–28.

25. The executive director at that time was Florence Brown.

26. Twins placed together by LWS have never come forth or been identified.

27. As I indicated in chapter 2, the literature, cited by Abrams (1986), consisted of only several case studies and a summary. Bernard does not cite any relevant studies in her publications.

28. Viola W. Bernard, interview with Lawrence Wright.

29. Marjorie R. Leonard, "Twins: The Myth and the Reality." *Child Study* 30, no. 2 (1953): 9–13, 38–41; Betsy H. Gehman, *Twins: Twice the Trouble, Twice the Fun* (New York: J.B. Lippincott Co., 1965); Helen L. Koch, *Twins and Twin Relations* (Chicago: University of Chicago Press, 1966).

30. Emma N. Plank, "Reactions of Mothers of Twins in a Child Study Group." *American Journal of Orthopsychiatry* 28, no. 1 (1958): 196–204; Twins Mothers Club of Bergen County, New Jersey, *And Then There Were Two: A Handbook for Mothers and Fathers of Twins* (New York: Child Study Association of America, 1959); Isabel G. Barker, Janice L. Fanelli, Marion P. Meyer, and June V. J. Moten, *Twins . . . A Guide to Their Education* (West Chester, PA: Main Line Mothers of Twins Club, 1961).

31. Samuel Abrams, "Disposition and the Environment." *The Psychoanalytic Study of the Child* 41, no. 1 (1986): 41–60.

32. Dorothy T. Burlingham, *Twins: A Study of Three Sets of Identical Twins with 30 Charts* (London: Imago, 1952).

33. Abrams, "Disposition and the Environment."

34. Unnamed source, interview with Nancy L. Segal, 2019; Wardle, *Three Identical Strangers*.

35. Nancy L. Segal, *Twin Mythconceptions: False Beliefs, Fables, and Facts About Twins* (New York: Elsevier, 2017).

36. Kevin J. Mitchell, *Innate: How the Wiring of Our Brains Shapes Who We Are* (Princeton, NJ: Princeton University Press, 2018).

37. Lawrence Perlman, interview in *The Twinning Reaction*, documentary film by Lori Shinseki, 2017.

38. Esther R. Goshen-Gottstein, "The Mothering of Twins, Triplets and Quadruplets." *Psychiatry* 43, no. 3 (1980): 189–204. The LWS-CDC twin study is not referenced.

39. Bernard, interview with Lawrence Wright.

40. Lawrence Wright, *Twins and What They Tell Us About Who We Are* (Hoboken, NJ: John Wiley, 1997); Wardle, *Three Identical Strangers*.

41. Vivian Bregman, mother of separated twin Sharon Morello. Interview in *The Twinning Reaction*, documentary film by Lori Shinseki, 2017.

42. Diane Bell, "Column: Documentary Outs Secret Twin Study, But Mystery Remains." *The San Diego Union Tribune*, July 25, 2018, https://www.sandiego uniontribune.com/news/columnists/diane-bell/sd-me-bell-20180726-story.html.

43. Hoffman and Oppenheim, "*Three Identical Strangers and The Twinning Reaction.*"

44. Email correspondence, Nancy L. Segal and Jewish Board of Family and Children's Services, 2019.

45. Eugene Mahon, interview with Nancy L. Segal, 2019.

46. Paula Kreech, interviews with Nancy L. Segal, 2018, 2019.

47. Lois Oppenheim, interview with Nancy L. Segal, 2019.

48. Hoffman and Oppenheim, "*Three Identical Strangers and The Twinning Reaction.*"

49. Lois Oppenheim, "The Facts About the Neubauer Twin Study: An Interview About Controversy or a Controversial Interview?" *International Journal of Controversial Discussions* 1 (2020): 171–88.

50. Lawrence M. Perlman, "Memories of the Child Development Center Twin Study of Adopted Monozygotic Twins Reared Apart: An Unfulfilled Promise." *Twin Research and Human Genetics* 8, no. 3 (2005): 271–75.

51. Drs. Patricia Nachman and Susannah Falk Shopsin Lewis, interviews with Nancy L. Segal, 2019.

52. European Advertising Academy, "Krems," http://www.europeanadvertis ingacademy.org/2019/krems/.

53. "Austrian-Jewish Immigrants in the USA." *The Austrian Heritage Collection* (New York: Leo Baeck Institute, September 9, 1999).

54. "Blau-Weiss." *Encyclopaedia Judaica. Encyclopedia.com*, September 9, 2019, https://www.encyclopedia.com.

55. "Hashomer Hatzair World Movement," 2019, http://www.hashomer-hatzair.net/cgi-webaxy/item?181.

56. Peter B. Neubauer, answers to the *Leo Baeck Self-Report Questionnaire*, September 9, 1999.

57. Neubauer, answers to the *Leo Baeck Self-Report Questionnaire*.

58. The *Leo Baeck Self-Report Questionnaire* does not provide details about how Neubauer's father's experience affected his study abroad. It is likely that Neubauer was aware of how the dangerous conditions in Austria affected his father and chose to remain out of the country.

59. Annie Pleshette Murphy, interview with Nancy L. Segal, 2019.

60. Jeremy Pearce, "Peter B. Neubauer, 94, Noted Child Psychiatrist, Is Dead." *New York Times*, March 3, 2008, B7.

61. Jack Novick and Kerry Kelly Novick, "Atruistic Analysis." In *The Anna Freud Tradition: Lines of Development—Evolution of Theory and Practice Over the Decades*, edited by Norka T. Malberg and Joan Raphael-Leff, 365–68 (London: Routledge, 2018).

62. In 1978, the Jewish Board of Guardians merged with Jewish Family Services to become the Jewish Board of Family and Children's Services. Aaron H. Esman, "The Diffusion of American Psychoanalysis: The JBG as Case Study." *Journal of Clinical Psychoanalysis* 12, no. 2 (2003): 191–99.

63. Peter B. Neubauer, ed., *The Process of Child Development* (Lanham, MD: Jason Aronson, 1976); Peter B. Neubauer, ed., *Children in Collectives: Child-Rearing Aims and Practices in the Kibbutz* (Springfield, IL: Charles C Thomas, 1965).

64. "Paid Notice: Deaths Neubauer, Peter, M.D." *New York Times*, February 18, 2008, https://archive.nytimes.com/query.nytimes.com/gst/fullpage-9504E3D7143AF93BA25751C0A96E9C8B63.html.

65. Jeremy Pearce, "Peter B. Neubauer, 94, Noted Child Psychiatrist, Is Dead." *New York Times*, March 3, 2008, B7.

66. Harry Belafonte, with Michael Schnayerson, *My Song: A Memoir of Art, Race and Defiance* (New York: Alfred A. Knopf, 2011).

67. Lawrence Wright, "Double Mystery." *The New Yorker*, August 7, 1995, 45–62. Wright, *Twins and What They Tell Us About Who We Are*.

68. Robert Plomin, *Nature and Nurture: An Introduction to Human Behavioral Genetics* (Pacific Grove, CA: Brooks/Cole, 1990).

69. Thomas J. Bouchard Jr., David T. Lykken, Matthew McGue, Nancy L. Segal, and Auke Tellegen, "Sources of Human Psychological Differences: The Minnesota Study of Twins Reared Apart." *Science* 250, no. 4978 (1990): 223–28; Nancy L. Segal, *Born Together—Reared Apart: The Landmark Minnesota Twin Study*.

70. Peter B. Neubauer, interview with Lawrence Wright, 1993.

71. Nancy L. Segal, "Commentary: More Thoughts on the Child Development Center Twin Study." *Twin Research and Human Genetics* 8, no. 3 (2005): 276–81.

72. Segal, "Commentary: More Thoughts on the Child Development Center Twin Study."

73. Nicholas L. Tilney, "Renal Transplantation Between Identical Twins: A Review." *World Journal of Surgery* 10, no. 3 (1986): 381–88; Nancy L. Segal, *Twin Mythconceptions: False Beliefs, Fables, and Facts About Twins* (New York: Elsevier, 2017).

74. John P. Merrill, Joseph E. Murray, J. Hartwell Harrison, and Warren R. Guild, "Successful Homotransplantation of the Human Kidney Between Identical Twins." *Journal of the American Medical Association* 160, no. 4 (1956): 277–82; John P. Merrill, Joseph E. Murray, J. Hartwell Harrison, Eli A. Friedman, James B. Dealy Jr., and Gustave J. Dammin, "Successful Homotransplantation of the Kidney Between Nonidentical Twins." *New England Journal of Medicine* 262, no. 25 (1960): 1251–60.

75. Peter B. Neubauer and Alexander Neubauer, *Nature's Thumbprint: The New Genetics of Personality* (New York: Addison-Wesley Publishing Co., 1990), p. 66.

76. Geoffrey A. Machin and Louis G. Keith, *An Atlas of Multiple Pregnancy: Biology and Pathology* (New York: Parthenon, 1999).

77. David T. Lykken, "The Diagnosis of Zygosity in Twins." *Behavior Genetics* 8, no. 5 (1978): 437–73.

78. Aaron Esman, interview with Nancy L. Segal, 2019.

79. I met Dr. Serlin when she invited me to participate in a panel discussion of *The Twinning Reaction*, as part of the American Psychological Association's 2019 film festival.

80. Arnold Richards, MD, interview with Nancy L. Segal, 2019.

81. Bernard, interview with Lawrence Wright.

82. Trudy Festinger, interview with Nancy L. Segal, 2019.

83. Elizabeth Cady Brown, "Wise Demise: Foster Care Group Closes Under Fire." *City Limits*, March 1, 2004, https://www.google.com/search?q=Wise+Demise%3A+Foster+Care+Group+Closes+Under+Fire&oq=Wise+Demise%3A+Foster+Care+Group+Closes+Under+Fire&aqs=chrome..69i57j69i60.1710j0j7&sourceid=chrome&ie=UTF-8.

84. Adam Dickter, "Home Found for Louise Wise Records." *The New York Jewish Week*, December 10, 2004, https://jewishweek.timesofisrael.com/home-found-for-louise-wise-records/.

85. Mark Weiner (June 20, 2019), "NY Lawmakers Pass Adoption Bill Championed by Pam Hunter, Ending Decades of Secrecy," https://www.syracuse.com/politics/2019/06/ny-lawmakers-pass-adoption-bill-championed-by-pam-hunter-ending-decades-of-secrecy.html.

86. Unnamed source, 2019.

87. Dr. Viola Bernard, interview with Dr. Nellie Thompson, December 11, 1985. Abraham A. Brill Library, New York Psychoanalytic Society and Institute.

88. Hoffman and Oppenheim, "Three Identical Strangers and The Twinning Reaction."

89. Interview with Dr. Lois Oppenheim by Nancy Segal, 2019.

90. Michael John Burlingham, *The Last Tiffany: A Biography of Dorothy Tiffany Burlingham* (New York: Atheneum, 1989).

91. Michael John Burlingham, interview with Nancy L. Segal, November 21, 2019.

92. Marty Babits, "Remember Anna Freud? A New Exhibit Brings Her Brilliance Into Focus." *Psychology Today*, May 15, 2017, https://www.psychology today.com/us/blog/the-middle-ground/201705/remember-anna-freud.

93. Interview with unnamed colleague by Nancy L. Segal, 2019.

94. Burlingham, interview with Nancy L. Segal, 2019.

95. Burlingham, *Twins*.

96. Elisabeth Young-Bruehl, *Anna Freud: A Biography* (New York: W.W. Norton & Co., 1988). Dorothy Burlingham to Anna Freud, November 15, 1939.

97. Michael John Burlingham, *The Last Tiffany: A Biography of Dorothy Tiffany Burlingham*.

98. "Some Notes Taken by Viola W. Bernard at Meeting with Mike Wallace at his Office, Monday, October 26, 1981." Viola W. Bernard Archives, Columbia University.

CHAPTER 3

1. "Doing it Better: The Twin Study, NYC—1960s," October 16, 2015, http://www.sdnews.com/view/full_story/26913001/article-DOING-IT-BETTER--The-Twin-Study--NYC---1960s?instance=update1.

2. "Analyzed Data," Yale University Archives, https://archives.yale.edu/repositories/12/top_containers/134627.

3. Nancy L. Segal, "A Possible Twin: The 1960s Twin Study Revisited." *Twin Research and Human Genetics* 21, no. 2 (2018): 155–62.

4. The twins' names have been disguised in the interest of privacy.

5. Lisa Banks is a pseudonym given to one of the twins in the interest of privacy.

6. Viola W. Bernard, interview with Lawrence Wright, 1993.

7. Viola W. Bernard, "Note for Records of Twins (or Triplets) Placed for Adoption Separately in Infancy." Spence-Chapin, December 18, 1978, courtesy of Sharon Morello; Viola W. Bernard, interview with Lawrence Wright, 1993.

8. Lawrence M. Perlman, "Memories of the Child Development Center study of Adopted Monozygotic Twins Reared Apart: An Unfulfilled Promise." *Twin Research and Human Genetics* 8, no. 3 (2005): 271–75.

9. Nancy L. Segal, *Born Together—Reared Apart: The Landmark Minnesota Twin Study* (Cambridge, MA: Harvard University Press, 2012),

10. The twins' names have been disguised in the interest of privacy.

11. Douglass W. Orr, "A Psychoanalytic Study of a Fraternal Twin." *The Psychoanalytic Quarterly* 10, no. 2 (1941): 284–96.

12. Nancy L. Segal, *Twin Mythconceptions: False Beliefs, Fables, and Facts About Twins* (New York: Elsevier, 2017).

13. Nancy L. Segal, "'Biracial'-Looking Twins: A New Twin Type?" *Twin Research and Human Genetics* 20, no. 3 (2017): 260–65.

14. National Forensic Science Technology Center, *A Simplified Guide to DNA Evidence*, 2013, http://www.forensicsciencesimplified.org/dna/principles.html. A DNA sample is usually obtained from saliva, from blood, or from a buccal smear, in which cells are obtained by gently rubbing the inner cheek with a special swab. Identical twins are assigned as such with 99.9 percent certainty, not 100 percent, because of the very remote chance that fraternal twins could independently inherit the same STRs.

15. Viola W. Bernard, interview with Larry Wright.

16. Ruth J. Loos, Catherine Derom, Robert Derom, and Robert Vlietinck, "Birthweight in Liveborn Twins: The Influence of the Umbilical Cord Insertion and Fusion of Placentas." *British Journal of Obstetrics and Gynaecology* 108, no. 9 (2001): 943–48. The chorion, the outer fetal membrane, forms at about day 7 of pregnancy.

17. Aaron R. Rausen, Masako Seki, and Lotte Strauss, "Twin Transfusion Syndrome: A Review of 19 Cases Studied at One Institution." *The Journal of Pediatrics* 66, no. 3 (1965): 613–28; Martin G. Bulmer, *The Biology of Twinning in Man* (Oxford: Oxford University Press, 1970).

18. Segal, *Twin Mythconceptions.*

19. David T. Lykken, "The Diagnosis of Zygosity in Twins." *Behavior Genetics* 8 no. 5 (1978): 437–73. Fifteen major blood groups had been identified by 1961, seventeen by 1965; Dariush D. Farhud and Marjan Zarif Yeganeh, "A Brief History of Human Blood Groups." *Iranian Journal of Public Health* 42, no. 1 (2013): 1–6.

20. Elinor W. Demarest and Muriel Chaves Winestine, "The Initial Phase of Concomitant Treatment of Twins." *The Psychoanalytic Study of the Child* 10, no. 1 (1955): 336–52.

21. Herbert J. Cronin, "An Analysis of the Neuroses of Identical Twins." *Psychoanalytic Review* 20 no. 4 (1933): 375–87. Note: The New York Psychoanalytic Society, founded in 1911, and the New York Psychoanalytic Institute, founded in 1931, merged in 2003 to form the New York Psychoanalytic Society and Institute (NYPSI). NYPSI, "New York Psychoanalytic Society and Institute: History," https://nypsi.org/history/, accessed July 2021.

22. Edward D. Joseph and Jack H. Tabor, "The Simultaneous Analysis of a Pair of Identical Twins and the Twinning Reaction." *The Psychoanalytic Study of the Child* 16, no. 1 (1961): 275–99.

23. Andrea K. Foy, Phillip A. Vernon, and Kerry Jang, "Examining the Dimensions of Intimacy in Twin and Peer Relationships." *Twin Research and Human Genetics* 4, no. 6 (2001): 443–52; Caroline M. Tancredy and R. Chris Fraley, "The Nature of Adult Twin Relationships: An Attachment-Theoretical Perspective." *Journal of Personality and Social Psychology* 90, no. 1 (2006): 78–93; Segal, *Twin Mythconceptions*.

24. Celia A. Brownell and Earnestine Brown, "Peers and Play in Infants and Toddlers." In *Handbook of Social Development: A Lifespan Perspective*, edited by Vincent B. Van Hasselt, 183–200 (Boston: Springer, 1992); Carol O. Eckerman and Karen Peterman, "Peers and Infant Social/Communicative Development." In *Blackwell Handbook of Infant Development*, edited by Gavin Bremner and Alan Fogelman, 326–50 (Malden: Blackwell, 2001).

25. T. Berry Brazelton, "It's Twins." *Redbook Magazine* 60 (1980): 83–84.

26. Peter B. Neubauer and Alexander Neubauer, *Nature's Thumbprint: The New Genetics of Personality* (New York: Addison-Wesley Publishing Co., 1990).

27. Janette Logan, "Birth Mothers and Their Mental Health: Uncharted Territory." *The British Journal of Social Work* 26, no. 5 (1996): 609–25.

28. Hedda Schacter Abbott, interview with Nancy L. Segal, 2019.

29. Mother of twins, interview with Nancy L. Segal, 2019.

30. Mother of a separated twin (requested anonymity), interview with Nancy L. Segal, 2019.

31. Viola W. Bernard, curriculum vitae, May 22, 1987. Abraham A. Brill Library, New York Psychoanalytic Society and Institute.

32. Florence Kreech, "An American Experience in Child Care Services." In *Social Work and Ethnicity*, edited by Juliet Cheetham, 112–21 (London: Gordon Allen & Unwin, 1982).

33. Ellen Herman, "Justine Wise Polier (1903-1987)," The Adoption History Project, Department of History, University of Oregon, https://pages.uoregon.edu/adoption/people/polier.html. But see chapter 2, footnote 10.

34. ROSS vs. Louise Wise Services Inc., 2007, https://caselaw.findlaw.com/ny-court-of-appeals/1280063.html.

35. ROSS vs. Louise Wise Services Inc.

36. Andy Tanenbaum, interview and email correspondence with Nancy L. Segal, 2018, 2019, 2020. Bernie's middle name was Sidney and many people, including Florence, called him "Sid." Bernie's son Edwin passed away in 2005 at age seventy-two.

37. Paula Kreech, interviews and email communication to Nancy L. Segal, 2018, 2019.

38. Viola W. Bernard, "Note for Records of Twins (or Triplets) Placed for Adoption Separately in Infancy." Spence-Chapin, December 18, 1978, courtesy of Sharon Morello.

39. Viola W. Bernard, letter from Florence Brown, Columbia University Archives and Special Collections.

40. Florence Kreech, memo to professional staff, March 4, 1971, Viola W. Bernard Archives, Columbia University Archives and Special Collections.

41. Mignon Krause, "Call From Dr. John Kliever," November 11, 1964; Viola W. Bernard, memo to Mignon Krause. December 16, 1964, Viola W. Bernard Archives, Columbia University.

42. Memo to Viola W. Bernard; likely source: Florence Kreech. December 2, 1964, Viola W. Bernard Archives, Columbia University.

43. Viola W. Bernard, letter to Dr. J. Winston Sapp. March 4, 1976; Florence Kreech, letter to Viola W. Bernard, March 17, 1976; Viola W. Bernard, letter to Florence Kreech, March 22, 1976, Viola W. Bernard Archives, Columbia University.

44. American Psychiatric Association, "Recent Deaths of APA Members Announced." *Psychiatric News*, May 16, 1997, https://psychnews.org/pnews/97-05-02/deaths.html.

45. Viola W. Bernard, letter to Dr. J. Winston Sapp, March 4, 1976, Viola W. Bernard Archives, Columbia University.

46. Samuel Abrams and Peter B. Neubauer, "Object Orientedness: The Person or the Thing." *The Psychoanalytic Quarterly* 45, no. 1 (1976): 73–99.

47. Former twin study assistant—anonymous, interview with Nancy L. Segal, 2019.

48. Thomas J. Bouchard Jr., "The Study of Mental Ability Using Twin and Adoption Designs." In *Twin Research 3: Part B. Intelligence, Personality, and Development*, edited by Luigi Gedda, Paolo Parisi, and Walter E. Nance, 21–23 (New York: Alan R. Liss, Inc., 1981); Elke D. Eckert, Leonard L. Heston, and Thomas J. Bouchard Jr., "MZ Twins Reared Apart: Preliminary Findings of Psychiatric Disturbances and Traits." In *Twin Research 3: Part B. Intelligence, Personality, and Development*, edited by Luigi Gedda, Paolo Parisi, and Walter E. Nance, 179–88 (New York: Alan R. Liss, Inc., 1981); Thomas J. Bouchard Jr., Leonard L. Heston, Elke D. Eckert, Margaret Keyes, and Susan Resnick, "The Minnesota Study of Twins Reared Apart: Project Description and Sample Results in the Development Domain." In *Twin Research 3: Part B. Intelligence, Personality and Development*, edited by Luigi Gedda, Paolo Parisi, and Walter E. Nance, 227–33 (New York: Alan R. Liss, Inc., 1981).

49. Sharon Morello, interview with Nancy L. Segal, 2019.

50. Viola W. Bernard, interview with Larry Wright.

51. "Staff Meeting of Adoption Department," January 20, 1964, Viola W. Bernard Archives, Columbia University.

52. Eliot Slater and A. W. Beard, "The Schizophrenia-Like Psychoses of Epilepsy: I. Psychiatric Aspects." *The British Journal of Psychiatry* 109, no. 458 (1963): 95–112.

53. Jessica Resnick, "Franz Kallman (1987-1956)." *The Embryo Project Encyclopedia*, https://embryo.asu.edu/pages/franz-josef-kallmann-1897-1965.

54. Franz J. Kallman, "The Genetic Theory of Schizophrenia." *American Journal of Psychiatry* 103, no. 3 (1946): 309–22. Kallman's twin similarity rates may be too high, given that he sampled his cases from a hospital residence and applied a broad characterization of the disorder. Nevertheless, a genetic risk for the disorder was demonstrated. Also see David Rosenthal, *Genetics of Psychopathology* (New York: McGraw-Hill Book Co., 1971).

55. Viola W. Bernard, "Memo to Morton Rogers," January 30, 1985, Viola W. Bernard, Columbia University Archives and Special Collections, November 30, 1961.

56. Niki Erlenmeyer-Kimling, interview with Nancy L. Segal, 2019.

57. David E. Sobel, letter to Viola W. Bernard, Viola W. Bernard Archives, Columbia University Archives and Special Collections, November 30, 1961.

58. Adoption Committee Minutes, October 11, 1960, Viola W. Bernard Archives, Columbia University.

59. The JCCA continues to offer support to children and families in need. Adoptive homes are found for children who cannot return safely to their families; https://www.jccany.org/our-programs/foster-care/csnyc/.

60. Henry Nunberg, interview with Nancy L. Segal, May 2, 2019.

61. Andrew L. Yarrow, interview and email correspondence with Nancy L. Segal, 2019.

62. Caroline A. Chandler, Reginald S. Lourie, Anne DeHuff Peters, and Laura L. Dittman (eds.), *Early Child Care: New Perspectives* (New York: Atherton Press, 1968).

63. Leon J. Yarrow, "Theoretical Implications of Adoption Research." *Child Welfare* 44, no. 2 (1965): 65–72.

64. US Department of Health, Education, and Welfare, *Research Grants Index*, 2, 1656 (Bethesda, MD: NIMH, 1965).

65. National Institutes of Health, "Eunice Kennedy Shriver National Institute of Child Health and Human Development (NICHD)," *The NIH Almanac*, June 19, 2018, https://www.nih.gov/about-nih/what-we-do/nih-almanac/eunice-kennedy-shriver-national-institute-child-health-human-development-nichd#director.

66. NICHD Information Resource Center, Communication September 26, 2019.

67. Barry Coburn, presentation at *The Twinning Reaction: Science and Deception*, University of Virginia Law School, Charlottesville, VA, March 29, 2019; Adam M. Kelmenson, interview with Nancy L. Segal, 2019.

68. A grant from the National Institute of Mental Health was awarded in 1971 to University of California, Los Angeles, researchers for studying Genie, the "wild child." The grant was not renewed in 1975, due to poor organization and lack of results; see Susan Donaldson James, "Wild Child Speechless After Tortured Life." *ABC News*, May 15, 2008, https://abcnews.go.com/Health/story?id=4804490&page=1.

69. Vivian S. Goldman, Catherine E. Harris, Jean M. Johnson, William H. Trayfors, and Cynthia A. Wiggins, *Research Relating to Children*, 17 (Washington, DC: Welfare Administration: Children's Bureau, 1963–1964), 8-U-29, 155. This bulletin included recently completed research and research in progress. It attempted to be comprehensive, but also relied on information from submitted abstracts.

70. A therapeutic nursery is designed to help preschool children who face behavioral challenges. Children's Crisis Treatment Center, "Therapeutic Nursery," 2019, http://cctckids.org/programs-services/at-our-center/therapeutic-nursery/.

71. Goldman, Harris, Johnson, Trayfors, and Wiggins, *Research Relating to Children*.

72. Florence Brown, letter to Viola Bernard, March 2, 1965, Viola W. Bernard Archives, Columbia University.

73. Adoption Study Records of the Child Development Center, Yale University Archives, https://archives.yale.edu/repositories/12/resources/3434.

74. Samuel Abrams, "Disposition and the Environment." *The Psychoanalytic Study of the Child* 41, no. 1 (1986): 41–60.

75. Wolfgang Saxon, "Philip A. Straus, 88, Financier and Patron of Art and Education." *New York Times*, Section A, February 13, 2004, 17.

76. Lynn Straus, interview with Nancy L. Segal, 2020; Philip A. Straus Jr., email correspondence with Nancy L. Segal, 2020; "Miss Lynn Gross Married July 17." *Scarsdale Inquirer* XXXI no. 30 (29 July 1949), 5.

77. Big Online. "Philip & Lynn Straus Foundation, Inc.," http://www.bigdatabase.com/Big-DB/USFoundation-profiles/PHILIP%20&%20LYNN%20STRAUS%20FOUNDATION%20INC-136161223.HTML.

78. Jewish Board of Family and Children's Services, "Annual Report of 08," https://jewishboard.org/wp-content/uploads/2016/02/jb_report_2008.pdf. According to former assistant Larry Perlman, the LWS-CDC twin study had received a donation from an anonymous donor who was a twin; see Perlman (2005), note 8.

79. Dr. Susannah Falk Lewis, interview with Nancy L. Segal, 2019.

80. Samuel Abrams, interview with Lawrence Wright, 1993.

81. Abrams, interview with Lawrence Wright.

82. Segal, *Twin Mythconceptions*.

83. In classic usage, drive would refer to a need behind a behavior expressed to reduce tension. For example, thirst propels an individual to drink. See *Encyclopedia Britannica*, "Drive: Behaviour," https://www.britannica.com/topic/drive.

84. *New York Times*, "Samuel Abrams, M.D.," September 19, 2016, https://www.legacy.com/obituaries/nytimes/obituary.aspx?n=samuel-abrams&pid=181453648. When Neubauer passed away in 2008, Abrams's acknowledgment of Neubauer's work in Neubauer's *New York Times* obituary didn't mention the twin study either; see Jeremy Pearce, "Peter B. Neubauer, 94, Noted Child Psychiatrist, Is Dead." *New York Times*, March 3, 2008, https://www.nytimes

.com/2008/03/03/nyregion/03neubauer.html. The Hampstead Clinic is now the Anna Freud International Center for Children.

85. Kimberly J. Saudino, Stacey S. Cherney, and Robert Plomin, "Parent Ratings of Temperament in Twins: Explaining the 'Too Low' DZ Correlations." *Twin Research and Human Genetics* 3, no. 4 (2000): 224–33.

86. Perlman, "Memories of the Child Development Center Study of Adopted Monozygotic Twins Reared Apart."

87. Former twin study assistant—anonymous, interview with Nancy L. Segal, 2019.

88. Projective tests assume that people have both unconscious and conscious motivations, attitudes, and needs. The Thematic Apperception Test asks subjects to analyze a series of scenes. The Rorschach Test asks subjects to interpret a series of inkblots. The Bender-Gestalt Test asks subjects to reproduce a series of drawings; this test is used to diagnose brain injury and behavioral disturbances, but has also been used projectively to assess various aspects of personality. Wisestep, "Projective Tests," https://content.wisestep.com/projective-tests-theory-types-advantages-disadvantages/; *Gale Encyclopedia of Medicine,* "Bender-Gestalt Test," September 11, 2019, https://www.encyclopedia.com/medicine/division-diagnostics-and-procedures/medicine/bender-gestalt-test; Max L. Hutt, "The Projective Use of the Bender-Gestalt Test." In *Projective Techniques in Personality Assessment,* edited by Albert I. Rábín, 397–420 (Berlin, Heidelberg: Springer, 1968).

89. Julie Edwards and Bill Edwards, interviews with Nancy L. Segal, 2004; Perlman, "Memories of the Child Development Center Study of Adopted Monozygotic Twins Reared Apart."

CHAPTER 4

1. Nancy L. Segal, *Someone Else's Twins: The True Story of Babies Switched at Birth* (Amherst, NY: Prometheus Books, 2011).

2. The Pepsi Company was one of several sponsors of the congress.

3. Viola W. Bernard, memo to colleagues, presumably to executive director at that time, Mr. Morton Roger, and Dr. Peter Neubauer, regarding twin placements. This memo resulted from Mike Wallace's efforts to produce a segment about the LWS twins for *60 Minutes.* More will be said about this segment in a subsequent chapter. Viola W. Bernard Archives, Columbia University (Box 76: 4, September 19, 1982). Twins placed together by LWS have never come forth.

4. Susan J., interview with Nancy L. Segal, 2012.

5. Viola W. Bernard, memo to colleagues (Box 76: 4, September 19, 1982). In her last sentence, she states that withholding knowledge of an infant's multiple birth status from adoptive parents "was in accordance with general adoptive

practice." This only suggests that the confidentiality of any information about the biological family was paramount. It does not indicate that agencies followed an established procedure regarding twins and triplets. However, "selective" information about the biological family was sometimes provided to the adoptive family such as the birth mother's artistic inclinations, as told to me in regard to a particular case. This was apparently done at the discretion of the LWS social workers or other staff members; see Viola W. Bernard (this reference); unnamed source, interview with Nancy L. Segal, 2019.

6. Martin Bryant, "20 Years Ago Today the World Wide Web Opened to the Public." August 6, 2011, https://thenextweb.com/insider/2011/08/06/20-years-ago-today-the-world-wide-web-opened-to-the-public/.

7. Edwin Chen, "Twins Reared Apart: A Living Lab." *New York Times*, December 9, 1979, 14, 16, 18, 22, 26, 112, 120. Constance Holden, "Twins Reunited: More Than the Faces Are Familiar." *Science* 80, no. 1 (1980); Donald D. Johnson, "Reunion of Identical Twin Raised Apart, Reveals Some Astonishing Similarities." *Smithsonian* (October 1980): 48–56.

8. Susan J., interview with Nancy L. Segal, 2012.

9. Thomas J. Bouchard Jr., interview with Nancy L. Segal, November 14, 2019.

10. Arthur Sorosky, Annette Baron, and Reuben Panor, *The Adoption Triangle: Sealed or Open Records: How They Affect Adoptees, Birth Parents, and Adoptive Parents* (New York: Doubleday, 1984).

11. Barbara Miller, memo to Morton S. Rogers and Viola W. Bernard, August 11, 1982. Columbia University Archives (Box 76: 4, September 19, 1982).

12. Susan J., interview with Nancy L. Segal, 2012.

13. Stephen Wise Tulin is an attorney and the son of Justine Polier and her first husband Arthur Tulin. He was involved in various litigation with LWS during the 1960s to 1990s. He also served as Secretary-Treasurer of Dr. Bernard's Tappanz Foundation for forty years and was on the Board of Directors of the Tappanz Foundation and its successor, the Viola W. Bernard Foundation, from approximately 1972 to 2016 when the latter disbanded; Stephen W. Tulin, interview and correspondence with Nancy L. Segal, 2019, 2020; Eric Brettschneider, interview with Nancy L. Segal, 2019.

14. Barbara Miller, memo to Morton S. Rogers and Viola W. Bernard, August 11, 1982, Columbia University Archives (Box 76: 4, September 19, 1982).

15. Susan J., interview with Nancy L. Segal, 2019.

16. Barbara Miller, memo to Morton S. Rogers and Viola W. Bernard, August 11, 1982, Columbia University Archives (Box 76: 4, September 19, 1982).

17. Susan J., interviews with Nancy L. Segal, 2012, 2018.

18. Drew N., interview with Nancy L. Segal, 2018.

19. Kelly: transcript of a message from Barbara Miller of LWS, August 6, 1982, Viola W. Bernard Archives, Columbia University.

20. Ilene, telephone call with Nancy L. Segal, 2019.

21. Susan J., interview with Nancy L. Segal, 2012, 2018.

22. Memo: "Sixty Minutes Program," August 16, 1982, Viola W. Bernard Archives, Columbia University (Box 76: 4).

23. Nancy L. Segal, Scott L. Hershberger, and Sara Arad, "Meeting One's Twin: Perceived Social Closeness and Familiarity." *Evolutionary Psychology* 1, no. 1 (2003): 70–95.

24. Elyse Schein and Paula Bernstein, *Identical Strangers: A Memoir of Twins Separated and Reunited* (New York: Random House, 2007); Nancy L. Segal, Scott L. Hershberger, and Sara Arad, "Meeting One's Twin: Perceived Social Closeness and Familiarity."

25. Nancy L. Segal, *Born Together—Reared Apart: The Landmark Minnesota Twin Study* (Cambridge: Harvard University Press, 2012).

26. Susan J., interview with Nancy L. Segal, 2012.

27. Susan J., interview with Nancy L. Segal, 2019.

28. Telephone call to Nancy L. Segal from Tim M., 2019.

29. Neither twin wished to participate. The information in this chapter comes from interviews with Tim's former wife Susan, Tim and Susan's son Drew, archival material at Columbia University, and my contact with the twins prior to their decision to decline.

30. Barbara Gonyo, "Genetic Sexual Attraction." *Decree* 4 no. 2 (Washington, DC: American Adoption Congress, Winter 1987): 1, 5.

31. Martha Beasley, "Sibling Shocker: After 30 Years of Marriage, Couple Discover They're Brother and Sister." *Sun* 8, no. 18 (May 1, 1990): 23.

32. *Daily Mail*, "Heartbreak of Married Twins," August 23, 1997.

33. Diane Amery, "Couple Wed 20 Years Discover They're Twins." *Sun* 3, no. 51 (December 17, 1985): 19.

34. Thomas McMillan, "Newlyweds Learn They Are Brother and Sister!" *Weekly World News* 7, no. 17 (February 4, 1986).

35. Associated Press, "Twins Separated at Birth Meet, Get Married," January 11, 2008, http://www.msnbc.msn.com/id/22612314/?gt1=10755.

36. Lord David Alton of Liverpool, email correspondence with Nancy L. Segal, November 21, 2019.

37. Fiona Barton, "Shock for the Married Couple Who Discovered They Are Twins Separated at Birth," January 11, 2008, https://www.dailymail.co.uk/news/article-507588/Shock-married-couple-discovered-twins-separated-birth.html.

38. Dr. Neville Cobbe, email correspondence with Nancy L. Segal, November 27, 2019; House of Lords Debates, "Official Report." 698, part no. 45 (2008): column 904.

39. Lord Bethell, "In Vitro Fertilisation: Questions for Department of Health and Social Care," September 22, 2020, https://questions-statements.parliament.uk/written-questions/detail/2020-09-14/hl8042.

40. Children resulting from the union of full siblings have a 25 percent chance of inheriting two copies of the same detrimental recessive gene if each of their

parents carries that gene in a single form. Examples of such conditions are hemo-chromatosis (excess iron absorption) and sickle cell anemia (red blood cell dis-order); also see footnote 47. Individuals with just one copy of the relevant gene are called carriers and are unaffected. Everyone carries single copies of various unfavorable gene forms.

41. Matt Ridley, *The Red Queen: Sex and The Evolution of Human Nature* (New York: Penguin Books, 1993); Debra Lieberman, John Tooby, and Leda Cosmides, "The Architecture of Human Kin Detection." *Nature* 445, no. 7129 (2007): 727–31.

42. Valerie S. Knopik, Jenae M. Neiderhiser, John C. DeFries, and Robert Plomin, *Behavioral Genetics*, seventh edition (New York: Worth Publishers, 2017). Interestingly, positive assortment is greater for behavioral traits than for physical traits; see Nancy L. Segal, Brittney A. Hernandez, Jamie L. Graham, and Ulrich Ettinger, "Pairs of Genetically Unrelated Look-Alikes." *Human Nature* 29, no. 4 (2018): 402–17, and references therein.

43. Dante Cicchetti, "Development and Psychopathology." In *Developmental Psychopathology*, edited by Dante Cicchetti and Donald J. Cohen, 1, second edition, 1–23 (New York: Wiley, 2006); Ville-Juhani Ilmarinen, Mari-Pauliina Vainikainen, Markku Johannes Verkasalo, and Jan-Erik Lönnqvist, "Homophilous Friendship Assortment Based on Personality Traits and Cognitive Ability in Middle Childhood: The Moderating Effect of Peer Network Size." *European Journal of Personality* 31, no. 3 (2017): 208–19.

44. Philippe J. Rushton and Trudy Ann Bons, "Mate Choice and Friendship in Twins: Evidence for Genetic Similarity." *Psychological Science* 16, no. 7 (2005): 555–59.

45. Segal, *Born Together—Reared Apart;* also see references therein.

46. Eli Badan-Lasar and Susan Dominus, "A Family Portrait: Brothers, Sisters, Strangers." *New York Times*, June 26, 2019, 31–51 (photographs); 52–54 (essay).

47. Knopik, Neiderhiser, DeFries, and Plomin, *Behavioral Genetics*. Phenylketonuria, Tay-Sachs disease, and cystic fibrosis are examples of medical conditions that are expressed when individuals inherit two copies of a recessive detrimental gene, one from each parent. There is a 50 percent chance that a common parent transmits a particular gene to a half-brother, a 50 percent chance that the gene is also transmitted to a half-sister, and a 25 percent chance that the same two genes are transmitted to their child: $(.50)(.50)(.25) = 6.25$ percent. Considering parental transmission of the same gene to half-siblings, a child conceived by half-siblings has a 6.25 percent chance of being affected. See also note 49.

48. Rosanna Hertz, Margaret K. Nelson, and Wendy Kramer, "Donor Sibling Networks as a Vehicle for Expanding Kinship: A Replication and Extension." *Journal of Family Issues* 38, no. 2 (2017): 248–84.

49. Jean-Louis Serre, Anne-Louise Leutenegger, Alain Bernheim, Marc Fellous, Alexandre Rouen, and Jean-Pierre Siffroi, "Does Anonymous Sperm Donation Increase the Risk for Unions Between Relatives and the Incidence of Autosomal

Recessive Diseases Due to Consanguinity?" *Human Reproduction* 29, no. 3 (2013): 394–99. It is estimated in France that 1.2 half-sibling unions would occur every ten years and that their children account for 0.01 percent of genetic recessive diseases in that nation. See also note 47.

50. Brenda Galland, wife of Eddy Galland who ended his life at age thirty-eight years. *Three Identical Strangers* (London, UK: Raw Documentary, 2018).

CHAPTER 5

1. Kathy Jo Mazlish, letter to Bruce Mayo, 1991.
2. Liz Mazlish, interview with Nancy L. Segal, 2019.
3. Viola W. Bernard, "Board Meeting." January 3, 1962. Handwritten note, Viola W. Bernard Archives, Columbia University.
4. LWS's 1960 policy of placing separated twins with families that had an older child may have been a more important requirement for the identical twins who were in the study. Fraternal twins like Kathy and Betsy were not studied and were placed prior to 1960.
5. L. Mazlish, interview with Nancy L. Segal, 2019.
6. Adele Faber and Elaine Mazlish, *Liberated Parents, Liberated Children* (New York: Avon Books, 1975); Adele Faber and Elaine Mazlish, *How to Talk So Kids Will Listen & Listen So Kids Will Talk* (New York: Avon, 1982); Adele Faber and Elaine Mazlish, *Siblings Without Rivalry* (New York: W.W. Norton & Co., 1987). The dates listed here are the original printings; these books were reprinted subsequently, most recently in 2004.
7. L. Mazlish, interview with Nancy L. Segal, 2019.
8. Letter to Kathy Jo Mazlish, from Spence-Chapin, March 10, 2008. Courtesy of Liz Mazlish. Kathy had dark brown eyes as an adult, but most non-Hispanic Caucasian babies are born with blue eyes that darken over the first three years; Burt Dubow, "Eye Color: Why It Develops and Why It Changes." *All About Vision*, 2020, https://www.allaboutvision.com/conditions/eye-color.htm, 2020.
9. "Edith Leon in Verona, NJ." Spokeo.com. Email communication from Liz Mazlish, December 26, 2019.
10. Letter to Kathy Jo Mazlish, from Spence-Chapin, March 10, 2008. Courtesy of Liz Mazlish.
11. Unnamed source, Nancy L. Segal, 2019.
12. "Governor Cuomo Signs Legislation Allowing Adoptees to Receive a Certified Birth Certificate at Age 18," https://www.governor.ny.gov/news/governor-cuomo-signs-legislation-allowing-adoptees-receive-certified-birth-certificate-age-18.

13. The name Ruth Crain was listed first in the New York Public Library records where birth certificates are stored. Kathy was the first-born twin, so it is likely that her first given name was Ruth.

14. Ulla Sankilampi, Marja-Leena Hannila, Antti Saari, Mika Gissler, and Leo Dunkel, "New Population-Based References for Birth Weight, Length, and Head Circumference in Singletons and Twins From 23 to 43 Gestation Weeks." *Annals of Medicine* 45, no. 5-6 (2013): 446–54.

15. The letter from Spence-Chapin indicates that the twins' birth mother was "surprised and delighted" by the birth of her babies. It is unknown whether a multiple pregnancy had been diagnosed in advance of her delivery.

16. Letter to Kathy Jo Mazlish, from Spence-Chapin, March 10, 2008. Courtesy of Liz Mazlish.

17. Letter to Kathy Jo Mazlish, from Spence-Chapin.

18. Bruce Mayo, email correspondence to Nancy L. Segal, 2019.

19. Letter to Kathy Jo Mazlish, from Spence-Chapin.

20. Michele Mordkoff, interview with Nancy L. Segal, 2019. Michele's birth mother was not given a choice; she was told that her twins would be separated.

21. Hedda Schacter Abbott, interview with Nancy L. Segal, 2019.

22. Letter to Kathy Jo Mazlish, from Spence-Chapin.

23. L. Mazlish, interview with Nancy L. Segal, 2019. Kathy had had her DNA analyzed with 23andme. Steven did, as well, and the results showed that Kathy and Steven were half-siblings. Steven is a fictitious name, used to protect the half-brother's privacy.

24. L. Mazlish, interview with Nancy L. Segal, 2019.

25. "Overview: Coeliac Disease," December 4, 2016, https://www.nhs.uk/conditions/coeliac-disease/. Coeliac disease differs from colic in which infants cry and may bring their knees to their tummy. It usually stops by six months of age. The cause of colic is unknown, but may result from digestive difficulties. "Colic," November 9, 2018, https://www.nhs.uk/conditions/colic/.

26. LWS document signed by adoptive parents upon receipt of a child from LWS. One line reads, "We have the right to return the child to LOUISE WISE SERVICES if, for any reason, we decide that we should not, or that we cannot keep the child." Source: Ellen Carbone, LWS separated twin.

27. Nancy L. Segal, *Twin Mythconceptions: False Beliefs, Fables, and Facts About Twins* (New York: Elsevier, 2017).

28. Betsy Caren Leon, state-issued New Jersey death certificate, US Social Security Death Index (SSDI).

29. Forgotten New York, "Meatpacking District, Manhattan," February 10, 2006, https://forgotten-ny.com/2006/02/meatpacking-district-manhattan/; Dana Schulz, "The Urban Lens: Travel Back to the Gritty Meatpacking District of the '80s and '90s," May 12, 2017, https://www.6sqft.com/the-urban-lens-travel-back-to-the-gritty-meatpacking-district-of-the-80s-and-90s.

30. Individuals who knew Betsy.

31. Mayo, email correspondence to Liz Mazlish, 2020. The poetry magazine was run by a friend in the day treatment program that Kathy later attended.

32. Individuals who knew Betsy.

33. Mayo, interviews with Nancy L. Segal, 2019; Elaine Mazlish as told to Liz; individuals who knew Betsy.

34. Mayo, interviews and email correspondence with Nancy L. Segal, 2019, 2020; individuals who knew Betsy.

35. John Mazlish; Liz Mazlish, interviews with Nancy L. Segal, 2019.

36. L. Mazlish, interview with Nancy L. Segal, 2019.

37. L. Mazlish, interview with Nancy L. Segal, 2019.

38. "Haim G. Ginott, Quotes." Goodreads, Inc., 2020, https://www.goodreads .com/author/quotes/212291.Haim_G_Ginott; also see Ginott, *Between Parent and Child* (London: Macmillan & Co. Ltd., 1961).

39. L. Mazlish, interview with Nancy L. Segal, 2019.

40. Mayo, email correspondence to Nancy L. Segal, 2019; Liz Mazlish, interview with Nancy L. Segal, 2019.

41. Mayo, email correspondence to Nancy L. Segal, 2019.

42. Mayo, interview with Nancy L. Segal, 2019; letter from Kathy to Bruce, circa 1992.

43. ALMA, http://almasociety.org/.

44. Florence Fisher, *The Search for Anna Fisher* (New York: A. Fields Books, 1973).

45. Letter from Kathy to Bruce Mayo, circa 1982–1983. Courtesy, Bruce Mayo.

46. Mayo, email correspondence, 2019. Kathy shared this information with Bruce Mayo on several occasions, but was unsure of the details.

47. Nancy L. Segal, *Born Together—Reared Apart: The Landmark Minnesota Twin Study* (Cambridge: Harvard University Press, 2012); Nancy L. Segal and Yesika S. Montoya, *Accidental Brothers: The Story of Twins Exchanged at Birth and the Power of Nature and Nurture* (New York: St. Martin's Press, 2018).

48. Segal, *Twin Mythconceptions*. Physical resemblance questionnaires have been designed to show high agreement with results from DNA testing and blood group analyses.

49. Relatives and friends of the twins. Multiple sources, 2019, 2020.

50. Nancy L. Segal, "Zygosity Diagnosis: Laboratory and Investigator's Judgment." *Acta Geneticae Medicae et Gemellologiae: Twin Research* 33 no. 3 (1984): 515–20.

51. Mayo, interview with Nancy L. Segal, 2019. Bruce is fairly certain that Madeline Amgott was the producer; his recollection was confirmed by Amgott's son, Seth, over the course of two interviews with me in 2019.

52. Mayo, interview and email correspondence with Nancy L. Segal, 2019, 2020.

53. L. Mazlish, interview with Nancy L. Segal; unnamed relatives. The twins' birth father was placed in a cast for eight months on a wooden plank with weights; it was the 1930s.

54. Robert T. Sataloff, "Genetics of the Voice." *Journal of Voice* 9, no. 1 (1995): 16–19.

55. Edwik Kiester Jr., "Accents Are Forever." *Smithsonian Magazine*, January 2001, https://www.smithsonianmag.com/science-nature/accents-are-forever-35886605/; Caroline Floccia, Claire Delle Luche, Samantha Durrant, Joseph Butler, and Jeremy Goslin, "Parent or Community: Where Do 20-Month-Olds Exposed to Two Accents Acquire Their Representation of Words?" *Cognition* 124, no. 1 (2012): 95–100.

56. L. Mazlish, interview with Nancy L. Segal, 2019.

57. Patrick F. Sullivan, Kenneth S. Kendler, and Michael C. Neale, "Schizophrenia as a Complex Trait: Evidence From a Meta-Analysis of Twin Studies." *Archives of General Psychiatry* 60, no. 12 (2003): 1187–92.

58. Valerie S. Knopik, Jenae M. Neiderhiser, John C. DeFries, and Robert Plomin, *Behavioral Genetics*, seventh edition (New York: Worth Publishers, 2017).

59. Mayo, interview with Nancy L. Segal, 2019.

60. Mayo, interview with Nancy L. Segal, 2019.

61. L. Mazlish, interview with Nancy L. Segal, 2019.

62. Segal, *Born Together—Reared Apart.*

63. L. Mazlish, interview with Nancy L. Segal, 2019.

64. Elaine Mazlish, as told to Liz Mazlish, interview with Nancy L. Segal, 2019.

65. Individuals who knew Betsy, 2020.

66. Matthew K. Nock, Irving Hwang, Nancy A. Sampson, and Ronald C. Kessler, "Mental Disorders Comorbidity and Suicidal Behavior: Results from the National Comorbidity Survey Replication." *Molecular Psychiatry* 15, no. 8 (2010): 868–76; Martin Voracek and Lisa Mariella Loibl, "Genetics of Suicide: A Systematic Review of Twin Studies." *Wiener Klinische Wochenschrift* 119, no. 15–16 (2007): 463–75.

67. Kathy Jo Mazlish, letter to Bruce Mayo, undated, but circa 1982–1983.

68. Mayo, email correspondence to Nancy L. Segal, 2019.

69. Viola W. Bernard, "Memorandum: Possible Wallace/Rather CBS Broadcasts on Twins," Viola W. Bernard Archives, Columbia University.

70. Florence Fisher, interview with Nancy L. Segal, 2019.

71. L. Mazlish, interview with Nancy L. Segal, 2019.

72. Lori Shinseki, email correspondence to Nancy L. Segal, 2020.

73. Lori Shinseki, text message to Nancy L. Segal, 2019; L. Mazlish, interview with Nancy L. Segal, 2020.

74. Mayo, email correspondence to Liz Mazlish, 2020.

75. Kathy Mazish, letter to Bruce Mayo, undated.

76. Kathy Mazish, letter to Bruce Mayo, undated.

77. According to her sister Liz, Bruce said that Kathy changed her name to Katherine to sound less like a little girl.

78. Elyse Schein and Paula Bernstein, *Identical Strangers: A Memoir of Twins Separated and Reunited* (New York: Random House, 2007).

79. J. Mazlish, email correspondence to Nancy L. Segal and Liz Mazlish, 2020.

80. Obituary, Katherine Jo Mazlish, Riverside-Nassau North Chapels, https://www.dignitymemorial.com/obituaries/great-neck-ny/katherine-mazlish -7750100.

81. L. Mazlish, interview with Nancy L. Segal, 2019.

82. L. Mazlish, letter to Bruce Mayo, undated.

83. Cecilia Tomassini, Knud Juel, Niels V. Holm, Axel Skytthe, and Kaare Christensen, "Risk of Suicide in Twins: 51 Year Follow Up Study." *British Medical Journal* 327, no. 7411 (2003): 373–74.

84. Kristin C. Doney, Thomas Chauncey, and Frederick R. Appelbaum, "Allogeneic Related Donor Hematopoietic Stem Cell Transplantation for Treatment of Chronic Lymphocytic Leukemia." *Bone Marrow Transplantation* 29, no. 10 (2002): 817–23.

85. Amazon.com, "Mike Wallace Is Here," https://www.amazon.com/Mike -Wallace-Here/dp/B07VCMLR7Q.

86. In addition to the 382 boxes, the collection includes five oversize boxes and three folders. It spans 129.65 cubic feet. Viola W. Bernard Papers, Columbia University, https://www.library-archives.cumc.columbia.edu/finding-aid/ viola-wertheim-bernard-papers-1918-2000.

CHAPTER 6

1. "Note RE: Calls from Madeline Amgott of CBS News to Dr. Bernard, May 15, 1981," Viola W. Bernard Archives, Columbia University.

2. It is likely that this program was part of Walter Cronkite's science series, *Universe*. The series began in 1980 but was cancelled in 1982. Sally Bedell, "'Cronkite's *Universe*' Is Cancelled." *New York Times*, August 12, 1982, C27.

3. "Some Notes Taken by Viola W. Bernard at Meeting with Mike Wallace at his Office, Monday, October 26, 1981," Viola W. Bernard Archives, Columbia University. Dr. Holly Atkinson is currently an assistant clinical professor in the Department of Medical Education at the Ichan School of Medicine, at Mt. Sinai Hospital in New York. She has been a medical correspondent for CBS, NBC, and PBS. "Holly Atkinson," https://www.leadingauthorities.com/speakers/holly-atkinson. Dr. Atkinson did not respond to several telephone and email requests for an interview.

4. Letter from Viola Bernard to Morton Rogers, July 30, 1981, Viola W. Bernard Archives, Columbia University.

5. Ellen Herman, "Justine Wise Polier (1903-1987)." The Adoption History Project, 2012, https://pages.uoregon.edu/adoption/people/polier.html; also see footnote 6 (Frey).

6. Debra Bradley Ruder, interview with Nancy L. Segal, 2019. Ruder, who examined her grandmother's papers, donated by Polier to the Schlesinger Library at Radcliffe's Institute for Advance Study at Harvard University, has no recollection of seeing twin-related materials. This was confirmed by a Schlesinger librarian who indicated, "I do not see any reference to twins or a twin study in the Papers of Justine Wise Polier MC 413." The finding aid to the collection lists "Adoptions, 1973-1979," correspondence with Dr. Viola Bernard, and LWS various documents (including 1980 correspondence and history) that might have twin-related material. The pandemic prevented my planned visit to the library in April 2020 and library policy gave priority to requests from Harvard University faculty, staff, and students in 2020 and 2021. However, in April 2021 I received Bernard's correspondence with Polier and other documents from Polier's collection. None of these materials referenced the twin study.

7. Stephanie C. Frey, secretary, "Minutes: The Board of Directors," October 6, 1982, Viola W. Bernard Archives, Columbia University; Note from "Guy," most likely a secretary, to Dr. Bernard, May 20, 1981. Viola W. Bernard Archives, Columbia University. Guy is the individual who referred to the situation as the "CBS Affair."

8. Viola W. Bernard, transcript of post-interview conversation with Justine W. Polier, May 20, 1981, Viola W. Bernard Archives, Columbia University.

9. Viola W. Bernard, "Initial Memo Upon Receiving from Mr. Rogers a Copy of Mike Wallace's Letter of September 14, 1982, to Him," September 15–16, 1982, Viola W. Bernard Archives, Columbia University.

10. Note from "Guy," most likely a secretary, to Dr. Bernard, May 20, 1981. Viola W. Bernard Archives, Columbia University.

11. Note from "Guy."

12. Viola W. Bernard, "Explanatory Statement for Use by Public-Relations Consultant in Preparing a Reaction to CBS News Program About LWS-CDC Twin Placement and Research," March 22, 1982, Viola W. Bernard Archives, Columbia University. This document was marked "CONFIDENTIAL: NOT FOR CIRCULATION."

13. Bernard, "Explanatory Statement for Use by Public-Relations Consultant in Preparing a Reaction to CBS News Program About LWS-CDC Twin Placement and Research."

14. Jack Solomon, letter to CBS. June 12, 1981. "*Universe*-General-1981," Box 2M665. Walter Cronkite Collection, University of Texas, Austin. The letter bears Dr. Thomas J. Bouchard Jr.'s handwritten note at the top: "FYI Original to Jon Ward 6/16." Bouchard cannot recall Ward's identity, but Ward may have been a producer and/or photographer interested in the subject.

15. Letter from Viola Bernard to Morton Rogers, July 30, 1981, Viola W. Bernard Archives, Columbia University. The show aired at a date later than August 13.

16. "Twins," *Walter Cronkite's Universe, III* (11). August 31, 1982, University of Rochester Library.

17. Letter from Viola Bernard to Morton Rogers, July 30, 1981, Viola W. Bernard Archives, Columbia University. The show aired at a date later than August 13.

18. Telephone message for Viola Bernard from Mrs. Solo at the Jewish Board, October 21, 1981. Dr. Neubauer called to say that Mike Wallace wanted to set up a meeting, October 6, 1982, Viola W. Bernard Archives, Columbia University.

19. "Some Notes Taken by Viola W. Bernard at Meeting with Mike Wallace at his Office, Monday, October 26, 1981," Viola W. Bernard Archives, Columbia University.

20. Sir Cyril Burt of Great Britain published several papers reporting the results of IQ resemblance in reared-apart twins (1943–1966), yielding consistent correlations of .771. These unusual findings were exposed in 1974 by Princeton University professor Leon Kamin who, along with many others, considered them suspect. It has generally been concluded that Burt's data were not fraudulent—possibly a function of clerical error, although suspicions linger among some. Burt's research is no longer cited in the psychological literature; see Segal (2012; note 39) and references therein.

21. "Some Notes Taken by Viola W. Bernard at Meeting with Mike Wallace at his Office, Monday, October 26, 1981." C1 and C2 indicate Child-1 and Child-2, respectively.

22. Wendy Doniger, "What Did They Name the Dog?" *London Review of Books* 20, no. 6 (March 19, 1998); Peter Neubauer, "Letters." *London Review of Books* 20, no. 9 (May 7, 1998).

23. Saul Z. Cohen, "Meeting with Mike Wallace on Monday, October 26, 1981," October 30, 1981, Viola W. Bernard Archives, Columbia University.

24. Sheldon Fogelman Agency, Inc., 2006, http://sheldonfogelmanagency .com/.

25. Sheldon Fogelman, interview with Nancy L. Segal, 2019.

26. Saul Z. Cohen and Sheldon Fogelman, letter to Mike Wallace, November 16, 1981. Fogelman is listed as president of LWS. "Officers of the Board," January 1985, and "Board of Directors," July 1985 lists Fogelman as president; "Officers of the Board," December 2, 1985, lists Fogelman as president and chair, Executive Committee; a handwritten note on that pages reads, "for 85-86." A later document, "Officers of the Board," August 28, 1987, lists Jerome R. Feniger as president and Fogelman as a member of the Finance and Personnel Practice Committees. Fogelman resigned from the board and LWS in 1989; see Sheldon Fogelman, letter of resignation. November 6, 1989, and "LWS Executive

Committee," Viola W. Bernard, handwritten note, June 4, 1981, Viola W. Bernard Archives, Columbia University.

27. Fogelman, interview with Nancy L. Segal, 2019.

28. Fogelman, interview with Nancy L. Segal, 2020.

29. Fogelman, interview with Nancy L. Segal.

30. *60 Minutes*, telephone message to Viola Bernard, November 9, 1981, Viola W. Bernard Archives, Columbia University. There is reference to someone named "Stone," apparently associated with Spence-Chapin. It is possible that the comment "I'll be damned" was uttered by this individual—or by Bernard. Spence-Chapin has had custody of LWS's adoption records since 2004.

31. Saul Z. Cohen and Sheldon Fogelman, letter to Mike Wallace, November 16, 1981, Viola W. Bernard Archives, Columbia University.

32. Viola W. Bernard, "Memo, Re: Mike Wallace," December 30, 1981, Viola W. Bernard Archives, Columbia University.

33. Viola W. Bernard, "CONFIDENTIAL MEMO," April 28, 1982, Viola W. Bernard Archives, Columbia University.

34. Barbara Miller, telephone message to Viola Bernard, August 6, 1982, Viola W. Bernard Archives, Columbia University.

35. Miller, telephone message to Viola Bernard, August 6, 1982.

36. Barbara Miller, "*60 Minutes* Program," August 11, 1982. Viola W. Bernard Archives, Columbia University.

37. "Twins," *Walter Cronkite's Universe, III* (11). August 31, 1982, University of Rochester Library.

38. Sari Aviv produced a program featuring my study of young Chinese twins adopted separately due to their nation's former One-Child Policy (1979–2015). The program, "Just Alike: Twins Separated at Birth," aired on *CBS Sunday Morning*, February 5, 2017.

39. Nancy L. Segal, *Born Together—Reared Apart: The Landmark Minnesota Twin Study* (Cambridge, MA: Harvard University Press, 2012).

40. Viola W. Bernard, letter to Morton Rogers (handwritten note in the margin). The letter is dated July 30, 1981, but the note must have been added in August or September after she saw the show.

41. Mike Wallace, letter to Morton Rogers, September 14, 1982. Viola W. Bernard Archives, Columbia University.

42. Viola W. Bernard, "Adoption." *Encyclopedia of Mental Health* (New York: Franklin Watts, 1963), 70–108.

43. Viola W. Bernard, "Initial Memo Upon Receiving from Mr. Rogers a Copy of Mike Wallace's Letter of September 14, 1982, to Him."

44. Susan Engel, interviews with Nancy L. Segal, 2019, 2020.

45. Viola W. Bernard, "Memo to Mr. Morton Rogers, and Mr. Shelly Fogelman From Viola Bernard," September 29, 1982, Viola W. Bernard Archives, Columbia University.

46. Viola W. Bernard, "Dear Mr. Wallace" (two drafts), September 1982, Viola W. Bernard Archives, Columbia University.

47. Bernard, "Memo to Mr. Morton Rogers, and Mr. Shelly Fogelman From Viola Bernard."

48. Viola W. Bernard, "Re Adoptive Twin Placement: Reversal of Outdated Board Policy," October 6, 1982, Viola W. Bernard Archives, Columbia University.

49. Viola W. Bernard, "Memorandum," October 5, 1982, Viola W. Bernard Archives, Columbia University; Viola W. Bernard, "Re Adoptive Twin Placement: Reversal of Outdated Board Policy," October 6, 1982, Viola W. Bernard Archives, Columbia University.

50. Bernard, "Memo to Mr. Morton Rogers, and Mr. Shelly Fogelman From Viola Bernard."

51. Viola W. Bernard, untitled memo regarding recommendation to the LWS board of directors, September 29, 1982, Viola W. Bernard Archives, Columbia University.

52. Frey, secretary, "Minutes: The Board of Directors," October 6, 1982, Viola W. Bernard Archives, Columbia University.

53. A "CONFIDENTIAL" 1983 draft of a statement for CBS approximates the year 1968 as the end of the twin separation policy. Viola W. Bernard, "Explanatory Statement for Use by Public-Relations Consultant in Preparing a Reaction to CBS News Program About LWS-CDC Twin Placements and Research," March 22, 1983, Viola W. Bernard Archives, Columbia University. A pair of identical twins was separated and studied after that date, in 1969.

54. Elyse Schein and Paula Bernstein, *Identical Strangers: A Memoir of Twins Separated and Reunited* (New York: Random House, 2008).

55. Schein and Bernstein, *Identical Strangers*.

56. Viola W. Bernard, letter to Christa Balzert, PhD. November 9, 1978; Viola W. Bernard, letter to Dorothy Krugman, October 27, 1982, Viola W. Bernard Archives, Columbia University.

57. Viola W. Bernard, transcript of post-interview conversation with Justine W. Polier, May 20, 1981, Viola W. Bernard Archives, Columbia University.

58. Viola W. Bernard, list of twin placements, circa October 1982, Viola W. Bernard Archives, Columbia University.

59. /p is the medical symbol for "after."

60. Viola W. Bernard, letter to Sheldon Fogelman, October 27, 1982, Viola W. Bernard Archives, Columbia University.

61. "Director's Report to the 225th National Advisory Mental Health Council Meeting - May 14, 2010." https://www.nimh.nih.gov/about/advisory-boards-and-groups/namhc/reports/directors-report-to-the-225th-national-advisory-mental-health-council-meeting-may-14-2010.shtml.

62. Zero to Three, "Stanley I. Greenspan." The original name of this organization was National Center for Clinical Infant Programs. https://www.zerotothree.org/our-team/stanley-i-greenspan.

63. Letter from Phyllis to Viola W. Bernard. Undated; Viola W. Bernard, letter to Phyllis, December 8, 1982, Viola W. Bernard Archives, Columbia University.

64. Viola W. Bernard, "Memorandum," February 7, 1983, Viola W. Bernard Archives, Columbia University.

65. HarperCollins Speakers Bureau, "Richard Cohen." https://www.harpercollinsspeakersbureau.com/speaker/richard-cohen/.

66. The Hastings Center, founded in 1969, was instrumental in establishing the field of bioethics. It is now headquartered in Garrison, New York. https://www.thehastingscenter.org/who-we-are/.

67. Richard M. Cohen, interview with Nancy L. Segal, January 14, 2019.

68. Lori Shinseki, email correspondence to Nancy L. Segal, January 6, 2020; Louise Wise Services, *News & Views*, circa 1989. Dr. Dabbs worked closely with Barbara Miller in post-adoption services and was with LWS for over fourteen years.

69. LWS, *News & Views*, circa 1989.

70. LWS, "80th Anniversary Celebration" Program. The date is most likely 1996, eighty years after the 1916 founding of the Child Adoption Committee of the Free Synagogue in 1916, by Louise Waterman Wise. The committee became the Louise Wise Services in 1949, a change made by Wise's daughter, Justine Wise Polier.

71. Jack Drescher, "An Interview with E. Gerald Dabbs, MD." *Journal of Gay & Lesbian Mental Health* 22, no. 2 (2018): 196–202; email correspondence to Dr. Nancy L. Segal, January 16, 2020; Lori Shinseki, email correspondence to Nancy L. Segal, January 6, 2020; E. Gerald Dabbs, interview and email correspondence with Nancy L. Segal, 2020.

72. Dabbs could provide no further details about this case.

73. CBS did not have offices in the Flatiron Building.

74. "Wanted," *Sunday New York Times*. February 18, 1983, Viola W. Bernard Archives, Columbia University.

75. Viola W. Bernard, "Possible Wallace/Rather CBS Broadcasts on Twins," March 17, 1983, Viola W. Bernard Archives, Columbia University.

76. Fogelman, interview with Nancy L. Segal.

77. Viola W. Bernard, "Explanatory Statement for Use by Public-Relations Consultant in Preparing a Reaction to CBS News Program About LWS-CDC Twin Placements and Research" (draft), March 22, 1983, Viola W. Bernard Archives, Columbia University.

78. Viola W. Bernard, "Copies Distributed of Draft," March 22, 1983, Viola W. Bernard Archives, Columbia University.

79. Viola W. Bernard, "Abbreviation of Main Ideas in Explanatory Statement of March 23, 1983 Re: CBS News Program Attacking LWS/CDC," April 11,

1983, Viola W. Bernard Archives, Columbia University. The last half page was either missing from the file or I overlooked it.

80. Viola W. Bernard, "Re: CBS/LWS/CDC," April 13, 1983, Viola W. Bernard Archives, Columbia University.

81. Sheldon Fogelman, letter to Viola W. Bernard, May 5, 1983, Viola W. Bernard Archives, Columbia University. The four enclosures are handwritten at the end of the letter by Bernard—all are related to her professional activities, not to the explanatory statement.

82. Debra Ruder, email correspondence to Nancy L. Segal, 2020.

83. Viola W. Bernard, untitled notes, March 23, 1983, Viola W. Bernard Archives, Columbia University.

84. Florence Kreech, letter to Viola W. Bernard, April 17, 1983, Viola W. Bernard Archives, Columbia University.

85. Tony Schwartz, "Lessons of the '60 Minutes Case.'" *New York*, June 20, 1983, 30–34.

86. Don Singleton, "TV News Queries: "Legal Woes for '60 Minutes,'" *Daily News*, May 8, 1983, Viola W. Bernard Archives, Columbia University.

87. John Corry, "When Form Dictates Content, What Happens to the News?" *New York Times*: TV View, Section 2, June 26, 1983.

88. Charlottesville, VA, March 29, 2019; "A Discussion of the Film: *Three Identical Strangers*," Yale Pediatric Ethics Program and Program for Biomedical Ethics, March 2, 2020.

89. Nancy L. Segal, notes from telephone conversations with Stephanie Saul. May 30, 1997; June 26, 1997. We met on September 29, 1997, at Jojo's restaurant on New York's upper east side.

90. Seth Amgott, interview with Nancy L. Segal, 2019.

91. Joyce Gramza, interview with Nancy L. Segal, 2019; unpublished tribute to Madeline Amgott.

CHAPTER 7

1. Martha Birnbaum, interview with Nancy L. Segal, 2019.

2. Susan Engel, Anne Adler, and Martha Birnbaum, interviews with Nancy L. Segal, 2019, 2020.

3. Becky Read, text and email messages to Nancy L. Segal, December 2019.

4. Susan Golomb, interview with Nancy L. Segal, 2020.

5. Peter B. Neubauer Collection. Yale University Archives, https://archives.yale.edu/repositories/12/top_containers/134627.

6. Viola W. Bernard, "Initial Memo Upon Receiving from Mr. Rogers a Copy of Mike Wallace's Letter of September 15, 1982, to Him," September 15, 1982,

Viola W. Bernard Archives, Columbia University. Copies were sent to Neubauer, Balzert, Rogers, and Miller.

7. Babies are born feet first in breech deliveries. Laura E. Berk, *Child Development*, ninth edition (Boston: Pearson, 2013).

8. Engel, interview with Nancy L. Segal.

9. Birnbaum, interview with Nancy L. Segal, 2019; Engel, interview with Nancy L. Segal, 2019.

10. Anne Adler, interview with Nancy L. Segal, 2019.

11. Amy Tubbs, interview with Nancy L. Segal, 2020.

12. Tubbs, interview with Nancy L. Segal.

13. Bruce Fleishaker, interview with Nancy L. Segal, 2020.

14. Engel, interview with Nancy L. Segal, 2019.

15. Birnbaum, interview with Nancy L. Segal, 2019.

16. Viola W. Bernard, interview with Lawrence Wright, 1993; Anne Adler, interview with Nancy L. Segal, 2019.

17. Adler, interview with Nancy L. Segal, 2019.

18. Adler, interview with Nancy L. Segal.

19. An ectopic pregnancy is one in which the fertilized egg develops outside the uterus where it cannot survive. The pregnancy may prove life-threatening for the mother. Mayo Clinic, "Ectopic Pregnancy," 2020, https://www.mayoclinic.org/diseases-conditions/ectopic-pregnancy/symptoms-causes/syc-20372088.

20. Hugo Lagercrantz and Jean-Pierre Changeux, "The Emergence of Human Consciousness: From Fetal to Neonatal Life." *Pediatric Research* 65, no. 3 (2009): 255–60.

21. Nancy L. Segal, *Twin Mythconceptions: False Beliefs, Fables, and Facts About Twins* (New York: Elsevier, 2017).

22. Lagercrantz and Changeux, "The Emergence of Human Consciousness: From Fetal to Neonatal Life."

23. Berk, *Child Development*.

24. Nancy L. Segal, *Born Together—Reared Apart: The Landmark Minnesota Twin Study* (Cambridge, MA: Harvard University Press, 2012).

25. Birnbaum, interview with Nancy L. Segal, 2019.

26. Sharon Morello (LWS twin who received partial papers from Yale), interview with Nancy L. Segal, 2019.

27. Engel, Birnbaum, Barry Kostrinsky, interviews with Nancy L. Segal, 2019, 2020.

28. Engel, Birnbaum, interviews with Nancy L. Segal, 2019.

29. Separation anxiety may escalate among infants six to fifteen months of age, as they become aware that their caregiver exists even if absent. Anne may have also experienced some stranger anxiety, the fear of unfamiliar adults that may begin during the second half of the first year of life. Berk, *Child Development*.

30. Joyce M. Pavao, email correspondence to Nancy L. Segal, 2020.

31. Tubbs, interview with Nancy L. Segal, 2020.

32. Adler, interview with Nancy L. Segal, 2019.

33. Adler, interview with Nancy L. Segal, 2019.

34. Nancy L. Segal and Yesika S. Montoya, *Accidental Brothers: The Story of Twins Exchanged at Birth and the Power of Nature and Nurture* (New York: St. Martin's Press, 2018).

35. Heather Rockwell, interview with Nancy L. Segal, 2020.

36. Adler, email correspondence to Nancy L. Segal, 2020.

37. Rockwell, interview with Nancy L. Segal.

38. Segal and Montoya, *Accidental Brothers.*

39. Fleishaker, interview with Nancy L. Segal, 2020.

40. Golomb, interview with Nancy L. Segal, 2020.

41. Ann Rubin, interview with Nancy L. Segal, 2020.

42. Engel, Birnbaum, interviews with Nancy L. Segal.

43. Birnbaum, interview with Nancy L. Segal, 2019.

44. Viola W. Bernard, "Explanatory Statement for Use by Public-Relations Consultant in Preparing a Reaction to CBS News Program About LWS-CDC Twin Placement and Research," March 22, 1982, Viola W. Bernard Archives, Columbia University. This document was marked "CONFIDENTIAL: NOT FOR CIRCULATION."

45. Viola W. Bernard, "Explanatory Statement for Use by Public-Relations Consultant in Preparing a Reaction to CBS News Program About LWS-CDC Twin Placement and Research," March 22, 1982, Viola W. Bernard Archives, Columbia University. This document was marked "CONFIDENTIAL: NOT FOR CIRCULATION."

46. Birnbaum, interview with Nancy L. Segal, 2019.

47. Iris E. C. Sommer, Nick F. Ramsey, René C. W. Mandl, and René S. Kahn, "Language Lateralization in Monozygotic Twin Pairs Concordant and Discordant for Handedness." *Brain* 125, no. 12 (2002): 2710–18.

48. Segal, *Born Together—Reared Apart*; Ziada Ayorech, Eva Krapohl, Robert Plomin, and Sophie von Stumm, "Genetic Influence on Intergenerational Educational Attainment." *Psychological Science* 28 no. 9 (2017): 1302–10A.

49. Viola W. Bernard, "Initial Memo Upon Receiving from Mr. Rogers a Copy of Mike Wallace's letter of September 14, 1982, to Him," September 15–16, 1982, Viola W. Bernard Archives, Columbia University.

50. Bernard, "Initial Memo Upon Receiving from Mr. Rogers a Copy of Mike Wallace's letter of September 14, 1982, to Him."

51. When mothers have an Rh- (Rhesus) blood group factor and their fetus is Rh+, mothers may build up antibodies to the foreign protein. This puts babies at risk for difficulties such as mental retardation and even death. First-born children are at little risk compared to later born children. Berk, *Child Development.* Both Anne and Susan are Rh negative, so they were not at risk.

52. Nancy L. Segal, Brittney A. Hernandez, Jamie L. Graham, and Ulrich Ettinger, "Pairs of Genetically Unrelated Look-Alikes." *Human Nature* 29, no. 4 (2018): 402–17.

53. David T. Lykken and Auke Tellegen, "Is Human Mating Adventitious or the Result of Lawful Choice? A Twin Study of Mate Selection." *Journal of Personality and Social Psychology* 65, no. 1 (1993): 56–68.

54. J. Phillippe Rushton and Trudy A. Bons, "Mate Choice and Friendship in Twins: Evidence for Genetic Similarity." *Psychological Science* 16, no. 7 (2005): 555–59.

55. Yoon-Mi Hur, Thomas J. Bouchard Jr., and Elke Eckert, "Genetic and Environmental Influences on Self-Reported Diet: A Reared-Apart Twin Study." *Physiology & Behavior* 64, no. 5 (1998): 629–36.

56. Yoon-Mi Hur, Thomas J. Bouchard Jr., and David T. Lykken, "Genetic and Environmental Influence on Morningness–Eveningness." *Personality and Individual Differences* 25, no. 5 (1998): 917–25.

57. Lawrence Wright, "Double Mystery." *The New Yorker*, August 7, 1995, 45–62.

58. Adler, interviews and emails with Nancy L. Segal, 2019, 2020; Engel, interviews with Nancy L. Segal, 2019, 2020; Samuel Abrams, "Disposition and the Environment." *The Psychoanalytic Study of the Child* 41, no. 1 (1986): 41–60.

59. Peter B. Neubauer and Alexander Neubauer, *Nature's Thumbprint: The New Genetics of Personality* (New York: Addison-Wesley Publishing Company, 1990).

60. Engel, email correspondence to Nancy L. Segal, June 7, 2020.

61. Peter Neubauer, Samuel Abrams, and Christa Balzart, "Findings 1: The Individual Children" (sample chapter from *Identical Twins Reared Apart; A Longitudinal Study*, p. 17, unpublished), circa 1987, Viola W. Bernard Archives, Columbia University.

62. Female twin, interview with Nancy L. Segal, 2020.

63. David E. Sobel, letter to Viola W. Bernard, November 30, 1961, Viola W. Bernard Archives, Columbia University. "Mrs. F" refers to Mrs. Fichandler, who appears to be a case worker or other intermediary.

64. Gertrude Sandgrund, letter to Viola W. Bernard, December 16, 1963, Viola W. Bernard Archives, Columbia University.

65. Viola W. Bernard, "Staff Meeting of Adoption Department," January 20, 1964, Viola W. Bernard Archives, Columbia University.

66. Engel, interview with Nancy L. Segal, 2020; Associated Press, "Arthur Bloom, 63; News Director Helped Get '60 Minutes' Ticking in '68." *Los Angeles Times*, January 29, 2006, https://www.latimes.com/archives/la-xpm-2006-jan-29-mc-bloom29-story.html.

67. Jacques Steinberg, "Ed Bradley, TV Correspondent, Dies at 65." *New York Times*, November 10, 2006, https://www.nytimes.com/2006/11/10/arts/television/10bradley.html.

68. Kostrinsky, interview with Nancy L. Segal, 2020.

CHAPTER 8

1.The IHOP restaurant chain started in 1958. It currently operates nearly eighteen hundred restaurants worldwide. Jordan Valinsky, "Happy 61st Birthday, IHOP. Here's How the Chain Still Rakes in Millions." *CNN Business*, https://www.cnn.com/2019/07/16/business/ihop-history/index.html.

2. Arlene Lippel, interviews with Nancy L. Segal, 2019.

3. Lippel, interviews with Nancy L. Segal.

4. Lippel, interviews with Nancy L. Segal.

5. Lippel, interviews with Nancy L. Segal

6. Melanie Mertzel, interviews with Nancy L. Segal, 2019, 2020.

7. Ellen Carbone, interviews with Nancy L. Segal, 2019, 2020

8. Laura Lee Hope, *The Bobbsey Twins* (series) (Multiple publishers, 1904–2005).

9. M. Mertzel and Carbone, interviews with Nancy L. Segal, 2019, 2020.

10. Nancy L. Segal, *Twin Mythconceptions: False Beliefs, Fables, and Facts About Twins* (New York: Elsevier, 2017).

11. M. Mertzel and Carbone, interviews with Nancy L. Segal, 2019, 2020.

12. Melanie recalls that only her mother was present at that time, whereas Alice believes that she and Bert were told of the twinship at the same time.

13. Carbone, interviews with Nancy L. Segal, 2019, 2020.

14. Alice Mertzel, interviews with Nancy L. Segal, 2019; M. Mertzel, interviews with Nancy L. Segal, 2019, 2020.

15. A. Mertzel, interviews with Nancy L. Segal, 2019.

16. A. Mertzel, interviews with Nancy L. Segal, 2019.

17. Alice could not recall which *New York Times* article described the separated twin study. It is possible that she saw it in different sources that drew considerable attention to the story: Lawrence Wright, "Double Mystery." *The New Yorker,* August 7, 1995, 45–62, or Stephanie Saul, "In the Name of Research: Identical Brothers Separated at Birth Were Studied, But Truth Was Hidden." *Newsday,* October 12, 1997, A5, A52–53.

18. A. Mertzel, interviews with Nancy L. Segal, 2019.

19. M. Mertzel, interviews with Nancy L. Segal, 2019, 2020.

20. Nancy Mertzel, interview with Nancy L. Segal, 2020.

21. Lisa Belkin, "What the Jumans Didn't Know About Michael." *New York Times*, March 14, 1999: 42–49, https://www.nytimes.com/1999/03/14/magazine/what-the-jumans-didn-t-know-about-michael.html.

22. The hardware store was in Manhattan, on Second Avenue, between East 37th and 38th Streets. The Corinthian Building where the Mertzels owned property is on East 38th Street.

23. A. Mertzel, interviews with Nancy L. Segal, 2019, 2020

24. Thelma Lieber, interview with Nancy L. Segal, 2019.

25. Carbone, interviews with Nancy L. Segal, 2019, 2020.

26. Lieber, interview with Nancy L. Segal, 2019.

27. Elyse Schein and Paula Bernstein, *Identical Strangers: A Memoir of Twins Separated and Reunited* (New York: Random House, 2007).

28. Lieber, interview with Nancy L. Segal.

29. Lieber, interview with Nancy L. Segal.

30. Robert Plomin, *Blueprint: How DNA Makes Us Who We Are* (London: Allen Lane, 2018).

31. Intelligence2 Debates, "Parenting Is Overrated," October 29, 2019, https://www.intelligencesquaredus.org/debates/parenting-overrated.

32. Lieber, interview with Nancy L. Segal, 2019.

33. Carbone, interviews with Nancy L. Segal, 2019, 2020.

34. M. Mertzel, interviews with Nancy L. Segal, 2019, 2020.

35. Nancy L. Segal, Joseph L. Nedelec, and Vanessa A. Costello-Harris, "Differences in Development in Monozygotic Twins." In *Why Are Monozygotic Twins Different: From Genetics to Environment*, edited by Alexandra Matias and Issac Blickstein, 285–95 (New York: Elsevier, 2020).

36. When I spoke with Melanie on March 8, 2020, she had not had a cigarette for one week.

37. Nancy L. Segal, *Born Together—Reared Apart: The Landmark Minnesota Twin Study* (Cambridge: Harvard University Press, 2012); Tag Archives, "Identical Twins Who Were Separated at Birth: Amazing Similarities," https://lornareiko.wordpress.com/tag/identical-twins/.

38. M. Mertzel, interviews with Nancy L. Segal, 2019, 2020.

39. Nancy L. Segal and Franchesca A. Cortez, "Born in Korea-Adopted Apart: Behavioral Development of Monozygotic Twins Raised in the United States and France." *Personality and Individual Differences* 70 (2014): 97–104.

40. Nancy L. Segal, "Laboratory Findings: Not Twins, Twins, not Twins." *Twin Research and Human Genetics* 9 no. 2 (2006): 303–08.

41. Twins cannot be classified as identical with 100 percent certainty because it is possible, albeit extremely unlikely, for two siblings to share exactly the same DNA markers. Therefore, twins are classified as identical with greater than 99 percent certainty when they have matching DNA markers; in contrast, twins can be classified as fraternal with complete certainty if any of their DNA markers differ. The 2015 documentary film *Twinsters* captured my telling Samantha and Anaïs that they are identical twins and Samantha's dropping of her wine glass when she heard the news.

42. M. Mertzel, interviews with Nancy L. Segal, 2019, 2020.

43. Nancy L. Segal and Yesika S. Montoya, *Accidental Brothers: The Story of Twins Exchanged at Birth and the Power of Nature and Nurture* (New York: St. Martin's Press, 2018).

44. M. Mertzel, birth document and interviews with Nancy L. Segal, 2019, 2020.

45. Carbone, birth certificate.

46. A. Mertzel, interview with Nancy L. Segal, 2020.

47. J. P. Triseliotis, *In Search of Origins* (London: Kegan Paul, 1973).

48. Ralph R. Greenson, "On Sexual Apathy in the Male." *California Medicine* 108, no. 4 (1968): 275–79; Emma N. Plank, "Reactions of Mothers of Twins in a Child Study Group." *American Journal of Orthopsychiatry* 28, no. 1 (1958): 196–204.

49. M. Mertzel, interviews with Nancy L. Segal, 2019, 2020.

50. N. Mertzel, interviews with Nancy L. Segal, 2019, 2020.

51. Nancy L. Segal, Dina A. N. Arch, Kathleen S. J. Preston, and William D. Marelich, "Social Closeness Revisited in Monozygotic and Dizygotic Twin Families: Aunt/Uncle-Niece/Nephew Relations." *Personality and Individual Differences* 157C (April 2020): article 109815.

52. Albert A. Raphael Jr., letter to Sol and Thelma Lieber. October 25, 1967. Courtesy: Ellen Carbone.

53. Melanie Mertzel, interviews with Nancy L. Segal, 2019, 2020.

54. Louise Wise Services, adoption document. The witness appears to be "Esther R"; the handwritten last name is illegible. Courtesy: Ellen Carbone.

55. Viola W. Bernard, "Explanatory Statement for Use by Public-Relations Consultant in Preparing a Reaction to CBS News Program About LWS-CDC Twin Placement and Research," March 22, 1982, Viola W. Bernard Archives, Columbia University. This document was marked "CONFIDENTIAL: NOT FOR CIRCULATION."

56. "Belmont Report: Ethical Principles and Guidelines for the Protection of Human Subjects of Research, Report of the National Commission for the Protection of Human Subjects of Biomedical and Behavioral Research," *Federal Register* 44, no. 76 (April 18, 1979): 23192–97. However, on July 12, 1974, Congress signed the National Research Act into law, which established the National Commission for the Protection of Human Subjects of Biomedical and Behavioral Research. Approval by an Institutional Review Board of human subjects research at any institution receiving Department of Health, Education and Welfare funding was now required; see Joseph L. Breault, "Protecting Human Research Subjects: The Past Defines the Future." *Ochsner Journal* 6, no. 1 (2006): 15–20.

57. "Separated at Birth, 19-Year-Old Triplets Reunited." *The Record*, September 24, 1980; Stephanie Saul, "In the Name of Research." *Newsday 58* (October 12, 1997): A5, A48.

58. The study was variously funded by the Philip A. and Lynn Strauss Foundation, the Tappanz Foundation (Dr. Bernard's Foundation) and one grant from the National Institute of Mental Health (HD01625-1). Samuel Abrams, "Disposition and the Environment." *The Psychoanalytic Study of the Child* 41, no. 1 (1986): 41–60; National Institutes of Health, *Research Grants Index* 2, (1965): 1656. There were other sources such as private donations.

59. Peter B. Neubauer, interview with Lawrence Wright, 1993.

60. There were originally five twin pairs and one triplet set, but recall that one pair—Susan and Anne—had been dropped from the study. However, Susan and Anne did not leave the study until they were young children and their data were retained. However, another pair discussed in chapter 15 was completely eliminated after a very brief period. It is possible that the 1969 return date on Melanie's consent form was a typographical error that should have read 1978. I did not view this document; it was included in a list titled, "Signed Consent and Release Forms." Viola W. Bernard Archives, Columbia University.

61. M. Mertzel, email correspondence to Nancy L. Segal, February 25, 2020.

62. Child Development Center, consent and release, September 21, 1878, Viola W. Bernard Archives, Columbia University.

63. Carbone, interviews and email correspondence with Nancy L. Segal, 2019, 2020.

64. M. Mertzel, interviews with Nancy L. Segal, 2019, 2020.

65. Janet Audrain-McGovern and Neal L. Benowitz, "Cigarette Smoking, Nicotine, and Body Weight." *Clinical Pharmacology & Therapeutics* 90, no. 1 (2011): 164–68; Adam D. Gepner, Megan E. Piper, Heather M. Johnson, Michael C. Fiore, Timothy B. Baker, and James H. Stein, "Effects of Smoking and Smoking Cessation on Lipids and Lipoproteins: Outcomes From a Randomized Clinical Trial." *American Heart Journal* 161, no. 1 (2011): 145–51; Mohammad R. Hayatbakhsh, Alexandra Clavarino, Gail M. Williams, Maryam Sina, and Jake M. Najman, "Cigarette Smoking and Age of Menopause: A Large Prospective Study." *Maturitas* 72, no. 4 (2012): 346–52.

66. Schein and Bernstein, *Identical Strangers*.

67. Lawrence Wright, "Double Mystery." *The New Yorker*, August 7, 1995, 45–62.

68. "Zombie Walk," https://en.wiktionary.org/wiki/zombie_walk.

69. The twins' Halloween plans were foiled by an event held near to where the party was to take place: Melanie preferred not to drive in that area.

70. Samuel Abrams, "Disposition and the Environment"; Wright, "Double Mystery."

71. A. Mertzel, interview with Nancy L. Segal, 2020.

72. Abrams, "Disposition and the Environment"; Peter B. Neubauer and Alexander Neubauer, *Nature's Thumbprint: The New Genetics of Personality* (New York: Addison-Wesley, 1990).

73. Nancy L. Segal, "The Paths Not Taken." *The New Yorker*, January 25, 2021, 3.

CHAPTER 9

1. Lori Shinseki (director), *The Twinning Reaction*, Fire Horse Pictures, 2017.

2. Shinseki, *The Twinning Reaction.*

3. Howard Burack, email correspondence to Nancy L. Segal, May 20, 2019.

4. Twins Days, Inc., "Twins Days Festival," 2020, https://twinsdays.org/.

5. Richard T. Sunderland, "Twinsburg, Ohio: Sesquicentennial," http://twinsburg200.com/wp-content/uploads/2016/05/Twinsburg-Sesquicentennial-Booklet.pdf.

6. Twins Days, Inc., "Twins Days Festival," 2020, https://twinsdays.org/.

7. Andrew Paparella, Eric M. Strauss, Lauren Effron, and Alexa Valiente, "Twins Make Astonishing Discovery That They Were Separated Shortly After Birth and Then Part of a Secret Study." *ABC News*, March 9, 2018, https://abcnews.go.com/US/twins-make-astonishing-discovery-separated-birth-part-secret/story?id=53593943; Shinseki, *The Twinning Reaction.*

8. Shinseki, *The Twinning Reaction*; Paparella, Strauss, Effron, and Valiente, "Twins Make Astonishing Discovery That They Were Separated Shortly After Birth and Then Part of a Secret Study."

9. Shinseki, *The Twinning Reaction.*

10. Shinseki, *The Twinning Reaction.*

11. Shinseki, *The Twinning Reaction.*

12. Shinseki, *The Twinning Reaction.*

13. Shinseki, *The Twinning Reaction.*

14. Paparella, Strauss, Effron, and Valiente, "Twins Make Astonishing Discovery That They Were Separated Shortly After Birth and Then Part of a Secret Study."

15. Paparella, Strauss, Effron, and Valiente, "Twins Make Astonishing Discovery That They Were Separated Shortly After Birth and Then Part of a Secret Study."

16. Paparella, Strauss, Effron, and Valiente, "Twins Make Astonishing Discovery That They Were Separated Shortly After Birth and Then Part of a Secret Study."

17. Shinseki, *The Twinning Reaction.*

18. T. Berry Brazelton, "It's Twins." *Redbook Magazine*, February 1980, 80–84.

19. Paparella, Strauss, Effron, and Valiente, "Twins Make Astonishing Discovery That They Were Separated Shortly After Birth and Then Part of a Secret Study."

20. Laura E. Berk, *Child Development*, ninth edition (Boston: Pearson, 2013).

21. Esther Thelen, "Determinants of Amounts of Stereotyped Behavior in Normal Human Infants." *Ethology and Sociobiology* 1, no. 2 (1980): 141–50.

22. Shinseki, *The Twinning Reaction.*

23. Susan Farber, interview and email correspondence with Nancy L. Segal, 2019, 2020.

24. Susan Farber, "Sex Differences in the Expression of Adoption Ideas: Observations of Adoptees from Birth Through Latency." *American Journal of Orthopsychiatry* 47, no. 4 (1977): 639–50.

25. Susan Farber, "Sex Differences in Working Through Adoption Issues: Male and Female Children from Birth Through Latency." Paper presented at the American Psychoanalytic Association, Bethesda, MD, Spring 1976.

26. P. Neubauer, V. Bernard, S. Abrams, and C. Balzert were twin study investigators. V. Wolsk and S. Kofman made home visits to the separated twins, including Doug and Howard. Lynn Kelly worked at the CDC. Samuel Abrams, "Disposition and the Environment." *The Psychoanalytic Study of the Child* 41, no. 1 (1986): 41–60; Viola Bernard, "Memorandum: Publication of Twin Book," May 5, 1986, Viola W. Bernard Archives, Columbia University; Lori Shinseki, unpublished film notes; Lynn Kelly, "Adoption Study Meetings," October 10, 1984, Viola W. Bernard Archives, Columbia University.

27. Herschel Alt, Peter Neubauer, and John Mann, "18-Y-14: A Program of Child Welfare Research at the Jewish Board of Guardians." *Research Relating to Children* 17, no. 191; study duration: July 1964–June 1965. The study's four goals were to assess children's personality and well-being, family factors affecting nurturing and protection, availability of community resources, and standards and norms of the placement agency itself and as a surrogate of the community.

28. Susan L. Farber, *Identical Twins Reared Apart; A Reanalysis* (New York: Basic Books, 1981).

29. Farber, *Identical Twins Reared Apart*.

30. Farber, interview with Nancy L. Segal, 2019; "Dr. Susan Farber, Ph.D.," https://www.healthgrades.com/providers/susan-farber-ypp8v.

31. Office for Human Research Protections, "The Belmont Report." https://www.hhs.gov/ohrp/regulations-and-policy/belmont-report/index.html.

32. Viola W. Bernard, letter to Florence Kreech, March 22, 1976, Viola W. Bernard Archives, Columbia University.

33. George Rausch, letter to Dr. Vivian Wolsk, October 27, 1978, Viola W. Bernard Archives, Columbia University. In Shinseki's film *The Twinning Reaction* Rausch complained that nothing had been published from twin study—adding that even if the findings were good the study was bad.

34. Viola W. Bernard, "Explanatory Statement for Use by Public-Relations Consultant in Preparing a Reaction to CBS News Program About LWS-CDC Twin Placement and Research," March 22, 1983, Viola W. Bernard Archives, Columbia University. This document was marked "CONFIDENTIAL: NOT FOR CIRCULATION."

35. Shinseki, *The Twinning Reaction*.

36. Shinseki, *The Twinning Reaction*.

37. Shinseki, *The Twinning Reaction*.

38. Shinseki, *The Twinning Reaction*; Shinseki, email correspondence to Nancy L. Segal, June 2018. The twins appear to be opposite-handed.

39. Richard D. Arvey, Brian P. McCall, Thomas J. Bouchard Jr., Paul Taubman, and Marcie A. Cavanaugh, "Genetic Influences on Job Satisfaction and Work Values." *Personality and Individual Differences* 17 (1994): 21–33; Nicos

Nicolaou and Scott Shane, "Entrepreneurship and Occupational Choice: Genetic and Environmental Influences." *Journal of Economic Behavior & Organization* 76, no. 1 (2010): 3–14.

40. Nancy L. Segal, Dina Arch, Kathleen S. J. Preston, and William D. Marelich, "Social Closeness Revisited in Monozygotic and Dizygotic Twin Families: Aunt/Uncle-Niece/Nephew Relations." *Personality and Individual Differences* 157C (April 2020): article 109815.

41. Nancy L. Segal, "A Tale of Two Sisters." *Psychology Today* 88 (November/December 2015): 68–75.

42. Kaisu Keskitalo, Karri Silventoinen, Hely Tuorila, Markus Perola, Kirsi H. Pietiläinen, Aila Rissanen, and Jaakko Kaprio, "Genetic and Environmental Contributions to Food Use Patterns of Young Adult Twins." *Physiology & Behavior* 93, no. 1-2 (2008): 235–42.

43. Michele Mordkoff, interview with Nancy L. Segal, 2019.

44. Barry Coburn, interview with Nancy L. Segal, 2019; Shinseki, *The Twinning Reaction*. Coburn is a friend of both Lori Shinseki and her husband, Tim Heaphy, an attorney who was initially involved with the case.

45. Notes, Saturday, July 13; the year is not given. Dorothy Krugman was closely involved with the separated twins. Viola W. Bernard Archives, Columbia University.

46. Shinseki, *The Twinning Reaction*.

47. Lawrence M. Perlman, "Memories of the Child Development Center Study of Adopted Monozygotic Twins Reared Apart: An Unfulfilled Promise." *Twin Research and Human Genetics* 8, no. 3 (2005): 271–75.

48. Shinseki, *The Twinning Reaction*; Paparella, Strauss, Effron, and Valiente, "Twins Make Astonishing Discovery That They Were Separated Shortly After Birth and Then Part of a Secret Study."

49. Shinseki, *The Twinning Reaction*. The 1985 and 1986 documents have the typed initials and notation "PBN, SA and CB reviewed"; they stand for Peter B. Neubauer, Samuel Abrams, and Christa Balzert. The 1987 document is most likely a first draft for a book that was being planned.

50. Gareth Harvey, *60 Minutes–Australia* producer, email correspondence with Nancy L. Segal, 2019; *Three Identical Strangers*, "The Experiment," interview with *60 Minutes–Australia,* August 9, 2020, https://www.youtube.com/watch?v=UQI LXtd3ZOM&feature=youtu.be.

51. Shinseki, *The Twinning Reaction*.

52. Shinseki, *The Twinning Reaction*.

CHAPTER 10

1. Farrell Hirsch, interview with Nancy L. Segal, 2019.

2. State University of New York, "Sullivan County Community College." https://www.suny.edu/campuses/sullivan/.

3. Tim Wardle, *Three Identical Strangers*, Raw Films, London, UK, 2018.

4. Judy Gould, "What Happens When Three Young Men Find Out They're Triplets? It's Not as Simple as 1-2-3." *People Magazine*, October 13, 1980, https://people.com/archive/what-happens-when-three-young-men-find-out-theyre-triplets-its-not-as-simple-as-1-2-3-vol-14-no-15/.

5. *New York Post*, September 1980. The *New York Post* article reporting a twins reunion is referenced in another *New York Post* article that appeared several days later; see Kiernan Crowley, "Amazing Twins Are Now Seeing Triple as a Third Brother Surfaces." *New York Post*, September 23, 1980, p. 3.

6. Minnesota Study of Twins Reared Apart (MISTRA): Personality, *ABC News*, *Nightline*, October 2, 1989.

7. MISTRA, *ABC News*, *Nightline*.

8. Wardle, *Three Identical Strangers*.

9. MISTRA, *ABC News*, *Nightline*.

10. Wardle, *Three Identical Strangers*. Two mothers and three fathers were present; Bob's mother was ill at the time. The attorney was a family friend of the Shafrans. Robert Shafran, "The Unbelievable Way 3 Men Found Out They Were Triplets Separated as Babies." *The Today Show*, July 12, 2018, https://www.youtube.com/watch?v=J30G5RaoWNk.

11. Viola W. Bernard, "CBS Affair: Confidential," May 20, 1981, Viola W. Bernard Archives, Columbia University.

12. Viola W. Bernard, "Some Notes Taken by Viola W. Bernard at Meeting with Mike Wallace at His Office," October 26, 1981, Viola W. Bernard Archives, Columbia University.

13. Wardle, *Three Identical Strangers*.

14. Ellen Handler Spitz, "Documentary Danger: Reflections on Three Identical Strangers." *Bulletin of the Association for Psychoanalytic Medicine* 53 (Fall 2018): 22–29.

15. "Minutes of the Board Meeting," LWS, May 5, 1982, Viola W. Bernard Archives, Columbia University.

16. Wardle, *Three Identical Strangers*. Eddy's words were recalled by then *Newsday* Assistant Managing Editor Howard Schneider.

17. "Edward Scott 'Eddy' Galland." *Find a Grave*, June 16, 1995, https://www.findagrave.com/memorial/79439251/edward-scott-galland; "Eddy Galland, Robert Shafran and David Kellman Said Friday . . .," *UPI*, https://www.upi.com/Archives/1980/09/26/Eddy-Galland-Robert-Shafran-and-David-Kellman-said-Friday/6750338788800/; MISTRA, *ABC News*, *Nightline*.

18. Robert E. Kessler and Alan Finder, "The Face Looked Familiar." *Newsday*, September 17, 1980, 3, 23.

19. Howard Schneider, interview with Nancy L. Segal, 2020.

20. Lori Shinseki, *The Twinning Reaction*, Fire Horse Pictures, United States, 2017.

21. Ellen Cervone, interview in Wardle, *Three Identical Strangers*.

22. Sara Stewart, "Separated-at-Birth Triplets Met Tragic End After Shocking Psych Experiment." *New York Post*, June 23, 2018, https://nypost.com/2018/06/23/these-triplets-were-separated-at-birth-for-a-twisted-psych-study/.

23. Stephanie Saul, "Separated Triplets Had Been Studied Since Birth." *Newsday*, October 27, 1997.

24. Schneider, interview with Nancy L. Segal.

25. Phyllis C. Richman, "Triplets—A Tall, But True, Tale." *The Washington Post*, September 21, 1988, https://www.washingtonpost.com/archive/lifestyle/food/1988/09/21/triplets-a-tall-but-true-tale/deadd1c3-db84-48e3-b3e9-e1cd4753ce8f/; Film Arts Focus, "Split at Birth." *Global Times*, January 23, 2018, http://www.globaltimes.cn/content/1086154.shtml. The triplets' restaurant has been referred to as both the Triplets Old New York Restaurant and the Triplets Roumanian Steakhouse.

26. Nancy L. Segal, *Indivisible by Two: Lives of Extraordinary Twins* (Cambridge, MA: Harvard University Press, 2005).

27. "Mistaken Identity Leads to a Surprising Discovery," *New York Times*, September 19, 1980.

28. Nancy L. Segal, *Born Together—Reared Apart: The Landmark Minnesota Twin Study* (Cambridge, MA: Harvard University Press, 2012).

29. Dr. Thomas J. Bouchard Jr., noted that none of the parents brought up the LWS-CDC study, further evidence that they were unaware of its scope. Thomas J. Bouchard Jr., interview with Nancy L. Segal, 2020.

30. Jack Solomon, letter to Dr. Thomas J. Bouchard Jr., December 4, 1980. Courtesy of Dr. Thomas J. Bouchard Jr.

31. "Secret Siblings." *20/20*, March 9, 2018.

32. Samuel Abrams, "Disposition and the Environment." *The Psychoanalytic Study of the Child* 41, no. 1 (1986): 41–60; Peter B. Neubauer and Alexander Neubauer, *Nature's Thumbprint: The New Genetics of Personality* (New York: Addison-Wesley Publishing Co., 1990).

33. Peter B. Neubauer, Samuel Abrams, and Christa Balzert, "Findings 1: The Individual Children" (book proposal chapter). Viola W. Bernard Archives, Columbia University. Circa 1987.

34. Niels Juel-Nielsen, *Individual and Environment: Monozygotic Twins Reared Apart* (New York: International Universities Press, 1965/1980 rev).

35. European Commission, "Europeans and Their Languages." *Special Eurobarometer 243* (February 2006), https://ec.europa.eu/commfrontoffice/publicopin°ion/archives/ebs/ebs_243_en.pdf.

36. Niels Juel-Nielsen, *Individual and Environment*; see 151–52.

37. Thomas J. Bouchard Jr., interview with Nancy L. Segal, 2019.

38. The SJR is based on the number of citations received by a journal and the importance of the journals from where these citations come. In 2017, the score range for psychology journals with non-zero rankings was 00.10 to 12.03. "Oncotarget Rank and SCImago Journal Rank (SJR)," https://www.resurchify .com/all_ranking_details_2.php?id=2064; "Psychoanalytic-Study-of-the-Child: Impact Factor Trend 2000-2017," https://www.scijournal.org/impact-factor-of -Psychoanalytic-Study-of-the-Child.shtml; "Scimago Journal and County Rank," https://www.scimagojr.com/journalrank.php?area=3200&year=2017&type=j&p age=23&total_size=1159.

39. Wardle, *Three Identical Strangers*.

40. Lawrence Wright, "Double Mystery." *The New Yorker*, August 7, 1995, 45–62; Lawrence Wright, *Twins: And What They Tell Us About Who We Are* (New York: John Wiley & Sons, 1997); Saul, "Separated Triplets Had Been Studied Since Birth."

41. Saul, "Separated Triplets Had Been Studied Since Birth."

42. Saul, "Separated Triplets Had Been Studied Since Birth." Elsa Shafran, an attorney, passed away. Dr. Shafran remarried Alice Shafran, who appears in *Three Identical Strangers*.

43. Based on Susan Farber, "Sex Differences in the Expression of Adoption Ideas: Observations of Adoptees From Birth Through Latency." *American Journal of Orthopsychiatry* 47, no. 4 (1977): 639–50; David Kellman, "Journalist On Discovering the Study of the 'Three Identical Strangers' Triplets," *Today Show*, July 12, 2018, https://www.youtube.com/watch?v=A-WByPZuWqQ.

44. Internet searches; multiple sources.

45. Wardle, *Three Identical Strangers*; Wright, *Twins*; multiple sources.

46. "Bubala," Urban Dictionary, https://www.urbandictionary.com/define .php?term=bubala.

47. A March 9, 1967, letter from LWS Executive Director Florence (Brown) Kreech to Viola Bernard says that Kreech tried to contact Mrs. Galland, but without success. She promised to keep trying and to let Bernard "know the results." Eddy would have been six years old at that time. The reason for the contact was not given.

48. Farber, "Sex Differences in the Expression of Adoption Ideas."

49. "Signed Consent and Release Forms," Viola W. Bernard Archives, Columbia University.

50. Lois Oppenheim, "The Facts About the Neubauer Twin Study: An Interview About Controversy or a Controversial Interview?" *International Journal of Controversial Discussions* 1 (March 2020): 171–98. Eddy's absence from the study was confirmed by a former twin study assistant. Former twin study assistant Larry Perlman believes that one of the triplets left the study. He tested only two of them when he arrived in 1968, when the triplets would have been six or seven years old; see Lawrence M. Perlman, "Memories of the Child Development Center Study

of Adopted Monozygotic Twins Reared Apart: An Unfulfilled Promise." *Twin Research and Human Genetics* 8, no. 3 (2005): 271–75.

51. Justine Wise Polier, interview from previous footage, in *Three Identical Strangers*, 2018. The actual interview most likely took place in the early 1980s; see chapter 6.

52. James F. A. Traniello and Theo C. M. Bakker, "Minimizing Observer Bias in Behavioral Research: Blinded Methods Reporting Requirements for *Behavioral Ecology and Sociobiology*." *Behavioral Ecology and Sociobiology* 69 (2015): 1573–74.

53. Samuel Abrams and Peter B. Neubauer, "Object Orientedness: The Person or the Thing." *The Psychoanalytic Quarterly* 45, no. 1 (1976): 73–99.

54. "Adoption Study Meeting." May 13, 1975. Courtesy of Becky Read, document provided by surviving triplets.

55. MISTRA, *ABC News*, *Nightline*.

56. Dr. Paul Billings is currently chief medical officer at Natera, a company that uses new technologies to help manage disease worldwide. Natera, "About Us," https://www.natera.com/natera-our-people.

57. Auke Tellegen, David T. Lykken, Thomas J. Bouchard, Kimerly J. Wilcox, Nancy L. Segal, and Stephen Rich, "Personality Similarity in Twins Reared Apart and Together." *Journal of Personality and Social Psychology* 54, no. 6 (1988): 1031–39.

58. Bouchard, interview with Nancy L. Segal, 2020.

59. MISTRA, *ABC News*, *Nightline*.

60. Bob's score indicated left-handedness, whereas Eddy's and David's scores indicated right-handedness. Attempts were made to shift Bob's handedness from left to right when he learned to write in school, but they were unsuccessful. Outline of proposed book, "Chapter I: The Individual Children." Viola W. Bernard Archives, Columbia University. Eddy and David's scores varied slightly; multiple sources.

61. See Nancy L. Segal, *Twin Mythconceptions: False Beliefs, Fables and Facts About Twins* (New York: Elsevier, 2017). There is a photograph that hangs in the hallway of Elliott Hall, the building that houses the Department of Psychology at the University of Minnesota. It shows the triplets' faces arranged in vertical order, from top to bottom. Reversals can be seen in the smile and bone structure across the different dyads: Bob-Eddy; Bob-Dave; Eddy-Dave. For example, the smile appears higher on the left side of one triplet (Dave) and higher on the right side of another (Eddy).

62. Laura E. Berk, *Child Development*, ninth edition (Boston: Pearson, 2013).

63. *CNN*, "Unseen Footage From '*Three Identical Strangers*.'" https://www.cnn.com/videos/tv/2019/01/21/three-identical-strangers-never-seen-footage-orig.cnn.

64. Wardle, *Three Identical Strangers*.

65. "'It Was Extreme': Story Behind Twisted Triplet Experiment." *Sunshine Coast Daily*, June 24, 2018, https://www.sunshinecoastdaily.com.au/news/these-triplets-were-separated-at-birth-for-a-twist/3450241/.

66. Robert Shafran, "Journalist on Discovering the Study of the 'Three Identical Strangers' Triplets." *Today Show*, July 12, 2018, https://www.youtube.com/watch?v=A-WByPZuWqQ.

67. Shafran, "Journalist on Discovering the Study of the 'Three Identical Strangers' Triplets."

68. Segal, *Born Together—Reared Apart*.

69. Pauline Bouchard, interview with Nancy L. Segal, 2020.

70. Leonard L. Heston, interview with Nancy L. Segal, 2020.

71. "Edward Scott 'Eddy' Galland." *Find a Grave*, June 16, 1995, https://www.findagrave.com/memorial/79439251/edward-scott-galland; "Eddy Galland, Robert Shafran and David Kellman Said Friday . . ." UPI, https://www.upi.com/Archives/1980/09/26/Eddy-Galland-Robert-Shafran-and-David-Kellman-said-Friday/6750338788800/.

72. Kevin Haroian, interview with Nancy L. Segal, 2020.

73. Elizabeth Bouchard Penning, interview with Nancy L. Segal, 2020.

74. The *Twin Film* was to be made for Educational Media, Inc., a non-profit corporation based in Minneapolis. Photographer Jill Siegel-Greer is married to Ken Greer.

75. Wardle, *Three Identical Strangers*.

76. MISTRA, *ABC News, Nightline*; Kelly Schorr, "Interest in Firefighting Brings Together Identical Twins." *The Oklahoman*, September 9, 1987, https://oklahoman.com/article/2198193/interest-in-firefighting-brings-together-identical-twins.

77. "Some Notes Taken by Viola W. Bernard at Meeting with Mike Wallace at his Office, Monday, October 26, 1981," Viola W. Bernard Archives, Columbia University.

78. Letter from Viola W. Bernard to Morton Rogers, July 39, 1981, Viola W. Bernard Archives, Columbia University.

79. Minutes of the LWS Board Meeting, May 5, 1982, Viola W. Bernard Archives, Columbia University.

80. Untitled list (of issues). The list is undated, but it appears to have been compiled in March 1983, based on similar documents. Viola W. Bernard Archives, Columbia University.

81. Viola W. Bernard, letter to Sheldon Fogelman, September 23, 1981, Viola W. Bernard Archives, Columbia University.

82. Saul, "Separated Triplets Had Been Studied Since Birth."

83. UJA-Federation of New York, "List of Affiliated Agencies," 2021 https://ajhs.org/uja-federation-new-york-list-affiliated-agencies. The list was compiled from documents in their collection and other relevant materials. *Newsday* was not pressured to withhold the name of the UJA as a funding source for LWS. If they had been pressured, they would not have yielded to that pressure; Lonnie Isabel,

former deputy managing editor for *Newsday*, email correspondence to Nancy L. Segal, April 3, 2020; Howard Schneider, former managing editor for *Newsday*, interview with Nancy L. Segal, 2020.

84. Shinseki, *The Twinning Reaction.*

85. Hana Zouk, Alexander McGirr, Véronique Lebel, Chawky Benkelfat, Guy Rouleau, and Gustavo Turecki, "The Effect of Genetic Variation of the Serotonin 1B Receptor Gene on Impulsive Aggressive Behavior and Suicide." *American Journal of Medical Genetics Part B: Neuropsychiatric Genetics* 144, no. 8 (2007): 996–1002.

86. Stewart, "Separated-at-Birth Triplets Met Tragic End After Shocking Psych Experiment."

87. Shafran, "Journalist on Discovering the Study of the 'Three Identical Strangers' Triplets."

88. Wardle, *Three Identical Strangers.*

89. Shafran, "Journalist on Discovering the Study of the 'Three Identical Strangers' Triplets."

90. Wardle, *Three Identical Strangers.* In the film, Dave says that the triplets' birth mother had "minor problems," then suggested that these problems were "not so minor."

91. Wardle, *Three Identical Strangers*; Stewart, "Separated-at-Birth Triplets Met Tragic End After Shocking Psych Experiment."

92. Zucker-Hillside Hospital is one of three campuses that are part of the Long Island Jewish Medical Center, which dates back to 1954, https://lij.northwell .edu/about; Dr. Alec Roy, email correspondence to Nancy L. Segal, April 7, 2020. Also see Nicholas Bakalar, "1940: Electroshock Therapy." *New York Times,* August 17, 2015, https://www.nytimes.com/2015/08/18/science/1940-electro shock-therapy.html.

93. E. Fuller Torrey, Ann E. Bowler, Edward H. Taylor, and Irving I. Gottesman, *Schizophrenia and Manic-Depressive Disorder: The Biological Roots of Mental Illness as Revealed by the Landmark Study of Identical Twins* (New York: Basic Books, 1994); also see Jan Scott, Yvonne McNeill, Jonathan Cavanagh, Mary Cannon, and Robin Murray, "Exposure to Obstetric Complications and Subsequent Development of Bipolar Disorder: Systematic Review." *The British Journal of Psychiatry* 189, no. 1 (2006): 3–11.

94. G. Kuratomi, Kazuya Iwamoto, M. Bundo, I. Kusumi, N. Kato, Nakao Iwata, N. Ozaki, and T. Kato, "Aberrant DNA Methylation Associated With Bipolar Disorder Identified From Discordant Monozygotic Twins." *Molecular Psychiatry* 13, no. 4 (2008): 429–41; Emma L. Dempster, Ruth Pidsley, Leonard C. Schalkwyk, Sheena Owens, Anna Georgiades, Fergus Kane, Sridevi Kalidindi, et et al., "Disease-Associated Epigenetic Changes in Monozygotic Twins Discordant for Schizophrenia and Bipolar Disorder." *Human Molecular Genetics* 20, no. 24 (2011): 4786–96.

95. J. Thomas Noga, Katlin Vladar, and E. Fuller Torrey, "A Volumetric Magnetic Resonance Imaging Study of Monozygotic Twins Discordant for Bipolar Disorder." *Psychiatry Research: Neuroimaging* 106, no. 1 (2001): 25–34.

96. Wardle, *Three Identical Strangers*. Bob went on to become a lawyer; Dave and Eddy worked in the restaurant until Eddy's death, after which Dave became an insurance producer and independent general agent; see https://www.linkedin .com/in/robert-shafran-917-306-2975-7931a212 and https://www.linkedin.com/ in/david-kellman-4967a394.

97. Walter Bogdanich and Stephanie Saul, interviews with Nancy L. Segal, 2019.

98. Kinney Littlefield, "How 60 Minutes' Ethics Went Up in Smoke." *Sun Sentinel*, November 2, 1999, https://www.sun-sentinel.com/news/fl-xpm-1999 -11-02-9911010352-story.html. Wigand had told Wallace that the tobacco industry's executives at Brown & Williamson said privately that tobacco was addictive, but publicly said it was not. Brown & Williamson threatened a lawsuit if the segment aired.

99. Walter Bogdanich with Mike Wallace, "Secrets and Lies." *60 Minutes*, CBS, 1998, https://www.worldcat.org/title/60-minutes-secrets-lies/oclc/ 934521137.

100. Lisa Belkin, "What the Jumans Didn't Know About Michael." *New York Times Magazine*, March 14, 1999, 42–49, https://www.nytimes.com/1999/03/14/ magazine/what-the-jumans-didn-t-know-about-michael.html.

101. Lisa Belkin, interview with Nancy L. Segal, 2020.

102. Wardle, *Three Identical Strangers*.

103. Nancy L. Segal and Yesika S. Montoya, *Accidental Brothers: The Story of Twins Exchanged at Birth and the Power of Nature and Nurture* (New York: St. Martin's Press, 2018).

CHAPTER 11

1. Sharon Morello, interview with Nancy L. Segal, 2019.

2. Lori Shinseki, *The Twinning Reaction*, Fire Horse Pictures, United States, 2017; Sharon Morello, interviews with Nancy L. Segal, 2019, 2020.

3. Sharon Morello, interviews with Nancy L. Segal, 2019, 2020.

4. Shinseki, *The Twinning Reaction*; "Janet David," Linkedin, 2020, https:// www.linkedin.com/in/janet-david-2112a9b/; Shinseki, personal communication to Nancy L. Segal, May 10, 2021.

5. "Twins Separated at Birth (Secret Twin Study), *20/20*, March 9, 2018.

6. Janet David, email correspondence to Vivian Bregman, March 2015. Courtesy of Sharon Morello.

7. Twin study documents, courtesy of Sharon Morello; "Twins Separated at Birth (Secret Twin Study)," *20/20*, March 9, 2018, https://twitter.com/abc2020/status/972363171565465600?lang=en.

8. "Janet David," Linkedin. It is likely that Janet David did leave the CDC in 1967 because that is the last year that she visited the Bregman family; if so, then the "1967–1978" date in her email message to Vivian Bregman is a typographical error and should read "1967–1968." It is also possible that David continued to work as an administrative assistant at the CDC from 1967 to 1978, and that she could have assessed other twins during that eleven-year period. See Janet David, email correspondence to Vivian Bregman, March 2015. Courtesy of Sharon Morello.

9. Sharon Morello, interviews with Nancy L. Segal.

10. Dr. Levi, "Denise and Danielle: Observations." Yale University Records, courtesy of Sharon Morello.

11. New York State Department of Health, "Adoption Information Registry," 2020, https://www.health.ny.gov/vital_records/adoption.htm. The waiting time for receipt of materials can take months or years. Identifying information can be released if all parties consent.

12. Elyse Schein and Paula Bernstein, *Identical Strangers: A Memoir of Twins Separated and Reunited* (New York: Random House, 2007). Birth records are currently held for individuals born in New York City from 1866 to 1909, although it varies by borough. Individuals born between 1949 and 1965 can access the online Ancestry Library Edition; New York Public Library, "Vital Records," 2020, https://www.nypl.org/about/divisions/milstein/vital-records.

13. Sharon Morello, interview with Nancy L. Segal.

14. Vivian Bregman and Janet David, email exchange, March 2015. Courtesy of Sharon Morello.

15. Sharon Morello, interviews with Nancy L. Segal.

16. Spence-Chapin, Narrative: Sharon Morello. Courtesy of Sharon Morello.

17. Spence-Chapin, Narrative: Sharon Morello; Sharon Morello, interview with Nancy L. Segal.

18. WebMD, "Preeclampsia," 2020, https://www.webmd.com/baby/preeclampsia-eclampsia#1. Symptoms of preeclampsia are high blood pressure, protein in urine, and swelling of legs, hands, and feet. The treatment is delivery.

19. Forceps deliveries are those in which the baby is delivered with the assistance of metal tongs. In a low forceps delivery, the baby's head is visible at the outlet of the birth canal. Sharon was in the preferred occiput anterior position in which the head is down and the fetus is facing the mother's back. See Merriam-Webster Dictionary, "Low Forceps," 2020, https://www.merriam-webster.com/medical/low%20forceps; MedlinePlus "Delivery Presentations," September 25, 2018, https://medlineplus.gov/ency/patientinstructions/000621.htm; "History of the Delivery." Yale University Records, courtesy of Sharon Morello.

20. Ulla Sankilampi, Marja-Leena Hannila, Antti Saari, Mika Gissler, and Leo Dunkel, "New Population-Based References for Birth Weight, Length, and Head Circumference in Singletons and Twins from 23 to 43 Gestation Weeks." *Annals of Medicine* 45, no. 5-6 (2013): 446–54. Apgar scores express the physical condition of the newborn; scores of seven and higher are considered to be good; ten is the highest possible score. Laura E. Berk, *Child Development*, ninth edition (Boston: Pearson, 2013).

21. Spence-Chapin, narrative.

22. Ronald S. Wilson, "Concordance in Physical Growth for Monozygotic and Dizygotic Twins." *Annals of Human Biology* 3, no. 1 (1976): 1–10. The greater identical twin birthweight difference in this study was mainly due to a few pairs with large differences. A more recent study found that identical twins showed smaller birth weight differences than fraternal twins; see Elena C. Tore, Evangelia E. Antoniou, Keith Reed, Taunton R. Southwood, Luc Smits, Joseph P. McCleery, and Maurice P. Zeegers, "The Association of Intrapair Birth-Weight Differences With Internalizing and Externalizing Behavior Problems." *Twin Research and Human Genetics* 21, no. 3 (2018): 253–62.

23. "Observation," June 13, 1966. Sharon weighed ten pounds, three ounces, whereas her sister weighed ten pounds, seven ounces. Also see Ronald S. Wilson, "Concordance in Physical Growth for Monozygotic and Dizygotic Twins." *Annals of Human Biology* 3, no. 1 (1976): 1–10.

24. Nancy L. Segal, *Twin Mythconceptions: False Beliefs, Fables, and Facts About Twins* (New York: Elsevier, 2017).

25. Spence-Chapin, narrative.

26. S. Schneer, "Placement Summary," June 3, 1966. Courtesy of Sharon Morello.

27. Schneer, "Placement Summary."

28. Names on twins' records released from Dr. Neubauer's archives at Yale University are redacted unless signed consent is provided by all individuals whose names appear.

29. Jewish Board, "The Jewish Board's History," 2020, https://jewishboard .org/about-us/our-history/. The Jewish Board of Guardians merged with the Jewish Board in 1978; Jeremy Pearce, "Peter B. Neubauer, 94, Noted Child Psychiatrist, Is Dead." *New York Times*, March 3, 2008, https://www.nytimes .com/2008/03/03/nyregion/03neubauer.html. Dr. Peter Neubauer directed the board's CDC from 1951 to 1985.

30. "Face Sheet," note made on July 18, 1966: "Re Danielle after her twin was adopted." No other notes, such as "Observation of Baby" or "Films" that were listed for the other foster home and adoptive home visits, were listed. Courtesy of Sharon Morello; Morello, interview with Nancy L. Segal, 2019.

31. Myron Bregman, interview with Nancy L. Segal, 2019.

32. Spence-Chapin, narrative.

33. "Twins Separated at Birth (Secret Twin Study)," *20/20*, March 9, 2018.

34. V. Bregman, interview with Nancy L. Segal, 2019. Vivian told me that I was the first person to hear her thoughts about Sharon's low birth weight possibly being caused by being born a twin.

35. Nancy L. Segal and Yesika S. Montoya, *Accidental Brothers: The Story of Twins Exchanged at Birth and the Power of Nature and Nurture* (New York: St. Martin's Press, 2018).

36. Viola W. Bernard, interview with Lawrence Wright, 1993.

37. Bernard, interview with Lawrence Wright.

38. Louise Wise Services, "Adoption Fees." Courtesy of Sharon Morello.

39. "Dollar Times." H Brothers, Inc., Seattle, WA, 2020, https://www.dollar times.com/inflation/inflation.php?amount=1&year=1966.

40. Valentina P. Wasson, *The Chosen Baby* (Philadelphia: J.B. Lippincott, 1950).

41. Florence Rondell and Ruth Michaels, *The Adopted Family* (New York: Crown Publishers, 1951).

42. Rose Wagschal, letter to Mrs. Myron Bregman, June 7, 1973. Courtesy of Sharon Morello.

43. Dr. Esther R. Goshen-Gottstein, interview with Nancy L. Segal, 2020.

44. V. Bregman, interview with Nancy L. Segal, 2019; Morello, interviews with Nancy L. Segal, 2019, 2020.

45. Sharon Morello, interview with Nancy L. Segal.

46. Breast cancer risk is elevated in identical twins whose twin sisters are diagnosed with the disease. See Julian Peto and Thomas M. Mack, "High Constant Incidence in Twins and Other Relatives of Women with Breast Cancer." *Nature Genetics* 26, no. 4 (2000): 411–14.

47. Dana Stallard, letter to Sharon Morello, March 31, 2015. Stallard, a social worker at Spence-Chapin, referred to the New York State Adoption Information Registration Form from the New York State Adoption Information Registry, in Albany, New York. This is the "twins' application" Sharon referenced. Courtesy of Sharon Morello.

48. Sharon Morello, email communication to Barry, Kara, Jackie, Dana. May 19, 2015. Courtesy of Sharon Morello. Kara Allen is currently an attorney advisor at the Consumer Financial Protection Bureau, in Washington, DC. "Kara Allen," Linkedin, 2020, https://www.linkedin.com/in/kara-allen-91b54b14/.

49. Scott Morello, interview with Nancy L. Segal, 2019.

50. Peter Watson, *Twins: An Uncanny Relationship?* (Chicago: Contemporary Books, Inc., 1981).

51. Veronique Bataille, Harold Snieder, Alex J. MacGregor, Peter Sasieni, and Tim D. Spector, "Genetics of Risk Factors for Melanoma: An Adult Twin Study of Nevi and Freckles." *Journal of the National Cancer Institute* 92, no. 6 (2000): 457–63.

52. Scott Morello, interview with Nancy L. Segal.

53. The combined index was 2,547,946,490:1; prior probability = 0.50.

54. Scott Morello, interview with Nancy L. Segal; Sharon Morello, interview with Nancy L. Segal.

55. Justia Lawyers, "Robert Michael Shafran," 2020. Dave and Eddy ran Triplets after Bob's departure; the restaurant closed in 2000 several years after Eddy's suicide on June 16, 1995. Also see Neta Alexander, "A Triple Whammy: 'Three Identical Strangers' Asks Disturbing Questions." *Haaretz*, July 15, 2018, https://www.haaretz.com/us-news/.premium.MAGAZINE-a-triple-whammy-three-identical-strangers-asks-disturbing-questions-1.6265707gers-asks-disturbing-questions-1.626570. The triplets' restaurant has been referred to as both the Triplets Old New York Restaurant and the Triplets Roumanian Steakhouse.

56. Nancy L. Segal, *Indivisible by Two: Lives of Extraordinary Twins* (Cambridge, MA, Harvard University Press, 2005).

57. Nancy L. Segal, Scott L. Hershberger, and Sara Arad, "Meeting One's Twin: Perceived Social Closeness and Familiarity." *Evolutionary Psychology* 1, no. 1 (2003): 70–95.

58. Sharon Morello, interview with Nancy L. Segal.

59. Sharon Morello, interview with Nancy L. Segal.

60. Sharon Morello, interview with Nancy L. Segal.

61. Sharon Morello, interview with Nancy L. Segal.

62. Scott Morello, interview with Nancy L. Segal.

63. A "confidential" 1983 draft of a statement for CBS approximates the year 1968 as the end of the twin separation policy. Viola W. Bernard, "Explanatory Statement for Use by Public-Relations Consultant in Preparing a Reaction to CBS News Program About LWS-CDC Twin Placements and Research," March 22, 1983, Viola W. Bernard Archives, Columbia University.

64. "Twins Separated at Birth (Secret Twin Study)," *20/20*.

65. M. Bregman, email message to family and friends, March 3, 2018. Courtesy of Sharon Morello.

66. *20/20*, "Former Researcher Questioned About Secret Study With Separated Identical Siblings." March 9, 2020, https://www.facebook.com/ABC2020/videos/10155734111014934/?comment_id=10155735524024934&comment_tracking=%7B%22tn%22%3A%22R0%22%7D.

67. Sharon Morello, interview with Nancy L. Segal.

68. V. Bregman, interview with Nancy L. Segal.

69. "Face Sheet," Yale University Archives, courtesy of Sharon Morello.

70. The Cattell Infant Intelligence Test, developed in 1950, measures motor control and verbalization in children between three and thirty months of age, "Cattell Infant Intelligence Scale," *Encyclopedia of Childhood and Adolescence*, http://www.bookrags.com/research/cattell-infant-intelligence-scale-geca/#gsc.tab=0, 2005-2006. The Merrill-Palmer Scales include nineteen mental tests for assessing language skills, motor skills, manual dexterity, and matching ability in children between eighteen months and four years of age. "Merrill-Palmer Scales of Mental Tests," *Psychology Encyclopedia: Psychological Tests and Methods*, 2020, https://

psychology.jrank.org/pages/415/Merrill-Palmer-Scales-Mental-Tests.html. The Standford-Binet, developed in 1985 and now in its fifth edition, includes fifteen subtests that assess children's verbal reasoning, abstract/visual reasoning, quantitative reasoning, and short-term memory. It is given to children at age two, as well as to adults. "Stanford-Binet Intelligence Scale," https://www.ency clopedia.com/medicine/psychology/psychology-and-psychiatry/stanford-binet -intelligence-scale.

71. Sibylle K. Escalona and Harvey H. Corman's Albert Einstein Scales of Sensorimotor Development measure prehension (grasping), object permanence, and space. They can be used with typically developing infants and infants and adults with mental difficulties. James V. Kahn, "Cognitive Assessment of Mentally Retarded Infants and Preschoolers." In *Assessment of Young Developmentally Disabled Children*, edited by Theodore Wachs and Robert Sheehan (Boston: Springer, 1988). Also see Sibylle K. Escalona and Harvey H. Corman, "Albert Einstein Scales of Sensorimotor Development." Unpublished manuscript, Department of Psychiatry, Albert Einstein College of Medicine, New York, 1969.

72. The Bender-Gestalt Test examines visual-motor functioning, visual-perceptual skills, neurological impairment, and emotional disturbances in children and adults ages three and older. "Bender-Gestalt Test," 2020, https://www .encyclopedia.com/medicine/divisions-diagnostics-and-procedures/medicine/ bender-gestalt-test.

73. The Human Figure Drawing Test, developed in 1926, can be given to individuals of any age. The literature indicates that it can be used as an additional assessment of children's intelligence, but not as a substitute for standardized tests. Ratanotai Plbrukarn and Somchit Theeramanoparp, "Human Figure Drawing Test: Validity in Assessing Intelligence in Children Aged 3-10 Years." *Journal of the Medical Association Thai* 86, no. S3 (2003): S610–11; Eleanor Holtz-Eakin and Ida Sue Baron, "Human Figure Drawing Tests." In *Encyclopedia of Clinical Neuropsychology*, edited by Jeffrey S. Kreutzer, John DeLuca, and Bruce Caplan (New York: Springer, 2011).

74. The Children's Apperception Test (CAT) is a projective test for assessing children's personality, maturity level, and psychological health. The CAT, created by Leopold Bellak and Sonya Sorel Bellak in 1949, was based on the Thematic Apperception Test (TAT) created by Henry A. Murray. Stephen Pines, "Children's Apperception Test," *Encyclopedia of Children's Health*, 2020, http://www .healthofchildren.com/C/Children-s-Apperception-Test.html.

75. The Three Wishes tasks and Sentence Completion are semi-projective tests designed to assess self-perceptions. Elisabeth M. Dykens, K. Schwenk, Melissa A. Maxwell, and B. Myatt, "The Sentence Completion and Three Wishes Tasks: Windows into the Inner Lives of People with Intellectual Disabilities." *Journal of Intellectual Disability Research* 51, no. 8 (2007): 588–97.

76. The Rorschach Inkblot Test, developed in the 1920s, is a performance-based personality test. Individuals look at ten inkblots and say what they see. There

has been controversy surrounding the reliability and validity of the scores. Joni L. Mihura and Gregory J. Meyer, "Rorschach Inkblot Test." *The Encyclopedia of Clinical Psychology* (2014): 1–6.

77. The Mental Age IQ score, calculated as Mental Age/Chronological Age x 100, was used in the 1960s. Difficulties with that score led to the development of the Deviation IQ score, by David Wechsler. Wechsler revised IQ testing with the Wechsler-Bellevue test in 1939, updated as the Wechsler Adult Intelligence Scale in 1955. The currently used Deviation IQ is a standardized score, based on the child's standing within his or her narrow age band; see "Alfred Binet and the History of IQ Testing," 2020, https://www.verywellmind.com/history-of-intelligence-testing-2795581; "Wechsler Test and Intelligence Scale," https://iqtestprep.com/wechsler-intelligence-scale/. The twin study children would have completed the Wechsler Intelligence Scale for Children (WISC), developed in 1949. On subsequent visits some twins may have received the revised version, the WISC-R, that appeared in 1974.

78. Sharon Morello and V. Bregman, interviews with Nancy L. Segal.

79. Peter B. Neubauer, letter to Dr. S. B. Gusberg. March 8, 1966. Courtesy of Sharon Morello.

80. Ellen Herman, "Viola Wertheim Bernard (1908-1998)." Dr. Viola W. Bernard directed the Division of Community and Social Psychiatry at Columbia University's Medical School from 1956 to 1969. The Adoption History Project, 2012, https://pages.uoregon.edu/adoption/people/bernard.htm.

81. It is highly unlikely that any of the twins' blood samples were preserved. In the early 1960s, twin testing might have been done on the following independent blood group systems: A_1A_2BO, MN, rhesus, haptoglobin and the Gm-serum system; see Rune Cederlöf, Lars Friberg, Erland Jonsson, and Lennart Kaij, "Studies on Similarity Diagnosis in Twins with the Aid of Mailed Questionnaires." *Acta Genetica et Statistica Medica* 11 (1961): 338–62.

82. Rondell and Michaels, *The Adopted Family.*

83. Lawrence Wright, *Twins: And What They Tell Us About Who We Are* (New York: John Wiley & Sons, 1997).

84. Viola W. Bernard, "Note for Records of Twins (or Triplets) Placed for Adoption Separately in Infancy." Spence-Chapin, 1978. Courtesy of Sharon Morello; Bernard, interview with Lawrence Wright.

CHAPTER 12

1. Peter B. Neubauer, "Twins." In *Comprehensive Textbook of Psychiatry*, edited by Alan M. Freedman and Harold I. Kaplan, 2301–3 (Baltimore: Williams & Wilkins, 1975).

2. Lawrence M. Perlman, "Memories of the Child Development Center Study of Adopted Monozygotic Twins Reared Apart: An Unfulfilled Promise." *Twin Research and Human Genetics* 8, no. 3 (2005): 271–75; Nancy L. Segal, "Commentary: More Thoughts on the Child Development Center Twin Study." *Twin Research and Human Genetics* 8, no. 3 (2005): 276–81.

3. New York University's Institute for Psychoanalytic Education is now known as the Psychoanalytic Association of New York. https://med.nyu.edu/psych/affiliates/institute-psychoanalytic-education.

4. Jeremy Pearce, "Peter B. Neubauer, 94, Noted Child Psychiatrist, Is Dead." *New York Times*, March 3, 2008, https://www.nytimes.com/2008/03/03/nyregion/03neubauer.html; Center for Psychoanalytic Training and Research, *Digital Historical Collections*, Columbia University Health Sciences Schools, https://www.library-archives.cumc.columbia.edu/digital-collections-columbia-university-health-science-schools. Neubauer lectured at Columbia University between 1984 and 2007.

5. "Peter B. Neubauer," Zero to Three, 2020, https://www.zerotothree.org/our-team/peter-b-neubauer.

6. Note that Yale University rarely accepts archived material from its faculty members unless the work is extraordinary or relates to university activities. Yale University archivist, 2020.

7. Viola W. Bernard Papers, Archives & Special Collections, Columbia University Health Sciences Library; Stephen E. Novak, email correspondence with Nancy L. Segal, June 1, 2021. The deed of gift was signed by Kathleen L. Kelly, Cary A. Koplin, and Joan Wofford as executors of the estate of Viola W. Bernard, and by Perry Ottenberg as president of the Viola W. Bernard Foundation. The typed date is Sept. 14, 2000 but it is unclear if any or all of them signed on that actual date. Columbia University archivist Stephen E. Novak's counter-signature is dated Oct. 13, 2000; therefore, the others would have signed some time before that because the actual paper document would have been mailed to Novak for his signature.

8. William McCormack, "Records from Controversial Twin Study Sealed at Yale Until 2065." *Yale News*, October 1, 2018, https://yaledailynews.com/blog/2018/10/01/records-from-controversial-twin-study-sealed-at-yale-until-2065/.

9. Stephen E. Novak, email correspondence to Nancy L. Segal, May 12, 2020. Novak thanked me for reminding him that a decision was needed by 2021.

10. Novak, email correspondence to Nancy L. Segal, May 19, 2021. Owing to the pandemic, visits to the library holding Viola W. Bernard's archive have been restricted to members of Columbia University.

11. Samuel Abrams and Peter B. Neubauer, "Object Orientedness: The Person or the Thing." *The Psychoanalytic Quarterly* 45, no. 1 (1976): 73–99; Samuel Abrams, "Disposition and the Environment." *The Psychoanalytic Study of the Child* 41, no. 1 (1986): 41–60; Peter B. Neubauer and Alexander Neubauer, *Nature's*

Thumbprint: The New Genetics of Personality (New York: Addison-Wesley Publishing Co., 1990); Samuel Abrams and Peter B. Neubauer, "Hartmann's Vision: Identical Twins and Developmental Organizations." *The Psychoanalytic Study of the Child* 49, no. 1 (1994): 49–59.

12. Lois Oppenheim, "The Facts about the Neubauer Twin Study: An Interview about a Controversy or a Controversial Interview?" *International Journal of Controversial Discussions* 1 (2020): 171–88.

13. Peter Neubauer and Christa Balzert, "Genetik und Psychotherapie" ("Genetics and Psychotherapy"), in *Der Psychoanalytische Prozeß*, edited by Sylvia Zwettler-Otte and Albrecht Komarek, 169–83 (Vienna: Turia & Kant, 1996).

14. Christa Balzert, "Genetic Findings and Their Impact on the Psychoanalytic Theory of Development." Presented at the Institute for Child, Adolescent and Family Studies, New York City, NY; Peter B. Neubauer and Christa Balzert, "Genetics and Psychotherapy." Presented at the American Academy of Psychoanalysis, Miami, FL, May 1995. The dates of these conferences were not provided in Oppenheim's interview, but the date and location of the Neubauer and Balzert paper were indicated in other sources.

15. Susan L. Farber, *Identical Twins Reared Apart: A Reanalysis* (New York: Basic Books, 1981).

16. Neubauer and Neubauer, *Nature's Thumbprint.*

17. George L. Engel, "The Death of a Twin: Mourning and Anniversary Reactions. Fragments of 10 Years of Self-Analysis." *International Journal of Psycho-Analysis* 56 (1975): 23–40. I had the pleasure of hearing Dr. Engel deliver an early version of this paper at the Chicago Psychoanalytic Institute, Helen Ross Lecture, 1974.

18. Abrams, "Disposition and the Environment."

19. Susan Farber, "Sex Differences in the Expression of Adoption Ideas: Observations of Adoptees From Birth Through Latency." *American Journal of Orthopsychiatry* 47, no. 4 (1977): 639–50.

20. "Matched samples" is a statistical term. It refers to participant samples in which each member of one sample is matched with a member of all other samples, except for the measure under study. *Glossary of Statistical Terms*, April 7, 2004, https://stats.oecd.org/glossary/detail.asp?ID=3709.

21. International University of Berlin, "Linked Through Orthodoxy and Internationalism," https://www.ipu-berlin.de/en/harald-leupold-loewenthal-im-portraet/.

22. Oppenheim, "The Facts about the Neubauer Twin Study."

23. "Mag. means, I studied first Latin and German to teach as a 'Magister,' but then I made a 2nd study, Psychology, to become Doctor and psychoanalyst." Sylvia Zwettler-Otte, email correspondence to Nancy L. Segal, April 30, 2020, May 1, 2020.

24. Abrams and Neubauer, "Hartmann's Vision"; Neubauer and Balzert, "Genetik und Psychotherapie."

25. Viola W. Bernard, letter to Florence Kreech, March 22, 1976, Viola W. Bernard Archives, Columbia University.

26. Samuel Abrams, interview with Lawrence Wright, 1993.

27. Dr. Leon Hoffman, interview with Nancy L. Segal, 2020; A former student, email correspondence with Nancy L. Segal, June 19, 2019.

28. The Behavior Genetics Association was established in 1970, bga.org; the International Society for Twin Studies was established in 1974, https://twinstud ies.org.

29. These studies were conducted or were being conducted by Drs. James Shields in England (1962), Niels Juel-Nielsen in Denmark (1965, 1980), and Thomas J. Bouchard Jr. in the United States (1979; data collection continued until 1999 and papers are still being written). A fourth major study conducted in the United States by Horatio H. Newman and colleagues had been completed in 1937. Another comprehensive reared-apart twin study took place in Sweden, beginning in 1984, several years after the LWS-CDC twin study ended their data collection. However, Dr. Neubauer and colleagues were processing their materials and thinking about writing a book; thus, collaborations would have been possible.

30. "Identical Twins Reared Apart: A Longitudinal Study." Proposal to Yale University Press, circa 1986. Viola Wertheim Bernard Papers, Archives & Special Collections, Columbia University Health Sciences Library.

31. Niels Juel-Nielsen, *Individual and Environment: Monozygotic Twins Reared Apart* (New York: International Universities Press, 1965), 28. I contacted several of Juel-Nielsen's colleagues to determine if there were letters or notes from his association with Neubauer, but there were none.

32. Nancy L. Segal, *Entwined Lives: Twins and What They Tell Us About Human Behavior* (New York: Plume, 2000); Nancy L. Segal, *Born Together—Reared Apart: The Landmark Minnesota Twin Study* (Cambridge, MA: Harvard University Press, 2012).

33. "Belmont Report: Ethical Principles and Guidelines for the Protection of Human Subjects of Research, Report of the National Commission for the Protection of Human Subjects of Biomedical and Behavioral Research." *Federal Register* 44, no. 76 (April 18, 1979): 23192–97.

34. Viola W. Bernard, letter to Dr. Christa Balzert, November 9, 1978, Viola Wertheim Bernard Papers, Archives & Special Collections, Columbia University Health Sciences Library.

35. Viola W. Bernard, letter to Stephen W. Tulin. June 11, 1986; George Rausch, letter to Dr. Vivan Wolsk, October 27, 1978, Viola W. Bernard Archives, Columbia University.

36. Child Development Center, Consent and Release, September 21, 1978, Viola Wertheim Bernard Archives, Columbia University.

37. Lynn Kelly, "Adoption Study Meetings." Memo to Dr. Bernard. October 10, 1984. Viola Wertheim Bernard Papers, Archives & Special Collections, Columbia University Health Sciences Library.

38. Peter Neubauer, "Endangerment from Publication of Twin Study." Inter-office memo to Professor Bertram J. Black, JBFCS, October 9, 1984.

39. Viola W. Bernard, "Handwritten Note to Peter Neubauer," July 9, 1986, Viola Wertheim Bernard Papers, Archives & Special Collections, Columbia University Health Sciences Library.

40. Viola W. Bernard, "Joint Meeting, re: Publication of Adopted Twin Study," January 30, 1985, Viola Wertheim Bernard Papers, Archives & Special Collections, Columbia University Health Sciences Library.

41. Viola W. Bernard, "Publication of Adopted Twin Study." February 20, 1985, Viola Wertheim Bernard Papers, Archives & Special Collections, Columbia University Health Sciences Library.

42. Robert Mcg. (McGill) Thomas Jr., "William J. Curran, 71, Dies; Developed Health Law Field," *New York Times*, September 25, 1996, https://www.nytimes.com/1996/09/25/us/william-j-curran-71-dies-developed-health-law-field.html.

43. "Institutional Review Board Meeting," March 7, 1985, Viola Wertheim Bernard Papers, Archives & Special Collections, Columbia University Health Sciences Library. Neubauer is listed as a member, but this could be in reference to his membership in the CDC because he was presenting the twin project to the committee for approval. Drs. Christa Balzert and Bertram Black were among the guests.

44. An assurance of compliance is a document submitted by an institution that engages in human subjects' research conducted or supported by the Department of Health and Human Services. Through the assurance of compliance, an institution commits to the Department of Health and Human Services that it will adhere to the requirements specified in the regulations for the protection of human subjects. https://www.hhs.gov/ohrp/regulations-and-policy/guidance/faq/assurance-process/index.html. On May 4, 2020, I sent a message to Dr. Bruce Grellong, chairperson of the Centers for Disease Control and Prevention's IRB, asking for an interview and inquiring about the document on informed consent. On May 19, I received a reply in which he apologized for the delay and requested a copy of the document with which he said he was unfamiliar; I sent it. I did not receive a response to my follow-up message sent in July.

45. Professor Bertram J. Black, memo to Dr. Peter Neubauer, March 14, 1985, Viola Wertheim Bernard Papers, Archives & Special Collections, Columbia University Health Sciences Library.

46. "Publication and Liability," Adoption Study Meeting, April 15, 1986, Viola Wertheim Bernard Papers, Archives & Special Collections, Columbia University Health Sciences Library.

47. Drs. Bernard and Neubauer joked that they would probably never publish the twin study findings unless they disguised their work as a Japanese study. Unnamed source, interview with Nancy L. Segal, 2020.

48. "Publication of Twin Book," memorandum to Neubauer, Abrams, and Balzert, May 5, 1986; "Addendum," May 7, 1986, Viola Wertheim Bernard

Papers, Archives & Special Collections, Columbia University Health Sciences Library.

49. Viola W. Bernard, "Copy of Phone Talk," May 27, 1986, Viola Wertheim Bernard Papers, Archives & Special Collections, Columbia University Health Sciences Library.

50. Bernard, letter to Stephen W. Tulin.

51. Viola W. Bernard, letter to Peter Neubauer, July 9, 1986, Viola Wertheim Bernard Papers, Archives & Special Collections, Columbia University Health Sciences Library.

52. L. Erlenmeyer-Kimling and Barbara Cornblatt, "Biobehavioral Risk Factors in Children of Schizophrenic Parents." *Journal of Autism and Developmental Disorders* 14, no. 4 (1984): 357–74; L. Erlenmeyer-Kimling, Clarice Kestenbaum, Hector Bird, and Ulla Hilldoff, "Assessment of the New York High-Risk Project Subjects in Sample A Who Are Now Clinically Deviant." In *Children at Risk for Schizophrenia: A Longitudinal Perspective*, edited by Norman F. Watt, E. James Anthony, Lyman C. Wynne, and Jon E. Rolf, 227–39 (New York: Cambridge University Press, 1984); L. Erlenmeyer-Kimling and Barbara A. Cornblatt, "The New York High-Risk Project: A Followup Report." *Schizophrenia Bulletin* 13, no. 3 (1987): 451–61.

53. Barbara Fish, "Characteristics and Sequelae of the Neurointegrative Disorder in Infants at Risk for Schizophrenia: 1952-1982." In *Children at Risk for Schizophrenia: A Longitudinal Perspective*, edited by Norman F. Watt, E. James Anthony, Lyman C. Wynne, and Jon E. Rolf, 423–39 (New York: Cambridge University Press, 1984); Sarnoff Mednick and Fini Schulsinger, "Some Premorbid Characteristics Related to Breakdown in Children with Schizophrenic Mothers." In *The Transmission of Schizophrenia*, edited by David Rosenthal and Seymour S. Kety, 267–91 (Oxford: Pergamon Press, 1968).

54. Dr. Bernard noted that she had mailed the letter to Curran on October 10, 1986. However, she referred to a letter dated October 18 that was originally sent on October 10, so it was not mailed again.

55. Robert Mcg. (McGill) Thomas Jr., "William J. Curran, 71, Dies; Developed Health Law Field," *New York Times*, September 25, 1996, https://www.nytimes.com/1996/09/25/us/william-j-curran-71-dies-developed-health-law-field.html.

56. Viola W. Bernard, letter to Professor William Curran. Bernard learned that Curran's appointment was in the School of Public Health, not the Law School, which may have explained the difficulty in reaching him. October 10, 1986, Viola Wertheim Bernard Papers, Archives & Special Collections, Columbia University Health Sciences Library.

57. This document, dated May 23, 1983, was largely excerpted from one dated April 11, 1983; see chapter 6.

58. "Outline of Legal Questions," October 31, 1986, Viola Wertheim Bernard Papers, Archives & Special Collections, Columbia University Health Sciences Library.

59. Viola W. Bernard, "Adoption." In *Encyclopedia of Mental Health* (New York: Franklin Watts, 1963).

60. Jonathan Kraus, "Predicting Success of Foster Placements for School-Age Children." *Social Work* 16, no. 1 (1971): 63–67; Martha J. Aldridge and Patricia W. Cautley, "Placing Siblings in the Same Foster Home." *Child Welfare* 55, no. 2 (1976). These studies, while published in the 1970s, included children placed in the 1960s.

61. Exactly who these "40 or so individuals" are is not specified, but are most likely the eleven twins, their adoptive parents, and possibly some siblings or biological mothers.

62. Documents retrieved from Viola Wertheim Bernard Papers, Archives & Special Collections, Columbia University Health Sciences Library.

63. Viola W. Bernard, "Addendum to 10/31/1986 Outline of Legal Questions," Viola Wertheim Bernard Papers, Archives & Special Collections, Columbia University Health Sciences Library.

64. Peter B. Neubauer and Viola W. Bernard, letter to Professor William Curran, November 3, 1986, Viola Wertheim Bernard Papers, Archives & Special Collections, Columbia University Health Sciences Library.

65. Viola W. Bernard, letter to Peter B. Neubauer, November 5, 1986, Viola Wertheim Bernard Papers, Archives & Special Collections, Columbia University Health Sciences Library.

CHAPTER 13

1. "Identical Twins Reared Apart: A Longitudinal Study," proposal to Yale University Press, July 1985; Viola W. Bernard, letter to Peter Neubauer, June 11, 1986, Viola Wertheim Bernard Papers, Archives & Special Collections, Columbia University Health Sciences Library.

2. "Identical Twins Reared Apart: A Longitudinal Study" proposal.

3. John G. Ryden, "Letter of Agreement," Yale University Press, December 19, 1986, Viola Wertheim Bernard Papers, Archives & Special Collections, Columbia University Health Sciences Library.

4. Ryden, "Letter of Agreement," Bernard Papers, Archives & Special Collections, Columbia University Health Sciences Library. The 1987 letter of agreement states that it superseded the contract of December 22, whereas the previous contract is dated December 19, 1986. It is unlikely that two contracts would have been drafted three days apart.

5. The additions and adjustments have been paraphrased and the italics are mine.

6. Peter B. Neubauer, letter to William Curran. December 29, 1986, Viola Wertheim Bernard Papers, Archives & Special Collections, Columbia University Health Sciences Library.

7. Peter B. Neubauer, letter to William Curran, April 9, 1987, Viola Wertheim Bernard Papers, Archives & Special Collections, Columbia University Health Sciences Library.

8. Viola W. Bernard, letter to Justine Polier, February 27, 1987, Viola Wertheim Bernard Papers, Archives & Special Collections, Columbia University Health Sciences Library.

9. The words "book" and "monograph" are used interchangeably in the twin study letters and documents. They are quite similar; however, a book is a work of fiction or nonfiction, whereas a monograph is a detailed study or paper on a limited topic. https://www.dictionary.com/browse/book?s=t; https://www.dictionary.com/browse/monograph.

10. Viola W. Bernard, letter to Samuel Abrams, March 6, 1987, Viola Wertheim Bernard Papers, Archives & Special Collections, Columbia University Health Sciences Library.

11. Viola W. Bernard, "Child Development Center Project" (meeting of the members of the Tappanz Foundation, Inc. Board of Trustees), June 1, 1987, Viola Wertheim Bernard Papers, Archives & Special Collections, Columbia University Health Sciences Library.

12. Peter Neubauer, "Summary of Conversation with Sheldon Fogelman, re: Contract," July 15, 1987, Viola Wertheim Bernard Papers, Archives & Special Collections, Columbia University Health Sciences Library.

13. The Sheldon Fogelman Agency was established in 1975 for the publication of children's books.

14. Ronald S. Wilson, "The Louisville Twin Study: Developmental Synchronies in Behavior." *Child Development* 54, no. 2 (1983): 298–316.

15. Eric N. Turkheimer, "Gene-Environment Interaction and Correlation in the Louisville Twin Study." National Institutes of Health, https://grantome.com/grant/NIH/R03-AG048850-01, 2014-2016.

16. Kid Sense Child Development Corporation, "Gross Motor Skills," https://childdevelopment.com.au/areas-of-concern/gross-motor-skills/; "Fine Motor Skills," https://childdevelopment.com.au/areas-of-concern/fine-motor-skills/.

17. The motor-function areas were listed from one to fifteen; either item fourteen was not listed or was inadvertently labeled as fifteen.

18. Nancy L. Segal, *Born Together—Reared Apart: The Landmark Minnesota Twin Study* (Cambridge, MA: Harvard University Press, 2012).

19. Ryden, interview and email correspondence with Nancy L. Segal, 2020.

20. Paid Notice, "Deaths: Topkis, Gladys Susman." *New York Times*, September 28, 2009, https://archive.nytimes.com/query.nytimes.com/gst/fullpage-9901EEDF1E3AF93BA1575AC0A96F9C8B63.html.

21. Ms. Jean E. Thomson Black, email correspondence to Nancy L. Segal, 2020.

22. Paid Notice, "Deaths: Topkis, Gladys Susman." *New York Times*, September 28, 2009, https://archive.nytimes.com/query.nytimes.com/gst/fullpage

-9901EEDF1E3AF93BA1575AC0A96F9C8B63.html; "Felony & Mayhem," https://felonyandmayhem.com/pages/about-us.

23. Maggie Topkis, email correspondence to Nancy L. Segal, May 12, 2020.

24. Staff Member, Yale University Press Acquisitions Department, email correspondence to Nancy L. Segal, 2020; Ms. Jean E. Thomson Black, email correspondence to Nancy L. Segal, 2020.

25. Yale University Press, email correspondence to Nancy L. Segal, 2020.

26. Peter B. Neubauer, interview with Lawrence Wright, 1993.

27. Peter B. Neubauer and Alexander Neubauer, *Nature's Thumbprint: The New Genetics of Personality* (New York: Addison-Wesley Publishing Company, 1990).

28. Leon Hoffman and Lois Oppenheim, "*Three Identical Strangers and The Twinning Reaction*—Clarifying History and Lessons for Today from Peter Neubauer's Twins Study." *Journal of the American Medical Association* 322, no. 1 (2019): 10–12.

29. Lois Oppenheim, "The Facts about the Neubauer Twin Study: An Interview about a Controversy or a Controversial Interview?" *International Journal of Controversial Discussions* 2020 (1): 2020, 171–88.

30. "Book Draft and Dictation," Yale University Archives, circa 1960-1980, https://archives.yale.edu/repositories/12/archival_objects/1202637.

31. Pamela Bernstein, interview with Nancy L. Segal, 2020.

32. Manta Media, Inc., "Pamela Bernstein," 2019, https://www.manta.com/c/mm51fsb/pam-bernstein.

33. S. Yoshimasu, "Psychopathie und Kriminialität." *Psychiatric Neurology—Japan* 45 (1941): 455–531.

34. Bernstein, interview with Nancy L. Segal.

35. Neubauer and Neubauer, *Nature's Thumbprint*.

36. Ms. Jane Isay, interview with Nancy L. Segal, 2020.

37. Jane Isay, "How I Found Alice Miller, and Lost Her." *Huffington Post*, May 25, 2011, https://www.huffpost.com/entry/how-i-found-alice-m iller_b_554297?guccounter=1&guce_referrer=aHR0cHM6Ly93d3cuZ29vZ2xl LmNvbS8&guce_referrer_sig=AQAAADnbwuhryzX1WP1TdLM-e0tw8uAxa CLWYtV5Xpve_zGuh8K8hB2HbTZV0RSHC3jMuyqUVZazwD1pZZtWIM vvpOX6nMqW1ZN4xaSnf7V9BLq5HmeGKa0X8choEBsFs0Qcrx0mCAtnV _Q_aht541f7Rw9kZCmmyn3sr4K3f51ng8IF; "Jane Issay," https://www.audible .com/author/Jane-Isay/B001JS0ET4.

38. "Jane Isay," *New York Journal of Books*, https://www.nyjournalofbooks .com/reviewer/jane-isay.

39. Ms. Isay, interview with Nancy L. Segal, 2020.

40. Ms. Isay, interview with Nancy L. Segal, 2020.

41. Bob Roehr, "Richard Isay: Cured Psychonanalysis of Its Phobia." *British Medical Journal* 345 (2012): 28; Isay, interview with Nancy L. Segal.

42. Ms. Isay, interview with Nancy L. Segal.

43. Orbis, Yale University Library Catalog, https://orbis.library.yale.edu/ vwebv/holdingsInfo?bibId=910175.

44. Albert Solnit was director of the Yale Child Study Center from 1966 to 1983. He passed away in 2002. "In Memoriam: Renowned Yale Child Psychiatrist Albert J. Solnit," *Yale News*, June 25, 2002, https://news.yale.edu/2002/06/25/memoriam-renowned-yale-child-psychiatrist-albert-j-solnit.

45. Lois Oppenheim, email correspondence to Nancy L. Segal, April 22, 2020.

46. Unnamed source, interview with Nancy L. Segal, 2019.

47. Yale University archivist, 2020. The love letters sent by poet T. S. Eliot to Emily Hale were given by Hale to Princeton University in 1969, with the stipulation that the material not be released until fifty years after their deaths. The file was opened in January 2020; Maria Gramer, "The Love Song of T.S. Eliot." *New York Times*, Section C, p. 3, January 6, 2020.

48. The Health Insurance Portability and Accountability Act, passed in 1996, is a federal law requiring the establishment of national standards to protect against disclosure of sensitive health information without a person's knowledge or consent. Centers for Disease Control and Prevention, September 14, 2018, https://www.cdc.gov/phlp/publications/topic/hipaa.html. The Family Educational Rights and Privacy Act is a federal law protecting the privacy of student education records. It was updated in 2011. US Department of Education, https://www2.ed.gov/policy/gen/guid/fpco/ferpa/index.html; "Student Privacy 101: What is FERPA and Why Does it Matter?" Pam Dixon, World Privacy Forum, https://www.worldprivacyforum.org/2015/01/a-brief-history-of-ferpa-reform-and-why-it-matters/.

49. Yale University archivist, comment to Nancy L. Segal, 2020. The donations were presumably those made to the Yale Child Study Center, directed by Donald J. Cohen from 1983–2001.

50. Tim Wardle, *Three Identical Strangers*, Raw Films, United Kingdom, 2018; Megyn Kelly *Today*, "The Unbelievable Way 3 Men Found Out They Were Triplets Separated as Babies." NBC, July 12, 2018, https://www.youtube.com/watch?v=J30G5RaoWNk.

51. *20/20 Saturday*, "What the Jewish Board Now Says to Twins in the Study," June 2, 2018, https://www.facebook.com/watch/?v=10155935218429934.

52. Andrew Paparella, Eric M. Strauss, and Alexa Valiente, "Twins Make Astonishing Discovery That They Were Separated Shortly After Birth and Then Part of a Secret Study." *ABC News*, March 9, 2018, https://abcnews.go.com/US/twins-makeastonishing-discovery-separated-birth-part-secret/story?id=53593943.

CHAPTER 14

1. Charlotte Goldberg, video produced by Justin Goldberg, 2017, https://www.adultbehavior.org.

2. Erika Hayasaki, "Identical Twins Hint at How Environments Change Gene Expression." *Atlantic Monthly*, May 15, 2018, https://www.theatlantic.com/science/archive/2018/05/twin-epigenetics/560189/.

3. Bruce Haring, "Justin Goldberg's Search for Long-Lost Twin Is Story Made for Hollywood." *Deadline*, November 24, 2017, https://deadline.com/2017/11/justin-goldberg-hollywood-executive-twin-brother-search-adoption-12022 13641/.

4. Julie Goldberg Maniha, interview with Nancy L. Segal, 2020.

5. Justin Goldberg, interview with Nancy L. Segal, 2020.

6. Rema Goldberg, interview with Nancy L. Segal, 2020.

7. One of these articles Justin came across was Lawrence Wright's "Double Mystery," published in the *New Yorker* magazine in 1995. The article is shown in Justin's online video.

8. Justin Goldberg, interviews with Nancy L. Segal, 2017, 2018, 2020; video produced by Justin Goldberg, https://www.adultbehavior.org, 2017.

9. Justin's sister Julie lives in northern California, approximately four hundred miles from Los Angeles.

10. Justin Goldberg, interviews with Nancy L. Segal and *ABC News*, 2017.

11. Julie was born on December 10, 1969.

12. Nancy L. Segal, *Entwined Lives: Twins and What They Tell Us About Human Behavior* (New York: Plume, 2000).

13. J. Goldberg Maniha, interview with Nancy L. Segal.

14. R. Goldberg, interview with Nancy L. Segal.

15. Jay Goldberg, interview with Nancy L. Segal, 2020.

16. Eric M. Strauss, interview with Nancy l. Segal, 2017.

17. Justin Goldberg, interviews with Nancy L. Segal.

18. R. Goldberg, interview with Nancy L. Segal.

19. Segal, *Entwined Lives*.

20. Segal, *Entwined Lives*.

21. J. Goldberg Maniha, interview and email correspondence with Nancy L. Segal, 2020.

22. NBCUniversal Media Village, "*SYFY*: About," https://www.nbcumv.com/programming/syfy/about?network=33143.

23. Lori Shinseki (director), *The Twinning Reaction*, Fire Horse Pictures, United States, 2017.

24. Bruce Haring, "Justin Goldberg's Search for Long-Lost Twin Is Story Made for Hollywood." *Deadline*, November 24, 2017; Bruce Haring, email correspondence to Nancy L. Segal, November 26, 2017.

25. "Jay Goldberg," http://www.jaygoldberg.com/.

26. Marquis Who's Who, "Jay Goldberg Honored for Excellence in Civil and Criminal Law," October 11, 2016, https://www.24-7pressrelease.com/press-release/429371/jay-goldberg-honored-for-excellence-in-civil-and-criminal-law.

27. Jay Goldberg, *The Courtroom Is My Theater: My Lifelong Representation of Famous Politicians, Industrialists, Entertainers, Men of Honor, and More* (New York: Post Hill Press, 2018).

28. "Rema Goldberg," Linkedin, https://www.linkedin.com/in/rema-goldberg-39ba15168/; "Rema Goldberg: Artist," remagoldberg.com.

29. Justin Goldberg, interviews with Nancy L. Segal; R. Goldberg, interview with Nancy L. Segal.

30. Justin Goldberg, interviews with Nancy L. Segal. Jay Goldberg claims that he never encouraged Justin to enter the legal profession.

31. "Justin Goldberg," Linkedin, https://www.linkedin.com/in/justingoldberg2/.

32. "Justin Goldberg," Linkedin, https://www.linkedin.com/in/justingoldberg2/.

33. Justin Goldberg and Eric M. Strauss, interviews with Nancy L. Segal, 2017, 2018.

34. Justin Goldberg and J. Goldberg Maniha, interviews with Nancy L. Segal.

35. Karen March, "Who Do I Look Like? Gaining a Sense of Self-Authenticity Through the Physical Reflections of Others." *Symbolic Interaction* 23, no. 4 (2000): 359–73.

36. Nancy L. Segal, *Born Together—Reared Apart: The Landmark Minnesota Twin Study* (Cambridge, MA: Harvard University Press, 2012).

37. Adoption Search Reunion, "Locating Records," January 28, 2010, http://www.adoptionsearchreunion.org.uk/search/righttosearch/accessinfo.htm.

38. Christina Bryan Fitzgibbons, "My Hoodie Project," 2017, https://www.myhoodieproject.com/.

39. Christina Bryan Fitzgibbons, interviews with Nancy L. Segal, 2017, 2020.

40. Joseph M. Hall, post-adoption coordinator, letter from Spence-Chapin to Justin Goldberg, February 16, 2018. Courtesy of Justin Goldberg.

41. Fitzgibbons, interviews with Nancy L. Segal.

42. R. Goldberg, interview with Nancy L. Segal.

43. According to traditional Jewish Law, children born to Jewish mothers whose partners are not Jewish are considered to be Jewish; however, children are not recognized as being Jewish if their fathers are their only Jewish parent. Tzvi Freeman and Yehuda Shurpin, "Why Is Jewishness Matrilinial?" https://www.chabad.org/library/article_cdo/aid/601092/jewish/Why-Is-Jewishness-Matrilineal.htm

44. The Spence-Chapin narrative indicated that Joan's age at Justin's birth was nineteen.

45. Justin Goldberg, interviews with Nancy L. Segal.

46. François Brunelle, "I'm Not a Look-Alike!" http://www.francoisbrunelle.com/webn/e-project.html.

47. Nancy L. Segal, Brittney A. Hernandez, Jamie L. Graham, and Ulrich Ettinger, "Pairs of Genetically Unrelated Look-Alikes: Further Tests of Personality Resemblance and Social Affiliation." *Human Nature* 29, no. 4 (2018): 402–17.

48. Christine Hauser, "Meet Your Art Twin: A 400-Year-Old with an Oily Complexion." *New York Times*, Section C, January 17, 2018, 1; Jessica Grimaud,

"Do You Have a Look-alike? Find Your Doppelgänger," November 20, 2019, https://www.familysearch.org/blog/en/find-your-doppelganger/; also see twin strangers.net.

49. Daniel G. Freedman, *Human Sociobiology: A Holistic Approach* (New York: Free Press, 1979).

50. Segal, Hernandez, Graham, and Ettinger, "Pairs of Genetically Unrelated Look-Alikes."

51. ABC News, "Twins Separated at Birth (Secret Twin Study)," *20/20*, March 9, 2018.

CHAPTER 15

1. Elyse Schein and Paula Bernstein, *Identical Strangers: A Memoir of Twins Separated and Reunited* (New York: Random House, 2007).

2. Schein and Bernstein, *Identical Strangers*.

3. Schein and Bernstein, *Identical Strangers*.

4. "Types of Schizoaffective Disorder and Treatment Strategies," http://www.mentalhealthcenter.org/types-of-schizoaffective-disorder-and-treatment-strategies/. The twins' birth mother had been in and out of psychiatric institutions.

5. Emily Nussbaum, "Sliding Doors," *New York Magazine*, October 11, 2007, https://nymag.com/arts/books/features/39290/.

6. Nancy L. Segal, *Entwined Lives: Twins and What They Tell Us About Human Behavior* (New York: Plume, 2000); Nancy L. Segal, *Born Together—Reared Apart: The Landmark Minnesota Twin Study* (Cambridge, MA: Harvard University Press, 2012).

7. Denise Flaim, "Two Sisters, Lost and Found," *Newsday*, October 17, 2007, https://www.newsday.com/lifestyle/two-sisters-lost-and-found-1.876887.

8. Schein and Bernstein, *Identical Strangers*.

9. Flaim, "Two Sisters, Lost and Found."

10. Schein and Bernstein, *Identical Strangers*.

11. Joe Richman, "The Story of Two Women Who Found Out They Were Identical Strangers," *Radio Diaries*, March 22, 2016, https://whyy.org/segments/the-story-of-two-women-who-found-out-they-were-identical-strangers/.

12. Krista Carothers, "Twins Separated at Birth: 12 Real Stories That Will Give You Goosebumps," *Reader's Digest*, 2018, https://www.rd.com/culture/twins-separated-at-birth/; Aviva Patz, *Reader's Digest* editor, email correspondence to Nancy L. Segal, August 6, 2018.

13. "Elyse Schein," Open Path Psychotherapy Collective, https://openpathcollective.org/clinicians/elyse-schein/.

14. "Paula Bernstein, https://www.paulabernstein.com/.

15. Schein and Bernstein, *Identical Strangers*.

CHAPTER 16

1. Hedda Schacter Abbott, interviews with Nancy L. Segal, 2019, 2020.

2. Ulla Sankilampi, Marja-Leena Hannila, Antti Saari, Mika Gissler, and Leo Dunkel, "New Population-Based References for Birth Weight, Length, and Head Circumference in Singletons and Twins From 23 to 43 Gestation Weeks." *Annals of Medicine* 45, no. 5-6 (2013): 446–54.

3. Abbott, interview in *The Twinning Reaction*, Lori Shinseki (director), Fire Horse Pictures, United States, 2017.

4. Abbott, interview with Nancy L. Segal.

5. Blake Apgar, "Suspended Las Vegas Lawyer Jacob Hafter Dies at Age 42," *Las Vegas Review-Journal*, April 18, 2018, https://www.reviewjournal.com/news/suspended-las-vegas-lawyer-jacob-hafter-dies-at-age-42/.

6. Celia Silverman, interviews with Nancy L. Segal, 2019, 2020.

7. Adam S. Sherman, interview and email correspondence with Nancy L. Segal, 2020.

8. C. Silverman, interviews with Nancy L. Segal.

9. Ronald S. Wilson, "Analysis of Longitudinal Twin Data: Basic Model and Applications to Physical Growth Measures." *Acta Geneticae Medicae et Gemellologiae: Twin Research* 28, no. 2 (1979): 93–105.

10. Nancy L. Segal, *Twin Mythconceptions: False Beliefs, Fables, and Facts About Twins* (New York: Elsevier, 2017).

11. A. Sherman, interview and email correspondence with Nancy L. Segal.

12. Laura E. Berk, *Child Development*, ninth edition (Boston: Pearson, 2013); T. Berry Brazelton, "It's Twins." *Redbook Magazine*, February 1980, 80–84.

13. Leo Silverman, interview with Nancy L. Segal, 2020; Paula Sherman, interview in *The Twinning Reaction*.

14. Caption, *The Twinning Reaction*.

15. A. Sherman, interview and email correspondence with Nancy L. Segal.

16. L. Silverman, interview and email correspondence with Nancy L. Segal, 2020; C. Silverman, interview with Nancy L. Segal, 2019, 2020; Janet Silverman, interviews with Nancy L. Segal, 2020.

17. L. Silverman, email correspondence with Nancy L. Segal; C. Silverman, interviews with Nancy L. Segal.

18. C. Silverman, interview with Nancy L. Segal.

19. J. Silverman, interview with Nancy L. Segal.

20. J. Silverman, interview with Nancy L. Segal.

21. Martin Silverman, interview with Nancy L. Segal.

22. George Silverman, interview with Nancy L. Segal.

23. L. Silverman and C. Silverman, interviews with Nancy L. Segal, 2020.

24. In the 1970s, few female students in the United States were enrolled in industrial arts classes that were traditionally "male," such as carpentry and

woodworking. William A. Horn, Gertrude Mitchell, and Mark Travaglini, eds., *American Education* (Washington, DC: US Department of Health, Education, and Welfare, Office of Education, 1977).

25. C. Silverman, interviews with Nancy L. Segal.

26. L. Silverman, email correspondence to Nancy L. Segal.

27. Shinseki, *The Twinning Reaction*.

28. Benjamin N. Cardozo was Justice of the US Supreme Court and Chief Judge of the New York Court of Appeals The school, located in Bayside, Queens, is a public institution known for its academic excellence. "About Benjamin N. Cardozo," *Cardozo Law*, https://cardozo.yu.edu/about/about-benjamin-n-cardozo.

29. Jeff Noreman, interview with Nancy L. Segal, 2020.

30. Sitting shiva is a Jewish custom of mourning in which relatives gather for seven days, usually in the home of the deceased.

31. Abbott, interviews with Nancy L. Segal, 2019, 2020; C. Silverman, interviews with Nancy L. Segal; Paula Sherman, interview in *The Twinning Reaction*.

32. Dylan Sherman, interview with Nancy L. Segal, 2020.

33. Paula's "sister-friend," interview with Nancy L. Segal, 2020.

34. A. Sherman, interview and email correspondence with Nancy L. Segal.

35. A. Sherman, interview and email correspondence with Nancy L. Segal.

36. Abbott, interviews with Nancy L. Segal.

37. A. Sherman, interview and email correspondence with Nancy L. Segal. In Shinseki's film *The Twinning Reaction*, Paula struggled with the knowledge that she and Marjorie had shared a crib for three months, even when the researchers planned to separate them.

38. According to Marjorie's brother Leo, Marjorie's date of death was June 30, 1988. The New Montefiore Cemetery list Marjorie's date of death as June 29, 1988; see http://newmontefiorecemetery.org/search/.

39. C. Silverman, interview in *The Twinning Reaction*; interviews with Nancy L. Segal.

40. Holly Hedegaard, Sally C. Curtin, and Margaret Warner, "Increase in Suicide Mortality in the United States, 1999–2018." *National Center for Health Statistics Date Brief* no. 362 (April 2020): 1–7.

41. William Feigelman, "Are Adoptees at Increased Risk for Attempting Suicide?" *Suicide and Life-Threatening Behavior* 35, no. 2 (2005): 206–16; Margaret A. Keyes, Stephen M. Malone, Anu Sharma, William G. Iacono, and Matt McGue, "Risk of Suicide Attempt in Adopted and Nonadopted Offspring." *Pediatrics* 132, no. 4 (2013): 639–46.

42. Abbott, interview in *The Twinning Reaction*; interviews with Nancy L. Segal.

43. A. Sherman, interview with Nancy L. Segal.

44. Nancy L. Segal, *Entwined Lives: Twins and What They Tell Us About Human Behavior* (New York: Plume, 2000); Nancy L. Segal, "Twin Data: The Lives That Drive the Findings." *Twin Research and Human Genetics* 2, no. 1 (2020): 61–65.

45. There is a line in Hebrew that runs across the top of the grave that reads, "Here lies buried Minna daughter of Reb (rabbi) Yosef." Minna is actually a Yiddish name.

46. Paula Sherman, interview in *The Twinning Reaction*. The yew bush symbolizes immortality and everlasting life, rebirth, changes and regeneration after difficult times, and protection; see Leah H. Bostwick, "Yew Tree Symbolism," https://www.sunsigns.org/celtic-yew-tree-symbolism-meanings/. Jewish tradition does not allow flowers to be placed on a grave. Pebbles are used to mark one's presence; see Zalman Goldstein, "14 Jewish Ways to Honor the Soul of a Deceased Loved One," https://www.chabad.org/library/article_cdo/aid/372952/jewish/14-Jewish-Ways-to-Honor-the-Soul-of-a-Deceased-Loved-One.htm.

47. L. Silverman, interviews with Nancy L. Segal. Mensch is a Yiddish term for someone who has integrity and does the right thing.

48. L. Silverman, interviews with Nancy L. Segal.

49. A. Sherman, interview with Nancy L. Segal.

50. J. Silverman, interview with Nancy L. Segal.

51. Abbott, email correspondence to Nancy L. Segal, 2020. Hedda's late son and brother were over six feet tall. Hedda's currently reduced height of five feet, five inches tall is a function of aging.

52. A. Sherman, interviews with Nancy L. Segal, 2020.

53. C. Silverman, interviews with Nancy L. Segal.

54. A. Sherman, interview with Nancy L. Segal.

55. C. Silverman, interviews with Nancy L. Segal.

56. A. Sherman, interview with Nancy L. Segal, 2020.

57. Paula's best friend, telephone discussion with Nancy L. Segal, 2020.

58. D. Sherman, interview with Nancy L. Segal, 2020.

59. Cecilia Tomassini, Knud Juel, Niels V. Holm, Axel Skytthe, and Kaare Christensen, "Risk of Suicide in Twins: 51 Year Follow Up Study." *British Medical Journal* 327, no. 7411 (2003): 373–74.

60. "Brain Aneurysm," https://www.healthline.com/health/aneurysm-in-the-brain.

61. G. Silverman, interview with Nancy L. Segal, 2020.

62. D. Sherman, interview with Nancy L. Segal, 2020.

CHAPTER 17

1. Michele Mordkoff, interview by Tim Wardle, "Adult Twins, Separated at Birth, Have Emotional Reunion." *The Atlantic*: Short Documentary Films; Emily Buder, "Twins, Separated at Birth, Reunite as Adults." *The*

Atlantic, October 3, 2018, https://www.theatlantic.com/video/index/571867/two-identical-strangers/.

2. Mark Silverschotz, email correspondence to Nancy L. Segal, October 3, 2018; Wardle; Buder, "Adult Twins, Separated at Birth, Have Emotional Reunion."

3. Elyse Schein and Paula Bernstein, *Identical Strangers: A Memoir of Twins Separated and Reunited* (New York: Random House, 2007).

4. Buder, "Twins, Separated at Birth, Reunite as Adults."

5. Michele Mordkoff, interviews with Nancy L. Segal, 2018, 2019, 2020; Wardle; Buder, "Adult Twins, Separated at Birth, Have Emotional Reunion."

6. Lisa Belkin, "What the Jumans Didn't Know About Michael." *New York Times Magazine,* March 14, 1999, 42–49, https://www.nytimes.com/1999/03/14/magazine/what-the-jumans-didn-t-know-about-michael.html.

7. M. Mordkoff, interviews with Nancy L. Segal.

8. 23andMe, "23andMe and Ancestry.com Partner to Extend Access to Genetic Ancestry Expertise," September 9, 2008, https://mediacenter.23andme.com/press-releases/23andme-and-ancestry-com-partner-to-extend-access-to-genetic-ancestry-expertise/. In a March 25, 2012, email, a representative from 23andme's communications department provided clarification regarding the linking of relatives. Michele had submitted a DNA sample to both companies, first sending her sample to 23andme.

9. Allison Kanter, interviews with Nancy L. Segal, 2018, 2019, 2020.

10. A. Kanter, interviews with Nancy L. Segal.

11. "Secret Siblings." *ABC 20/20,* March 9, 2018.

12. A. Kanter, interviews with Nancy L. Segal.

13. A. Kanter, interviews with Nancy L. Segal.

14. A. Kanter and M. Mordkoff, interviews with Nancy L. Segal. The twins' birth information is based on the narrative sent to Michele by Spence-Chapin. I have not reviewed the original document.

15. Nancy L. Segal, *Twin Mythconceptions: False Beliefs, Fables, and Facts About Twins* (New York: Elsevier, 2017).

16. Ulla Sankilampi, Marja-Leena Hannila, Antti Saari, Mika Gissler, and Leo Dunkel, "New Population-Based References for Birth Weight, Length, and Head Circumference in Singletons and Twins from 23 to 43 Gestation Weeks." *Annals of Medicine* 45, no. 5-6 (2013): 446–54. The twins' relatively high birth weights suggest that the length of their mother's pregnancy was underestimated.

17. A. Kanter, interviews with Nancy L. Segal.

18. Segal, *Twin Mythconceptions.* Also note that many people incorrectly assume that one placenta signifies identical twinning; however, separate placentae fuse about 50 percent of the time.

19. Nancy L. Segal, "More Thoughts on the Child Development Center Twin Study." *Twin Research and Human Genetics* 8, no. 3 (2005): 276–81.

20. Segal, *Twin Mythconceptions.*

21. A. Kanter and M. Mordkoff, interviews with Nancy L. Segal.

22. A. Kanter and M. Mordkoff, interviews with Nancy L. Segal.

23. A. Kanter, interviews with Nancy L. Segal.

24. M. Mordkoff, interviews with Nancy L. Segal,

25. A. Kanter, interviews with Nancy L. Segal.

26. "Shop Tempt." https://www.facebook.com/pg/shoptempt/about/.

27. A. Kanter, interviews with Nancy L. Segal.

28. Constance Krauss, interview with Nancy L. Segal, 2020.

29. "Allison Kanter," September 2013, https://twitter.com/alli_kanter?lang=en.

30. Iris and Allan Wolk, interviews with Nancy L. Segal, 2019; M. Mordkoff, interviews with Nancy L. Segal.

31. A. Wolk, interview with Nancy L. Segal; M. Mordkoff, interviews with Nancy L. Segal.

32. I. Wolk and A. Wolk, interview with Nancy L. Segal; M. Mordkoff, interviews with Nancy L. Segal.

33. Intelligence2 Debates, "Parenting Is Overrated," October 29, 2019, https://www.intelligencesquaredus.org/debates/parenting-overrated.

34. M. Mordkoff, interviews with Nancy L. Segal, 2018, 2019, 2020; Andrew Mordkoff, interview with Nancy L. Segal, 2020.

35. Ohio State University, "Statistical Summary," 2019, https://www.osu.edu/osutoday/stuinfo.php.

36. M. Mordkoff, interviews with Nancy L. Segal.

37. Nancy L. Segal and Yesika S. Montoya, *Accidental Brothers: The Story of Twins Exchanged at Birth and the Power of Nature and Nurture* (New York: St. Martin's Press, 2018).

38. *New York Times*, "Michele Wolk and Allan Mordkoff, Lawyers, Wed," October 15, 1990, https://www.nytimes.com/1990/10/15/style/michele-wolk-and-allan-mordkoff-lawyers-wed.html.

39. M. Mordkoff, interviews with Nancy L. Segal, 2018, 2019, 2020.

40. Natalie M. Baptista, Kurt D. Christensen, Deanna Alexis Carere, Simon A. Broadley, J. Scott Roberts, and Robert C. Green, "Adopting Genetics: Motivations and Outcomes of Personal Genomic Testing in Adult Adoptees." *Genetics in Medicine* 18, no. 9 (2016): 924–32.

41. Sheldon Fogelman, interview with Nancy L. Segal, 2019.

42. M. Mordkoff, interviews with Nancy L. Segal, 2018, 2019, 2020.

43. As an attorney, Michele believes that the twins' records were easily available. She explained that LWS had undergone past legal proceedings that would have required granting lawyers access to documents. Michele believes the delay was linked to the controversies surrounding the twins' separations. M. Mordkoff, interviews with Nancy L. Segal, 2018, 2019, 2020.

44. M. Mordkoff, interviews with Nancy L. Segal, 2018, 2019, 2020; A. Mordkoff, interview with Nancy L. Segal, 2020.

45. US Birth Certificates, "Birth Certificate Number Definition," https://www .usbirthcertificates.com/glossary/birth-certificate-number. Current US birth certificates add a six-digit number at the end.

46. M. Mordkoff, A. Kanter, and Kyle Kanter, interviews with Nancy L. Segal, 2018, 2019, 2020.

47. M. Mordkoff, interviews with Nancy L. Segal.

48. US Legal.com, "Immediate Family Law and Legal Definition," 1997–2019, https://definitions.uslegal.com/i/immediate-family/. Stepchildren and adopted children and their spouses are also considered immediate family members.

49. DNA services update their databases and formats from time to time. When Michele looked at her Ancestry.com pages a year later, Allison was listed as a "sister." M. Mordkoff, interview with Nancy L. Segal, 2019. Full siblings and fraternal twins have the same degree of genetic relatedness, or 50 percent of their genes, on average. However, the genetic overlap between specific pairs of full siblings and fraternal twins may be above or below that average. It is believed that their range of genetic relatedness is between 42 to 58 percent; see Segal, *Twin Mythconceptions*.

50. Annelie Hansen, "Untangling the Centimorgans on Your DNA Test," April 6, 2020, https://www.familysearch.org/blog/en/centimorgan-chart-under standing-dna/; Blaine T. Bettinger, "The Shared cM Project: Version 4.0.," March 2020, https://thegeneticgenealogist.com/wp-content/uploads/2020/03/ Shared-cM-Project-Version-4.pdf.

51. Kyle Kanter is Allison Kanter's son.

52. M. Mordkoff and I. Wolk, interviews with Nancy L. Segal.

53. Wardle; Buder, "Adult Twins, Separated at Birth, Have Emotional Reunion."

54. Allison Kanter, interview by Wardle; Buder, "Adult Twins, Separated at Birth, Have Emotional Reunion."

55. M. Mordkoff, interviews with Nancy L. Segal.

56. Franz J. Neyer, "Twin Relationships in Old Age: A Developmental Perspective." *Journal of Personality and Social Relationships* 19, no. 2 (2002): 155–77.

57. I. Wolk, A. Wolk, M. Mordkoff, and A. Kanter, interviews with Nancy L. Segal.

58. A. Kanter, interviews with Nancy L. Segal.

59. A. Kanter and M. Mordkoff, interviews with Nancy L. Segal.

60. Emily Lavin, "Twins Reunited After a Lifetime Apart." *Calabasas Courier Online*, December 13, 2018, https://chscourier.com/features/2018/12/13/ twins-reunited-after-a-lifetime-apart/.

61. Some studies have reported higher levels of parenting quality (e.g., emotional involvement and quality of interaction among adoptive parents than biological parents, as well as greater parenting satisfaction); see Susan Golombok, Rachel Cook, Alison Bish, and Clare Murray, "Families Created by the New Reproductive Technologies: Quality of Parenting and Social and Emotional Development of the Children." *Child Development* 66, no. 2 (1995): 285–98; Cosario Ceballo, Jennifer E.

Lansford, Antonia Abbey, and Abigail J. Stewart, "Gaining a Child: Comparing the Experiences of Biological Parents, Adoptive Parents, and Stepparents." *Family Relations* 53, no. 1 (2004): 38–48; Joan T. D. Suwalsky, Christina M. Padilla, Cynthia X. Yuen, E. Parham Horn, Alexandra L. Bradley, Diane L. Putnick, and Marc H. Bornstein, "Adoptive and Nonadoptive Mother–Child Behavioral Interaction: A Comparative Study at 4 Years of Age." *Adoption Quarterly* 18, no. 3 (2015): 196–216.

62. Nancy L. Segal, *Born Together—Reared Apart: The Landmark Minnesota Twin Study* (Cambridge, MA, Harvard University Press, 2012).

63. M. Mordfoff and A. Mordkoff, interview by Wardle; Buder, "Adult Twins, Separated at Birth, Have Emotional Reunion"; A. Mordkoff, interview with Nancy L. Segal.

64. Josh Mordkoff, interview with Nancy L. Segal, 2020.

65. J. Mordkoff, A. Mordkoff, A. Kanter, and M. Mordkoff, interviews with Nancy L. Segal, 2020.

66. A. Mordkoff, email correspondence to Nancy L. Segal, 2020.

67. A. Wolk, interview with Nancy L. Segal.

68. A. Kanter, interviews with Nancy L. Segal.

69. A. Kanter and M. Mordkoff, interviews with Nancy L. Segal.

CHAPTER 18

1. Daniel Engber, "*Three Identical Strangers* Has a Long-Lost Twin." *Slate*, June 28, 2018, https://slate.com/culture/2018/06/the-new-doc-three-identical -strangers-has-a-long-list-twin-the-twinning-reaction.html.

2. Michele Mordoff, interviews with Nancy L. Segal, 2018, 2019, 2020; Josh Mordkoff, interview with Nancy L. Segal, 2020.

3. "David Kellman," https://www.linkedin.com/in/david-kellman-4967a394.

4. Lois Oppenheim, interview with Nancy L. Segal, 2019. Dr. Arnold (Arnie) Richards first told me that the letter had been written and sent.

5. Lois Oppenheim did not indicate if the letter was sent to the Academy by mail or by email. Dr. Arnold Richards, one of the signatories, thought that the letter had been sent to the Motion Picture Academy three months in advance of the award announcements; interview with Nancy L. Segal, 2019.

6. Lois Oppenheim and signatories, "Twin Research—Correcting Falsehoods," January 25, 2019, https://www.facebook.com/Twin-Research-Correcting -Falsehoods-287346895517330/. Dr. Oppenheim mentioned that the letter had been posted on Facebook, but I do not know who posted it.

7. Academy for Motion Picture Arts and Sciences, "The Academy and ABC Announce Key Dates for 91st Oscars," April 23, 2018, https://www.oscars.org/ news/academy-and-abc-announce-key-dates-91st-oscars.

8. Natalie Kojen, "91st Oscars ® Shortlist in Nine Award Categories Announced." Oscars, December 17, 2018.

9. Academy for Motion Picture Arts and Sciences, "The Academy and ABC Announce Key Dates for 91st Oscars," April 23, 2018, https://www.oscars.org/news/academy-and-abc-announce-key-dates-91st-oscars.

10. Rudie Obias, "9 Oscar Nominations That Were Revoked," February 23, 2019, https://www.mentalfloss.com/article/73722/8-oscar-nominations-were -revoked. The film *Young Americans* proved to be ineligible for the 1969 award because it was first released in 1967. Eligible films can only be released during the year prior to its consideration.

11. Pacella Parent Child Center, "Our Staff: Leon Hoffman, M.D." http://www.theparentchildcenter.org/our-staff.

12. Academy, email correspondence, July 2020.

13. Leon Hoffman, "*Three Identical Strangers*: Precluding a Real Conversation About the Ubiquity of Self-Deception," August 20, 2018, https://www.psychologytoday.com/us/blog/beyond-freud/201808/three-identical -strangers; Lois Oppenheim, "The Truth About 'Three Identical Strangers': Does Every Good Story Need a Villain?" *Psychology Today*, February 7, 2019, https://www.psychologytoday.com/us/blog/psychoanalysis-unplugged/201902/the-truth-about-three-identical-strangers.

14. I believe that this article is the one referenced in the protest letter: Daniel Engber, "*Three Identical Strangers* Has a Long-Lost Twin." *Slate*, June 28, 2018, https://slate.com/culture/2018/06/the-new-doc-three-identical-strangers-has-a -long-list-twin-the-twinning-reaction.html.

15. Nancy L. Segal, *Born Together—Reared Apart; The Landmark Minnesota Twin Study* (Cambridge, MA: Harvard University Press, 2012).

16. Joyce M. Pavao, interview with Nancy L. Segal, 2019.

17. Nancy L. Segal, "Commentary: More Thoughts on the Child Development Center Twin Study." *Twin Research and Human Genetics* 8, no. 3 (2005): 276–81.

18. Peter Neubauer and Christa Balzert, "Genetik und Psychotherapie" ("Genetics and Psychotherapy"), in *Der Psychoanalytische Prozeß*, edited by Sylvia Zwettler-Otte and Albrecht Komarek, 169–83 (Vienna: Turia & Kant, 1996). I had this chapter translated from German into English.

19. Lois Oppenheim, "The Facts about the Neubauer Twin Study: An Interview about a Controversy or a Controversial Interview?" *International Journal of Controversial Discussions* 1 (2020): 171–88.

20. Jonathan Moreno, interview with Nancy L. Segal, 2019. The former LWS social work intern is his family friend.

21. The 1996 edition of *Nature's Thumprint* is identical to the 1990 edition, with the exception of a new preface and acknowledgments. As in the 1990 volume, there are no mentions of Dr. Viola Bernard, LWS, Sam Abrams, or Christa Balzert, and Neubauer's twin-related papers published prior to 1996 are not referenced. According to a former book editor, poor sales are often responsible for

book transfers between publishers, although the reason it was done in this case (from Addison-Wesley to Columbia University Press) is unknown.

22. Sharon Morello, email correspondence to Nancy L. Segal, July 2020.

23. Those who agreed to an interview spoke freely and most agreed to be tape-recorded. I provided material I intended to use to the individuals requesting it.

24. The original interviews and email correspondence are retained in my files.

25. The letter was provided to me by the author, who requested anonymity.

26. This individual, while named in the letter, asked to remain anonymous.

27. Paul Sheehan, "2019 Emmys Calendar: Two-week Voting Begins June 10, Nominations on July 16, Ceremony on September 22." *Gold Derby*, June 10, 2019, https://www.goldderby.com/article/2019/2019-emmys-calendar-dates-nominations-ceremony/.

28. TV Academy, "*Three Identical Strangers*—Awards and Nominations," 2019, https://www.emmys.com/shows/three-identical-strangers.

29. IMDb, "Tim Wardle: Awards," https://www.imdb.com/name/nm226 8736/awards.

30. Jim Yeager, telephone conversation with Nancy L. Segal, December 2019. Yeager dictated his response to me which I repeated back to him for accuracy.

31. Daniel Wikler, email correspondence to Debra Ruder, forwarded to Nancy L. Segal, October 2019; interview with Nancy L. Segal, 2020.

CHAPTER 19

1. Catherine Ross, presentation at *The Twinning Reaction: Science and Deception*, University of Virginia Law School, Charlottesville, VA, March 29, 2019.

2. Alice Bussiere, "The Development of Adoption Law." *Adoption Quarterly* 1, no. 3 (1998): 3–25.

3. New York State, "Principles of Adoption Services." 178 CRR-NY 421.2, 2020; historical note; filed April 26, 1978; repealed, new filed September 30, 1981; Elyse Schein and Paula Bernstein, *Identical Strangers: A Memoir of Twins Separated and Reunited* (New York: Random House, 2007).

4. Bussiere, "The Development of Adoption Law."

5. Professor Bertram J. Black, memo to Dr. Peter Neubauer. March 14, 1985, Viola Wertheim Bernard Papers, Archives & Special Collections, Columbia University Health Sciences Library.

6. Arnold (Arnie) Richards, interviews with Nancy L. Segal, 2019.

7. Bussiere, "The Development of Adoption Law."

8. Thomas Mack, email communication to Nancy L. Segal, August 4, 2020.

9. "Publication/Legal Issues." Adoption Study Meeting. October 2, 1984, Viola W, Bernard Archives, Columbia University.

10. Barbara Jones, "Do Siblings Possess Constitutional Rights." *Cornell Law Review* 78, no 6 (1993): 1187–220.

11. Jones, "Do Siblings Possess Constitutional Rights." See footnote 59 in her article.

12. L. v. G., 497 A.2d 215, 218 (New Jersey Superior Court. Ch. Div. 1985); cited in Jones, "Do Siblings Possess Constitutional Rights."

13. Nancy L. Segal, *Someone Else's Twin: The True Story of Babies Switched at Birth* (Amherst, NY: Prometheus Books, 2011); Nancy L. Segal and Yesika S. Montoya, *Accidental Brothers: The Story of Twins Exchanged at Birth and the Power of Nature and Nurture* (New York: St. Martin's Press, 2018).

14. William M. Grove, Elke D. Eckert, Leonard Heston, Thomas J. Bouchard, Nancy Segal, and David T. Lykken, "Heritability of Substance Abuse and Antisocial Behavior: A Study of Monozygotic Twins Reared Apart." *Biological Psychiatry* 27, no. 12 (1990): 1293–304.

15. Mignon Kraus, "Call from Dr John Kliever." November 11, 1964, Viola W. Bernard Archives, Columbia University.

16. American Psychological Association, "Ethical Principles of Psychologists and Code of Conduct," 2016, https://www.apa.org/ethics/code.

17. American Psychological Association, *Ethical Standards of Psychologists* (Washington, DC: APA, 1953). This document was revised and updated eleven times and was published in widely read professional sources, such as the *American Psychologist* and *APA Monitor*. See American Psychological Association, "Ethical Principles of Psychologists and Code of Conduct."

18. Robert J. Lifton, *The Nazi Doctors: Medical Killing and the Psychology of Genocide* (New York: Basic Books, 1986); "The Nuremberg Trials," June 7, 2019, https://www.history.com/topics/world-war-ii/nuremberg-trials. Subsequent Nuremberg trials lasted until 1949.

19. Adil E. Shamoo and David B. Resnik, *Responsible Conduct of Research* (Oxford, UK: Oxford University Press, 2003); Evelyne Shuster, "Fifty Years Later: The Significance of the Nuremberg Code." *New England Journal of Medicine* 337, no. 20 (1997): 1436–40.

20. Jochen Vollmann and Rolf Winau, "Informed Consent in Human Experimentation Before the Nuremberg Code." *British Medical Journal* 313, no. 7070 (1996): 1445–47; Adil E. Shamoo and David B. Resnik, *Responsible Conduct of Research* (Oxford: Oxford University Press, 2003).

21. Vollmann and Winau, "Informed Consent in Human Experimentation Before the Nuremberg Code."

22. David Rothman, "Research, Human: Historical Aspects." In *Encyclopedia of Bioethics*, third edition, edited by Stephen G. Post, 2316–26 (New York: MacMillan, 1995).

23. National Institutes of Health, *Handbook for Patients at the Clinical Center*, publication no. 315 (Bethesda, MD: National Institutes of Health, 1953).

24. "Ethical Directives for Human Research." In *Encyclopedia of Bioethics*, third edition, edited by Stephen G. Post, 2815–906 (New York: MacMillan, 1995).

25. World Medical Association, "Declaration of Helsinki." *Bulletin of the World Health Organization* 79 (no. 4): 373–74.

26. Paul A. Buelow, "The Institutional Review Board: A Brief History of Attempts to Protect Human Subjects in Research." *Clinical Nurse Specialist* 25, no. 6 (2011): 277–80; Kelly Schindelholz, "How the National Research Act of 1974 Enhanced Trial Safety." *IMARC*, April 16, 2019, https://www.imarcresearch.com/blog/the-national-research-act-1974. The requirement for IRBs is stated in Federal Regulations 45C (1981, 1983, 1989, 1991); see Adil E. Shamoo and Dianne N. Irving, "Accountability in Research Using Persons with Mental Illness." *Accountability in Research* 3, no. 1 (1993): 1–17.

27. "The Belmont Report uses the term 'justice' to refer to 'fairness in distribution.' This is different from the word›s common association with enforceable rights and penalties within a legal system, but consistent with general usage in the field of bioethics." See Michael D. Smith, "Major Issues in Ethics of Aging Research." In *Handbook of Models for Human Aging*, edited by P. Michael Conn, 69–78 (New York: Academic Press, 2006).

28. Phoebe Friesen, Lisa Kearns, Barbara Redman, and Arthur L. Caplan, "Rethinking the Belmont Report?" *The American Journal of Bioethics* 17, no. 7 (2017): 15–21.

29. Paul A. Buelow, "The Institutional Review Board: A Brief History of Attempts to Protect Human Subjects in Research." *Clinical Nurse Specialist* 25, no. 6 (2011): 277–80. The Common Rule, the standard ethics, is found at title 45, part 46, subpart A of the Code of Federal Regulations; Jeremy Sugarman, Anna C. Mastroianni, and Jeffry P. Kahn, *Ethics of Research with Human Subjects: Selected Policies and Resources* (Frederick, MD: University Publishing Group, Inc., 1998).

30. Adil E. Shamoo and David B. Resnik, *Responsible Conduct of Research*; Rachita Narsaria, "The Hippocratic Oath: The Original and Revised Version," *The Procto Blog for Doctors*, March 10, 2015, https://doctors.practo.com/the-hippocratic-oath-the-original-and-revised-version/. However, reciting this oath is less standard than in the past—some medical students compose a personal version as part of the education process; Dr. Stephen Latham, interview with Nancy L. Segal, 2019. Dr. Latham directs Yale's Interdisciplinary Center for Bioethics. He holds a doctoral degree in jurisprudence and social policy, and a degree in law.

31. Leon Hoffman and Lois Oppenheim, "*Three Identical Strangers and The Twinning Reaction*—Clarifying History and Lessons for Today from Peter Neubauer's Twins Study." *Journal of the American Medical Association* 322 no. 1 (2019): 10–12; Susan Kolod and Edith McNutt, interviews with Nancy L. Segal, 2019.

32. Leon Hoffman, "Three Identical Strangers: Precluding a Conversation About the Ubiquity of Self-Deception." *Psychology Today*, August 20, 2018, https://www.psychologytoday.com/us/blog/beyond-freud/201808/three-identical-strangers. The actual wording of that comment is "retrofits today's values

and scientific knowledge about the importance of sibships and twinships onto the past" (italics are mine).

33. Mark Mercurio, interview with Nancy L. Segal, 2019.

34. Jonathan Moreno, interview with Nancy L. Segal, 2019.

35. Jewish Board of Guardians, "Institutional Review Board Meeting." March 7, 1985, Viola W. Bernard Collection, Columbia University Archives.

36. Jewish Board of Guardians, "Institutional Review Board Meeting."

37. William Spivak, "60 Years On, Twin/Triplet Study Still Raises Questions." *Medpage Today*, July 3, 2019, https://www.medpagetoday.com/psychiatry/gener alpsychiatry/80829?pop=0&ba=1&xid=fb-md-lmtm-id-gsv&rt=rtc3676&trw=n o&scrf=1&fbclid=IwAR29guy6dIpqWaJnk833PKfwmsu9QCQptsWqcmNp84S bxhqGEocpFZEVXec.

38. William Spivak, interview with Nancy L. Segal, 2019.

39. Robert L. Klitzman and Adam M. Kelmenson, "Experiment on Identical Siblings Separated at Birth: Ethical Implications for Researchers, Universities, and Archives Today." *Journal of Medical Ethics* (2020); Barron H. Lerner, "'Three Identical Strangers': The High Cost of Experimentation Without Ethics." *Washington Post*, January 27, 2019.

40. Jonathan Moreno, interview with Nancy L. Segal, 2019.

41. Ilene Wilets, interview with Nancy L. Segal, 2019.

42. Ellen Handler Spitz, "Documentary Danger: Reflections on *Three Identical Strangers*." *Bulletin of the Association for Psychoanalytic Medicine* 53 (Fall 2018): 22–29.

43. Daniel Wikler, interview with Nancy L. Segal, 2020.

44. Ross, presentation at *The Twinning Reaction: Science and Deception*.

45. Lois Oppenheim, "The Facts About the Neubauer Twin Study: An Interview About Controversy or a Controversial Interview?" *International Journal of Controversial Discussions* 1 (2020): 171–88; Adam M. Kelmenson and Ilene Wilets, "Ethical Questions Remain in Controversial Twins Study: Further information and Sources Are Required to Find Resolve." *International Journal of Controversial Discussions* 1 (2020): 189–96.

46. Viola W. Bernard, "VB—Re: CDC Material." The proposed book on the twin study was to include "C-5 and C-5: one complete set of data and discussions. Plus: 2 sets of partial duplicates." The parents of C-5 and C-6 had not provided signed consent. March 24, 1987, Viola W. Bernard Archives, Columbia University.

47. Adam M. Kelmenson and Ilene Wilets, "Historical Practice of Separating Twins at Birth." *Journal of the American Medical Association* 322, no. 18 (2019): 1827–28.

48. Kelmenson and Wilets, "Ethical Questions Remain in Controversial Twins Study: Further information and Sources Are Required to Find Resolve."

49. US Food and Drug Administration, "Additional Protections for Children." *Federal Register* 66, no. 79, April 24, 2001, https://www.fda.gov/science-research/ clinical-trials-and-human-subject-protection/additional-protections-children; University of California Los Angeles, "Guidance and Procedures: Child Assent

and Permission by Parents or Guardians." Office of the Research Protection Program, June 9, 2016, https://ora.research.ucla.edu/OHRPP/Documents/Policy/9/ChildAssent_ParentPerm.pdf.

50. Henry K. Beecher, "Ethics and Clinical Research." *New England Journal of Medicine* 274, no. 24 (1966): 1354–60; Jack El-Hai, "Henry Knowles Beecher, Brief Life of a Blooming Ethicist: 1904-1976." *Harvard Magazine*, March–April (2017), https://www.harvardmagazine.com/2017/03/henry-knowles-beecher.

51. Willard Gaylin, interview with Nancy L. Segal, 2020.

52. Mark Mercurio, Ilene Wilets, and Adam M. Kelmenson, interviews with Nancy L. Segal, 2019, 2020.

53. Erin Blakemore, "30,000 People Were 'Disappeared' in Argentina's War. These Women Never Stopped Looking." *History.com*, https://www.history.com/news/mothers-plaza-de-mayo-disappeared-children-dirty-war-argentina; Malin Fezehei, "The Disappeared Children of Israel." *New York Times*, February 20, 2019, https://www.nytimes.com/2019/02/20/world/middleeast/israel-yemenite-children-affair.html; Nick Poppy, "This Woman Stole Children From the Poor to Give to the Rich." *New York Post*, June 17, 2017, https://nypost.com/2017/06/17/this-woman-stole-children-from-the-poor-to-give-to-the-rich/.

54. Barry Coburn, presentation at *The Twinning Reaction: Science and Deception*, University of Virginia Law School, Charlottesville, VA, March 29, 2019.

55. Nancy L. Segal, "More Thoughts on the Child Development Center Twin Study." *Twin Research and Human Genetics* 8, no. 3 (2005): 276–81; Schein and Bernstein, *Identical Strangers*.

56. Florence Brown, letter to Viola Bernard. March 2, 1965, Viola W. Bernard Archives, Columbia University.

57. Viola W. Bernard, letter to Florence Kreech. March 22, 1976, Viola W. Bernard Archives, Columbia University.

58. Nancy L. Segal, *Entwined Lives: Twins and What They Tell Us About Human Behavior* (New York: Plume, 2000).

59. Peter B. Neubauer and Alexander Neubauer, *Nature's Thumbprint: The New Genetics of Personality* (New York: Addison-Wesley, 1990).

60. Mercurio and Latham, interviews with Nancy L. Segal, 2019, 2020.

61. Latham, interviews with Nancy L. Segal, 2019, 2020. Interestingly, Dr. Christa Balzert, one of three co-authors of the unpublished manuscript, noted that if the same genetically-based disorder had been seen in both separated twins, this information would have been disclosed to the families. As I indicated, there is no evidence that this was done; see footnote 45, chapter 19.

62. Mack, email correspondence to Nancy L. Segal, August 4, 2020.

63. Nancy L. Segal, *Twin Mythconceptions: False Beliefs, Fables, and Facts About Twins* (New York: Elsevier, 2017).

64. Viola W. Bernard, "Copy of Phone Talk." May 27, 1986, Viola Wertheim Bernard Papers, Archives & Special Collections, Columbia University Health Sciences Library.

65. Ross, presentation at *The Twinning Reaction: Science and Deception*.

66. Austen Garwood-Gowers, *Medical Use of Human Beings: Respect as a Basis for Critique of Discourse, Law and Practice* (London: Routledge, 2020).

67. Janet Silverman (cousin of separated twin Marjorie Silverman), interview with Nancy L. Segal, 2020.

68. Lori Shinseki, *The Twinning Reaction*, Fire Horse Pictures, United States, 2017; Tim Wardle, *Three Identical Strangers*, Raw Films, United Kingdom, 2018; Francine Woldisz, "*Three Identical Strangers* Director: Their Lives Were Like the Truman Show." *Jewish News*, December 12, 2018, https://jewishnews.times ofisrael.com/three-identical-strangers-director-their-lives-were-like-the-truman -show/; parents' interviews with Nancy L. Segal, 2019. In the early nineteenth and twentieth centuries, the Aryans became a mythical "race" that some scholars believed was superior to others. The Nazis promoted this false notion, claiming that the German people were members of the superior "Aryan race." See United States Holocaust Memorial Museum, "Aryan." Holocaust Encyclopedia, https:// encyclopedia.ushmm.org/content/en/article/aryan-1 (accessed May 2021).

69. US Holocaust Memorial Museum, "Nazi Medical Experiments." *Holocaust Encyclopedia*, 2006, https://encyclopedia.ushmm.org/content/en/article/ nazi-medical-experiments; Jewish Virtual Library, "Nazi Medical Experiments: Background and Overview." *Encyclopaedia Judaica*, 2008, https://www.jewishvir tuallibrary.org/background-and-overview-of-nazi-medical-experiments; Nancy L. Segal, "The Twin Children of Auschwitz-Birkenau: Conference on Nazi Medicine." *Twin Research and Human Genetics* 16, no. 3 (2013): 751–57; Andy Walker, "The Twins of Auschwitz," January 28, 2015, bbc.com/news/maga zine-30933718; David G. Marwell, *Mengele: Unmasking the Angel of Death* (New York: W.W. Norton & Co, 2020); 9NOW, "The Experiment: Interviews on *60 Minutes–Australia*," August 9, 2020, https://www.youtube.com/watch?v=UQIL Xtd3ZOM&feature=youtu.be.

70. David G. Marwell, *Mengele: Unmasking the Angel of Death* (New York: W.W. Norton & Co, 2020).

71. Arthur L. Caplan, Mark Mecurio, and Daniel Wikler, interviews with Nancy L. Segal, 2019, 2020.

72. Former twin study assistant—anonymous, interview with Nancy L. Segal, 2019.

73. Lawrence Wright, *Twins and What They Tell Us About Who We Are* (New York: John Wiley & Sons. Inc., 1997).

74. Beecher, "Ethics and Clinical Research"; Henry K. Beecher, "Consent in Clinical Experimentation: Myth and Reality." *Journal of the American Medical Association* 195, no. 1 (1966): 34–35.

75. Joan Wofford, Jen Wofford, and Martha Wofford, interview with Nancy L. Segal, 2020.

76. Kimberly Springer, "In Tribute—First African-American Psychoanalyst, Margaret Lawrence Dies at 105." *News from Columbia's Rare Book and Manuscript*

Library, December 16, 2019, https://blogs.cul.columbia.edu/rbml/2019/12/10/
in-tribute-first-african-american-psychoanalyst-margaret-lawrence-dies-at-104/.

77. M. Wofford, interview with Nancy L. Segal, 2020.

78. Trudy Festinger, interview with Nancy L. Segal, 2019.

79. Debra Bradley Ruder, interview with Nancy L. Segal, 2019.

80. Staff member, Schlesinger Library, email correspondence to Nancy L. Segal, 2021.

81. Jen Wofford, interview with Nancy L. Segal, 2020.

82. Joan Wofford and Jen Wofford, interview with Nancy L. Segal, 2020.

83. Justine Wise Polier, "Letter to Viola W. Bernard," November 6, 1981, Viola W. Bernard Collection, Columbia University Archives.

84. Jen Wofford, interview with Nancy L. Segal, 2020.

85. Lawrence Hartmann, "In Memoriam: Viola W. Bernard, M.D. (1907-1998)." *Journal of the American Academy of Child and Adolescent Psychiatry* 39, no. 1 (2000): 131.

86. Lawrence Hartmann, email correspondence to Nancy L. Segal, 2020; see Samuel Abrams and Peter B. Neubauer, "Hartmann's Vision: Identical Twins and Developmental Organizations." *The Psychoanalytic Study of the Child* 49, no. 1 (1994): 49–59. Dr. Hartmann is the younger brother of the late psychoanalyst and sleep researcher Ernst Hartmann.

87. Joan Wofford and Jen Wofford, interviews with Nancy L. Segal, 2020.

88. M. Wofford, interview with Nancy L. Segal, 2020. In my 2020 interview with Lawrence Hartmann, he recalled that Bernard's nieces shared stories about their aunt at her informal memorial. "She was always interested in you and was very adaptable and available. But within ten minutes, even if you were seven years old, she'd want to know what you thought about the Vietnam War."

89. Dr. Viola Bernard, interview with Dr. Spafford Ackerly, May 30, 1973; Dr. Viola Bernard, interview with Dr. Milton J. E. Senn, March 16, 1977; Dr. Viola Bernard, interview with Dr. Nellie Thompson, December 11, 1985. Abraham A. Brill Library, New York Psychoanalytic Society and Institute.

90. Viola W. Bernard, Curriculum Vita. Abraham A. Brill Library, New York Psychoanalytic Society and Institute.

91. Hartmann, "In Memoriam."

92. Unnamed colleague and friend of Dr. Peter Neubauer, interview with Nancy L. Segal, 2019.

93. Caplan, interview with Nancy L. Segal.

94. Schein and Bernstein, *Identical Strangers*.

95. Dorothy Krugman, interview with Nancy L. Segal, 2005. Krugman passed away in 2011.

96. Samuel Abrams, "Disposition and the Environment." *The Psychoanalytic Study of the Child* 41, no. 1 (1986): 41–60.

97. Dorothy Krugman, interview with Nancy L. Segal and Larry Perlman, May 25, 2005.

98. Peter B. Neubauer, interview with Milton J. E. Senn, Jewish Board of Guardians, Child Development Center, April 8, 1977. Courtesy of John P. Rees, National Library of Medicine.

99. Susan Sherkow, interview with Nancy L. Segal, 2020. In psychoanalytic theory, the primary object is the first person you are in contact with, usually the mother. The mother-child relationship is considered central to development; see Rafael Sharón, "What Is Object Relation Theory in Psychoanalysis?" *Modern Psychoanalyst*, https://modernpsychoanalyst.com/what-is-object-relations-theory -in-psychoanalysis/#:~:text=Another%20psychoanalytic%20theory%20is%20 the,the%20giver%20of%20the%20law.

100. Hartmann, email correspondence to Nancy L. Segal, 2020.

101. Drs. Harold P. Blum, Deanna Holtzman, John and Munder Ross, "Peter B. Neubauer." *New York Times*, February 19, 2008, https://www.legacy.com/ obituaries/nytimes/obituary.aspx?n=peter-b-neubauer&pid=103776155.

102. Harry Belafonte with Michael Schnayerson, *My Song: A Memoir* (New York: Alfred A. Knopf, 2011).

103. Neubauer, interview with Milton J.E. Senn.

104. Sheldon Fogelman, telephone conversation with Nancy L. Segal, 2020.

105. Suzanne Bachner, interview with Nancy L. Segal, 2019.

106. Schein and Bernstein, *Identical Strangers*.

107. Wright, *Twins and What They Tell Us About Who We Are*.

108. Austen Garwood-Gowers, email correspondence to Nancy L. Segal, 2020.

109. Wikler, interview with Nancy L. Segal.

110. Mercurio, interview with Nancy L. Segal.

111. Nancy L. Segal, Scott L. Hershberger, and Sara Arad, "Meeting One's Twin: Perceived Social Closeness and Familiarity." *Evolutionary Psychology* 1 (2003): 70–95.

112. Jessica Bernstein, email correspondence with Nancy L. Segal, 2020.

113. Segal, *Entwined Lives: Twins and What They Tell Us About Human Behavior*.

114. Lawrence Hartmann, interview with Nancy L. Segal, 2020.

115. Nancy L. Segal, *Born Together—Reared Apart: The Landmark Minnesota Twin Study* (Cambridge, MA: Harvard University Press, 2012).

116. Constance Krauss, interview with Nancy L. Segal, 2020.

117. Barron H. Lerner and Arthur L. Caplan, "Judging the Past: How History Should Inform Bioethics." *Annals of Internal Medicine* 164, no. 8 (2016): 553–57. Caplan, interview with Nancy L. Segal, 2019.

118. Beecher, "Ethics and Clinical Research"; Beecher, "Consent in Clinical Experimentation: Myth and Reality."

CHAPTER 20

1. Leon Hoffman and Lois Oppenheim, "*Three Identical Strangers and The Twinning Reaction*—Clarifying History and Lessons for Today from Peter Neubauer's Twins Study." *Journal of the American Medical Association* 322, no. 1 (2019): 10–12.

2. Susan P. Sherkow, interview with Nancy L. Segal, 2019; Susan P. Sherkow, "Susan P. Sherkow, M.D." Curriculum vitae, http://sherkowcenter.org/cv.pdf.

3. Esther R. Goshen-Gottstein, "The Mothering of Twins, Triplets and Quadruplets." *Psychiatry* 43, no. 3 (1980): 189–204.

4. Mother-infant attached is generally assessed when infants are between one and two years of age. The method used by Goshen-Gottstein was not described.

5. Samuel Abrams, "Disposition and the Environment." *The Psychoanalytic Study of the Child* 41, no. 1 (1986): 41–60.

6. A paradigm shift is a profound change in how natural phenomena or other events are viewed or interpreted. It originated in a book by Thomas Kuhn, *The Structure of Scientific Revolutions* (Chicago: University of Chicago Press, 1962).

7. Dorothy Burlingham, *Twins: A Study of Three Pairs of Identical Twins* (New York: International Universities Press, 1952).

8. Dr. Susannah Falk Shopsin Lewis, interview with Nancy L. Segal, 2019. According to Bernard, "We are unaware of research studies that compare the development of identical twins reared in their biological homes from infancy on with those reared apart under the conditions studied by CDC." See Viola Bernard, "CONFIDENTIAL: Explanatory Statement for Use by Public Relations Consultant [text has been removed] and Research." March 22, 1983, Viola W. Bernard Archives, Columbia University. Note that this comment is in a single paragraph, separate from the longer version of the statement. Also note that longitudinal studies of reared-together identical (and fraternal) infant twins had been published when the LWS-CDC study was in progress; see, for example, Daniel G. Freedman and Barbara Keller, "Inheritance of Behavior in Infants." *Science* 140, no. 3563 (1963): 196–68. This study was less comprehensive than the LWS-CDC study and followed twins periodically for just one year. However, the Louisville Twin Study, a comprehensive behavioral and physical investigation started in the late 1950s, followed reared-together twins from infancy until age fifteen. See Sally Ann Rhea, "Reviving the Louisville Twin Study: An Introduction." *Adoption Quarterly* 45, no. 6 (2015): 597–99.

9. Marjorie R. Leonard, "Problems in Identification and Ego Development in Twins." *The Psychoanalytic Study of the Child* 16, no. 1 (1961): 300–20; Amram Scheinfeld, *Twins and Supertwins* (Philadelphia, PA: J.B. Lippincott Company, 1967); Goshen-Gottstein, "The Mothering of Twins, Triplets and Quadruplets."

10. Mary Foley, "Organizations for Parents of Twins." *Twins List FAQs*, 2007, http://www.twinslist.org/resparentorgs.html#:~:text=%2C%20Inc%20(NOMO TC),Description%3A,specifically%20to%20multiple%20birth%20children.

11. "ICOMBO," https://icombo.org/about/.

12. Michele Mordkoff, interview with Nancy L. Segal, 2020.

13. Nancy L. Segal and Francisca J. Niculae, "Fullerton Virtual Twin Project: Overview and 2019 Update." *Twin Research and Human Genetics* 22, no. 6 (2019): 731–34.

14. Adoption Study Meeting, "Publication/Legal Issues." October 2, 1984, Columbia University Health Sciences Library: Archives and Special Collections. "Viola Wertheim Bernard Papers."

15. James Shields, *Monozygotic Twins: Brought Up Apart and Together* (London: Oxford University Press, 1962).

16. Nancy L. Segal, "Reared-Apart Chinese Twins: Chance Discovery." *Twin Research and Human Genetics* 20, no. 2 (2017): 180–85; CBS, "Just Alike: Twins Separated at Birth." *CBS Sunday Magazine,* February 5, 2017; Nancy L. Segal, Francisca J. Niculae, Erika N. Becker, and Emmy Y. Shih, "Reared-Apart/ Reared-Together Chinese Twins and Virtual Twins: Evolving Research Program and General Intelligence Findings." *Journal of Experimental Child Psychology* 207 (2021): article 105106; https://www.sciencedirect.com/science/article/abs/pii/ S0022096521000230.

17. Nancy L. Segal, Joanne Hoven Stohs, and Kara Evans, "Chinese Twin Children Reared Apart and Reunited: First Prospective Study of Co-Twin Reunions." *Adoption Quarterly* 14, no. 1 (2011): 61–78.

18. Columbia University Health Sciences Library: Archives and Special Collections, "Viola Wertheim Bernard Papers." Box 5.4: *Child Development Center (CDC): Twin Study [Twins Reared Apart]*, 1953–1997.

19. Single page from a document provided by Spence-Chapin to separated twin Sharon Morello. Columbia University Archives and Special Collections. "The Papers of Viola W. Bernard, M.D." December 18, 1978; Memo, September 29, 1982, Columbia University Archives and Special Collections. "The Papers of Viola W. Bernard, M.D." Box 76.4: Child Development Center-Twin Study (Twins Reared Apart).

20. Viola W. Bernard, interview with Lawrence Wright, 1993.

21. Luigi Pirandello and Mark Musa, *Six Characters in Search of an Author and Other Plays* (New York: Penguin Modern Classics, 1996).

22. Michele Mordkoff, interview with Nancy L. Segal, 2019.

23. Aaron Esman, interview with Nancy L. Segal, 2019. In Wardle's film *Three Identical Strangers,* journalist Lawrence Wright suggested that the twins were intentionally separated for the study.

24. Hoffman and Oppenheim, *"Three Identical Strangers and The Twinning Reaction*—Clarifying History and Lessons for Today from Peter Neubauer's Twins Study."

25. Lois Oppenheim, interview with Nancy L. Segal, 2019; Hoffman and Oppenheim, *"Three Identical Strangers and The Twinning Reaction*—Clarifying History and Lessons for Today from Peter Neubauer's Twins Study."

26. Hugh Lytton, Dorice Conway, and Reginald Sauve, "The Impact of Twin-ship on Parent-Child Interaction." *Journal of Personality and Social Psychology* 35, no. 2 (1977): 97–107.

27. Michelle E. Barton and Randi Strosberg, "Conversational Patterns of Two-Year-Old Twins in Mother–Twin–Twin Triads." *Journal of Child Language* 24, no. 1 (1997): 257–69; Hélène Tremblay-Leveau, Sophie Leclerc, and Jacqueline Nadel, "Linguistic Skills of 16-and 23-Month-Old Twins and Singletons in a Tri-adic Context." *First Language* 19, no. 56 (1999): 233–54; Johanna Rendle-Short, Louise Skelt, and Nicolette Bramley, "Speaking to Twin Children: Evidence Against the 'Impoverishment' Thesis." *Research on Language and Social Interaction* 48, no. 1 (2015): 79–99.

28. Nancy L. Segal, *Twin Mythconceptions: False Beliefs, Fables, and Facts About Twins* (New York: Elsevier, 2017).

29. Nancy L. Segal, "Commentary: More Thoughts on the Child Development Center Twin Study." *Twin Research and Human Genetics* 8, no. 3 (2005): 276–81.

30. Joan Wofford, interview with Nancy L. Segal, 2020.

31. Hoffman and Oppenheim, "*Three Identical Strangers and The Twinning Reaction*—Clarifying History and Lessons for Today from Peter Neubauer's Twins Study."

32. Viola W. Bernard, "Draft for CBS News" (CONFIDENTIAL: NOT FOR PUBLICATION OR CIRCULATION). March 22, 1983, Viola W. Bernard Archives, Columbia University. Hoffman and Oppenheim, "*Three Identical Strangers and The Twinning Reaction*—Clarifying History and Lessons for Today from Peter Neubauer's Twins Study."

33. Adam M. Kelmenson and Ilene Wilets, "Historical Practice of Separating Twins at Birth." *Journal of the American Medical Association* 322, no. 18 (2019): 1827–28.

34. Peter Neubauer, interview with Lawrence Wright, 1993.

35. Peter B. Neubauer Collection, "Intra-Twin Comparisons." Yale University Archives, https://archives.yale.edu/repositories/12/archival_objects/1202631.

36. Proposal to Yale University Press, "Identical Twins Reared Apart: A Lon-gitudinal Study." July 1985, Viola W. Bernard Archives, Columbia University.

37. Viola W. Bernard, "Abbreviation of Main Ideas in Explanatory Statement of March 23, 1983. Re: CBS News Program Attacking LWS/CDC," April 11, 1983, Viola W. Bernard Archives, Columbia University. There is also a reference in 1983 to twin separations ending ten to fifteen years ago.

38. Bernard, interview with Lawrence Wright.

39. As I indicated in chapter 9, Doug and Howard learned in 2000 that they were twins because an ailing LWS staff member went against regulations. How-ever, as I also explained in chapter 16, one year earlier Paula Sherman had con-tacted LWS to learn more about her biological family. She was invited to visit the agency because an administrator believed that the news she wished to tell Paula was best disclosed in person—it was during this visit that Paula learned she was a

twin. It is possible that the administrator had the authority to reveal this information, whereas the staff member in Doug and Howard's case did not.

40. Segal, *Twin Mythconceptions*.

41. Case Western Reserve University, "Oral Contraceptive Pill," 2010, https://case.edu/affil/skuyhistcontraception/online-2012/pill.html#:~:text=The%20U.S.%20Food%20%26%20Drug%20Administration,of%20birth%20control%20in%201960.

42. Martha J. Bailey, Melanie Guldi, Allison Davido, and Erin Buzuvis, "Early Legal Access: Laws and Policies Governing Contraceptive Access, 1960–1980." Unpublished manuscript (2011). Martha J. Bailey is professor of economics at the University of California, Los Angeles.

43. William H. James, "Coital Frequency and Twinning—A Comment." *Journal of Biosocial Science* 24, no. 1 (1992): 135–36.

44. Florence G. Brown, letter to Dr. Viola Bernard, November 14, 1961, Viola W. Bernard Archives, Columbia University.

45. Myra Kahn, interview with Nancy L. Segal, 2020; Louise Wise Adoptees, Facebook, https://www.facebook.com/search/top/?q=louise%20wise%20adoptee&epa=SEARCH_BOX.

46. Kenneth S. Kendler, "A Joint History of the Nature of Genetic Variation and the Nature of Schizophrenia." *Molecular Psychiatry* 20, no. 1 (2015): 77–83.

47. Robert Kolker, *Hidden Valley Road: Inside the Mind of an American Family* (New York: Doubleday, 2020).

48. Franz J. Kallmann, "The Genetic Theory of Schizophrenia: An Analysis of 691 Schizophrenic Twin Index Families." *American Journal of Psychiatry* 103, no. 3 (1946): 309–22; David Rosenthal, ed., *The Genain Quadruplets: A Case Study and Theoretical Analysis of Heredity and Environment in Schizophrenia* (New York: Basic Books, 1963); Leonard L. Heston, "Psychiatric Disorders in Foster Home Reared Children of Schizophrenic Mothers." *British Journal of Psychiatry* 112, no. 489 (1966): 819–25.

49. Ellen Handler Spitz, "Documentary Danger: Reflections on Three Identical Strangers." *Bulletin of the Association for Psychoanalytic Medicine* 53 (Fall 2018): 22–29.

50. Lisa Belkin, interview with Nancy L. Segal, 2020.

51. Peter Neubauer, Alexander Neubauer, Viola Bernard, and Samuel Abrams, interviews with Lawrence Wright.

52. Lois Oppenheim, "The Facts about the Neubauer Twin Study: An Interview about a Controversy or a Controversial Interview?" *International Journal of Controversial Discussions* 2020 (1): 171–88.

53. Lawrence Wright, "Journalist on Discovering the Study of the 'Three Identical Strangers' Triplets." *Today Show with Megyn Kelly*, July 12, 2018, https://www.youtube.com/watch?v=A-WByPZuWqQ.

54. Viola Bernard, interview with Nellie Thompson, December 11, 1985. Abraham A. Brill Library, New York Psychoanalytic Society and Institute.

55. Stephen Wise Tulin, interview with Nancy L. Segal, 2019.

56. Tulin, handwritten letter to Nancy L. Segal, October 7, 2020.

57. Viola Bernard, memo to members of Tappanz Foundation, Inc. Board of Trustees. June 1, 1987. Courtesy of Becky Read.

58. Perry Ottenberg, psychiatrist (deceased, 2017), University of Pennsylvania; Eric Brettschneider, now first deputy commissioner at the NYC Administration for Children's Services; Cary A. Koplin, attorney; Stephen Wise Tulin, retired attorney; Joan Wofford, retired organizational consultant and trainer; Jennifer Wofford, clinical social worker; Carrie Wofford, attorney; Tim Ross, applied child welfare researcher; Marta Siberio, organizational development and strategic management consultant; and Gretchen Buchenholz, children and family advocate.

59. Eric Brettschneider, interview and email correspondence with Nancy L. Segal, September 27, 2019, June 1, 2021. Brettschneider was First Deputy Commissioner of the New York City Administration for Children from 2014 until his retirement in April 2021.

60. "Fund Will Help Child Study Center Innovate, Increase Access." *Medicine@ Yale*, Yale School of Medicine, September-October, 2016, https://medicine.yale .edu/news/medicineatyale/fund-will-help-child-study-center-innovate-increase/.

61. Cary A. Koplin, interview and email correspondence with Nancy L. Segal, 2019, 2020.

62. Brettschneider, personal communication, 2019.

63. Stephen E. Novak, email correspondence with Nancy L. Segal, 2020.

64. Brettschneider, interview with Nancy L. Segal.

65. Brettschneider, interview with Nancy L. Segal. During his conversation with David Rivel, Brettschneider wasn't certain if Rivel had referenced Bernard's or Neubauer's materials. Or course, he meant Neubauer's because the JBFCS had donated the collection to Yale and maintained control over it. Bernard's associates had set up her archives at Columbia.

66. Christine Weideman, email correspondence with Nancy L. Segal, 2019; also see the finding aid for Neubauer's collection.

67. Barry Coburn is a personal friend of Tim Heaphy; Heaphy is married to Lori Shinseki, the director and producer of the 2017 documentary film, *The Twinning Reaction*. Heaphy left the Hunton Andrews Kurth's firm in 2015 to become university counsel and senior assistant attorney general at the University of Virginia in Charlottesville.

68. "Mark Barnes," https://law.yale.edu/mark-barnes; "David Peloquin," https://www.ropesgray.com/en/biographies/p/david-peloquin.

69. Unnamed sources, 2020.

70. Yale University Archives, email communication to Nancy L. Segal, 2020.

71. Barry Coburn, interview in *The Twinning Reaction*, Lori Shinseki (director), Fire Horse Pictures, United States, 2017; Mark Mercurio, Stephen Latham, and Arthur Caplan, interviews with Nancy L. Segal, 2019, 2020; Kelmenson and Wilets, "Historical Practice of Separating Twins at Birth."

72. Susan Kolod, interview with Nancy L. Segal, 2019; also see Spitz, "Documentary Danger: Reflections on Three Identical Strangers" and *Category 4* commentaries in chapter 18.

73. Adam M. Kelmenson and Ilene Wilets, "Ethical Questions Remain in Controversial Twins Study: Further information and Sources Are Required to Find Resolve." *International Journal of Controversial Discussions* 1 (2020): 189–96.

74. Latham, interviews with Nancy L. Segal, 2019, 2020.

75. Coburn, presentation at The Twinning Reaction: Science and Deception, University of Virginia Law School, Charlottesville, VA, March 29, 2019.

76. Stephen E. Novak, email correspondence to Nancy L. Segal, 2020. In 2003, Stephen E. Novak and Kathleen L. Kelly co-wrote the Finding Aid for Bernard's collection. Some additional materials were discovered in 2016. "Viola Wertheim Bernard Papers." https://www.library-archives.cumc.columbia.edu/sites/default/files/finding-aids/M-0020_Bernard%2520finding%2520aid%2520temporary%2520complete%2520web%2520version.pdf.

77. Megyn Kelly, "Journalist on Discovering the Study of the 'Three Identical Strangers' Triplets." *Today Show with Megyn Kelly*, July 12, 2018, https://www.youtube.com/watch?v=A-WByPZuWqQ.

78. Dr, Michael Alpert, interview with Nancy L. Segal, 2019; Michael Alpert, "Yale Ethics Meeting Re: Neubauer-Bernard Twin Study," Yale University, July 25, 2013. Courtesy of Lori Shinseki.

79. Bernard, interview with Lawrence Wright.

80. Lori Shinseki, email correspondence to Nancy L. Segal, 2020.

81. Stephen Saito, "Interview: Tim Wardle on Making All the Connections in '*Three Identical Strangers*.'" Reviews, June 27, 2018, http://moveablefest.com/tim-wardle-three-identical-strangers/.

82. William McCormack, "Records from Controversial Twin Study Sealed at Yale Until 2065." *Yale Daily News*, October 1, 2018, 3.

83. William McCormack, email correspondence to Nancy L. Segal, 2019.

84. 9NOW, *Three Identical Strangers*, and "The Experiment." *60 Minutes–Australia*, August 9, 2020, https://www.youtube.com/watch?v=UQILXtd3ZOM&feature=youtu.be.

85. Mind Brain Behavior Interfaculty Initiative, "Three Identical Strangers: Virtual Panel Discussion," Harvard University, March 29, 2021, https://mbb.harvard.edu/event/three-identical-strangers.

86. Catherine Ross, presentation at The Twinning Reaction: Science and Deception, University of Virginia Law School, Charlottesville, VA, March 29, 2019.

87. Caplan, interviews with Nancy L. Segal, 2019, 2020. Furthermore, Hoffman and Oppenheim's assertion that "In fact, any participant can access records pertaining to their own information by contacting the Jewish Board" belies the difficulties of this process; see Hoffman and Oppenheim, "Three Identical Strangers and the Twinning Reaction—Clarifying History and Lessons for Today from Peter Neubauer's Twins Study."

Bibliography

PRIMARY SOURCES

Details concerning the specific papers, documents, and individuals I have consulted appear in the endnotes to each chapter.

Archived Collections

Archives & Special Collections, Augustus C. Long Health Sciences Library, Columbia University, New York, NY.
Viola Wertheim Bernard papers, 1918–2000.
New York Psychoanalytic Society and Institute, New York, NY.
Viola Wertheim Bernard papers.
Peter B. Neubauer papers.

Films and Television Programs (listed in chronological order)

Walter Cronkite's Universe, III. "Twins," (11). August 31, 1982, University of Rochester Library.
ABC. "Minnesota Study of Twins Reared Apart (MISTRA): Personality," *ABC News, Nightline,* October 2, 1989.
Walter Bogdanich with Mike Wallace. "Secrets and Lies." *60 Minutes,* CBS, 1998.
Shinseki, Lori. *The Twinning Reaction.* Fire Horse Pictures, 2017.
CBS. "Just Alike: Twins Separated at Birth." *CBS Sunday Magazine,* February 5, 2017.
Bruce Haring. "Justin Goldberg's Search for Long-Lost Twin Is Story Made for Hollywood." *Deadline,* November 24, 2017.
Tim Wardle. *Three Identical Strangers.* Raw, 2018.
ABC. "Twins Separated at Birth (Secret Twin Study)." *20/20,* March 9, 2018.

Tim Wardle. "Adult Twins, Separated at Birth, Have Emotional Reunion." *The Atlantic:* Short Documentary Films, October 3, 2018.

Gareth Harvey. *Three Identical Strangers*: "The Experiment." *60 Minutes–Australia,* August 9, 2020.

Personal Interviews

Colleagues and family members of Drs. Bernard and Neubauer, and separated twins and their family members.

Professionals in the fields of psychology, bioethics, medicine, law, adoption, journalism, editing, and publishing.

SELECTED SECONDARY SOURCES CITED

The most important secondary sources are presented here (listed in alphabetical order). All secondary sources cited appear in the endnotes to each chapter.

Abrams, Samuel. "Disposition and the Environment." *The Psychoanalytic Study of the Child* 41, no. 1 (1986): 41–60.

Abrams, Samuel, and Peter B. Neubauer. "Object Orientedness: The Person or the Thing." *The Psychoanalytic Quarterly* 45, no. 1 (1976): 73–99.

Abrams, Samuel, and Peter B. Neubauer. "Hartmann's Vision: Identical Twins and Developmental Organizations." *The Psychoanalytic Study of the Child* 49, no. 1 (1994): 49–59.

American Psychological Association. "Ethical Principles of Psychologists and Code of Conduct." https://www.apa.org/ethics/code, 2016.

Amery, Diane. "Couple Wed 20 Years Discover They're Twins." *Sun* 3, no. 51 (December 17, 1985): 19.

Beasley, Martha. "Sibling Shocker: After 30 Years of Marriage, Couple Discover They're Brother and Sister." *Sun* 8, no. 18 (May 1, 1990): 23.

Bedell, Sally. "'Cronkite's *Universe*' Is Cancelled." *New York Times*, August 12, 1982, C27.

Beecher, Henry K. "Ethics and Clinical Research." *New England Journal of Medicine* 274, no. 24 (1966): 1354–60.

Beecher, Henry K. "Consent in Clinical Experimentation: Myth and Reality." *Journal of the American Medical Association* 195, no. 1 (1966): 34–35.

Belafonte, Harry, with Michael Schnayerson. *My Song: A Memoir of Art, Race and Defiance* (New York: Alfred A. Knopf, 2011).

Belkin, Lisa. "What the Jumans Didn't Know About Michael." *New York Times*, March 14, 1999, 42–49.

Berk, Laura E. *Child Development*, ninth edition (Boston: Pearson, 2013).

Bernard, Viola W. "Adoption." *Encyclopedia of Mental Health* 1 (New York: Franklin Watts, Inc., 1963), 70–108.

Blatz, William E., et al. *Collected Studies on the Dionne Quintuplets* (Toronto: University of Toronto Press, 1937).

Bouchard, Jr., Thomas J. "The Study of Mental Ability Using Twin and Adoption Designs." In *Twin Research 3: Part B. Intelligence, Personality, and Development*, edited by Luigi Gedda, Paulo Parisi, and Walter E. Nance, 21–23 (New York: Alan R. Liss, Inc., 1981).

Bouchard, Jr., Thomas J., Leonard L. Heston, Elke D. Eckert, Margaret Keyes, and Susan Resnick. "The Minnesota Study of Twins Reared Apart: Project Description and Sample Results in the Development Domain." In *Twin Research 3: Part B. Intelligence, Personality and Development*, edited by Luigi Gedda, Paolo Parisi, and Walter E. Nance, 227–33 (New York, Alan R. Liss, Inc., 1981).

Bouchard, Jr., Thomas J., David T. Lykken, Matthew McGue, Nancy L. Segal, and Auke Tellegen. "Sources of Human Psychological Differences: The Minnesota Study of Twins Reared Apart." *Science* 250, no. 4978 (1990): 223–28.

Brady, Joyce A., E. Hamilton, Michele J. K. Osterman, Anne K. Driscoll, and Patrick Drake. "Births: Final Data for 2017." *National Vital Statistics* Reports 67, no. 8 (November 7, 2018): 1–50.

Brazelton, T. Berry. "It's Twins." *Redbook Magazine* 60 (1980): 83–84.

Breault, Joseph I. "Protecting Human Research Subjects: The Past Defines the Future." *Ochsner Journal* 6, no. 1 (2006): 15–20.

Buelow, Paul A. "The Institutional Review Board: A Brief History of Attempts to Protect Human Subjects in Research." *Clinical Nurse Specialist* 25, no. 6 (2011): 277–80.

Bulmer, Martin G. *The Biology of Twinning in Man* (Oxford: Oxford University Press, 1970).

Burlingham, Dorothy T. *Twins: A Study of Three Sets of Identical Twins with 30 Charts* (London: Imago, 1952).

Burlingham, Michael John. *The Last Tiffany: A Biography of Dorothy Tiffany Burlingham* (New York: Atheneum, 1989).

Bussiere, Alice. "The Development of Adoption Law." *Adoption Quarterly* 1, no. 3 (1998): 3–25.

Chen, Edwin. "Twins Reared Apart: A Living Lab." *New York Times*, December 9, 1979, 112–23.

Cronin, Herbert J. "An Analysis of the Neuroses of Identical Twins." *Psychoanalytic Review* 20, no. 4 (1933): 375–87.

Demarest, Elinor W., and Muriel Chaves Winestine. "The Initial Phase of Concomitant Treatment of Twins." *The Psychoanalytic Study of the Child* 10, no. 1 (1955): 336–52.

Diamond, Milton, and H. Keith Sigmundson. "Sex Reassignment at Birth: Long-Term Reviews and Clinical Implications." *Archives of Pediatric and Adolescent and Medicine* 151, no. 3 (March 1997): 298–304.

Dickter, Adam. "Home Found for Louise Wise Records." *The New York Jewish Week* (December 10, 2004).

Doniger, Wendy. "What Did They Name the Dog?" *London Review of Books* 20, no. 6 (March 19, 1998).

Eckert, Elke D., Leonard L. Heston, and Thomas J. Bouchard Jr. "MZ Twins Reared Apart: Preliminary Findings of Psychiatric Disturbances and Traits." In *Twin Research 3: Part B. Intelligence, Personality, and Development*, edited by Luigi Gedda, Paolo Parisi, Walter E. Nance, 179–88 (New York: Alan R. Liss, Inc., 1981).

Erlenmeyer-Kimling, L., and Barbara A. Cornblatt. "The New York High-Risk Project: A Followup Report." *Schizophrenia Bulletin* 13, no. 3 (1987): 451–61.

Esterberg, Michelle L., and Michael T. Compton. "Causes of Schizophrenia Reported by Family Members of Urban African American Hospitalized Patients with Schizophrenia." *Comprehensive Psychiatry* 47, no. 3 (2006): 221–26.

Farber, Susan. "Sex Differences in the Expression of Adoption Ideas: Observations of Adoptees from Birth Through Latency." *American Journal of Orthopsychiatry* 47, no. 4 (1977): 639–50.

Farber, Susan L. *Identical Twins Reared Apart; A Reanalysis* (New York: Basic Books, 1981).

Feigelman, William. "Are Adoptees at Increased Risk for Attempting Suicide?" *Suicide and Life-Threatening Behavior* 35, no. 2 (2005): 206–16.

Friesen, Phoebe, Lisa Kearns, Barbara Redman, and Arthur L. Caplan. "Rethinking the Belmont Report?" *The American Journal of Bioethics* 17, no. 7 (2017): 15–21.

Galton, Francis. "The History of Twins, as a Criterion of the Relative Powers of Nature and Nurture." *Fraser's Magazine* 12, no. 71 (1875): 566–76.

Garwood-Gowers, Austen. *Medical Use of Human Beings: Respect as a Basis for Critique of Discourse, Law and Practice* (London: Routledge, 2020).

Gehman, Betsy H. *Twins: Twice the Trouble, Twice the Fun* (New York: J.B. Lippincott Co., 1965).

Goldman, Vivian S., Catherine E. Harris, Jean M. Johnson, William H. Trayfors, and Cynthia A. Wiggins. *Research Relating to Children* 17 (Washington, DC: Welfare Administration: Children's Bureau, 1963–1964), 8-U-29: 155.

Gonyo, Barbara. "Genetic Sexual Attraction." *Decree* 4, no. 2 (Washington, DC: American Adoption Congress, Winter, 1987), 1, 5.

Goshen-Gottstein, Esther R. "The Mothering of Twins, Triplets and Quadruplets." *Psychiatry* 43, no. 3 (1980): 189–204. The LWS-CDC twin study is not referenced.

Hartmann Lawrence. "In Memoriam: Viola W. Bernard, M.D. (1907-1998)." *Journal of the American Academy of Child and Adolescent Psychiatry* 39, no. 1 (2000): 131.

Herman, Ellen. "The Difference Difference Makes: Justine Wise Polier and Religious Matching in Twentieth-Century Child Adoption." *Religion and American Culture* 10, no. 1 (2000): 57–98.

Herman, Ellen. *Kinship by Design: A History of Adoption in the Modern United States* (Chicago: University of Chicago Press, 2008).

Hoffman, Leon, and Lois Oppenheim. "Three Identical Strangers and The Twinning Reaction—Clarifying History and Lessons for Today from Peter Neubauer's Twin Study." *Journal of the American Medical Association* 322, no. 1 (July 2019): 10–12.

Jewish Board of Family and Children's Services. "Adoption Study Records of the Child Development Center." *Yale University Archives* call no. MS 1585 (circa 1960–1980).

Kallman, Franz J. "The Genetic Theory of Schizophrenia." *American Journal of Psychiatry* 103, no. 3 (1946): 309–22.

Kelmenson, Adam M., and Ilene Wilets. "Ethical Questions Remain in Controversial Twins Study: Further Information and Sources Are Required to Find Resolve." *International Journal of Controversial Discussions* 1 (2020): 189–96.

Kelmenson, Adam M., and Ilene Wilets, "Historical Practice of Separating Twins at Birth." *Journal of the American Medical Association* 322, no. 18 (2019): 1827–28.

Keyes, Margaret A., Stephen M. Malone, Anu Sharma, William G. Iacono, and Matt McGue. "Risk of Suicide Attempt in Adopted and Nonadopted Offspring." *Pediatrics* 132, no. 4 (2013): 639–46.

Klitzman, Robert L., and Adam M. Kelmenson. "Experiment on Identical Siblings Separated at Birth: Ethical Implications for Researchers, Universities, and Archives Today." *Journal of Medical Ethics* (2020).

Knopik, Valerie S., Jenae M. Neiderhiser, John C. DeFries, and Robert Plomin. *Behavioral Genetics* (New York: Macmillan Higher Education, 2017).

Jones, Barbara. "Do Siblings Possess Constitutional Rights." *Cornell Law Review* 78, no. 6 (1993): 1187–220.

Juel-Nielsen, Niels. *Individual and Environment: A Psychiatric-Psychological Investigation of Monozygotic Twins Reared Apart* (Copenhagen: Munksgaard, 1965).

Kessler, Robert E., and Alan Finder. "The Face Looked Familiar." *Newsday*, September 17, 1980, 3, 23.

Koch, Helen L. *Twins and Twin Relations* (Chicago: University of Chicago Press, 1966).

Kolker, Robert. *Hidden Valley Road: Inside the Mind of an American Family* (New York: Doubleday, 2020).

Kreech, Florence. "An American Experience in Child Care Services." In *Social Work and Ethnicity*, edited by Juliet Cheetham, 112–21 (London: Gordon Allen & Unwin, 1982).

Krueger, Robert F., Kristian E. Markon, and Thomas J. Bouchard Jr. "The Extended Genotype: The Heritability of Personality Accounts for the Heritability of Recalled Family Environments in Twins Reared Apart." *Journal of Personality* 71, no. 5 (2003): 809–33.

Leonard, Marjorie R. "Twins: The Myth and the Reality." *Child Study* 30, no. 2 (1953): 9–13, 38–41.

Logan, Janette. "Birth Mothers and Their Mental Health: Uncharted Territory." *The British Journal of Social Work* 26, no. 5 (1996): 609–25.

Lykken, David T. "The Diagnosis of Zygosity in Twins." *Behavior Genetics* 8, no. 5 (1978): 437–73.

Lytton, Hugh, Dorice Conway, and Reginald Sauve. "The Impact of Twinship on Parent-Child Interaction." *Journal of Personality and Social Psychology* 35, no. 2 (1977): 97–107.

Machin, Geoffrey A., and Louis G. Keith. *An Atlas of Multiple Pregnancy: Biology and Pathology* (New York: Parthenon, 1999).

Martin, J. A., and Michelle J. K. Osterman. "Is Twin Childbearing on the Decline? Twin Births in the United States, 2014–2018." *NCHS Data Brief*, no. 351 (October 2019).

Marwell, David G. *Mengele: Unmasking the Angel of Death* (New York: W.W. Norton & Co., 2020).

McCormack, William. "Records from Controversial Twin Study Sealed at Yale Until 2065." *Yale News* (October 1, 2018).

McMillan, Thomas. "Newlyweds Learn They are Brother and Sister!" *Weekly World News*, 7, no. 17 (February 4, 1986).

Mednick, Sarnoff, and Fini Schulsinger, "Some Premorbid Characteristics Related to Breakdown in Children with Schizophrenic Mothers." In *The Transmission of Schizophrenia*, edited by David Rosenthal and Seymour S. Kety, 267–91 (Oxford: Pergamon Press, 1968).

Merrill, John P., Joseph E. Murray, J. Hartwell Harrison, and Warren R. Guild. "Successful Homotransplantation of the Human Kidney Between Identical Twins." *Journal of the American Medical Association* 160, no. 4 (1956): 277–82.

Mitchell, Kevin J. *Innate: How the Wiring of Our Brains Shapes Who We Are* (Princeton: Princeton University Press, 2018).

National Commission for the Protection of Human Subjects of Biomedical and Behavioral Research. "Belmont Report: Ethical Principles and Guidelines for the Protection of Human Subjects of Research, Report of the National Commission for the Protection of Human Subjects of Biomedical and Behavioral Research." *Federal Register* 44, no. 76 (April 18, 1979): 23192–97.

Neubauer, Peter B. (ed.). *Children in Collectives: Child-Rearing Aims and Practices in the Kibbutz* (Springfield, IL: C.C. Thomas, 1965).

Neubauer, Peter B. "Twins." In *Comprehensive Textbook of Psychiatry*, edited by Alan M. Freedman and Harold I. Kaplan, 2301–3. Baltimore: Williams & Wilkins, 1975.

Neubauer, Peter B. (ed.). *The Process of Child Development* (Lanham, MD: Jason Aronson, 1976).

Neubauer, Peter, Samuel Abrams, and Christa Balzart. "Findings 1: The Individual Children." (Sample chapter from *Identical Twins Reared Apart; A Longitudinal Study*, p. 17, unpublished.) Circa 1987, Viola W. Bernard Archives, Columbia University.

Neubauer, Peter, and Christa Balzert, "Genetik und Psychotherapie" ("Genetics and Psychotherapy"), in *Der Psychoanalytische Prozeß*, edited by Sylvia Zwettler-Otte and Albrecht Komarek, 169–83. Vienna: Turia & Kant, 1996.

Neubauer, Peter B., and Alexander Neubauer. *Nature's Thumbprint: The New Genetics of Personality* (New York: Addison-Wesley Publishing Co., 1990).

Newman, Horatio N., Frank N. Freeman, and Karl J. Holzinger. *Twins: A Study of Heredity and Environment* (Chicago: University of Chicago Press, 1937).

Novick, Jack, and Kerry Kelly Novic. "Atruistic Analysis." In *The Anna Freud Tradition: Lines of Development—Evolution of Theory and Practice Over the Decades*, edited by Norka T. Malberg and Joan Raphael-Leff, chapter 31, 365–68 (London: Routledge, 2018).

Oppenheim, Lois. "The Facts About the Neubauer Twin Study: An Interview About Controversy or a Controversial Interview?" *International Journal of Controversial Discussions* 1 (2020): 171–88.

Orr, Douglass W. "A Psychoanalytic Study of a Fraternal Twin." *The Psychoanalytic Quarterly* 10, no. 2 (1941): 284–96.

Pearce, Jeremy. "Peter B. Neubauer, 94, Noted Child Psychiatrist, Is Dead." *New York Times*, March 3, 2008, B7.

Pedersen, Nancy L., Gerald E. McClearn, Robert Plomin, and Lars Friberg. "Separated Fraternal Twins: Resemblance for Cognitive Abilities." *Behavior Genetics* 15, no. 4 (1985): 407–19.

Perlman, Lawrence M. "Memories of the Child Development Center Twin Study of Adopted Monozygotic Twins Reared Apart: An Unfulfilled Promise." *Twin Research and Human Genetics* 8, no. 3 (2005): 271–75.

Plank, Emma N. "Reactions of Mothers of Twins in a Child Study Group." *American Journal of Orthopsychiatry* 28, no. 1 (1958): 196–204.

Plomin, Robert. *Nature and Nurture: An Introduction to Human Behavioral Genetics* (Pacific Grove, CA: Brooks/Cole, 1990).

Plomin, Robert. *Blueprint: How DNA Makes Us Who We Are* (London: Allen Lane, 2018).

Polderman, Tina J. C., Beben Benyamin, Christiaan A. De Leeuw, Patrick F. Sullivan, Arjen Van Bochoven, Peter M. Visscher, and Danielle Posthuma. "Meta-Analysis of the Heritability of Human Traits Based on Fifty Years of Twin Studies." *Nature Genetics* 47, no. 7 (2015): 702–09.

Rendle-Short, Johanna, Louise Skelt, and Nicolette Bramley. "Speaking to Twin Children: Evidence Against the 'Impoverishment' Thesis." *Research on Language and Social Interaction* 48, no. 1 (2015): 79–99.

Ridley, Matt. *The Red Queen: Sex and The Evolution of Human Nature* (New York: Penguin Books, 1993).

Rooks-Rapport, Joe. "Notable American Jewish Women: A Computer Aided Study in Collective Biography." Rabbinic thesis, Hebrew Union College (1984), cited in Joe Rooks-Rapport, "Louise Waterman Wise." *Jewish Women: A Comprehensive Historical Encyclopedia (Jewish Women's Archive)* February 7, 2009.

Rosenthal, David. *Genetics of Psychopathology* (New York: McGraw-Hill Book Co., 1971).

Schein, Elyse, and Paula Bernstein. *Identical Strangers: A Memoir of Twins Separated and Reunited* (New York: Random House, 2007).

Sankilampi, Ulla, Marja-Leena Hannila, Antti Saari, Mika Gissler, and Leo Dunkel. "New Population-Based References for Birth Weight, Length, and Head Circumference in Singletons and Twins from 23 to 43 Gestation Weeks." *Annals of Medicine* 45, no. 5-6 (2013): 446–54.

Saul, Stephanie. "In the Name of Research: Identical Brothers Separated at Birth Were Studied, But Truth Was Hidden." *Newsday* (October 12, 1997), A5, A52, A 53.

Schwartz, Tony. "Lessons of the '60 Minutes Case.'" *New York* (June 20, 1983), 30–34.

Segal, Nancy L. "Cooperation, Competition, and Altruism Within Twin Sets: A Reappraisal." *Ethology and Sociobiology* 5, no. 3 (1984): 163–77.

Segal, Nancy L. "Zygosity diagnosis: Laboratory and Investigator's Judgment." *Acta Geneticae Medicae et Gemellologiae: Twin Research* 33, no. 3 (1984): 515–20.

Segal, Nancy L. "Holocaust Twins: Their Special Bond." *Psychology Today* (August 1985): 52–58.

Segal, Nancy L. *Entwined Lives: Twins and What They Tell Us About Human Behavior* (New York: Plume, 2000).

Segal, Nancy L. *Indivisible by Two: Lives of Extraordinary Twins* (Cambridge: Harvard University Press, 2005).

Segal, Nancy L. "Commentary: More Thoughts on the Child Development Center Twin Study." *Twin Research and Human Genetics* 8, no. 3 (2005): 276–81.

Segal, Nancy L. (2006). "Laboratory Findings: Not Twins, Twins, not Twins." *Twin Research and Human Genetics* 9, no. 2 (2006): 303–08.

Segal, Nancy L. *Someone Else's Twins: The True Story of Babies Switched at Birth* (Amherst, NY: Prometheus Books, 2011).

Segal, Nancy L. *Born Together—Reared Apart: The Landmark Minnesota Twin Study* (Cambridge: Harvard University Press, 2012).

Segal, Nancy L. *Twin Mythconceptions: False Beliefs, Fables, and Facts About Twins* (New York: Elsevier, 2017).

Segal, Nancy L. "Reared-Apart Chinese Twins: Chance Discovery." *Twin Research and Human Genetics* 20, no. 2 (2017): 180–85.

Segal, N. L. "A Possible Twin: The 1960s Twin Study Revisited." *Twin Research and Human Genetics* 21, no. 2 (2018): 155–62.

Segal, Nancy L. "Co-Twin Control Studies: Natural Events, Experimental Interventions and Rare Happenings." *Twin Research and Human Genetics* 22, no. 4 (2019): 272–76.

Segal, Nancy L., and Franchesca A. Cortez. "Born in Korea-Adopted Apart: Behavioral Development of Monozygotic Twins Raised in the United States and France." *Personality and Individual Differences* 70 (2014): 97–104.

Segal, Nancy L., Brittney A. Hernandez, Jamie L. Graham, and Ulrich Ettinger. "Pairs of Genetically Unrelated Look-Alikes." *Human Nature* 29, no. 4 (2018): 402–17.

Segal, Nancy L., Joanne Hoven Stohs, and Kara Evans. "Chinese Twin Children Reared Apart and Reunited: First Prospective Study of Co-Twin Reunions." *Adoption Quarterly* 14, no. 1 (2011): 61–78.

Segal, Nancy L., Scott L. Hershberger, and Sara Arad. "Meeting One's Twin: Perceived Social Closeness and Familiarity." *Evolutionary Psychology* 1, no. 1 (2003): 70–95.

Segal, Nancy L., and Yesika S. Montoya. *Accidental Brothers: The Story of Twins Exchanged at Birth and the Power of Nature and Nurture* (New York: St. Martin's Press, 2018).

Segal, Nancy L., Joseph L. Nedelec, and Vanessa A. Costello-Harris. "Differences in Development in Monozygotic Twins." In *Why Are Monozygotic Twins Different: From Genetics to Environment*, edited by Alexandra Matias and Issac Blickstein, 285–95 (New York: Elsevier, 2020).

Segal, Nancy L., and Francisca J. Niculae. "Fullerton Virtual Twin Project: Overview and 2019 Update." *Twin Research and Human Genetics* 22, no. 6 (2019): 731–34.

Shamoo, Adil E., and David B. Resnik. *Responsible Conduct of Research* (Oxford: Oxford University Press, 2003).

Shields, James. *Monozygotic Twins: Brought Up Apart and Together* (London: Oxford University Press, 1962).

Slater, Eliot, and A. W. Beard. "The Schizophrenia-Like Psychoses of Epilepsy: I. Psychiatric Aspects." *The British Journal of Psychiatry* 109, no. 458 (1963): 95–112.

Sorosky, Arthur, Annette Baron, and Reuben Panor. *The Adoption Triangle: Sealed or Open Records: How They Affect Adoptees, Birth Parents, and Adoptive Parents* (New York: Doubleday, 1984).

Stewart, Ellen A. *Exploring Twins: Towards a Social Analysis of Twinship* (New York: Palgrave Macmillan, 2000).

Sullivan, Patrick F., Kenneth S. Kendler, and Michael C. Neale. "Schizophrenia as a Complex Trait: Evidence from a Meta-Analysis of Twin Studies." *Archives of General Psychiatry* 60, no. 12 (2003): 1187–92.

Tellegen, Auke, David T. Lykken, Thomas J. Bouchard, Kimerly J. Wilcox, Nancy L. Segal, and Stephen Rich. "Personality Similarity in Twins Reared Apart and Together." *Journal of Personality and Social Psychology* 54, no. 6 (1988): 1031–39.

Thomas, Alexander, Stella Chess, and Herbert G. Birch. *Temperament and Behavior Disorders in Children* (New York: New York University Press, 1968).

Thomas, Alexander, Stella Chess, and Herbert G. Birch. "The Origin of Personality." *Scientific American* 227, no. 2 (1970): 102–09.

Tomassini, Cecilia, Knud Juel, Niels V. Holm, Axel Skytthe, and Kaare Christensen. "Risk of Suicide in Twins: 51 Year Follow Up Study." *British Medical Journal* 327, no. 7411 (2003): 373–74.

Torrey, E. Fuller, Ann E. Bowler, Edward H. Taylor, and Irving I. Gottesman. *Schizophrenia and Manic-Depressive Disorder: The Biological Roots of Mental Illness as Revealed by the Landmark Study of Identical Twins* (New York: Basic Books, 1994).

Triseliotis, John P. *In Search of Origins* (London: Kegan Paul, 1973).

U.S. Department of Health, Education, and Welfare. Research Grants Index, 2 (Bethesda: NIMH, 1965), 1656.

Visscher, Peter M., Naomi R. Wray, Qian Zhang, Pamela Sklar, Mark I. McCarthy, Matthew A. Brown, and Jian Yang. "10 Years of GWAS Discovery: Biology, Function, and Translation." *The American Journal of Human Genetics* 101, no. 1 (2017): 5–22.

Voracek, Martin, and Lisa Mariella Loibl. "Genetics of Suicide: A Systematic Review of Twin Studies." *Wiener Klinische Wochenschrift* 119, no. 15-16 (2007): 463–75.

Vollmann, Jochen, and Rolf Winau. "Informed Consent in Human Experimentation Before the Nuremberg Code." *British Medical Journal* 313, no. 7070 (1996): 1445–47.

Weiner, Mark. "NY Lawmakers Pass Adoption Bill Championed by Pam Hunter, Ending Decades of Secrecy" (June 20, 2019).

Wilson, Ronald S. "Analysis of Longitudinal Twin Data: Basic Model and Applications to Physical Growth Measures." *Acta Geneticae Medicae et Gemellologiae: Twin Research* 28, no. 2 (1979): 93–105.

World Medical Association. "Declaration of Helsinki." *Bulletin of the World Health Organization* 79 (no. 4): 373–74.

Wright, Lawrence. "Double Mystery." *The New Yorker* (August 7, 1995): 45–62.

Yarrow, Leon J. "Theoretical Implications of Adoption Research." *Child Welfare* 44, no. 2 (1965): 65–72.

Young-Bruehl, Elisabeth. *Anna Freud: A Biography* (New York: W.W. Norton & Co., 1988).

Index

Page references for figures are italicized.

About the Author

Dr. Nancy L. Segal is professor of psychology at California State University, Fullerton, and director of the Twin Studies Center. She has authored over 250 articles and six books on twins and twin development. Her 2012 book, *Born Together—Reared Apart: The Landmark Minnesota Twin Study*, won the 2013 William James Book Award from the American Psychological Association. Her other books include *Twin Mythconceptions: False Beliefs, Fables and Facts About Twins* (2017), *Someone Else's Twin: The True Story of Babies Switched at Birth* (2011), *Indivisible by Two: Lives of Extraordinary Twins* (2007), and *Entwined Lives: Twins and What They Tell Us About Human Behavior* (2000). Her most recent book, *Accidental Brothers* (April 2018), follows the life histories of two sets of identical Colombian twins who were inadvertently exchanged at birth. She has appeared on *CBS This Morning*, CNN, and the *Oprah Winfrey Show*, and been featured in the *New York Times* and *Wall Street Journal*. She lives in southern California.

Please see Nancy Segal's website for reviews, photographs, and other information about *Deliberately Divided* as these items become available: http://drnancy segaltwins.org/deliberately-divided.

OTHER BOOKS BY NANCY L. SEGAL

Entwined Lives: Twins and What They Tell Us About Human Behavior

Indivisible by Two: Lives of Extraordinary Twins

Someone Else's Twin: The True Story of Babies Switched at Birth

Born Together—Reared Apart: The Landmark Minnesota Twin Study
(2013 William James Book Award, American Psychological Association)

Twin Mythconceptions: False Beliefs, Fables, and Facts About Twins

Accidental Brothers: The Story of Twins Exchanged at Birth and the Power of Nature and Nurture